The Earnest Christian:

Devoted to the Promotion of Experimental and
Practical Piety

B.T. Roberts, A.M., Editor
Volume 1

First Fruits Press
Wilmore, Kentucky
c2016

First Fruits Press
The Academic Open Press of Asbury Theological Seminary
204 N. Lexington Ave., Wilmore, KY 40390
859-858-2236
first.fruits@asburyseminary.edu
asbury.to/firstfruits

THE

EARNEST CHRISTIAN:

DEVOTED TO THE PROMOTION OF

EXPERIMENTAL AND PRACTICAL PIETY.

B. T. ROBERTS, A. M., EDITOR.

Strait is the Gate, and Narrow is the Way, that leadeth unto Life.—Jesus.

VOLUME I.

BUFFALO, N. Y.
PUBLISHED BY BENJAMIN T. ROBERTS.
1860.

CLAPP, MATTHEWS & CO'S STEAM PRINTING HOUSE,
OFFICE OF THE BUFFALO MORNING EXPRESS.

INDEX.

Title	PAGE
Are you Holy? *By the Editor*	14
A Single Eye. *By Mrs. M. F. Kendall,*	84
A Solemn Thought,	234
"And Then." *Archdeacon Hare,*	238
Alone at the Judgment. *Dr. Cumming,*	243
Art thou Christ's? *Baxter,*	244
Are you Safe? *Krummacher,*	268
A Bitter but Healthful Morsel. *By Rev. Wm. Arnot,*	269
An Awful Warning,	271
A Beautiful Thought,	275
A Place for Prayer,	302
Abounding in Faith. *Rev. F. D. Huntingdon,*	306
A Hint to Mothers. "*Golden Rule,*"	342
A Worthy Confessor,	344
A Wonderful Mission,	346
Are you Saved? *By M. N. Downing,*	351
Amazing Grace,	372
A Witness for Jesus,	374
Be Thorouh, but be in Haste. *By Rev. J. W. Redfield,*	11
Be in Earnest. *By Rev. A. A. Phelps,*	45
Backsliding in Old Age. *By the Editor,*	181
Backwoods Preachers,	184
Bluebeard—An Allegory for Children,	221
Burning and Shining. *By Rev. A. A. Phelps,*	240
Baptism of the Holy Ghost and of Fire. *Judd,*	244
Bigotry. *By Thomas Quinton Stowe,*	281
Be Definite. *By Alexander,*	302
Backsliders. *By Finney,*	347
Costly Attire. *By Dr. Judson,*	52
Consecration. *By President Edwards,*	87
Courage. *By Flavel,*	88
Compromising. *By the Editor,*	151
Church, a Pure. *By Olin,*	157
Consecration, Personal. *By J. Wesley,*	157
Christian Simplicity. *By Upham,*	187
Christian Comfort. *By Lavington,*	242
Censoriousness. *By Rev. A. A. Phelps,*	245
China,	254
Confirmation of Scripture,	299
Called to Preach. *By the Editor,*	318
Closing with Christ. *By Cumming,*	362
Dancing. *By Adam Clarke,*	207
Divine Guidance. *By Whately,*	276
Difficulties,	276
Dead Worship. *By Berridge,*	281
Deeds. *By Carlyle,*	286
Difference between Sanctification and Regeneration. *By Rev. W. Cooley,*	293
Decision of Mrs. Fletcher,	306
Discouragement. *By the Editor,*	316
Drinking Poison,	344
Dispute with the Devil,	356
Do Duty. *By Dr. Annesley,*	356
Defective Religion. *Howe,*	373
Drunken Women,	377
Energy,	159
Experience of Mrs. Minerva Cooley,	173
Evil Company,	214
Education. *By Coleridge,*	239
Evil Whisperings. *By John Wesley,*	243
Enthusiasm. *By Dr. Jenkyn,*	276
Experience of Frances D. Byrns,	277
Eternity,	354
Experience of Mrs. Eunice Cobb,	379
Formal Ministers. *By Archbishop Leighton,*	85
Faith. *By Cecil,*	148
Fullness of Joy. *By Mrs. B. M. Gilley,*	155
Fanaticism. *By Fletcher,*	178
Free Churches. *By the Editor,*	
Essential to Reach the Masses,	6
Needed to Save the Rich,	37
Required to Prevent Religious Aristocracy,	39
Required by Apostolic Precepts,	40
Free Churches. *By the Editor,*	
Can be Sustained,	69
Required by the Saviour's teaching,	71
Required by the Dedication Service,	72
Rewards Promised to those who Build and Sustain them,	73
Freshness of the Bible,	234
Faith. *By Berridge,*	281
Fate of the Apostles,	332
Formalism,	355
Fault Finding,	376
Godly Letter of John Bradford,	147
Gospel Preacher, Melancthon's Portrait of a	183
God's Presence. *By Olin,*	206
Growth in Grace. *By Doddridge,*	271
High Profession. *By M. N. Downing,*	145
Holy Life, Rules for a. *By Archbishop Leighton,*	159
Healing Slightly. *By Whitfield,*	172
Holy Ghost, Substitutes for the. *By Rev. A. A. Phelps,*	178
How Far is it to Canaan,	189
Hints to Preachers,	215
Heaven a Home,	223
Hypocrisy. *By Flavel,*	254
He that Winneth Souls is wise. *By Rev. James Mathews,*	300
Humility,	301
I'll Rest when I get Home,	234
"Irrepressible Conflict," The. *Rev. J. A. Wells,*	248
"It is Written,"	305
Industry in Ministers. *By Dr. Murray,*	350
James Brainerd Taylor. *By the Editor,*	229
Justification, The Bible View of. *By Rev. W. Cooley,*	234
Letter from England. *By W.C. and P. Palmer. C. A. and J.*	84
Literary Notices.	
Slavery in the M. E. Church. *By E. Bowen, D. D.*—Shouting, Genuine and Spurious. *By G. W. Henry,*	86
Life of Mrs Fanny L. Bartlett. *By Rev. A. A. Phelps,*	160
Look and Live. *By S. K. J. Chesbrough,*	58
Laurence Saunders, the Martyr. *By Fox,*	144
Light of the Spirit, The. Central Idea,	209
Lean on Jesus,	276
Loss of the Soul. *By Edward Irving,*	381
Moral Individuality. *By Rev. L. Stiles, Jr.,*	17
Millenium, The. *By Bishop Hamline,*	21
Making Fun,	94
Moral Miracles,	149
Meekness,	207
Methodist Meeting in 1775. *By Rev. T. Rankin,*	208
Messages of Dying Saints,	218
Mysteries. *By Archbishop Whately,*	276
No Alternative. *By M. H. Freeland,*	213
No Repentance—No Peace. *By J. C. Ryle,*	239
No Middle Course in Religion,	242
No Compliments in Prayer,	243
Nobody Saved. *By Rev. A. A. Phelps,*	303
Now!	356
Object and Scope of this Magazine. *By the Editor,*	5
Order and Confusion. *By Rev. W. Cooley,*	81
Outside and Inside. *By Flavel,*	242
Obedience the Price of Freedom. *By S. K. J. Chesbrough,*	247
One in Jesus. *By Mrs. M. F. Kendall,*	266
One Brick Wrong,	284
Origin of the Free Methodist Church,	360
Opinions of Eminent Men Respecting the Bible,	371
Persecuted but not Forsaken. *By the Editor,*	15
Preaching Perfection. On *By Rev. W. C. Kendall,*	46
Purity and Peace. *By Rev. W. Cooley,*	42

INDEX.

	PAGE.
Prejudice. *By Larke,*	61
Prayer, Answer to,	156
Preaching Holiness. *By Bishop George,*	158
Persecution. *Ryle,*	158
Pride. *Edwards,*	172
Preaching. *By Rev. Napoleon Russell,*	180
Preacher's Defects,	190
Preaching in Another's Parish. *Asbury,*	208
Preparation for Death,	212
Pitcairn's Island,	219
Paternal Duty,	233
Partiality. *Milward,*	246
Presumption. *By J. G. Terrill,*	265
Power of the Holy Ghost. *Arthur,*	274
Paul's Estimate of Heaven. *By Hannah Moore,*	347
Pic-Nic Religion,	358
Poetry.	
Would you be Young Again,	20
Rest in Heaven. *By H. T. Lyte,*	30
Let me Stay. *By M. N. Halsey,*	41
Forget me Not. *By P. C. Lavant,*	75
I Hold Still,	95
Watching for Morning,	137
The Bank of Heaven,	137
The Crown of Thorns. *Translated from the German,*	207
Always Rejoicing,	217
Mildly Judge ye of Each Other,	233
The Pass of Death,	239
The Awakening. *By J. G. Clark,*	251
Trusting in Jesus. *By Alfred Sully,*	268
Beauties of the World to Come,	296
Come to Jesus,	301
God Known by Loving Him. *By Madame Guyon,*	315
Think Gently of the Erring,	319
The Joy of the Cross. *By Madame Guyon,*	341
Preaching,	367
Please your Husband,	370
Prayer. *By Rev. John B. Graham,*	375
Quarterly Meeting of Olden Time. *Bang's Hist. M. E. C.*	31
Redemption. *Rev. J. W. Redfield,*	26
Regrets too Late,	49
Reproving Ministers. *Baxter,*	49
Repentance. *By the Editor,*	76
Religious Experience of D. W. Tinkham,	79
Righteousness. *By the Editor,*	101
Rules for a Holy Life *Archbishop Leighton,*	159
Religious Sensibility. *By the Editor,*	165
Religious Sensibility. *By the Editor,*	197
Rules for Moral Warfare. *By Rev. T. L. Cuyler,*	241
Reflections. *By Rev. James Mathews,*	345
Rev. John Winnebrenner. *By the Editor,*	358
Reading *Fenelon,*	376
Revivals. *By the Editor,*	32
A Village Converted,	33
True Ministers promote them,	62
Arthur's Tracts for Revivals,	64
Awful Gardner's Story of Himself,	66
Revival in the Church,	95
Lay Preaching,	96
Convention at Olean,	97
The Country Ripe for a Revival,	129
Matters of Experience,	160
The Revival in England,	162
Moral Enthusiasm,	168
Dedication at Albion,	224
General Conference of the M. E. Church,	226
Appeal Cases,	226
Immuring a Woman for being Converted,	227
The Revival in Ireland,	191
The Revival in Ireland,	228
Revival in France,	193
Tidings from an Old Pilgrim,	193
To Our Friends,	193
Persecution,	194
Dying Grace,	195
Does Christ Dwell Here,	196
Bergen Camp Meeting,	255
St. Charles Camp Meeting,	255
Letter from Dr. Bowen,	256
Free Methodist Church in Buffalo,	258
Notice for Convention at Pekin,	259
Western Convention,	260

	PAGE.
Our Selections,	260
Pekin Camp Meeting,	287
Church Festivals,	288
Convention at Pekin,	291
Rushford Camp Meeting,	320
Aurora Camp Meeting,	320
A Brave Boy,	323
Dedication of the Second Free Methodist Church, Buffalo,	363
Spiritual Manifestations,	13
Scene in the Late Episcopal General Convention,	18
Salvation and Pew-renting. *By J. A. Latta,*	19
Supernatural in Christianity, The. *Arthur,*	20
Saving Faith. *Judson,*	20
Self-Deception, Ministers in Danger of. *Hedding,*	25
Shouting among Scotch Seceders. *Gaddis,*	28
Spirit of Jesus in the Church. *By Rev. J. A. Wells,*	47
Scriptural Conviction. *By Mrs. M. H. Freeland,*	50
Self-Deception. *By Mrs. Emeline Smith,*	89
Satan in White. *Christmas Evans,*	93
Salvation from Sin. *By the Editor,*	133
Spiritual Freedom. *By M. A. H.*	136
Sin. *Edwards,*	144
Self-Examination. *Jay,*	148
Singing in Church,	177
Satan's Arts. *Upham,*	181
Sectarian Strife. *Rev. S. Colley,*	209
Small Sins. *By D. C.*	210
Scraps from Dr. Redfield,	237
Sensible Prayer. *By a Boy,*	242
Secret Religion, *Cecil,*	244
Seed to the Sower,	251
Self-Examination. *By Flavel,*	254
Sanctification not Identical with Regeneration. *By E. Bowen, D. D.*	261
Scope of Miracles,	270
Strive to enter in at the Strait Gate. *By J. Wesley,*	273
Stand to your Post. *By M. N. Downing,*	285
Spiritual Liberty. *Upham,*	309
St. Patrick no Romanist,	315
Sanctification Experienced. *By Rev. Wm. Cooley*	325
Some one must Pray,	341
Strong Believers,	370
Secret Prayer,	374
The kind of Preaching we need. *By Mrs. E. L. Roberts,*	59
The Divine Promises. *By Rev. C. D. Burlingham,*	86
The Spirits Power. *Rev. W. Arthur,*	92
The Wedge of Gold,	211
The Mysteries of the Fall. *Spurgeon,*	216
Trials. *Flavel,*	217
The Sword of the Spirit. *Simeon,*	238
The Cause *By M. H. Freeland,*	252
The Boy Martyr,	282
The Boy Preacher of Louisiana,	283
Temptation. *Bunyan,*	284
The True Wisdom. *Dr. Guthrie,*	298
The Land of Ruins,	304
True and False Humility,	313
True Radicalism,	316
The Roman Sentinel,	318
Turned out, are you? "*Golden Rule,*"	319
The Quarter-Dollar Sin,	373
The World. *Mason's Remains,*	376
Village Converted. *A.*	33
Work of the Spirit *President Edwards,*	20
Where are we drifting? *By an old Methodist,*	30
Worldly Society. *Payson,*	57
William Clowes. *By the Editor,*	188
Who are the children of God? *By Nelson C. Lyon,*	171
With Christ *By Rev. Wm. Hart,*	182
Who should Preach. *Dr. Wayland,*	188
Worldly Amusements,	220
Wesley's Journal, extract from	246
Woman's Influence. *By Miss L. C. Clement,*	272
Worship. *By the Editor,*	343
Which will you have?	348
Warning. *Bunyan,*	357
Worldliness. *Cheever,*	362
Wesleyan Methodism,	383

THE EARNEST CHRISTIAN.

VOL. I. JANUARY, 1860. NO. 1.

OBJECT AND SCOPE OF THIS MAGAZINE.

BY THE EDITOR.

THERE are many sincere and earnest persons throughout the land, anxiously inquiring "for the old paths." Dissatisfied with being outer-court worshippers, they are desirous of "dwelling in the secret place of the MOST HIGH."

Upon their minds God often lets the light from Heaven shine. They see that repentance is something more than a vague conviction that the past life has not been entirely right. Conversion as they, illuminated by the SPIRIT, view it, is a work far more radical than is implied in simply a "change of purpose." At times they are tremblingly alive to the fact, that a religion of fashion and parade, of pomp and show, and circumstance, cannot save their souls. The Holy Ghost presses home the truth that Christ's disciples are characterized by self denial, humility, and love.

It is for this increasing class of persons that we write—for those who are IN EARNEST to gain Heaven, and anxious to know the conditions upon which eternal happiness can be secured.

EXPERIMENTAL RELIGION, as the foundation and life of practical piety, as well as the indispensable condition of final salvation, will be explained, illustrated, and enforced in all its stages, from the first awakening of the sinner to his conversion, his deliverance from sin, his crucifixion to the world, and his baptism with the Holy Ghost, *till he is filled with all the fulness of God.*

We shall insist upon a *conversion* that makes a man willingly part with his sins—that makes the proud humble, the churl liberal, the selfish generous, the slaveholder anxious "to break every burden and to let the oppressed go free;" that changes the rumseller into an industrious and useful citizen, that transforms the dishonest and unjust, into the righteous and upright.

The doctrine of Christian Holiness, as taught by Wesley and Fletcher, being, as we conceive, plainly enforced in the Word of God, and constituting the real strength and power for good of the Church of Christ, will occupy a prominent place in our columns.

The claims of the neglected poor, the class to which Christ and the Apostles belonged, the class for whose special benefit the Gospel was designed, to all the ordinances of Christianity, will be advocated with all the candor and ability we can command. In order that the masses, who have a peculiar claim to the Gospel of Christ may be reached, the necessity of plain Churches, with the seats free, of plainness of dress, of spirituality and simplicity in worship, will, we trust, be set forth with convincing arguments. We shall endeavor to keep free from controversey, and to avoid all offensive personalities. We hope never to infringe upon the sacred right of private judgment. Should it ever be necessary to correct any misrepresentations that may be made, we promise our friends that it shall be done with all possible mildness, and in the spirit of candor and love.

In short our object is to publish a revival journal; our aim shall be to set up the Bible standard of religion. We hope by our catholic spirit, by an uncompromising advocacy of "righteousness, peace and joy in the Holy Spirit," to make our magazine a favorite and welcome visitor to every family where pure religion and morality are inculcated.

And now we ask you, Christian friends of every name, to aid us in our undertaking. This you can do by praying for us. Our enterprise has been commenced after much pleading for Divine direction, with the hope of being able to contribute somewhat to the promotion of the cause of Christ. To succeed we must have the help of the HOLY SPIRIT. Be importunate, then, in your supplications for us, that we may be governed by *the wisdom that cometh from above.*

We need subscribers. The expense of publishing such a magazine is necessarily considerable. From all parts of the country we have received encouraging promises of support. Let us have, in the outset, a large list of subscribers. We are satisfied that it can be easily secured. Will you assist in doing it? Please show this number to persons of your acquaintance, induce them to subscribe; and send on their names and Post Office address without delay.

FREE CHURCHES.

BY THE EDITOR.

Mankind need nothing so much, as the universal prevalence of the Christian religion, in its purity. This would allay the evils under which humanity is groaning, by removing their cause. It would bring Paradise back to earth. For the blessings of the Gospel of Christ there is no substitute. He who enjoys them, in their fulness, has all he needs to make him happy. In their absence, man is "wretched, and miserable, and poor, and blind, and naked."

Things, trifling in themselves, become important when they affect the accomplishment of some great, beneficent enterprise. A glass of wine overthrew the Orleans dynasty, resulted in the horrors of civil war, and deluged France with the best blood of her children. A passing cloud suggested to Franklin the theory of electricity, and led to the transmission of messages upon the swift wing of the trained lightning. A small file may render worthless the heaviest piece of artillery, and decide the battle on which the fate of nations is suspended.

The question of free churches derives its importance from its influence upon the purity and the progress of Christianity. It has a greater bearing upon both, than many imagine. The world will never become converted to Christ, so long as the Churches are conducted upon the exclusive system. It has always been contrary to the economy of the Methodist church, to build houses of worship with pews to sell or rent. But the spirit of the world has encroached upon us by little, and little, until in many parts of the United States, not a single free church can be found in any of the cities or larger villages. The pew system generally obtains among all denominations. We are thoroughly convinced that this system is wrong in principle, and bad in its tendency. It is a corruption of Christianity. This we propose to show. We claim the indulgence of expressing ourself strongly. We cannot adopt the cautious language of doubt, for we have no misgivings. We do not believe merely that there should be free churches, but that *all* churches should be free. Not merely that some unmarketable seats should not be rented or sold, but that no seat in the House of God should be rented or sold. Respected readers, we ask your candid attention to the arguments that may be presented in these pages. Weigh them well. You may have given your countenance to the pew system, as many have, simply because you found it in practice. If you have thought upon the question at all, you may have regarded it merely as one of expediency. We hope to show that the pew system is both inexpedient and wrong. We design to prove that our houses of worship should be, like the grace we preach, and the air we breathe, free to all.

Free Churches are essential to reach the masses.

The wealth of the world is in the hands of a few. In every country the poor abound. The most prudent are liable to misfortunes. Sickness may consume the earnings of the industrious. Death may take from the helpless wife, and dependent children, the heart that loved, and the hand that filled the house with plenty. Man is depraved. Sin has diffused itself every where, often causing poverty and suffering.

God assured his ancient people, favored above all others with precautions against want, that "the poor shall never cease out of the land." These are the ones upon whom the ills of life fall with crushing weight. Extortion wrings from them their scanty pittance. The law may endeavor to protect them; but they are without the means to obtain redress at her courts. If famine visits the land, she comes unbidden to their table, and remains their guest until they are consumed.

The provisions of the gospel are for all. The "glad tidings" must be proclaimed to every individual of the human race. God sends the TRUE LIGHT to illuminate and melt every heart. It visits the palace and the dungeon, saluting the king and the captive. The good news falls soothingly upon the ear of the victim of slavery, and tells him of a happy land, beyond the grave, where the crack of the driver's whip, and the baying of blood-hounds are never heard. The master is assured, that though he be a sinner above all other sinners, yet even he, by doing works meet for repentance, may be forgiven, and gain heaven. To civilized and savage, bond and free, black and white, the ignorant and the learned, is freely offered the great salvation.

But for whose benefit are special efforts to be put forth?

Who must be *particularly* cared for? Jesus settles this question. He leaves no room for cavil. When John sent to know who he was, Christ charged the messengers to return and show John the things which they had seen and heard. "The blind receive their sight, and the lame walk, the lepers are cleansed, and the deaf hear, the dead are raised up," and as if all this would be insufficient to satisfy John of the validity of his claims, he adds, "AND THE POOR HAVE THE GOSPEL PREACHED TO THEM. This was the crowning proof that He was the ONE THAT SHOULD COME. It does not appear that after this John ever had any doubts of the Messiahship of Christ. He that thus cared for the poor must be from God.

In this respect the Church must follow in the footsteps of Jesus. She must see to it, that the gospel is preached to the poor. With them, peculiar pains must be taken. The message of the minister must be adapted to their wants and condition. The greatest trophies of saving grace must be sought among them. This was the view taken by the first heralds of the cross. Paul wrote to the Corinthians, "for ye see your calling, brethren, how that not many wise men after the flesh, not many mighty, not many noble, are called. But God hath chosen the foolish things of the world to confound the wise; and God hath chosen the weak things of the world to confound the things which are mighty; and base things of the world, and things which are despised, hath God chosen, yea, and things which are not, to bring to naught things that are: that no flesh should glory in his presence."

Similar statements in regard to the rich are not to be found in the Bible. On the contrary, the Apostle James asks the brethren, "do not rich men oppress you, and draw you before the judgment seats? Do not they blaspheme that worthy name by which ye are called?" He also refers to it, as an undeniable fact, that the poor are elected to special privileges under the gospel dispensation. "Hearken my beloved brethren, hath not God chosen the poor of this world rich in faith, and heirs of the kingdom which He hath promised to them that love him?"

Thus the duty of preaching the gospel to the poor is enjoined, by the plainest precepts and examples. This is the standing proof of the Divine mission of the Church. In her regard for the poor, Christianity asserts her superiority to all systems of human origin. The pride of man regards most the mere accidents of humanity; but God passes by these, and looks at that which is alone essential and imperishable. In his sight, position, power, and wealth, are the merest trifles. They do not add to the value or dignity of the possessor. God has magnified man by making him free and immortal. Like a good father, he provides for all his family, but in a special manner for the largest number, and the most destitute. He takes the most pains with those that by others are most neglected.

Hence, as that great, good man, Dr. Olin, says: "The Gospel is preached to the poor—to the masses. It is made for them—it suits them. Is it not for the rich, for the cultivated, the intellectual? Not as such. They must become as the poor, as little children, as fools. They must come down to the common platform. They must be saved just like so many plowmen, or common day laborers. They must feel themselves sinners, must repent, trust in Christ, like beggars, like publicans. Sometimes we hear men prate about preaching that may do for common people, while it is good for nothing for the refined, and the educated. This is a damning heresy. It is a ruinous delusion. All breathe the same air. All are of one blood. All die. There is precisely one gospel for all; and that is the gospel that the poor have preached to them. The poor are the favored ones. They are not called up. The great are called down. They may dress, and feed, and ride, and live in ways of their own choosing; but as to getting to heaven, there is only God's way, the way of the poor. They may fare sumptuously every day, but there is only one sort of manna.

That *is* the gospel which is effectually preached to the poor, and which converts the people. The result shows it. It has demonstration in its fruits. A great many things held, and preached, may be above the common mind—intricate—requiring logic and grasp of intellect to embrace them. They may be true, important, but they are not the gospel, not its vital, central truths. Take them away, and the gospel will remain. Add them and you do not help the gospel. That is preached to the poor. Common people can understand it. This is a good test. All the rest is, at least, not essential.

There are hot controversies about the true Church. What constitutes it, what is essential to it, what vitiates it? These may be important questions, but there are more important ones. It may be that there cannot be a Church without a bishop, or that there can. There can be none without a gospel, and a gospel for the poor. Does a church preach the gospel to the poor—preach it effectively? Does it convert and sanctify the people? Are its preaching, its forms, its doctrines, adapted *specially* to these results? If not, we need not take the trouble of asking any more questions about it. It has missed the main matter. It does not do what

Jesus did, what the Apostles did. Is there a church, a ministry, that converts, reforms, sanctifies the people? Do the poor really learn to love Christ? Do they live purely, and die happy? I hope that Church conforms to the New Testament in its government and forms, as far as may be. I trust it has nothing anti-republican, or schismatic, or disorderly in its fundamental principles and policy. I wish its ministers may be men of the best training, and eloquent. I hope they worship in goodly temples, and all that; but I cannot think or talk gravely about these matters on the Sabbath. They preach a saving gospel to the poor, and that is enough. It is an Apostolic church. Christ is the corner stone. The main thing is secured, thank God."

If the gospel is to be preached to the poor, then it follows, as a necessary consequence, that all the arrangements for preaching the gospel, should be so made as to secure this object. There must not be a mere incidental provision for having the poor hear the gospel; this is the main thing to be looked after.

There is a feeling of independence in man that prompts him not to go where he fears he shall be regarded as an intruder. This is especially true of our American people. They will not accept as a gratuity, what others claim as a right. Their poverty does not lessen their self-respect. Let them be treated at a social visit as objects of charity, rather than equals, and they will not be very likely to repeat it. Hence, houses of worship should be, not like the first class car on a European railway, for the exclusive, but like the streets we walk, free for all. Their portals should be opened as wide for the common laborer, or the indigent widow, as for the assuming, or the wealthy. All who behave themselves in a becoming manner, should feel at perfect liberty to attend on all occasions of public worship.

The requirement of the gospel is not met by setting apart a certain number of free seats, for those who are too poor, or too indifferent to rent or purchase. As Bishop Morris says: "We know it is the custom in many pewed chapels, to leave certain seats free for the accommodation of such as cannot buy or rent, but it seems to answer almost no purpose, except to give offence. Who is willing, thus publicly, to advertise his poverty or misfortune, his want of ability, or inclination to afford himself a place in the church, by taking the 'poor seats?' Such humility is not to be expected in those who need the instruction of the gospel most. Besides, to require it, is not only uncharitable and unwise, but unscriptural."

If it be said that seats would be freely given to those who are unable to pay for them, we answer, this does not meet the case. But few are willing, so long as they are able to appear at church, to be publicly treated as paupers. Neither is it true, as is sometimes assumed, that those who are too poor, too indifferent to religion, to pay for a seat in the House of God, would not be likely to be benefited by its ordinances. Had not such persons been reached, the conquests of the gospel would have been limited indeed. Christianity would have died out long ago. The greatest number of her adherents, and the ablest champions that ever stood up in her defense, were once of this class.

The pew system, wherever it prevails, not only keeps the masses from attending church, but alienates them, in a great degree, from Christianity itself. They look upon it as an institution for the genteel, and the fashionable; and upon Christians as a proud and exclusive class. "When I came to this city," said a respectable mechanic, "I was a member of a Christian church. I rented a seat, and attended worship regularly. But I found that I could not hire a seat, and attend church at an expense of less than fifty dollars a year, without having my family looked down upon with contempt. This expense I could not afford; so we do not any longer attend religious meetings." His experience is that of multitudes. Many who, on going to the cities, are favorably inclined to religion, finding themselves virtually excluded from the churches, become at first indifferent, and then ready to drink in any error that comes along. Hence the ease with which the advocates of Millerism, and Spiritualism have found hearers and converts.

Perhaps no part of our country has greater religious advantages, than New England. In some portions laws formerly existed, requiring, under penalty, attendance upon church. A habit of church-going was formed. The influence of the immigration of foreigners is less there than in any other section of the Union. There the pew system was first introduced. There it almost universally prevails. What is the result? Says the Report on Home Missions, presented to the Massachusetts General Association, 1858: "From reliable statistics it appears, that in Maine, New Hampshire, Vermont, and Massachusetts, not more than one quarter of the population are in the habit of attending church. There are one million, three hundred thousand people in New England, who, so far as attending church is concerned, are practically like the heathen."

Says the Rev. Edward Stuart, a clergyman in London, "The pew system, which has introduced so unchristian a distinction in the House of God, between the sittings of the rich and the poor, is (there can be little doubt) doing more to alienate the hearts of tens of thousands in every large town in England from the Church of CHRIST, than any other thing that could be named." He tells us that the large churches in London are filled almost exclusively with the rich, and adds, "In some cases it is all but impossible for a poor man to find a place in the House of CHRIST—of CHRIST, who himself, lived all his life amongst the poor." The editor of the *English Guardian*, remarks that the system of pews "has eaten, and is eating, the very life out of the church."

Take a city nearer home. Says the Buffalo *Christian Advocate:* "We have in Buffalo, about forty Protestant churches. These reach, and influence, more or less, about twenty thousand of our eighty thousand people. This leaves sixty thousand either unprovided for, or to Catholic influence. It may be safe to calculate that forty thousand of our inhabitants attend no place of worship whatever."

Friends of Jesus, we call upon you to take this matter into serious consideration. The Gospel is committed to your trust. Your business is to save souls—first your own, then the souls of others. You are to dig for rough diamonds amid the ruins of fallen humanity, and polish them up for jewels in the crown of your Redeemer. The church edifice is your workshop. Do not, we beseech you, convert it into a show room, to display, not the graces of Christians, but the vain fashions of the world.

Politicians teach us an important lesson. How do they reach the masses? The places for their public gatherings, often rough and uncomfortable, are always free. The rich and poor associate as equals. What party could long survive, should they build splendid temples for the propagation of their principles, and then sell, at a high rate, the right to the occupancy of their seats? It is no feeble proof of the Divine origin of Christianity, that it has been able to survive a practice so absurd. But it can never spread with the rapidity with which we are authorized —from its sublime doctrines affecting man's highest interests for time and for eternity, from the beneficent influence it ever exerts upon society, and from the gracious efficacious assistance which God has promised to those who labor, as He directs, for its promotion—to expect it should, until all its houses of worship are free.

SLOTHFULNESS in the service of God is as damning as open rebellion.—PRES. EDWARDS.

BE THOROUGH, BUT BE IN HASTE.

BY REV. J. W. REDFIELD.

In taking a view of the work to be done by the Church for the world, the vast interests involved, the very narrow limit to the time within which it must be done; the very few to whom *God* and the Church can look to as helpers in this mighty enterprise involving the world's redemption, I feel to ask, and with an emphasis that would stir the bones of the dead, *Who, who* will act; *act now;* act with a purpose to succeed at any cost? Enter the list with *God* and *Jesus* and the *Holy Ghost,* for the accomplishment of this grand object—a world's redemption?

THE WORK TO BE DONE.

We have upon our globe eight hundred and fifty millions of deathless souls to be saved—souls once bearing the image of the great *Father*, but now in ruins, and yet capable of a re-creation and an elevation above angels. "We shall judge angels." Imagination grows dizzy in the attempt to penetrate the vast future of an interminable life; a life bounded only in its duration by the coming years of God. And every one of this great throng is now, while I write, passing away to *Heaven* or to *Hell.* The average of human life has been variously estimated at from twenty-five to forty-three years; but to silence all cavil, we may say, that this vast congregation will be dead in fifty years. Eight hundred and fifty millions added to the list of mortality! Eight hundred and fifty millions more of dead men, women and children putrifying in the grave! And eight hundred and fifty millions of souls begin a destiny of joy or sorrow, never—no never —to be changed in its character, however high the good may rise, or however low the bad may sink. Their fate is sealed, and sealed forever. Is the Bible true? How overwhelming the contemplation of their fate, would we realize the length and breadth, nay, the immensity of interests involved! Then measure, if we can, the value that any one soul must put upon its individual concern—foot up every hope of heaven, every item of value in the world to come—now dashed to atoms, and forever; then look at every foreboding of the lost roused by the rehearsal of the fate of rich *Dives;* and, all realized, what a sense of loss, when first sent utterly out of sight of every token of *God's* approval; of crowns, thrones and mansions! What elements of anguish in the uncounted items of torture, with no relief but in the change of one sorrow for another; and, to drive each sting deeper, to know it is forever. No turn, no change, no hope, no mitigation forever! If but one soul should ever be thus lost, and the universe of intelligent beings were convened to make a demonstration worthy of so sad a fate, what wails could give vent to becoming sorrow! What badges of mourning could image forth the solemn story! What awful shrieks could jar to discord the dead march of one soul's obsequies! What length of funeral train would shadow forth by any or every token of agony the magnitude of such a tragedy! Now multiply this unspoken suffering eight hundred and fifty millions of times, and we have the sum of interest involved in only half a century.

The soul sickens at the thought. Imagination staggers under the burden. We utterly faint at the sight and seek relief by ceasing to think.

Not to admit this tale of sorrow as possible, is to assume that we can grasp the utmost of what it is to be lost—is to deny the plain declaration of the Bible.

Eight hundred and fifty millions of souls will be lost or saved within fifty years.

God's way of saving the world is by the instrumentality of the Church.

Let us now compare the number of the army to be conquered and the army to conquer, if we may use a military figure. At least eight hundred millions are arrayed against *God*. Now the army to meet this great host is as Gideon's only. We have, probably, about eight millions of evangelical Christians, for we must leave out the Roman and Greek Churches. It is probably safe to say, that not more than six millions, though orthodox in creed, believe in any change of heart. It is not harsh judgment to suppose that three millions of the six, have only the form of godliness, and are more concerned to maintain church order and popularity, than to get sinners converted to Christ; and all these are worse than enemies out of the church. But alas, we must more than decimate again! Reduced to three millions, full two millions of these have no sense of responsibility, and no courage to act for God, only when and where a trifling victory in a narrow limit has rendered Jesus temporally popular. They shout Hosanna to-day, and to-morrow cry out *Crucify Him! Crucify Him!* Of the remaining one million, will one half, ministers or members, "shut the doors of God's house for naught?" Position, salary, and church order sway them effectually, and bring them to a dead halt—or more frequently to an open or secret opposition to the few whose fidelity to God, and whose fruits are eclipsing them before the world. See them watching for a flaw in a devoted brother, ready to fire their heaviest artillery at the faithful worker, when they will not discharge a single arrow at the real enemies of God. How willingly they allow to pass uncontradicted, any slander which may be hurled against the little band who are doing almost all that is effectually done for the true church of Christ. Pamper and flatter these men, and they will work, as doth the hireling, for position, popularity and money; but will they go alone, like an apostle, use their own means, make tents for living, if need be, carry the Gospel amid opposition and perils uncounted, even amid false brethren? Will they not effectually, though secretly, try to reduce the true laborers for God to their own level, when the cost of coming up to the true position is too expensive?

I ask, have we more than half a million who have religion enough? Who have so much of the spirit of Jesus as to go amid scorn, and face the very light persecution which the law permits? To go unpaid, if need be, go without even the meed of flattery, go against wind and tide, make every energy bend, bring every force of their being to work, work for the redemption of a lost world—weep, pray, fast, and exhort everybody, and everywhere it is consistent, and have no reward but in heaven and in seeing souls won to Christ?

Ministers may live of the gospel if they can, but nothing more. And what if they cannot? shall souls perish? shall Christ's interests be disregarded? Who will go, if need be, without fee or reward—without even the poor man-conferred title of D. D.? Go, too, with only idea, *Christ Crucified;* meet the hostile army of more than eight hundred and forty-nine millions, amid *abuses, slanders, persecutions*, and get nothing for it till they pass away to hear the "Well done, good and faithful servant?"

How many can be found in America who are actually doing this work, and enduring rebuffs?

Shall we call this an overdrawn picture of facts, or of the obligation now pressing upon the churches with all the solemn weight of eternal interests?

Is it above, or beyond the labors of the primitive disciples? And do not the wants of the present generation appeal for relief from the church, with equal clamor, in this noon of the nineteenth century.

Do not ten, nay one hundred, die without hope, and unwept by the church in our nation, where one only is soundly converted to God?

Should God call for another army of martyrs, (the seed of the church,) to win a victory for primitive piety, to burn willingly at the stake, to give emphasis to their mission, *where* could be found enough to form the first platoon?

How pertinent then is our motto, "BE THOROUGH BUT BE IN HASTE."

"SPIRITUAL MANIFESTATIONS."

A FEW WORDS RESPECTING ALLEGED "EVILS" CONNECTED WITH CERTAIN MEETINGS.

It is assumed, that "screaming," "leaping," "falling," and such like exercises, in religious meetings, are not the result of a divine influence, but are proofs of "fanaticism;" and therefore, disgraceful to the church, and offensive to God.

It is also assumed, that the alleged "evils" are *general*—the prominent traits—in such meetings. But this is a mistake. The "reports" of such meetings are usually exaggerated, or caricatured; the "evils" occuring only to a very limited extent, not sufficient to give character to the meetings.

The "evils," so called, when the real truth respecting them is known, are found, generally, to be only such as have usually been connected with the work of God. In the process of salvation, in the extending the cause of Christ, the *divine* and the *human* are combined; and though it is desirable that the compound should be very largely divine, and but slightly human, yet facts prove that in all cases where there is a deep, thorough work of the Divine Spirit, there will be more or less of the distinctly human manifestations. And we should no more decry the whole work as "fanatical," or something worse, because of such results, than we would ascribe the distinctly human, in spiritual exercises, to the Divine Being; though the agony of the Divine Spirit in the heart and among the people, is the occasion of such human manifestations. Hence, what are usually denominated "evils," in this connection, are not "evils;" but considering the weakness, and infirmities, and prejudices, and depravity of human nature, these "evils," so called, are the *certain*, and may I not say, the *necessary* accompaniments of the mighty operations of the Divine Spirit, in renovating our moral nature, that we "might be filled with all the fulness of God?" In all religious meetings that continue for several hours or days, where there is a deep work of the Holy Spirit on the hearts of the people, the manifestations of the human spirit, under the influence of the divine, will necessarily take their coloring from those constitutional, or other peculiarities, with which they are connected, as evinced by moderate liveliness, or deep solemnity, or excessive weeping, or extreme joyousness; the occasional extravagance and excess of such manifestations being as natural and necessary as the spray and foam of the deep, mighty, majestic Niagara.

It is quite possible that some of these manifestations are of *merely* human prompting; and some the result, in part, of habit, and therefore, to a certain extent, voluntary; but then, such like manifestations are the ordinary accompaniments of the deep and thorough searchings of the Divine Spirit. It is assumed that the leaders, in such meetings, labor to produce said manifestations, in all their variety, and then argue to defend them as the marked proofs of genuine and desirable spiritual results. No, brethren, you mistake the character of such labors. Those men labor, as gospel instrumentalities, to advance the cause of Christ; and when the blessing of God attends their work, and candid persons who are willing, or cavilers who desire to find an "occasion," urge objections to the work, or its results, because some things are not in harmony with their models of propriety; then these men, as in duty bound, argue to defend the general work, as the work of God, notwithstanding the occasional extravagances and excesses, so called, that usually accompany the process of salvation.

That such meetings are not fanatical, but in harmony with our church usages, from the beginning, is evinced by an incident at Hartland Corners, in 1818, as given by Rev. Dr. Paddock, in a recent article in the *N. C. Advocate*, under the heading, "Ridgeway Circuit."

The Doctor says: "Supper was now announced, and all were invited to 'set by.' When the meal was ended, the preacher (that is, himself,) drew back from the table, and, perhaps forgetting that he had sung it before, sang the same verse again. Ere it was concluded, however, a lady screamed out in unutterable agony, and falling to the floor, called upon the preacher to pray for her. He was soon on his knees, and all the company with him, each one crying for mercy. The whole scene was not only unique, but quite indescribable. But the struggle was brief, for in the course of some twenty or thirty minutes, all was calm again; when one after another arose and said, 'The Lord has spoken peace to my soul!' All were saved, and all were soon after formed into a class."

Dec. 8, 1859.   D.

ARE YOU HOLY?

BY THE EDITOR.

Do not evade the question. Press it home upon your conscience. Ponder it, weigh it, consider it, revolve it. Keep it in your mind until an honest and correct conclusion is reached.

You readily admit that there would be reason for uneasiness were you justly in doubt as to whether or not you were converted. *The obligation to be converted is no stronger than the obligation to be holy.* Both rest on the same foundation—THE COMMAND OF GOD. This is no less explicit in the one case than in the other.

Why should we be born of the Spirit? The ready answer is, Jesus says, *Ye must be born again.* Why OUGHT we to be holy? The same Divine Teacher declares, *This is the will of God, even your sanctification.* Is the one essential to salvation? The infallible Guide which says, "*except* ye be converted and become as little children, ye can in no case enter into the kingdom of heaven," says also, WITHOUT HOLINESS, NO MAN SHALL SEE THE LORD. If you are indifferent as to your personal sanctity, you have reason to doubt the genuineness of your conversion. *Truly regenerated souls aspire after holiness.* Even where the system of theology in which they have been educated denies its attainableness, they still long for it as something desirable. With the pious Watts they exclaim.

"Could we but climb where Moses stood,
   And view the landscape o'er,
Not Jordan's stream nor death's cold flood
   Could fright us from the shore."

This is the longing of a converted soul. "*Could we but climb,*' how gladly would we do it. Were we satisfied that it is within the reach of possibility, we would make a desperate effort." Well, earnest Christian, you may ascend, even here, to Pisgah's summit. You may dwell in the land of Beulah, where the sun always shines. *Holiness is possible.* Consider. Would you impose upon your tender child of ten years age, a load which would require the utmost strength of a full grown man to carry? Would you require your son, so far recovered from a protracted sickness, as to be able to sit up an hour at a time, to do a day's work that none but an able-bodied man could accomplish? "If ye then being evil" would not require impossibilities, how much less would "your Father in Heaven?" God commands us BE YE HOLY. Pharaoh may demand the full tale of brick without furnishing material, but God never imposes a duty without providing every needed help for its fulfilment.

Were we obliged to obtain a holy heart by our own efforts, we might despair. If we were "to grow up" into holiness by habits of obedience, discouragement might take place. BUT A HOLY HEART IS AS MUCH THE WORK OF GOD AS IS CONVERSION. The WORD says, IF WE CONFESS OUR SINS, HE IS FAITHFUL AND JUST to forgive us our sins, and TO CLEANSE US FROM ALL UNRIGHTEOUSNESS. Who forgives sins? God only. Who cleanses from ALL unrighteousness? *The same* ALMIGHTY BEING. None, then, need despair. Do not limit the

Holy One of Israel. If you meet the conditions, God will make even you holy. If holiness be God's work, try ever so long and earnestly, and you cannot grow up into it. Ask him now *to sprinkle clean water upon you, and ye shall be clean, to put his Spirit* within you, and cause you to walk in his statutes.

As Dr. Adam Clark says: "In no part of the scriptures are we directed to seek holiness *gradatim*, (that is, *step by step, gradually*). We are to come to God as well for an instantaneous and complete purification from all sins, as for an instantaneous pardon. Neither the *seriatim* pardon nor the *gradatim* purification exists in the Bible. It is when the soul is purified from all sin that it can properly grow in grace, and in the knowledge of our Lord Jesus Christ. As the field may be expected to produce a good crop, and all the seed vegetate, when the thorns, thistles, briars, and noxious weeds of every kind are grubbed out of it."

Come to God, then, in faith to make you holy; and soon, exulting, you shall sing—

Rejoicing now in earnest hope,
I stand, and from the mountain top
See all the land below.

PERSECUTED, BUT NOT FORSAKEN.

BY THE EDITOR.

THE minutes of the Genesee Conference for 1859, contain the following record: "Who have been expelled? L. Stiles, Jr., J. A. Wells, W. Cooley, C. D. Burlingham."

These brethren are, all of them, able, zealous, faithful laborers for the spread of earnest Christianity. They are also honest anti-slavery men, opposed to the continuance of slaveholders in the church. This accounts for their expulsion. Timid, compromising men never reach the honors of martyrdom.

Rev. L. STILES, the first upon the list, has for eleven years faithfully discharged the duties of a minister of Jesus Christ. As a preacher, he is fearless, pointed, clear and eloquent. The editor of the *Northern Independent*, himself a preacher of no ordinary grade, said of Mr. Stiles after hearing him at the Auburn Camp Meeting: "He takes rank with the first pulpit orators of the age." Living near to God, with an honest, upright purpose to do his will, incapable of being bought with favors or of being intimidated by proscription, Mr. Stiles has been highly favored with the Divine approbation upon his labors. His charges have always prospered under his administration. We have been assured, from reliable sources, that the Pearl Street Church in Buffalo has never flourished so highly as under his labors. He filled with great acceptability the office of Presiding Elder of Genesee District, one year. We doubt if a Presiding Elder in that time ever intrenched himself more firmly in the affections of the people. They were urgent for his return. But some thirty preachers conspired together not to take work unless he was removed from the cabinet. His success in promoting earnest Christianity was too great for endurance. The plot succeeded. He was stationed at Union Chapel, Cincinnati. At the close of the year he was transferred back at the solicitation of the people and a large number of the preachers to the Genesee Conference. He well knew he was exposing himself to danger, but he felt it his duty to stand by the oppressed children of God. He is in labors more abundant, preaching since his expulsion with still greater power than ever.

Rev. J. A. WELLS has been seven years a successful laborer in the Genesee Conference. He is a good preacher, studious in his habits, entirely devoted to the service of God, a man of honest intention and straight forward integrity. We strongly suspect that what caused him to be selected as a victim of proscription, was the wonderful success which attended the Laymen's Camp Meeting held in the bounds of his charge, with his approval.

He is now laboring at Brockport, and

in the vicinity, for the salvation of souls. He feels that God has called him to this work, and who shall forbid him?

Rev. WM. COOLEY has been for seventeen years a diligent, faithful and acceptable preacher in the Genesee Conference. He is a quiet, peaceable and unoffending man. This may be said of all the expelled ministers. We doubt if there is one of them that has an enemy in the world save those that were made such by their fidelity of God and the souls of man. Mr. Cooley is more than an ordinary preacher. His sermons are clear, scriptural and searching. He always makes the impression that he is thoroughly in earnest. He professes, lives as we believe, and preaches full salvation. He labors at present in Niagara county.

Rev. C. D. BURLINGHAM has, for nineteen years, devoted his energies to the service of the Methodist Church, as a traveling preacher in the Genesee Conference. He has labored much beyond his physical ability. With a broken down constitution, a large and dependent family, he is thrown out of a work to which he has given the best years of his life, and to which he was ardently attached. He is a superior preacher, original in his thoughts, happy in his illustrations, never failing to secure the unwearied attention of his audience. For four years he filled, to the satisfaction of his preachers and people, the office of Presiding Elder of the Olean District. All the departments of his work were carefully looked after, and the District was never in so flourishing a condition as when he left it. He was a delegate to the last General Conference.

Mr. Burlingham has decided not to preach till after the next session of the General Conference. His object is to prevent the existence of any excuse for rejecting his appeal. His continuing to preach *not by virtue of any authority from the M. E. Church*, but BY VIRTUE OF HIS CALL FROM GOD, could not prejudice his appeal before any impartial tribunal. It is probable that a partisan spirit will prevail in the General Conference to some extent. But we have no doubt but that among its members will be found many honest and upright men, who, whatever their party predilections, will be disposed to "judge righteous judgment," and it should be assumed that the body will be composed mainly of such.

A preacher of talent in the Presbyterian Church was a few years since deposed from the ministry, as he conceived, unjustly. He joined the Methodists, and continued to preach. Lately the Presbyterians became convinced that they had done him an injustice, and in the true spirit of Christians, they reinstated him as a minister, though at the *same time he was holding a license in another church!*

This was undoubtedly right. If a man called of God to preach, has the license which he received from man taken from him wrongfully, the responsibility of the irregularity of his subsequent course, while he discharges his duty to God, rests, not upon himself, but upon those who have done him the wrong. It would have been treason to God for Luther to have desisted from preaching when excommunicated by the church to which he belonged.

In the second Conference held by Wesley it was asked: "Is not the will of our governors a law?" The answer was emphatic, "No; not of any governor, temporal or spiritual. Therefore if any bishop wills that I should not preach the Gospel, his will is no law to me. But what if he produce a law against your preaching? *I am to obey God rather than man.*"*

Yet any other person called and commissioned of God to preach, has the same authority for discharging his duty as Luther and Wesley had for executing the work intrusted to them.

We think, then, Mr. Burlingham errs in remaining silent when God has not silenced him. If men lived to the age of Methuselah, if sinners were not dying all around us, and going to perdition, we might better afford to lose

* Stevens' History of Methodism, vol. i, p. 312.

a year or two at the dictation of a party.

May HE who "suffered without the gate" be with these brethren beloved, who have gone "without the camp bearing his reproach," comfort their hearts, make them exceeding joyful in all their tribulations and abundantly bless their labors.

MORAL INDIVIDUALITY.

BY REV. L. STILES, JR.

Moral individuality stands in striking contrast with a decided tendency of the age to amalgamation of mind, and an ignoring and relinquishing in moral actions, of personal responsibilities.

Thousands seem to have no positive opinions of their own, because they shun the responsibility incidental to the avowal of a definite belief. They constitute others the trustees and guardians of their opinions, from a conscious inability to support their own feeble bantlings of thought. Such are mere society automatons, burdens to themselves, victims of knaves, pitied by the good, and despised by the bad. If they avow an opinion, it is with the understanding, that with *your consent* they *believe* thus and thus. Cowper has well daguerreotyped this opinionless being, in the following lines:

> "He would not with a clear decided tone,
> Assert the nose upon his face, his own;
> With hesitation admirably slow,
> He humbly hopes, presumes it may be so;
> Knows what he knows as if he knew it not,
> What he remembers, seems to have forgot;
> His sole opinion whatsoe'er befall,
> Centering at last in having none at all."

Now this negation of humanity is of the least possible consequence in the sum total of responsible existence. The demand of the age is for men of action, and nerve, and moral perpendicularity. The cry of the necessity of the age is, "give us positive men, with positive characters, faith, opinions and actions." Give us such men, although they may occasionally be in an error, rather than noncommittal, neutral beings, with doubtful faith, wavering opinions, undecided actions, and fluttering hearts.

Such is the present disposition to yield opinions, rather than provoke opposition, that the waters of virtue, morality, and religion, are in danger of stagnation, for want of rocks to break their quiescence. "Anything for union," is the cry of the persistent, impudent minority. "Anything for *peace*," is the echo of the yielding, impressible majority. The soul that would preserve a moral individuality, in this age of mind amalgamation, must squander no time in calculating chances of loss and gain in the path of life's activities. Duty is ours, results are God's. "Do right though the heavens fall." Fear not, God will never let the heavens fall on the path of duty. Go straight forward in the path of duty. Do not dodge though the lightnings smite you. "Sanctified by lightning," I believe is an old Latin proverb, for those who suffer in virtue's cause. Be not too anxious to tread a beaten path. Inquire not what is the "vox populi," but listen to the voice of duty. In the path of duty, you may often meet with the fiercest blasts of adverse elements. Murky clouds may drift above you, and darken your sky, but blessings will be shaken from those very clouds that are rifted by the storm that beats upon you, and you may shout a harvest home of good deeds, that a cloudless sky might never have shed upon you. Duty and real interest are never antagonistic. They are wedlocked by the unalterable fiat of Heaven. The path of duty should be chosen as men *used* to take their wives, "for richer or for poorer, for better or for worse." Such a union is very likely to be a happy one. What cheering and noble examples do we find in the history of God's people, of moral individuality! Job, forsaken by every friend, exclaiming, "Though He slay me, yet will I trust in him." Joshua saying, "As for me and my house, *we will* serve the Lord." The three worthies hurling defiance in the face of regal power, and saying to the king, "We are not careful to answer thee in this matter. Be it known unto thee, O king, that we will not serve thy gods." Paul declaring his purpose "To know nothing among men, but Jesus Christ, and him crucified," and Luther avowing his determination to go to Worms, "although they should build a fire that might reach from Wittenburg to Worms, and flame up to heaven." All these are examples of moral individuality that put to blush the moral cowardice and fawning, favor majority seeking, of the present age. Let us heed well the voice of the Master, "Thou shalt not follow the multitude to do evil." God never made a slave, moral or physical. This is all man's work. Soul freedom is man's inalienable birthright. He who sells this for a mess of pottage of popular, political, or ecclesiastical favor, barters that away which robs him of his manhood, if not his hope of heaven.

A SCENE
IN THE LATE EPISCOPAL GENERAL CONVENTION.

We have alluded to the great feeling manifested at different times in our late Convention. The question was as to the sending forth of missionary Bishops, and after different speakers had occupied the floor, Dr. Creighton, the president, put the question. But as a writer of the Mobile Tribune has so graphically described the scene, we let him speak:

Dr. Creighton rose in his place and called for the expression of the House in the usual way. "Those who are in favor, &c., will say aye."

"*Aye!*" rolled through the vast church in one deep, strong voice, as the voice of one man!

"Contrary minded," said the President. Unbroken silence all over the House was the only response.

It was not yet the hour of adjournment by half an hour. All debate on lesser subjects that would have followed seemed out of place after such a triumph of right feeling in the right direction. Rev. Dr. Stephens, under the influence of this reflection, rose amid the silence and said:

"Such an extraordinary occasion as this ought not to pass without some expression of gratitude to the great Head of the Church for this unity of the House on so momentous a question. Let us all rise my brethren, and chant the Te Deum, and at once adjourn!"

"Not the Te Deum, but the *Gloria in Excelsis!*" cried an earnest voice.

"Let some one of the Delegates raise it!" said another, with emotion in his tones.

The Rev. Dr. Talbot, of Indiana, then rose with the mighty "Gloria" on his lips, and two hundred and fifty voices joined in and swelled the sublime chant.

"Glory be to God on high, on earth peace, good will towards men! We praise thee, we bless thee, we worship thee, we give thanks to thee," &c., &c.

After the first few words many of the voices gradually dropped down, and faces were buried in hands and handkerchiefs; tears choked the utterance of many, and in the midst of the profoundest emotion, which no pen can describe, no tongue do justice to, the Gloria went on, now rising, now falling, now kindling with rapture, now muffled and lowered with weeping; but as one after another subdued his emotions, and joined in again, the sacred song rose louder and louder, with woman's trembling treble intermingled, until at length with the full anthem of all the voices, rich and tremulous, every one of them with tears, this grand chant, sung as it was never sung before on earth, ended. Every eye was shining with tears, yet beaming with serene joy! It seemed as if the Holy Spirit had descended, upon his Church, as aforetime in the day of Pentecost, moving all hearts as one heart towards each other and to God.

"The Benediction from the chair!" cried some one.

The President had stood all the while deeply moved, his handkerchief in his hand, while the tears coursed down his cheeks. He said, (as soon as he could command himself sufficiently to trust his voice,) "Let us pray."

The whole Delegation fell upon their knees, and the President offered up the beautiful and appropriate prayer, the last in the Institution Office, which seemed as if written for this very scene and hour. The Benediction was then pronounced with pathos most touching, and for a long time the House remained upon its knees in silent, solemn thanksgiving.

The members then rose calmly, every eyelid wet, and retired with the gravity of eternity impressed upon their countenances, as if they had seen God face to face. Such, faintly, was the scene which I have felt myself incompetent to describe so as to convey any just outline of the reality, and so as fully to impress you with its extraordinary character.

The Bishops in the other House, hearing the singing, were filled with surprise, and several came in to see what was passing, and stood in the church looking on with wonder, not knowing what had gone before.

This day will never be forgotten in the Church.—*Christian Witness.*

SALVATION AND PEW RENTING.

[WE publish the following with pleasure. We shall be glad to insert any incidents with which our correspondents may furnish us, illustrating the uncompromising devotion of Methodist preachers in other years to the work of saving souls.—*Ed.*]

DEAR BRO. ROBERTS: I have before me a Prospectus for a new Monthly, "THE EARNEST CHRISTIAN." I like the name, not for its newness, but for Earnest Christianity is no new thing. There have been Earnest Christians in the M. E. Church in by-gone days, as the following incident, which I give from memory, after the lapse of about thirty years, will prove.

When the Rev. G. F——e was stationed at the first M. E. Church in Rochester, a great revival occurred under his labors. The whole city was moved, and hundreds were converted. A new and large church edifice was built. When the time came for renting the pews, the revival still continuing, the trustees came to the preacher, just before the opening of the services one Sabbath evening, and desired him to give notice that the pews would be rented on a certain day of that week. "And," said they, in a confidential manner, "as we are deeply in debt, and need all the assistance we can get, we hope you will have as little noise and excitement this evening, as possible; so that some respectable persons who feel favorably disposed towards us may not be deterred from taking seats." The minister gave no direct reply, but went into the pulpit, and, as was his wont, preached a powerful and moving discourse. At the close of the sermon, those who were willing to seek salvation were invited forward, and the altar was surrounded with weeping penitents. After the penitents had come to the altar, Brother F. arose and repeated what the Trustees had said to him—and then said, "Now, brethren, what shall we do? We have a good basement, and, if we should go down into it, and invite these penitents to go, some that feel the need of religion most would go; others would leave the house, and lose their convictions, and perhaps their souls. The Trustees want the money, and these souls want salvation. I tell you what we will do. All you that can pray come in and about the altar, and we will have a camp meeting time, and all pray. If the friends rent pews afterwards, they will do so with their eyes open. And if we make a noise at any time, they cannot say we deceived them."

This exhortation, given with the unction of the Holy Spirit, was nobly responded to by the members who crowded the altar. We had a camp meeting time, and many souls were saved. J. A. LATTA.

THE SUPERNATURAL IN CHRISTIANITY.—Instead of seeking to keep down spiritual movements to the level of natural explanations, in an age when natural marvels reach almost to miracles, we ought rather to be impelled to pray that they may put on a more striking character of supernatural manifestation. To-day, more, by far, is necessary to carry into the mind of the multitude a clear conviction, "It is the hand of God," than was necessary in other ages. When men saw few wonders from natural science, they readily ascribed each wonder to Divine agency; but now that they are accustomed to see them daily, moral wonders must swell beyond all pretext of natural explanations, before they are felt to be from God. Is our footing firm? Do we stand, or do we tremble? Is Christianity to seat herself in the circle of natural agency, or to arise from the dust, and prove that there is a God in Israel? Are we to shrink from things extraordinary? Are we to be afraid of anything that would make skeptical or prayerless men mock? Are we to desire that the Spirit shall use us and work in us to just such a degree as will never bring a sneer upon us—to pray, as a continental writer represents some as *meaning*, "Give us of the Holy Spirit, but not too much, lest the people should say that we are full of new wine."—REV. WM. ARTHUR.—*Tongue of Fire, page* 203.

SAVING FAITH.—Let us depend upon it, that nothing but real faith in Christ proved to be genuine by a holy life, can support us at last. That faith which consists merely in a correct belief of the doctrines of grace, and prompts to no self denial—that faith which allows us to spend all our days in serving self, content with merely refraining from outward sins, and attending to the ordinary duties of religion—is no faith at all.

O, it is a solemn thing to die—an awful thing to go into eternity, and discover that we have been deceiving ourselves.—DR. JUDSON.

WOULD YOU BE YOUNG AGAIN?

Composed by Carolina, Baroness Nairn, in 1742, in her 76th year.

Would you be young again?
  So would not I—
One tear to memory given,
  Onward I'd hie.
Life's dark flood forded o'er,
All but at rest on shore,
Say, would you plunge once more,
  With home so nigh?

If you might, would you now
  Retrace your way?
Wander through stormy wilds,
  Faint and astray?
Night's gloomy watches fled,
Morning all beaming red,
Hope's smiles around us shed,—
  Heavenward—away!

Where, then, are those dear ones,
  Our joy and delight!
Dear and more dear, though now
  Hidden from sight?
Where they rejoice to be,
There is the land for me;
Fly time, fly speedily—
  Come, life and light!

WORK OF THE SPIRIT.—To rejoice that the work of God is carried on calmly, without much ado, is in effect to rejoice that it is carried on with less power, or that there is not so much of the influence of God's Spirit; for though the degree of the influence of the Spirit of God, on *particular persons*, is by no means to be judged of by the degree of external appearances, because of the different constitutions, tempers and circumstances of men; yet if there be a very powerful influence of the Spirit of God on a mixed multitude, it will cause some way or other, a great visible commotion.—PRESIDENT EDWARDS.

WE cannot vex the Devil more than by teaching, preaching, singing and talking of Jesus.—LUTHER.

THE MILLENIUM.

BY BISHOP HAMLINE.

[THE following article copied from the third volume of the *Ladies' Repository*, is so appropriate to the conflict at present going on in the Church between spirituality and formalism, that we conclude to give it entire to our readers. To most of them it will be new, and those who have read it will be glad to give it another perusal.—*Ed*.]

THE word millenium, signifies a thousand years. In theology it denotes a coming period, of the universal spread and prevalence of holiness. As to its manner, there are two differing opinions. The first is, that Christ will reign personally on the earth, and that the martyrs and eminent Christians will rise from the dead, and share in his terrestrial reign. Others argue that Christ will not appear in person, but will come by the power of the Holy Spirit, and that the resurrection of the martyred saints denotes only the restoration of their holy, self-denying tempers to the hearts of Christians.

The former opinion has been embraced by thousands of learned and pious men. Justin Martyr, who wrote in the second century, earnestly supports it. He claims that in his day it was the commonly received opinion. In modern times, Dr. Gill, Bishop Newton, Mr. Kett, and others of equal eminence, adopted this view of the subject. Recently, some of the most respectable divines in Europe and America have become converts to the same faith. It is said that in England, such men as Baptiste Noel and Bickersteth are its firm adherents. The opinion is gaining advocates amongst learned American divines.

If we are correctly informed, Mr. Wolff, the converted Jew, now a presbyter of the Church of England, and a sincere and zealous minister of Christ, has extensively propagated this view of the millenium in the English Church. To him, more than to any other, may its present currency be traced. It is said that he deems this view of the prophecies important in regard to the conversion of the Jews.

Some of the ablest living expositors of Scripture in the west agree with this opinion. A few openly advocate it. Whether it gains or loses ground amongst the clergy, we cannot say. Our clerical acquaintances hold for the most part, that the millenium will be a period of unexampled religious prosperity, in which Christ will have spiritual dominion from sea to sea, and from the rivers to the ends of the earth. This is our own opinion, and for the following reasons.

1. The prophecies which relate to Christ's millenial reign are highly figurative in their style. This is the case with the Book of Revelation. To interpret the fourth verse of the twentieth chapter as simply implying a restoration of the *spirit* of the martyrs to the Church, seems to us a warrantable license, taking into view the *genius of the Apocalypse*. Should we insist on the literal sense of this text, why not also on the passages which describe the binding of Satan with a great chain, or the flight of the woman into the wilderness.

2. The personal reign of Jesus on earth is hardly consistent with some portions of Scripture, especially those texts which speak of his second advent. "And it is appointed unto men once to die, but after this the *judgment;* so Christ was once offered to bear the sins of many; and unto them that look for him shall he appear the *second time* without sin unto salvation." Here the judgment and the "second coming" are connected, in a way that precludes the millenial advent.

3. The passage in Revelation xx, 4, speaks not of the bodies, but of the *souls* of the martyrs. "I saw the *souls* of them that were beheaded for the witness of Jesus, and for the word of God; and they lived and reigned with Christ a thousand years." How natural to interpret this as denoting the restoration to the Church, in her millenial

state, of the purity and zeal which glowed in the hearts of her ancient confessors. As Elijah was restored to the world in the person of John the Baptist, of whom the Saviour said, "Elias hath already come;" so the ancient witnesses will return in the persons of many holy ministers, who shall not count their lives dear unto them, if they may but minister as becomes the Gospel, and finish their course with joy. Happy Church, and blessed period, when a martyr's spirit shall glow in every pious bosom! And "the time is at hand." There are signs which none need mistake, of the near approach of the Saviour's universal dominion. He shall soon " take to himself his great power, and reign King of nations, as he is King of saints."

As to the commencement of this happy period, we have little to say concerning it. It is near at hand. Of this there can be no doubt. How near— whether at the door, or one, twenty-five, or one hundred and fifty-eight years distant, can be of little consequence. Too much may have been written already on this point. It is important to believe firmly that it is near; but what practical benefit could result from knowing the day or the year?

It seems to us unadvised to draw the attention of the Church to what may properly be called curious and unlearned questions. And have we not done it in regard to the millenium? Its exact period, its mode of commencing, its implications as it regards the personal coming of Christ, are of no great practical moment, or they would have been revealed so clearly as not to admit of *pros* and *cons*. These are unlearned questions—that is, they are unlearnable, not being set forth with certainty in the Scriptures. The fact that they are not, is a hint to man. He should let them alone, or at least touch them lightly and diffidently. Over and above mere hints, we are admonished to "avoid" them. "It is not for us to know the times and seasons which God hath put in his own power." Creatures cannot tell us the *when* of these things, nor the *how* in any precise detail. Why should we, launching on the sea of God's providence, attempt to navigate regions which the chart he has given does not cover? Let us explore where he offers pilotage and anchorage. Let us bear away from courses uninvited and unwarranted, and betake ourselves to the voyage on which he sends us. He commissions us to sail in the regions of repentance, and afterwards in the regions of faith and love. When we have circumnavigated these fields, and have no more discoveries to make or depths to sound, let us strive how many we can take in convoy over the regions we have so thoroughly explored. When we have the world in our wake, and not a craft on its surface is heading towards perdition, then—no, not even then may we launch beyond the limits of our commission! Then we will cast anchor, and wait for further orders.

Some think these things are revealed. If revealed, why so much labored argument? why so many and different opinions? If revealed, they are facts, and should be presented as clearly as the facts of history. What orthodox couplet of high or low Churchman ever debated whether there shall be a resurrection and a judgment—whether there is a heaven or a hell? These are Gospel postulates with all but infidels. So is the millenium; but not its period, nor the manner of Christ's coming to dwell among his saints; whether in person, or by the presence of the Comforter. Let us hold on to the postulate then, and make good use of it, but leave all else where God is pleased to leave it. Let us hold on to the postulates, that courage and zeal may not be wanting in the warfare whose issues involve this holy, blessed millenium.

Some other things are revealed which it deeply concerns us to ponder. We should know that perilous times are at hand. Dread darkness will go before the sunrise of the millenium. This is told us for a warning. Shall we stir curious questions, and pass admonitions by? He would be a reckless officer, who should disregard the reports of faithful spies. "An ambush," say they, "is in your van. A fearful foe lurks in the fastnesses of yonder heights, at the base of which you are leading your thronging legions." The commander hears, calls a halt, draws up his troops, and when they wait to hear a spirit-stirring appeal to their courage and ambition, and warnings to beware, their General entertains them with lively and graphic descriptions of the cities they shall conquer, and the booty they shall win. Is this the way to triumph? It is the way to disaster and defeat. Is it not our way? What, sing and shout in millenial tones, while ambuscades are thickening all around us, and shutting Zion in on every side! An army of formalists presses her on one side, and hosts of errorists on the other side. These mix and sweeten poisons to destroy her—those waft upon her the spirit of slumber. Under both, she nods and sickens. And shall we fall to and entertain her drowsy, enfeebled senses, with things sweet and savory to her palate? She wants music. Give it to her; but let it be none of your soft, cozening symphonies about a "millenium at hand." Sound an alarm in God's holy mountain. The foe! the foe! should be exclaimed by all her watchmen along the extended walls of Jerusalem. Yet she is putting off her armor, as though her enemy were finally and for ever repulsed. Repulsed! There never was an hour in fifteen centuries so full of brooding mischief to the Church, as is this very hour. Her own zeal has inspirited her foes, and her own providence has taught them. Would to God that she could profit by her own experience, as they do by her example!

One thing is certain. Ours will be a day of conflict. The Scriptures which admonish us of perilous times, are so near being fulfilled, that the event begins to interpret the prophecy. The millenium, as is generally supposed, may be near—that is, within two centuries of us. But in the meantime, there are waiting for sudden development the elements of fiercer persecutions than ever yet raged on earth. These the Church must endure, and she should be making ready for the travail.

Is this unwelcome intelligence? It ought to be most welcome. Persecutions are precursory of the millenium. "In the last days, perilous times shall come." And if perils are to herald the reign of the Messiah, shall we dread their approach? They are graves which lie between us and the augured triumphs of the cross. They are shadows which we are assured must gather around us, that out of their deepest gloom may spring, to our transport, the intense, abiding light. Shall we lament the trials, which however they involve us, are harbingers of Zion's universal conquests? No. We hail the era of persecution. If we must pass through this strait gate to the millenium, thank God that we begin to feel its pressure. Let the enemy exult upon us—let the kindling fires burst forth—let blood flow like rivers. These violences are the throes of a new birth, and shall result in the regeneration of a world.

But in the meantime, what should be the attitude of the Church? It should be *boldly offensive*. No effort should be relaxed, no emprise of charity abandoned. Otherwise, her zeal and toil should be increased a thousand-fold. She should be above past example, a praying, laboring, suffering witness for Jesus and his truth.

First, she should be a praying witness. We continually forget the power of prayer; or if not, we are indolent and worldly, and do not apply this power to help on the conquests of Zion. If you were now called upon to select the most efficient of Christ's militant followers, to whom more than to any others, Zion is indebted for her advances and her victories, where would you look for them? In the pulpit? You might mistake. Would you fix your eye on a public-spirited professor, who gives ten thousand dollars to a college, ten thousand to a theological seminary, ten thousand to the missions, and ten thousand to the Bible society? You might greatly err. I would not go to the pulpit, or to the list of charities to make this selection; but I would go to the closet. Give me access to the devotions of the closet, and power to ascertain who spends most time in secret prayer, and wrestles with most faith and fervor for God's blessing on a perishing world, and I will, with bold assurance, point out the most efficient of Christ's militant followers. The humblest subaltern in Zion's armies may be the bravest of her warring bands—her champion in God's sight, who seeth not as man seeth—who judges not from the outward or formal organization of the Church, but looketh on the heart. Probably such a champion might be found in some undistinguished mother in Israel, who for fifty years has been drawing nearer and nearer to God, and now with almost open vision, a faith clear as sight, wrestles day and night for the revival of God's work, exclaiming, O, that the salvation of Israel were come out of Zion!

And this is emphatically woman's sphere. Does she ask what she can do for Zion? I answer, pray. Pray as Abraham did for Sodom, and with more perseverance. Do this and you shall stand in the front of battle. The invincibles in Immanual's army are those who, with uplifted weapons, receive the enemy on their knees. Woe to them who make an onset in this direction. They will meet the captain of the Lord's host, and will be scattered like chaff before the wind.

And when the whole Church awakes to prayer—when each of her members thirsts after God, and weeps day and night for perishing sinners, the world will be moved. A heavenly power will descend and sway the minds of its perishing millions, and like the multitudes on the day of Pentecost, these millions will exclaim with one voice, "Men and brethren, what shall we do?"

But the Church must be a *laboring* witness for God. She must no longer busy herself about the world. She must turn her energies into another channel. Her enterprise must be directed towards the relief of the spiritual, not merely the temporal wants of our nature. She must evidence that her treasure is truly in heaven, and that her business is to accumulate riches there. She must prosecute her work of saving souls with a zeal proportionate to her avowed estimate of the value of the soul. She is, even now, a busy Church. What a bustling scene does she present to the observer! But what is she doing? Buying and selling, and getting gain—hoarding up silver and gold, and lavishing both in extravagant outlays for sumptuous dwellings and prideful display. The disciple of Jesus, with successful emulation, rivals the vainest and most profligate of the world; and from their manner and apparel, who can distinguish the Church from the world—the modest bride of Christ from the bold and flaunting harlot? O, what a stripping of herself will there be from the disguises she hath so long worn! What a putting off of pride and its coverings—what aversions from sin and its indulgences—what a dressing herself in the decent attire of a humble, laboring, blood-bought Church, whose business it is to come out from the world, and bring the world out from itself to serve the living God. The hour is at hand when prince and princess will turn exhorters in the cause of God, and the saloons of the palace will witness the birth and halleluiahs of converts to righteousness.

And why not now? Why not enter at once on the blessed avocations of piety and charity? Why not to-day commence the labors which are to bless the perishing nations with a millenium? Let the reader and the writer make two of the number who shall toil henceforth to *millenialize* the world. Let us, in this holy cause, do what our hands—our lips—find to do, with our might. We may stir up others to join us in these labors. It may expose us to some reproach; but Jesus will not frown—it may cost us sufferings; but we should remember that the Church must also become a *suffering* witness for Jesus. What will be the mode or amount of her sufferings we cannot well determine. Scorn and derision from her foes, and treachery from her friends, will greatly annoy and waste her. Her enemies have scarcely yet commenced their assaults. The Church has done little to provoke derision. She is now so like the world, that the world, which loves its own, can tolerate her with great comfort. When her example becomes reproving, and the world is frowned from her fellowships, we shall see a change. Then men will be provoked to ancient proofs of the malignant wickedness of the heart. It will then be seen that God and his Son are not less abhorred than when Noah built the ark, and Christ was " crucified and slain."

But the severest sufferings of the Church will flow from direct and cruel persecution. Let none suppose for a moment that no more trials of this sort await us. Look for sanguinary scenes. The spirit of past ages is rolling back upon us, and already we can see the swell and hear the surge. Zion has endured sharp conflicts, and has won hard-fought fields. In certain periods of her militant career, she has been bold and faithful. Sometimes she might have been addressed,

"Servant of God, well done; well hast thou fought!"

But to her it cannot be said, as to Abdiel—

"The easier conquest now remains to thee!"

Like Satan and his discomfited legions, after the first day's onset, her enemies have invented new weapons of war, and

"Not distant far, with heavy pace, the foe Approaching gross and huge,"

trains his infernal enginery, compasses the camp of the saints about, and is waiting to lay waste the beloved city. Our business should be to prepare to witness for Jesus by meek and patient suffering. The approaching conflict will call for the exercise of all the passive virtues. True, we must remit no holy enterprise. Our missions must be sustained, our revivals encouraged, our benevolent associations all cherished and multiplied a thousand fold; but while we act, we must also be ready to die for Jesus.

In conclusion, if all the Church were to assume the attitude of a *praying, laboring, suffering* witness for Jesus, we need not look far forward to the millenium. We should suddenly find ourselves making our triumphant entrance upon its opening scenes of light and joy.

MINISTERS IN DANGER OF SELF-DECEPTION.— "Examine yourselves whether ye be in the faith," is an admonition necessary for ministers as well as for people. Men are liable to be deceived with regard to their own conversion, and to satisfy themselves with a work of the imagination instead of the work of the Spirit. Let us, therefore, compare our experience with the Word of God, and satisfy ourselves that we are truly born of the Spirit.

We are in danger of being deceived in another way. Having been really born of God, we may backslide in heart, lose the Spirit we then received from Heaven, and yet retain the form, the morals, and the profession of Christianity, and still persuade ourselves that we are as pious as when we were warm in our first love! Let us look into this matter, and see whether we are, indeed, as near to Christ as when we were first made partakers of his love. We ought to be nearer; we should be growing in grace, and in the knowledge of our Lord Jesus Christ. —BISHOP HEDDING. *Address to Genesee Conference, in* 1842. *Hedding's Life, page* 575.

ADMINISTERING DISCIPLINE.— It is better to let many vicious persons go unpunished, or uncensured, when we want full evidence, than to censure one unjustly, which we may easily do if we go upon presumptions, which is sure to bring on the pastors the scandal of partiality, and of unrighteous and injurious dealing, and thereby cause all their reproofs and censures to become contemptible.—BAXTER.

REDEMPTION.

BY REV. J. W. REDFIELD.

We are compelled to indorse the doctrine that redemption must cover the entire evil resting on our race resulting from the fall. And, if we accept Christ as our second Adam, to fill the place of our first progenitor, vested with full power to repair the whole wrong, we must likewise own that doctrine in detail, and in its application to the parts of man's interests to be repaired.

To deny power, capability, or design to cover the whole, is to undeify Christ—is to reduce him to a second-rate god, and make him inadequate to meet the exigencies of the case. The term redemption means the ransom, deliverance, and restoration of a lost or captive being, to a condition equal to that which has been lost. In duration it must reach from Adam to the last man that shall die. In breadth it must cover our moral nature, and our mental faculties; embracing reason, memory, and all else pertaining to a thinking, designing, and independent, yet responsible being. In extent, it must span the tomb, and go down to the utmost limits of the wasteless ages of eternity.

We take all these positions thus far to be granted, and proceed to elaborate the points as to the time and conditions of redemption. To get a fair starting point, we must make the statement, that our progenitor Adam, by one act of disobedience, cut us loose, and set us adrift far from God, the only fountain of life; so that the only life we have, out of and from God, is due to the unspent forces used in our creation; and the result is, death will terminate our career in every sense, except that immortality which could not become extinct, because our powers, primarily given, were never placed under its control. Nor could they be; for any effort on our part to extinguish being, would but add a life-sustaining effort. Try, for example, to cease thinking, and you will only increase power and concentration of thought. The question now is, how can we get back to the life-giving and life-perpetuating fountain? The chasm that separates us, in our fallen condition, from Deity, is too broad for mortal to cross; our Babel towers are too insignificant to enable us to climb to Heaven. Nor could we bear the approach, for "God is a consuming fire." Nor could God endure us, but must spurn us from his presence. For aught we can see, God had but one possible way to put us in connection with the fountain; and that was to open the communication by means of His Son, whose right hand of Divinity could be laid on the only true God, and then attach to that a pure, unpolluted humanity, that might touch us and impart to us the quickening principle, from the life-giving fountain. If Christ, then, is to be our Adam, our Redeemer, he must not simply heal, but resuscitate. He takes not Adam's children to mend them, but to make them over, and we become the children of God, being the children of the resurrection. It follows, that if Christ undertakes our cure, only after death has done its work, that each and every part must first suffer death before we are proper subjects of resurrection or redemption. What more natural then, than that Christ should begin to redeem where our ruin began? The beginning, then, is with us, as trangressors, and we must first die to active sin, before we can be brought to spiritual life.

The conditions of this are—that we stop sinning, repent of sin, pray to conquer—deliberately take the cross, the instrument of death, (ceasing to sin does not kill us nor bring us to life,) and confess to the world our want of Christ, and thus a final blow is given to our reasoning, our vain philosophy, and our plans of saving ourselves. We are now dead to active sin, and to the opinions of the enemies of God. The last act of faith in Christ touches the crucified human nature, and instantly life is imparted, guilt is gone, and we are redeemed from the pangs of condemnation, and adopted into the family of God.

But is this all that was lost through Adam, and restored through Christ? I answer, this is not the death caused by Adam. We have thus far spoken only of redemption from the death due to known transgressions. The tendencies of our natures to evil, for which we feel no condemnation, and which we inherited from Adam, still lie masked; and they will struggle for ascendency. They naturally incline us away from God. Our next work then, is to secure the restoration of the image of God. And here again the death pangs must precede the resurrection of our moral natures. We need only try our remodeling energies in forcing good fruits, hoping to discipline ourselves into harmony with God, to find out that something above the human must be brought to bear, if we succeed. What then more appropriate than that we begin, item by item, to starve the wrong tendencies and affections to death; to take them in their order, and make of them all a burnt offering before the Lord? Whatever we have on earth, which causes us to swerve from hearty love and obedience to God, give up, crucify. Resolve to die, rather than furnish a single supply for one passion that diverts from God. And now reach out the shriveled hand of faith and lay hold of Jesus, and we are so restored in our moral tendencies, that we feel that God's will and our wills harmonize. But who will say that a change in our affections, and moral tendencies, back to harmony with God, completes the full restoration to what was lost in the fall? We must have had senses capable of appreciating spiritual things. These have been closed. But the Gospel on the day of Pentecost, developed capacities rather than created them. But as the death blow must precede the restoration, the sufferings preceding the restoration are usually the burdens borne in doing the duties devolving upon us.

We may look in this direction for the reasons why even the state of holiness ceases to supply the wants of the soul fully, so that those in that state lose the freshness of the joys of full salvation. Our nature is ever on the stretch for progress, and how natural that each acquisition should cease to satisfy, when well understood and enjoyed. Each acquisition increases the longing for more. An innate presentiment possesses all minds, that onward and upward is our interminable course. Who does not feel, that to make a limit, however distant in the world to come, to the possible progress of the soul, cripples our energies and depresses our aspirations? Intellect must be redeemed, and then the things of God are open to our comprehension. So must the body first pass to dust before it can be resurrected. The earth, too, shall be consumed, and then shall redemption bring back from its ashes a new world, and Christ shall see of the travail of his soul and be satisfied.

TARRY AT JERUSALEM.—Dr. P. said to me a few hours after receiving the fullness of salvation, "Mr. Wesley says that one sanctified person is equal to ten conversions, as it will result in that." So I have found, that in due proportion to the extent and depth of the work of holiness in the church, has the extent and permanency of the work of conversion been among sinners.—REDFIELD.

I FIND it impossible to avoid offending guilty men; for there is no way of avoiding it but by our silence or their patience; and silent we cannot be, because of God's commands; and patient they cannot be, because of their guilt and partiality.—BAXTER.

WHEN God contemplates some great work he begins it by the hand of some poor weak human creature, to whom he afterwards gives aid, so that the enemies who seek to obstruct it are overcome.—LUTHER.

NOTHING we do for God, in the cause of humanity is lost, either to the cause or to ourselves.—BISHOP OF CALCUTTA.

SHOUTING AMONG SCOTCH SECEDERS.

MAXWELL P. GADDIS, in his Footprints of an Itinerant, gives an interesting account of the conversion of his mother, who was, at the time, a staunch member of the old Scotch Seceders' Church. Her son John had been converted at a Methodist Camp Meeting, and thus, in the estimation of the parents, brought disgrace upon the family. The mother positively forbade his going again among the Methodists. She said "she felt it to be her duty, as a parent, if possible, to restrain him from bringing any additional obloquy upon the family. She would *compel* him to obey her commands at all hazards." That evening a Methodist meeting was held at a neighbor's, and missing John, she concluded he had gone, contrary to her injunction. She resolved to follow, and to compel him to return. She left the house in a great rage, breathing out terrible threatenings against the Methodists, and all who attended their meetings. Passing the barn she heard the voice of her son John praying. She stood and listened, and was at once powerfully convicted by the Spirit of God. She was seized with trembling, her whole frame shook, and her strength left her in a moment. She had to take hold of the logs of the old barn to keep from falling to the earth. With difficulty she reached the house, and retired to rest.

"My father," continues Mr. Gaddis, "had fallen into a deep sleep. However, the agony of my mother soon became so great that she "cried out in the night watches upon her bed." This aroused my father, and spread alarm through all that part of the house. Father sprang out on the floor, lighted a candle, and cried out, "Mary! Mary! do tell me what is the matter with you!" My mother made him no reply, but with her hands clasped upon her breast, with streaming eyes, continued, in the in the most plaintive manner, to plead with God for Christ's sake to have mercy upon her soul. My father was alarmed and bewildered. He ran into the other part of the dwelling and awoke my brother John, and said, "Come! O, come quickly into my room; your mother has an attack of the 'hysterics!' Come, get up and go for the doctor, I fear she will die soon, unless she gets relief."

John arose and concluded to go and see his mother before he started for the physician. On entering her bedroom he soon discovered that she had no need of medical assistance. Christ, the physician of the sin-sick soul, was all she wanted now. As soon as mother discovered my brother, she entreated his forgiveness, and asked him to get down and pray to God to forgive her also, and change her nature, too. My brother instantly fell upon his knees and cried to God to set her soul at liberty. Oh! it was a time of deep anguish. The conflict lasted several hours. She continued to cry, "Lord help me." At last the Comforter came, and said to the weeping Mary, "Daughter, be of good cheer, thy sins which are many, are all forgiven thee; go in peace, and sin no more." It was in that hour,

Her tongue broke forth in unknown strains,
And sang redeeming love.

My mother shouted aloud for joy, and my brother rejoiced with her. The balance of the night was nearly all spent in prayer and praise. My father, who had been an eye witness of all that passed, said the only thing that comforted him at the time, was the reflection, that it had all occurred in the night—the neighbors would not know it, and the family would be saved from disgrace. I have often heard him state he thought they were both partially deranged, and would be restored to their senses by the light of the morning. This, however, was a delusive hope. The following morning father assembled the family as usual for worship. He read a psalm, and then sung it, and kneeled down to pray; but soon after he commenced, mother began to praise God, in an audible voice. This was a breach of decorum that my father could not endure. He ceased praying at once, rose up from his knees, and left the house. He did not return again till called in to breakfast. This was of frequent occurrence during the week.

On the following Sabbath the family, as usual, went to their own church. The services were unusually solemn, on that day. The Sacrament of the Lord's Supper was administered. The sermon was well adapted to the occasion, and long before its close my mother was very happy. She shouted aloud for joy. The consternation of both minister and people was very great, as mother continued to "bless God in the Sanctuary." At last the minister was overwhelmed with confusion, and took his seat in the pulpit; a part of the congregation fled from their seats toward the door, with great fear and trembling; the services were speedily brought to a close, and as the congregation returned home, they said one to another, "We have seen strange things to-day." Among all of them that retired from the house that day, none were so deeply chagrined as my father. Mother was now considered partially deranged, and, if not restored, would soon be a fit subject for the Insane Asylum.

In the mean time, the news had spread throughout the neighborhood, like fire in dry stubble, that the good old-fashioned, psalm-singing Seceders had caught the *Methodist fire*, and were actually engaged in shouting in the public congregation. This strange news brought together a large congregation to see and hear for themselves. Our family repaired to their own place of worship as usual. The services were commenced, and conducted in the usual manner about half way through, when, on a sudden, the Spirit of God filled the heart of my mother, and she broke out in joyful strains of "halleluiah to God" for what he had done for her soul. The congregation was thrown into great confusion, and the minister remarked that he would sit down for a while, and as soon as quiet was restored, he would try to proceed with his discourse. The ecstacy of my mother was very great, and it was some time before she ceased to praise the God of her salvation. The excitement in the audience was indescribable; all present seemed to be overwhelmed with a sense of the majesty and power of God. I have often heard my father remark that, at that time he would cheerfully have given all he possessed to be free from the odium thus brought upon the family and upon his own church by these strange religious exercises of my mother.

The third Sabbath arrived, and a greater crowd assembled at the church to see for themselves. The minister had not preached long before my mother commenced praising God in an audible manner. The minister was sorely displeased, and cried out at the top of his voice, ORDER! Order! Order! But mother heeded not the words, but continued to praise the Lord with a loud and clear voice. Her pastor, finding that she disregarded his commands, called upon the elders of the church, in the most imperative manner, to go and remove her from the pew. But alas for the poor elders! although they loved their minister, not one of them even arose from their places to attempt to execute his orders. Their courage was not equal to the task; they seemed to act as though they were much more safe to keep at a respectful distance. Mother continued to shout till the whole congregation was melted to tears. After she had desisted, the minister arose and dismissed the congregation, which retired hastily, in the greatest possible confusion; some crying, others scoffing.

Things had now come to a crisis. The minister was very angry. In the early part of that week mother received a written notification to "attend trial" before the "session," to answer the charge of "disorderly conduct in the house of God;" specification, for *shouting three successive Sabbaths*. When the period for the trial arrived, both my parents repaired to the church. The session reported that after "mature deliberation, we have concluded not to examine Mrs. Gaddis upon the charge preferred against her, or to inquire any further at present into the peculiar nature of her religious exercises. We also have unshaken confidence in her piety and integrity, and do not wish to throw any obstacles in her way. We will not even pass an OFFICIAL CENSURE upon her late conduct at church."

Soon after, Mrs. Gaddis joined the Methodist Episcopal Church, in which shouting was in order, and she was not long after followed by almost all of her family.

REST IN HEAVEN.

BY H. T. LYTE.

My rest is in Heaven, my home is not here,
Then why should I murmur at trials severe?
Be hushed, my sad spirit, the worst that can come,
But shortens thy journey, and hastens thee home.

It is not for me to be seeking my bliss,
Or building my hopes in a region like this;
I look for a city that hands have not piled,
I pant for a country by sin undefiled.

No scrip for my journey, no staff in my hand,
A pilgrim and stranger, I press for that land;
My way may be rough, but it cannot be long,
So I'll smooth it with hope, and I'll cheer it with song.

The thorn and the thistle around me may grow;
I would not lie down upon roses below;
I ask not my portion, I seek not my rest,
'Till I find them forever, eternally bless'd.

Afflictions may damp me, they cannot destroy,
One glimpse of his love turns them all into joy;
And the bitterest tears if he smile but on them,
Like dew in the sunshine, turn diamond or gem.

Let troubles and dangers my progress oppose,
They'll only make Heaven more sweet at the close;
Come joy, or come sorrow, whate'er may befall,
One moment in glory will make up for all.

We grieve the Holy Spirit by little sins, and thus lose our only support.— DR. JUDSON.

WHERE ARE WE DRIFTING?

BY AN OLD METHODIST.

Every worldly fashion has its day. So have religious fashions; by which we mean the phases which meet the casual observer, and give him the first abiding impression of the nature, quality, and design of religion. Once our church, as a whole, made the impression everywhere, that we ministers and members believed the Bible, and believing it, saw the world lying in the wicked one, and having only to die to be lost. With the love of Christ in our souls we could no more trifle with religion, joke or jest with sinners, than we could trifle with the poor convict on his way to the gallows.

The Bible was true to us, for we believed it. Religion was a reality, and we knew it. Our work was before us, and our plans to accomplish our work, (the salvation of sinners,) were natural, and suggested by the difficulties to be overcome, and the noble end to be gained.

Knowing the corrupt tendencies of the heart, we did not dare to pander to a corrupt taste by remodeling the severe demands of the law, and converting half-way outward obedience into a conventional rule, by which to make an honorable distinction between gentlemen and lady professors, from the unmannerly and uncouth poor. Our churches were plain and a free seat for everybody. Every man felt, if a stranger even, "there is a shelter and a seat for me in a Methodist church." It was felt that every real christian would extend courtesies to the stranger; yes, a Methodist church was a bethel to the wayfaring man. *It was the fashion;* GOD *made that fashion*; true piety fostered it. The plain preacher knew there was a stranger in the house. The leader was sure that not idle curiosity, but heartfelt interest, would induce him to come into a despised Methodist church. Preacher, leader and member had a kind look, and a vigorous shake of the hand was enough; the stranger is at home. Sinners saw nothing to mar the symmetry of Bible religion. They were convinced of the truth of Bible religion, sought it, obtained it, lived it, and died triumphantly. The end was gained. The grand impression was made on the world that a Methodist church was the place where honest hearts communed with God.

That fashion is changing fast. What mean those towering steeples? Is it to vie in stateliness with ambitious neighbors? Go inside. What is the minister trying to do? To win applause or sinners? Which? Where is the poor man's seat? Who has monopolized the gallery? and who presides at the worshipping machine? Who welcomes the stranger, and tries to win him to Jesus? Where are the members? Surely these cannnot be Methodists, so thoughtless, sleepy, and so gaudily attired. Where are the Methodists? Where? the answer comes. And where are we drifting?

QUARTERLY MEETING OF OLDEN TIME.—In Upper Canada a gracious revival had commenced in 1797, chiefly through the instrumentality of Calvin Wooster, whose fervency of spirit led him forth in the work of reformation in a most remarkable manner, and with singular success. In company with Samuel Coate, he volunteered his services as a missionary to this distant field of labor, and after enduring almost incredible hardships on their way, for they lodged no less than twenty-one nights in the wilderness, they arrived just in time to attend a quarterly meeting on the Bay of Quinte circuit. After the preaching on Saturday, while the presiding elder, Darius Dunham, retired with the official brethren to hold the Quarterly Meeting Conference, Brother Wooster remained in the meeting to pray with some who were under awakenings, and others who were groaning for full redemption in the blood of Christ. While uniting with his brethren in this exercise, the power of the Most High seemed to overshadow the congregation, and many were filled with joy unspeakable, and were praising the Lord aloud for what he had done for their souls, while others, "with speechless awe, and silent love," were prostrate on the floor.

When the presiding elder came into the House, he beheld these things with a mixture of wonder and indignation, believing that "wild-fire" was burning among the people. After gazing for a while, with silent astonishment, he kneeled down and began to pray to God to stop the "raging of the wild-fire," as he called it. In the meantime, Calvin Wooster, whose soul was burning with the "fire of the Holy Spirit," kneeled by the side of Brother Dunham, and while the latter was earnestly praying for God to put out the wild-fire, Wooster softly whispered out a prayer in the following words, "Lord, bless Brother Dunham! Lord, bless Brother Dunham!" Thus they continued for some minutes; when, at length, the prayer of Brother Wooster prevailed, and Brother Dunham fell prostrate on the floor; and ere he arose, received a baptism of that very fire which he had so feelingly deprecated, as the effect of a wild imagination. There was now harmony in their prayers, feelings, and views; and this was the commencement of a revival of religion, which soon spread through the entire province; for as Brother Dunham was the presiding elder, he was instrumental in spreading the sacred flame throughout the district, to the joy and salvation of hundreds of immortal souls—*Bangs' Hist. M. E. C.*

RELIGIOUS EXCITEMENT.—Eternal things are so great, and of such vast concern, that there is great absurdity in men's being but moderately moved by them. And when was there ever such a thing since the world stood, as a people, in general, being greatly affected in any affairs whatsoever, without noise or stir? The nature of man will not allow it.—PRES. EDWARDS.

REVIVALS.

BY THE EDITOR.

The Lord has enabled us, in His good Providence during the year past, to travel some six thousand miles, and participate in, as nearly as we can judge, some four hundred religious meetings. In over half that number it was our privilege to preach the Gospel of the grace of God. The interest every where is beyond what we ever saw before. In places where it was formerly difficult to secure a respectable audience on a week day, to listen to our ablest preachers, large congregations have come out in dark nights, over muddy roads, to hear the plain, searching truths of God's Word applied to their consciences. From two to four thousand persons have attended common grove meetings held in the busiest season of the year.

We have seen, too, what we hope may yet be a common thing, souls awakened and clearly saved, in the first meeting we held in a place.

Early in the spring it was our privilege to spend several weeks with the brethren at St. Louis. Here the previous winter, under the labors of that faithful servant of God, Rev. J. W. Redfield, a deep and thorough revival of God's work had taken place. Many felt that henceforth they must live and labor for the salvation of souls. Finding a determined opposition from some in the church to which they belonged, and judging from the past that it was likely to continue, they thought it best for those who were of one heart and one mind, to go together and form a new M. E. Church. They were encouraged by the Presiding Elder of the district, to expect that they would be regularly organized and cared for. But he afterwards refused to do any thing for them. They organized as a "Free Methodist Church," adopting the old Methodist Discipline as far as applicable to their circumstances, *making non-slaveholding one of the conditions of membership.* Their enemies predicted that they would go down as soon as Dr. Redfield left them. But Jesus had given them *life in themselves.* For about six months they were without preacher, presiding elder or bishop. But the GOOD SHEPHERD was with them. A lively interest was kept up in their meetings. Souls were converted all along.

Rev. E. W. Dunbar, from New Bedford, Mass., is laboring with them at present, with great acceptability and success. Some twenty-five have taken letters and removed from the city, but their membership has increased from ninety to one hundred and eighty-eight. Their Sabbath school is prosperous, with an average attendance of from one hundred and fifty to one hundred and seventy-five. Their place of worship, a large room capable of holding four or five hundred persons, has become too small. They have hired a large church, and also, as we understand, the St. Louis Theatre for religious meetings. God bless the pilgrims of St. Louis.

At Albion, a large majority of the members have resolved to stand by Bro. Stiles, and the truth God has commissioned him to proclaim. They could have kept the church property; for the law of this State gives the control of church property to a majority of the corporators. But the brethren dreaded strife and litigation, and the loss of spirituality consequent thereon. So they gave up all, "taking joyfully the spoiling of their goods." With an energy equal to that exhibited by the pioneers of Methodism they purchased a lot, raised a subscription, and proceeded at once to the erection of a new house of worship. They are building a large, plain, and commodious edifice. The audience room is to be fifty-five feet by eighty. An airy, pleasant basement, the whole size of the building, will afford ample room for class and prayer meetings.

They now hope to have it dedicated in February next. Their meetings, held at present in the Academy Hall, are full of interest. The hall is crowded to its utmost capacity.

Buffalo has not been unvisited by mercy drops. The calls away to labor have been so many and so urgent, that we could not devote that attention to home work which we desired to. More has been realized from the amount of labor expended, than could have been reasonably anticipated. Quite a number of precious souls have found the "peace that passeth all understanding." Through the liberality of Mr. Jesse Ketchum, of the Congregationalist church, we have a commodious house of worship furnished for us, free of cost. We have an interesting congregation, gradually increasing in size; a flourishing Sabbath school, and three or four prayer meetings a week, well attended. We are looking for "showers of blessings" from the hand of the Lord.

AT BROCKPORT, some six or seven devoted Christians, who had struggled with opposition and persecution in the church, feeling that they must go where they could worship God in spirit, without giving offence, assembled in February last in the Village Hall, to hold a prayer meeting. The Lord was with them. They have kept up Sabbath services since. The little praying band has increased to over fifty, most of the additions being persons who have been converted through their instrumentalities. Daniel Sinclair has labored with them most of the time. Finding the hall too small to accommodate the congregation, they have rented the Free Will Baptist church. They have a flourishing Sabbath school, and are making their influence felt for good upon the community.

AT PEKIN, several souls have found peace, within the past few days, as the result of some extra meetings held in Temperance Hall.

AT TONAWANDA a strong religious influence prevails. Several have been converted of late. The Lord gives Bros. Sinclair and Chesbrough favor in the eyes of the people; their meetings are crowded, and sinners are coming to the Saviour.

THE WONDERFUL REVIVAL IN IRELAND is still in progress. It is carried on in a manner that confounds formalism and false philosophy. Stalwart men of all temperaments, hardened in sin, with nerves of iron; wild young men, women and children, in the midst of their work, by the roadside, in the market places, as well as in the meetings, are suddenly arrested and struck down by the power of God. In the deepest agony they cry for mercy, till the wail of penitence is succeeded by the shout of deliverance. These "physical manifestations" are common among all denominations, Episcopalians, Presbyterians and Methodists. At the first breaking out of this revival, the enemies of earnest Christianity among us, attempted to throw ridicule upon it, stigmatizing it as a "Nazarite revival." May such a work of God sweep all over our land.

A VILLAGE CONVERTED.

The Ayrshire *Express*, Scotland, gives an interesting account of a work of grace in a Scottish village, in which conversions occurred in nearly every house.

Fifteen months since, some friends belonging to a coal-pit at Drumclare, a village near Slamanan, eighteen miles east of Glasgow, wrote to Mr. Abercrombie to come over from America to his native country, and become the teacher of the children belonging to the pitmen. He came, but soon had reason to regret the step; and heartily did he wish and pray that God in his all-wise Providence would open to him the way to escape. He had been useful as a teacher, and also as a certified preacher in the States: and here he found no congenial spirits, but was imprisoned in a small hamlet of three hundred souls, who seemed to be sunk far below the moral level of his countrymen. The filth of the houses, the degradation of the entire people; the cursing, obscenity, drunkenness, open Sabbath desecration, and the incidental poverty and misery, were too much for him. He opened a meeting for prayer and preaching; almost no one would attend. At length, resolved while he was there that he would work, he began to preach outside, and near enough to the houses to be heard by the inmates. Thus he continued preaching, exhorting and praying; and when he was well nigh weary—about six months ago—he found two or three evincing much concern, who were ultimately led to trust in the Saviour, and rejoice in Him—these with great heartiness helped on the work. Mr. Abercrombie is a Baptist, and as soon as a few, six or seven, gave evidence of a change of heart, he invited Mr. Dunn, a Baptist minister of Airdrie, to go over, and they were baptized in the Black Loch. At this ordinance, at which there were many witnesses, great solemnity prevailed; many were pricked to their hearts, and very shortly afterwards, a goodly number desired to confess Christ, and were also baptized into his name. Last Saturday, August 13, twenty-three were added to the number; in all about sixty souls, out of an adult population of about one hundred.

LETTER FROM ENGLAND.

North of England—Great Revival—Newcastle-on-Tyne—Miners converted—A new Element—Sunderland—Wonderful Work.

Here in the north of England the Lord has commenced a work which, we have no doubt, will spread over the whole kingdom, if all holy carefulness is observed on the part of the hosts of the Lord as workers together with God in promoting it. The battle is the Lord's. But God works through human agencies and with prepared instrumentalities. Church communities are made up of individuals. Zion has might. The time is come when, in the most emphatic sense, the God of battles would have her arise and put on her strength, and in her individual and collective capacity come up to the help of the Lord against the mighty. Day and night are we being penetrated yet more deeply with the solemnity of our position, as we by an eye of faith see the Captain of the hosts of Israel, with drawn sword, standing as the conqueror of his foes, for the defense of his own glory, and we hear him saying to us: "The place whereon thou standest is holy."

Newcastle-on-Tyne is a place noted for its stoical coolness and apathy, if not worse, even infidelity; nothing has ever before seemed to make an impression on the public mind or move the masses. The population is about 120,000. But here God began to pour out his Spirit in a wonderful manner. The ministers and official and leading men of the Church sought and obtained the baptism of fire, even as the early disciples on the day of Pentecost, and pentecostal blessings brought pentecostal results, as we believe they ever will. The whole town seemed to be moved. The Brunswick-place Chapel, that will hold about 3,000 persons, was generally crowded, and we were told that hundreds at times had to leave, unable even to find standing room. Members from all the different evangelical Churches very largely mingled with us, and many of them were blest with full salvation, and carried the influence to their own Churches. In one Episcopal Church, where the usual number of communicants was about sixty, at a recent communion they had over two hundred; at another (Independent) they had one hundred and thirty new communicants. A note received a few nights since, states that in a place a few miles distant from Newcastle, from which place a number of miners came in every Saturday, and many of them received this full baptism of the Spirit, a work has broke out, and upwards of four hundred miners have been converted. The note ends with the exclamation, "Glory be to God!" in which, I am sure, you will join.

You will see by our address that we are now in Sunderland. It is two weeks yesterday since we left Newcastle. It was difficult to tear ourselves away. We were there thirty-eight days, and gladly would have remained thirty-eight more had not our engagements elsewhere prevented. The revival flame broke out the first day after our arrival, and kept steadily and most rapidly extending its more fervent, all pervading, and penetrating influences during our stay. Meetings were held both afternoon and evening during the whole time, (neither Saturday nor Sabbath afternoons were excepted,) and during the whole time the interest increased and the flame rose higher. The last afternoon and evening exceeded all. The presence of the High and Holy One was so manifestly realized, truth was felt in its deep spirituality, and everything seemed naked and open to the eyes of Him with whom we had to do. Surely the place was awful, yet glorious, on account of the felt presence of God. During the period of our visitation in Newcastle the secretaries of the meeting took over thirteen hundred names among the newly blessed.

In an official document, which we received by post since we left, of resolutions passed at a meeting of the ministers, stewards, leaders, etc., of Newcastle, the second resolution reads thus:

"2. This meeting records, with sincere gratitude to Him to whom alone is the glory, that during the thirty-eight days' labor of Doctor and Mrs. Palmer in this place, very many Church members received the baptism of the Holy Ghost, and not fewer than *thirteen hundred* persons decided for God, and besought the prayers of his people. Many of these were from the world, the others from different sections of the Church; and it is hoped that the largest portion of them obtained peace with God through our Lord Jesus Christ."

Rev. Mr. Young speaks of this revival in the *Watchman*, which you perhaps have seen, as an "Evangelical Alliance Revival," and truly we seem to have come to a point where "Ephriam shall not envy Judah, and Judah shall not vex Ephriam." Frequently from five to six ministers, and people of different denominations, would take part in the prayer-meeting exercises. The chief notices of this revival have been given to the public by an honored gentleman of this community who is known as an Independent, and much devoted to the interests of his own Church community. He has published tracts on the subject, which have been largely diffused, and is weekly furnishing notices of the work in the *British Standard*, published in London, and is applying to us for facts, ect., connected with the revival, which we are unable to furnish for want of time. The revival in Newcastle is still most graciously progressing. The day meetings have been discontinued, but the evening meetings are still being held, and the Saviour of sinners is gloriously present. On the evening we closed our labors, Rev. Mr. Young announced that he would bring in a new element.

Some young men of remarkable promise had been made partakers of saving grace, and now it was announced that evening after evening it might be expected that some of these young converts might enter within the communion rail and testify for Jesus. This proved to be eminently of God. To use the expression of one, "The young men of Newcastle are coming in by shoals!" We are informed that about twenty persons are being saved nightly.

And now what shall we say of Sunderland? The work exceeds any thing we have ever before witnessed either in America or Ireland. It seems as if the whole community is being moved. Surely it is "not by might, nor by power, but by my Spirit, saith the Lord." Two or three nights in succession the secretaries of the meeting have recorded the names of one hundred and over, who have been made recipients of grace. The number of seekers seems to be only bounded by the accommodations we are able to furnish them on presenting themselves for prayer. It is now Tuesday. We commenced our labors here on Sabbath afternoon two weeks since. We talked about the full baptism of the Holy Ghost, as received by the early disciples on the day of Pentecost, as the absolute necessity of believers of the present day. Many resolved that they would come out and definitely seek this endowment of power. Among the first to approach the communion rail, as openly seeking the baptism of fire, was one of the able ministers of this town. I need not say that many followed him. And thus the work went on. On Monday afternoon the leading men in the Church, with their wives, came forward in well-nigh a body, and such an outpouring of the Spirit as we then received I cannot describe. Pentecostal blessings, as before observed, bring pentecostal results. In the evening we had an overwhelming congregation. The chapel is very large here, as in Newcastle. It was estimated that as many as 3,000 were present. I believe we should speak truly if we should say hundreds were pricked to the heart. There was a rush to the altar when the invitation was given. The communion rail and all its surroundings being filled, and not being able to find places for more under the circumstances, I said, as there was no more room around the altar, that all who desired to seek the Lord and wished the prayers of God's people, would manifest it by raising the right hand, and keeping it uplifted till the recording angel had made the record. Hundreds of hands were uplifted in every part of the house. What a scene was this; never shall I forget it! The place was filled with the solemn, awful presence of the Triune Deity. We had endeavored to ask in faith that every person in the house might be arrested by the power of the Spirit, and it is our belief it was even so. The next evening not only was the communion rail and other surroundings filled, but the vestry was also crowded. The next evening the upper vestry, which is used as the lecture-room, was also filled, and about one hundred were blessed. For several evenings past we have three vestries engaged for persons seeking the Lord to retire to, one of them especially for the children, and they are mostly filled, sometimes crowded, besides the communion rail. Over one thousand names have been recorded the past fifteen days, and still the work seems only to have begun. "Halleluiah, the Lord God Omnipotent reigneth." "Not unto us, not unto us, but unto thy name give glory for thy mercy and thy truth's sake."

WALTER C. AND PHOEBE PALMER.
—*Christian Advocate and Journal.*

LITERARY NOTICES.

SLAVERY IN THE METHODIST EPISCOPAL CHURCH. BY ELIAS BOWEN, D. D. Auburn, William J. Moses, Printer, 1859.

The slavery question is one that can never lose its interest until the oppressed go free. God will raise up men who will bear their testimony, at any peril, against what John Wesley calls "the sum of all villainies." Dr. Bowen's book is a strong, able, and emphatic rebuke of the sin of slaveholding in the Church. We wish his book might be read by every minister and member of the M. E. Church. He shows that the Church is responsible for slavery—that the anti-slavery cause in the M. E. Church is declining, and that for this fearful state of things the bishops are mainly responsible. He says: "The last General Conference developed the humiliating fact, that as a Church, we had greatly deteriorated in our anti-slavery character, especially for the last few years; and that the slave-power had been rapidly gaining ground among us, riveting our chains, and deluding us with the idea of progress, in the very face of our anti-slavery hopes and efforts. The bishops, whose equivocal silence had long and justly been regarded as evidence of their sympathy with the slave power, here laid aside their wonted reserve, and openly espoused the cause of Church slavery, by throwing the full weight of their influence in the way of prohibitory legislation upon the subject."

This work is the more remarkable from the fact that its venerable author has long occupied a prominent position in the Church. He has counted the cost of speaking out in behalf of humanity, for he says in the Introduction, "The liberty of speech and of the press, and the rights of conscience, if not wholly taken from us by the slave power which has usurped the control of the Church, can no longer be exercised with safety. Persecution and proscription, the sure harbingers of fire and faggot in those countries where religion is enabled to avail itself of the civil arm, are forever staring us in the face; and reminding us of the difficulties and perils that await our anti-slavery enterprise."

This book is a 12 mo. of 317 pages, and may be had, we presume, at Auburn, or of the author, at Cortland, Cortland Co., N. Y.

SHOUTING: GENUINE AND SPURIOUS. In all ages of the Church, from the birth of Creation, when the Sons of God shouted for joy, until the shout of the Arch-angel: with numerous extracts from the Old and New Testaments, and from the works of Wesley, Evans, Edwards, Abbott, Cartwright and Finley. Giving a history of the outward demonstrations of the Spirit, such as Laughing, Screaming, Shouting, Leaping, Jerking, and Falling under the power, &c. With extensive comments, numerous anecdotes, and illustrations, by G. W. HENRY, author of "Trials and Triumphs, or Travels in Egypt," "Twilight and Beulah," "Wedlock and Padlock, temporal and spiritual," "Camp Meeting Hymn Book," &c. With steel engraving of author and son. Published and bound by the author. Oneida, Madison Co., N. Y., 1859.

The above is the title in full, of a work intended, and destined, we doubt not, to do good service in promoting earnest Christianity, written by a remarkable man. Blind Henry is a genius. His conceptions are original. His mode of advocating truth is peculiar. Though without the advantages of an early literary training, and in later life suffering from the still greater disadvantage of being entirely blind, he has nevertheless written several books that have had a wide circulation and been made a a blessing to thousands.

The work before us is an able defence of emotional religion. His statements are clear, and sustained by arguments that cannot easily be answered, even by those who refuse to be convinced by them. The book abounds in interesting incidents, and cannot fail to be read with pleasure and profit. It contains 425 pages 12 mo., and as a mechanical production is highly creditable to the skill of a blind man, not brought up to the business of book making.

In the characteristic preface the author says: "We expect to give an account in the judgment for every word we have written. Our book is a child of prayer. Unceasingly have we prayed for the Spirit's direction; the need of which we have felt especially, because our blindness compelled us to the unnatural method of writing through our son or daughter.

Oh! Lord, if the book please Thee, give it the wings of a carrier dove, and prepare its way to the firesides of thousands; and may it win many souls to Christ after we are dead. Amen!"

THE EARNEST CHRISTIAN.

VOL. I. FEBRUARY, 1860. NO. 2.

FREE CHURCHES.

BY THE EDITOR.

Free Churches are needed to save the rich.

THE Bible recognizes the existence of special difficulties in the way of the salvation of the rich. "How hardly," says Jesus, "shall they that have riches enter into the kingdom of God! For it is easier for a camel to go through a needle's eye, than for a rich man to enter into the kingdom of God." "They that will be rich," writes Paul, "fall into temptation, and a snare, and into many foolish and hurtful lusts, which drown men in destruction and perdition."

It would be easy to multiply quotations on this point; but these are sufficient. They show that wealth interposes serious obstacles to the eternal salvation of its possessor. One great difficulty is the comparative ease with which the rich may commit and cover up transgressions. Many a man yields to sinful passions if the means to gratify them are at hand, when he would not do so if gratification were more difficult. The certainty of present exposure and disgrace, has often strengthened the faltering resolution of the lowly; while the hope of sinning with impunity lures the wealthy on into the jaws of destruction. The readiness with which the influential find apologists for their misdeeds is a great injury to them. Many a rich transgressor is kept in the church and encouraged to maintain a christian profession; when, if he were poor, he would soon be shown his true position. A keen observer of human nature says—

"Through tattered clothes small vices do appear
Robes and furred gowns hide all."

We are sorry that this saying finds its application in the church as well as in the world.

But the chief danger of riches is found in their tendency to beget and foster pride. The Holy Ghost recognizes this tendency in the injunction to the ministry, "charge them that are rich that they be not high-minded." Every one has observed it, either in himself or in others. A secret enemy is the most dangerous. A small force, concealed in ambush, overcomes an army that it would not dare to face in the open field. Pride is an insidious foe. It reigns in many a heart where its existence is hardly suspected. It comes in a garb so tasteful and attractive, and meets with so many compliments and favors from the world, and withal is treated with such consideration from the church, that when it is found to be a tenant of the soul, its residence there is hardly regretted. Yet pride is a dangerous and damning sin. It sinks its victim to the depths of hell, and leaves him there in untold agonies forever. "For the day of the Lord of hosts shall be upon every one that is proud and lofty, and upon every one that is lifted up; and he shall be brought low."

Notwithstanding the difficulties, the rich may be saved. For them, also, Christ died. With them the Holy Spirit strives. But in order to be saved, they must, like the poor, yield an unconditional submission to all the terms of the Gospel. Those who have been accustomed to make conditions for others, will find, on coming to Christ, that they have a new lesson to learn. They must come to His terms. Nothing short of the most perfect compliance will be accepted. None but an unreserved consecration of all a man has, and is, for all coming time, will be received. As of old, any blemish, however small, unfitted an animal for a sacrifice, so any reservation, however trifling, on the part of him who would come to Christ, will cause his rejection. We must go to the warfare at His charges. We cannot "eat our own bread, and wear our own apparel," and still be called by his name, "to take away our reproach."

We must be allowed to give here another quotation from Dr. Olin. We do this the more readily as it is not generally known how deeply he felt and mourned the increasing disposition to depart from the ancient landmarks.

He says that multitudes of professing Christians "give law to religion. They retain as many indulgencies, and concede as many sacrifices, as may fall in with their tastes. They make provision for pride, and ambition, and sensuality and self-will, and 'put on the Lord Jesus Christ' only in so far as they think he may set off their own purple and fine linen to the best advantage. But my business is with the sincere, who wish to be made holy, and to be saved by Christ, and who really desire to know the conditions of success. I take it upon me to warn all such to beware of admitting *any worldly or selfish motive or consideration whatever* into the settlement of this great question between God and their souls. I take it upon me to proclaim that all such tampering in the business of religion will certainly prove fatal to any well-founded hopes of success in the Christian career.

Whoever stops to inquire whether it may cost him sacrifices to be a Christian, with any intention to hesitate if it does, has admitted a consideration utterly incompatible with his becoming a Christian at all. Whoever chooses his creed or his church with any, the slightest, reference to the honor, or the ease, or the emolument it may give or withhold, does by such an admission, utterly vitiate all his claim to have any part or lot in the matter of saving piety. I do not speak of those who knowingly, and deliberately make these their chief ground of preference, but I affirm that it is wholly anti-Christian and an insult to the crucified Saviour to yield any, the smallest, place to wordly motives in choosing the christian position which we will occupy. Let Christ and conscience decide this matter. 'Put ye on the Lord Jesus Christ, and make not provision for the flesh to fulfill the lusts thereof.' The Gospel will admit of no compromise here. This is its point of honor, which it cannot, and will not yield by a single iota. I feel called upon to use the language of unmeasured denunciation against a mistake so often fatal to hopeful beginnings in religion."

The rich man should feel, as he enters the house of God, that he is in the presence of that dread Being, in whose sight worldly distinctions are of no account whatever. Any concession to his pride will be likely to inflict an injury that all the services cannot repair. Every arrangement of the sanctuary of God should be such as to teach, impressively, the essential equality of man. Here it should be the case, now, as formerly, that the rich and poor meet together, and every one should be made to realize that the Lord is the maker of them all.

That the tendency of the pew system is the reverse of all this, must be admitted by those who have witnessed its workings. The unregenerate man finding a still greater deference paid to him in the house of God, on account of his wealth, than he is accustomed to meet with in the world, naturally comes to think that he is by no means in as bad a spiritual condition as common sinners; and after, perhaps, a feeble effort to seek the Lord on terms of his own proposing, either concludes that he is good enough without religion, or takes up with an experience exceedingly superficial and unsatisfactory. Thus is his danger increased. To his partially awakened soul he cries, peace, peace! when God hath not spoken peace. Others are ready to echo the cry, and the delusion is confirmed. In examining revivals of religion, one who has not made it a subject of thought, will be surprised at the small number of pew-holders that give satisfactory evidence of being thoroughly converted to God. It has been remarked by the veterans of the Methodist Episcopal Church, that in years gone by, when the pew system was unknown among us, a much larger proportion of men of influence became converted and attached to the church, than do under existing arrangements.

I know it is said that many, if they cannot have their pew, will not hear the gospel at all. But this is a great mistake. Who ever staid away from a literary or political lecture, because he could not have his "pew" so as to be free from all danger of contact with the vulgar throng? It is a burning shame to the followers of Him who "had not where to lay His head," that they pay, in their solemn assemblies, a homage to wealth and pride, that is stoutly refused by the literary and political world. The Master did not so.

The pew system tends to introduce unchristian distinction into the House of God.

Christianity knows no difference between her votaries, except what is based on personal piety. In many a college may be found young men of opposite conditions in life. One belongs to a wealthy, honored, aristocratic family. Another is the son of a common day laborer, battling bravely for a thorough education. He sits side by side with the favored child of fortune, listens to the same instructions, has access to the same libraries, enjoys the same rights. The Alma Mater, in distributing her honors, knows no distinction among her children, but those founded on literary excellence. She says to the high born as they enter her walls,

"Forget you now, your state and lofty birth;
Not titles here, but works must prove your worth."

In a still more eminent degree, shines forth the impartiality of the Church of Jesus Christ, wherever her true spirit is carried out. She has but one altar, one baptism, one communion, one salvation, for all her children. Has a person renounced the world, the flesh, and the devil; does he believe in Christ, and is he saved through the virtue of His blood from sin? She inquires no farther. She welcomes him to her embrace. Here is an immortal soul, trying to get to Heaven, that needs her help. She will know no more respecting him. She treats him with all the kindness possible.

"Our mother, the Church, hath never a child,
 To honor before the rest ;
But she singeth the same for mighty kings,
 And the veriest babe on her breast;
And the Bishop goes down to his narrow bed,
 As the ploughman's child is laid ;
And alike she blesseth the dark-browed serf,
 And the chief in his robe arrayed."

"It is," writes Dr. Olin, "the peculiar glory of the Gospel, that even under the most arbitrary governments, it has usually been able to vindicate and practically exemplify the essential equality of man. It has had one doctrine and one hope for all its children; and the highest and the lowest have been constrained to acknowledge one holy law of brotherhood in the common faith of which they are made partakers." He says the gospel is a leveler, and will have all classes "mingle before a common altar, and bow before a common Saviour. It abhors caste, and is ambitious of bringing together in one vast brotherhood of faith, and feeling, and co-operation, all blood bought souls." This would be accomplished but for human inteference. "Now the pride of man comes in to thwart this benevolent design. It will have an aristocracy, where Heaven can, least of all, tolerate it." The aristocracy, brought into the house of God by the pew system, is the most contemptible of all; an aristocracy of wealth. This prominent pew is occupied by the family of a noted rum seller—that one by a professional gambler. They pay liberally for the consideration shown them by the church; and she says she has no right to inquire how they came by their money.

Very different from this was the order observed in the primitive church. Mosheim says that in the first century, "all the members of the Christian community considered themselves as being on a footing of the most perfect equality." In their public worship, the faithful, as would naturally be the case, occupied the places nearest the altar, and in rear of them the congregation was seated promiscuously, without the slightest regard being paid to rank or wealth. But if the Apostles and the Seventy were to visit some modern churches, they would find themselves unceremoniously sent to the gallery or some obscure corner, for they were poor, unassuming men. Such are some of the absurdities of the Pew System. It honors those whom God abhors, and treats the special objects of His regard with neglect. As Bishop Morris truly says, "It begins, progresses, and terminates in aristocracy."

The system of Free Seats is imperatively required by the precept given through St. James.

His language is explicit. He condemns, as will be seen, the Pew System *in toto*. He could not have done so more pointedly if he had written on purpose. He says, "My brethren, have not the faith of our Lord Jesus Christ, the Lord of glory, with respect of persons. For if there come unto your assembly, a man with a gold ring, in goodly apparel, and there come in also a poor man in vile raiment; and ye have respect to him that weareth the gay clothing, and say unto him, Sit thou here in a good place; and say to the poor, Stand thou there, or sit here under my footstool: Are ye not then partial in yourselves, and are become judges of evil thoughts? * * If ye fulfill the royal law, according to the Scripture, Thou shalt love thy neighbor as thyself, ye do well. But if ye have respect to persons, ye commit sin, and are convinced of the law as transgressors. For whosoever shall keep the whole law and yet offend in one point, he is guilty of all." The repetition of a sinful act, does not render it any the less sinful. He who steals from your drawer every day in the year, is certainly as much a thief as when he committed the first offence. It must be admitted that this precept of St. James can be violated. There is as much choice now in the places for sitting in the Christian assemblies, as there was in his day. Two persons enter a church, the one rich, the other poor. The rich man, because of his wealth, is conducted to an eligible seat, the poor man is shown to an undesirable seat in an obscure corner. Here, all will concede, is a violation of the Apostolic injunction. But where the pews are rented or sold, the "brethren" virtually say to him who is able and willing to pay the most for the privilege, "You shall have the exclusive right to the occupancy of the best seat in the house, every Sabbath in the year." Does then an action, which, when committed once, is a sin, become right when it is virtually performed fifty-two times or more in a year? By no means. Thus, wherever pews are rented or sold, is one of the plainest injunctions of sacred writ systematically and regularly trampled upon.

The Pew System is not only based upon a plain violation of an express command of God, but, wherever it obtains, it involves special transgressions from Sabbath to Sabbath. There is not a sexton of a pewed church in the land, that does not feel obliged to have respect to persons in seating a congregation. He knows that it would not do to put any other than genteel persons into certain pews. A poor man, in vile raiment, might consider himself fortunate, if in some churches he was not hastily showed to the door, with a charge to go about his business!

It is true that respect to persons may be had in a Free Church. But there is no necessity for it. The system does not require it. But in a pewed church there *must* be respect to persons. It is an essential element of the system. This is the consideration for which the rent is paid. When one pays for a pew "in a good place," it is with the understanding that he shall have the right to say who shall occupy it.

Nor is any regard had to moral character. The rich man may be a rum seller, a gambler, and an infidel. The one qualification for the occupancy of the seat of distinction in a pewed house, is the possession of money to purchase it! No matter how the money was obtained. The "poor man in vile raiment" may be a sincere follower of the Saviour, but this does not secure him, in the House of his Master, equal privileges with the wealthy scoffer. When the sale of pews takes place, the auctioneer never restricts his sales to men of "good, moral character." In fact, the reason generally given for the adoption of the Pew System is, that more money can be obtained from irreligious men, for the support of the gospel, than in any other way. Thus plainly does the Word of God prohibit the system of Pewed Churches.

POTHINUS, Bishop of Lyons, was put to death in the fourth general persecution of Christians. He was ninety years of age, of great weakness and infirmity of body, but his soul was in no respect decayed. The desire of being deemed worthy of martyrdom, gave him vigor. When brought to the governor, this captious question was asked: "Who is the God of the Christians?" He replied, "If you be worthy you shall know." Regardless of both age and humanity, he was barbarously dragged up and down, and unmercifully beaten, being kicked by those who were nearest, and pelted by those more distant with anything offensive which they could seize. He was at length taken from the ground, almost breathless, and cast into prison, where in two days after he died.

LET ME STAY.

BY M. N. HALSEY.

The Christian in Divine Communion, the world calls him away.

Let me stay! my soul is feasting
 On Immanuel's saving grace—
Let me stay! I now behold Him
 In my spirit, face to face.

Let me stay! His charms pervade me
 With a bliss beyond control;
Now His rapturous love, all vital,
 Streams into my panting soul.

I *will* stay! The union's perfect,
 I in Christ, and Christ in me!
Henceforth I will draw my being,
 Every instant, Lord, from Thee.

Now the radiant scenes of Glory
 Move around me clear and bright;
Here the beings pure and perfect,
 Bask and sing in living light.

Deep and full their songs seraphic
 Swell the atmosphere divine;
And I echo high their chorus,
 "Life! Eternal Life! is mine!"

I will stay! O this is Heaven!
 Glorious mansion of the blessed!
Now my worn and weary spirit
 Finds in Christ its perfect rest.

THERE is a two-fold perfection, the perfection of the work, and that of the workman. The perfection of the work is, when the work does so exactly and strictly answer the holy law of God, that there is no irregularity it it. The perfection of the workman, is nothing but inward sincerity and uprightness of the heart towards God, which may be where there are many imperfections and defects intermingled. It is not so much what our works are, as what our heart is, that God looks at and will reward. Yet know, also, that if our hearts are perfect and sincere, we shall endeavor, to the utmost of our power, that our works may be perfect, according to the strictness of the law.— BISHOP HOPKINS.

ON PREACHING PERFECTION.

BY REV. WILLIAM C. KENDALL, A. M.

[The following article from the pen of our lamented brother Kendall, will, we trust, be perused with interest by all our readers. Those whose privilege it was to sit under his ministry, will readily testify how perfectly his own practice corresponded with the views here set forth. This article was prepared by him a few years before his death, to be read at the Preachers' Association, and has never before appeared in print.—ED.]

The commission of our Lord to his apostles, "Go ye into all the world and preach the gospel to every creature," points out in unmistakable terms, the work of his ministers. The gospel, without addition or diminution, is their message. It has pleased God by the foolishness of proclaiming it to save the lost. To this end, all parts of the gospel contribute their quota, yet no one will maintain that the influence of each is the same. The effect of setting aside portions of truth will be more or less disastrous, as they are fundamental or otherwise. The Quaker may renounce the obligation of the Sabbath and water baptism, and be a pious man; while the Universalist, leaving out of his creed the "faith that works by love," is as truly a child of the devil as before. A limb may perish with disease, and the man still live and act; but let the heart be attacked, and before destruction commences, death will ensue.

We may readily ascertain the comparative necessity of preaching perfection by examining its position in the gospel scheme. We call it a doctrine of the Bible, but need only glance at revelation to know that it is *the doctrine of the Bible*. Upon this requirement of the law hang all the law and the prophets. Pluck away this, and the whole system falls. It matters not what our attainments are, without this, all will be ruin. As faith is the one condition of salvation, so is perfect holiness the only fitness for eternal blessedness. It is the sun of the Christian system, without which, all would be dark and dead.

Glance at redemption's plan, and you will see this truth every where standing out. Mark those toil-worn apostles facing every difficulty of land and sea, counting all things but loss, not even reckoning their lives dear unto themselves. And for what end? It may be answered, to preach Christ. True, but was this the final cause of their efforts? Hear St. Paul answer, "Whom we preach warning every man and teaching every man in all wisdom, that we may present every man perfect in Christ Jesus; whereunto I also labor, striving according to his working, which worketh in me mightily." This, then, was the one aim of their teaching and labor, to present every man perfect, and for this Paul strove mightily, God working with him. Again hear him: "He gave some apostles, and some prophets, and some evangelists, and some pastors and teachers, for the perfecting of the saints for the work of the ministry for the edifying of the body of Christ, till we all come in the unity of the faith and of the knowledge of the son of God unto a perfect man, unto the measure of the stature of the fullness of Christ." This, then, was the express design of these orders in the ministry. Open again the sacred volume, examine its doctrines, its precious promises, its commands and awful threatenings, and mark, if you will, the one design running through the whole. No doubt exists here. "God is his own interpreter." "All scripture is given by inspiration of God, and is profitable for doctrine, for reproof, for correction, for instruction in righteousness, that the man of God may be perfect, thoroughly furnished unto all good works." In a still wider view, survey as a whole that fearful tragedy occupying the attention of all ages. Heaven, Earth and Hell are actors. For four thousand years altars are smoking with their slain victims. At length Jesus, disrobed of glory, appears within the arena and falls in the conflict. A world's wickedness crushes the innocent one; but he rises again, heralds run to and fro, martyrs bleed, angels are flying, and God the Spirit moving. What is the mighty motive that stirs the universe? What sustains Christ amid the most fearful sufferings? Why, simply the fulfillment of the "righteousness of the law in us." "Christ gave himself for the church, that he might sanctify and cleanse it with the washing of water by the word, that He might present it to himself a glorious church, not having spot or wrinkle, or any such thing; that it should be holy and without blemish." Perfection, then, is the central idea of christianity, and as ministers of the New Testament, shall we pass it by, neglecting our one work, or at best give it a subordinate place in our ministrations? This course has already aided fearfully in filling the world with backsliders. All the energies of our religion have been paralyzed by leaving out the main spring. As a late writer remarks, "As well might you tear out the heart and then attempt to give value to the veins, and arteries, and blood, as to reject *holiness*, and still hope to save the gospel scheme. As well might you burn up your towns and leave your guide-boards standing, as to destroy *holiness*, and insist on justification by faith or any other great doctrine of christianity." No, it must be the one work of every preacher to establish a full salvation, and to this end every sermon should be framed and uttered.

This, we are happy to say, has been the economy of Methodism. Wesley declared himself called of God, especially to this work. After more than thirty years experience in the ministry, he, with holy zeal, affirms, "all our preachers should make a point of preaching perfection *constantly, strongly*, explicitly." Such was his practice and the practice of his co-laborers, who were most successful in soul-saving.

Again and again he attributes declension in societies to the neglect of preachers on this point. Speaking of one, he says: "I hope he is not afraid to preach full salvation *receivable now by faith*. This is the word which God will always bless and which the devil peculiarly hates, therefore he is constantly stirring up his own children and the weak children of God against it." Mr. Asbury, the Wesley of American Methodism, says: "I am divinely impressed to preach sanctification in *every* sermon." A Garretson and an Abbott were found thundering the same sentiments to all, wherever they went. George Pickering, of a later date, after fifty years in the ministry, in his semi-centennial sermon, exhorts his brethren to "preach to the people the blessed doctrine of holiness," adding, "this is the only thing that will hold the Methodist Church together." When on his dying bed, being visited by all the ministers of Boston, grasping the hand of the brother who was acting as spokesman for the whole, he exclaimed: "Tell, O tell the brethren to preach Christ and him crucified, an all-able, all-powerful, all-willing, all-ready Saviour, a present Saviour, saving now. Preach, now is the accepted time, now is the day of salvation. O tell them to preach holiness. Holiness is the principal thing. Preach holiness, holiness, holiness! God help you to preach holiness!" His feelings here overcame him, and thus ended the dying charge of that holy man. We have cause of gratitude that Methodism has yet some such spirits within her bosom. Without this distinguishing characteristic, our communion would compare favorably indeed with other denominations, but in this respect she has towered far above them. It is our earnest prayer that if they are ever on a footing with us, it may be by their coming up to our position, and not by our sinking. Instead of yielding one iota from the stand taken, let us in every movement write on all our banners, "Holiness to the Lord."

Having thus seen the preacher's duty, let us look for a moment at the manner of its performance. The divine direction is, "Thou shalt hear the word at my mouth and warn them from me." As God has preached it, so must we, not merely as a privilege, but as a solemn command. Does the Most High, with awful authority, forbid murder? With the same he enjoins full salvation. The same voice that says "Thou shalt not kill," says also "Thou shalt love the Lord thy God with all thy heart." If we may neglect the enforcement of the one, so we may of the other, and of all the commands of God.

With the obligation should be proclaimed the promises. Speaking of this day, the prophet says, "Then will I sprinkle clean water upon you, and ye shall be clean." St. Paul writes expressly of this, "Faithful is he who hath called you, who also will do it." O, how does God long to do the work, and all his messages should impress this truth upon the people, that He is infinitely able and willing to save to the utmost them that come to Him.

The inquirer should know also the conditions. There is only one condition of this work, which is FAITH. St. Peter declares of the Gentiles, God "put no difference between us and them, purifying their hearts by faith." Faith sees the work to be wrought—the obligation—the blessed Saviour waiting to save. By faith, the Christian ventures on Him, reckoning himself dead indeed unto sin, but alive unto God, believing that the blood of Christ cleanseth from all sin. Not believing that the blood *has* cleansed in order to *be* cleansed, but relying on Christ as a present Saviour saving now, and he is that moment saved. With the work he receives the spirit's witness, and the language of his whole heart is, "thou dost this moment save, with full salvation bless." Then will he cry with the psalmist, "draw near all ye that fear God, and I will declare what he hath done for my soul." His whole being exclaims:

"O, that the world might taste and see
The riches of his grace,
The arms of love that compass me,
Would all mankind embrace."

There is nothing so important as *definiteness* on this subject. A confused indefinite attack, firing in no particular direction, would never enable an army to conquer the foe. The minister must Nathan-like with the sharp sword of the spirit, cut in pieces the "man of sin." If he would be successful, let things be called by their proper names—the names God has given them, and let the people feel the infinite necessity of immediate action. But says one, "This would cause divisions in the church." Did Christ come to send peace on the earth? Nay, but a sword; and this close work on holiness is the sword that strikes at the root of carnality in the church as well as out of it. The man who holds on to his carnal propensities must, of necessity, take his stand against perfection. But would you have the martyr renounce his religion to escape the stake? Would you have the herald of the cross draw back, lest opposition arise? God says, "If any man draw back my soul shall have no pleasure in him."

Finally, preaching must be experimental. How can a man expect to be relied upon as a safe pilot amid the rocks and shoals of a sea he has never traversed? Shall the diseased person set himself up as competent to remove from his brother the malady under which himself continues to groan? His withering rebuke would be, "Physician, heal thyself." Can the blind lead the blind, and escape the ditch in spite of Omniscience? If ministers would successfully lead the children of God to the possession of entire holiness, they must first experience it. Then will they no longer be exposed to the imputation which St. Paul heaps upon teachers of his day, of "not understanding what they say, nor whereof they affirm." But in the language of the poet of Methodism—

"What we have felt and seen,
With confidence we tell,
And publish to the sons of men
The signs infallible."

They would send conviction to many hearts and awaken them to action.

O, if the ministers of the Methodist Episcopal Church would all become fully alive on this subject, and breathe that life into all their ministrations, how would the church gird herself with strength, and the world hasten to its millennial day!

BE IN EARNEST.

BY REV. A. A. PHELPS.

That Christians should be *in earnest*, is but the common conviction of the great heart of humanity, and the spontaneous confession of all who have any just claims to orthodoxy. If the Christian system is true, "it is *tremendously* true!" If it is true, then heaven, with its speechless glories, is all a *reality*, and will one day open its bright portals for the admission of all the blood-washed millions that shall eternally swell the anthems of the skies! If it is true, then *hell*, with its dark and endless horrors, will be the portion of every rebel against God! If it is true, then none can avoid perdition, and escape to the mansions above, but those that give up their sins, renounce the world, deny themselves and follow Jesus according to all the light that streams upon their pathway. If it is true, then all this preparation must be made within the brief span of human life, *or never be made at all!* If it is true, then millions on millions are dropping into the whirlpool of despair, where their cup will be filled with wrath without mercy, and ruin without remedy! If it is true, then everybody that has any light, any conscience, any love for souls, any desire to help hedge up the way to hell, and to people heaven with souls redeemed by blood, ought to be all alive and all astir from this very hour! There is enough in the scheme of salvation to move a man to action, if his heart is not made of adamant, and his conscience so "seared" as to be forever impervious to the impressions of the Holy Ghost. Does the reader still want motives to earnestness? Look over the churches, and mark their general lethargy, their frigid formality, their love of the world, their exhibitions of vanity, their policy-working management, their general contentedness with the mere *politics* of religion, with scarcely any of its *purity and power!* Look out upon the wants of the world, and gather up arguments that cannot fail to move an honest soul to diligence and duty. See the ignorance to be dispelled, the sufferings to be alleviated, the sinners to be converted, or lost forever! Look into heaven, and hear the sweet music, and see the white robed company basking in the mellow light of "one eternal day." Is there anything desirable in such a vision? and is it sufficiently so to make you in sober earnest to participate in those blissful scenes yourself, and enlist your energies to help others there? Look into hell, and hear them groan in everlasting agony! Is there anything in such a scene that makes you shrink back in horror, and fills you with deep desires to avoid so fearful a destiny? And have you no indescribable yearnings of heart to snatch your friends and neighbors from the "fiery pool?" O be *earnest*, in spirit and in life, and thus demonstrate to all that you *believe in God.*

POLYCARP, when being led out for martyrdom, being required to swear by the genius of Cæsar, gave this spirited answer: "Four score and six years have I served my master Christ, and he never did me any injury; how then shall I now blaspheme my King and my Saviour?" The same day he was committed to the flames.

To allow yourself deliberately to sit down satisfied with any imperfect attainments in religion, and to look upon a more confirmed and improved state of it as what you do not desire, nay, as what you secretly resolve that you will not pursue, is one of the most fatal signs we can well imagine, that you are an entire stranger to the first principles of it.—DODDRIDGE.

PURITY AND PEACE.

BY REV. WILLIAM COOLEY.

Peace is really desirable. It has many attractions to make it an object of interest. It can hardly be esteemed too highly. Christ is the Prince of peace, the gospel is the gospel of peace, and the peace makers are commended. The early, angelic announcement, was "peace on earth and good will to men." It is also our duty to pray for the peace of Jerusalem. The error into which many fall is that peace is a means to an end, rather than an end or result to be achieved. Purity is the cause, and peace the effect. "But the wisdom that is from above is first pure, then peaceable, gentle."—James iii, 17. "Follow righteousness, faith, charity, *peace*, with them that call on the Lord out of a pure heart."—2d Tim. ii, 22. "And the work of righteousness shall he peace; and the effect of righteousness, quietness and assurance forever."—Isa. xxxii, 17. Christ said, "Think not that I am come to send peace on earth; I am come not to send peace, but a sword. For I am come to set a man at variance against his father, and the daughter against her mother, and the daughter-in-law against her mother-in-law, and a man's foes shall be they of his own household."—Matt. x, 34, 36. The true ground of peace is purity, and peace resting on any other foundation is false and dangerous. False peace is the result of stupidity, or of a seared conscience, or of error, and is rather the precursor of coming ruin, than an element of happiness. Agitation is better than false peace. Purity is the condition of peace with the individual, the society, the church or the nation. Sin and holiness, truth and error, are eternal antagonisms, and there can never be true peace until sin and error are removed. In doing this work, there will be agitation and commotion, but this agitation is a sure indication that the light is shining, and that the lash of conscience is felt somewhere. It becomes our duty to expose and oppose every wrong and sinful practice, and this is what causes agitation. Men are obliged to become the cause of agitation, and to fight even, in order to secure peace. It is not with carnal weapons or bitter strife that we secure the peace of God to the souls of men, but by proclaiming the plain piercing truth of God's word. The Bible enjoins upon us to "Cry aloud, and spare not, lift up thy voice like a trumpet, and show my people their transgressions, and the house of Jacob their sins."—Isa. lviii, 1. "Have no fellowship with the unfruitful works of darkness, but rather reprove them."—Eph. v, 11. "Them that sin rebuke before all, that others also may fear."—1 Tim. v, 20. "Reprove, rebuke, exhort with all long suffering and doctrine."—2 Tim. iv, 2.

Elijah was a great agitator and troubler in Israel. Our Saviour, by his purity, his plain preaching, and uncompromising opposition to sin, made a great stir in his day, and well deserved the title of agitator. He disturbed the peace and quiet of the formal, wordly and hypocritical Pharisees, and was by them in return slandered, opposed and put to death. Paul was an agitator, and so was Martin Luther, and John Wesley. They greatly disturbed the peace of the churches to which they belonged. What is now wanted, is an agitation that shall rock all the churches in Christendom, so that the chaff of formalish, worldly policy, and worldly conformity, shall blow away forever, and the moral atmosphere become freed from the deadly vapors of sin, so that spiritual life, vitality and power, may be felt in every department and branch of this great Zion, and purity and evangelical peace everywhere prevail.

If love be sincere, it is accepted as the fulfilling of the law. Surely we serve a good Master, that has summed up all our duty in one word, and that a short word, and a sweet word, *love*, the beauty and harmony of the Universe. God is love; and love is his image upon the soul.—Henry.

THE SPIRIT OF JESUS IN THE CHURCH.

BY REV. J. A. WELLS.

The attempt to substitute electricity for the vital forces in the human system will be about as likely to succeed in bringing the dead to life, as the effort, now so generally made, to carry on the operations of the Church by worldly policy, without the Spirit of Jesus, will be to succeed in converting the world to God. When worldly policy, in any form, awakens the church to a realization of the condition of the unsaved world, gives it melting sympathies for the perishing, and tongues of fire to cut its way through the myriad foes of God, we may expect also that galvanic forces will cause the dead man to feel, think, speak, act and perform all the functions of the human soul. As one is impossible, so is the other. What a wonder that such an absurdity as seeking, without the Spirit of Jesus, to promote christianity should be so persistently followed! Only a few men ever tried to raise the dead by means of electricity, and they had no hearty expectation of success; but almost the whole professed christian world have persevered, from age to age, in trying to resuscitate a formal and dead church by means of money, worldly greatness, show and pageantry. Let us notice some of the errors that have contributed to the adoption and perpetuation of this absurd and fatal policy.

1. *Mistakes concerning the character of the Church of Christ.* Want of spiritual vision calls for the use of carnal vision. Men who believe that Christ has a church, but who are not able to discern the spiritual, will look for something temporal. Hence the world-wide mistake of confounding the church of Christ with ecclesiastical organizations.

The church of Jesus knows no parochial limits; it cannot be hemmed in by theological formularies. It is as wide as redeemed humanity. It knows no limit but the limit of the spirit. But men have supposed that their organization and creed were the limit of the church. They have practically regarded all in the organization as Christians, all out of it as sinners. That first principle of the kingdom of heaven that the church of Christ is the union of the kindred spirits of believers, is forgotten. With such a mistake as this, how could it otherwise happen, than that worldly policy should be resorted to, to carry on the work of the church. If men suppose that the church is of the world, they will carry on its operations by worldly means.

All the labors of the church, proceeding from such a mistake, are abortive. They are attempts to reach the hearts of men by organizations, by mere ecclesiastical machinery. It is wholly forgotten that an organization, as such, has no human sympathy. It cannot feel for the lost. The work of saving souls is a work of the heart. Sympathy is the only human instrument that can be used in the case.

Christianity is a character rather than an organization. Men who have the spirit of Christ are drawn into society by the force of mutual affection. They are baptized by one spirit into one body. The unity of the spirit is the bond of the church. When this fundamental principle is forgotten, and organizations are substituted for the unity of the spirit, it is perfectly natural that the whole interior life of the church should be discarded, and that worldly policy should be called in to supply its place. When will the church learn that it is the character of a Christian that constitutes a Christian? When will the prayer of Jesus, "That they may all be one, as Thou Father art in me, and I in Thee, that they also may be one in us," be realized in the recognized spiritual unity of the church? Jesus is one with the Father spiritually. We are made one with Jesus and the Father spiritually. So the whole church of Christ is one spiritually. When this doctrine shall be fully recognized, and men shall labor in accordance with it, to build up the church, then God will dwell in the church in awful majesty, and her victories will be glorious. The nations will know that Jehovah is God.

2. *Mistakes concerning the nature of religion.* True religion is nothing less than such a change in the heart, that the spirit of the world gives place to the spirit of Christ. The real Christian is actuated by the same spirit that actuated Jesus in all the labors and sufferings of his life. The man of the world, on the other hand, is actuated by the same spirit that persecuted Jesus and put him to death. The transition from the state of a sinner to that of a true Christian, is fundamental, and consists in the substitution of the spirit of Christ, as the ruling principle of life, for a spirit in every sense the opposite. But this radical change of heart and spirit is lost sight of, to an alarming extent, by nominal Christians. They are ever disposed to put on some of the accidents of religion and retain the spirit of the world. The carnal mind will be allowed to live and rule, on condition that it do homage to the name of Christianity. Instead of yielding the heart to Jesus, there is an effort to educate the spirit of the world into religion.

Some suppose that training the intellect, and cultivating the moral sentiments, will answer the terms of Christianity, and save the soul. Others believe that there is some virtue inhering in the means of grace, and the forms of religion, which, when they are diligently used, will secure eternal salvation. Others believe that there is a power in the church that can save them. They, accordingly, bend all their energies to securing the favor of what they conceive to be the church. There are still others, who, ignoring the corruption and fall of human nature, or in other words, its unlikeness to the spirit of Jesus, build their hopes of salvation on that indefinite thing, called by the world "morality."

All these ideas are of the world. Their prototypes are worldly and not heavenly. They are realized by worldly means. They set aside true Christianity, and leave men to run a fruitless chase after a phantom of the world bearing the name only of Christianity. Throughout all the land do our eyes, with pain, witness the desolation of God's heritage in consequence of these mistakes and follies. When will a pure Christianity prevail?

3. *Mistakes concerning the aim of the ministry.* The true aim of the ministry is to get sinners converted, and to build believers up in that holiness, without which no man can see the Lord. Ministers are sent to speak in Christ's stead, and beseech men to be reconciled to God. But many lose sight of the true object of the ministry, and go astray from its appropriate labor. The disposition to look at temporal things rather than spiritual, leads many a minister, even some who have once been successful in saving souls, to spend his time and talents in labor aside from his true work. Some labor merely to increase their own importance and extend their influence. Some work for fame. To have their praise in all the churches is of primary importance with them. There are those who rise no higher in their aims than the securing of their own support. All these motives, and any others that are not true gospel motives, are of the world. They lead to the adoption of worldly policy, and the use of worldly means. The minister who thus loses sight of the true aim of his work, will be characterized by want of power in proclaiming the Gospel. He will be constantly endeavoring to make up for that want of power by the use of some worldly thing in support of the gospel. All this use of some shining worldly excellence, instead of the simple power of the truth, this catering to the tastes of the ungodly, this patronizing air and demeanor towards sinners, this compromising with sin, and this weak, bashful spirit and manner in dealing with the wrongs of the day, which are everywhere seen, as the reproach of the church—all these show but too

plainly that the occupants of our pulpits are losing sight of the true work of Christ's ministers. Worldly means prevail for the accomplishment of worldly ends, instead of the spirit of Jesus actuating the church for the salvation of souls.

The sure antidote to all these errors and mistakes is the spirit of Jesus in the church. Where Christ reigns in the hearts of his people, there is spiritual life, and souls are saved. May God hasten the day when the church shall return from her wanderings and follow Jesus.

REGRETS TOO LATE.—It is stated that Lord Byron was at one time conversing in regard to his daughter with a distinguished lady of rank, whose influence over him checked his continuing the glaring immoralities of one of his worst poems, when she told him that if he loved his child, he should never write a line that would bring a blush of shame to her cheek or a sorrowing tear to her eye. He replied that the book was written to beguile hours of wretchedness, and to loosen her hold upon his affections, but added, "I will write no more of it. Would that I had not written a line." Referring in conversation with the same lady to his unhappy temperament, he said, "Depend upon it, people's tempers must be corrected while they are children; for not all the good resolutions in the world can enable a man to conquer habits of ill-humor or rage, however he may regret having given way to them.

SAID a very promising young minister of a few years standing in the Conference, (on witnessing the work of God follow in conversions of sinners as the fruit of a holy church,) "I verily believed that the world's redemption was to be secured by metaphysics; but I see it is a spiritual church, a holy ministry, that is to be thus honored.

I doubt we are not explicit enough, in speaking on full sanctification, either in public or private.—WESLEY.

REPROVING MINISTERS.—A free confession is a condition of a full remission; and when the sin is public, the confession must be public. If the ministers of England had sinned only in Latin, I would have made shift to have admonished them in Latin, or else have said nothing to them. But if they will sin in English, they must hear of it in English. Unpardoned sin will never let us rest nor prosper, though we be at ever so much care and cost to cover it. Our sin will surely find us out though we find not it.

Too many who have set their hand to this sacred work (the ministry) are, notwithstanding, still addicted to self-seeking, negligence, pride and other sins, so that it is our duty to admonish them. To give them up as incurable, were cruel, as long as there are other means to be used. We must not hate them, but plainly rebuke them, and not suffer sin upon them, (Lev. xix, 17.) To bear with the vices of the ministers is to promote the ruin of the church. For what more speedy way is there to deprave and undo the people than the depravity of their guides? And how can we more effectually farther a reformation than by endeavoring to reform the leaders of the church? Surely, brethren, if it be our duty to endeavor to cast out those ministers that are negligent, scandalous, and unfit for the work, it must be our duty to endeavor to heal the sins of others, and to use a much gentler remedy to them that are less guilty.—BAXTER, 1656.

HE, therefore, who loves God with his whole heart, and his neighbor as himself, although he may be the subject of involuntary imperfections and infirmities, which, in consequence of his relation to Adam, require confession and atonement, is nevertheless, in the Gospel sense of the terms, a holy or sanctified person.—UPHAM.

AFTER all, one touch of the Spirit of God is worth more than all our plans and contrivances for the promotion of church order.—DR. JUDSON.

SCRIPTURAL CONVICTION.

BY MRS. MARIETTE HARDY FREELAND.

The subject before us opens a field for investigation of no ordinary importance. Underlying, as it does, the religious experience of every Christian, and thus forming a basis upon which the glorious superstructure is reared, conviction in its true character cannot be too closely examined by such as would win souls to God. However extensive may be the oneness of *theory* among theologians, respecting this subject, it is nevertheless true that there does exist a very great *practical* difference among them, both as respects conviction itself, and the means by which it is produced.

True conviction, as taught by the holy scriptures, is not sympathy with Christ or his followers. The unawakened sinner may have his sympathies enlisted, and his feelings powerfully wrought upon by the rehearsal of real or imaginary suffering, but this is not conviction for sin. A sympathy for friends, who deeply desire one's salvation, may prompt to identify one's self as a seeker of salvation, but it is not conviction. Therefore the minister or private member who deeply desires the salvation of souls, should beware how he dwells upon subjects calculated to arouse the sympathies rather than enlighten the understanding and convict the heart, for in so doing he is in danger of deceiving souls respecting their real condition.

Neither is scriptural conviction a mere intellectual perception of the truthfulness of God's word. Men may be convinced without being convicted, the will remaining fully set to do evil. They may admit that it is right to love and serve God; that men ought to be moral; but at the same time be nurturing the most deadly hatred to righteousness. Let but the hearts of such men be penetrated by the two edged sword of gospel truth, and it would at once be evident there was a nest of vipers slumbering there, ready coiled to inflict the mortal wound upon any who should dare disturb their peace.

Conviction for sin is not remorse. The soul all hardened in guilt may suffer the keenest pangs of bitter remorse and still not have one penitent thought. He feels the horrors of retribution, but curses the hand of justice. Remorse is, undoubtedly, often mistaken for conviction, when experienced by those near the eternal world. Hence, the instances are not unfrequent where individuals are restored to health, who have professed repentance on the sick bed, when no evidence is given of a real change. Their's was not a godly sorrow. They sorrowed for the *consequences* of transgression, but not for the transgression itself.

"The heart is deceitful above all things, and desperately wicked," is the declaration of God's word, but how slow are we to believe. Sin has so interwoven itself with every fibre of our being, that it will not relax its grasp without a death struggle. And so far gone from original righteousness is the unrenewed heart, that it comes to regard sin as an indispensable part of itself—a real friend and source of everlasting joy. Indeed, the heart of man, while thus unchanged, is the abode of darkness, anarchy and death. It is lost to all good, and utterly incapable of self renovation. Much as the doctrine of total depravity is scouted at and rejected, even by many who are professedly orthodox, nevertheless it still remains true that "from the crown of the head to the sole of the foot, there is no soundness in" man. He is in a *lost* condition; lost to every element of righteousness. But what makes his condition far more deplorable, is the fact that he thinks himself safe; he knows not that he is *lost*, but as has been remarked, he regards his direst enemy, sin, as his real friend, and madly clings to it as his only hope. While the whole human family were thus lost to all good, and plunged into the darkness of sin in its varied form, God was pleased to undertake for us.

"He laid help upon one that is mighty to save and strong to deliver," at that moment "when there was no eye to pity, nor arm to save." Glory be to God! Jesus died to redeem the lost race of man from the thraldom of sin; and by his death purchased the gift of the Holy Ghost, which is freely bestowed upon man. The office of this Spirit is to enlighten the understanding and convince the heart that it is thus lost. This work of the Spirit is scripturally termed conviction for sin. In the light thus given, man sees the folly of trusting in the pleasures of sense for permanent enjoyment. He awakes, as it were, from the sleep of moral death, to a realization of his true condition. Ah! how empty and unreliable everything of earth in which he has so fondly trusted, now appears! He sees, too, the awful guilt of ingratitude that rests upon his soul, for thus neglecting salvation in his vain pursuit of creature joys; and he deeply feels the infinite justice of the decree, "The soul that sinneth, it shall die," and feels also that it would be *just* for him to suffer the penalty of a broken law to all eternity. With sighs and groans he confesses his transgressions, and his sins are ever before him. Like Bunyan's Pilgrim, he puts his fingers in his ears and cries "Life! life! eternal life!" as his former companions seek to dissuade him from his newly formed purposes to live for God and heaven. The sinner, thus keenly alive to his condition, does not stop for the more honorable of his companions in sin to accompany him, but he is ready to bow with the veriest beggar to supplicate for mercy.

The genuineness of conviction, when cherished, is also evidenced by a universal hatred to sin, especially the sin that has been the greatest snare to the individual, and the source of the most sinful pleasure. The convicted miser scatters his golden store as mere bubbles on the murmuring stream. The drunkard dashes his cup to the earth and vows eternal abstinence, while the guilty vender of the intoxicating draught, trembles and turns away from the scenes of traffic with human souls, to seek a more congenial employment. The airy belle of fashion lays aside her gilded baubles and robes of vanity, and, like a Hester Ann Rogers, rips them up, or consumes them in the flames, lest they should tempt her from her purpose to be right with God. Such are some of the fruits of scriptural conviction, or such conviction for sin as the Holy Scriptures pronounce genuine. Talk of men or women being under conviction for sin, and earnestly seeking salvation, and still *enjoying* the vain fooleries of fashionable life, or finding satisfaction in sinful pursuits, and you talk absurdities. Nay, sooner would the man of correct morals *love* to mingle in scenes of drunkenness and vice, than a convicted sinner in scenes of frivolity and mirth. His language is

"The world can never give
The bliss for which I sigh."

But what do some professed teachers in our Israel affirm by their instructions and practice, but that the circle of fashionable pleasure is a fit place, not only for the convicted sinner, but also for the converted soul? Else why the festive scenes so frequently witnessed in our churches and parsonage? Ah! may it not be said of such "They be blind leaders of the blind," and shall not both fall into the ditch? Let awakened souls beware how they mingle in such scenes, though patronized by ministry and membership, and even by dignified "D. D's." No marvel that there is confusion in our ranks, for all are not Christians who bear the name, as all are not meet for the kingdom of heaven who say Lord, Lord. May the time soon come when the abominations which make desolate shall be done away, and mourning souls find proper instructions to guide them into the narrow way.

Thus we see it means something more to be under conviction than is usually supposed. Indeed, it is not uncommon to find those who have for years professed to be followers of Jesus, who are, notwithstanding, practically ignorant of genuine conviction, having never felt its penetrating power upon their hearts. It is not strange that such individuals should still pursue to a greater or less extent the same round of worldly pleasures that they did previous to professing religion, decorating their bodies according to the latest fashion, and frequenting places of vain amusement, for their tastes and inclinations remain unchanged. Conviction must precede conversion, hence an individual that has never borne the fruits of conviction, viz: universal hatred to sin, cannot be a converted man or woman, however high the profession may be. In view of such facts, it becomes a subject of deep and thrilling interest, how this state of things has been brought about, or in other words, how have individuals found their way within the pale of the Christian Church, without so much as a practical or experimental knowledge of genuine conviction for sin, and destitute of a personal knowledge of sins forgiven. For this, as we have remarked, must be the case, if the first is wanting, and it is not unfrequently true where conviction, deep and pungent, has been felt upon the soul. But as an investigation of this subject would naturally involve reference to the means or instrumentality divinely authorized to lead lost sinners home to God, we will defer such investigation to a future article; meanwhile praying that the numerous readers of *The Earnest Christian* may look well to the important matter of laying the foundation of a religious experience in accordance with the word of God. And hoping, too, that all who labor for the salvation of others may be watchful here, and not point souls away to the wounds of the Crucified before they are sufficiently sensible of their need of a Saviour.

WATCHFULNESS.—When we are alone we have our thoughts to watch; in the family, our tempers; in company, our tongues—H. MORE.

LETTER ON ORNAMENTAL AND COSTLY ATTIRE.

[The following letter from the devoted Apostle of Burmah, now gone to his reward will, we trust, receive the prayerful attention of all our readers. We see from this, that the extravagance of dress indulged in by too many of the professed followers of the Meek and the Lowly One, and countenanced by too many ministers that stand up in the sacred desk in *His* holy name, exerts its baleful influence upon the minds of poor benighted heathens in far off lands. That soul must be hardened indeed, that can read unmoved this touching appeal, and go away and worship at the altar of vanity.—ED.]

To the Female Members of Christian Churches in the United States of America.

DEAR SISTERS IN CHRIST:—Excuse my publicly addressing you. The necessity of the case is my only apology. Whether you will consider it a sufficient apology for the sentiments of this letter—unfashionable, I confess, and perhaps unpalatable—I know not. We are sometimes obliged to encounter the hazard of offending those whom, of all others, we desire to please. Let me throw myself at once on your mercy, dear sisters, allied by national consanguinity, professors of the same holy religion, fellow-pilgrims to the same happy world. Pleading these endearing ties, let me beg you to regard me as a brother, and to listen with candor and forbearance to my honest tale.

In raising up a church of Christ in this heathen land, and in laboring to elevate the minds of the female converts to the standard of the gospel, we have always found one chief obstacle in that principle of vanity, that love of dress and display—I beg you will bear with me—which has, in every age and in all countries, been a ruling passion of the fair sex, as the love of riches, power, and fame, has characterized the other. That obstacle lately became more formidable, through the admission of two or three fashionable females into the church, and the arrival of several missionary sisters, dressed and adorned in that manner which is too prevalent in our beloved native land. On my meeting the church, after a year's absence, I beheld an appalling profusion of ornaments, and saw that the demon of vanity was laying waste the female department. At that time I had not maturely considered the subject, and did not feel sure what ground I ought to take. I apprehended, also, that I should be unsupported, and, perhaps, opposed, by some of my coadjutors. I confined my efforts, therefore, to private exhortation, and with but little effect. Some of the ladies, out of regard to their pastor's feelings, took off their necklaces and ear ornaments before they entered the chapel, tied them up in a corner of their handkerchiefs, and on returning, as soon as they were out of sight of the mission house, stopped in the middle of the street to array themselves anew.

In the mean time I was called to visit the Karens, a wild people, several days' journey to the north of Maulmain. Little did I expect there to encounter the same enemy, in those "wilds, horrid and dark with o'ershadowing trees." But I found that he had been there before me, and reigned with a peculiar sway, from time immemorial. On one Karen lady I counted between twelve and fifteen necklaces, of all colors, sizes, and materials. Three was the average. Brass belts above the ankles; neat braids of black hair tied below the knees; rings of all sorts on the fingers; bracelets on the wrists and arms; long instruments of some metal, perforating the lower part of the ear, by an immense aperture, and reaching nearly to the shoulders; fancifully-constructed bags enclosing the hair, and suspended from the back part of the head; not to speak of the ornamental parts of their clothing—constituted the fashions and the ton of the fair Karenesses. The dress of the female converts was not essentially different from that of their countrywomen. I saw that I was brought into a situation that precluded all retreat—that I must fight or die.

For a few nights I spent some sleepless hours, distressed by this and other subjects, which will always press upon the heart of a missionary in a new place. I considered the spirit of the religion of Jesus Christ. I opened to 1 Tim. ii. 9, and read these words of the inspired apostle: "I will, also, that women adorn themselves in modest apparel, with shamefacedness and sobriety; *not with broidered hair, or gold, or pearls, or costly array.*" I asked myself, can I baptize a Karen woman in her present attire? No. Can I administer the Lord's supper to one of the baptized in that attire? No. Can I refrain from enforcing the prohibition of the apostle? Not without betraying the trust I have received from him. Again: I considered that the question concerned not the Karens only, but the whole Christian world; that its decision would involve a train of unknown consequences; that a single step would lead me into a long and perilous way. I considered Maulmain and the other stations; I considered the state of the public mind at home. But "*what is that to thee? follow thou me,*" was the continual response, and weighed more than all. I renewedly offered myself to Christ, and prayed for strength to go forward in the path of duty, come life or death, come praise or reproach, supported or deserted, successful or defeated in the ultimate issue.

Soon after coming to this resolution, a Karen woman offered herself for baptism. After the usual examination, I inquired whether she could give up her ornaments for Christ? It was an unexpected blow! I explained the spirit of the gospel. I appealed to her own consciousness of vanity. I read her the apostle's prohibition. She looked again and again at her handsome necklace—she wore but one—and then, with an air of modest decision that would adorn, beyond all outward ornaments, any of my sisters whom I have the honor of addressing, she quietly took it off, saying, *I love Christ more than this.* The news began to spread. The Christian women made but little hesitation. A few others opposed, but the work went on.

At length the evil which I most dreaded came upon me. Some of the Karen men had been to Maulmain, and seen what I wished they had not; and one day, when we were discussing the subject of ornaments, one of the Christians came forward, and declared that at Maulmain he had actually seen one of the great female teachers wearing a string of gold beads around her neck.

Lay down this paper, dear sisters, and sympathize a moment with your fallen missionary. Was it not a hard case? However, though cast down, I was not destroyed; I endeavored to maintain the warfare as well as I could, and when I left those parts, the female converts were, generally speaking, arrayed in modest apparel.

On arriving at Maulmain, and partially recovering from a fever which I had contracted in the Karen woods, the first thing I did was to crawl out to the house of the patroness of the gold necklace. To her I related my adventures, and described my grief. With what ease, and truth too, could that sister say, notwithstanding this necklace, "I dress more plainly than most ministers' wives and professors of religion in our native land! This necklace is the only ornament I wear; it was given me when quite a child, by a dear mother, whom I expect never to see again, (another hard case,) and she begged me never to part with it as long as I lived, but to wear it as a memorial of her." O ye Christian mothers! what a lesson you have before you! Can you, dare you give injunctions to your daughters directly contrary to apostolic commands? But to the honor of my sister, be it recorded, that, as soon as she understood the merits of the case, and the mischief done by such example, off went the gold necklace, and she gave decisive proof that she loved Christ more than father or mother. Her example, united with the efforts of the rest of us at this station, is beginning to exercise a redeeming influence in the female department of the church.

But notwithstanding these favorable signs, nothing, really nothing, is yet done. And why? This mission, and all others, must necessarily be sustained by continual supplies of missionaries, male and female, from the mother country. Your sisters and daughters will continually come out, to take the place of those who are removed by death, and to occupy numberless stations still unoccupied. And when they arrive they will be dressed in their usual way, as Christian women at home are dressed. And the female converts will run around them, and gaze upon them, with the most prying curiosity, regarding them as the freshest representatives of the Christian religion from that land where it flourishes in all its purity and glory. And when they see the gold and jewels pendent from their ears, the beads and chains encircling their necks, the finger rings set with diamonds and rubies, the rich variety of ornamental head-dress, "the mantles, and the wimples, and the crisping pins." (see Is. iii. 19, 23,) they will cast a reproachful, triumphant glance at their old teachers, and spring, with fresh avidity, to repurchase and resume their long-neglected elegances; the cheering news will fly up the Dah-gyne, the Laing-bwai, and the Salwen; the Karenesses will reload their necks, and ears, and arms, and ankles; and when, after another year's absence, I return and take my seat before the Burmese or the Karen church, I shall behold the demon of vanity enthroned in the centre of the assembly more firmly than ever, grinning defiance to the prohibitions of apostles, and the exhortations of us who would fain be their humble followers. And thus you, my dear sisters, sitting quietly by your firesides, or repairing devoutly to your places of worship, do, by your example, spread the poison of vanity through all the rivers, and mountains, and wilds of this far-distant land; and while you are sincerely and fervently praying for the upbuilding of the Redeemer's kingdom, are inadvertently building up that of the devil. If, on the other hand, you divest yourselves of all meretricious ornaments, your sisters and daughters, who come hither, will be divested of course; the further supplies of vanity and pride will be cut off, and the churches at home being kept pure, the churches here will be pure also.

Dear Sisters: Having finished my tale, and therein exhibited the necessity under which I lay of addressing you, I beg leave to submit a few topics to your candid and prayerful consideration.

1. Let me appeal to conscience, and inquire, what is the real motive for wearing ornamental and costly apparel? Is it not the desire of setting off one's person to the best advantage, and of exciting the admiration of others? Is not such dress calculated to gratify self-love, and cherish sentiments of vanity and pride? And is it not the nature of those sentiments to acquire strength from indulgence? Do such motives and sentiments comport with the meek, humble, self-denying religion of Jesus Christ? I would here respectfully suggest, that these questions will not be answered so faithfully in the midst of company as when quite alone, kneeling before God.

2. Consider the words of the apostle, quoted above, from 1 Tim. ii. 9,— "I will also that women adorn themselves in modest apparel, with shamefacedness and sobriety, *not with broidered hair, or gold, or pearls, or costly array*." I do not quote a similar command, recorded in 1 Pet. iii. 3, because the verbal construction is not quite so definite, though the import of the two passages is the same. But cannot the force of these two passages be evaded? Yes, and nearly every command in Scripture can be evaded, and every doctrinal assertion perverted, plausibly and handsomely too, if we set about it in good earnest. But preserving the posture above alluded to, with the inspired volume spread open at the passage in question, ask your hearts, in simplicity and godly sincerity, whether the meaning is not just as plain as the sun at noonday. Shall we then bow to the authority of an inspired apostle, or shall we not? From that authority shall we appeal to the prevailing usages and fashions of the age? If so, please to recall the missionaries you have sent to the heathen; for the heathen can vindicate all their superstitions on the same ground.

3. In the posture you have assumed, look up and behold the eye of your benignant Saviour ever gazing upon you with the tenderest love—upon you, his daughters, his spouse, wishing above all things, that you would yield your hearts entirely to him, and become holy as he is holy, rejoicing when he sees one after another accepting his pressing invitation, and entering the more perfect way.

4. Anticipate the happy moment, "hastening on all the wings of time," when your joyful spirits will be welcomed into the assembly of the spirits of the just made perfect. You appear before the throne of Jehovah; the approving smile of Jesus fixes your everlasting happy destiny; and you are plunging into "the sea of life and love unknown, without a bottom or a shore." Stop a moment; look back on yonder dark and miserable world that you have left; fix your eye on the meagre, vain, contemptible articles of ornamental dress, which you once hesitated to give up for Christ, the King of glory; and on that glance decide the question instantly and forever.

Surely you can hold out no longer. You cannot rise from your knees in your present attire. Thanks be to God, I see you taking off your necklaces and ear-rings, tearing away your ribbons, and ruffles, and superfluities of head-dress, and I hear you exclaim, "What shall we do next?"—an important question, deserving serious consideration. The ornaments you are removing, though useless, and worse than useless, in their present state, can be so disposed of as to feed the hungry, clothe the naked, relieve the sick, enlighten the dark-minded, disseminate the Holy Scriptures, spread the glorious gospel throughout the world. Little do the inhabitants of a free Christian country know of the want and distress endured by the greater part of the inhabitants of the earth. Still less idea can they form of the awful darkness which rests upon the great mass of mankind in regard to spiritual things. During the years that you have been wearing these useless ornaments, how many poor creatures have been pining in want! How many have languished and groaned on beds of abject wretchedness! How many children have been bred up in the blackest ignorance, hardened in all manner of iniquity! How many immortal souls have gone down to hell, with a lie in their right hand, having never heard of the true God and the only Saviour! Some of these miseries might have been mitigated; some poor wretch have felt his pain relieved; some widow's heart been made to sing for joy; some helpless orphan have been taught in the Sabbath school, and trained up for a happy life here and hereafter. The Holy Bible and valuable tracts might have been far more extensively circulated in heathen lands had you not been afraid of being thought unfashionable, and not "like other folks;" had you not preferred adorning your persons, and cherishing the sweet seductive feelings of vanity and pride.

O Christian sisters, believers in God, in Christ, in an eternal Heaven, and an eternal Hell, can you hesitate, and ask what you shall do? Bedew those ornaments with the tears of contrition; consecrate them to the cause of charity; hang them on the cross of your dying Lord. Delay not an instant. Hasten with all your might, if not to make reparation for the past, at least to prevent a continuance of the evil in future.

And for your guidance, allow me to suggest two fundamental principles—the one based on 1 Tim. ii, 9—*all ornaments and costly dress to be disused; the other on the law of general benevolence—the avails of such articles, and the savings resulting from the plain dress system, to be devoted to purposes of charity.* Some general rules in regard to dress, and some general objects of charity, may be easily ascertained; and free discussion will throw light on many points at first obscure. Be not deterred by the suggestion that in such discussions you are concerned about *small* things. Great things depend on small; and, in that case, things which appear small to short-sighted man are great in the sight of God. Many there are who praise the principle of self-denial in general, and condemn it in all its particular applications as too minute, scrupulous, and severe. The enemy is well aware that, if he can secure the minute units, the sum total will be his own. Think not anything small which may have a bearing upon the kingdom of Christ and upon the destinies of eternity. How easy to conceive, from many known events, that the single fact of a lady's divesting herself of a necklace for Christ's sake may involve consequences which shall be felt in the remotest parts of the earth, and in all future generations to the end of time—yea, stretch away into a boundless eternity, and be a subject of praise millions of ages after this world and all its ornaments are burned up.

Beware of another suggestion made by weak and erring souls, who will tell you that there is more danger of being proud of plain dress and other modes of self-denial than of fashionable attire and self-indulgence. Be not insnared by this last, most finished, most insidious device of the great enemy. Rather believe that He who enables you to make a sacrifice is able to keep you from being proud of it. Believe that He will kindly permit such occasions of mortification and shame as will preserve you from the evil threatened. *The severest part of self-denial consists in encountering the disapprobation, the envy, the hatred of one's dearest friends.* All who enter the straight and narrow path in good earnest soon find themselves in a climate extremely uncongenial to the growth of pride. The gay and fashionable will, in many cases, be the last to engage in this holy undertaking. But let none be discouraged on that account. Christ has seldom honored the leaders of worldly fashion by appointing them leaders in his cause. Fix it in your hearts that in this warfare *the Lord Jesus Christ expects every woman to do her duty.* There is, probably, not one in the humblest walks of life but would, on strict examination, find some article which *might* be dispensed with for purposes of charity, and *ought* to be dispensed with in compliance with the apostolic command. Wait not, therefore, for the fashionable to set an example; wait not for one another; listen not to the news from the next town; but *let every individual go forward,* regardless of reproach, fearless of consequences. The eye of Christ is upon you. Death is hastening to strip you of your ornaments, and to turn your fair forms into corruption and dust. Many of those for whom this letter is designed will be laid in the grave before it can ever reach their eyes. We shall all soon appear before the judgment seat of Christ, to be tried for our conduct, and to receive the things done in the body. When placed before that awful bar, in the presence of that Being whose eyes are as a flame of fire, and whose irrevocable fiat will fix you forever in Heaven or in Hell, and mete out the measure of your everlasting pleasures and pains, what course will you then wish you had taken? Will you then wish that, in defiance of His authority, you had adorned your mortal bodies with gold, and precious stones, and costly attire, cherishing self-love, vanity, and pride? Or will you wish that you had chosen a life of self-denial, renounced the world, taken up the cross *daily,* and followed Him? *And as you will then wish you had done,* DO NOW.

Dear sisters, your affectionate brother in Christ, A. JUDSON.

WORLDLY SOCIETY.—After long doubting the propriety, and even the lawfulness, of mixing at all in society where duty does not call, and after smarting a number of times for indulging myself in it—more, however, through fear of offending, than for any pleasure I find in it—I am at length brought to renounce it entirely; and it is not a needless scrupulosity. It does appear a duty to shun all communication with the world, when there is no well-grounded reason to hope to do good. There are, to be sure, many plausible reasons, but I doubt whether they will bear the test of Scripture.

Can a man walk on pitch, and his feet not be defiled? Can a man take coals of fire in his bosom and his clothes not be burned? If he can, then he may mix freely with the world, and not be contaminated. But I am not the one who can do it.

I speak only for myself. Others may experience no bad effects; but, for myself, when I go into company, if it is pleasant and agreeable, it has a tendency only to fix my thoughts on earth, from which it is my duty and my desire to turn them; to give me a distaste for serious duties, especially prayer and meditation; and to render me desirous of the applause and approbation of those with whom I associate. I cannot avoid feeling some desire for its friendship; and this friendship, the apostle assures us, and my own experience feelingly convinces me, is enmity with God.—PAYSON.

IT requires a great degree of watchfulness to retain the perfect love of God; and one great means of retaining it is, frankly to declare what God has given you, and earnestly to exhort all the believers you meet with to follow after full salvation.—WESLEY.

POLITENESS is the religion of the heart, as piety is that of the soul. It is good nature in action. It renders whoever may be its object contented and happy under its softening influence. It consists in acts which show their source—the heart.

LOOK AND LIVE—BELIEVE AND ENTER IN—OBEY AND POSSESS.

BY S. K. J. CHESBROUGH.

How simple is the plan of Salvation. Yet how many stumble at this very thing. Does not much of the power of Salvation lie in the simplicity of the Gospel plan? Was not this simplicity a stumbling block to the self-righteous Jew, and foolishness to the proud and learned Greek? God has seen fit in His wisdom so to confound the wisdom of this world as to hide these things from the wise and prudent, and to reveal them into babes. How very repugnant to the carnal heart this simple way of faith! The heart convicted of sin, sinking beneath the weight of guilt, looks all around for some other way to be saved, endeavoring, though vainly, by works, to gain Salvation; and it frequently happens that the soul, that is thus seeking Jesus, mourns for weeks, before it learns, like Peter, to repeat the simple prayer of utter helplessness, "*Lord save me, or I perish.*" How simple was the remedy God provided for the poor sinning Israelite when bitten by the "fiery serpent." It was simply to look upon the "brazen serpent" Moses had lifted up, and they were healed; it was but to "look and live." Thus, dear sinner, has Jesus been lifted up, that whosoever looks upon Him may live. Look up, sinner, poor backslider in heart or life, "look and live." "Well," says one, "I have looked and I have been saved." Then there is another step to be taken. The land of Canaan, or of perfect love, lies close to this "wilderness" where you have been wandering. God has brought you up out of Egypt, through the Red Sea; the Egyptians who followed hard after have been drowned. Now you are come to Kadish Barnea; God says go over, enter in. That mighty foe, Unbelief, now confronts you, whispers to you that there are giants there. You have been conscious that you felt that there are roots of bitterness yet within you. You have felt the risings of pride, anger, selfishness, impatience, fretfulness, peevishness; you have seen that they dwelt in "walled cities;" you are almost discouraged. Unbelief whispers to you and says, "you are but as a grasshopper, do not venture."

What does GOD *say?* "See, I have set the land before thee, go over and possess it, in the length of it and in the breadth of it." How many, from this point, shrink and go back, vainly hoping that by wandering around forty years they will at last enter in over against Jericho, instead of Kadish Barnea. Ah! how many carcasses lie scattered here and there. These inward foes have proved to be too mighty. Reader, is this your condition? I entreat you to consecrate all to God, and by simple faith claim the promised land, "the rest from inbred sin," "perfect love which casts out fear." We are to walk by the same rule and mind the same things in every step of the Divine life. Simple faith, and trust in God—letting go of self, and falling into the arms of Jesus, and He will save you. Can you not now say "Lord, I believe?" Says one, "Now we are over. What remains to be done?"

Obey and possess. As the Israelites only possessed as much and as far as they obeyed God, so it will be with us. Our "Jericho," and our "Ai," are to be taken, the Seven Nations are to be destroyed, the thirty and one Kings are to be overthrown—all, all, to be utterly destroyed.

We must contend for a "*clean victory.*" If we permit any to remain, we shall find this man-fearing and compromising spirit will be "pricks in our eyes," shutting out the clear light; "thorns in our sides," causing us pain and fearful anxiety. God demands perfect obedience. Oh! my brother and sister, what an inheritance is before us. Are you striving earnestly, yea contending for every foot of your possessions? Do not commence as soon as Jericho is taken, and you gain one victory, to sing "There is rest for the weary." The battle has just commenced. In this day, when a compromising, man-fearing, and man-pleasing spirit abounds, and professed soldiers of the cross are seeking for worldly honors, positions in Church and State, conforming to the world, sighing for the day to come "when the offence of the cross shall cease," "fearing the Lord and serving their own gods;" we need to arise, and shake ourselves from the dust, gird on our armor, and in Jesus' might go forth to glorious war against "spiritual wickedness in high places." If the "*Sauls*," who stand head and shoulders above the people, dare not fight with the formidable Goliaths, God will raise up Davids, who, with the simple sling of faith, and the smooth stones—the pure yet simple testimony—will go up against the enemies of our Israel.

Who will this day consecrate himself to God, gird on all the armor, cut off every retreat, and cry, "I mean to die in the army of the Lord?"

To prove the sincerity of our humiliation and repentance, instead of cloaking and extenuating our manifold sins, let us confess them with deep sorrow, and return to the Lord with mourning and prayer, as well as with fasting; bearing each of us the load of our own private iniquities, the additional load of the iniquities of our families, and the immensely accumulated load of the iniquities of our country at large.—FLETCHER.

IF you cannot relieve, do not grieve the poor; give them soft words, if nothing else; abstain from either sour looks or harsh words. Let them be glad to come, even though they should go empty away. Put yourself in the place of every poor man; and deal with him as you would God should deal with you.—WESLEY.

THESE professors, (unstable ones,) have more of the moon than of the sun, little light, less heat, and many changes.—FLAVEL.

THE KIND OF PREACHING WE NEED.

BY MRS. ELLEN L. ROBERTS.

How many in these days are groaning under the feeling, "Woe is me if I preach not the Gospel." They look at themselves—the few advantages they have had for the cultivation of their minds—their limited knowledge of rhetoric and grammar, and say, "How can I do it?" They glance, too, at the style of preaching which prevails at the present day, and the response is, "Who is sufficient for these things?" They try to think either that they are mistaken, or else that God will perhaps excuse them; or perchance they endeavor to compromise the matter so as not to go quite as far as the Holy Spirit leads them, and thus they bring barrenness and leanness upon their own souls and render themselves inefficient in the cause of God. When we see a cross, will God bless us in an attempt to take a part of that cross, or in substituting a cross of our own for the one He lays upon us? We say to a soul, seeking pardon or purity, take the *whole* cross; we say the same to that person who is called to preach the Gospel. Let us get in the dust and ask Jesus to show us what kind of preaching He requires of us. What does the world demand, and the multitudes call for? Not dry essays, nor theological dissertations, nor doctrinal discussions; the masses have starved on these, and are now asking for holy lives, a living, burning experience; men and women that can pilot them from conviction for sin, into justification, sanctification, and on into the ocean of God's love. If you have the qualification of a Gideon Oursley, "a knowlege of the disease and remedy," you may, like him, be instrumental in saving thousands from the death that never dies.

Call to mind the eloquent sermons to which you have listened, from the most gifted ministers, and you may find the impression they made soon wore away, while the simple story of a child who had just passed from death unto life, or the words of some father or mother in Israel, as they testified to the power of grace which enabled them to triumph in the midst of suffering, privation and the loss of all things, left an arrow in your soul which was never removed till you became savingly acquainted with Jesus. We have trembled like an aspen leaf under the burning appeals of an Olin and a Hamline, and yet they did not make the impression upon our minds that the simple relation of their experience did. The *way* they came in possession of justifying and santifying grace, we remembered longer than their sermons upon those subjects.

But do you say, "Must I go into the pulpit with this simple kind of preaching?" We answer, *take the whole cross*. In Ireland little children are placed upon the stand to tell what Jesus has done for them; sinners are convicted, and they melt and yield to the claims of God while listening to them. If God should lead you farther, to talk about any portion of His word, or simply to read a command or threatening, we believe He could give you so much of the holy unction that it would sink deeper in some hearts than any learned exposition of the word. It is not the head we need to reach, but the heart. When we get into some upper room, and wait for the baptism of the Holy Ghost, *paying the price for it which the disciples paid*, laying our wisdom in the dust, and continuing with one accord in prayer and supplication, "until we too are endowed with the same" power from on high—then shall we prove that "God has chosen the foolish things of the world to confound the wise;" and "the weak things of the world to confound the things which are mighty."

WHERE God's Word is taught, pure, and undefiled, there is also poverty. Superstition, idolatry and hypocrisy have ample wages, but truth goes a begging.—LUTHER.

THE blessed apostle John, living at Ephesus to extreme old age, being carried to the church, was wont to say nothing but this, "Little children, love one another." The brethren, tired with hearing so often the same thing, said, "Sir, why do you always say this?" He replied, "Because it is the Lord's command; and if that alone be done, it is sufficient."—JEROME, A. D. 392.

WHEN Ongin was seventeen years of age, his father was cast into prison for being a Christian. The son fearing that his father, distressed for the destitute condition of his family, might be induced to compromise his religion, wrote to him as follows: "Take heed, father, that you do not change your mind for our sakes."

No holy word, no righteous act can ever die. Strike the cords of influence with a manly hand! Their vibration will ring on forever. Be hopeful! We are moving on toward high noon; hardly out of the twilight yet, it may be, but thank God it is the twilight of the morning and not of the evening, and the hour hand on the great dial plate of time never goes back. Slowly and silently, except when it strikes at long intervals the progressive epochs of the world, it advances toward the meridian.

IT is possible that one's suffering and privation may be numbered among his poorest pleasures. He who foregoes a luxury for the sake of those he loves, or turns away from the gifts of fortune to discharge a duty, finds in that self denial his highest happiness.

GLORIOUS is the destiny of the real martyr; there is a sublimity in his voluntary sacrifice, that pertains not to triumphs in arts and arms, when the soul is girded, and equipped to suffer and be strong.

GIVE to a grief a little time, and it softens to regret, and grows beautiful, at last, and we cherish it as we do some old, dim picture of the dead.—B. F. TAYLOR.

PREJUDICE.

Every one is forward to complain of the prejudices that mislead other men or parties, as if he were free, and had none of his own. This being objected on all sides, it is agreed that it is a fault and an hindrance to knowledge. What now is the case? No other but this, that every man should let alone others' prejudices and examine his own. Nobody is convinced of his by the accusation of another; he recriminates by the same rule, and is clear. The only way to remove this great cause of ignorance and error out of the world, is for every one, impartially, to examine himself. If others will not deal fairly with their own minds, does that make my errors truths? or ought it to make me in love with them, and willing to impose upon myself? If others love cataracts in their eyes, should that hinder me from couching of mine as soon as I can? Every one declares against blindness, and yet who almost is not fond of that which dims his sight, and keeps the clear light out of his mind, which should lead him into truth and knowledge? False or doubtful positions, relied upon as unquestionable maxims, keep those in the dark from truth who build on them.

To those who are willing to get rid of this great hindrance of knowledge, to those who would shake off this great and dangerous impostor, prejudice, who dresses up falsehood in the likeness of truth, and so dexterously hoodwinks men's minds, as to keep them in the dark, with a belief that they are more in the light than any that do not see with their eyes, I shall offer this one mark whereby prejudice may be known.

He that is strongly of any opinion, must suppose, (unless he be self-condemned,) that his persuasion is built upon good grounds; and that his assent is no greater than what the evidence of the truth he holds forces him to; and that they are arguments, and not inclination, or fancy, that make him so confident and positive in his tenets. Now, if after all his professions, he cannot bear any opposition to his opinions, if he cannot so much as give a patient hearing, much less examine and weigh the arguments on the other side, does he not plainly confess it is prejudice governs him? And it is not the evidence of truth, but some lazy anticipation, some beloved presumption, that he desires to rest undisturbed in. For if what he holds be, as he gives out, well fenced with evidence, and he sees it to be true, what need he fear to put it to the proof? If his opinion be settled upon a firm foundation, if the arguments that support it and have obtained his assent, be clear, good, and convincing, why should he be shy to have it tried, whether they be proofs or not? He whose assent goes beyond this evidence, owes this excess of his adherence only to prejudice, and does in effect own it when he refuses to hear what is offered against it; declaring thereby that it is not evidence he seeks, but the quiet enjoyment of the opinion he is fond of, with a forward condemnation of all that may stand in opposition to it, unheard and unexamined; which, what is it but prejudice?—Locke.

Sanctus, a deacon of Vienna, sustained excessive torments, and would neither tell his name, condition, nor habitation, but constantly answered, "*I am a Christian.*" Red hot plates of brass were then applied to the tenderest parts of his body, which was all over full of wounds and stripes, besides being so bowed down as to have lost the external shape of a man. In the amphitheatre he was afflicted with every torment, as if he had suffered nothing before; sometimes being placed on a red hot iron chair; and at other times dragged and torn by wild beasts to satiate the fury of the people, until his life was closed.

Love and humility are two things the most contrary to the spirit of the devil of any thing in the world; for the character of that evil spirit, above all things, consists in pride and malice.—Edwards.

REVIVALS.

BY THE EDITOR.

When the human body is in a healthy condition, every part performs its appropriate functions. So of the Church of Jesus Christ, which is termed His "body." Its peculiar work is, instrumentally, to save the souls of men. A revival signifies, literally, a restoration from death to life. Men, by nature, are dead in trespasses and sins. The conversion of sinners and the quickening of believers constitute a revival of religion. When a Church is in a healthy state, one or both, and usually both of these works, is carried on. When months and years pass away in the history of a Church, without either of these results being achieved to any considerable degree, something is as evidently out of place, as when a steamer fails to make progress, having on a full head of steam, and all hands at work, or as when a farm yields no harvest at the end of the year. A living Church is a revival Church. If no revival takes place, if no souls are saved through its instrumentality, it fails to accomplish the end for which it was instituted. Its organization may be perfect, its ceremonies duly performed, its seats filled with respectful hearers, its temporalities in a flourishing condition; but if sinful hearts are not purified and fitted for Heaven, its main business is neglected. However good its influence as a social organization, as a Church it is worthless. The money laid out in keeping it up had better be expended in feeding the hungry and clothing the naked.

Ministers are agents employed by God to promote revivals. They are the servants of Jesus Christ. He employs them. As distinctly as Aaron was called of God to minister at the altar, so are they divinely called to labor for the salvation of immortal souls. They have their commission from Heaven written in characters of living fire upon their hearts. A necessity is upon them. A divine impulse is impelling them to go forth to lead their fellow men to Christ. They cannot keep still if they would. The word of the Lord is "as a fire shut up in their bones." They are ordained by the imposition of an Almighty hand to proclaim the gospel. Opposition may be encountered, tumults may be excited, authorities may forbid them "to speak any more in this name," but feeling that they must "obey God rather than man," they double their diligence and press forward in their work. Where there is an open door to do good, they enter it; where there is none, they make one. Let others sigh for ease and seek worldly honors and emoluments, they are striving for immortal crowns. A burning love for sinners infused into their hearts by Christ, constrains them

"To seek the wandering souls of men,
  With cries, entreaties, tears to save,
  To snatch them from the gaping grave."

Entirely consecrated to God, He fits them for his service by touching their "lips with a live coal from off his altar," purging away their sins. As they wait upon him in all prevailing prayer, he bestows upon them the Holy Ghost, giving them

"Hearts and tongues of fire
  To pray, and praise and love."

Men thus called, commissioned, and furnished for the ministry, cannot be otherwise than successful in their appropriate work. This is to promote revivals—to save souls. Laborers sent into the harvest field are expected, not to flourish their sickles, and boast how bright and sharp they are, but to gather wheat. So Jesus looks to have his servants, sent forth to gather souls in the whitening fields of humanity, employ all their time, and bend all their energies, not in making a display of their literary or scientific attainments, but in "turning many to righteousness," in "converting sinners from the error of their ways."

It is as much the business of a minister to promote revivals, as it is of a physician to cure his patients. How many would patronize a doctor, who, in his professional visits, invariably, with urbane manner and soft words, flatters the sick, pampers their appetites, and gives them anodynes, till even those, who, left alone, might recover, pass into eternity under his kind treatment? What sane person would employ a surgeon whose custom it is to apply a cosmetic when a caustic is needed, and who to save the pain of amputating a finger allows the body to perish?

Yet is not a parallel course pursued by too many of the professed ministers of Jesus? Do they not sing the lullaby of repose, when they should sound the note of alarm? If any, under their influence, are partially awakened to the strictness of God's claims, and the narrowness of the way of life, do they not assure them that their scruples are needless, and bid them beware of "fanaticism," when their real danger arises from a spirit of indifference? Instead of applying God's scorching truth to the torpid conscience, until the awakened soul cries out,

> "What shall be done
> To save a wretch like me,
> How shall a trembling sinner shun
> That endless misery,"

do they not rather attempt to quiet his fears and allay his excitement? In the place of preaching as God directs, "hearing the word at his mouth," and giving "warning from him," do they not

> "Smooth down the stubborn text to ears polite,
> And snugly keep damnation out of sight?"

Ministers who pursue such a course will not have revivals. They do not want them. They are looking for their reward here, in popular applause, and good salaries. Whenever they can "do better," in a worldly sense, at some other employment, they are ready to leave the ministry. Whatever "call" promises to be most lucrative and honorable, whether it be to a teacher's chair, a legislator's seat, or a more fashionable pulpit, they readily persuade themselves it is from Heaven!

There is always something wrong with ministers who are not instrumental in the salvation of souls. Usually there is a want of personal piety. Men who daily walk with God, and who go into the pulpit "full of faith and of the Holy Ghost," will so preach Christ, that some of their hearers will be "pricked to the heart." He then that is not instrumental in saving souls should be diligent to search out the cause. He should give himself no rest till God works through him. If he will not pay the price of spiritual power, let him leave the work for those who will. He has no right to stay in the ministry. He is like a fig tree in the vineyard, which eats up the fatness of the soil, and shades the ground, but bears no fruit. Earnest Christians, let us pray that God's dear ministers—the ambassadors of Christ—may be clothed with soul-saving power!

AT TONAWANDA the Lord is still carrying on his work in power. Brother Sinclair has been holding extra meetings for a few weeks past. The Church is crowded with attentive hearers, and awakenings are general. An old resident of the village told us that he had never seen the place so shaken by the Spirit of God. From forty to fifty profess to have passed from death unto life, and conversions are still occurring in almost every meeting. Some very interesting cases of conversion, which we may speak of more definitely hereafter, have fallen under our notice.

THE GENERAL QUARTERLY MEETING AT NORTH PARMA was attended with the Holy Spirit's seal of approbation. Though held on week days, the Church was filled—galleries, porch, and aisles; and a Divine influence seemed to pervade the entire throng of human beings. All felt that God was there. The work of revival commenced, which is still going on. An esteemed Brother of that place, inviting us a day or two since to go and assist them, says, "God is at work among us, and some of us already have confessed and forsaken our sins, and obtained *full salvation*. Backsliders are coming out from the world, and sinners are getting interested to learn about this salvation. God has commenced, and is making a clean sweep in the Church. Hallelujah to his name!" May the work go on till multitudes are redeemed from sin!

FROM MANY PLACES IN THE WEST we are receiving cheering accounts of the progress of Earnest Christianity. Many professing Christians, tired of empty forms, are renouncing the world in reality, and coming to Christ for that full salvation which alone can satisfy the longings of an awakened soul.

One Brother writes us from Illinois, "I take pleasure in informing you that there are pilgrim bands springing up in every direction in this country."

Another Brother, a local preacher, writing us respecting those who, in another place, are striving to walk in the narrow way, says, "I was with them last Sabbath, and tried to preach to them; for which I expect to suffer martyrdom at the hands of the old Church. But my happy heart and redeemed spirit say Amen to it. Brother Redfield was refused the Methodist pulpit; so some of his friends hired the Universalist Church, and went and heard him preach; *for which some fourteen were read out of the Church without any trial.* They went and fitted up a hall, and now hold meetings in it with crowded congregations. The preacher in charge of the old Church told me last Monday morning that he should read out twenty-seven names more next Sunday morning at the Love Feast. How can they call it a Love Feast, when they read out of the Church the vitality of religion?"

Another Brother, sending us a good list of subscribers, says, "May the Lord abundantly bless you in attempting to revive the old-fashioned Methodist thunder and fire. We used to have it here in the West twenty-five years ago. Until a few years since it has been somewhat dimmed by the influence of some of your eastern regency preachers. We poor laymen out here want something besides worldly wisdom to feed our poor souls. We must have it. None of your milk-and-water preaching is going to save American sinners, or be the means of sanctifying believers. If our Church can have a holy ministry, the western world will be taken."

THE REVIVALS IN IRELAND.

The English and Irish newspapers continue to have many descriptions of the great revival—Rev. F. A. WEST writes an excellent article to the *London Morning Star* on the subject, from which we extract the following:—*Zion's Herald.*

Whatever may be said of some localities, the broad case is too public and general to admit of dispute—that there is a great moral reform; and that there have been multiplied sudden conversions; as sudden as the primitive Christian types, given in an undoubted history of the workings of divine power. The moral aspect of towns and villages, and neighborhoods, has been completely changed by the only sure and permanent reform—that of individual conversion. It is, in my humble judgment, a grand manifestation of the power of Christianity; a divine rebuke of those who say that it has served its purpose—has become effete, and must now be substituted by more perfect knowledge, and institutions and influences more adapted to the genius of the age. God calls men to see that it retains its power to accomplish its original design. Personal salvation is the end of Christianity, or it is without a purpose; and there cannot be two ways of being saved. And here, strong men in the midst of their work, or in the throng of the market place, or by the roadside, as well as women in the hum of domestic duties, and girls while busy in the factory—young men gay and frolicsome, "fast young men"—and the profane mocker at that religion which is man's only solace and hope—all these are arrested; all these are brought to prayer; all seek mercy of an offending God; all plead one atonement as their only refuge from the fears of guilt; and eventually, as they have before all used one Litany, now employ one *Te Deum* on their deliverance. And this is agreeable to truth. The articles and homilies of the Church of England and the confession of all Protestant Churches, agree in the truths which vitally concern the revival. Error and wickedness cannot be the honored instruments of saving men; and yet God may occasionally bless truth mixed with venial error, and administration accompanied by much human infirmity. The effects of the revival are too good to be the work of our prime Deceiver, or his kingdom is divided against itself; and too great to be the product of man's best device and highest power. Nor is that to be denounced as a mere disease which yet, whatever its accidental evils, heals the soul. Sudden moral changes from ill to good are none the worse for being sudden; and, where so many are fitly fruitful, it behooves the psychologist, as well as the religious teacher, to be slow in judgment, and to wait for such a collection of facts as will enable him, by a true induction, to judge whether this is not, after all, the finger of God.

I am, sir, your obedient servant,
Hackney, Oct. 18.   F. A. WEST.

REV. WILLIAM ARTHUR'S "TRACTS FOR REVIVALS."

No. VI. of this series continues the author's account of the revival in Ballymena, and glances at the same gracious work in Coleraine. The facts recited are the more valuable as they appear to have been conscientiously pondered and in some instances personally investigated. From the remarks interwoven with the narrative, we transcribe the following extract:—*Christian Guardian.*

"The bodily affection attending some of the cases of conviction had now become an ordinary feature of the revival. Beforehand, every minister and religious man in the district would have recoiled from the idea of such scenes; the reproach certain to arise would have been one ground of fear, and the danger of fanaticism a more serious one. A revival, such as that lately witnessed in America, where the dry bones came together without any terrific shaking, was what all longed to see; and what now occurred could not have found a people less likely to welcome any thing boisterous, or forms of worship less likely to fan wildfire, than among the 'cold Presbyterians,' as they were so often called. But here, by no man's desire or effort, contrary to the wish of every one, was an uncontrollable, unaccountable, somewhat—influence? stroke? disease? what? human weakness? Satanic alloy? divine visitation? Perplexed, discomposed, awed, and startled, good men pondered much. One thing, and only one, was clear; but that shone like the sun—the moral result. The bad were suddenly good, the Ethiopian changed his skin, the leopard his spots. 'Instead of the thorn, came up the fir tree; instead of the briar, came up the myrtle tree.'

"The best of miracles, the moral miracle, by which deeds of righteousness spring from those whose natures had been deeply depraved—this miracle was hourly wrought before all men. The servants of God hailed it, wondering greatly, and rejoicing much. One and another, known as blind from their birth, always stumbling pitifully on the broad road, and making dreadful falls close to the edge of the precipice, 'went and washed, and came seeing; came with a firm tread into the strait and narrow road, and went on, day by day, saying to all who questioned them, 'One thing I know, that, whereas I was blind, now I see.' The fault found with this work wrought upon them was not that it was done on the Sabbath day, but that clay had been put on their eyes. Why was that? It could do no good; it was not dignified. It was very improbable that such a strange and humbling circumstance should be connected with a work really divine. There must be error. The result could only be a delusion. The only possible answer was, 'He put clay upon mine eyes, and I washed, and *do see.*'

"Some asserted that a revival, accompanied with similar affections, had never occurred in the Church of England. They were told, among others, of Jno. Berridge's Church, at Everton, in Bedfordshire, in the year 1759, just one hundred years ago. Others cried, 'It is all hysteria, its cause close air, and girls its subjects.' But the open fields, road sides, markets, and the cool of evening, often witnessed these prostrations. Only girls! why, bony working men, with arms like the handle of a spade, of lymphatic, bilious, and sanguine temperament, indifferently—men, the like of whom not three doctors living ever treated for hysteria—felt this influence. We do not explain it; but we are very sure some who imagine they do, ought to read what others attempted in the same line, respecting the 'preaching sickness' in Sweden, or the great revival in Cornwall, and then go to the scenes of those movements, and learn how far the lapse of years has accredited the imagined explanations.

"Others say that it is all produced through appeals to the base passion of fear. Fear is not base in itself. Love, ill-directed, often drags us through vile mire; and fear, ill-directed, drives us from right into wrong. But fear of God, fear of sin, who shall call that base? The voice of the Blessed never appealed to a base passion; and of all those implanted pure in my nature by his hand, and fouled by my first father's sin, no one is more frequently addressed by his voice than the fear of the Lord. Base! He lifts us up, as on eagle's wings, and sweeps heaven and earth, the caverns of death, the unfathomed sea, with the question, 'Where shall wisdom be found?' and returning from such a flight as the soul of man is no where else carried over (Job xxviii, 12, etc.) he sets us down with this everlasting lesson: 'Unto man he said, Behold the fear of the Lord, that is wisdom.' But were fear base, we declare that we heard no preaching on the scenes of the revival in which fear of damnation, of unquenchable fire, of body and soul being cast into hell, of weeping and wailing, and gnashing of teeth, of outer darkness, of many stripes, of torment in flame, of God's most terrible wrath against impenitent sinners, was appealed to, either with frequency or plainness, comparable with those found in the discourses of him who was the word of God; and who shall dare to call that which he did, appealing to base passion?

"To accuse the ministers of Ulster of 'getting up' these affections, is as rational as to suspect physicians of bringing an epidemic. The course taken by the Lancet, in charging them with 'rascality,' reminds me of what happened to a relative of my own, in a large English town, in 1832, when he was mobbed and pelted for spreading the cholera. The ministers were at first terrified by the affections, and became reconciled to them only after much evidence that, amid them—they at first thought, in spite of them—the Lord was manifesting his regenerating power in a way never seen in Ireland before.

"The popular speech now became affected by the feeling that the revival was a visitation from the hand of God, in the same sense as an epidemic. The common mind did not care to sift second causes in the one case more than in the other, but passed through them to the instinctive conclusion, that no matter to what extent they were employed, they did not originate and could not direct the visitation. In common parlance, a person 'affected' was 'a case;' being under conviction was being 'very bad;' finding peace was becoming 'better;' and so all the expressions describing sickness and recovery were adopted. But, notwithstanding this, the reformation of manners and morals proceeded with rapid steps. Each fresh convert became a soldier fighting against sin; the boldness of habitual transgressors forsook them; the public mind became pervaded with a conviction that God was directly dealing with his fallen creatures, for their salvation.

"The effect of teaching by facts instead of by words, was daily growing plainer. The primary lesson of Christ's ministry, 'Ye must be born again,' so hard to write upon the convictions of a community by mere language, now became part of the popular perceptions. A hundred cases of change from wicked to holy lives, taking place before every man's eye, among his neighbors and kinsfolk, made him feel that salvation from sin was not a dream, and preparation for heaven not a deathbed ceremony. In one thing all the dispensations agree; the ministry of the prophets, that of John, of Jesus, and of the apostles, all make God's first call to man, repent! Even in theory this had passed from the sight of many Christians; and books, not very old, may be found, in which men well placed in God's Church do not know where to fix repentance in Christian life, at the beginning, middle, or end. But the voice of Christ, and of his own messengers, 'Repent and believe the Gospel,' was re-echoed by every case of conversion which occurred, till, clear as day, the correspondence between the word written and the work wrought gave to theologians the clear conception, to the populace the prompt instinct, that the foundation of the Spirit's work in the soul of man is laid in repentance and faith—repentance from the dead works, and faith towards God; that the high office of Christ enthroned is as 'a Prince and Saviour to give *repentance* to Israel and remission of sins.'"

"AWFUL GARDNER'S STORY OF HIMSELF.

"Awful Gardner," the converted pugilist, was present on Sunday evening at a meeting in the Methodist Church, in Greene street, and narrated to the congregation the circumstances of his conversion, as follows:

I feel it my duty to tell you what God has done for me. I hope you will hear all I have to say. There are many here who have known me for ten years—have known me when I was fearfully wicked. Now I am on the Lord's side. I want it thoroughly understood that now I am on the Lord's side.

I was on a visit to my brother in the country, about twenty-eight miles away, at a town called Portchester. When I went there I had as much idea of getting religion as many of you have now—that is none at all. But I hope when you get home you cannot rest nor sleep till you get religion. I went to church in that town for accommodation, that's all, to the folks. The Saviour was there. The Lord's Spirit was powerfully displayed, and went from heart to heart all through the Church. It worked upon me three or four nights. The pastor of the Church came to me and asked me if I would not like to get religion and serve God. I answered, "No, I didn't care about it just then," and told him a lie, for I did; I felt as though I wanted religion.

I got dreadfully uneasy, and made up my mind I had better leave that part of the country; it was getting too warm for me. I told my brother I was going to New York in the morning. He said "Wait another day," and I made up my mind I would stay and attend another night. Some remarks were made to backsliders the next night, many of whom I knew; they sat there unmoved. The minister and my friends had been trying to get me to be a Christian, but the devil said, "Don't be taken in by those fellows." After church that night, as we were going home—the minister lived up our way—I made some remark about those backsliders, saying to him that if I were in their place I would come out like a man and seek religion over again.

The minister told me that he thought I was a very great sinner; that I stood in a critical condition, and was more likely to be lost than any of them. I said to my brother, if that was the way the minister was going to talk, I would go; I got my carpet bag ready next day and started. I opened the door; I wanted to go, and I didn't want to go; and I hoped my brother would urge me to stay; he did so, and I stayed. That was Saturday. After I had my dinner, I resolved that I would seek the Lord that night. I made a strong resolution; I felt where I stood, that perhaps it was the last time the Lord would strive with me. Saturday night the invitation was given to come forward to the altar—on my shoulders my load of sins—up I went with them, the cross of Christ upon my back. I got up and threw my sins down by the altar. I tried as hard as a man ever did, and I got no religion.

Sunday night I attended with a like result. That night I could not sleep, my sins looked so bad; they came up on every hand and looked at me; all the sins of my life crowded upon me, many I should never have thought of, had not the devil brought them before me. I could not sleep; I wiggled and waggled around the bed all night; the Lord was striving with me. Monday morning I got up and prayed; I did the best I could; I asked the Lord to take away the weight that bore me down so. There was a friend came to me that day and said he was going over to White Plains, and I could go with him. Knowing I would be in good company, I concluded to go, thinking he might do me some good. There was little said on the way, but he told me to keep looking for the Saviour; that I was trying to get religion, and had let everybody know it; the Lord was willing to bless me at any time or anywhere. I was riding along, singing a hymn, and in an instant I felt as though I was blessed. I am sure I gave up my soul and body. The first thing I knew, God spoke peace to my soul. It came like a shot—it came like lightning when I was not anticipating it, and the first thing I said, "Glory! God blessed me." My friend said he knew it; he felt the shock too. We rode against a stone fence two or three times, and came near tumbling on the ground. The change was surprising; the trees looked as though they had been blessed; everything appeared to have been blessed, even the horse and wagon. I felt strong. I could almost fly. Glory to God, this religion is good! The Lord has blessed me ever since. My faith in him grows stronger every day. I would face all the people that God ever put in the earth, and tell them all I am bound for heaven. My heart says see the scorner: I say, I will go and pray for him. Everything is pleasing. I love those I used to hate. Now, that shows pretty good for religion—don't it brothers? [Yes, yes.] Men that I used to seek to injure, I love now; I pray for them. I don't hate a soul that God ever put breath in. As I look around, you all look good to me; I love the Christian a little better than I do the sinner, but I love you too. I would not swap this religion for all New York city. I would rather have religion and live on bread and water till God calls me. They talk about noise here—what it will be when we get to heaven? I have tested the world's pleasures, but religion is the only thing that will make a man happy here, and the only thing that will make a man happy hereafter. There are a great many here that know me, and it is, no doubt, a mystery to them that God should accept such a creature. Now is the time to step to the altar. Don't say to God, let me accomplish this or that, and then I will seek you. When you receive the religion of Jesus Christ, you are the richest person on the earth. Come at once. Clear the way, here! Seats all around; allow yourselves to be led to Christ.—*N. Y. Tribune.*

NOTICES.

THE EARNEST CHRISTIAN.—The first number of a new Monthly Magazine, to be published in this city by the Earnest Christian Publishing Association, was laid on our table yesterday. It is under the editorial charge of Mr. B. T. Roberts, A. M. By the title page we are advised that this work is to be "devoted to the promotion of Experimental and Practical Piety" —than which, certainly, there can be no better or purer design. In the brief explanation by the editor of "the object and scope of this magazine," he announces that it is designed to aid those who are in search of a true and undefiled religion—of "those who are in earnest to gain Heaven, and anxious to know the conditions upon which eternal happiness can be secured." To this end, among other things, he says, "the doctrines of Christian holiness, as taught by WESLEY and FLETCHER, will occupy a prominent place" in the columns of the work. "In short," says he, "our object is to publish a revival journal."

From this notice, our readers may be able to judge better than we can, to what particular sect this new magazine is to be an assistant in enforcing their peculiar doctrines. The magazine contains 36 pages, and is very handsomely printed. The contents are of a diversified character, and appear to be upon many interesting subjects.—*Buffalo Com. Adv.*

THE EARNEST CHRISTIAN.—The first number of this new magazine has just come to hand. It makes a fine appearance, and is well filled. We have no doubt but it will be a success, and eminently deserving of patronage by the religious public. The editor, Rev. B. T. Roberts, is a mature scholar and Christian; "persecuted," it is true, "but not forsaken, cast down, but not destroyed."—*Nor. Independent.*

THE EARNEST CHRISTIAN.—Rev. B. T. Roberts, of this city, has commenced the publication of a new religious magazine, with the above title, the first number of which is before us. The magazine is a neat one in appearance, and promises much in the ability of its management and the interest of its articles, which, in the present number, are upon live topics and subjects of great importance.—*Buffalo Morning Express.*

MELROSE, Mass., Dec. 31st, 1859.
Your new monthly has just come to hand, and its pages have been examined with no ordinary interest. Its general appearance is at once attractive, expressive, and Methodistic: though we use the last epithet to convey no more than many are coming to endorse and love, in the various Christian denominations of the land. THE EARNEST CHRISTIAN is surely an appropriate title for a periodical designed to be a faithful exponent of the principles adopted in your "Prospectus," and set forth at greater length in your opening article on the "Object and Scope" of the newly issued magazine. The mechanical execution of your periodical is certainly respectable, but this is neither the best nor the most important part of it. I confess, *I like your matter exceedingly*, and only regret that such stirring truths cannot have a world-wide circulation from the the very start. Your theory and advocacy of "free churches," are but the echo of my own sentiments, entertained for years. Nothing short of this will make it possible for any particular church, or the church in general, to be the ever-living exemplification of New Testament piety, for which she was raised up by the hand of God. Dr. Redfield's first article is alone worth the subscription price of your periodical. The great need of the church to-day, is to have such vivid, soul-stirring views of truth and duty, as will effectually break her awful reverie, and send her out in one earnest, ceaseless march after human *souls*, that "must forever live, in raptures or in woe!"
A. A. PHELPS.

From Rev. D. W. THURSTON, P. E., of Cortland Dist.
CORTLAND, Jan. 2d, 1860.
MY DEAR BROTHER ROBERTS: I have read your magazine with intense pleasure. It is just the thing. Success to THE EARNEST CHRISTIAN. God's blessing on the noble band of ministers in Western New York, who will stand up for Jesus, cost what it may. I am grateful for the kind Providence which brought me into communion with them.
Yours affectionately,
D. W. THURSTON.

From Rev. E. BOWEN, D. D.
CORTLAND, Jan. 2nd, 1860.
I hope and trust your periodical will succeed. I like the object at which you aim, and your first number augurs well for the enterprise. May Heaven bless you in the much needed effort to promote the true interests and spirit of our holy religion. E. BOWEN.

EAST CLARKSON, Dec. 30th, 1859.
The first number of THE EARNEST CHRISTIAN has come to hand, and we are very much pleased with its contents. I think it is destined to be a favorite with those who are in favor of *Christianity in earnest*, and are striving to walk in the *narrow way*. Its position I think is the best that could have been taken. * * * * It has my warmest sympathies, and is, I trust, destined to be a blessing to the age. S. S. RICE.

MARENGO, Illinois.
I am much pleased with the way you have got up THE EARNEST CHRISTIAN. I see you are inclined to be as wise as a serpent, and as harmless as a dove. O. P. ROGERS.

YOUNGSTOWN, New York.
THE EARNEST CHRISTIAN.—I must say I am *highly pleased* with this number—*really* elated. It looks so plain and modest, and yet is so replete with the marrow of the gospel.
WILLIAM COOLEY.

THE EARNEST CHRISTIAN.

VOL. I.   MARCH, 1860.   NO. 3.

FREE CHURCHES.

BY THE EDITOR.

Free Churches can be sustained.

The practice of having the seats free in the house of God, must be admitted to be both Scriptural and rational. The pew system is resorted to, it is claimed, as a necessity. The Methodist discipline, which up to 1852 read, "Let all our churches be built plain and decent, and *with free seats*," now advises that the same system be carried out, whenever "practicable." This concedes, virtually, that the selling of pews is at least of doubtless propriety; to be tolerated only in extreme cases, as a wounded man submits to have a limb amputated to save his life.

The Gospel never requires that we should abandon its principles in order to sustain it. If a church could not be kept up in any particular locality without tolerating rumselling and gambling, every true Christian would say let it go down. As you had better be entirely destitute, than have a large supply of counterfeit money, so a community is better off without any religious services, than with those that give countenance to passions, the indulgence of which will result in the loss of the soul. If pride excludes men from Heaven, for a church to adopt a system that begets and fosters it, is as absurd as it would be for a father to place in the position of bar-keeper, an inebriate son whom he wished to reform. No possible necessity can justify the act. A Roman General, sent by the Senate upon a service that required him to cross the Tiber, when a storm was raging so violently that it seemed impossible for a boat to keep above the waves, said to friends who tried to dissuade him from the attempt, "It is not necessary that I should live, but it is necessary that I should obey my orders."

Do the churches sincerely desire the salvation of men more than to obtain their money? This should be so apparent as not to admit of question. The father of Cyrus the Great, when about to die and leave his kingdom to his son, said to him, "If you would have the cordial obedience of your officers, you must make them believe that you understand affairs better than they do." "But how," said the young man, "shall I make them believe so?" "By understanding them better in reality," replied the dying king. So, if the churches would produce the impression that they are laboring, instrumentally, to save souls from death and hell, rather than to gain money or applause, this must really be their aim. In all the arrangements that are made, this end will be kept steadily in view. In every place where a church is needed, a free church can be sustained. Do you ask, how? *We answer by the voluntary offerings of the people.* Those who attend church, generally believe the Bible. Now the Bible declares that whosoever gives a cup of cold water, in the name of a disciple, to one engaged in propagating Christianity, shall in no wise lose his reward. Says the Apostle, "God is not unrighteous to forget your work and labor of love, which ye have showed toward his name, in that ye have ministered to the saints, and do minister." Voluntary contributions for the support of the ordinances of religion, are then to be regarded in the light of acceptable offerings to the Most High. As such, they entitle the giver, by virtue of the promise, to look for a reward. We may then reasonably expect that every believer in revelation, and especially every lover of Jesus, will contribute more for the cause of God, when he looks to eternity for his reward, than when he receives an equivalent for his money in the use of a pew, and in the enjoyment of a certain degree of social distinction. In the days of the purity and poverty of the church, when this view prevailed, there was no difficulty in sustaining its ordinances without calling in the aid of worldly policy. Mosheim says, "The prayers of the first Christians were followed by oblations of bread, wine, and other things; and hence, both the ministers of the church and the poor derived their subsistence. Every Christian who was in an opulent condition, and indeed every one according to his circumstances, brought gifts and offered them, as it were, to the Lord." We have gained little and lost much by the unnatural divorce of praying and giving. Many do not contribute anything for the support of the Gospel. Some, feeling compelled to do it if they would not lose caste, pay for a seat much more than their just proportion; others not so much, as with their means they should devote to Christianity. The distribution of the burden is very unequal. Let every one give, as in apostolic days, "according as the Lord hath prospered him," and the church can be far more easily sustained than under the pew system. An average of ten cents per member, per week, would amount in a church numbering 200, to over $1000 per annum. God can take care of His cause without calling in the aid of mammon.

The tendency of Christianity is not to make men selfish. We are not left, however, to mere reasoning. The institutions of religion have, for six thousand years, been supported upon the voluntary principle. The patriarchal, the Mosaic, and the Gospel ordinances, have all been sustained, without the aid of the traffic in pews. It was the opinion of St. Chryrostom, and St. Austin, that the system of voluntary offerings, when practised, furnished a better provision for the support of the ministry, than the income from the lands and possessions of the church, with which, after the conversion of Constantine, she became endowed, by princely munificence. The Methodist church in this country has been, and still is, we believe, in a majority of places, sustained under the system of free seats. And shall it be said that those who worship in pews have less love for the institutions of Christ?

The experiment of free seats is being tried, at the present time, by the Protestant Episcopal Church. Many of their houses of worship have been made free, in accordance with resolutions passed by their conventions. Statistics have been collected, showing the effect of the free seat system upon the finances. We quote from a long list, almost at random. "The church of the Holy Communion, New York, seating but 500 persons, defrays all the expenses of public worship, with a Daily Service, and contributes more than any church of its size to the general purposes of the church. St. Pauls, Key West, Florida, seating but 250 persons, where the pews, if rented, would realize $800, receives from its offertory and subscriptions $1,150 per annum. Holy Innocents, Albany, New York, seating 250 persons, where the pews if rented, would realize $800, receives from its offerings $1,200 to $1,300 per annum. Christ church, Elizabeth Town, New Jersey, seating 250 persons, where the pews, if rented, would realize about $500 or $600, received last year from offerings and subscriptions for parish expenses, $1,066, besides $600 appropriated to the poor and general objects of the church. Grace church, Petersburgh, Va., seating 350 persons, realizes from subscriptions and offerings, $1,100 per annum. Christ church,

Vicksburgh, Miss., seating 500 persons, which had great difficulty in paying its expenses under the *pew system*, last year, the fifth since they adopted the *free system*, received through the offerings and sucscriptions for various objects, about $3000, exclusive of the Rector's salary, which is equal to about $2000. St. Stephen's church, Oxford, North Carolina, seating 150 persons, receives from subscriptions, $1,500 per annum. St. John's church, Knoxville Tenn., seating 250, receives from offerings and subscriptions, $1,200 per annum." We are willing to place these examples, taken from every portion of the country, by the side of the like number of churches of the same size, which have the pew system, without the least fear that the free churches will, in any way, suffer by the comparison.

Facts are stubborn things. These facts show conclusively, that in the Protestant Episcopal church, at the present day, the expenses of public worship can be better met under the free, than under the pew system. But does this denomination possess a monopoly of piety? Is there less of a spirit of consecration in the other churches? It is an insult to the piety of any congregation, to say that they will not sustain the Gospel, unless their pride and love of distinction can be flattered. A church composed of such members is not worth sustaining. For the honor of religion it had better go down. But we do not believe that such churches exist. It is our firm conviction, that there would still be found in all our churches enough of piety to sustain them without a resort to worldly policy.

We are forbidden to make the House of God a House of merchandise.

To the worst of sinners the Saviour was usually mild and forbearing. He had compassion and forgiveness for a repentant Magdalene. The dying thief, confessing his sins, and believing in Jesus, was promised a seat with him in Paradise. His tears flowed freely over the hardened apostates who killed the prophets, and stoned the holy men that were sent unto them. He met with the most violent opposition, and endured the most bitter persecution at the hands of men who should have been his warmest friends; his words were perverted, his motives were impugned, his character assailed; he was charged with being a glutton and a wine-bibber, a Sabbath-breaker, and a blasphemer, a friend of publicans and sinners; yet he bore all with calmness, and expiring on the cross, prayed for his merciless tormentors.

Of all the sins that he witnessed, one only aroused his holy indignation to such a degree, that he resorted to physical force. This was the profanation of the Temple. He cleansed it in a summary manner once, and probably twice. Dr. A. Clarke says, "The vindication of God's house from profanation was the *first* and the *last* care of our Lord; and it is probable he *began* and *finished* his public ministry by this significant act." This incident is one of the few in the life of our Saviour, recorded by all four of the Evangelists. The Holy Ghost regarded it as conveying too important a lesson to be omitted by any of his historians. Wherever the Gospel shall be sent in all coming time, there shall this forcible teaching of Christ go with it. We quote the account given by St. John. "And the Jews passover was at hand; and Jesus went up to Jerusalem, and found in the temple those that sold oxen, and sheep, and doves, and the changers of money, sitting: And when he had made a scourge of small cords, he drove them all out of the temple, and the sheep and the oxen; and poured out the changer's money, and overthrew the tables; and said unto them that sold doves, Take these things hence; make not my Father's house, an house of merchandise."

We should bear in mind that all these things were lawful articles of traffic. They were also indispensable to the Temple service. Many of the worshippers came from a great distance, and from far off countries. No one was permitted to appear empty handed before the Lord. They could not, without great inconvenience, bring from their distant homes the animals needed for offerings to the Most High. It was difficult to find in the public market those suitable for sacrifices, of the proper age, without spot and blemish. It was, then, a matter of great convenience, if not necessity, to have for sale, in the outer courts of the Temple, the cattle, sheep, and doves required in worship, by the law of Moses. The money changers enabled the devout to present to the treasury such sums as they wished, and in the current coin of Jerusalem.

All this trade was intended to facilitate religious worship. It was carried on with decency and propriety. But the Saviour would not tolerate it, however good the intention. He made a scourge of small cords and drove out the buyers and sellers. What would he have done, if he had found them selling by auction, to the highest bidder, parts of the temple itself? Would the traffic in pews, in the House of His Father, have excited his indignation less than did the traffic in sacrifices? The one had an immediate connection with the worship of God; the other is often a mere matter of speculation. Pews are offered for sale in the market, and advertised in the newspapers, the same as dry goods and groceries. Church stock rises in value, as religion becomes fashionable, and the minister of the Gospel popular among the proud and aspiring. Stock is sometimes purchased in churches, as it is in banks and railroads—to make money. We once heard a speculator boast that the money which he had invested in a certain church, brought him in fourteen per cent. Men of means buy pews in the house of the Lord and rent them, for their own benefit, for much more per year than the legal interest of the purchase money. This speculating in the house of the Lord, grows naturally out of the pew system, which is based on mercenary considerations.

The striking conduct of Christ in cleansing the Temple, could not have been recorded by the four Evangelists to prevent the repetition of the particular offence that he thus strongly condemned; for they knew that the Temple would soon be destroyed, and its typical ceremonials be abolished forever. Had the all-seeing eye of Jesus looked down through the vista of succeeding centuries and rested upon the pew system, the latest corruption of the religion which He came down upon earth to establish, He could hardly have condemned it more strongly than by the words and the actions which accompanied them. "Make not my Father's House an house of merchandise." A pew is a man's personal property. He sells it at his pleasure. It may be attached for his debts. How can God's house be made a house of merchandise, if the pew system does not do it?

It is a solemn mockery to dedicate a church to God, and then sell it off in parcels, like the estate of an insolvent, under the auctioneer's hammer.

When the Temple at Jerusalem was built, the people brought, in great abundance, gold, and silver, and precious stones, and gave them willingly to the Lord. They renounced the ownership in them as much as if they had received a material equivalent. The complaint against Ananias and Sapphira was, not that they gave too little, but that, having devoted their possessions to Christ, they kept back part of the price. Is not this same thing done whenever a church is dedicated to the service of Almighty God, without reserve, and then the pews sold, like any other articles of traffic? Wherever it is the intention to make merchandise of the seats of the Lord's house, the solemn rites of dedication should never be performed. "For," as the learned Wheatly says, "by these solemnities, the founders surrender all the right they have in them to GOD, and make God himself the sole owner of them. And formerly, whoever gave any lands or endowments to the service of God, gave them in a formal writing, sealed and witnessed, (as is now usual between man and man,) the tender of the gift being laid upon the altar by the donor on his knees. The antiquity of such dedications is evident, from its being a universal custom amongst Jews and Gentiles; and it is observable that amongst the former, at the consecration of both the Tabernacle and the Temple, it pleased the Almighty to give a manifest sign that He then took possession of them." What devout person ever attended the dedication of a church, when, a few hours after the officiating minister, in behalf of the donors, had solemnly cosecrated the pulpit, the altar, the seats, the galleries, and all, to the service of Almighty God, the shrill voice of the auctioneer, and the clamor of competing bidders filled the sacred courts, that so recently resounded with the voice of prayer and praise, without feeling shocked at the horrid profanation? It would be considered childish trifling, or criminal fraud, for a man to bestow a house or farm upon a friend, and then claim the rents of it for his own use. When Christians dedicate a church to the service of the Lord, it should be free for all who may wish to unite with them in His worship. To put the pews up for public sale, to any one, Jew or Gentile, believer or infidel, who may choose to become a purchaser, has the appearance of dedicating the house to God, in compliment, and then inviting and urging mammon, in earnest, to come and take possession.

The Pew System robs Christians of rewards promised by the Saviour for labors in His cause.

It is a glorious truth that he who dies in the faith is at once saved, without respect to any works of righteousness which he has done. But to escape hell, is not all that may be accomplished by the follower of Jesus. There is a wide difference in the condition and circumstances of the citizens of New York, though all reside in the same city, and receive the protection of the same laws. One may enjoy every comfort that wealth can purchase; another may, by unremitting toil, barely secure a scanty subsistence. So there is a diversity of state in Heaven, though all are happy. But there are degrees of happiness. As the sun, moon and stars differ in glory, so do those that share in the first resurrection. They that are wise shall shine as the firmament—but they that turn many to righteousness, as the stars for ever and ever. The stars outshine the firmament as much as the kingly palace excels the hut of poverty. The honors of the world soon fade away; the rich and the poor lie down alike in the grave; but those whom God especially honors, are honored for ever. Too little attention is paid by Christians to the degrees of bliss enjoyed by the redeemed above. Many appear to think, if they are barely admitted to the mansions of glory, it is sufficient. But no one should be satisfied with this. We cannot conceive how any earnest Christian can be. The voice of his ascended Lord is urging him on to take a seat near the throne. The strongest inducements are held out to every one, to lead a life of devotion to Christ.

Over and above participating in the common salvation of the redeemed, the faithful laborer shall be specially rewarded. No action, however trifling, performed out of love to Christ, shall be forgotten by Him, in the great day of eternity.

Building churches, for the worship of His followers, and the promotion of His cause, is a means of doing good that the Saviour will remember with special marks of approbation. Jesus performed but few miracles in behalf of any but the covenant people of God. "I am not sent," he said, "but unto the lost sheep of the house of Israel." To the Canaanitish woman, who besought him, with great earnestness, in behalf of her daughter, he replied, "It is not meet to take the children's bread and to cast it to the dogs." But when the elders of the Jews requested him to heal the servant of a Gentile centurion, and backed up the request by saying, *That he was worthy for whom he should do this; for he loveth our nation, and hath built us a synagogue,* without making a single objection, Jesus went with them. It was as if he said, "I will do any thing in my power, for one who, out of love for the people of God, hath built them a house of worship."

Now the Pew System steps in here, and robs those who contribute of their means for the erection of the church, of all expectation of being specially rewarded by Christ. *They have their reward here,* and in consequence are the losers to all eternity. They receive an equivalent for their money in the shape of church stock. It is true their money is invested in a house of worship. But this alone does not render the investment particularly acceptable to God. It is their property still. They might as well expect God to reward them for taking stock in a railroad, because bibles and ministers are transported upon it.

Special blessings are also promised to those who, out of love to Christ, aid in supporting his ambassadors, who are laboring to persuade men to become reconciled to God.

Here again the Pew System interposes, and by corrupting the motives of the giver, deprives him of the greatest benefits that would otherwise accrue from his gifts. Instead of bestowing his means directly for the support of the gospel, he rents a pew for his own convenience and that of his family, or, if he owns it, he pays the annual tax to which it is subjected, and which, in many instances, constitutes a lien upon it. As he pays the market price for the use of the property, the thought of being rewarded by the Great Judge, at the day of reckoning, never enters his mind. He would as soon think of being rewarded for buying a carriage for his family to ride in to church.

Thus the Pew System works an eternal loss to all Christians who give it their support. It leads many to do, out of selfish considerations, what under other circumstances, they would be ready to do from higher and holier impulses. Nor is the advantage which they receive sufficient to compensate for the loss. The advantage is temporary—the loss will be felt while eternity endures. The benefit is imaginary—the injury real.

When a Church is built upon the principles of worldly policy, which constitute an essential element of the Pew System, all its enterprises are too likely to be carried on in the same spirit. The taint spreads. If money is to be raised for any purpose connected with the Redeemer's Kingdom, those having the matter in charge proceed upon the assumption that the "perilous times" spoken of by the Spirit, when *men having the form of Godliness, shall be lovers of pleasure, more than lovers of God,* have already come. So instead of appealing to the love the people have for Christ, and the motives drawn from eternity, virtually acknowledging the weakness of these, they appeal to their love of pleasure. Does the church need repairs? a festival, with its lottery accompaniments, is gotten up, and the patronage of the world solicited. The servants of God, without scruple, resort to expedients for raising money, which when adopted by sinners, becomes an indictable offence.

If the Sabbath school library needs replenishing, an excursion is planned. And even the motives which should lead Christians to make liberal contributions for the conversion of the heathen would seem to be insufficient unless the attractions of a tea party are superadded! The love of pleasure must indeed be much stronger than the love of God, if after defraying the expenses of all these various contrivances for the support of His cause, a larger amount is realized than would have been obtained by appealing to higher principles. Such is the tendency of the Pew System. The shape of the foundation controls that of the superstructure. A Church built upon the expedients of worldly policy, will be very likely to be carried on in the same way. Whatever we do in the cause of God, should be done with a single eye. We should learn to act for eternity. *Let no man take thy crown.*

FORGET ME NOT.
BY P. C. LAVANT.

When from the east the morning breaks,
  And twilight gently flits away—
When from repose all nature wakes
  To praise her God at early day—
Unknown, unseen to mortal eye,
  Then hie thee to a lonely spot,
And meekly pray to God on high,
  And in thy prayer—*forget me not.*

When thou shalt see the sun's last rays
  Beam brightly from the golden west,
Go pour thy soul in prayer and praise—
  Go meet thy Maker, and be blest;
Oh, when to thee the blessing's given,
  And God smiles on thy happy lot,
When thou dost raise thy prayer to heaven,
  In thy request—*forget me not.*

When sore temptations thee beset,
  And darkness covers all thy day—
When evil spreads her wanton net,
  To lure thee from the "Living Way"—
Then turn thee from the tempter's power,
  To Him who hath salvation wrought;
Pray for deliverance in that hour,
  And in thy prayer—*forget me not.*

For I, temptations, too, must meet,
  Must overcome, if I would reign,
And never from the field retreat,
  'Till I the "heavenly rest" obtain;
Then oft at each returning day,
  Seek thee a lone secluded spot,
In solitude where thou canst pray,
  And in thy prayer—*forget me not.*

It is hardly credible of how great consequence before God, the smallest things are; and what great inconveniences sometimes follow those which appear to be light faults.

As a very little dust will disorder a clock, so the least grain of sin, which is upon the heart, will hinder its right motion towards God.—WESLEY.

There is no love of God without patience, and no patience without *lowliness* and sweetness of spirit.—WESLEY.

ENTHUSIASM IN RELIGION. — We need more of it, a hundred-fold more than we have. Enthusiasm in science, in trade, in politics, we have plenty of, and all that is done for the advance of business and learning is done by enthusiastic men.

The word needs to be guarded, but the prudent reader knows that enthusiasm is not fanaticism. The grandest subject in all the universe of God taking full possession of the soul, ought to fill with intense emotion. It shall profit a man nothing to gain the whole world and lose his own soul; and if we praise him who pursues business with so much industry and tact as to gain a million before he dies, shall we not much more admire the enthusiasm of him who gains heaven!

The world is to be saved. We ought to be in earnest about saving it. Our friends, children, neighbors, the heathen, are perishing. We can do something to save them. If they were on a ship wrecked off shore, or in a burning house, we would be enthusiastic to deliver them from death. May we not be enthusiastic in delivering them from hell?

The apostles were enthusiastic. The Saviour himself was filled with zeal. All the best men who have been mighty in pulling down error or building up truth, have been enthusiastic. God grant that the church may rise and shake herself from the dust. It is a time to be up and doing. Let us work while it is day.—*N. Y. Observer.*

IMMODERATE zeal is always to be suspected; especially when it appears in pursuing such measures as tend to injure or ruin an individual. A bad cause, which originated from hatred or malice, will almost always be carried on with more intemperate zeal, and bolder measures than a consciousness of acting right will ever produce. The pursuit of any end in view, when governed by the passions, is always more violent than when directed by reason and truth.—WHITEHEAD.

REPENTANCE.

BY THE EDITOR.

Have you ever truly repented of your sins? Do you now possess the Christian grace of repentance?

The apostle says, "Ye are God's building." Repentance is the foundation. A defect in this endangers the entire superstructure. The higher the edifice is reared, the more elaborately it is finished and adorned, the greater will be the loss, if, when "the rains descend and the winds blow," the foundation gives way.

Repentance is "the strait gate" spoken of by our Saviour as placed at the entrance of "the narrow way that leadeth unto life." The longer and the faster you travel, the farther you will be from Heaven unless your steps are in that way cast up for the ransomed of the Lord, upon which no one can possibly enter without passing through the "strait gate."

How important, then, that you truly repent! If you would not pass the endless years of eternity in hopeless agony among the lost in perdition, tormented by your own conscience, now terribly alive to reproach you for the sins of a life time, committed against a God of purity, vexed with the companions of your misery, and tortured by a remorseless Devil, whose victim you are, you must see to it that you repent; for He who never sounded an idle alarm, has said, "Except ye repent, ye shall all likewise perish." There is reason to fear that many who feel secure, dreaming of Heaven, have never yet taken this first step in the right direction.

Beloved friend, we would not needlessly afflict or grieve you, but we would help you to a correct understanding of your case, so that if you have been building upon the sand, you may, before the storms of eternity beat upon your structure, correct your mistake.

Repentance, literally signifies, "an after thought," "a change of mind or purpose on reflection." In the gospel sense it is "turning with penitential grief from all our sins to God."

When evangelical, repentance is always accompanied by deep anguish of spirit, because of the sins we have committed against God. Thus the Psalmist says: "There is no soundness in my flesh because of thine anger; neither is there any rest in my bones because of my sin. For mine iniquities are gone over mine head, as a heavy burden they are too heavy for me. I am troubled; I am bowed down greatly; I go mourning all the day long." What grief, what compunction is here expressed! Have you ever felt it? If you have ever drunk the wormwood and the gall of true repentance, you will not consider the language of the Psalmist as extravagant.

St. Paul says, "Godly sorrow worketh repentance." By the phrase "Godly sorrow," literally "sorrow in respect to God"—may be meant, "sorrow," because we, by our sins, have incurred the displeasure of God, and exposed ourselves to the penalties of his holy law. In this view, we shall mourn just as deeply for sins that are known to him only, as for those that have brought upon us exposure and disgrace. With penitential grief we shall cry out, "Against Thee, Thee *only* have I sinned and done this evil in thy sight."

Or the term "Godly sorrow,"—sorrow in respect to God—may be used as a term of comparison. Among the old Hebrews, the highest degree of comparison was expressed in this way: Thus "Ninevah was an exceeding great city," (Jonah iii, 3.) In the original, "a great city before God." "Nimrod was a mighty hunter before the Lord," (Gen. x, 9) that is, exceedingly expert in hunting. So also "Moses was exceeding fair," (Acts vii, 20) in the Greek, literally "fair before God." "Zacharias and Elizabeth were righteous before God," (Luke i, 6) that is, really and eminently pious. The reason for this mode of comparison doubtless is, that everything appears to be, in the sight of God, what it really is. The phrase, Godly sorrow, taken in this sense, would mean exceedingly great sorrow on account of our sins—a deep anguish of spirit that will not let us take pleasure in any thing until God's "anger is turned away," and He comforts us with the assurance that our iniquities are all forgiven. Such sorrow did Ezra feel when he prayed and confessed "weeping and casting himself down before the house of God," and "the people wept very sore." Job experienced it, when, upon a view of the God of purity, he exclaimed, "Wherefore I abhor myself and repent in dust and ashes." Peter felt it, when, after having denied Jesus, he "went out, and wept bitterly."

The same view is inculcated by the Church of England, which says, in the Homily on Fasting: "When men feel in themselves the heavy burden of sin, see damnation to be the reward of it, and behold with the eye of their mind the horror of hell, they tremble, they quake, and are inwardly touched with sorrowfulness of heart, and cannot but accuse themselves, and open their grief unto Almighty God, and call unto him for mercy. This being done seriously, their mind is so occupied, partly with sorrow and heaviness, partly with an earnest desire to be delivered from this danger of hell and damnation, that all desire of meat and drink is laid apart, and loathsomeness (or loathing) of all worldly things and pleasure cometh in place, so that nothing then liketh them more than to weep, to lament, to mourn, and both with words and behaviour of body, to show themselves weary of life."

This is the description of repentance given by a Church not considered fanatical. Who will say that such penitence is not Scriptural? Have you felt the *heavy burden of sin*, and seen *damnation* to be the reward of it? Have you *trembled* and *quaked* as you beheld with the eye of your mind *the horror of hell?* Has your mind been so occupied with *sorrow* and a desire to be delivered from the *danger of hell and damnation*, as to destroy your appetite for "meat and drink?" Alas! how few even of those who profess to repent, act as if they really believe there is any danger of their falling into hell!

Southey, the poet laureate of England, thus describes the emotions of the awakened soul when called by God to repent:

In awe I heard, and trembled and obeyed;
  The bitterness was even as of death;
I felt a cold and piercing thrill pervade
  My loosened limbs, and, losing sight and breath,
To earth I should have fallen in despair,
Had I not clasped the cross and been supported there.
My heart I thought was bursting with the force
  Of that most fatal fruit; soul-sick I felt,
And tears ran down in such continuous course
  As if the very eyes themselves should melt.
But then I heard my Heavenly Teacher say
Drink, and this mortal grief shall pass away.
I stooped and drank of that Divinest well,
  Fresh from the rock of ages where it ran;
It had a heavenly quality to quell
  My pain; I rose a renovated man,
And would not now when that relief was known
For worlds the needful suffering have foregone.

Men who have been eminent for piety and usefulness, have laid the foundation of their spiritual power in a deep repentance.

Luther's meditations, so says one of his biographers, "on the divine justice and wrath, awakened such terrors in him, that his bodily powers failed him, and he sometimes lay motionless, as if dead. He was, indeed, found one day on the floor of his cell without any signs of life." Whitfield, when awakened, was accustomed to go out into an open meadow upon a stormy night, exposed to the cold till his hands began to blacken. He fasted and prayed till, by "abstinence and inward struggles, he so emaciated his body as to be scarcely able to creep up stairs."

The Scriptures nowhere specify the degree of "Godly sorrow" that is essential to "work repentance." It must be sufficiently deep and lasting to induce a settled hatred of sin and a controlling desire to be delivered from its guilt and power. Any thing short of this will be utterly unavailing. When this exists, the flesh will be crucified, the appetites brought into subjection, and the pride of the heart will be subdued.

Confession of sin will always be made when repentance is genuine and evangelical. Perhaps no requirement which

God makes of the transgressor comes harder than this. It has sometimes seemed that men would sooner take the fearful plunge into perdition, than make a frank and open confession of their sins, especially if they were committed under the cloak of a religious profession. They will readily consent to make promises of amendment, when they will not consent to make a humble acknowledgment of guilt. Yet confession is an imperative condition of forgiveness.

"He that covereth his sins shall not prosper: but whoso confesseth and forsaketh them, shall have mercy." Confession must, in *all cases*, be made to God. Many, perhaps the greater number, of our sins are committed against Him directly. They consist in a violation of the obligations we owe to Him. But sin against any of His creatures is sin against God. So that every transgression, whether it be against the Divine Sovereignty only, or whether it involve a violation of the rights of our fellow creatures, must be penitently confessed to God. But the harder part, in many cases, is to go to our fellow men whom we have injured, and frankly confess the wrong, and make reparation to the best of our ability. But this must be done by all who would truly repent. Jesus says: "If thou bring thy gift to the altar, and there rememberest that thy brother hath aught against thee, leave there thy gift before the altar, and go thy way; *first be reconciled* to thy brother, and then come and offer thy gift." Both the Old and the New Testament insist upon restitution. Every truly awakened soul sees its necessity. When Freeborn Garrettson was aroused to the fact that he was a sinner on his way to hell, he was the owner, by inheritance, of a number of slaves. He says that he had never, up to that time, suspected that the practice of slave-holding was wrong, having neither read any thing on the subject, nor conversed with any persons respecting its sinfulness. As a true penitent he began to discharge, to the best of his ability, all the duties he owed to God. While engaged in conducting family worship, as he was giving out the hymn, the Holy Spirit said to him: "It is not right for you to keep your fellow creatures in bondage, you must let the oppressed go free." He says "after a minute's pause, I replied: Lord, the oppressed shall go free. I then addressed the slaves and told them, 'You do not belong to me; I will not desire your service without making you a sufficient compensation.' I now found liberty to proceed in family worship. After singing, I kneeled down to pray, but if I had the tongue of an angel, I could never fully describe what I felt. All that dejection and melancholy gloom which I had groaned under, vanished away in a moment. A divine sweetness ran through my whole frame. My soul was admitted into the depths of the Redeemer's love in an inexpressible manner." Thus will it be with every repenting sinner. He will "bring forth fruits meet for repentance," by restoring, as far as lies in his power, to even the meanest of his fellow creatures, their God-given rights. Let none hope that his sin is forgiven while he holds possession of the prize for which it was committed.

"May one be pardoned, and retain the offence?
In the corrupted currents of this world,
Offence's gilded hand may shove by justice;
And oft 'tis seen, the wicked prize itself
Buys out the law: But 'tis not so above;
There is no shuffling, there the action lies
In his true nature; and we ourselves compelled,
Even to the teeth and forehead of our faults,
To give in evidence."

For the want of this humiliating work of confession and restitution, many hopeful beginnings in religion have a disastrous issue.

In building up a Christian character, see to it then, that in laying the foundation you go down to the rock. Let all the rubbish be removed. You had better, by far, grieve too much over your sins, than grieve too little. If you err at all in this momentous matter, let it be upon the safe side. Your peril will be less if you should confess and restore in some cases where it was not called for, than if you should allow a single wrong that you have committed to pass without being rectified. May you have, dear reader, that "repentance unto salvation that nedeeth not to be repented of." Take all necessary pains, for you are doing work for eternity.

RELIGIOUS EXPERIENCE.

BY D. W. TINKHAM.

THE EARNEST CHRISTIAN! My soul is stirred within me as I write these words, and inquire of myself, am I an earnest Christian? Am I Christ-like? Do I rebuke sin of every kind, unbelief, wickedness in high places; and do I bear my testimony against all that robs God of His glory? An "earnest Christian" will seek to please God rather than men. The Bible and the Holy Ghost will be his teacher, and if, obedient to God's commands, he will be led into all truth, will walk "in the light" and become a living reproof of sin wherever he comes in contact with it, there will be point and edge to his words. His appearance and manners will send conviction to those who are walking in darkness. He fears to *offend* God. Flavel says, "If I let into my heart the slavish fear of man, I must let out the reverential awe and fear of God."

An earnest Christian is a true witness for Jesus. He feels it a privilege, though sometimes a cross, to declare what Jesus has done for his soul.

I lived in the Church 16 years, sinning and repenting; making my vows to God and breaking them; resolving from time to time to keep the commandments, and even writing down my resolutions, but all to no purpose. Occasionally I heard a sermon with a little salvation in it, and I would find some crumbs for my hungry soul. I attended the means of grace, gave liberally for the support of the Gospel; comforted myself that we had means and numbers; at times had a rejoicing—in others, was warmed by their fires; in short had a form of Godliness, knowing little of its power. The grave looked dark, and I could not rejoice in prospect of death. There was a longing for something I did not possess. My Heavenly Father permitted trials to come upon me. I felt I was wronged by those who professed to love Jesus, but though trying to my nature, it proved a blessing to my soul. I soon found it was hard to pray for my enemies, and I began to look and search my heart and to resolve I would be right with God, or die at the feet of Jesus. The evidence of my acceptance was restored to me, and I began to seek something more. I had not believed in holiness of heart as a distinct blessing. God showed me my inbred corruption—the inward foes of my heart, pride, anger, and love of the world. I began to read Wesley's Plain Account of Christian Perfection, and J. T. Peck's Central Idea of Christianity, which gave me great light on the subject. I saw the Bible *commanded* us *to be holy*. I began seeking to have the roots of bitterness all raked out by the fine harrow of the Gospel. Oh what a killing out, what a dying I experienced as the light shone on the truth. I saw the depravity and unbelief of my heart, the strength of my will, and I begged to know the worst of my case; I prayed for the mighty searching of God's Spirit, and the Gospel plough did go through and through my heart, till it was all broken up. Then it was harrowed till every root, and stump, and stone, seemed laid on the surface.

I looked the ground over, saw God demanded *all*—time, *property*, family, self, *all*. Satan withstood me at every step. I struggled, groaned, agonised at this point of yielding *all*—but I was enabled to surrender. The promises came to my relief, and I began to sink down on Jesus. Then came the enemy and told me if I had given *all* I would have the witness. I traveled the ground over again, reading the Bible and other books, and again laid all on Christ. It was the hardest to keep self on the altar. The enemy knowing where to take me, kept me looking at myself and the consecration. I was miserable, grew poor, could not work, and my determined will resolved to die begging, or find the promised land,

"The land of rest from inbred sin."

It was the month of February—I was in the woods trying to chop a little, when I became so uneasy I shouldered my axe, started for my barn, determined not to sleep till I found rest in Christ. I loathed myself, it seemed impossible for Jesus to receive me. The heavens seemed as brass, and I almost despaired of finding rest. I rose from my knees, went to the house where all had been peace and harmony, and everything was wrong—wife, children, and all. I took my Bible and Hymn-book and returned to the barn and knelt in the same place where I had received the pardon of my sins. I read about the baptism of the Holy Ghost. I laid down my book and began to talk to my Father as a helpless, dependent child; told Him I had done all I could—I would lay at his feet—if He showed me anything more I could do, I would do it. I began to feel a sinking down, and a voice said, *believe in Jesus*. A sweetness came over my soul as I repeated the words *believe in Jesus*. I seemed to fall at Jesus' feet as helpless as an infant. The promises were sweet, the name of Jesus precious to my soul. I did not want to think of anything but Jesus. I rested there five days and eight hours, watching the offering, hardly daring to move lest I should lose sight of Jesus. My faith was weak. About this time, while listening to a sermon from Bro. Stiles, and as he was speaking of Jacob's wrestling and prevailing with God, it struck me I had wrestled and prevailed, and Jesus was my Saviour and saved me now. Bless His name. My faith increased and I claimed all in Jesus as mine. Just then a bright light came down with the speed of lightning, and as it struck me I was filled with glory. I praised the Lord with all my soul and strength, and forgetting everything around me I was lost in praise. When I began to realize again where I was, I found myself lying on the floor, and the congregation singing. I was happy day and night for a long time. Then came trials, but I ran to Jesus in every time of danger, and He kept me safe. I was tried on every point; lost a considerable sum of money, had my property attached; death came to our family, but I saw the hand of my Father in it all. I needed to be tried to see whether the tree God had planted in my heart would bear all the fruits of the spirit. Bless the Lord, He has kept me for two years by the moment, and I believe He can keep me forty more in the same way. I don't love sin, especially the sin of unbelief. I have claimed many things at the hand of my Father, since he began to lead me, and I am this day strong in the faith-giving glory of God. I am in

"The land of corn and wine and oil,"

where the sun never goes down out of sight of Doubting Castle. My name is written in the Lamb's book of Life; indelibly stamped there in his own blood by the Holy Ghost, and I am on my way to the City of the living God. The Lord permits Satan to put new teeth into his harrow every few days, so as to keep the soil stirred up just enough to make new applications of the truth, which strengthens my love to God and man, and hatred to the enemy and all his works. I find it requires constant watching to keep the eye single. I ask for no ease or rest till I join the throng above.

"Knowing as I am known,
How shall I love that word,
And oft repeat before the throne
Forever with the Lord."

WE ought quietly to suffer whatever befalls us, to bear the defects of others and our own, to confess them to God in secret prayer or with groans which cannot be uttered; but never to speak a sharp or peevish word, nor to murmur or repine.—WESLEY.

ORDER AND CONFUSION.

BY REV. W. C. COOLEY.

Much is said about order and confusion. A little earnestness or noise is regarded as confusion, and with many is intolerable. Some seem to have strange notions of order. They appear to believe that entire regularity and stillness constitute true order in religious worship, and to prove it Paul's language in 1 Cor. xiv, is often quoted, "Let all things be done decently and in order." The confusion which is condemned here is, several prophesying or teaching at the same time in an ordinary assembly. Where the design is to instruct, what is said must be heard to do any good, but in a large assembly several may speak at the same time without interfering with each other; as at the Caneridge camp meeting in Kentucky, the Rev. J. B. Finley says he saw seven ministers preaching at the same time. But there were in the congregation about 25,000 people. For some to fall under the power of the Spirit, and others to pray with groanings that cannot be uttered, and others to shout, is God's order or He would not cause it. The great lesson many need to learn is, that God's order is very different from man's notion of order. Says Mr. Platt, "Order, indeed! what is order, if following the impulses of the Holy Spirit is not? Does God's Spirit need to be taught politeness by the cold, impassive frigidities of modern conventionalism?" The bible, the work of the Spirit, and nature, are the three sources of knowledge in relation to the divine order. The bible says much more about noise, than it does about stillness. There may be times when it is our strength to sit still, and when God's people should stand still and see the salvation of God, but the general rule is to be active, and stillness is the exception. It is true the Lord came to the prophet Elijah not in the great wind, nor in the earthquake, nor in the fire, but in the still small voice. But we must remember that the still small voice was preceded by great agitation and noise. The obvious design of God in this case, was to teach the prophet, who had complained of being alone in Israel, that victory does not depend upon numbers or great things, but upon simply trusting in the Lord. God comes into the hearts of some sinners, who have been lashed by the guilt of conscience into a storm of grief and agony, in a still small voice, and then all is quiet and serene, and the soul is filled with great peace. But God often comes in a manner quite different.

When He came down upon Mount Sinai, the record says, "And it came to pass on the third day in the morning, that there were thunders and lightnings, and a thick cloud upon the mount, and the voice of the trumpet exceeding loud; so that all the people that was in the camp trembled." "And Mount Sinai was altogether on a smoke, because the Lord descended upon it in fire; and the smoke thereof ascended as the smoke of a furnace, and the whole mount quaked greatly." God was in all this noise and commotion.

When the foundation of the second temple was laid, as recorded in the third chapter of the book of Ezra, there was what many would call great disorder, but the Lord approved of it. The account given is, "So that the people could not discern the noise of the shout of joy from the noise of the weeping of the people; for the people shouted with a loud shout, and the noise was heard afar off." When God came by the Spirit, among the disciples on the day of Pentecost, it was not in a still manner, for there was heard "suddenly a sound from heaven, as of a rushing mighty wind, and it filled all the house where they were sitting." In addition to this great noise, they were all filled with the Holy Ghost, and spake with tongues, and appeared as men intoxicated, and a multitude of the people were crying out, Men and brethren, what shall we do? Instead of this great confusion's hindering the work, three thousand souls were converted in one day under such power.

When Jesus rode into Jerusalem, the people spread their clothes in the way, "And when He was come nigh, even now at the descent of the Mount of Olives, the whole multitude of the disciples began to rejoice and praise God with a loud voice for all the mighty works that they had seen, saying, Blessed be the King that cometh in the name of the Lord: peace in heaven, and glory in the highest." But some of the Pharisees said to Jesus, Rebuke thy disciples; but his reply was, If these should hold their peace, the stones would immediately cry out. David said, "O clap your hands, all ye people; shout unto God with the voice of triumph. God is gone up with a shout, the Lord with the sound of a trumpet." Zechariah says, "Rejoice greatly, O daughter of Zion; shout, O daughter of Jerusalem; behold, thy King cometh unto thee." St. John says in the book of Revelation, "And a voice came out of the throne, saying, Praise our God, all ye His servants, and ye that fear Him, both small and great. And I heard as it were the voice of a great multitude, and as the voice of many waters, and as the voice of mighty thunderings, saying, Alleluia: for the Lord God omnipotent reigneth."

To ascertain what God's order is, as seen in the work of the Spirit, we will notice some of the revivals of religion in the past history of the Church.

The revival under Mr. Wesley was characterized by great power, deep convictions, thorough conversions, various manifestations, and much apparent disorder and confusion. We will give as an example the Fetter-lane baptism. Mr. Wesley's account of it is, "We acknowledged our having grieved Him by our divisions; 'one saying, I am of Paul, another, I am of Apollos;' by our leaning again to our own works, and trusting in them, instead of Christ; by our resting in those little beginnings of sanctification, which it had pleased Him to work in our souls; and, above all, by blaspheming His work among us, imputing it either to nature, to the force of imagination and animal spirits, or even to the delusion of the devil. In that hour, we found God with us as at the first. Some fell prostrate upon the ground. Others burst out, as with one consent, into loud praise and thanksgiving. And many openly testified, there had been no such day as this since January the first preceding."

Mr. Wesley speaks thus of another meeting at the same place. "Mr. Hall, Kinchin, Ingham, Whitfield, Hutchins, and my brother Charles, were present at our love-feast in Fetter-lane, with about sixty of our brethren. About three in the morning, as we were continuing instant in prayer, the power of God came mightily upon us, insomuch that many cried out for exceeding joy, and many fell to the ground. As soon as we were recovered a little from that awe and amazement at the presence of His Majesty, we broke out with one voice, We praise Thee, O God; we acknowledge Thee to be the Lord." Mr. Whitfield says, "After I had begun, the Spirit of the Lord gave me great freedom, till at length it came down like a mighty rushing wind, and carried all before it. Immediately the whole congregation was alarmed. Shrieking, crying, weeping and wailing were to be heard in every corner, men's hearts failing them for fear, and many falling into the arms of their friends."

President Edwards, speaking of the great revival in New England, says, "It was a very frequent thing to see a house full of outcries, faintings, convulsions and such like, both with distress, and with admiration and joy. There were some instances of persons lying in a sort of trance, remaining for perhaps a whole twenty-four hours motionless, and with their senses locked up; but in the meantime under strong imaginations, as though they went to Heaven, and had there a vision of glorious and delightful objects."

Mr. Finley, speaking of the Caneridge revival, says, "These meetings exhibited nothing to the spectator unacquainted with them but a scene of confusion, such as scarcely could be put in human language. They were generally opened with a sermon or exhortation, at the close of which there would be a universal cry for mercy—some bursting forth in loud ejaculations of prayer or thanksgiving for the truth; some breaking forth in strong and powerful exhortations, others flying to their careless friends with tears of compassion, entreating them to fly to Christ for mercy; some, struck with terror and conviction, hasting through the crowd to escape, or pulling away from their relations; others trembling, weeping, crying for mercy; some falling and swooning away, till every appearance of life was gone, and the extremities of the body assumed the coldness of death."

The great revival now in progress in Ireland, with all the manifestations and confusion of all other noted revivals, has a place in this testimony. The facts are so fully before the people, we will not make any quotations here. What we learn of God's order in the natural world, agrees with what we have shown in the preceding remarks and facts. Sometimes all is still and quiet in nature around us, then again all is commotion and the war of elements, the driving storm, the rattling hail, the pealing thunder, and the surging waters are heard. Some of the great powers in nature work silently, as gravitation, but its effects are not silent, as falling bodies prove.

Some hold that for more than one to pray vocally at the same time, is opposed to order, and is only confusion. Perhaps it is to the mere looker on, who ought to be praying, but God is no more confused than if they were miles apart. In teaching, "we are to prophesy one by one," but it is widely different in praying. As a general rule, the leading voice should be heard in the time of prayer, but there are exceptions to this rule, as when several penitents are in great distress of mind on account of their sins, they should wrestle with God for deliverance each for himself until salvation comes. For these, or for believers who are laboring for them, to wait for each other would be a waste of time. Also when a company of believers are seeking sanctification or a baptism of the spirit upon their own hearts, it is well for each to go earnestly to God for what he needs, and press his case until he gets it. *We should guard against doing this from habit or from a desire to have a noisy meeting*, for such a meeting, cannot bless us. It is Jesus, and not the meeting, whether still or noisy, that blesses the soul.

We have seen great displays of divine power when many have been calling earnestly upon God at the same time, which shows that God is not offended with this noise. When the Spirit presses us to pray, or to shout, we should do it with an eye to please God and not men. Several years ago in a revival the brethren were in earnest, and at times, several of them would pray, without waiting for each other, and some of the formal members were confused and offended. One of these went to the minister, who was an elderly man, and complained that he could not understand all that was said in the time of prayer, and he wanted him to correct these brethren. The minister put on the air of authority, and sternly replied, "Brother, I want you to understand we do not pray to you *at all.*"

How grossly do you delude yourselves, who make your hearts dens of pride, filthy lust, malice and envy, and thousands of vanities, and yet think to find a corner in them to lodge Christ too! Truly, you would both straiten him in room, and give him very bad neighbors. No: they that think not a whole heart too little for him, shall never enjoy him.—LEIGHTON.

IT is scarce conceivable how *strait the way* is, wherein God leads them that follow him; and how dependent on him we must be, unless we are wanting in our faithfulness to him.—WESLEY.

A SINGLE EYE.

BY MRS. M. F. KENDALL.

The want of a single eye makes vascillating church members.

There are multitudes of professing Christians who live year after year in doubts and darkness. Here began the backsliding of those who once did run well. They ceased to ask the question when anything doubtful came before the mind, "Will this please the Lord? Can I do this to the glory of God?" The Holy Spirit, so tender, given to lead them into all truth, was grieved and gradually withdrawn. At first a mist gathered over the mind so they could not see clearly, but after a time thick darkness came on, and they had no spiritual discernment left. At times they were melted down by the heat around them. By the light reflected from others, they saw that they were far from God, and they resolved to get back. Then the Holy Spirit began to draw them; and as they uttered their resolutions, it shed comfort into their hearts to encourage them to come back to Jesus. Perhaps it applied some promise that caused a degree of joy. They might even in the midst of rejoicing saints, sometimes rejoice aloud. But mistaking these evidences for the direct witness of the Spirit that they were free from *condemnation*, they rested short of saving faith. They found, when temptation came, they had no power to overcome—that with all their good resolutions, none were carried out—and their rejoicing was found to be, not in themselves alone, but in another. If they are ever saved, they will have to come back to the very spot where they refused to walk in all the light, repent of it, and again by faith in Christ obtain the witness of their adoption.

There is nothing hard to be understood in God's way of saving souls. It is so plain, that a "wayfaring man, though a fool, need not err therein." How presumptuous then—how *wicked*, for those who acknowledge they are not meeting all the claims of God, to assert over and over again, they are doing the best they know how to do—they would do this or that if they could only see it to be their duty—they *cannot believe*. Such may think themselves honest, but they are not. "Let God be true and every man a liar." True indeed, "ye cannot serve God," but why? "How can ye believe who receive honor one of another, and seek not that honor which cometh from God only."

Ceasing to act with a single eye, makes vascillating ministers.

Confusion is the consequence, not only in the class, and the prayer-meeting, but in every department of the church. So long as the minister's aim is to preach the gospel so as to *save* men, he has light in his own soul, and sheds it on others around him. The word he preaches, brings forth fruit. While he is resolved to hold his hearers to the standard of God's Word, and runs the risk of losing their favor and his support, determined to live of the Gospel or not at all, he finds the Holy Ghost is given to clothe his ministrations with power to lay open men's hearts, making them feel they have to do with *God*. Just as long as he seeks the glory of God, and the triumph of the cross of Christ as the *end* of his labors, he is never long in doubt as to the *means* to be employed in accomplishing that end. It matters not how many or how few are with him, he must please him whose servant he is. And whether men hear or forbear, he reiterates the warning, as a faithful watchman, that their "blood be not required at his hands."

Let him swerve from any one of these positions, he is shorn of his strength to the extent he deviates. When he seeks to please men he is left to his own understandings, and the mist of unbelief obscures the truth, if it does not lead into fatal error. He is left to wonder why conversions do not attend his preaching, or why they are so few and so weak. If he lowers the standard of truth a little, to suit the tastes and experience of the masses, and insure also a better living, he has to resort to the figures of rhetoric, and the fancies of imagination, to hold even the attention of his hearers. The Holy Spirit is not felt in all his words and prayers. The faithful mourn, and God forsakes the place! Should he so far forget his calling, and the injunction to seek to present every man perfect in Christ Jesus, as to seek the *pre-eminence* spoken of in John, he is ever in doubt as to what is the best course to build up "the church." He tries first one experiment and then another, till he loses sight entirely of the truth that God is to save men as *individuals* and not as churches; that the church of Christ can never be raised up or sustained, except by personal holiness; and he thus becomes an easy prey to practical infidelity.

He may contend for the *form* of a pure religion, with a zeal becoming a saint indeed, but his heart has no relish for the spirit of that form; and while he vehemently contends that he both loves and enjoys it, he will be the first to silence, or condemn, as possessed of the devil, that one who really gives utterance to that spirit which magnifies the Lord, or which maketh intercession for us with groanings which cannot be uttered, however holy in life that person may be. True, this is confusion and darkness indeed. Woe be to that man or woman who lends his or her influence to promote it! But whether we intend it or not, *we do it*, when we cease to act in all things with an eye single to the glory of God! What darkness, confusion, and *eternal ruin* might be shunned, if we would remember this one rule, "When thine eye is single, thy whole body also is full of light; but when thine eye is evil, thy body also is full of darkness." There is no excuse, no exempt case. *All* may know what God requires at their hands, both for their own well-being, and for the prosperity of Zion.

We need not be mistaken amidst all the commotion of church and state, as to what is our individual work. We have only to carry our case to God, with a sincere desire to know his will, and a fixed purpose to *do* it, and though opposing elements are on every side to bias our judgment, He will so cause the true light to shine on our heart and understanding, that we can do as Luther did, decide for truth, and right, and *God*, against the whole world.

FORMAL MINISTERS. — The Italian proverb says of preachers, "They do not hear their own voice."

They may grow hard by custom of speaking of Divine things without Divine affection; so that nothing themselves or others say, can work on themselves. Hence it is that so few formal dead ministers are converted, that one said, "*Raro vidi clericum poenitentem;*" (seldom have I seen a minister penitent) so hardened are they against the means of conviction, in which they have been speaking so often of heaven and hell, and of Jesus Christ, and feeling nothing of them that the words have lost their power, and they are grown hard as the skin of Leviathan, *esteeming iron as straw and brass as rotten wood*. And this may be a reason why that sin mentioned in the sixth chapter of the epistle to the Hebrews, is unpardonable: it is, in the nature of things, without such a miracle as God will not exert, *impossible* that they who have stood out such things in vain, *should be renewed*. This should make us who are ministers, especially to tremble at an unholy life, or at the thought of declining from those ways of religion of which we have known so much, and for which we have so many means of improvement.—ARCHBISHOP LEIGHTON.

CONSECRATION.—Offer all that thou hast, to be nothing, to use nothing of all that thou hast about thee and is called thine, but to His honor and glory; and resolve through His grace to use all the powers of thy soul, and every member of thy body, to His service, as formerly thou hast done to sin.

THE DIVINE PROMISES.

BY REV. C. D. BURLINGHAM.

2ND PETER, i. 4.—" Whereby are given unto us exceeding great and precious promises; that by these ye might be partakers of the divine nature, having escaped the corruption that is in the world through lust."

A very marked trait in the character of the inspired Scriptures is, the prominence given to experimental religion. This may be deemed the distinguishing characteristic of the apostolic witness. Certainly our doctrines, and ceremonies and ordinances, though excellent and important, can be of but little benefit to us, unless they tend to increase our spirituality—to advance us in our Christian experience. Saint Peter appears to entertain very elevated and comprehensive views respecting Gospel privileges and Christian attainments.

1. The character of Bible promises, the promises of God, are numerous, adapted, comprehensive, "exceedingly great," inconceivably "precious," free and unlimited in the benefits they proffer to man, conditional and discriminating in the blessings they secure to man.

2. The object they are designed to accomplish—salvation. Salvation is deliverance from all sin: "having escaped the corruption that is in the world through lust." "Lust," or desire, is the origin and conservator of depravity. This depravity pervades all minds and corrupts all hearts. Here is the fountain of moral evil, and the agent of eternal death! Salvation is deliverance from all moral depravity, and from the curse it entails. Salvation demands our mightiest energies as the condition of and preparation for it. Salvation requires the exertion of Almighty Power. Salvation is the elevation of the soul from the groveling and sensual to the ennobling and spiritual—the subjugation of the affections and desires, here denominated "lust," to the conscience and judgment: and the entire being—physical, intellectual and moral—pervaded by and assimilated to the Divine nature. "Partakers of the Divine nature;" that is, perfectly renewed in the Divine image, and living in God.

This is a very high state of grace: and does the Gospel provide for it? Does God require it? Do our interests demand it? Do the promises pledge it? Then it is practicable, and we may enjoy it.

3. The manner in which the Divine promises accomplish their object. The promises inspire confidence in the Mercy of God. They inspire the highest respect for the Divine veracity. God will dispense blessings according to his promises, and He will inflict curses according to His threatenings. The promises encourages repentance and prayer, as means of grace. The promises are the arguments for faith in Christ. The promises are the channels of grace to the soul, in every possible need: Ezek. xxxvi, 25–27. "Then will I sprinkle clean water upon you, and ye shall be clean: from all your filthiness, and from all your idols, will I cleanse you. A new heart also will I give you, and a new spirit will I put within you: and I will take away the stony heart out of your flesh, and I will give you a heart of flesh. And I will put my Spirit within you, and cause you to walk in my statutes, and ye shall keep my judgments and do them. And ye shall dwell in the land that I gave to your fathers; and ye shall be my people, and I will be your God."

IT is not one of the least fruits of righteousness to bear the reproach of Christ. The world will let you go on quietly enough if you have no more piety than what pleases them. While you follow the indifferent *rationality* of your neighbors, you will never be reproached; but strike out of the beaten path that leads to death, and you will be pointed at. And yet this must be so; a sense of the presence of God surrounding you and a view of eternity will always inspire you with singularity.—SUMMERFIELD.

CONSECRATION.

Great revivals are preceded by God's people consecrating themselves entirely to His service. President Edwards makes the following remarks relative to the great revival which took place in Northampton under his labors:

"I have been," he says, "particularly acquainted with many persons who have been the subjects of the high and extraordinary transports of the present day. Extraordinary views of Divine things, and religious affections are frequently attended with very great effect on the body, nature often sinking under the weight of divine discoveries, the strength of the body taken away, so as to deprive of all ability to stand or speak; sometimes the hands clinched and flesh cold, but senses still remaining; animal nature often in a great emotion and agitation, and the soul very often, of late, so overcome with great admiration, and a kind of omnipotent joy, as to cause the person (wholly unavoidably) to leap with all the might, with joy and mighty exultation of soul; the soul at the same time being so strongly drawn toward God and Christ in heaven that it seemed to the person as though soul and body would, as it were of themselves, of necessity mount up, leave the earth and ascend thither.

These effects on the body did not begin now in this wonderful season, that they should be owing to the influence of the example of the times, but about seven years ago; and began in a much higher degree, and greater frequency, near three years ago, when there was no such enthusiastical season, as many account this; but it was a very dead time through the land: they arose from no distemper catched from Mr. Whitfield or Mr. Tennent, because they began before either of them came into the country; they began as I said, near three years ago, in a great increase, upon an extraordinary self-dedication, and renunciation of the world, and resignation of all to God, made in a great view of God's excellency, and high exercise of love to Him, and rest and joy in Him; since which time they have been very frequent; and began in a yet higher degree, and greater frequency, about a year and a half ago, upon another new resignation of all to God, with a yet greater fervency and delight of soul; since which time the body has been very often fainting, with the love of Christ; and began in a much higher degree still, the last winter upon another resignation and acceptance of God as the only portion and happiness of the soul, wherein the whole world and the dearest enjoyments in it, were renounced as dirt, and all that is pleasant and glorious, and all that is terrible in this world, seemed perfectly to vanish into nothing, and nothing to be left but God, in whom the soul was perfectly swallowed up, as in an infinite ocean of blessedness. Since which time there have often been great agitations of body, and an unavoidable leaping for joy; and the soul as it were dwelling almost without interruption, in a kind of paradise; and very often, in high transports, disposed to speak of these great and glorious things of God and Christ, and the eternal world that are in view to others present, in a most earnest manner, and with a loud voice, so that it is next to impossible to avoid it; these effects on the body not arising from any bodily distemper or weakness, because the greatest of all have been in a good state of health. This great rejoicing has been a rejoicing with trembling, *i. e.* attended with a deep and lively sense of the greatness and majesty of God, and the persons own exceeding littleness and vileness. Spiritual joys in this person never were attended, either formerly or lately, with the least appearance of any laughter or lightness of countenance, or manner of speaking; but with a peculiar abhorrence of such appearances in spiritual rejoicings, especially since joys have been greatest of all. These high transports when they have been past, have had abiding effects in the increase of the sweetness, rest and humility that they have left upon the soul; and a new engagedness of heart to live to God's honor, and watch and fight against sin.—PRESIDENT EDWARDS.

COURAGE.—Be well satisfied that you are in the way of your duty, and that will beget holy courage in times of danger. "Who will harm you if you be followers of that which is good?" Or if any do attempt it, you may boldly commit yourselves to God in well-doing. It was this consideration that raised Luther's spirit above all fear. "In the cause of God," said he, "I ever am and shall be stout; herein I assume this title, "*Cedo nulli*"—I yield to none. A good cause will bear up a man's spirit bravely. Hear the saying of a heathen, to the shame of cowardly Christians. When the emperor Vespasian had commanded Fluidius Priscus not to come to the senate, or if he did, to speak nothing but what he would have him, the senator returned this noble answer; that, "as he was a senator, it was fit he should be at the senate; and if being there he were required to give his advice, he would speak freely that which his conscience commanded him." The emperor threatening that then he should die, he answered, "Did I ever tell you that I was immortal? Do you what you *will*, and I will do what I ought; it is in your power to put me to death unjustly, and in mine to die with constancy." Righteousness is a breastplate; the cause of God will sustain all you venture upon it: let them tremble whom danger finds out of the way of duty.—FLAVEL.

UNCONVERTED PROFESSORS.—Methodism as well as other Churches, is cursed with unconverted members, who live without salvation, who are just like the brutes that went into Noah's ark;—went in brutes, and they came out brutes;—they come among the Methodists unconverted, and they go into eternity in the same manner.—CAUGHEY.

BE silent when blamed and reproached unjustly, and under such circumstances that the reproachful and injurious person will be likely, from the influence of his own reflections, to discover his error and wrong speedily. Listen not to the suggestions of nature, which would prompt a hasty reply; but receive the injurious treatment with humility and calmness; and He in whose name you thus suffer, will reward you with inward consolation, while He sends the sharp arrow of conviction into the heart of your adversary.

Do not think it strange when troubles and persecutions come upon you. Rather receive them quietly and thankfully, as coming from a Father's hand. Yea, happy are ye, if in the exercise of faith you can look above the earthly instrumentality, above the selfishness and malice of men, to Him who has permitted them for your good. Thus persecuted they the Saviour and the prophets.—UPHAM.

MORTIFY all impatience in all pains and troubles, whether from the hands of God or men, all desire of revenge, all resentment of injuries; and by the pure love of God, love thy very persecutors as if they were thy dearest friend.

Mortify all bitterness of heart toward thy neighbors, and all vain complacency in thyself, all vain glory and desire of esteem, in words and deeds, in gifts and graces. To this thou shalt come by a more clear and perfect knowledge and consideration of thy own vileness, and by knowing God to be the fountain of all grace and goodness.—LEIGHTON.

To a worldly man, great gain sweetens the hardest labor; and to a Christian, spiritual profit and advantage may do much to move him to take those afflictions well which are otherwise very unpleasant. Though *they are not joyous for the present*, yet this allays the sorrow of them—the fruit that grows out of them—*that peaceable fruit of righteousness.*—ARCHBISHOP LEIGHTON.

SELF-DECEPTION.

BY MRS. EMELINE SMITH.

Among the most serious obstacles in the way of the work of God, are the unscriptural views of the Christian character entertained by a large proportion of those professing godliness. There is not, taking in *the whole range* of difficulties to be overcome, in the accomplishment of the great work for which the Church of Christ was instituted, anything so calculated to paralyze the energies, and grieve the very souls of God's *believing and obedient children* as the claims set up, and the practices indulged by many who professedly are engaged in carrying out the same object.

In our branch of the visible Church, we claim to be devoted to the spread of Scriptural holiness. Multitudes may be found in this, as in other branches of the Church, who, although they bring forth none of the fruits which spring from *real union with Christ*, seem confidently to expect a a participation in the blessedness, promised to those who *labor and suffer in His cause*. While the word of God is so full of *cautions* to take heed to ourselves, lest we deceive our own souls, and while the tests of discipleship are laid down on almost every page of the *New Testament*, it would seem impossible for one to mistake his spiritual condition. But we have only to glance at the mass of those who profess to be the disciples of Jesus, and to compare the hopes they entertain in their lives and labors, with the plain requirements of God's holy word, to be mournfully convinced that self-deception is not so rare as might be expected. Taking the professed followers of Christ in the aggregate, there is great reason to fear by far the largest proportion will refuse to test themselves by the rules laid down in the word of God. It is hard to say this, but will not the facts sustain us?

If we look into the New Testament we shall find several classes of persons accurately portrayed. Promises and warnings are given, differing as widely as the various classes of persons to whom they are addressed. To the children of God are made those promises and encouragements which the apostle speaks of as "exceeding great and precious." Then there is a class spoken of, who "say they are rich, and increased in goods, and have need of nothing." God says of these, they are neither cold or hot, and the admonition given to these is that unless they repent, and buy the gold tried in the fire, that He will spew them out of His mouth. And so the various classes of men are spoken of, and as *their characters vary*, so are the promises and admonitions made to each distinct class of persons varied. If we regard as a matter of any importance the knowledge of our true standing in the sight of God, we have only to study His word, and find under which class we come, and then we may ascertain, without any possibility of a failure, if we are but honest, whither we are tending. Having ascertained where we belong, we are prepared to apply to ourselves the portion of Scripture belonging to us. But here lies the difficulty. Persons coming to the word of God, without any reference to the conditions upon which the promises are based, claim the glorious ones made by the Almighty to His *believing and obedient children*. Too many, making this claim, answer to a far different description and inherit an entirely different class of promises. The true child of God is described all through the New Testament as one who is completely delivered from the bondage and dominion of sin. "Whosoever is born of God doth not commit sin." And on the other hand, "He that committeth sin is of the devil." "There is, therefore, now, no condemnation to them who are in Christ Jesus, who walk not after the flesh, but after the Spirit." "If our heart condemn us, God is greater than our heart." If we love God we are represented as "*keeping all His commandments;*" "Walking in the light;" "Denying self, and taking up the cross daily;" "Abiding in Christ and bringing forth much fruit to His glory;" "Gathering with Christ." As the fountain is pure, all the streams flowing therefrom are pure. And thus lineament after lineament of the Christian character is so plainly portrayed that none need be deceived but those who choose to be.

Yet, a class of persons, just as accurately described, and to whom a far different type of promises are made, boldly claim those precious encouragements that God in His written word holds out to those who walk with Him in white. True they will acknowledge they are living in the frequent neglect of known duty. Years ago, perhaps, there were crosses presented which they refused to bear. They are now almost daily brought under condemnation. Even at the bar of their own consciences, seared as they have become by long continued disobedience of God's requirements, they are constrained to admit that they are not walking in all the light, and keeping all the commands of God. With what propriety can such persons expect a part in the final reward of those who bear the burdens and perform the labor required of Christ's true disciples? The true believers show their faith by a cheerful obedience, an unfaltering pursuit of the prize held out to those who run in the way of God's commandments. To them the promises of God are yea and amen in Christ Jesus. But the other class who thus lay claim to the same prize, are running a far different race. The opinions of men form the bar at which they try the calls of God's Spirit and word. If not regarded as very fanatical, they will do some Christian duties; possibly speak and go through the form of prayer in a religious meeting, unless the cross is too heavy. But these never know what it is to labor successfully for those out of Christ. Their pride of heart is yet unsubdued, and self is just as truly reigning in such a heart as ever. If their circumstances in life are prosperous, they conclude the complacence they feel is religion. If God, by His providences, calls after them, and adversity becomes their teacher to win them back to the cross, they fail to discern the hand of God in the trials which are suffered to befall them. They see only *second causes*, and while they murmur and struggle against these providential dealings of God, they still talk of resignation to His will. But this resignation is compulsory. They are *submissive* because it is impossible for them to control or change the circumstances that hem them in. They are always persuading themselves that they are undervalued and misunderstood. Peevish, impatient, yielding to every temptation, it does not matter what such persons profess. Before they have any right to the encouragements given to the people of God, there must be a genuine repentance! a sorrow so deep and pungent as shall lead them at once to forsake every evil way! and a hearty confession, not to God only but to all who have seen in them these tempers and practices. A complete surrender of soul and bodies' powers into the hands of God! And a willingness, if God so requires, to forsake all that they have, whether it be reputation, or friends, or substance! When these steps have been taken, Jesus will be presented to them as the object of faith. Having met the conditions laid down in the word of God, He on his part will forgive their sins, renew their natures, and implant His Spirit in their hearts. They will find Christ the door by which they will enter the sheepfold. Entering through the door, their title to the promises is secured to them if they *continue to walk in the way*.

It is not enough for a person who has been living in the neglect of some duty once plainly presented, but now not clearly seen as duty, to plead that now they feel no condemnation for their neglect. This is not strange! Refusing to walk in the light that light has become darkness. Such persons will often talk of faith in Christ, and even of being blessed of God. At one time they had probably a measure of saving faith. But they saw a self denying path. They saw the reproach and contempt that might come upon them if they walked in that path. They were unwilling to have their names cast out as evil, and thus they refused to follow Jesus in the way. The Spirit was grieved, they felt the loss; but still persisting in their refusal to walk in the light, it has now become darkness. They *profess*, it may be, just as much religion as ever. Possibly they have persuaded themselves they enjoy more. I know some who say they have no fear of death, and who claim that they do believe in God to the salvation of their souls. Though they can look back to a point where they deliberately refused to do duty, when it was plainly presented, still they talk of joys and peace! Such persons are to be met in all the Churches. O if God would but enable me to say something that would reach and alarm such souls! What a snare of the devil is here. The enemy of souls is a wily foe. After a refusal to follow Christ, and the consequent withdrawal of the light of God's countenance, unless the adversary can substitute something in its place to lull the conscience, there is hope that we may become so much alarmed as to give over these wanderings, and again take up the cross. Satan knows this full well, and to such souls he gives something as near like their former experience as he possibly can, a sort of dead faith—a peace—but it is a peace with sin in our hearts. It is not necessary that we should be outbreakingly wicked. If one should fall into any great wickedness, he would be aroused to see that he had departed from his God. Satan can accomplish far more with one of these "good" people than with one who stands confessed a child of wrath.

This peace differs from God's peace so widely that none need be deceived, unless they refuse to come to the light, lest their deeds should be reproved. God's peace cannot exist where there is not obedience to all of God's requirements. But these deceived ones can fall into sin, and call it infirmity! temperament! anything but what *it is*—an infraction of the law of God. They do feel a degree of condemnation, for every violation of God's requirements, but here is another point of difference. A soul that has not rejected the light, if by any means it is led into any sin, or says, or does anything that brings condemnation, feels a loathing of sin AS *sin*. There is no disposition to palliate it, as a very little thing, hardly worthy of notice, but there is a willingness to confess, and the heart is fully set to forsake all such practices. And O how that point is guarded after such a stumble! But these who can hardly believe that God condescends to mark their omissions and commissions, unless they are of the grossest kind, feel in one sort condemned, but the sorrow they experience is, in fact, only a fear of punishment.

A confession of our faults one to another, is a serious business, and the soul that realizes, that if it yields to evil tempers it will have to confess the wrong to all who have witnessed it, finds that Sin is not such a cheap thing after all.

There is another strongly marked point of difference between those in the light, and those in whom the light has become darkness. Talk to the latter class of the mercies of God—of the glories of the heavenly world—the rewards of the blessed on high—charm them with singing! or with the beauties of poetry, and their natural sympathy will be excited; they will shed a few tears perhaps, and profess and believe, they are happy in God! As well might the sentimentalist, weeping over the last new novel! The feeling is precisely the same. But you talk to such souls of a God of infinite purity, of unbending justice. Hold the truth upon their heart and conscience, that God's people are an obedient working people! Present the fields all white to the harvest, and call for the laborers! Urge the truth that no man is following Christ, who is not bearing the cross; repeat in their hearing, Whosoever will live godly in Christ Jesus, shall suffer persecution; and do they get happy? Try them once more. The word says, "The kingdom of God is righteousness and peace and joy in the Holy Ghost." Have they these constituent elements of the kingdom of God? But they say they have peace and joy even. "But the joy of the Lord is our strength." Is there any strength in the joy of which such persons speak? Have they strength to overcome temptation? Have they strength to work for God any where? Are they enabled to win souls to Christ? Is not their joy like the crackling of thorns under a pot, destitute of heat. To such a talent has been entrusted, but they have not improved upon it. Looking upon those who have made the effort to improve upon what God has given, they have been tried with their extravagant zeal, and high professions, and have rejoiced in their own fancied humility. What a fearful awaking as they come up to the very entrance of the Celestial City, and say, "Lord, Lord, open unto us," &c. Here they stand, still self deceived, confidently expecting to be admitted into the Kingdom. And here at last, when too late to rectify the fatal mistake, the Judge of quick and dead startles them in their fancied security, by declaring, "Depart from me, I never knew you—ye that work iniquity." Take the talent from the unprofitable servant, and cast him into outer darkness." May the Holy Spirit search our hearts, that we may know on what foundation our hopes are based.

THE SPIRIT'S POWER.

In this age of faith in the natural, and disinclination to the supernatural, we want especially to meet the whole world with this *credo*, "I believe in the Holy Ghost." I expect to see saints as lovely as any that are written of in the Scriptures—because I believe in the Holy Ghost. I expect to see preachers as powerful to set forth Christ evidently crucified before the eyes of men, as powerful to pierce the conscience, to persuade, to convince, to convert, as any that ever shook the multitudes of Jerusalem, or Corinth, or Rome—because I believe in the Holy Ghost. I expect to see Churches, the members of which shall be endued with spiritual gifts, and every one moving in spiritual activity, animating and edifying one another, commending themselves to the conscience of the world by their good works, commending their Saviour to it by a heart-engaging testimony—because I believe in the Holy Ghost. I expect to see villages where the respectable people are now opposed to religion, the proprietor ungodly, the nominal pastor worldly, all that take a lead, set against living Christianity—to see such villages summoned, disturbed, divided, and then re-united, by the subduing of the whole population to Christ —because I believe in the Holy Ghost. I expect to see cities swept from end to end, their manners elevated, their commerce purified, their politics Christianized, their criminal population reformed, their poor made to feel that they are among brethren—righteousness in the streets, peace in the homes, an altar at every fireside—because I believe in the Holy Ghost. I expect the world to be overflowed with the knowledge of God; the day to come when no man shall need to say to his neighbor, "Know thou the Lord;" but when all shall know Him, "from the least unto the greatest;" east and west, north and south, uniting to praise the name of the one God, and the one Mediator —because I believe in the Holy Ghost. —Rev. William Arthur.

To ridicule old age is like pouring cold water into the bed in the morning, in which you have to sleep at night.

Never forget the kindness which others do for you, nor remind others of the kindness which you do for them.

SATAN IN WHITE.

Satan perceived that it would be convenient and advantageous for him to have two suits of clothes. A suit of flaming, impurpled, and blackish red was his raiment since he instigated the rebellion in heaven: this he wears at home. This is the garment that is emblatic of his wrath and cruelty against El-Shaddai. He transformed himself when he tempted the first Adam, and succeeded in casting him down. The Second Adam knew him, when he required him to obey his command, and worship him instead of the true God. The Second Adam would die, rather than eat bread made out of a stone by the command of Satan.

It was in his flaming, bloody, black-red garb that Satan appeared among the persecutors, both pagan and popish, lighting up the funeral fires of the Martyrs. But he soon found it necessary to have a suit of white, descriptive of his cunning and hypocrisy; and he ordered white garments for his servants also, to wear upon certain occasions, when from home upon his expeditions. He met with reception in his white robe, angel-like, in many places where he would not have been received at all in his suit of flaming red-black, in which he took the lead at pastimes, Sabbath plays, in taverns, and horse-races. But in his white robe he had an early admittance into many a cathedral, and he appointed some of his servants to offices there.

He also, in his white suit, found his way into the houses of evangelical dissenters, though they profess to have a book which exhibits his devices. Notwithstanding all the watching that had been at the doors, he rushed in to the communion table, as he had done to the consecrated altar of the cathedral, and sowed discord between the minister and the deacons; and he himself undertook the managing matters between them, seated in his chair and vested in his white robe. He forced many to assume a profession, like tares of the field; and some also of his best beloved servants, who were utterly destitute of the love of Christ and the fear of God, he raised into the pulpit, while they were living in secret sins; but they all had a white robe, as white as the sepulchres of the Pharisees, covering all these things. Satan held these up to deceive before the eye of God, and all the terrors of eternity. To sustain them from fainting, he administers unto them his potions from the pitcher of presumption; and hardened their consciences with the hot iron of hypocrisy, heated in the fire of hell. He taught them to persecute religion in the garb of an angel.

Let us not give room to the devil in his white raiment! When he attempts to destroy the character of a brother, he assumes his white robe, and not his murdering garment, pretending to vindicate the glory of God and the cause of justice, asserting that the cause of religion must be cleared; while all this time envy rankles in his heart, notwithstanding his fair pretences, as when the Jews delivered Jesus to be crucified. It was his white garment that Satan wore in the court of Caiaphas, when he charged the true God with blasphemy. This garb, also, his servant Judas wore, when he displayed such zeal and sympathy for the poor, in the case of the ointment at Bethany. Let us ask grace, that we may be able to recognise the devil in his white raiment, as well as in his old black-red garb. He is not so easily distinguished in his borrowed white, as in his own proper suit. Let us cleanse out hypocrisy. Such is our instruction.
—Christmas Evans.

The saints are as in a common butchery in the world; yea, not only "as sheep for the slaughter," but sometimes as sheep for the altar, men thinking it a sacrifice. "They that kill you," says our Saviour, "shall think they do God service. Yet even this pulls not from Him. They part with life? ay, why not? This life is but a death, and He is our life for whom we live it.—Archbishop Leighton.

MAKING FUN.

Once when traveling in a stage-coach, I met a young lady who seemed to be upon the constant look out for something laughable; and not content with laughing herself, she took great pains to make others do the same.

Now traveling in a stage-coach is rather prosy business. People in this situation are very apt to show themselves peevish and selfish; so the young lady's good humor was, for a time, very agreeable. Every old barn was made the subject of a passing joke, while the cows and hens looked demurely on, little dreaming that folks could be merry at their expense. All this perhaps, was harmless enough. Animals are not sensitive in that respect. They are not likely to have their feelings injured because people make fun of them; but when we come to human beings, that is quite another thing. So it seemed to me, for after a while an old lady came running across the fields, swinging her bag at the coachman, and in a shrill voice begging him to stop. The good-natured coachman drew up his horses, and the old lady, coming to the fence by the road-side, squeezed herself through two bars which were not only in a horizontal position, but very near together. The young lady in the stage-coach made some ludicrous remark, and the passengers laughed. It seemed very excusable; for in getting through the fence the poor woman had made sad work with her old black bonnet, and now, taking a seat beside a well dressed lady, really looked as if she had been blown there by a whirlwind. This was a new piece of fun, and the girl made the most of it. She caricatured the old lady upon a card; pretended, when she was not looking, to take patterns of her bonnet; and in various other ways sought to raise a laugh. At length the poor woman turned a pale face toward her.

"My dear," she said, "you are young, healthy and happy; I have been so too, but that time is past. I am now old, decrepit, and forlorn. This coach is taking me to the death-bed of my only child. And then, my dear, I shall be a poor old woman, all alone in a world where merry girls will think me a very amusing object. They will laugh at my old-fashioned clothes, forgetting that the old woman has a spirit that has loved, and suffered, and will live forever."

The coach now stopped before a poor looking house, and the old lady feebly descended the steps.

"How is she?" was the first trembling inquiry of the poor mother.

"Just alive," said the man who was leading her into the house.

Putting up the steps, the driver mounted his box, and we were on the road again. Our merry young friend had placed the card in her pocket. She was leaning her head upon her hand; and you may be assured I was not sorry to see a tear upon her fair young cheek. It was a good lesson, and one which we greatly hoped would do her good.

It is pleasant to see a smiling face. We should encourage our hearts to look on the sunny side of things, and there is no harm in being merry where no one is injured by it; but in this, as in every other thing, let us be conscientious. The wise man has said,—"There is a time to laugh;" but remember, dear children, If we would not displease our heavenly Father, we must take care and not be merry when conscience tells us it is wrong. I have heard children excuse themselves for laughing in the house of God, by saying they couldn't help it. Now what is to be done when children can't help doing wrong? When they kneel before God in prayer, do they say, "I have done wrong, but I couldn't help it?" No, they would not dare say that. Let us, then, teach our hearts to be very honest, for unto Him who *searcheth* the heart *we must tell the whole truth.*

"I HOLD STILL."

Pain's furnace heat within me quivers,
  God's breath upon the flame doth blow,
And all my heart in anguish quivers,
  And trembles at the fiery glow;
And yet I whisper, As God will!
And in his hottest fire hold still.

He comes and lays my heart, all heated,
  On the hard anvil, minded so
Into His own fair shape to beat it
  With His great hammer, blow on blow;
And yet I whisper, As God will!
And at his heaviest blows hold still.

He takes my softened heart and beats it,
  The sparks fly off at every blow.
He turns it o'er and o'er, and heats it,
  And lets it cool, and makes it glow;
And yet I whisper, As God will!
And in His mighty hand hold still.

Why should I murmur? for the sorrow
  Thus only longer lived would be;
Its end may come, and will, to-morrow,
  When God has done His work in me.
So I say, trusting, As God will!
And, trusting to the end, hold still.

He kindles for my profit purely
  Affliction's glowing fiery brand,
And all His heaviest blows are surely
  Inflicted by a Master hand;
So I say, praying, As God will!
And hope in Him, and suffer still.

In the afternoon, an old friend (now with the Moravians) labored much to convince me that I could not continue in the church of England, because I could not implicitly submit to her determinations; "For this," he said, "was essentially necessary to the continuing in any church." Not to the continuing in any but that of the Brethren; if it were, I would be a member of no church under heaven. For I must still insist on the rights of private judgment. I dare call no man, Rabbi. I cannot yield implicit faith or obedience to any men, or number of men, under heaven.—WESLEY.

REVIVALS.

BY THE EDITOR.

THE natural tendency of the human heart is to depart from God. This tendency exists, though in greatly diminished force, even after conversion has truly taken place. It remains until the obedient disciple is fully "crucified with Christ," dead unto sin, and "alive to God." As comparatively few in any of the churches are led into the enjoyment of this state of grace, there is apparent every where a proneness to backsliding. The revival ceases, and the faith, and love, and zeal, of too many die away. The Holy Spirit is grieved, and gradually withdraws His support, worldly conformity ensues, sinful passions are indulged, and the tone of piety is lessened down far below the Gospel standard. With such a state of things, a revival, to be a blessing, must commence with the professed children of God. They are the models after which the new recruits will naturally fashion their experience and their lives. Unless the leading members of the church are obediently walking in God's commandments, and living free from condemnation, the converts, in the mass, will be almost certain to fall below the requirements of the Bible. A class-leader in a fashionable Methodist church stated in our hearing, that out of a large number who had united with the church, as the fruit of a "splendid revival," he had not known one to cease to "adorn themselves with gold and pearls and costly array," but he had known some who had not previously worn jewelry, to put it on upon uniting with the church! It is one of the greatest injuries that can be inflicted upon an individual, to persuade him to take up with any thing short of a Gospel hope. His profession serves as a shield to ward off the arrows of truth. The self-complacency naturally resulting from a discharge of what are considered religious duties, he mistakes for the approbation of God; the conviction, felt occasionally, of the necessity of a more radical change of heart, he is taught to regard as a morbid scrupulousness of conscience which must be repressed; and the melting influences of the Spirit given to him, at times, to encourage him to come to Christ, he looks upon as an assurance from Heaven that he is in the right way. Thus his condition is far more hopeless than when he made no profession of religion. He is rather a proselyte than a convert, and happy is he if he does not become "two-fold more the child of hell" than before! A revival, then, should commence with the church. Let every one that has named the name of Christ repent in dust and ashes before the Lord, depart from all iniquity, and be filled with "faith, and with the Holy Ghost," and God's work will be carried on through their instrumentality. Difficulties will vanish, or be overcome, resources will be created or dispensed with, and souls will be converted, not to a party or an opinion, but to CHRIST.

LAY PREACHING.

As churches become rich, ministers clothe themselves with importance. They arrogate high-sounding titles, and, without any regard to their personal sanctity, claim a superstitious reverence, by virtue of their office as "ambassadors of Christ." God, who chooses "the weak things of the world to confound the mighty," passes by these consequential ones, and selects persons of no pretensions as the chosen instrumentalities for promoting His work. He leaves the professional warrior unnoticed, and takes a Deborah from the cares of her family, or a Gideon from the threshing floor, to lead his marshalled hosts to battle and to victory. In all the great revivals that have taken place, private members have acted a conspicuous part. One of the objections most strongly and frequently urged against the work of God, carried on in Wesley's day, was the fact that the instruments chiefly employed in promoting it were laymen. To those who pressed this objection, and urged that he must be sensible of its strength, as he had not attempted to answer it, Wesley replied:

"It was not distrust of my cause, but tenderness to you, which occasioned my silence. I had something to advance on this head also; but I was afraid you could not bear it. I was conscious to myself that, some years since, to touch this point, was to touch the apple of my eye; and this makes me almost unwilling to speak now, lest I should shock the prejudices I cannot remove.

"Suffer me, however, just to intimate to you something which I would leave to your further consideration. The scribes of old, who were the ordinary preachers among the Jews, were not priests; they were not better than laymen. Yea, many of them were incapable of the priesthood, being of the tribe of Simeon, not of Levi. Hence, probably it was that the Jews themselves never urged it as an objection to our Lord's preaching, (even those who did not acknowledge or believe that he was sent of God in an extraordinary character,) that he was no priest after the order of Aaron, nor, indeed, could be, seeing he was of the tribe of Judah.

"Nor does it appear that any objected this to the Apostles; so far from it, that at Antioch in Pisidia, we find the rulers of the synagogue sending unto Paul and Barnabas, strangers just come into the city, "Saying, men and brethren, if ye have any word of exhortation for the people, say on."—Acts xiii. 15.

"If we consider these things, we shall be the less surprised at what occurs in the eighth chapter of the Acts: "At that time there was a great persecution against the Church; and they were all scattered abroad, (that is all the church, all the believers in Jesus) throughout the regions of Judea and Samaria," verse 1. "Therefore they that were scattered abroad went everywhere preaching the word," verse 4. Now what shadow of reason have we to say, or think, that all these were ordained before they preached?"

"If we come to later times; was Mr. Calvin ordained? Was he either priest or deacon? And were not most of those whom it pleased God to employ in promoting the reformation abroad, laymen also? Could that great work have been promoted at all in many places, if laymen had not preached? And yet how seldom do the very Papists urge this as an objection against the reformation! Nay, as rigorous as they are in things of this kind, they themselves appoint, even in some of their strictest orders, that, "if any lay brother believes himself called of God to preach as a missionary, the superior of the order, being informed thereof, shall immediately send him away."

"In all Protestant churches it is still more evident that ordination is not held a necessary prerequisite for preaching; for in Sweden, in Germany, in Holland, and I believe in every reformed church in Europe, it is not only permitted but required, that before any one is ordained, (before he is admitted even into deacon's orders, wherever the distinction between priests and deacons is retained.) he should publicly preach a year or more, *ad probandum facultatem* (on trial.) And for this practice they believe they have the authority of an express command of God. "Let them first be proved; then let them use the office of a deacon, being found blameless."—1 Tim. iii. 10."

At the present time, in the church which Mr. Wesley founded, about the same importance is attached to the necessity of being licensed, to authorize one to call sinners to repentence, that there was in his day to being ordained to preach the Gospel. Many are troubled about a license. Give yourself no anxiety about it. Does God call you to preach? Up and at it. Go to your neighbors and warn them faithfully to flee from the wrath to come. Are they awakened? Lead them to Christ. Is an interest in religion excited? Appoint meetings, bear your testimony to the power of Christ to save, exhort, sing, pray, as the Holy Spirit leads, and encourage others to do the same. But is this preaching? Wesley says, "What is it to preach, but *prædicare verbum Dei*, to publish the word of God. And this, laymen do all over England."

Do not then be anxious about a license. Obey God. Be filled with the Spirit. We have tried to spread the Glad Tidings without license and with license; we have been ordained and we have been unordained, but we never could discover that any of these things affected our ability to preach one way or the other. The one essential qualification we have found to be the baptism of the Holy Ghost, inspiring the heart with love to God and love to the souls of men. If you have this, go forward. Do your whole duty. Turn to righteousness as many of your erring fellow men as possible.

The discipline of the Methodist Church implies plainly that persons shall preach before they are licensed In the section entitled, "Of the trial of those who think they are moved by the Holy Ghost to preach," the question is asked, "Have they fruit? Are any truly convinced of sin, and converted to God, by their preaching?" How can men be converted "by their preaching" until they preach?

Again, the General Rules—the constitution of the church—say that all who have "a desire to flee from the wrath to come, and to be saved from their sins," should evince this desire "by instructing, reproving or exhorting all they have any intercourse with." What is this but preaching? What preacher does more than this? How few do as much! God gives you, earnest Christian, a license to do all the good you can.

SALVATION BANDS.

One of the most important measures adopted by the late Laymen's Convention of Genesee Conference, was that recommending the formation of praying bands. The design is to induce those in sympathy with earnest Christianity to put forth direct, systematic and persevering efforts for the salvation of souls. Wherever there are three or more believers in Christ, of one heart and one mind, who feel the worth of souls, let them form a Band, adopting the directions to the Band Societies, found in all the Methodist Disciplines published prior to 1852. Let them choose a leader who shall give direction, under God, to the meetings. Guided by the Holy Spirit, select some locality where a revival of religion is specially needed. Procure some place—a church, school-house, hall, shop, any place where the people can be comfortably convened —and go to work. Sing, pray, exhort, "with hearts and tongues of fire." At each meeting let one or more who has a living experience relate it as the spirit directs. Clear, burning testimonials of the power of Christ to save, are the "sling-stones" before which the enemies of God will fall. As souls are awakened pray with them and lead them to Jesus. As they are converted, set them to work for the salvation of others. Let this be done all over the land, and a mighty revival of religion would take place.

LAYMEN'S CONVENTION OF THE GENESEE CONFERENCE.

A very interesting session was held at Olean the first and second of February. Its proceedings have been published so widely in the weekly papers that we deem it best to give only a general outline.

The Love Feast on Tuesday evening was a season of great spiritual profit.

The Convention was opened on Wednesday morning by Abner I. Wood, Esq., of Parma, President, who presided with his usual ability. The attendance was large, and the action emphatic and harmonious. The delegates pledged themselves personally, and in behalf of their constituents, to stand by the work of God and the men who are laboring to promote it. The intelligence, Christian firmness, kindness and devotion to the great interests of the Redeemer's Kingdom, manifested by the Convention, must have favorably impressed all who witnessed their proceedings.

On Wednesday evening the Rev. L. Stiles preached an able and spiritual sermon, and administered the Sacrament of the Lord's Supper to a large number of communicants. It was a solemn occasion. Most of the members of the Presbyterian and Methodist churches present, came together at the common board of our common Lord.

On Thursday, measures were taken to circulate a petition asking the General Conference to exclude slaveholders from the church, and also one asking the General Conference to give a patient hearing to the difficulties of Genesee Conference.

The delegates went home from the Convention to labor with renewed zeal, and increased faith, for the salvation of souls.

THE WORK OF REVIVAL GOING ON.

An esteemed brother, in the regular work, formerly a member of the Genesee Conference, writes us from Illinois. "We are now enjoying a glorious outpouring of salvation of the earnest type. Sinners *seek* in earnest, and God *converts* in earnest. Where Christ reveals himself, it sometimes happens to the penitent as it did to Daniel by the river Hiddekel—to the three on the mount—to Saul on his way to Damascus, and to John on Patmos—"There remains no strength in them." Between sixty and seventy have been converted, and "the Lords adds to their number daily." In addition, some forty rose last night and requested prayers, and the end is not yet." H. E.

A Local Preacher writing from Illinois, says, "I have been laboring here a few weeks in connection with another pilgrim preacher, and more than one hundred have passed from death unto life. Many are witnesses to the work of holiness, and the work is still going on."

A Brother writes us from central Illinois, "We are more than pleased with the February number of the Earnest Christian, and if you should issue no more, we have got more than paid. "Hallelujah to God and the Lamb forever, that you have been directed by the Spirit of God to tear away the rubbish, dig up and bring to light the thunders of Methodism that shook old England and America more than a century ago. We can smell the smoke of the old artillery in your last number. May the Lord help you to bring out more of the old fire, and let the world have it. There is richness, dignity and glory about it, that eclipse all modern improvements." L. J.

A devoted Local Preacher, who is evidently determined to have "a starry crown" on the other shore, writes us, "I thought I would let you know something how we are getting along 'out west.' As a general thing, the work is deepening, the more and the harder the efforts to stop it, the faster it rolls. Like the flame Bunyan saw, the more water they turn on, the more the flame increases. But the mystery is solved; somebody 'the other side the wall,' is turning on oil. The Lord is raising up a host in the west, to battle for God and the right; raising up preachers, and firing up the laity. At one camp meeting, last fall, a brother and I counted twenty young men then on the ground, all young converts, called to preach, and going 'the straight way.' They all are 'rowing against wind and tide,' but it is having the happy effect to make them the more firm and uncompromising. Fathers and mothers, that have grown gray in Methodism, are taking a bold stand for the 'old paths.' Looking on and beholding the desolation of Zion, they have come to the conclusion, something must be done. A Presiding Elder in the Rock River Conference asked a Brother, 'Who would you like to have for your next preacher?' 'Well, anybody that's got religion; and if we can't have one of that kind, do send us one that's seriously inclined.' Oh! such stabs. From all parts we hear of the great stir, the proceedings of Genesee Conference, and the spirit manifesting itself in our own, has produced. The inquiry arises, 'What evil hath he done?' Why, they will halloo and shout in meeting. Every effort put forth to stop the work, only rings the bell for everybody to come. The people are anxious to see how we look, but they invariably get the impression that we are what their fathers used to call *Methodists.* 'Well, don't you believe they're honest?' 'Yes *sir.*' 'Well, the only trouble I find with them, they draw the light so straight.'

"At Clinton, a short distance above us on the river, there has been a glorious work. There were, to begin with, some three or four living members in the place. One hundred and twenty have been converted, and that in a place where there are two distilleries. It was a place thrown away by the Conference. The pastor of the adjoining charge hearing of the success of two *little* local preachers, who didn't try to be anybody, was very much concerned to know whether they had license to preach or not; and spent nearly a day trying to find out the facts.

"A few days ago I received a letter from Mt. P. where Brother R. and I labored in the fall. One Sabbath one of their class leaders took a number of "Pilgrims," and went over to a neighboring school-house and commenced operations. The teacher of the school arose the first opportunity, and told them he wanted this kind of religion. So the fire rolls. Another Brother writes, 'The work of the Lord is progressing among us. The work of Holiness has been increasing steadily ever since the fourth of July last. We hold a meeting expressly for Holiness every Monday eve, where we get empowered to work for the Lord; and then we go out into the highways where the people have been neglected by the regular ministry for the last fifteen years. We have adopted a system peculiar to ourselves, viz.: I try to preach a short sermon, always insisting on the absolute necessity of Holiness in order to salvation, and then the truth is backed by the testimony of a number of living witnesses, as the spirit giveth utterance; and the stouthearted are made to bend, and yield to be saved, and as soon as they are soundly converted, we lead them right to the 'Fountain,' and thus our army is increased. There are so few preachers that go straight for God, it is hard getting a supply, so we use our lay members.

Some of our Sisters are becoming powerful preachers, and all they need is liberty to use their talents, and the Lord will make them mighty to move the people. We have one young sister, (M. R.) who is worth a score of some preachers. May she live forever."

"Here in this place the Lord is leading out the Sisters, in prophecying. Some of them speak in power. We number about fifty at present, and are gradually increasing. Members from the old church come over to our meetings to seek for Holiness. Everything seems to be moving right." J. G. T.

A beloved brother who has been weeping for years over the spiritual desolation of Zion, writes us from New York: "I have read the first number of the *Earnest Christian* with interest and profit. Without being invidious I may say one article is worth the price of the volume. Its appearance is decidedly creditable, while its matter is not only creditable but profitable; and very forcibly reminds an old pilgrim like myself of the days when we had but one periodical in our entire connection in this country, and that one teemed with thrilling relations of God's power in the salvation of sinners. The *Earnest Christian* rekindles the hope that the time is rapidly approaching when the mountain of the Lord's house shall be established in the mountains, and all men shall flow unto it.

The article on Free Churches has touched a chord to which my soul vibrates. My soul agonizes for the salvation of the poor as I pass them in the street in my rounds of duty on the Sabbath, and reflect how industrious they are in their efforts to make the most of the time in such unlawful pursuits as affords them a momentary gratification, and leaves a sting behind like the sting of the scorpion. What adds greatly to my agony for them is the reflection that they, or many of them are shut out from the house of God by the alliance formed between the Church and the world, which is worse than the re-established friendship of Pilate and Herod. It is like an agreement with Hell and a league with damnation. Its avowed object is to draw the wealthy into the Church. For what? If I answer the question as I have been often answered, 'For the purpose of building up and sustaining' fashionable "Churches," which must of course be expensive Churches, what is the result? Are these fashionable and rich pew-holders saved? The day of judgment will reveal how many noble, mighty or rich ones are saved. But one of the apparent results we shall not have to wait until the day of judgment to learn; that is, the poor do not have the Gospel preached to them. The mission of Christ in this respect is thwarted, and that by His professed friends and followers. There is a fearful responsibility resting upon some body, and the inquiry may be made by more than it was at the last supper, 'Lord, is it I?'"

J. A. O.

A SISTER writing us from a locality where we held a grove meeting last summer, says: "A short time since a stranger came to Mr. B. with the question, 'Are you a holy man?' and taking his hand with such joyful eagerness that at first my husband thought he might be insane, but it did not take long to understand him. He was the sexton of the Presbyterian church, and was just converted. He said that the Spirit had been striving with him for a long time—mentioned your meeting—repeated your text, etc.—all of which convinces me that he was then awakened. Since then his sister came to our meeting. She is now clearly converted, and her husband was forward for prayers last Sunday evening. We have now four in our meetings recently converted."

N. S. B.

The meetings referred to are in a private house. These are but the first fruits of a great harvest of souls which we trust will be gathered to Christ in the band meetings which are being instituted in many places.

I have read the two numbers of the *Earnest Christian*, especially the last, with pleasure and profit. The articles, generally, are not only good specimens of Essaying, but they are eminently *practical* and *energetic*,—meeting the demands of the times.

The following are worthy of special attention for their appropriateness and excellency:

Scriptural Conviction, Be in Earnest, Look and Live, On Preaching Perfection, The Spirit of Jesus in the Church, Purity and Peace, and Doctor Judson's Address. The Lord make the Magazine a blessing to thousands.

C. D. BURLINGHAM.

LITERARY NOTICES.

THE LIFE OF MRS. FANNY L. BARTLETT, Consort of the late DR. OLIVER C. BARTLETT. Containing copious extracts from her Journal, and eminently calculated to lead to a holy life. BY REV. A. A. PHELPS. "*The righteous shall be in everlasting remembrance.*"—Ps. cxii. 6. Boston, Published by H. V. Degen, 1860.

Mrs. BARTLETT was a Christian of the primitive stamp She was for twenty-five years a resident of Lima. She retained, till the close of her useful life, that Gospel simplicity and spiritual power, for which the early Methodists were distinguished. She became acquainted with many of the young preachers students—and her influence over them was most salutary, as the writer of this can cheerfully testify. She encouraged them not to rest without a deep experience in the things of God. Her exhortation to the preachers, at the last Bergen Camp meeting she attended, to hold up the self denying doctrines of the cross, whatever the consequences to them personally, will not soon be forgotten.

In the interesting volume before us we have a faithful record of her experience, her struggles, and her victories. Our friend, Rev. A. A. PHELPS, of the Genesee college, has performed his part well. His style is pleasing and attractive, and his subject is presented to us as she appeared to those whose privilege it was to enjoy a personal acquaintance with her. As stated in the title, we believe this book is "eminently calculated to lead to a holy life" all who shall give it a careful perusal.

It is a neat volume of 295 pages, got up in good style, and embellished with a portrait of Mrs. BARTLETT. It may be had of the publisher at Boston, or of the author at Lima, Livingston Co., N. Y. You can have a copy sent to you by mail, postage paid, by enclosing 15 three cent postage stamps to the author as above.

DR. BOWEN'S BOOK ON SLAVERY.

We have procured a few copies of this sterling work, and any of our readers can have a copy sent to them by mail, postage paid, by sending 27 postage stamps to B. T. Roberts, Buffalo, N. Y.

THE EARNEST CHRISTIAN.

VOL. I.   APRIL, 1860.   NO. 4.

RIGHTEOUSNESS.

BY THE EDITOR.

EVERY material substance has its essential properties. These distinguish it from every other body, and without them it could not exist. Gold possesses the quality of being drawn into thin sheets when sufficiently beaten, while iron pyrites, of nearly the same external appearance, fly into fragments under the hammer.

Christianity is something positive. It is not a mere negative. It has an actual existence, and possesses its positive elements. First and foremost among them is RIGHTEOUSNESS. The religion of Christ appears before the world with so many appendages, that we almost look upon these as the thing itself. Like the birds in the cornfield, we mistake the coat and the hat, carefully adjusted upon a bundle of straw, for the man himself. Forms and ceremonies do not make the performer a disciple of Christ. Tall-steepled temples, decorated in the highest style of art, do not constitute Christian churches; and the singing of devout hymns by undevout vocalists, hired for the purpose, and the reading, in solemn tone to a polite congregation by a grave-looking gentleman, of a moral, historical or philosophical essay, do not constitute Christian worship. There may be Christianity with or without churches, bishops, ministers or choirs, but there can be none without righteousness. "Ye are," says Paul, of Christians, "the temple of God." Righteousness is the frame-work, without which the entire structure will fall to ruins before the fierce blast of the tempest. Righteousness is the breast-plate of the soldier of the cross, and if he goes into battle without it, the first arrow from his skillful adversary will lay him prostrate upon the field, mortally wounded. It is the warp of the white robe, in which the redeemed saint shall be presented to the court of Heaven.

In its most comprehensive sense, righteousness denotes that state of the heart which enables one faithfully to discharge all the duties he owes to God and man. This is the signification in which it is used by our Saviour when He says, "Blessed are they which do hunger and thirst after righteousness: for they shall be filled"—they shall have such a fullness of grace, that, like Enoch of old, they will "walk with God." In this sense it corresponds most nearly to the Latin *justitia, ex qua una virtute* says Cicero, *boni viri appellantur*—"From which virtue alone, men are called good." In the more limited signification in which it is generally used in the Bible, it denotes that gracious disposition of the soul, which leads to the fulfilling of all moral obligations—which prompts one to perform all the acts affecting our fellow men that God requires, and to exercise suitable dispositions towards them.

In particular it implies, *strict honesty in all business transactions*. Men are in haste to get rich. With many, wealth is the grand object of pursuit. The disciples of Christ, thrown into competition with those who prosper by dishonesty, are tempted to pursue a course which they see generally practised, though it involve a deviation from the strict principles of integrity. But the righteous resist the temptation. They are honest not merely when "honesty is the best policy," but when it involves a sacrifice of pecuniary interests. They serve Christ: and the requirement "to do justly" they consider binding upon them at all times.

Open opposition to all wrong and injustice is another element of Scriptural righteousness. Many who would not do wrong themselves will countenance it, at least indirectly, in others. This is usually the first step towards a loss of virtue. He who, for the sake of party interests, personal friendship, or any other cause, is silent when he should reprove, will soon apologize for, then justify, then approve, and, if occasion serves, perpetrate the wrong from which, at first, his moral sensibilities revolted. Well has it been said:

> Vice is a monster of so frightful mien,
> As to be hated needs but to be seen;
> But seen too oft, familiar with her face,
> We first endure, then pity, then embrace.

The teaching of the Bible, little as it is heeded, is very emphatic upon this point. Prov. xvii. 19—"He that justifieth the wicked, and he that condemneth the just, even they both are abomination to the LORD." Isa. v. 23—"Wo unto them which justify the wicked for reward, and take away the righteousness of the righteous from him! therefore as the fire devoureth the stubble, and the flame consumeth the chaff, so their root shall be as rottenness, and their blossom shall go up as dust: because they have cast away the law of the LORD of hosts, and despised the word of the Holy One of Israel. Therefore is the anger of the LORD kindled against His people." It would be well for those who look in silence, construed into approbation, upon gigantic oppression and enormous wrong, to ponder these and similar passages. Lot would never have come out of Sodom alive had not that "righteous man," dwelling among the wicked, "vexed his righteous soul from day to day with their unlawful deeds."

Connected with the condemnation of wickedness, and necessarily implied in it, is the vindication of the innocent. The penitent thief upon the Cross manifested the genuineness of his repentance, not only by a confession of his own guilt, but by declaring the innocence of Jesus. "We receive the due reward of our deeds, but this man hath done nothing amiss." It is not conclusive evidence that an individual is wicked, because some man, or body of men, however respectable their position, have pronounced him guilty of crime. It is possible that the guilt attaches to the tribunal rendering the verdict. Christ was crucified, the apostles were put to death, the martyrs burned, Luther was excommunicated and the Wesleys indicted by the proper authorities! Righteousness recognizes virtue upon the gallows or in the dungeon, just as readily as when she walks forth among her votaries the admired of all beholders.

Rigid impartiality is another element of righteousness.

There is no respect of persons with God. With Him the distinctions that men make among themselves, pass for nothing. To His eyes of purity, sin perpetrated in a palace, in the most refined manner possible, presents as revolting an appearance as when it is committed in a hovel by the coarse and ignorant. "He hath appointed a day in which He will judge the world in righteousness," that is, with impartiality. A degree of this attribute He gives to all His children as soon as He adopts them into His family. Their new nature disposes them to look at things as they are, irrespective of the circumstances by which they are surrounded. They remember the command, "Ye shall do no unrighteousness in judgment; thou shalt not respect the person of the poor, nor honor the person of the mighty: but in righteousness shalt thou judge thy neighbor."

Were this principle generally prevalent, what a change would be produced in the administration of justice! Neither the man of passion, though seated in Congress, nor the wealthy planter, could murder, in open day, with impunity. Juries, civil and ecclesiastical, would decide cases according to their merits, and not as partisan inclination or personal bias should dictate.

This Scriptural righteousness prompting to do right under all circumstances is not inherent in man. By nature there is none righteous, no, not one. But by grace, righteousness is possible to humanity. Here and there one may be found who is righteous before God. The Bible speaks of such a class.

Ceremonial righteousness has its foundation in fallen human nature. It is an artificial growth from a degenerate stock. The unconverted man, influenced by education or a partially awakened conscience, commences the performance of some religious rites, and when his lesson is learned so that he can go through the prescibed routine, with comparative ease, he persuades himself that he is a child of God! He makes a conscience of discharging what he is pleased to call religious duties, but still lives, as before, the life of nature.

Evangelical righteousness is the result of the operation of the Spirit of God upon the human heart. None possess it save those who have been born again. To obtain it we must "put off the old man which is corrupt according to the deceitful lusts, and put on the new man which after God is created in righteousness and true holiness." There must be, not a polishing up of the old nature, but a new CREATION, bringing into being that which had no existence before. God puts into the human heart a principle which was lost by the fall. Man is transformed by the renewing of his mind, before righteousness can dwell in his heart.

Allow me to ask you, respected reader, do you possess this righteousness? You may be orthodox in your creed—we trust you are—but it matters not how correct your conceptions of the doctrines of the Bible are, or with what clearness you may state them, or with what ability you may defend them, if you are defective in personal righteousness at that dread hour when God shall bring the secrets of man into judgment, your eternal ruin will be inevitable. No substitute for this will be allowed. No scrupulous observance of rites—not even of those ordained of God—neither fervent numerous prayers, nor study of the Bible, nor fastings, nor bestowment of money to build churches, or support ministers or missionaries, nor attendance upon the preaching of the word, nor going to sacraments—neither one nor all of these, can compensate, in the slightest degree, for the lack of righteousness.

In particular, are you honest? especially in small matters? Do you never practice deception? Do you claim as your own, property that rightfully belongs to others? It makes no difference whether you obtained it before or since you made a profession of religion. God never pardons a soul until that person has done all he can to make right the wrongs which he has committed.

Are you as careful to give to others their due as you are to exact your claims of them? Do you never take advantage of the ignorance or necessities of men? The heathen standard of honesty was higher than that of some professed Christians! Cicero proposes a case. He says, Antisthenes brings a ship load of grain to Rhodes at a time of great scarcity. The Rhodians flock about him to buy. He knows that five other ships, laden with grain, will be there to-morrow. Ought he to tell the Rhodians this before he sells his own grain? "Undoubtedly he ought," says this honest heathen, "otherwise he makes a gain of their ignorance, and so is no better than a thief or a robber!" Let now memory and conscience do their offices, and if you can discover any dishonest act that you have committed in the past, give yourself no rest till, by repentance, confession, and restitution, you have done all in your power to have the guilt of the wrong blotted out. Perhaps you may satisfy *yourself* in an easier way, but you cannot obtain the favor of God on any other terms. Praying is good, but it can never answer as a substitute for honesty.

Again, do you in your decisions upon the conduct of your fellow-men discountenance vice and encourage virtue? Or do you "justify the wicked for reward?" To incur the "wo" pronounced against such, it is not necessary that you should be openly bribed. Satan is too skillful a fisher for the souls of men to throw out a bait so gross. The reward you anticipate may be the approval of those in position and power, or the promoting of the success of a party, or of the "unity of the Church!" A professed Christian was asked what he knew against one whom he had loved as a devoted and eminent servant of Christ, that he would not hear him preach. "All I wish to," was the prompt reply. "What is it?" was urged. "Why, that a majority voted against him!" This was all he wished to know! No matter how the majority was obtained. How unlike is this to righteous Job, who said, "The cause which I knew not I searched out." Had such men lived in the days of the Apostles, they would not have professed Christianity, for this was proscribed by the unanimous verdict of the authorities of "the Church!"

Were slaveholding abolished in our country how few would be found among us who would apologize for its existence in Turkey or Algiers! But on the side of the oppressor there is power, and when grave doctors of divinity and venerable bishops give oppression their sanctions, too many, who would be Christians, are led away by such examples.

See to it, then, that you are righteous. If you have it not, make haste to get that unbending integrity, which will not let you do wrong under any temptation. What an enemy said of an old Roman ought to be true of every Christian. "It would be easier to turn the sun from his course than Fabricius from the path of honesty." Remember the words of our Lord: "Except your righteousness shall exceed the righteousness of the Scribes and Pharisees ye shall in no case enter into the kingdom of Heaven."

HAVE you the love of God in your soul, the Spirit of God in you? How dare you cross the threshold of a theatre or tavern any more? What! the Spirit of God amid the wanton songs of a theatre, or the boisterous merriment of a tavern! Shame on such practical blasphemy! No: leave them, dear friends, to be cages for devils, and every unclean and hateful bird. You must never cross their threshold any more. What shall I say of games, cards, dice and dancing? I will only say this, that if you love them, you've never tasted the joys of the new creature. If you feel the love of God and the Spirit, you will not lightly sin these joys away amid the vain anxieties of cards, or the rattling of senseless dice. What shall I say of simpering tea-parties, the pleasures of religious gossiping, and useless calls, without meaning, sincerity or end? I will only say, they are the happiest of God's children who have neither time nor heart for these things. I believe there cannot be much of the Spirit where there is much of these.

What shall I say of dress? A young believer, full of faith and joy, was offered a present of flowers for her hair. She would not take them. She was pressed to accept them; still she refused. Why will you not? Ah, she said, how can I wear roses on my brow, when Christ wore thorns on his? The joy of being in Christ is so sweet that it makes all other joys insipid, dull, lifeless. In his right hand are riches and honors; in his left are length of days. His ways are ways of pleasantness. What, then, have I to do any more with idols?—McCheyne.

To what purpose dost thou reason profoundly concerning the Trinity, if thou art without humility, and thereby displeasest that Trinity?—Kempis.

THE CHARACTER OF A METHODIST.

1. THE distinguishing marks of a Methodist are not his opinions of any sort. His assenting to this or that scheme of religion, his embracing any particular set of notions, his espousing the judgment of one man or of another, are all quite wide of the point. Whosoever, therefore, imagines that a Methodist is a man of such or such an opinion, is grossly ignorant of the whole affair; he mistakes the truth totally. We believe, indeed, that "all Scripture is given by the inspiration of God;" and herein we are distinguished from Jews, Turks, and infidels. We believe the written word of God to be the only and sufficient rule both of Christian faith and practice; and herein we are fundamentally distinguished from those of the Romish Church. We believe Christ to be the eternal, supreme God; and herein we are distinguished from the Socinians and Arians. But as to all opinions which do not strike at the root of Christianity, we think and let think. So that, whatsoever they are, whether right or wrong, they are no distinguishing marks of a Methodist.

2. Neither are words or phrases of any sort. We do not place our religion, or any part of it, in being attached to any peculiar mode of speaking, any quaint or uncommon set of expressions. The most obvious, easy, common words, wherein our meaning can be conveyed, we prefer before others, both on ordinary occasions, and when we speak of the things of God. We never, therefore, willingly or designedly, deviate from the most usual way of speaking; unless when we express Scripture truths in Scripture words, which, we presume, no Christian will condemn. Neither do we affect to use any particular expressions of Scripture more frequently than others, unless they are such as are more frequently used by the inspired writers themselves. So that it is as gross an error to place the marks of a Methodist in his words, as in opinions of any sort.

3. Nor do we desire to be distinguished by actions, customs, or usages, of an indifferent nature. Our religion does not lie in doing what God has not enjoined, or abstaining from what he hath not forbidden. It does not lie in the form of our apparel, in the posture of our body, or the covering of our heads; nor yet in abstaining from marriage, or from meats and drinks, which are all good if received with thanksgiving. Therefore, neither will any man, who knows whereof he affirms, fix the mark of a Methodist here,—in any actions or customs purely indifferent, undetermined by the word of God.

4. Nor, lastly, is he distinguished by laying the whole stress of religion on any single part of it. If you say, "Yes, he is; for he thinks 'we are saved by faith alone:'" I answer, You do not understand the terms. By salvation he means holiness of heart and life. And this he affirms to spring from true faith alone. Can even a nominal Christian deny it? Is this placing a part of religion for the whole? "Do we then make void the law through faith? God forbid! Yea, we establish the law." We do not place the whole of religion, (as too many do, God knoweth,) either in doing no harm, or in doing good, or in using the ordinances of God. No, not in all of them together; wherein we know by experience a man may labor many years, and at the end have no religion at all, no more than he had at the beginning. Much less in any one of these; or, it may be, in a scrap of one of them: like her who fancies herself a virtuous woman, only because she is not a prostitute; or him who dreams he is an honest man, merely because he does not rob or steal. May the Lord God of my fathers preserve me from such a poor, starved religion as this! Were this the mark of a Methodist, I would sooner choose to be a sincere Jew, Turk, or Pagan.

5. "What then is the mark? Who

is a Methodist, according to your own account?" I answer: A Methodist is one who has "the love of God shed abroad in his heart by the Holy Ghost given unto him;" one who "loves the Lord his God with all his heart, and with all his soul, and with all his mind, and with all his strength." God is the joy of his heart, and the desire of his soul; which is constantly crying out: "Whom have I in Heaven but thee? and there is none upon earth that I desire beside thee! My God and my all! Thou art the strength of my heart, and my portion for ever!"

6. He is therefore happy in God, yea, always happy, as having in him "a well of water springing up into everlasting life," and overflowing his soul with peace and joy. "Perfect love" having now "cast out fear," he "rejoices evermore." He "rejoices in the Lord always," even "in God his Saviour;" and in the Father, "through our Lord Jesus Christ, by whom he hath now received the atonement." "Having" found "redemption through his blood, the forgiveness of his sins," he cannot but rejoice, whenever he looks back on the horrible pit out of which he is delivered; when he sees "all his transgressions blotted out as a cloud, and his iniquities as a thick cloud." He cannot but rejoice, whenever he looks on the state wherein he now is; "being justified freely, and having peace with God through our Lord Jesus Christ." For "he that believeth, hath the witness" of this "in himself;" being now the son of God by faith. "Because he is a son, God hath sent forth the Spirit of his Son into his heart, crying, Abba, Father!" And "the Spirit itself beareth witness with his spirit, that he is a child of God." He rejoiceth also, whenever he looks forward, "in hope of the glory that shall be revealed;" yea, this his joy is full, and all his bones cry out, "Blessed be the God and Father of our Lord Jesus Christ, who, according to his abundant mercy, hath begotten me again to a living hope—of an inheritance incorruptible, undefiled, and that fadeth not away, reserved in Heaven for me!"

7. And he who hath this hope, thus "full of immortality, in everything giveth thanks;" as knowing that this (whatsoever it is) "is the will of God in Christ Jesus concerning him." From him, therefore, he cheerfully receives all, saying, "Good is the will of the Lord;" and whether the Lord giveth or taketh away, equally "blessing the the name of the Lord." For he hath "learned, in whatsoever state he is, therewith to be content." He knoweth "both how to be abased, and how to abound. Everywhere and in all things he is instructed both to be full and to be hungry, both to abound and suffer need." Whether in ease or pain, whether in sickness or health, whether in life or death, he giveth thanks from the ground of his heart to Him who orders it for good; knowing that as "every good gift cometh from above," so none but good can come from the Father of lights, into whose hand he has wholly committed his body and soul, as into the hands of a faithful Creator. He is therefore "careful" (anxiously or uneasily) "for nothing;" as having "cast all his care on Him that careth for him," and "in all things" resting on him, after "making his request known to him with thanksgiving."

8. For indeed, he "prays without ceasing." It is given him "always to pray, and not to faint." Not that he is always in the house of prayer; though he neglects no opportunity of being there. Neither is he always on his knees, although he often is, or on his face, before the Lord his God. Nor yet is he always crying aloud to God, or calling upon him in words: for many times "the Spirit maketh intercession for him with groans that cannot be uttered." But at all times the language of his heart is this: "Thou brightness of the eternal glory, unto thee is my heart, though without a voice, and my silence speaketh unto thee." And this is true prayer, and this alone. But his heart is ever lifted

up to God, at all times and in all places. In this he is never hindered, much less interrupted, by any person or thing. In retirement or company, in leisure, business, or conversation, his heart is ever with the Lord. Whether he lie down or rise up, God is in all his thoughts; he walks with God continually, having the loving eye of his mind still fixed upon him, and everywhere "seeing him that is invisible."

9. And while he thus always exercises his love to God, by praying without ceasing, rejoicing evermore, and in everything giving thanks, this commandment is written in his heart, "That he who loveth God, love his brother also." And he accordingly loves his neighbor as himself; he loves every man as his own soul. His heart is full of love to all mankind, to every child of "the Father of the spirits of all flesh." That a man is not personally known to him, is no bar to his love; no, nor that he is known to be such as he approves not, that he repays hatred for his good will. For he "loves his enemies;" yea, and the enemies of God, "the evil and the unthankful." And if it be not in his power to "do good to them that hate him," yet he ceases not to pray for them, though they continue to spurn his love, and still "despitefully use him and persecute him."

10. For he is "pure in heart." The love of God has purified his heart from all revengeful passions, from envy, malice, and wrath, from every unkind temper or malign affection. It hath cleansed him from pride and haughtiness of spirit, whereof alone cometh contention. And he hath now "put on bowels of mercies, kindness, humbleness of mind, meekness, long suffering:" so that he "forbears and forgives, if he had a quarrel against any; even as God in Christ hath forgiven him." And indeed all possible ground for contention, on his part, is utterly cut off. For none can take from him what he desires; seeing he "loves not the world, nor" any of "the things of the world;" being now "crucified to the world, and the world crucified to him;" being dead to all that is in the world, both to "the lust of the flesh, the lust of the eye, and the pride of life." For "all his desire is unto God, and to the remembrance of his name."

11. Agreeable to this his one desire, is the one design of his life, namely, "not to do his own will, but the will of Him that sent him." His one intention at all times and in all things is, not to please himself, but Him whom his soul loveth. He has a single eye. And because "his eye is single, his whole body is full of light." Indeed, where the loving eye of the soul is continually fixed upon God, there can be no darkness at all, "but the whole is light; as when the bright shining of a candle doth enlighten the house." God then reigns alone. All that is in the soul is holiness to the Lord. There is not a motion in his heart, but is according to his will. Every thought that arises points to him, and is in obedience to the law of Christ.

12. And the tree is known by its fruits. For as he loves God, so he keeps his commandments; not only some, or most of them, but all, from the least to the greatest. He is not content to "keep the whole law, and offend in one point;" but has in all points, "a conscience void of offence toward God and toward man." Whatever God has forbidden, he avoids; whatever God hath enjoined, he doeth; and that whether it be little or great, hard or easy, joyous or grievous to the flesh. He "runs the way of God's commandments," now he hath set his heart at liberty. It is his glory so to do; it is his daily crown of rejoicing, "to do the will of God on earth, as it is done in Heaven;" knowing it is the highest privilege of "the angels of God, of those that excel in strength, to fulfil his commandments, and hearken to the voice of his word."

13. All the commandments of God he accordingly keeps, and that with all his might. For his obedience is in proportion to his love, the source from

whence it flows. And therefore, loving God with all his heart, he serves him with all his strength. He continually presents his soul and body a living sacrifice, holy, acceptable to God; entirely and without reserve devoting himself, all he has, and all he is, to his glory. All the talents he has received, he constantly employs according to his Master's will; every power and faculty of his soul, every member of his body. Once he "yielded" them "unto sin" and the devil, "as instruments of unrighteousness;" but now, "being alive from the dead, he yields" them all "as instruments of righteousness unto God."

14. By consequence, whatsoever he doeth, it is all to the glory of God. In all his employments of every kind, he not only aims at this, (which is implied in having a single eye,) but actually attains it. His business and refreshments, as well as his prayers, all serve this great end. Whether he sit in his house or walk by the way, whether he lie down or rise up, he is promoting, in all he speaks or does, the one business of his life; whether he put on his apparel, or labor, or eat and drink, or divert himself from too wasting labor, it all tends to advance the glory of God, by peace and good will among men. His one invariable rule is this: "Whatsoever ye do, in word or deed, do it all in the name of the Lord Jesus, giving thanks to God and the Father by him."

15. Nor do the customs of the world at all hinder his "running the race that is set before him." He knows that vice does not lose its nature, though it becomes ever so fashionable; and remembers, that "every man is to give an account of himself to God." He cannot, therefore, "follow" even "a multitude to do evil." He cannot "fare sumptuously every day," or "make provision for the flesh to fulfil the lusts thereof." He cannot "lay up treasures upon earth," any more than he can take fire into his bosom. He cannot "adorn himself," on any pretence, "with gold or costly apparel."

He cannot join in or countenance any diversion which has the least tendency to vice of any kind. He cannot "speak evil" of his neighbor, any more than he can lie either for God or man. He cannot utter an unkind word of any one; for love keeps the door of his lips. He cannot speak "idle words;" "no corrupt communication" ever "comes out of his mouth," as is all that "which is" not "good to the use of edifying," not "fit to minister grace to the hearers." But "whatsoever things are pure, whatsoever things are lovely, whatsoever things are" justly "of good report," he thinks and speaks, and acts, "adorning the Gospel of our Lord Jesus Christ in all things."

16. Lastly. As he has time, he "does good unto all men;" unto neighbors and strangers, friends and enemies; and that in every possible kind; not only to their bodies, by "feeding the hungry, clothing the naked, visiting those that are sick or in prison;" but much more does he labor to do good to their souls, as of the ability which God giveth; to awaken those that sleep in death; to bring those who are awakened to the atoning blood, that, "being justified by faith, they may have peace with God;" and to provoke those who have peace with God to abound more in love and in good works. And he is willing to "spend and be spent herein," even "to be offered up on the sacrifice and service of their faith," so they may "all come unto the measure of the stature of the fullness of Christ."

17. These are the principles and practices of our sect; these are the marks of a true Methodist. By these alone do those who are in derision so called, desire to be distinguished from other men. If any man say, "Why, these are only the common, fundamental principles of Christianity!" Thou hast said; so I mean; this is the very truth; I know they are no other; and I would to God both thou and all men knew, that I, and all who follow my judgment, do vehemently refuse to be distinguished from other men, by any but the common principles of Chris-

tianity,—the plain, old Christianity that I teach, renouncing and detesting all other marks of distinction. And whosoever is what I preach, (let him be called what he will, for names change not the nature of things,) he is a Christian, not in name only, but in heart and in life. He is inwardly and outwardly conformed to the will of God, as revealed in the written word. He thinks, speaks, and lives, according to the method laid down in the revelation of Jesus Christ. His soul is renewed after the image of God in righteousness and in all true holiness. And having the mind that was in Christ, he so walks as Christ also walked.

18. By these marks, by these fruits of a living faith, do we labor to distinguish ourselves from the unbelieving world, from all those whose minds or lives are not according to the Gospel of Christ. But from real Christians, of whatsoever denomination they be, we earnestly desire not to be distinguished at all; not from any who sincerely follow after what they know they have not yet attained. No: "Whosoever doeth the will of my Father which is in Heaven, the same is my brother, and sister, and mother." And I beseech you, brethren, by the mercies of God, that we be in no wise divided among ourselves. Is thy heart right, as my heart is with thine? I ask no farther question. If it be, give me thy hand. For opinions, or terms, let us not destroy the work of God. Dost thou love and serve God? It is enough. I give thee the right hand of fellowship. If there be any consolation in in Christ, if any comfort of love, if any fellowship of the Spirit, if any bowels and mercies; let us strive together for the faith of the Gospel; walking worthy of the vocation wherewith we are called; with all lowliness and meekness, with long suffering, forbearing one another in love, endeavoring to keep the unity of the Spirit in the bond of peace; remembering, there is one body, and one Spirit, even as we are called with one hope of our calling; "one Lord, one faith, one baptism; one God and Father of all, who is above all, and through all, and in you all."—JOHN WESLEY.

HE that resolves to live well when a danger is upon him, or a violent fear, or when the appetites of lust are newly satisfied, or newly served, and yet when the temptation comes again, sins again, and then is sorrowful, and resolves once more against it, and yet falls when the temptation returns, is a vain man, but no true penitent, nor in the state of grace; and if he chance to die in one of these good moods, is very far from salvation; for if it be necessary that we resolve to live well, it is necessary we should do so. For resolution is an imperfect act, a term of relation, and signifies nothing but in order to the actions; it is as a faculty is to the act, as spring is to the harvest, as eggs are to birds, as a relative to its correspondent, nothing without it. No man, therefore, can be in a state of grace and actual favor, by resolutions and holy purposes; these are but the gate and portal toward pardon; a holy life is the only perfection of repentance, and the firm ground upon which we can cast the anchor of hope in the mercies of God, through Jesus Christ.—JEREMY TAYLOR.

THERE is no man in this world without temptation. In the time of prosperity, we are tempted to wantonness, pleasures, and all lightness; in the time of adversity to despair of God's goodness. Temptation never ceases. There is a difference between being tempted, and entering into temptation. He bids them therefore, not to pray that they be not tempted, but that they "enter not into temptation." To be tempted is no evil thing. For what is it? It is no more than when the flesh, the devil and the world solicit and move us against God. To give place to their suggestions, and to yield ourselves, and suffer ourselves to be overcome by them, this is to enter into temptation.—BISHOP LATIMER.

THE REFINER OF SILVER.

Some months ago, a few ladies, who met together in Dublin, to read the Scriptures and make them the subject of conversation, were reading the 3d chapter of Malachi. One of the ladies gave it as her opinion, that the Fuller's soap, and the Refiner of silver, were the image, both intended to convey the same view of the sanctifying influence of the grace of Christ; while another observed :—there is something remarkable in the expression in the third verse:—" He shall sit as a refiner and purifier of silver."

They agreed that possibly it might be so; and one of the ladies promised to call on a silversmith, and report to them what he said on the subject. She went accordingly, and without telling the object of her errand, begged to know from him the process of refining silver, which he fully described to her, "But, sir," said she, "do you *sit* while the work of refining is going on?" "O yes, madam," replied the silversmith, "I must sit with my eye steadily fixed on the furnace, for if the time necessary for refining, be exceeded in the slightest degree, the silver will be injured." She saw at once the beauty, and the comfort too of the expression. " He shall sit as a refiner and purifier of silver." Christ sees it needful to put his children into the furnace, but he is seated by the side of it, his eye is steadily intent on the work of purifying, and his wisdom and love are both engaged in the best manner for for them. Their trials do not come at random; the very hairs of their head are all numbered. As the lady was leaving the shop, the silversmith called her back, and said he had still further to mention that he only knew when the process of purifying was complete, by seeing his own image reflected in the silver. Beautiful figure! When Christ shall see his own image in his people, his work of purifying will be accomplished.

Eternal Life.—The following sentiment from one of the Christians of the third century, we commend to the careful consideration of all, especially of those who think to gain Heaven without difficulty or self-denial :

Whosoever prefers the life of the soul, must of necessity despise that of the body; nor can he aspire to the highest good, unless he despise advantages of an inferior kind. For the All-wise God did not choose that we should attain to immortality in a soft, indolent way, but that we should gain that inexpressible reward of eternal life, with the highest difficulty and severest labor.—Lactautius.

Our offences sometimes are of such nature, as required that particular men be satisfied, or else repentance to be utterly void and of none effect. For if either through open rapine or cloaked fraud, if through injurious or unconsciable dealings, a man have wittingly wronged others to enrich himself; the first thing evermore in this case required (ability serving) is restitution. For let no man deceive himself: from such offences we are not discharged, neither can we be, till recompense and restitution to man accompany the penitent confession we have made to Almighty God.—Hooker.

Those whom Christ know He Conforms to His Image.—An unrenewed person, whatever be his education, talents, or natural temper, can never fall in with Christianity as it is taught in the New Testament. If, therefore, he occupies a station in the church, he will be almost certain to transform religion so as to suit himself. This was the grand source of the Romish apostacy.—Andrew Fuller.

That is not saving faith which can be separated, even in theory, from good works and evangelical obedience.—Dr. Hopkins.

ENTIRE CONSECRATION TO GOD.

Know, therefore, that the Lord thy God, he is God," (Deut. vii., 9.) "that keepeth covenant and mercy for them that love him and observe his commandments;" (Nehemiah i., 5.) "And if thou wilt love the Lord, and serve him," (Deuteronomy x., 12; x., 20; xi., 13; xiii., 4.) "And keep the charge of the Lord thy God, to walk in his ways, to keep his statutes, and his commandments, and his judgments, and his testimonies." (1st Kings, ii., 3.) "Then shall thy light break forth as the morning, and thy health shall spring forth speedily: And thy righteousness shall go before thee; the glory of the Lord shall be thy reward." (Isaiah lviii, 8.) "And he shall guide thee continually, and thou shall be as a watered garden, and like a spring of water whose waters fail not." (Isaiah lviii., 11.)

FORM OF CONSECRATION.

Eternal and ever-blessed Lord, deeply impressed with the solemnity and importance of the step I am taking, I humbly crave and implore divine assistance.

In obedience to the word of inspiration and the dictates of conscience, and desiring to occupy a position where I may receive and enjoy the precious blessings and privileges so graciously provided and freely offered to those who enter into and keep covenant with thee, *I present myself to thee a living sacrifice, with full confidence in thy truth and faithfulness, and firm reliance in the virtue of the atonement,* for acceptance.

Feelingly alive to my utter unworthiness of any favor at thy hand, and desiring nothing so much as to be thine, and *thine altogether,* I solemnly and willingly, *fully* surrender and consecrate to thee all that I am, and all that I have, *soul, body and spirit,* my time, talents and influence, together with my worldly possessions, all to be resolutely employed in obedience to thy commands, *as long as I live*—holding all in readiness to know, to do, or to suffer thy holy and righteous will.

Helpless of myself, I look to thee for aid, and trust in the assurance "*My grace is sufficient for thee.*" Yielding thus my *all* to thee, I nothing claim or have as my own, but, being brought into covenant union with the Sovereign of the world, I have thy promise that my wants shall be supplied. Condescend, O my father! to use me as an instrument of thy service, and number me with thy "peculiar people." Sprinkle me ever with the purifying blood of thy dear Son; transform me more and more into his image; impart to me, through him, all needful influences of thy spirit, and let my life be passed under the approving smile of thy gracious countenance, as my Father and my God. And when the solemn hour of death shall come, and heart and flesh shall fail, be thou my confidence and my strength. Sustained in thy everlasting arms, may I triumph over the "King of terrors," and receive an abundant entrance into the kingdom of thy glory, to go out no more forever. And to thee, O Father! to Jesus, the Mediator of the new covenant, and to thy Holy Spirit, be eternal glory. Amen.

RULES FOR HOLY LIVING.

"If ye live after the flesh, ye shall die; but if ye through the spirit do mortify the deeds of the body, ye shall live."—Rom. viii. 13.

1. I will endeavor to render perfect obedience to the revealed will of God.
2. Religion shall be my chief concern, and the business of my life.
3. I will begin each day with God, by consecrating myself anew to his service.
4. In resuming my daily cares, I will endeavor to aim at the glory of God.
5. I will improve my time to the best of my ability.
6. I will observe *three stated seasons each day* for private devotion.

7. When I have the privilege, I will puruse the word of God *on my knees*.

8. I will watch over myself with godly jealousy, carefully inspecting my thoughts, motives and desires.

9. I will practice self-denial in various ways, and fast each week, as health and circumstances permit.

10. I will pay strict regard to truth.

11. I will resolutely oppose all inclination to fictitious and unprofitable reading.

12. I will, when possible, punctually attend the stated means of grace, ready and willing to bear the cross.

13. Inclination shall in no case prevent compliance with known duty.

14. As far as circumstances shall permit, I will do to others as I would they should do unto me.

15. I will observe plainness and simplicity in dress, avoiding useless expenditure and ornament.

16. I will shun idle and unprofitable conversation and foolish jesting.

17. I will join no association likely to injure my religious influence.

18. I will take no recreation that I may not in the name of the Lord.

19. I will neither make nor attend large "tea parties."

20. I will be scrupulous in observance of the Sabbath day, and enter the sanctuary prayerfully and seriously.

21. I will endeavor, by divine grace, in all things to be exemplary, that my influence may be a savor of life unto life.

22. I will close each day with self-examination and prayer, and will not suffer myself to close my eyes in sleep in a state of condemnation before God.

23. *Love to God* and filial fear shall be my motive in the discharge of every Christian duty.

A HELP TO SELF-EXAMINATION.

"Ponder the path of thy feet, and let all thy ways be established."—Prov. iv. 26.

Question.—1. Did I rise this morning with a grateful sense of the goodness of God?

2. Did I offer myself anew to him in consecration?

3. Did I do it thoughtfully, as in the presence of duty?

4. Has the reading of the Scripture profited me?

5. Have I been firm and resolute in doing my duty?

6. Has no part of my time run to waste?

7. Have I governed my thoughts well?

8. Have I indulged no wrong tempers or dispositions?

9. Have I improved opportunities for doing or getting good?

10. Have I been strong in faith toward God?

11. Have I seen the goodness of God in little things which have a tendency to disquiet me?

12. Have I been resigned to the will of God, as indicated in His providences.

13. Have I been much in prayer?

14. Has my life corresponded with my profession?

15. Have I held sweet communion with my Saviour?

16. Have I met and overcome temptation?

17. Have I knowingly done anything to grieve another?

18. Have I broken any of my "Rules?"

19. Do I close this day with gratitude to God, and a consciousness of His favor and approbation.

20. Do I feel a firm unwavering confidence in God as my Father and my God.

A professed Christian, whether a private member or an officer in the church, or a minister of the gospel, who enjoys the fullness of the love of God in his heart, by his daily walk and conversation, may bind the golden chain of divine love around scores by the bright light emanating from his own character; or by a manifest disregard of vital piety, either in sentiment or example, by making *his own elevation* tower above the promotion of *God's glory*, may lose the respect and confidence of all, and thus become the *gilded vessel* sailing under false colors, bearing a cargo of immortal souls to the dark ocean of eternal ruin.

As the sense, so the motion, of him that liveth the life of God hath a peculiar kind of excellency. His hands are not stretched out towards his enemies, except it be to give them alms: his feet are slow save only when he travelleth for the benefit of his brethren. When he is railed upon by the wicked, his voice is not otherwise heard than the voice of Stephen—"Lord lay not this thing to their charge."—HOOKER.

THE circumstances of the Christian profession vary; but the Christian spirit is the same in every age. There must be the same essential feature of character in all the servants of God, amid all their diversified experience in passing through this world to heaven, and that feature is spirituality.—ROBERT HALL.

Cursed are all preachers that in the the church aim at high, hard, and neat things, and (neglecting the saving health of the poor unlearned people,) seek their own honor and praise, therewith to please one or two ambitious persons.—LUTHER.

Let prayer be not only the key that opens the day, and the lock that shuts out the night; but let it be also, from morning to night, our staff and stay in all our labors, and enable us to go cheerfully up into the mount of God.—LEIGHTON.

The most unprofitable piece of the world, is either a profane, a carnal, or a formal, dead minister; he is good for nothing—unsavory salt, of all things the most unsavory.—LEIGHTON.

Why are ye fond of those earthly things, which are neither true riches, nor are they yours? If they are yours, take them with you.—LT. BERNARD.

REV. JAMES B. FINLEY.

BY THE EDITOR.

WE have seldom been more entertained with any book than with the autobiography of this pioneer of the west. He was born in the year 1781, while the war of the revolution was raging, and died some year or two since, honored and beloved. He contributed as much perhaps as any other man to the establishment and spread of Methodism at the west. His father was a graduate of Princeton College and Presbyterian preacher. In 1788, he removed with his family to the wilds of Kentucky. The Indians were still hostile, and the voyage of the emigrants down the Ohio in an open boat was full of danger. They however reached their destination in safety, and went to work and made them a home in the wilderness. After some years of toil, having cleared up the land, and rendered themselves comfortable, defects in the title of their farm, occasioned them to remove into the wilds of Ohio.

Amid the excitements, hardships and perils of pioneer life, augmented by the hostilities of the savages, young Finley was brought up. His father, however, gave him a good classical education. He studied for the medical profession, and was duly admitted to practice, but the attractions of a backwoods hunter's life were too powerful for the young physician: he threw aside his books and medicines, and plunged into all the excitements of border life. "Occasionally," he says, "I would take a spree; would swear when angry; and fight when insulted, at the drop of a hat."

In the midst of his wild career the young backwoodsman was arrested by the Spirit of God. Reports reached his ears of a great revival of religion that had commenced in the State of Kentucky. It was attended with such physical manifestations as spread terror and alarm all over the country.

"It was reported," he says, "that hundreds who attended the meeting were suddenly struck down, and would lie for hours, and sometimes for days, in a state of insensibility; and that when they came out of that state, they would commence praising God for his pardoning mercy and redeeming love.

Hearing that a great meeting was to be held in his father's old congregation in Kentucky, he concluded to go, and see and hear for himself. On the way he said to his companions, "now if I fall it must be by physical power, and not by singing and praying;" and, he proceeds to say, "as I prided myself upon my manhood and courage, I had no fear of being overcome by any nervous excitability, or of being frightened into religion." But no one can tell what he will do when he comes under the influence of the Spirit of God. Physical strength can be turned into corruption in a moment, as in the case of Daniel, and prejudices as deeply rooted as the oaks upon the mountains may be overturned in the twinkling of an eye, as in the case of Saul of Tarsus.

Finley describes this camp-meeting, held in 1801, in the following language: "We arrived upon the ground, and here a scene presented itself to my mind not only novel and unaccountable, but awful beyond description. A vast crowd, supposed by some to have amounted to twenty-five thousand, was collected together. The noise was like the roar of Niagara. The vast sea of human beings seemed to be agitated as if by a storm. I counted seven ministers, all preaching at the same time, some on stumps, others in wagons, and one was standing on a tree, which had in falling, lodged against another. Some of the people were singing, others praying, some crying for mercy in the most piteous accents, while others were shouting most vociferously. While witnessing these scenes, a peculiarly strange sensation, such as I had never felt before, came over me. My heart beat tumultuously, my knees trembled, my lip quivered, and I felt as though I must fall to the ground. A strange supernatural power seemed to pervade the entire mass of mind there collected. I became so weak and powerless that I found it necessary to sit down. Soon after I left and went into the woods, and there I strove to rally, and man up my courage. My pride was wounded, for I had supposed that my mental and physical strength and vigor could most successfully resist these influences."

"After some time I returned to the scene of excitement the waves of which, if possible, had risen still higher. The same awfulness of feeling came over me. I stepped up on to a log, where I could have a better view of the surging sea of humanity. The scene that then presented itself to my mind was indescribable. At one time I saw at least five hundred swept down in a moment, as if a battery of a thousand guns had been opened upon them, and then immediately followed shrieks and shouts that rent the very heavens. My hair rose upon my head, my whole frame trembled, the blood run cold in my veins, and I fled for the woods a second time and wished I had staid at home. While I remained here my feelings became intense and insupportable. A sense of suffocation and blindness seemed to come over me, and I thought I was going to die. I cautiously avoided my companions fearing lest they should discover something the matter with me. In this state I wandered about from place to place in and around the encampment. At times, it seemed as if all the sins I had ever committed in my life were vividly brought in array before my terrified imagination, and under this awful pressure I felt that I must die if I did not get relief. Then it was that I saw clearly through the thin veil of Universalism, and this refuge of lies was swept away by the Spirit of God. Then fell the scales from my sin-blinded eyes, and I realized in all its force and power, the awful truth that if I died in my sins I was a lost man forever. O how I dreaded the death of the soul, for

"There is a death whose pang
Outlasts the fleeting breath,
O what eternal horrors hang
Around the second death!"

Notwithstanding all this, my heart was so proud and hard that I would not have fallen to the ground for the whole State of Kentucky."

The next day he started for home, feeling that he was a "ruined man." The spirit of the Lord followed him, and his trouble on account of his sins continued to increase. Putting up at the close of the day, he passed the night in weeping and promising God that if he would spare him till morning, he would pray and "mend his life" and abandon his wicked practices. As soon as the day broke he went to the woods to pray, and no sooner had his knees touched the ground than he cried aloud for mercy and fell prostrate. His cries attracted the neighbors and they gathered around him. Among them was a German who enjoyed religion. He had him carried to the house and then prayed for his salvation in Dutch and broken English. He continued singing and praying till nine o'clock, when "suddenly," says Finley, "my load was gone, my guilt removed, and presently the direct witness from heaven shone full upon my soul. Then there flowed such copious streams of love into the hitherto waste and desolate places of my soul, that I thought I should die with excess of joy. I cried, I laughed, I shouted, and so strangly did I appear to all but my Dutch brother, that they thought me deranged."

He continued happy in the Lord until his mind became exercised upon the subject of preaching; he resisted the call as a temptation; had no rest day nor night, till from a state of robust health he was reduced almost to "a walking skeleton." His comfort was gone—he gave up his religious exercises and gradually relapsed to his former practices.

In this backsliden state he remained for about three years, when he again yielded to the strivings of the spirit and resolved to return to the Lord. While on his way to the barn to pray, he says, "suddenly God poured upon me the Holy Spirit in such a manner, and in such measure, that I fell my whole length in the snow, and shouted and praised God so loud that I was heard over the neighborhood. As soon as I was able to rise I returned to the house, and caught my wife in my arms and ran round the house, shouting Salvation! Salvation! God has again blessed me with his pardoning love. No doubt many would have said, had they seen me, "This man is drunk or crazy." But I was not "drunk with wine, wherein is excess," but I was filled with the spirit." For an hour I could do nothing but praise the Lord. While thus exercised, I felt as though some one had spoken to me, "Go preach my Gospel." I instantly replied, "Yes, Lord, if thou wilt go with me." He started at once; went to his nearest neighbor, called all the family together and told them what God had done for his soul. From this time, without waiting for a license, he commenced holding meetings in his own house. In less than a month nineteen of his relatives and neighbors experienced religion. From this time to the close of his life, he made the salvation of men his one business.

He filled prominent positions in the church, always with credit and acceptability. He was Presiding Elder for a number of terms, Chaplain to the State Penitentiary of Ohio, and a delegate to many of the General Conferences. We conclude this sketch by giving the account which he has published of

A REMARKABLE VISION.

"During my labors on the Dayton District, an incident occurred which I must relate.

It was in the summer of 1842, worn down with fatigue, I was completing my last round of quarterly meetings, and winding up the labors of a very toilsome year. I had scarcely finished my work till I was most violently attacked with bilious fever, and it was with great difficulty I reached home. The disease had taken so violent a hold on my system that I sank rapidly under its power. Everthing that kind attention and medical skill could impart was resorted to, to arrest its ravages; but all was in vain and my life was despaired of. On the seventh night, in a state of entire insensibility to all around me, when the last ray of hope had departed, and my weeping family and friends were standing around my couch waiting to see me breathe my last, it seemed to me that a heavenly visitant entered my room. It came to my side, and, in the softest and most silvery tones, which fell like rich music on my ear, it said, "I have come to conduct you to another state and place of existence." In an instant I seemed to rise, and, gently borne by my angel guide, I floated out on the ambient air. Soon earth was lost in the distance, and around us, on every side, were worlds of light and glory. On, on, away, away from world to luminous worlds afar, we sped with the velocity of thought. At length we reached the gates of Paradise; and O, the transporting scene that fell upon my vision as the emerald portals, wide and high, rolled back upon their golden hinges! Then in its fullest extent, did I realize the invocation of the poet:

> Burst, ye emerald gates, and bring
> To my raptured vision
> All the ecstatic joys that spring
> Round the bright Elysian.

Language, however, is inadequate to describe what then, with unveiled eyes, I saw. The picture is indelibly pictured on my heart. Before me, spread out in beauty, was a broad sheet of water, clear as crystal, not a single ripple on its surface, and its purity and clearness indescribable. On each side of this lake, or river, rose up the most tall and beautiful trees, covered with all manner of fruits and flowers, the brilliant hues of which were reflected in the bosom of the placid river.

While I stood gazing with joy and rapture at the scene, a convoy of angels was seen floating in the pure ether of that world. They all had long wings, and, although they went with the greatest rapidity, yet their wings were folded close by their sides. While I gazed I asked my guide who they were, and what their mission. To this he responded, "They are angels, dispatched to the world from whence you came, on an errand of mercy." I could hear strains of the most entrancing melody all around me, but no one was discoverable but my guide. At length I said "Will it be possible for me to have a sight of some of the just made perfect in glory?" Just then there came before us three persons; one had the appearance of a male, the other a female, and the third an infant. The appearance of the first two was somewhat similar to the angels I saw, with the exception that they had crowns of the purest yellow, and harps in their hands. Their robes, which were full and flowing, were of the purest white. Their countenances were lighted up with a heavenly radiance, and they smiled upon me with ineffable sweetness.

There was nothing with which the blessed babe or child could be compared. It seemed to be about three feet high. Its wings, which were long and most beautiful, were tinged with all the colors of the rainbow. Its dress seemed to be of the whitest silk, covered with the softest white down. The driven snow could not exceed it for whiteness or purity. Its face was all radiant with glory; its very smile now plays around my heart. I gazed and gazed with wonder upon this heavenly child. At length I said, "If I have to return to earth, from whence I came, I should love to take this child with me, and show it to the weeping mothers of earth. Methinks, when they see it, they will never shed another tear over their children when they die." So anxious was I to carry out the desire of my heart, that I made a grasp at the bright and beautiful one, desiring to clasp it in my arms, but it eluded my grasp, and plunged into the river of life. Soon it rose up from the waters, and as the drops fell from its expanding wings, they seemed like diamonds, so brightly did they sparkle. Directing its course to the other shore, it flew up to one of the topmost branches of one of life's fair trees. With a look of most seraphic sweetness it gazed upon me, and then commenced singing in heaven's own strains, "To Him that hath loved me, and washed me from my sins in His own blood, to Him be glory both now and forever. Amen." At that moment, the power of the eternal God came upon me, and I began to shout, and, clapping my hands, I sprang from my bed, and was healed as instantly as the lame man in the beautiful porch of the temple, who "went walking, and leaping, praising God." Overwhelmed with the glory I saw and felt, I could not cease praising God. The next Sabbath I went to camp-meeting, filled with the love and power of God. There I told the listening thousands what I saw and felt, and what God had done for me, and loud were the shouts of glory that reverberated through the forests.

Though years have rolled away since that bright, happy hour, yet the same holy flame in burning in my heart, and I retain the same glorious victory. "Hallelujah! for the Lord God omnipotent reigneth."

THE POWER OF CHRIST.—When Napoleon, on St. Helena, contemplated the wreck of his own empire, he was filled with awe of this mysterious power of Christ. "With all my power," said he, "I have only made men fear me; but this carpenter, without an army, has made men love him for eighteen hundred years.

"I have so often inspired multitudes that they would die for me. God forbid that I should form any comparison between the enthusiasm of the soldier and Christian charity, which are as unlike as their cause. But after all, my presence was necessary; the lightning of my eye, my voice, a word from me, then the sacred fire was kindled in their hearts. I do, indeed, possess the secret of this magical power, which lifts the soul, but I could never impart it to any one. None of my generals ever learned it from me; nor have I the means of perpetuating my name, and love for me, in the hearts of men, and to effect these things without physical means. Now that I am alone, chained upon this rock, who fights and wins empires for me? who are the courtiers of my misfortunes? who thinks of me? who makes efforts for me in Europe? Where are my friends?

"CHRIST speaks, and at once generations become his by stricter, closer ties than those of blood—by the most sacred, the most indissoluble of all unions. He lights up the flame of a love which consumes self-love, which prevails over every other love. The founders of other religions never conceived of this mystical love, which is the essence of Christianity, and is beautifully called Charity. In every attempt to effect this thing, namely, *to make himself beloved*, man deeply feels his own impotence. So that Christ's greatest miracle undoubtedly is the reign of Charity."

LIVING TO GOD.—I am laboring to live as near to God as any one I have ever known; yea, as near as Saint Paul himself. I read more frequently his character, and study more closely his deadness to the world, his zeal, his love to souls, his labor, his being always ready for his change, and his desiring *rather to be with Christ*. But I am more than ever convinced, that to accomplish this, I must redeem time to the uttermost; I must sleep no more, eat and drink no more than nature requires; and this calls for daily self-denial, such as I believe our Lord meant in his Divine Instructions. The Testament, the Book of God is more precious than ever. I read it, and am lost in wonder, love and praise. I find that to be cleansed from sin is one thing; but to be filled with God is much more. Dr. Clarke's note on that expression, "*the fullness of* GOD," never leaves me.—BRAMWELL.

THE eyes of the Lord are in every place, beholding the evil and the good.

THE EARLY CONVERSION OF CHILDREN.

BY REV. D. W. THURSTON.

The relation between parents and children is deeply interesting and important. It was designed by Infinite Wisdom to form a source of the richest earthly enjoyment; yet it often becomes the occasion of unmingled sorrow; a result originating almost invariably from a violation of the obligations growing out of this relation. The extent of these obligations we apprehend is not properly appreciated.

Parents, generally, deem it an imperative duty to instruct their children in good morals; to present before their minds the beauty and rewards of virtue, and the tendency and fruits of vice. Many sustaining the parental relation go further. They would feel condemned did they not impress upon the minds of their offspring the precepts of the Christian religion. These they inculcate diligently during the hours of family devotion. To aid them in this work, they secure for their children the instructions of the Sabbath School, and the stated ministration of the sanctuary. Over the associations of their tender charge they exercise untiring vigilance, promptly checking their evil propensities, encouraging and rewarding every virtuous manifestation.

There is reason to fear, however, that even of Christian parents, there is a small minority only, who employ direct and efficient means to secure the early conversion of their children to God. That this is the imperative duty of all having the charge of childhood, we shall endeavor to establish. It is argued—

1. From the obscurity attending the period when children become accountable to God.

That there is a period in the existence of every human being, when he is irresponsible for his conduct, is a point generally conceded. To controvert it is to impeach the justice and mercy of God, and to pervert the plain precepts of his word. We allude to the period of infancy. The Scriptures fix its termination in early life, yet the exact period when man enters upon his trial for eternity is one of those secret things which belong to the Lord our God. We infer, however, that in its determination he is influenced by the native strength of the mind's powers, and by the circumstances favoring their development. Now, whenever this boundary is passed by the youthful candidate for eternity, he becomes exposed to the torments of a dreadful hell, unless he immediately yields his heart to God. For he resists the Holy Ghost—refuses to love God—and thereby transgresses the divine laws; which is sin, of which the wages are death.

Since, then, the child becomes accountable to God at a period unknown to parents, and therefore becomes, at that time, subject to the awful penalties of a violated law, is it not their manifest duty to labor earnestly to bring his mind under the renewing power of the Holy Spirit as early as possible? Suppose the captain of a vessel, finding it necessary to send some one to the top of the mast, calls upon his son for the performance of the required service; he has reason to believe that, after ascending to a certain height, the boy will become dizzy, and can keep from falling only by looking aloft. If he loves his son, will he neglect earnestly and repeatedly to instruct and caution him in these things, so essential to his safety? Will not the anxious father vociferate, even before his child reaches the point of supposed danger, look up, my son! look up! look up!

This duty is argued—

2. From the corruption of human nature.

The Scriptures lucidly teach that a depraved nature is inherited by every child of apostate Adam. "Who," says Job, "can bring a clean thing out of an unclean? Not one." Says the inspired David: "Behold, I was shapen in iniquity, and in sin did my mother conceive me." In proof of this point, which is confirmed by universal experience, other passages might be adduced, but those already quoted are sufficient.

This inherent depravity of children, predisposes their minds to the embraces of error, and to the pursuits of vice. It invests with fearful potency the influence of vicious example, with which their minds are in frequent contact, and affords for the success af Satanic agency peculiar advantages.

Besides, the evil propensities of children grow with their growth, and strengthen with their strength. Their enmity to God—their love of the world, and their corrupt inclinations strike their roots deeper and deeper into the heart, while the increasing power of habit—of vicious associations, and the consequent fierce assaults of fallen spirits, urge the youthful probationer with uniformly accelerated velocity towards the gulf of perdition.

It is alarming to observe with what fearful rapidity the tender sensibilities of the child are merged into the cold indifference and daring recklessness of the hardened sinner! The transition is often complete long before the unsuspecting parent detects the first premonitions of the awful change!

Is it not the duty of parents to employ every instrumentality for the rescue of their children from the impending danger to which we have referred? Within the whole range of parental obligations, we can discover none more weighty than this. But against this danger religious instructions afford an insufficient safeguard. It may prevent the commission of overt acts of wickedness, yet nothing but the regenerating energy of the Divine Spirit can stay the rapid tide of inbred corruption.

That it is the duty of parents to attempt the early conversion of their children, is argued—

3. From the constitution of the human mind.

God has endowed man with a capacity for the exercise of various passions and emotions. Whenever the excitement of these is followed by corresponding actions, their original susceptibility gains strength. On the other hand, their power is always enfeebled by exercise when we fail to act in accordance with their direction.

In the perusal of fictitious narratives, which usually abound in scenes of sorrow, the sympathies of the soul become powerfully excited; but their excitement can be followed by no corresponding effort to relieve the sufferings contemplated, for they have no real existence. As a consequence, these sympathies are weakened, and a cold barren sentimentalism, which is unmoved by real misery, inevitably ensues.

It is a notorious fact, that a few years' residence in slaveholding communities, destroys in many minds their former deep-rooted aversion to human oppression. Why are their tender sensibilitities so soon struck down? Were the sufferings which first awakened them imaginary? No, they beggar all description. They surpass in horror the images of the liveliest imagination. The reason is obvious. The legal enactments of pro-slavery communities prohibits the performance of those duties which the wretchedness of the slave demands, and to which the feelings of the heart urgently prompt. Thus, the lover of his species first endures, then pities, then embraces a system which crushes the noblest powers of man, sunders the most sacred ties, and forces from the bleeding hearts of oppressed millions the lamentations of despair.

Religious instruction awakens in the minds of children a sense of their obligations to love and serve God. When corresponding duties are performed, the more exquisite does this moral sense become by successive excitements. But when these are neglected, as in the case of those who refuse to dedicate their hearts to God, their impressions of duty diminish in power. Frequent neglect secures to them the appellation of "Gospel-hardened sinners." In this condition, appeals that bring to their knees unenlightened and vicious men, fall as idle tales upon their ears, and affect their hearts no more than the pale moon-beams the mountain ice-berg. This feature in the human constitution accounts for the fact so frequently observed, that the children of religious parents often excel others for indifference to religious things. The world attributes this fact to undue strictness in parental oversight, than which nothing is more false. The truth is, the harmony of the moral powers is destroyed by neglecting the emotions, and the duties corresponding with the impressions of duty. Parents should deal with their children as the Gospel does with sinners of adult age. Immediate repentance and faith should be urged by all the solemn motives which the Gospel affords. A neglect to do this will render their instructions the savor of death unto death. Those instructions had better be withheld.

The duty in question is urged—

4. From the uncertain tenure of the parental relation.

That the tie uniting parents and children is subject to premature dissolution, no argument is needed to prove. Mysterious, indeed, is that Providence which tears from the embrace of children those who alone appear qualified to nurture and guide their youthful minds. But it is one of frequent occurrence. Parents reading this article, will, long before their youthful charge reach the period of manhood, mingle with departed spirits. What Christian parent can bid adieu to sinful children without the most gloomy forebodings? As he gazes upon them for the last time. he reflects that they are making their way towards the chambers of unending night. He knows that no human being can exert the power over their minds that the God of nature has rendered him capable of wielding. He is conscious that none will succeed to his charge who can feel for it a parent's concern. But he must yield it, perhaps, to wicked minds. In view of these solemn considerations, is it not the manifest duty of the parent to lead his child to Christ in infancy? Should he not labor to place his child in a position in which he may be reached by mercy's arm the very moment he passes the line of accountability?

That it is the duty of parents to seek the early conversion of their children is inferred—

5. From the instructions of Scripture.

The Bible teaches that the precepts of the Divine law are within the comprehension of children. The inculcation of those precepts to children was enjoined upon parents under the Mosaic dispensation. When about taking leave of his countrymen, Moses, at the instigation of the Almighty, delivers to them this solemn charge: These words, which I command thee this day, shall be in thine heart: And thou shalt teach them diligently unto thy children, and thou shalt talk of them when thou sittest in thine house, and when thou walkest by the way; and when thou liest down, and when thou risest up." Deut. vi. 6–7. Says Saint Paul to Timothy, "From a child thou hast known the holy Scriptures, which are able to make thee wise unto salvation through faith which is in Christ Jesus." II Tim. iii. 15.

From the fact thus established, that children may know God's law, we infer that they are capable of transgression, and consequently subject to the judgment of the Almighty. This inference is justified by Scripture authority. In proof of this, an incident in the life of Elisha is in point. God sanctioned the curse pronounced by this holy man upon the children of Bethel, who had reproached him, by commissioning wild beasts to destroy them. Would this awful judgment have fallen upon these children if they had not been viewed by God as transgressors of his law? Will it be urged that they had passed the period of children? The records of this transaction state explicitly that these offenders were "little children." It being proved, then, that little children may render themselves obnoxious to the wrath of God, is it not the duty of those having charge of them to induce them to seek his pardoning mercy? Again, the Scriptures recognize children as acceptable worshippers. David calls upon "young men and maidens, old men and *children*, to praise the name of the Lord. Christ publicly sanctioned and encouraged the acts of worship presented to him by children in the Temple. He silenced those who rebuked these juvenile worshippers by a reference to the inspired record. "Have ye not read," says he, "Out of the mouth of babes and sucklings there hast perfected praise?" Children, then, being called upon to engage in divine worship, ought not parents to urge them to comply with God's call, and to seek the renewing favor of the Spirit essential to spiritual homage?

Once more. We are taught in the book of God that children are susceptible of renewing grace. "All thy children shall be taught of the Lord," is an expression referring most manifestly to the inward operation of the Spirit; and the "great peace" to the fruits of this internal work. The following exhortation of the Apostle establishes the same doctrine: "Bring up your children in the nurture and admonition of the Lord." These terms evidently embrace the whole of the Christian religion. The history of the church confirms the instruction of Scripture on this point. Children, even before they have passed the fifth year of their existence, have manifested deep contrition for sin—given clear evidence of regeneration, and have left the world in ecstacy and triumph. If, then, they are susceptible of converting grace, who dare say that they are not accountable for its fruits? If they may partake of the rich enjoyments of the Christian religion, where is the heart so unfeeling as to neglect the instruction that might lead them into the possession of those enjoyments? Seeing, then, that the inspired writings teach that children may be informed of the Divine will—that they are treated as sinners upon the violating of God's law—that they are capable of glorifying their Maker by acts of devotion, and that they are susceptible of gracious influences and of the sweet enjoyment thereof, are not parents solemnly bound to labor to bring their little ones to the Cross at the earliest period possible? They need not fear that their offspring will be induced to make too early a consecration of their powers to God. The disciples of Christ thought that the blunder of those parents who brought their infants to Jesus was so gross as to merit rebuke. But the action and remarks of the Great Teacher, on this occasion, should be matters of grateful recollection to every parent. He took these infants in his arms and blessed them, and said, "Suffer little children to come unto me, and forbid them not, for of such is the kingdom of God."

Upon this subject, there is much infidelity. The church itself, we fear, is not free from it. In seasons of revival, who has not witnessed clear manifestations of dejection on the part of God's people, because "none but children expressed a desire for salvation?" Yes, although a score of weeping children are around the altar, crying for mercy—although Heaven is filled with joyful acclaim for the penitence of these young prodigals, Christians are disheartened, and report a "poor meeting" to their absent brethren, for "Nobody but children were forward for prayers." We have never heard anything which sounds so much like blasphemy against the Holy Ghost as this. "Nobody but children!" Did not the Eternal Spirit awaken them? Must they not be converted or sink to an eternal hell? Are they not possessed of immortal spirits, panting for the enjoyments and hopes of the Christian religion? O! why interdict them from the inheritance of the saints? Why not bear them on the arms of wrestling faith to the Eternal Throne, until their little hearts are gladdened by the love of Jesus?

The unbelief from which this unconcern for the souls of children originates, has framed numerous objections against their early nurture in the things of religion. It is urged that "in matters of religion they should be left uninfluenced, to think and choose for themselves." They must think and choose for themselves, most certainly, before they are converted; but that they should be left to do so uninfluenced by the counsel of experience, is unreasonable and inhuman. The suggestions of their corrupt natures, of fallen spirits, and of a wicked world, powerfully influence them to act in a manner that would ruin them eternally. May not, *should* not the parent counteract the tendency of such influence, by giving a right direction to their inexperienced minds? What parent or guardian is willing to carry out the principle of this objection? To do so, he must learn his child to select his books of instruction, his teacher, and his associations. He must not dissuade his child from lying, drunkenness, theft or murder. He must not influence him to the practice of virtue. All interference with him in these things is as inconsistent as in the affairs of his soul; for certainly he cannot be educated, moral, or virtuous, without thinking and choosing for himself. The child left to think and act for himself in matters of religion, is almost sure to act wrong. God holds parents responsible for the proper guidance of the youthful mind, and woe to that parent who proves recreant to his solemn charge.

It is objected, again, that "importunate efforts to convert children, will render religious things objects of disgust to their minds." Were this objection founded in truth, it would not justify a neglect to press unceasingly and urgently the claims of religion upon the youthful mind. His exposure to ruin demands vigorous effort to effect his conversion at every hazard. But experience and the philosophy of mind are opposed to this objection. God has a witness in the minds of children, which secures respect for the ministrations of truth. Diligence on the part of the spiritual laborer has no tendency to destroy that respect, but will almost invariably result in early conversion.

We will mention but one objection more. It is urged that "Children are more liable to backslide than converts of mature years." If this is a fact, it must owe its existence to neglect on the part of those whose duty it is to watch over the spiritual interests of babes in Christ, or to some weakness or besetments peculiar to children. If the assumed fact originates in neglect, its existence may and should be avoided. But to say that circumstances incidental to childhood, render youthful piety precarious, is to impeach the mercy and veracity of God—to say that the Great Shepherd leaves the tender lambs of his flock without those provisions which their helplessness requires, and that the promise, "My grace is sufficient for you," is not fulfilled—which is blasphemy. But it remains to be proved, that a greater number of those converted in childhood apostatize from God, than of those reconciled to him in manhood. We believe the assertion to be utterly false.

O! what a vast addition of moral power might be secured—what an immense outlay of means might be saved; and O, how much more rapidly would the cause of Christ be extended, if parents would attend faithfully to the duty in question! A new era would dawn upon the world. Millennial glory would be ushered in, and the knowledge of God would cover the earth!

We entreat parents to ponder seriously and prayerfully this solemn subject. You do well to procure for your children the instructions of the Sabbath school, and the ministrations of the Gospel. You do well to expound to them the Scriptures of inspiration in the domestic circle; but O, do not stop here. They may endlessly wail with the lost, notwithstanding these instructions, and they certainly will, unless converted, if they have passed the line of accountability! Rest not until their little hearts receive the impress of

God's own image. Take them daily into the closet; agonize before the throne; teach them to agonize; urge them to repentance and faith, and God will give you the desire of your hearts. Look into the future. A few days more and you are on the dying bed, bidding farewell to those loved ones. O, what will they do without religion, in a wicked world, surrounded by wicked men, pursued by wicked spirits?

Praise God, parents, that your children are yet within the reach of your influence. Haste to apply yourselves more diligently and earnestly in leading them into the kingdom; and may God grant that you, with them, may form an unbroken circle in Heaven. Amen.

GOD'S WILL.—As living to God's will is in all things to be our end, so in all the way to that end it is to be the rule of every step. For we cannot attain this end but in his way; nor can we attain it without a resignation of the way to his prescription, taking all our directions from him, how we shall honor him in all. This is to live to him, to find it our life. That such a lust be crucified, is it thy will, Lord? Then, no more advising, no more delay. How dear soever that was when I lived to it, it is now as hateful, seeing I live to thee who hatest it. Wilt thou have me forget an injury, though a great one, and love the person that has wronged me? While I lived to myself and my passions, this had been hard. But now, how sweet is it! seeing I live to thee, and am glad to be put upon things most opposite to my corrupt heart; glad to trample upon my own will to follow thine. And this I daily aspire to and aim at, to have no will of my own, but that thine be in me, that I may live to thee as one with thee, and thou my rule and delight; yea, not to use the very natural comforts of my life, but for thee; to eat and drink and sleep for thee; and not to please myself, but to be enabled to revere and please thee; to make one offering of myself and all my actions to thee, my Lord!

Oh! it is the only sweet life to be living thus, and daily learning to live more fully thus! It is heaven this, a little scantling of it here, and a pledge of whole heaven. This is, indeed, the life of Christ, not only like his, but one with his; it is his spirit, his life, derived into the soul.—LEIGHTON.

WATCHMAN.

Watchman, tell me, does the morning
  Of fair Zion's glory dawn?
Have the signs that mark his coming,
  Yet upon my pathway shone?
Pilgrim, yes—arise, look 'round thee—
  Light is breaking in the skies;
Gird thy bridal robes around thee,
  Morning dawns—arise, arise!

Watchman, see, the light is beaming
  Brighter still upon the way;
Signs through all the earth are gleaming—
  Omens of the coming day.
When the Jubal trumpet sounding
  Shall awake from earth and sea
All the saints of God, now sleeping,
  Clad in immortality!

Watchman, hail the light ascending,
  Of the grand Sabbatic year;
All with voices loud proclaiming
  That the Kingdom's very near.
Pilgrim, yes, I see just yonder
  Canaan's glorious height arise;
Salem, too, appears in grandeur,
  Towering 'neath its sunlit skies!

Watchman, in the glorious city,
  Seated on his azure throne,
Zion's King, enthroned in beauty,
  Reigns in peace from zone to zone.
There, on sunlit hills and mountains,
  Golden beams serenely glow;
Purling streams and crystal fountains,
  On whose banks sweet flowerets grow!

Watchman, see, the land is nearing,
  With its vernal fruits and flowers;
On just yonder—O, how cheering,
  Bloom forever Eden bowers.
Hark! the choral strains there ringing,
  Wafted on the balmy air;
See the millions, hear them singing—
  Soon the pilgrims will be there!

GUIDANCE OF THE HOLY SPIRIT.

[We commend to the careful perusal of our readers, the following article from the pen of the late Justice Hale, of England, who was no less eminent as a man of deep piety than as a learned and impartial judge. That the doctrine of the inward direction of God's Spirit is susceptible of abuse we readily admit; and what doctrine of the Bible is not? But the greater danger in this day of self-sufficiency lies in our laying too little rather than too much stress upon the guidance of the Holy Spirit.—Ed.]

They who truly fear God, have a secret guidance from a higher wisdom than that which is barely human,—namely, the Spirit of truth and goodness, which does really, though secretly, prevent and direct them. Any man that sincerely and truly fears Almighty God, and calls and relies upon him for his guidance and direction, has it as really as a son has the counsel of his father: and though the voice be not audible, nor discernable by sense, yet it is equally as real as if a man heard a voice saying: "This is the way, walk ye in it."

Though this secret direction of Almighty God is principally seen in matters relating to the good of the soul; yet, even in the concerns of this life, a good man fearing God, and begging his direction, will very often, if not at all times, find it. I can call my own experience to witness, that even in the temporal affairs of my whole life, I have never been disappointed of the best direction, when I have, in humility and sincerity, implored it.

The observance of the secret admonition of this Spirit of God in the heart, is an effectual means to cleanse and sanctify us; and the more it is attended to, the more it will be conversant with our souls, for our instruction. In the midst of difficulties it will be our counsellor, in the midst of temptations it will be our strength and grace sufficient for us, in the midst of trouble it will be our light and our comfort.

It is impossible for us to enjoy the influence of this Good Spirit, till we are deeply sensible of our own emptiness and nothingness, and our own minds are thereby brought down and laid in the dust. The Spirit of Christ is indeed a humbling Spirit, and the more we have of it, the more we shall be humbled; and it is a sign that either we have it not, or that it is yet overpowered by our corruptions, if our heart be still haughty.

Attend, therefore, to the secret persuasions of the Spirit of God, and beware of quenching or grieving it. This wind that blows where it lists, if shut out or resisted, may never breathe upon us again, but leave us to be hardened in our sins. If observed and obeyed, it will on all occasions, be our monitor and director. When we go out, it will lead us; when we sleep, it will keep us; and when we awake, it will talk with us.—Hale.

THE BIBLE.

BY A. F. BROWN.

How comes it that this little volume, written by humble men, in a rude age, when art and science were in their childhood, has exerted more influence on the human mind and on the social system than all other books put together? Whence comes it that this book has achieved such marvelous changes in the opinions of mankind—has banished idol worship—has abolished infanticide—raised the standard of public morality—created for families that blessed thing, a Christian home? What sort of a book is this, that even the winds and waves of human passion obey it? What other engine of social improvement has operated so long, and yet lost none of its virtues? Since it appeared, many boasted plans of amelioration have been tried and failed—

many codes of jurisprudence have arisen, and run their course. Empire after empire has been launched upon the tide of time, and gone down, leaving no trace upon the waters. But this book, this blessed book is still going about doing good, learning society with its holy principles—cheering the sorrowful with its consolations—strengthening the tempted—encouraging the penitent, calming the troubled spirit—and smoothing the pillow of death. Should the Bible be taken from us, it would be to mantle the world with more than Egyptian darkness; it would be taking the moral chart by which alone the inhabitants of Earth are guided. Ignorant of the nature of God, and only guessing at their own immortality, the tens of thousands would be as mariners tossed on a wide ocean, without a pole-star and without compass. The loss of the Bible would dry up the fountain of human happiness; it would take the tide from our waters, and leave them stagnant; and the stars from our heavens, and leave them in sackcloth; and the verdure from our valleys, and leave them in barrenness; it would make the present all recklessness, and the future all hopelessness. It tells us of God; unveils immortality, instructs in duty, wooes on to glory. Such is the Bible. Prize it more and more. Prize it, as ye are immortal beings, for it guideth to the New Jurusalem. Prize it, as ye are intellectual beings, for it giveth light to the simple.

CONVERSION.

WE readily take any little slight change for true conversion, but we may see here that we mistake it. It doth not barely knock off some obvious apparent enormities, but casts all in a new mould, alters the whole frame of the heart and life, kills a man and makes him alive again. And this new life is contrary to the old; for the change is made with that intent, that he live no longer to the lusts of men, but to the will of God. He is now, indeed, a *new creature*, having a new judgment and new thoughts of things, and so, accordingly, new desires and affections, and answerably to these, new actions. Old things are passed away and dead, and all things are become new.

Political men have observed, that in states, if alterations must be, it is better to alter many things than a few. Things do so relate one to another, that except they be adapted and suited together in the change it avails not; yea, it sometimes proves the worse on the whole, though a few things in particular seem to be bettered. Thus, half-reformations in a Christian turn to his prejudice; it is only best to be reformed throughout; and to give up with all idols; not to live one half to himself and the world, and as it were, another half to God, for that is but falsely so, and, in reality, cannot be. The only way is, to make a heap of all, to have all sacrificed together, and to live to no lust, but altogether and only to God. Thus it must be, there is no monster in the new Creation, no half-new creature—either all, or not at all.

We have to deal with the Maker and the Searcher of the heart, and he will have nothing unless he have the heart, and none of that neither, unless he have it all. If thou pass over into his kingdom, and become his subject, thou must have him for thy only sovereign. *Omnisque potestas impatiens consortis.*

"ROYALTY can admit of no rivalry." and least of all the highest and best of all. If Christ be thy king, then his laws and sceptre must rule all in thee; thou must now acknowledge no foreign power; that will be treason.

And if he be thy husband, thou must renounce all others. Wilt thou provoke him to jealousy? Yea, beware how thou givest a thought or a look of thy affection any other way, for he will spy it, and will not endure it. The title of a husband is strict and tender.

Now, thou hast but One to serve, and that is a great ease; and it is no slavery, but true honor, to serve so excellent a Lord, and in so high services; for he puts thee upon nothing but what is neat and what is honorable. Thou art as *a vessel of honor* in his house, for his best employment. Now thou art not in pain how to please this person and the other, nor needest thou vex thyself to gain men, to study their approbation and honor, nor to keep to thine own lusts and observe their will. Thou hast none but thy God to please in all; and if he be pleased thou mayest disregard who is displeased. His will is not fickle and changing as men's are, and as thine own is. He hath told thee what he likes and desires, and he alters not; so that now thou knowest whom to please, and what will please him. This cannot but much settle thy mind and put thee at ease.—ARCHBISHOP LEIGHTON.

CONFESSION.

BY S. K. J. CHESBROUGH.

At the present day, the duty of confession is not held up before the Church as it should be. Too many make it a superficial work. *What is it* to confess our sins? One defines it thus: "To own, and lay open our sins and offences, either unto God in private, or in public confession." The work must be thorough, it must needs go to the very depths of the heart. We must not judge of our sins by our own judgment as to their sinfulness, but must acknowledge even the so called "little sins," as heinous and damning in the sight of the great God, "who seeth not as man seeth."

Why should we confess our sins? Because God commands it, and it must necessarily precede our salvation, "for he that confesseth and forsaketh his sins shall have mercy." When we see ourselves as sinners, we must confess, repent of and forsake them. The reason why many bow at our altars of prayer, night after night, and yet go away unblessed, is because they do not make thorough work of confessing their sins. When this work is commenced in earnest, and we let the light shine, we shall find such a work before us as we little thought of, and to our sorrow we shall find the "leprosy of sin lies deep within." Satan whispers to the ear, Omit this and that; but we must go through. "Strait is the gate." We had better die here to self, than to die eternally. Reader, make thorough work in this matter; a mistake here may prove fatal to thy soul.

To whom should we confess our sins? Undoubtedly, most of our sins should be confessed to God in our closets. But our public faults or sins must be publicly confessed. The sins committed against our families, our friends, our neighbors, must be confessed to them as well as to God. Here is a point at which many stumble. The word of God, which is Spirit and Life, becomes like a two-edged sword. We see ourselves in the Gospel mirror. We feel that "our hearts have been secretly enticed"—our walk, our conversation, or dealings one with the other, our conduct before our families, have not been consistent with our profession. We begin in good earnest to confess to God our wanderings—we feel some relief, but no clear evidence of our acceptance. Why not? "We must confess our faults one to another, that we may be healed." And here is where the great hue and cry is made the present day against an earnest Christianity. "What! must I confess to the Church, to my wife, to my husband, to my children, to my *hired servants*, to my neighbors? Yes, reader, if you have given way to impatience, anger, pride, to light and trifling conversation, you need to confess to God, and to those before whom you committed these sins; they remember them, you remember them, God remembers them. "But," says one, "if I do this I shall bring a reproach upon the Church." God help you, my friend, He says that you are already a reproach. You may meet the frowns of those who are in the same condition. Never mind: obey God, and shame the devil. But instead of its bringing a reproach upon the Church, it is just the reverse. Israel was put to flight, they turned their backs to their enemies; there was sin in their ranks—secret sin. God knew it. Hear what Joshua says: Joshua, vii. 19, 20—

"And Joshua said unto Achan, My son, give, I pray thee, glory to the Lord God of Israel, *and make confession unto Him*: and tell me now what thou hast done; hide it not from me. And Achan answered Joshua and said, Indeed I have sinned against the Lord God of Israel, and thus and thus have I done." Mark the expression—"Give glory to the Lord God"—how this puts to blush the teachings of some ministers and class leaders of the present day, who cry, "Hold thy peace." Oh, may God's Spirit search out the Achans of the camp, and raise up Joshuas who, amid the threatenings of "hireling shepherds" and dead formalists, will hold the people to this cross until they confess their secret backslidings from God. How many have hid in their hearts the "Babylonish garment and wedge of gold." God sees it. They have lost their power. The world knows it, and they know it. In vain will they strive to get around the Cross —this duty stands before them : "Confess your sins." How many are shutting out the light! How many have emerged into the clear light, by simply rising and confessing before the Church the true state of their backslidden heart! Others have had to go from house to house. But to-day they are free. Oh! glorious freedom! Reader, search your heart; have you confessions to make? Tarry not! confer not with flesh and blood, but go and make thy confession, and thou shalt find mercy.

He will gain wisdom who knocks by prayer; not he who by quarreling makes a noise at the gate of truth.— AUGUSTINE.

All the virtues are the daughters of faith.—CLEMENS ALEXANDRIUS.

SUBSTITUTES FOR THE HOLY GHOST.

BY REV. A. A. PHELPS.

IN the remarks which we are about to make, it is no part of our design to "slander the Church." Our inmost feeling is that of lamentation rather than of reproach. If our pen should run into a strain of seeming severity, the undying interest we feel for the prosperity of Zion must be our only apology. That there is *danger* of departing from the simplicity of the gospel, and of losing the real elements of our power and success, is admitted by all. That this loss has been actually *sustained* by all branches of the Christian Church, to an alarming extent, is equally obvious to every careful observer who has no favorite theory to establish on the opposite assumption. In the same proportion as the Church loses the *real* DIVINITY from her midst, she is sure to accept some other god. There is a *Divine philosophy* which God designed should regulate the Church; and that philosophy is both understood and adopted when her politics and purity are in harmony with the order of Heaven; but when and in so far as she loses her spiritual vision, the philosophy of this world becomes the platform of her action. Mark some of the things upon which the Church depends for success, and which are often substituted for the omnipotent energies of the Holy Ghost:

1. *Numbers.* How natural it is to measure our power by the multitudes that throng our altars, and to become elated over the reflection that we are the "biggest Church in the land!" A feeling of self-security arises within us on seeing ourselves surrounded by so many of the "same faith and order," and we are ready to believe that the ark of God will move on irrespective of our individual character and position. We forget that the thousands of members in any single denomination, or of all the denominations combined, are utterly incapable of converting a single

soul, without the accompanying agency of the Holy Spirit. If all who are admitted to Church fellowship were required to conform in all things to the Bible standard of piety, our numbers might be a more reliable measurement of our power. As it is, the saying of a former Bishop is doubtless true, "that we could part with ship-loads of members, and be better off." And even if the entire membership were deeply devoted, it would be dangerous to rely on our numbers as an element of success. God does not want *multitudes* to fight His battles, but He wants "valient hearted men who are not afraid to die!" Sometimes numbers are in the way—a thinning out is the first step to efficiency, as in the case of Gideon's army, which was reduced from thirty-two thousand to three hundred. These, with God Almighty assisting, were enough to gain the most signal victory.

2. *Wealth*. The highest ambition of some professed Christians, seems to be to influence the *rich* to profess religion, and identify themselves with the Church. The gospel to them is a sort of machinery which is to be run with money. Their attention is all absorbed in the outward—the mechanical of Christianity, while the underlying spirit seems hid from view. How low must be their ideas of God to suppose that He cares a whit more for a millionaire than for the veriest pauper that walks the streets! Money is good in its place, but money is not God, and it will never answer as a substitute for God. If any doubt our position, let them find a practical demonstration in the fact that our poorest Churches, taking the work as a whole, actually do more in getting sinners saved than those that roll in opulence and ease, for the two are generally united.

3. *Social position*. It is true that Christianity has numbered among her votaries some of the wisest and mightiest men that have ever lived; and this fact is not without weight and importance in recounting the evidences of the Christian system; but when these giant intellects are in any manner depended on to carry forward the practical operations of the gospel, defeat and dismay must be the result of our ill-directed confidence. Men of honor and position may give to the Church the influence of their greatness, but they cannot give her the power that breaks the sinner's heart, and prevails with God. It is insulting to the Most High to suppose that with social position the Church can succeed without the Holy Ghost, or that with the Holy Ghost she cannot succeed without social position! "The great and wise" are far from being the principal want of the Church. God rather wants, to slay the Goliaths of sin, the "little ones" of real devotion and awful power. Let a Church be clothed with the might of the Spirit, and it matters but little whether "any of the rulers have believed on" Christ or not. With such a baptism of pure fire, she has a weapon more effectual than a combination of the largest numbers, the greatest wealth and the highest position among men.

4. *Forms*. These are eminently appropriate when appropriately employed. They must, however, be regarded as helps to a real good, and not the good itself. They are the leading-strings of the gospel to assist us in our approaches to the Parent of all. If we recline upon these, and refuse to go beyond them, we shall never outlive the weakness of a spiritual infancy. Forms and ceremonies amount to nothing and worse than nothing, only so far as they point us to something above and beyond themselves. They never saved anybody, and never will. "It is the *Spirit* that giveth *life*." But alas! how many have no eyes to look beyond the types and shadows! They bury themselves up in a mass of frigid and stereotyped formularies, and consent to drag out a miserable existence, without any touches of heavenly power, or baptisms of Divine consolation. They make speeches, and say prayers, and go through the routine of ordinary Christian duties, but they see and feel but very little of God in them all!

It is true they "hold fast the form of sound words," but they do no more; they never seek the energizing influence of the Holy Ghost. And yet, nothing else will answer. We must have, *we must have it,* or this revolted world will never be redeemed to God! Let us have what we may of outward prosperity and favorable circumstantials, but never may we mourn the absence of the Infinite Spirit! Take away our numbers, our wealth, our reputation, our ceremonies, but leave us, O leave us the anointing that abideth—the baptism of refining fire—the spirituality of a living gospel—the presence of an indwelling Divinity—the unction of the Holy Ghost!

THE more I see and know of the world the less I esteem it, and the more I desire to be delivered from it: to live indifferent to its smiles and frowns. O, what vanity and vexation is the portion of those, at least many of them, that enjoy much of what are called its good things. My soul keep thou free from it! In God alone is true happiness to be found. It is a great thing to be altogether a Christian.—LADY MAXWELL.

I am not afraid that the people called Methodists, should ever cease to exist either in Europe or America. But I am afraid lest they should only exist as a dead Sect, having the form of religion without the power. And this undoubtedly will be the case, unless they hold fast both the Doctrine, Spirit and Discipline, with which they first set out.—WESLEY.

IT would be wrong to suppose that the way of holiness is a *miraculous* way. It is wonderful, but it is not miraculous. Those who are in it walk by simple faith alone. And perhaps there is nothing more remarkable or wonderful in it, than that a result so great as that of the purification of heart, should be produced by a principle so simple.—FENTON.

REVIVALS.

BY THE EDITOR.

NEVER, since our remembrance, have the fields been so white for a spiritual harvest as at the present. There is an element in man that cannot be satisfied with material objects. The summit of ambition may be reached—political power may be secured, competency and wealth may be gained, but still, man's nature is not satisfied—he craves something more. This is illustrated forcibly in the experience of Madame de Maintenon, who had been married to Louis the 14th, though, for political reasons she was not publicly acknowledged as his wife. She had his confidence as well as his affections. For many years the most important affairs of France depended upon her concurrence. Her power was felt to be hardly less than that of the King. The greatest men of the Kingdom paid her homage. Everything which wealth or art could furnish was put in requisition to make her happy.

In the height of her prosperity and power, writing to a friend, she says: "Why can I not make you sensible of that uneasiness which preys upon the great, and the difficulty they labor under to employ their time. Do you not see that I am dying with melancholy, in a height of fortune which once my imagination could scarce have conceived? I have been young and beautiful, have had a high relish of pleasure, and have been the universal object of love. In a more advanced age I have spent years in intellectual pleasures, I have at last risen to favor; but I protest to you, my dear Madame, that *every one of these conditions leaves in the mind a* DISMAL VACUITY."

So is it with mankind generally in all conditions of fortune. There is in the mind,

"An aching void
The world can never fill."

This hunger of the soul for fruit that does not grow on trees of nature's planting, Christianity was designed to satisfy. It has in it a supernatural element calculated to meet the highest wants of man's spiritual being. It proffers to him the highest and most substantial joys; flowing from a source unseen by mortal eye; and completely delivered from the influence of all external circumstances. But where the Churches, the guardians and representatives of the religion of Christ, settle down into a dead formalism this want is not met. The earnest soul turns away in disgust from dry speculations, barren forms and idle fancies. It asks for the bread of life, and is offered instead the painted flowers of rhetoric, and spiritual mummies (from which the vital spark has long since fled,) carefully embalmed, and superstitiously preserved.

Hence the rapidity with which modern Spiritualism—the latest emanation from the bottomless pit—swept, like a moral simoon, over the country, leaving the wrecks of ruined virtue and domestic happiness in its path. Had a proper tone of Spirituality prevailed in the Churches, the devil could not have thus deceived, with his enchantments. But the effects of this diabolical attempt to imitate the work of the finger of God are too terrible for the delusion to be lasting. Already the attention of the public is directed to the Christian religion as that which alone can satisfy the conditions of our being.

All that is wanting for a revival of earnest Christianity to sweep through the country is for men and women, *full of faith and the Holy Ghost*, to labor everywhere, as in apostolic times, for the salvation of souls, preaching to sinners and formalists "repentance from dead works," and urging believers to "go on to perfection." Wherever this has been done faithfully, no matter what obstacles have been in the way, good results, exceeding the anticipations of the most sanguine, have been realized. In the hope of stirring up others to a holy activity, we give a brief account of what the Lord is doing in reviving earnest Christianity in different parts.

A brother, writing us from Illinois, says:

"God has a little pilgrim band in St. Charles, Rock River, Con., numbering something over a hundred. Some twenty-five of their number were expelled from the M. E. Church, (if the *preacher* in *charge* can become *complainant, counsel, committee, chairman* and *quarterly conference*, and all at one and the same time, Others have risen up from the blood of these martyrs and enlisted for life or during the war for holiness.

But the best of all is "the Lord of Host is with us! The God of Jacob is our refuge"—and in our "own hired house" sinners are converted to God—backsliders restored to their "first love" and led out into the highway of holiness.

The sister Churches in the place are deeply feeling the lightings-down of the Spirit of grace, a goodly number receiving among us the "baptism of fire," to return, as we trust, and kindle the flame in their own homes. The entire place is moved, but whether the walls shall utterly tumble at the blowing of the crooked horns, remains to be seen.

Thus far, in the battle, "He that is for us has been more than all" that have been against us. We have greatly wanted for room, and the work has been evidently hindered from this cause. We expect soon to remedy this by erecting a house in which God can be "Spiritually" worshipped. I bless God for a stamp of salvation, that does not *congeal* in winter nor *evaporate* in summer, for a salvation that *lives, breathes, walks, talks,* and *thinks,* and *acts,* that has in it "mustard-seed faith," "leavening-power, Holy Ghost," energies, with fire shut up in the bones, with "immortality and eternal life."

Often have I looked upon these expansive prairies and seen the night receding before a pursuing lake of fire; but a far sublimer scene is here preparing to open to the admiration of Angels and the astonishment of men. Even now, all along Fox River, and on either side of it, and out upon the stretching prairies, the holy fires are kindling, and we only wait another sweeping breath of heaven and we stand upon "a sea of glass, mingled with fire," with many harpers harping with their harps. "Hallelujah to God and the Lamb!" The deep-toned thunders of early Methodism are beginning again to salute our ears, and her long hushed echoes to utter their voices. Again, the voice of the expring Jesus is rending the rocks and quaking the earth—the graves are opening and many of the saints which slept are rising to appear unto many.

Continue the voice, my Lord, until the Churches "shall give up their dead," and the world shall be blessed and redeemed by a living ministry and a holy people.

PARMA, N. Y.—A member of the Genesee Conference, who has not bowed the knee to Baal, writes:

"The Lord is working with us on this

charge, both in the Church and out. Believers have been sanctified, and upwards of thirty sinners converted since the Conference, and still the work goes on. The *Earnest Christian* is loved much by the earnest Methodists in these parts, and you know their number is legion."—C. D.

PORTER, N. Y.—Rev. Wm. Cooley, one of the preachers "expelled" from the Genesee Conference last fall, writes:

"The revival on the Randall Road goes on gloriously. Over fifty have been converted here and a number have been clearly sanctified. So about seventy-five have been converted since we came to Porter, and about twenty have been sanctified. It looks to me as though the Lord is about to sweep through all this region in great power. I am in for this war to the end."—W. C.

"P. S.—I understand a good work is going on in Pendleton, under brother J. Stacy. Bless the Lord."—W. C.

WALES, N. Y.—A good brother laboring for souls in Wales, Erie County, writes:

The Lord has not forgotton us. Notwithstanding, on the part of the oppressor, there is power, the God of Daniel still lives, and all we have to do, after having done our duty, is to stand still, and see the salvation of our God. I can say of a truth that earnest Christianity is on the increase. And we are nobly "contending for the faith once delivered to the Saints."

We've nailed our colors to the mast,
And firmly we declare
We never will strike while time shall last,
Or Jesus answers prayer.

Our congregations are increasing in numbers and sinners are enquiring what they shall do to be saved. At Spring Book, the Lord is evidently reviving his work. Black sliders have been reclaimed, and still the work goes on, to God be all the glory.

Yours, for an Earnest Christianity,
C. HUDSON.

BUFFALO.—A good revival has been in progress for some time in the Thirteenth Street Free Methodist Church, in this city. The Lord has been carrying on a work of grace there almost ever since we commenced holding meetings in Mr. Ketchum's Church.

The interest has been steadily upon the increase, and souls have been saved almost from the commencement of our labors. For some weeks past brother Daniel Sinclair has been carrying on a protracted meeting there with the best results. Some forty or over give good evidence of having passed from death unto life. Last Sabbath from fifty to sixty staid in class, each one of whom gave in a clear testimony, of the enjoyment of a present salvation. This is about double the number that composed the entire congregation when we began to preach there, about one year since. Now the house is often crowded to the utmost, many going away unable to find standing room. A general interest is excited, and we hope soon to hold meetings also in a more central portion of the city.

IN ROCHESTER, we held some meetings for the promotion of earnest Christianity the latter part of February and fore part of March. Much of the divine presence was realized in all the meetings and great good was done. Persons in the habit for years of neglecting religious services were constant in attendance—a number were clearly saved and conviction appeared to be general. Such was the interest that we were obliged the last Sabbath of the meeting to go to Corinthian Hall for room. This, too, was crowded. It was said by those knowing the capacity of the Hall that there were at least 1,400 persons in attendance. A good work is commenced there, which will, we trust, result in the conversion of thousands of souls.

AT SYRACUSE there is a small but choice band of pilgrims, who are "strong in the faith, giving glory to God." Our four days meeting with them, commencing the 8th of March, was thinly attended, but the Lord was with us, and we had a pleasant and profitable time.

AT CANANDAIGUA we held a four days meeting, commencing the 15th of March. We have seldom left a place with so many regrets at our being unable to continue our labors longer. The congregations were large, there being, it was estimated, eight hundred or one thousand people present at the last service—there were all that could be crowded into the large hall, and into the entrance leading to it. The word was listened to with marked attention. Several came out into the clear light of a present salvation, and others received impressions which will, we trust, lead them to a speedy and total surrender to the claims of Christ. We would gladly have staid there longer, but other and pressing engagements compelled us to leave.

AT ALBION we learn that an interesting state of things prevails in the "Free Methodist church, of which the Rev. L. Stiles is the pastor. They now worship in the basement of their new church. This is a large and commodious room, capable of seating some six or seven hundred persons. This, we are informed, is crowded from Sabbath to Sabbath. A good religious influence prevails, and additions are made to their membership from week to week, of such, we trust, as 'shall be saved.'"

PERRY, N. Y.—An esteemed brother writing us from this place, gives the names of seventeen of the old and reliable members of the Methodist Episcopal church who were "withdrawn" without their knowledge or consent. At the time the preacher thus unceremoniously "read out" these Christians from the church which they had helped by their labors and money to build up, he also read a resolution of the official board, (his own creation) the substance of which was, "that if, through insufficient evidence or wrong information, any had been unjustly 'withdrawn,' they might appear before the next official meeting and they would reverse their action and reinstate them to their former position." "Now," writes the brother, "if we had any knowledge what we were turned out for, we might appear before that august body. There is not one of us that has been reproved by pastor or class-leader. The pastor said the case of Brother J. was a very clear one; for about one year before, a Protestant minister had held a protracted meeting in the school-house in Brother J.'s neighborhood, and was instrumental in the conversion of some of his children. Brother J. paid something for his support, thinking it to be his duty to do so, and notwithstanding he has attended preaching and class-meeting as regularly as he ever did, he is now read out of the M. E. Church for that single act; and the pastor said this *was a very clear case.* There is Popery for you with a vengeance!

The official board voted sister R. out, but before the quarterly meeting, they found out that she had paid her quarterage—some *fifty cents.* So they held a special meeting and voted her in again!

But blessed be God, though we are cast out we are not forsaken, for God is with us of a truth. After the action of the official board we organized ourselves into a band. Our meetings continue to increase in numbers and in interest. Two young men have been converted and have joined, and others are seeking.
T. S. C.

THE EARNEST CHRISTIAN.

WE are truly thankful to our Heavenly Father for the favor which he gives our magazine in the eyes of His children. We commenced it from a conviction of duty, at quite a pecuniary risk. Subscribers have come in from all sections of the country, beyond our most sanguine expectations. It is no longer an experiment. Its success is established.

We are gratified with the many expressions of approbation it receives from those whose approbation we prize.

A preacher in Vermont, a stranger to us in the flesh, but partaker of the precious faith, writes:

"I am beginning to think much, very much, of the *Earnest Christian.* The January number did not impress me very favorably, but the February number was much better, and the last is better still—it is full of power. I have just finished reading its strongest articles, and they so perfectly harmonize with my views, feelings, and preaching, that I must sit down and speak a word of encouragement to you. And the great feeling of my heart is this: God bless Brother Roberts in his uncompromising fidelity to *pure Bible truth.* Your last article on PEW RENTING is just the thing for these times. I give it my unqualified and unshrinking approval. It will stand the fires of the last day. Sister Smith's article is characterized by directness and searching truth, and consequently power. It should be read by all professing Christians. All the articles of this number which I have read are excellent, and I shall make an effort right away to get some to subscribe for you."
J. F. C.

A local preacher of the Genesee Conference writes: "I am more and more pleased with the *Earnest Christian.* I have only one source of anxiety on its account, viz: How can it be sustained and continued as good as it is now? But God will inspire writers as well as speakers, and I pray God that all who write for its pages will have the inspiration in their souls of an Earnest Christianity."
W. H.

BACK NUMBERS.—We can supply back numbers for a few hundred new subscribers. Will our friends take a little pains, show the E. C. to their neighbors, induce them to subscribe for it and send on their names, with the money, without delay? We shall try to make each number of the Magazine as good or a little better than its predecessor.

DIRECTIONS.—Write proper names very plainly, giving Post Office, County and State. If you wish the direction of your Magazine changed, be sure to give the Post Office where you have received it as well as that to which you wish it sent.

THE EARNEST CHRISTIAN.

VOL. I.   MAY, 1860.   NO. 5.

SALVATION FROM SIN.

BY THE EDITOR.

Sin is always an injury. It is polluting in its nature, and damning in its effects. When "it is finished, it brings forth death." Every awakened soul longs for deliverance from its dominion. No one can be rescued from its power and guilt, without often feeling a strong desire to have every sinful temper that has brought him into bondage, completely destroyed. The prayer of his heart is,

"Break off the yoke of inbred sin,
And fully set my spirit free."

Does the Bible teach us the possibility of having every wrong propensity of the soul destroyed? We are aware that some passages look, at first view, as though the continuance of sin in the soul was unavoidable. Let us give the more prominent of these a careful and candid examination. The first to which we call attention is found in 1 Kings, viii, 46: "If they sin against thee, (for there is no man that sinneth not.)" In the original Hebrew the word that is translated "sinneth" is in the future tense. "This tense," says Stuart, in his Hebrew Grammar, page 207, "designates all those shades of meaning, which we express in English by the auxiliaries *may*, can, *must*, *might*, could, should, *would*," etc. Thus, Gen. iii, 2: "We may eat of the fruit of the trees of the garden." The term "may eat," is, in the original, in the future tense. So, also, 1 Kings, viii, 40: "That they may fear thee." The phrase "may fear," is in the future tense in the Hebrew. The same is true of the phrase "may know," in the 43d verse, "That all people of the earth may know thy name." Hence, a literal translation of the 46th verse would read "If they sin against thee, (for there is no man that may not sin.)" This teaches, not that every man does actually and necessarily sin, but that *every one is liable* to sin. There is a *possibility* but not a *necessity* that he should sin. So, also, the supposition, "*if they sin*," implies that they might sin, or they might not. It expresses a contingency that could not exist if sin were unavoidable. That they might not sin, is clearly implied in the declaration that if they did, God would be angry with them, and deliver them into the hands of their enemies, so that they should be carried into captivity. But as this was not necessary, it follows that it was not necessary that they should sin.

Most of the above remarks will apply to the passage found in Eccl. vii, 20: "For there is not a just man upon earth that doeth good and sinneth not." The word "sinneth," is in the original, in the future tense, and should also, be rendered "may sin." This passage teaches the doctrine that runs all through the Bible, that we are never secure from the danger of falling. In our best estate, when grace has done the most for us, we have great need to "watch and pray that we enter not into temptation," to "keep our bodies under and bring them into subjection,' lest we should "become castaways."

Prov. xx, 9: "Who can say, I have made my heart clean, I am pure from my sin." This passage is intended to reprove the boasting of a self-righteous, conceited Pharisee, who not only claims a goodness he does not possess, but ascribes his fancied purity to himself. If we offer up in fervent desire, and a faith that will not be denied, the prayer of David, "Create in me a clean heart, O God," who shall say that this prayer will not be answered? God alone is able to purify the soul. It is only by coming to Him in importunate supplication that we can obey the Apostle's direction, "Cleanse your hands, ye sinners, and purify your hearts, ye double-minded."

"I cannot wash my heart;
But my believing thee,
And waiting for thy blood t' impart
The spotless purity."

In this way alone can God's command be met. "O Jerusalem, wash thine heart from wickedness that thou mayst be saved."

Job ix, 20: "If I justify myself, mine own mouth shall condemn me; if I say I am perfect, it shall also prove me perverse."

In this chapter Job treats of the majesty and holiness of God. In the 15th verse he says: "Whom though I were righteous, yet would I not answer, but I would make supplication to my judge." Before the infinite purity of God he counted his righteousness as nothing, however he might lift up his head in the presence of his fellow man. Thus, in the verse above, we understand Job to say, "If I justify myself" before God "mine own mouth," in the prayers that I make for the mercy of the Lord, " shall condemn me." He did justify himself most triumphantly before man, and repelled the accusations which his friends, unable to reconcile his afflictions with the supposition of his innocence had brought against him. If I say "I am perfect" in God's sight of myself, " it shall also prove me perverse." His perfect humility here manifested justifies the testimony that the Lord, who cannot be deceived, gives in his favor. "Hast thou considered my servant Job, that there is none like him in the earth, a PERFECT *and an upright man, one that feareth God and escheweth evil?*"

Job xiv, 4: "Who can bring a clean thing out of an unclean? not one." This text refers to the natural depravity that belongs to every one that is born into the world—to what is commonly termed original sin. It teaches that all are by nature depraved, not that this depravity cannot be removed by grace. The Septuagint—the Greek version of the Old Testament, from which our Saviour and the Apostles generally quoted, thus renders it: "For who is pure from corruption? Not one, although his life upon the earth be but one day."

Isa. vi, 5: "Wo is me! for I am undone; because I am a man of unclean lips." This is true of all while in their natural unsanctified condition, yet let us read on and we shall see that the SPIRIT OF GOD, represented by "a live coal" "from off the altar" touched his lips, so that his "iniquity was taken away," and his "sin was purged."

Isa. lxiv, 6: "All our righteousnesses are as filthy rags." The Jews were exceedingly corrupted in the days of Isaiah. The prophet being humbled and alarmed at the general wickedness of his people, confesses it in the first person, as ministers generally do on such occasions. It is the hypocritical righteousness of the ungodly—a strict observance of the forms and ceremonies of religion while living in sin—that the prophet compares to filthy rags.

Rom. vii, 14: "I am carnal, sold under sin." In this connection, the Apostle speaks of himself in different stages of inward experience. 1. As an unawakened Jew: "I was alive without the law once." 2. As a convicted sinner: "But when the commandment came" to my comprehension, "sin revived, and I died." My hopes perished. 3. As a believer in Christ: "For the law of the Spirit of life in Christ Jesus, hath made me free from the law of sin and death." Now, " being made free from sin," and become truly the "servant of God," he had his "fruit unto holiness, and the end everlasting life." That the Apostle, in the above passage, refers to himself prior to his conversion, is the opinion of President Edwards, a Congregationalist divine, who, for learning and piety, and philosophical acumen, never had a superior in this country: who says, "The Apostle Paul, speaking of what he was *naturally*, says, "I am carnal, sold under sin."

1 John i, 8: "If we say that we have no sin, we deceive ourselves and the truth is not in us." That this refers to man in his *natural* condition, is evident. The Apostle is speaking about the power of Jesus' blood *to cleanse us from all sin*. It is those who falsely and dangerously trusting to their own morality and their naturally aimable dispositions, say that they do not need to be "cleansed from sin," that the Apostle applies the above verse. But being convinced that we are sinners, both by nature and by practice, he assures us that "If we confess our sins, he is faithful and just to forgive us our sins, and to CLEANSE US FROM ALL UNRIGHTEOUSNESS."

These, we believe, are the strongest passages ever brought forward to prove the necessary continuance of sin. Look at them candidly and you will be satisfied that we have given them their true meaning.

Let us ask you, beloved reader, are you at the present time saved from sin? You may have been once. That cannot help you now. It only makes your condition still more deplorable, if you are now under the dominion of sin. Seek deliverance at once. Give no quarters. Let every sin die. Salvation from sin can alone secure salvation in Heaven. As Toplady, a pious Calvinist, sings—

"The grace that saves the soul from hell,
Will save from present sin."

One house, one day's food, and one suit of raiment are sufficient for thee; and if thou die before noon, thou hast one-half too much.—ARABIC PROVERB.

Spiritual pride takes great notice of opposition and injuries that are received, and is apt to be often speaking of them, and to be much in taking notice of the aggravations of them, either with an air of bitterness or contempt: whereas, pure unmixed Christian humility disposes a person rather to be like his blessed Lord, when reviled, dumb, not opening his mouth, but committing himself in silence to Him that judgeth righteously. The eminently humble Christian, the more clamorous and furious the world is against him, the more silent and still will he be; unless it be in his closet, and there he will not be still. Our blessed Lord Jesus seems never to have been so silent as when the world compassed him round, reproaching, buffeting, and spitting on him, with loud and virulent outcries, and horrid cruelties.—EDWARDS.

A graceless heart is not quickly and easily brought to *see the hand of* GOD in those troubles that befall it, and to be duly affected with it. "Lord, when thy hand is lifted up, they will not see." When it has smitten, or is lifted up to smite, they shut their eyes. It is the malice of this man, or the negligence of that, or the unfaithfulness of another, that has brought all this trouble upon me. Thus, the creature is the horizon that terminates their Sight, and beyond that they usually see nothing. Sometimes, indeed, the hand of God is so convincingly manifested in affliction, that they cannot avoid the sight of it; and then they may, in their way, pour out a prayer before him; but ordinarily they impute all to second causes, and overlook the first cause of their troubles.—FLAVEL.

I am persuaded much of the credit and comfort of Christianity is lost, in consequence of its professors fixing their aims too low, and not conceiving of their high and holy calling in so elevated and sublime a view as the nature of religion would require and the Word of God would direct.—DODDRIDGE.

SPIRITUAL FREEDOM.

The following extract from a letter written in July last, by a lawyer in Michigan, of devoted piety, to a brother in Syracuse, though not intended for publication, is so pertinent to the present state of affairs that we have concluded to give it to our readers:

Mrs. H. and myself are lovers of the truth, and greatly rejoice in its progressive development in the human mind.

We entertain no hopes, however, of a Christian reform of the denominations now in operation. A *radical, moral* reform of an ecclesiastical organism is unknown in history. Therefore we regard the *exodus* of the Christian Pilgrims from the ecclesiastical Egypt, as a necessity, and of consequence irresistible. The army of the Lord is on its homeward march, and woe betide all its opposing forces. The powers of evil, both in the body, and out of the body, must give way for its upward advance. This army is returning to God, with shouts of " Liberty !" and " songs " of deliverance, and everlasting joy upon their heads.

The free and full development of the Divine life, in the female heart, presents to our mind scenes of the brightest moral grandeur. It is the key-note of that universal anthem which will be sung by all the inhabitants of the " new heavens and the new earth," saying, " Glory to God in the highest, on earth peace and good will towards men." Look at it, my brother, look at this appalling scene, and estimate, if you can, its awful, soul-destroying effect. For more than eighteen hundred years past, woman, Christian woman! has been and *is* the innocent victim of *Satanic prejudice*. Look into all the churches, or into any of them. Look, for example, into the " Discipline " of that church organization of which we are members (one of the most liberal in its polity of all the churches.) Look there and you will find no provision for the exercise and encouragement of the talents, gifts and graces of the female disciple of Jesus. No provision is there found authorizing a " Mary " to " go to my brethren and say unto them, I ascend unto my Father, and to your Father, and to my God and your God." No *authority* to the female soul that is in labor for the salvation of sinners to say, " Behold the Lamb of God, who taketh away the sins of the world."

No *man authority* in the churches to a Christian female to say any of the words of Jesus—however amply qualified she may be by nature and Divine Grace. Look at this appalling subject, my brother, for the heavens behold! How must the churches on earth appear in the eye of the Lord, as their " chief men and captains " are engaged in forging the chains of ecclesiastical despotism, and coiling those chains around the more delicate members of Christ's body ? How must it sound in the ears of the Lord, as He hears the dark, puny, ignorant spirit in man, dictating the Holy Ghost in His mighty workings in the human soul ! ! What awful presumption ! What Satanic arrogance ! Yet this is daily done by men denominating themselves Christians.

The Lord says, " Your sons and your *daughters* shall prophecy."

But Satan says Your *sons* may prophecy, but your daughters shall not prophecy ; and to this prohibition all the rulers in the churches say Amen ! All are, or appear to be, in league with Satan to suppress the Holy Spirit in women. All the church creeds and formulas seal the lips of Jesus in the heart of His female disciple—in the soul of His little ones. A majority of the members of Christ's body on earth, are paralyzed by Satanic prejudice—because Satan entertains and manifests a more deadly hatred of woman than he does of man, for the reason that woman gave birth to Satan's destroyer. Into the masculine element of human nature Satan infuses his own vile spirit, thus causing depraved man to bind and lacerate the members of Christ's body, knowing that truth (or Jesus) cannot triumph, while his disciples are at war with each other. At this day, "the Bride, the Lamb's wife," is agonizing and weeping tears of blood, to be released of this inferno—ecclesiastical oppression and suppression. Her cries have gone up, her tears are numbered, and I hear a voice sounding down from the heavens, saying, "Liberty to the captives!" O Power Divine! dissolve every chain and bond, that holds to evil.

Yours, in Christian freedom,
M. A. H.

Do not expect to be made happy by religion, unless you become *eminent Christians*. A *half-way* Christian can neither enjoy the pleasures of the world nor the pleasures of religion; for his conscience will not let him seek the one, and he is too indolent to obtain the other. The Christian may be the happiest man on earth, but he must be a *faithful, active and devoted Christian*.—BAXTER.

Reader, be on thy guard: thou mayest fall by comparatively small matters, while resolutely and successfully resisting those which require a giant's strength to counteract them. In every concern God is necessary: Seek him for the *body* and for the *soul*: and do not think that anything that concerns thy present or eternal peace is too small or insignificant to interest Him.—ADAM CLARKE.

The godly have found by experience, that prayer, with quiet waiting in the use of means, getteth comfortably through, where overcaring and carnal policy, in the use of all other shifts, hath been forced to stick.—FULFILLING OF THE SCRIPTURE.

It is the true character of a self-deceiver to make a religion to himself of the cheapest part of God's service, which he endeavors to reconcile with his selfish ends, and to reject the rest.—BAXTER.

WATCHING FOR MORNING.

I am watching for the morning;
  The night is long and dreary;
I have waited for the dawning
  Till I am sad and weary;
I am watching for the morning,
  When the sons of God shall show
All their beauteous adorning
  So dimly seen below.

I'm a stranger and sojourner,
  A pilgrim on the earth;
A sick and lonely mourner,
  Few own my noble birth:
But I am watching for the morning—
  Oh when will morning come—
And I change the world's rude scorning
  For the fellowship of home.

They call me strange and gloomy,
  But oh! they little dream,
Of the hopes that fill my bosom,
  For I am not what I seem—
I am watching for the morning
  When he who for me died,
In triumphant state returning,
  Shall claim the church his bride.

They often find me weeping
  When I cannot tell them why,
For they know not the deep meaning
  Of my spirit's sympathy;
I am watching for the morning
  Of a bright and glorious day,
That shall hush creation's groaning
  And wipe her tears away.

The earnest expectation
  Of all nature is abroad;
Waiting the manifestation
  Of the true sons of God;
And I'm watching for the morning
  That shall *set the captive free,*
And shall change the chains of bondage
  Into glorious liberty.

I will get me to the mountain
  Till the shadows flee away;
I will ask of all the watchmen
  For the *tokens of the day.*
I am watching for the morning,
  The night is *almost* gone;
I *hear* their note of warning,
  I will hie me to *my home.*

WILLIAM CLOWES.

BY THE EDITOR.

The human body possesses no inherent power of self-preservation. No matter how massive in its proportions, how symmetrical in its form, or how fair its aspects, no qualities can save it from corruption when vitality is fled. So it is with Christians. He is a living Christian in whom the Holy Ghost dwells. Let the Spirit be grieved by disobedience or neglect, until He takes his departure as a controlling power, and no correctness of creed, nor outward propriety of conduct can prevent the loss of spiritual life.

No quality or process has ever yet been discovered, by which churches may be preserved in purity and simplicity. As with individuals, so with associations, the natural tendency is to depart from God. Neither doctrines, nor government, nor ritual, can destroy this tendency. The church at Ephesus was planted under the most favorable auspices. The apostle Paul, traveling through Asia Minor, found at Ephesus a few disciples. He instructed them, and labored with them in the gospel, until they were fully saved, and were endowed with the Holy Ghost. With the church thus started he spared no pains, "to present them perfect in Christ Jesus," laboring with them night and day for the space of three years. He kept back "nothing that was profitable to them," but declared unto them "all the counsel of God." Of the piety of the church thus planted and established, he speaks in the highest terms. Yet in a few years Jesus pronounces this very church fallen! Though they still kept up the form, the profession, and the morals of Christianity, and were an orthodox working church, they had lost their first love, and had become objects of loathing to Christ! This great change took place in the life-time of the apostles.

There probably never was a church that had its foundation in greater irregularities than did the Methodist societies. John Wesley, a presbyter of the Church of England, openly and systematically violated the plainest of her canons. He utterly disregarded parochial limits, going from place to place proclaiming the Gospel, and when, as was often the case, the churches were closed against him, he went into the highways and places of public resort, with the messages of mercy. He organized societies and licensed ministers. Whenever his fellow clergymen endeavored to impair his usefulness, by exciting a prejudice against him, he meted out to them the severest reproof. To the archbishop of York, who, in a pastoral address, had warned his clergy against the Methodists, Wesley wrote, "O, my lord, what manner of words are these! Supposing candour and love out of the question, are they the words of truth? I dare stake my life upon it there is not one true clause in all this paragraph." The clergy he charged with "setting themselves with all their might against a glorious work of God," and said there were among them "ungodly and unholy men, openly, undeniably such—drunkards, gluttons, returners of evil for evil, liars, swearers, profaners of the day of the Lord." Notwithstanding all this, John Wesley was permitted to live and die, a member of the church whose rules he thus violated, and whose clergy he thus exposed to contempt!

Yet strange to say, the church he thus founded, expelled from her communion, within twenty years after the death of Wesley, a pious and useful preacher, for the crime of attending camp or field meetings, "contrary to the Methodist discipline!"

William Clowes, the preacher referred to, one of the founders, under God, of the "Primitive Methodist Connexion," was born in Staffordshire, England, on the 12th of March, 1780. His father, pious in early youth, lost his religion in consequence of reading a pernicious book and remained "wild and dissipated" till near the close of life. At the age of ten years, William was apprenticed to learn the potter's trade, the business which his father followed. His literary advantages were poor, and poorly improved. He plunged into vice, he became an expert at dancing, with which was associated banqueting, gambling, drinking, swearing and fighting. "In the exercise of the last," he says, "my body has often been so beaten, that I have been nearly covered with bruises. Indeed, on one occasion, I was carried out of the room where I had been fighting, apparently dead, and a medical man was sent for to ascertain whether any symptoms of life remained." A strange training this for the founder of a new religious denomination, which was to number its converts by thousands, and among them the celebrated Spurgeon! But God can send by whom he will.

The Spirit of God, a "manifestation" of which "is given to every man to profit withal," arrested him from time to time in his wild career. Once when assembled with a party to dance, God so impressed him with a consciousness that his life had been spent in flagrant sin, that "great distress of mind followed." He was so ashamed that he left the place at once without speaking a word to any person, fearing that unless he did so, the Lord would take away his life and send him to hell. Running home he aroused his parents, who, supposing his distress to arise from some sudden attack of disease, administered to him tobacco smoke and gin! This, as is generally the case with all such prescriptions for sin-sick souls, only increased the anguish it was intended to remove. He besought his mother to pray for him, prayed himself, and promised the Lord that if he would spare his life he would give body and soul to his service. But he soon forgot his vows and again plunged headlong into sin.

With the hope of aiding him in his reformation he married; but he found his disposition remained unchanged. Becoming offended with his wife and her mother, he left them to go into another part of the country. Taking his mother's prayer book without her knowledge, he read in it and wept over it, as he sat down to rest by the way. He took an oath to abstain from drinking, but yielded to almost the first temptation with which he was assailed. Again "the Spirit of God," he says, "wrought upon me in such a manner, that I expected every moment for the space of two hours my soul would have been hurled into hell." Again he promised God that if He would spare him he would love and obey Him, but in a few days was "the same reckless, violent and miserable creature" as before.

At length these terrible conflicts between the Spirit of God and strong passions confirmed by indulgence, were to have a glorious termination. In a love-feast, to which he gained admission by artifice, he saw the folly of trying to serve God in his own strength, and clinging to the society of dissipated and ungodly associates." He resolved to give up with his besetting sins, his wicked companions, and to attend religious meetings. The next morning at seven o'clock he went to a prayer-meeting. "The meeting," he says, "was what some would term a noisy one, but I was not affected on that account; I felt I had enough to do for myself. The power of heaven came down upon me, and I cried for help to Him who is mighty to save. It was towards the close of the meeting when I felt my bonds breaking; and when this change was taking place, I thought within myself, what is this? This I said is what the Methodists mean by conversion; yes, this is it—God is converting my soul. In an agony of prayer, I believed God would save me —then I believed he was saving me— then I believed he had saved me, and it was so. I said God has pardoned all my sins."

The grace thus received was severely tested. But it was from God, and so it nobly stood the trial. His evil habits were at once broken up, his passions, which had exercised such tyrannical sway over him, were subdued by a power far superior to human resolution, and from that period till the close of life, though "narrowly watched by the world's malignant eye," he lived without a stain upon his character. Soon after he received the pardon of his sins he was assailed by the temptation that he had deceived himself—that he had "mistaken the drawings of the Father for conversion." Satan now whispered in his ear, "It is all over with thee. Thou hast sinned against the Holy Ghost in telling the people thou art pardoned, whereas thou art not." Under these powerful temptations his heart almost died within him. He acquainted his class leader with his distress. While following his advice, and going to the Lord in fervent prayer, he says, "the glorious power came down upon my soul, and such was the manifestation, that I instantly sprang to my feet and shouted "Glory! Glory!" with all my strength. My wife tried to stop me in vain, by telling me that the neighbors would hear me, and conclude that I had gone beside myself."

From this period on, though strongly assailed at times by the adversary of souls, he was borne upon the wings of love and praise, "in the world but not of the world." He took his leave of all his wicked associates, joined the Methodists, and commenced at once reproving sin, and persuading all he could to seek that salvation which he had found to be

A sovereign balm for every wound,
A cordial for our fears.

The conversion of his wife followed soon after his own.

While pursuing his wicked career, he had contracted debts in different places, and then left without ever intending to pay them. These he set himself to work to cancel. As many of them were of long standing, his creditors had given up all hope of ever receiving any thing from him. But he did not leave them in doubt as to the motives that influenced him to make restitution. In the letters containing his remittances, he told his creditors that "God had converted his soul," a fact they were not disposed to question after the tangible evidence with which they were furnished.

His house was opened for prayer-meetings, which were attended by all that the room could hold. "They were," he says, "mighty meetings, times of refreshing from the presence of the Lord. God saved souls in every room of the house, and in the pantry also."

He toiled all day at his trade, and every evening attended meetings, in which he usually labored till his strength failed. His Sabbath labors were excessive, commencing with a prayer meeting at six o'clock, and continuing almost unceasingly till late at night. Yet in the midst of all this labor, he says, "I felt strong, active, and unspeakably happy in God. My peace flowed like a river. My soul enjoyed such ecstacy, both night and day, that the time I spent in sleep was comparatively trifling."

Appointed a class-leader at Kidsgrove, the class-meetings greatly increased in usefulness, and many of the roughest colliers were brought to God. At one of these meetings many of the wicked came in, some of whom were half drunk. In doubt at first as to what course to pursue, he began personally to address the ungodly, and, he says, "As I proceeded, some of them were struck with such terror and alarm that they jumped up and rushed out of the house." They confessed afterwards that they "thought they should have fallen into hell if they had remained any longer, and they should take care not to go to William Clowes' class again." "The meeting being thus tolerably cleared, a mighty shout of glory went through the house, and many were saved of the Lord."

Thus far everything had gone on smoothly. Happy in his soul, and encouraged by his brethren, he labored in harmony with the preachers, and was often sent out to fill the appointments of the local ministers. But now new trials awaited him. He came in conflict with church authority. The occasion was this. An association, of which he was a member, was formed for the suppression of Sabbath breaking. In carrying out their object, they complained of several inn-keepers who allowed tippling in their houses on the Sabbath, contrary to law, and had them fined. The anger of the publicans was aroused. They went to the circuit steward, a wine and spirit merchant, of whom they bought their liquors, and told him that unless he endeavored in future to prevent the operations of this association, they should withdraw their patronage. The steward, whose craft was in danger, conferred with the preacher in charge of the circuit, and a meeting was called to put a stop to the obnoxious proceedings. The members of the association were told that "their conduct gave general dissatisfaction," and that if they "went on any longer they should be considered forthwith as expelled from the Methodist Society." The wicked, encouraged by the rulers of the church, came upon the association with redoubled fury, and seeing that it was hopeless to attempt to stem so high a tide of opposition, it was abandoned.

The steward and preacher then went to a Mr. Smith, in whose house William Clowes, with others, held a prayer meeting, and persuaded him that it was very wrong to have such "noises made" in the prayer meeting; that "such loud praying should be put an end to," as it was "very inconsistent." Mr. Smith made a vigorous effort to obey the directions of his spiritual rulers, but the faith of the praying band was too mighty for him, and he gave up vanquished.

Assisted from above, Mr. Clowes labored with increasing power to promote the work of the Lord in the class, and prayer meetings. "Many a time," he says, "I felt humbled in the dust before God to hear the people in speaking their experience, attribute their conversion and getting good, under God, to my instrumentality. The feelings of gratitude, joy, and astonishment, filled my soul in such a manner, whilst I listened to the recital of these things, that I often gave vent to my intense feelings, and shouts of praise and glory my lips did utter. But there were several persons who did not relish these demonstrations, and I was occasionally told to cease my noise in the love-feasts, as by my shouts of glory I made the chapel like a cock-pit. But the more this sort of disapprobation was expressed towards me, the more the people who had been blessed through my labors rejoiced aloud, and the more I was also constrained to give glory to God."

In 1807, about two years after his conversion, Mr. Clowes was regularly licensed to preach. His name appeared on the preachers' plan with appointments. These appointments he punctually supplied, and in connection with Hugh and James Bourne, James Nixon and others, assisted at camp meetings, so called, held in different parts of the country.

These meetings generally lasted but one day—usually Sunday—commencing at six o'clock in the morning, and continuing till dark. No particular order appears to have been observed. They were held by men of strong faith, who believed in the Holy Ghost, and they preached, exhorted, prayed and sung as the "Spirit gave them utterance." Sometimes four or more would be preaching at once. Praying services were held in different parts of the ground, and direct efforts were put forth for the salvation of souls. Multitudes were attracted to these meetings, and many were saved.

But they were not popular with the formal professors. "Much uneasiness," he says, was manifested by certain parties in the Burslem circuit on account of the camp meetings, and my attending them. Accordingly in the June quarter of 1810, my name was omitted on the preachers' plan." This, according to the usages of the church, was a deposition from the ministry. This intolerant measure created quite an excitement, and invitations to preach were sent to him from all parts of the country.

In September following, without the useless formality of a trial, he was excluded from the society. When he inquired at the leader's meeting the cause of his expulsion, he was told that it was "because he attended camp meetings contrary to the Methodist discipline," and that he "could not be a preacher or leader amongst them unless he promised not to attend them any more." He assured them that he would "attend to all the appointments that might be given him, and to all the means of grace and ordinances of the church; but he could not promise not to attend any more camp meetings, as God had greatly blessed him in these meetings which he believed were calculated for great usefulness." He was then told that he was no longer with them—that the matter was settled. "I therefore," he adds, "immediately delivered up my class papers and became unchurched."

A few days after, some of the members of his late classes came to him, and desired him to continue to lead them in the way to Heaven. He told them that if they thought it was the will of the Lord, they might come to his house and he would give them such advice and instruction as he was able. They went accordingly, and James Nixon, Thomas Woodnorth, and two others, left the Methodist society and went with them. The number of members was between thirty and forty. The Mr. Smith referred to above, opened his kitchen for a preaching place.

Such was the position of affairs that James Nixon and Thomas Woodnorth proposed to William Clowes, that if he would devote his whole time to the work of saving souls, they would each give him for the support of his family, five shillings a week out of their wages. To this he and his wife readily consented, although he could make four or five times that amount at his trade. He then went out upon preaching excursions in different portions of the country, and was encouraged by seeing souls converted to God. The persecutions and hardships which he endured were cheerfully borne, for his was a joyous and triumphant faith.

Returning to Tunstall, the place of his residence, he found the work still progressing. Their first love feast was held in Mr. Smith's kitchen. Such was the feeling against them among their old friends, the Methodists, that they actually turned out one of their most influential members, a Mr. James Steele, the "leader of two classes, a chapel steward, and superintendent of a large Sunday school," upon the false supposition that he had attended this love feast! The Sunday after, Mr. Steele went to open the Sunday school as usual, when one of the officials ordered him out of the pulpit. He submitted, and withdrew from the house, when nearly all the teachers and scholars followed. He exhorted them to return, stating that perhaps something would be done in the course of the week. During the week, Mr. Boden, a master potter, offered a large unoccupied room to teach the school in, and his offer was accepted. He also gave them permission to have Sunday preaching in it, and regular services were established in Tunstall," a place famous in the annals of the primitive Methodists, and which place became the head of the first circuit in the Connexion."

Mr. Steele's two classes continued to go to him for spiritual instruction. Hugh and James Bourne had taken the charge of a class at Stanley, in March, 1810. These two brothers also supported a home missionary, James Crawfoot. These all labored together in harmony.

In July, 1811, a partial organization was effected, Mr. Steele was chosen circuit steward—the salaries of the traveling preachers or "missionaries" was fixed, contributions were raised for their support, preaching appointments were made and regularly filled, and quarterly tickets were given to all the members of their classes. They now had two traveling preachers, fifteen local preachers, two hundred members and seventeen preaching places.

When societies were formed and established, they were left in the care of the local preachers and class-leaders, and the "missionaries" sought new openings for preaching the Gospel. No special effort seems to have been put forth to form new societies, but a large share of the fruits of the labors of these men of God, was reaped by the Church that had so unkindly thrust them from her bosom.

These desultory labors were continued till the 2nd of May, 1820, when the first conference of the primitive Methodists was held. This was composed of six traveling preachers, and twelve laymen. The state and prospects of the body were considered very encouraging; the number in society being 7,842. They had, during the session of the conference, preaching morning and evening, and three "camp meetings" on the Sabbath.

From this period the work assumed a regular aspect, and spread with much greater rapidity. The opposition to them from their old friends remained unabated. Thus at Marton, says Mr. Clowes, "Mark Noble, a Wesleyan class-leader wished to help us in our work, and to lead one of our classes; but this course met with censure from head quarters. He was ordered to desist leading our class, or give up his own. He was unwilling to do either, and suffered judgment to be passed upon him, which was, his expulsion from the Wesleyan society. He then became one of us. We employed him in the office of a local preacher, and he went on his way rejoicing. His house, which had been a comfortable home for the Wesleyan preachers, was abandoned by them because we were admitted to share the hospitalities of the family. The result was, we then became the only guests, and two of the daughters joined us, and became useful in the cause."

The preachers of this new sect were opposed and ridiculed everywhere they went. Even the once despised name of "Methodist" was refused them, and the appellation of "ranters" was commonly applied to them to bring into reproach the earnestness with which their religious exercises were conducted.

They had no men of commanding talents or influence, but the Lord was with them, and gave them unparalleled prosperity in their humble earnest efforts to do good. At their third conference held in May, 1822, the number of members was found to be 25,218—an increase of 17,376, or over 300 per cent. in two years.

At the present time they number, according to an article carefully prepared by Rev. C. Prindle, editor of the *Wesleyan*, 116,216 members, 609 circuit preachers, and 10,533 local preachers. "They have been" says Mr. P., in formal existence for forty years, and number 126,358—not far from three times as many as the parent body did in the same number of years."

Their government is liberal, their conference being composed of one-third traveling preachers, the other two-thirds being local preachers or laymen. They hold, in practice as well as in theory, that the gifts of the Holy Ghost constitute the main elements for success in the work of saving souls; and the exercise of these they encourage wherever found, whether among men or women. Some of their earliest and most successful travelling preachers were females.

Their "General Minutes" or Discipline, contains the following provision:

"A female travelling preacher shall receive two guineas a quarter, for the first and second years of her travelling, and fifty shillings a quarter during every successive year; and for her board and lodgings there must be allowed the same amount as is allowed to single male preachers according to the rule."

Every preacher is required to employ all his time in saving souls; four hours a day being allowed to study; and the balance to be devoted to family "visiting, and other active ministerial labors." He is required to make at least thirty family visits a week, throughout the year. "He must not be a member of any society called 'Order of Odd Fellows,' 'Secret Order' or any other name of a similar kind."

The connexion has had, as is stated

in the preface to the "Deed Poll, or charter of incorporation," great trials, with little apparent prospect of standing its ground.

"But, by the providence and grace of God, it rose amidst its difficulties, and many were converted to God, and other communities gathered of the fruits of its labors."

"It has been a means in the hand of God, of reviving open-air worship."

"It has also been instrumental in assisting to set forth and maintain the doctrines of a free, full and present salvation, through and by faith in the Lord Jesus Christ."

LAURENCE SAUNDERS, THE MARTYR.—Bonner, the bishop of London, desired him to write what he believed of transubstantiation. This Saunders did, saying, "My Lord, you seek my blood, and you shall have it: I pray God you may be so baptised in it, that you may ever after loathe blood-sucking, and become a better man." When being closely charged with *contumacy*, the severe replies of Mr. Saunders to the bishop so irritated him, that he exclaimed, "Carry away this frenzied fool to prison!"

On the 8th of February, 1555, he was led to the place of execution, in the park, without the city; he went in an old gown and a shirt, bare-footed; and oftentimes fell flat on the ground, and prayed. When he was come nigh to the place, the officer appointed to see the execution done, said to Mr. Saunders, that he was one of those who marred the Queen's realm; but if he would recant, there was pardon for him. "Not I," replied the holy martyr, "but such as you, have injured the realm. The blessed gospel of Christ is what I hold; that do I believe, that have I taught, and that I will never revoke!" Mr. Saunders then slowly moved towards the fire, sank to the earth, and prayed; he then rose up, embraced the stake, and frequently said, "Welcome, thou cross of Christ! welcome, everlasting life!" Fire was then put to the fagots; and he was overwhelmed in the dreadful flames, and sweetly slept in the Lord Jesus.

What will the reader think, when he is told that this martyr was of a timid disposition! and yet here we see with what constancy he died. This is a strong proof that there must be an almighty power working through faith in the hearts of those who are punished for the truth.

This is strongly verified in a conversation which took place between Dr. Pendleton and Mr. Saunders. The Doctor encouraged his friend to act heroically, and die a martyr for the truth; urging that he should himself have much more to bear from the agonies of burning, being a larger and lustier man; but how are the mighty often humbled! This proud talker turned apostate, and the humble Saunders *acted* that brave holy character the other knew only to talk of.—Fox.

SIN.—One way of sin lived in will wonderfully keep you down in your spiritual prosperity, and in the growth and strength of grace in your hearts. It will grieve the Holy Spirit of God, and will, in a great measure, banish him from you; this will prevent the good influence of the word and ordinances of God to the causing of grace to flourish in you. It will be a great obstacle to their good effect. It will be like an ulcer within a man, which, while it remains, will keep him weak and lean, though you feed him with ever so wholesome food, or feast him ever so daintily.—EDWARDS.

My heart is so enlarged to the poor, especially the Lord's poor, that I am in danger of making myself poor. I find the more I am found in this labor of love, the more the Lord finds out ways and opportunities for it; and sometimes causes others, even the most unlikely, to assist me. O, it is sweet to act for my God; to give to the Lord through the medium of his own poor precious people.—LADY MAXWELL.

HIGH PROFESSIONS.

BY N. M. DOWNING.

Many professed Christians, among whom are some ministers of the Gospel, make a great ado about high professions—such as holiness, sanctification, and perfect love. They look suspiciously at those who make them, treat them coldly, and in some instances go so far as to impeach their moral character, while at the same time *they* profess to be Christians, thereby professing to be the "light of the world," and the "salt of the earth." We have been shocked to behold the irritation of some, while the redeemed of the Lord have spoken in humility, yet with holy boldness, of the triumphs of grace; declaring they had, through the blood of the Lamb, achieved a victory over the world, the flesh and the Devil, and that the Holy Ghost was their present sanctifier. These objectors to high professions dare not profess holiness themselves, for the sufficient reason that they have it not.

As there is such an aversion to high professions of religious attainment, we wish to ask the question, is the profession of holiness higher, and does it impose a greater individual responsibility to God, as far as ourselves are concerned, than the profession of being a Christian? We answer no; for every one who professes to be a Christian professes to live without *sin;* for Christ did *no sin*, neither was *guile* found in His mouth; and every one who professes to be a Christian, professes to be *like* Christ, in *spirit, word and deed*. This is all the professor of holiness claims, and this is the *lowest* state of *saving* grace. And, instead of such a life being peculiar to the sanctified soul alone, it is the life of all who walk in the light of justifying grace. Let us substantiate this somewhat controverted point by the Word of God. Rom. viii. 1. "There is, therefore, now, no condemnation to them who are in Christ Jesus, who walk not after the flesh but after the Spirit." Now, they who knowingly commit sin are condemned; consequently they are not in Christ Jesus. Therefore, if they are not in Christ Jesus, they are out of Christ Jesus, and if out of Christ Jesus, they cannot be in the "narrow way," for Christ is the way. If not in the narrow way, they must be in the broad way that leads to death, there being no middle path. Again, "whosoever is born of God doth not commit sin." 1 Jno. iii. 9. Observe, "whosoever *is* born of God;" not whosoever *was*, a few months or years ago, but "whosoever *is* born of God," i. e., now "born of God," *now* a Christian, *now* enjoying the love of God, "doth not commit sin," "for his seed remaineth in him, and he cannot sin, because he is born of God." Now, this passage does not teach the impossibility of sinning, but that we cannot sin and enjoy the love of God at the same time. He that knowingly sins, realizes the immediate result, viz: a condemned heart and a guilty conscience. Therefore, he *cannot* sin, in the sense that he *cannot* put his hand in a flame of fire. He knows what the consequence will be. Neither does the justified soul any more *desire* to sin than a man desires to put his hand in the fire; for he who really desires to sin, is condemned, for he only needs opportunity to fulfill his desire. We ask, again, is the profession of holiness higher than the profession of living without even a desire to sin?

Again, "He that committeth sin is of the Devil." 1 John iii, 8. This being true, we ask where is there room for the sinning Christian? Nay, where is the sinning Christian to be found? Nowhere.

Again, "He that saith he abideth in Him, ought himself also to walk even as He walked." 1 John, ii, 6. Now, whoever professes to be a Christian, professes to abide in Christ. But why ought he to walk as Christ walked? That he may not give a lie to his profession. If he would enjoy the approbation of God, or have men believe what he says, he must walk as Christ walked. But how did Christ walk?

He certainly did not walk in sin. He was a pattern of *purity* in *deed, word* and *heart.*

In *deed* Christ was pure. Purity was stamped on all His actions. He was not a wine-bibber, nor a gluttonous person. He walked not in the paths of the wicked, neither did He mingle with them in their unholy pleasures. He did not conform to the world in spirit and practice. Hear Him, "My kingdom is not of this world." He was not a member of any secret society. Hear Him again, "What I tell you in darkness, that speak ye in light, and what ye hear in the ear, that *preach* ye on the housetops." Neither was He pro-slavery. Listen, "As ye would that others should do unto you do ye even so unto them." Is there any slavery in that?

In *word* Christ was pure. He was not deceitful. He did not say one thing and mean another. No guile was found in His mouth. His conversation was heavenly. When reviled He reviled not again. He did not speak evil of another. Though He rebuked sin in strong terms, yet it was in the spirit of love.

In *heart* Christ was pure. He indulged in no angry tempers, no impure desires, no unholy jealousies. He harbored no hardness towards any for abuse of any kind. He was kind, gentle, patient, loving, full of good works, without partiality, and without hypocrisy. This is how Christ walked, and he who professes to be a Christian, professes to walk the same way. And now, we ask, is the profession of holiness a higher profession than the profession of abiding in Christ? We answer, no.

Again, to profess to be a Christian, is to profess to be *holy*, for Christ was holy. We are aware this is a nice as well as a controverted point. We believe with all true Methodists, that at conversion the soul is not entirely sanctified, and yet at conversion all the graces of the Spirit are implanted *in* the soul. The power of sin is broken, the guilt incurred by actual transgression is wiped away, thereby removing condemnation, and the justified soul stands as clear before God, as far as guilt and condemnation is concerned, as though it had never sinned. And yet, the Bible and experience declare that there remains in the justified soul what is expressed by the use of various phrases, such as the "remains of the carnal mind," "inclination to sin," and "native depravity." These terms are used to denote what experience says remains in the newly born soul. This manifests itself in the inclination to gratify pride, to indulge in angry feelings and unholy desires. In the hour of temptation the justified soul feels the wrangling of these to his sorrow. But they do not gain the ascendancy, he does not yield to them, while he calls on God for help. As soon as he yields to them, he forfeits his justification. The difference, therefore, between the justified and the sanctified, in this respect, is this: While the former feels these things and has to war against them, the latter *does not* feel them. Then we say the justified soul is *holy* in the sense that it yields to no unholy desires, or tempers, is all consecrated to God, and has peace with Him. Then what is gained by sneering at high professions, since every one who professes the religion of Jesus Christ, professes to live without committing known sin?

In conclusion, we will remark, Christ is not faithfully confessed unless He is confessed all He is unto us. If He is unto us justification, He should be confessed so. If He is unto us sanctification, He should be confessed so. "He that is ashamed of me and my words, of him will I be ashamed before my Father and the holy angels."

The perfection we preach is nothing but perfect repentance, perfect faith and perfect love, productive of the gracious temper which Saint Paul himself describes in the 13th Chapter of First Corinthians.—FLETCHER.

GODLY LETTER

OF JOHN BRADFORD, THE HOLY MARTYR.

We have been highly entertained and instructed with looking over the 3d volume of the first edition of Fox's Book of Martyrs. It is a large folio volume of over 1,000 pages, weighing some fourteen pounds avoirdupois! It was printed in London in 1684, and is now owned by Rev. R. M. EVARTS, a worthy superannuated preacher, who has kindly consented to loan it to us. The following extract is taken from it.—ED.

MY DEARLY BELOVED IN THE LORD: As in Him I wish you well to fare, so I pray God I and you may continue in his true service, that perpetually we may enjoy the same welfare, as here in hope, so in Heaven indeed, and eternally.

You know this world is not your Home, but a Pilgrimage and place wherein God trieth his Children; and therefore as it knoweth you not, nor can know you, so I trust you know not it; that is, you allow it not, nor in any point will seem so to do, although by many you be occasioned thereto. For this hot sun, which now shineth, burneth so sore, that the corn which is sown upon sand and stony ground, beginneth to wither; that is, many which before times were taken for hearty Gospellers, begin now, for the fear of afflictions, to relent, yea to turn to their vomit again, thereby declaring that though they go from among us, yet they were never of us! or else they would have still tarried with us, and neither for sin nor loss have left us, either in word or in deed. As for their heart, (which undoubtedly is double, and therefore in danger of God's curse,) we have as much with us, as the Papist have with them, and more too by their own judgement. For they playing wily beguiling themselves, think it enough inwardly to favour the truth, though outwardly they curry favour. What though with my body, say they, I do this or that? God knoweth my heart is whole with him.

Ah, Brother, if thy heart be whole with God, why doest not thou confess and declare thyself accordingly by word and fact? Either that, which thou sayest thou believest in thy heart, is good or no. If it be good, why art thou ashamed of it? If it be evil, why dost thou keep it in thy heart? Is not God able to defend thee, adventuring thyself for his cause? Or will he not defend his worshipers? Doth not the Scripture say, that the eyes of the Lord are on them that fear him, and trust in his mercy? And whereto? Forsooth, to deliver their souls from death, and feed them in the time of hunger.

If this be true, as it is most true, why are we afraid of death, as though God could not comfort or deliver us, or would not, contrary to his promise? Why are we afraid of the loss of our goods, as though God leave them that fear him destitute of all things, and so do against his most ample promises? Ah, Faith! Faith! how few feel thee now-a-days! Full truely said Christ, that we should scarcely find Faith when he cometh on earth. For if men believed these promises, they would never do anything outwardly, which inwardly they disallow. No example of men, how many soever they be, or how learned soever they be, can prevail in this behalf; for the pattern which we must follow is Christ himself, and not the mere company or custom. His Word is the lantern to lighten our steps, and not learned men. Company and custom are to be considered according to the thing they allow.

Learned men are to be listened to and followed according to God's love and law; for else the more part goeth to the Devil. As custom causeth errour and blindness, so learning, if it be not according to the light of God's Word, is poison, and learned men most pernicious.

SELF-EXAMINATION.—In judging ourselves, the leaning should be to the side of severity. Let us be satisfied with nothing short of the real power of religion. Whatever we depend upon, while we are strangers to this, will be more than useless—it will issue in the most dreadful disappointment. It is better to err on the side of caution than of self-security. According to our Saviour, the delusion accompanies some to the very door of Heaven; they knock with confidence that they shall be admitted, and are surprised and confounded when they hear from within, I know you not, whence ye are. Do not place your religion in attending on divine ordinances; or in a mere belief of the truth; or in some outward reformation; or in some particular course of duty, to which you may have inducements that render it easy. Search and try your ways. See whether you have given God your whole heart, and can sacrifice every bosom lust. See whether your religion has anything in it above the efficiency of natural principles—whether it is flesh or spirit—whether you are under the law or under grace. Examine yourselves. If believers, does your faith work by love? And do you love in word and in tongue, or in deed and in truth? If penitents, have you said with Ephraim, what have I any more to do with idols? If worshippers, do you only draw nigh to Him with the mouth, and honor Him with your lips, while your heart is far from Him? If hearers, has the Gospel come to you, not in word only, but in power, and in the Holy Ghost, and in much assurance.—WM. JAY.

FREE CHURCHES.—Let all our churches be built plain and decent, and with free seats; but not more expensive than is absolutely unavoidable; otherwise the necessity of raising money will make rich men necessary to us. But if so, we must be dependent on them; yea, and governed by them. And then farewell to Methodist discipline, if not doctrine too.—OLD METHODIST DISCIPLINE.

FAITH.—God has marked implicitness and simplicity of faith with peculiar approbation. He has done this through the Scriptures, and he is doing it daily in the Christian life. An unsuspecting, unquestioning, unhesitating spirit, he delights to honor. He does not delight in a credulous, weak, and unstable mind. He gives us full evidence, when he calls and leads; but he expects to find in us a disposed heart. Though he gives us not the evidence of sense, yet he gives us such evidences as will be heard by an open ear, and followed by a disposed heart. "Thomas, because thou hast seen me, thou hast believed; blessed are they that have not seen, and yet believe!" We are witnesses what an open ear and a disposed heart will do in men of the world. If wealth is their pursuit; if a place presents itself before them; if their persons and families and affairs are the object; a whisper, a hint, a probability, a mere chance, is a sufficient ground of action. It is this very state of mind with regard to religion, which God delights in and honors. He seems to put forth hands, and to say, "Put thy hand into mine; follow all my leading; keep thyself attentively to every turn."—CECIL.

Whoever stops to inquire whether it may cost him sacrifices to be a Christian, with any intention to hesitate if it does, has admitted a consideration utterly incompatible with his becoming a Christian at all. Whoever chooses his creed or his church with any, the slightest, reference to the honor, or the ease, or the emolument it may give or withhold, does, by such an admission, utterly vitiate all his claim to have any part or lot in the matter of saving piety. I do not speak of those who knowingly and deliberately make these their chief grounds of preference; but I affirm that it is wholly anti-Christian, and an insult to the crucified Saviour, to yield any, the smallest, place to worldly motives in choosing the Christian position which we will occupy.—OLIN.

MORAL MIRACLES.

THE following extract from "The Gift of Power"—a work which we cannot commend too strongly to our readers, written by Rev. S. H. Platt, of the New York Conference, and printed at the Methodist Book Concern,—sets forth the privileges of believers in a stronger light than we have been accustomed to hear them advocated. Yet who can say that the view here presented is not fully warranted by the Scriptures? Let us claim by importunate prayer all that God has for us.—ED.

There can be no question that faith in prayer secures *all* blessings of the Spirit, whether miraculous or otherwise. I grant, indeed, that the prayer must be the inspiration of the Spirit—as are all pious desires—and that, consequently, if the Spirit never impels to prayers for miraculous works, they cannot be wrought. *But some promises of the Bible are utterly meaningless, or the Spirit does incite to such prayers, and such results may be realized!* To the denial of this proposition, I oppose simple *facts*.

I do not advocate this truth to encourage fanaticism, but to show the Church that she possesses a magazine of convicting energy, which, if brought forth and displayed, would astonish the world.

Upon the hypothesis of those who contend that this power was voluntarily withdrawn from the Church by her Lord—I ask *when* was it withdrawn? and when that is answered, *why* was it recalled? But the answer is at hand—"Because it was no longer necessary." But why was it no longer necessary? "Because Christianity was established, and the purpose for which it was given was accomplished!" Then I answer, it existed for three hundred years after the necessity for it had ceased;* for Christianity was established firmly as the pillars of Heaven, before the last Apostle went to his reward. And if it existed three hundred years, then why not eighteen hundred?

I contend that all the historical authorization that Christianity needed—all that could add one particle to its weight of evidence—was experienced in the days of the Apostles. Why, then, was it continued? Was it for the sake of impression? *The world never needed impression as it does to-day!*

Where, then, is the unreasonableness of the view which is here presented. But let us guard it from misapprehension. The Church may possess a miracle working power, so far as is necessary to produce the impression of its divinity; but it is held strictly upon the conditions of a holy life, and *faith in prayer!* This seems to be the doctrine of the Bible, and I have sought in vain for a well-grounded objection to it. There can be no danger in this view, so long as the qualifying clause is kept before the mind, viz.: That the incitements of the Spirit are necessary to such prayer and faith. I do not believe that a state of "*ordinary* piety" can claim it, for this is a most palpable misnomer. "Ordinary piety" is, in fact, gross impiety! and to such God will never vouchsafe the higher blessings with which he "honors those who honor him," by deep communings and unfaltering trust.

CHRIST saves those only who submit to his authority, and take His Spirit for the regulator of their heart, and His Word for the director of their conduct. How many do we find among those who would be sorry to be rated so low as to rank only with *nominal* Christians, talking of Christ as their prophet, priest and king; who are not taught by His word and Spirit; who apply not for *redemption in His blood*, and who *submit not* to His authority. —ADAM CLARKE.

TELL the *truth*, and shame the devil!

---

* According to Mosheim, miracles had not entirely ceased in the fourth century.

The record of the faith of Christ's people in Madagascar deserves to stand side by side with the highest triumphs of ancient martyrdom. For seventeen years the English missionaries were allowed to labor on that island, during that time completing and publishing a translation of the Scriptures. At the end of that time they were banished, and the profession of religion forbidden under the heaviest penalties. But there were fifty Christians on the island, and the translated Scriptures not easily to be blotted out. Among those Christians was a wealthy woman, privileged to become the first martyr for Christ. She was imprisoned, and her house given to plunder; it did not move her. She was renounced by her family; it did not move her. She was loaded with irons, and beaten; she continued to sing her hymns to Christ. She was led to execution; she said, "I care not if my blood be shed, so that the Word of God shall thereby prosper in this country." At the place of execution, she knelt calmly down and prayed. The queen forbid her to pray: but she continued to pray, and preached Christ to the crowds that surrounded her, until her constant soul was dismissed to heaven by a soldier's spear. Many were compelled to drink poisoned water. Some hid themselves in caves and forests. Some escaped to other lands. In 1840, sixteen who had been concealed were discovered. On being questioned, they replied, "We are not banditti or murderers; we are the praying people. This is our answer for life or death." Nine of them were slain. But Christianity was not destroyed. Let any one who is doubtful of the result of preaching a pure gospel among the heathen, look at the history of the Church in Madagascar. After only thirteen years' instruction, left absolutely without a school, a teacher, a minister, or a sacrament, with nothing but the Bible and a living faith, persecuted, cast out, reviled, more than half of them slain, yet through sixteen years that diminished band retained their love for Christ, and their devotion to him. At last the son of the queen herself, the heir to the throne, was converted under the powerful preaching of these martyrdoms; and happier days have begun to reward their constancy.—BP. BEARD.

ABOVE all, we need an inspiration, an indwelling spirit, that shall control, by a power outside of ourselves, the mind. This is the theme that I most love to dwell upon; my own faith that God's mind does not act upon ours through nature—though that is true; nor through the truth—though that is true; but by absolute contact, mind with mind — by inspiration coming from, springing from the very soul of God, being infused into our nature, resting in us, and acting upon us. When the power of God restrains our thoughts, guides our impulses, and inspires our affections, when God dwells in us, working in us to will and to do of his good pleasure—I need not say how secure we then are. God becomes the great author, as he will be the great finisher of our faith.—HENRY WARD BEECHER.

PRAYER. — When a pump is frequently used, but little pains are necessary to have water; the water pours out at the first stroke, because it is high. But if the pump has not been used for a long while, the water gets low, and when you want it you must pump a long while, and the water comes only after great efforts. It is so with prayer; if we are instant in prayer, every little circumstance awakens the disposition to pray, and desires and words are always ready. But if we neglect prayer, it is difficult for us to pray; for the water in the well gets low.—FELIX NEFF.

IT is easier to be wise for others than for ourselves. We have all sufficient strength to bear the evils which befall others.—TURKISH PROVERB.

A DIAMOND with some flaws is still more precious than a pebble that has none.—INDIAN PROVERB.

COMPROMISING.

BY THE EDITOR.

We often find ourselves in circumstances in which concession becomes a duty. In this world of conflicting interests, he who would obstinately stand upon his own rights, and never yield, will involve himself in serious and endless difficulties. To waive our own rights, in whole or in part, may be commendable; but to assume and exercise the authority of surrendering the rights of another, is an usurpation which admits of no apology or defence. We may give to the robber who demands it at the peril of our lives, all our money and be blameless, but when we authorize him to take a moiety of our neighbor's, without his consent, we become a participant in the crime.

With some show of propriety, we might commission the Southern master to drag us from our families, and condemn us to a life of unrequited toil, under the burning sun, and the stinging lash; but when we consent that he should take our helpless neighbor, whose only crime is being

"Guilty of a skin
Not colored like our own,"

and reduce him and his posterity to the condition of a brute, we become a partaker of his sin—"a sin which, among Christians," says Dr. Clarke, "is an enormity and a crime for which perdition has scarcely an adequate state of punishment."

The slavery compromises that we as a nation, have for years been making, are of this one-sided, despotic character. Comparatively no concession has been made, by the rulers either of the North or of the South, of their own rights or those of their constituents: We have preserved our own privileges intact. Every white man is at liberty to gain wealth and to enjoy it—to pursue whatever harmless avocation he chooses; and to go when and where he pleases. Our own rights are jealously guarded and always have been. The house of the poorest is his castle; and he and his family dwell in safety. But our colored brother has been the victim of our national compromises. We have assumed to give up one after another of his God-given rights until, at last, the declaration has been formally made by the highest judicial tribunal of the land, that "the colored race have no rights that the white man is bound to respect." The North is turned into one great hunting ground. Man, made in the image of God, is the game.

This compromising spirit has not confined itself to politicians. It is generally diffused. It has invaded the sacred desk. Ministers have drunk it in from the surrounding air. We too often manifest it when we stand up to speak in the name of Christ. We compromise His truth—a part is surrendered. We polish what God has left rough. We soften His hard sayings. Thus, unconsciously it may be, we treat God's truth as though it were our own.

We compromise, when, for the sake of pleasing men, we abandon the use of Scriptural terms.

This is often done in narrating religious experience. Some are prejudiced against the doctrine of holiness as taught in the Bible. To propitiate them we abandon the terms employed by the sacred writers to describe this state of grace. We then flatter ourselves that we have too broad views to adhere rigidly to mere phrases. Those who will not hear of "sanctification" or "perfect love," or "holiness," words dictated by the Holy Ghost, we exhort to seek "a deeper work of grace"— an expression no where to be met with in the Bible. "If people only experience the thing intended," it is said, "no matter by what name you call it." But it does matter. Jesus says, "If any man shall take away from the words of the book of this prophecy, God shall take away his part out of the book of life, and out of the holy city." It is dangerous to be ashamed of the words of Jesus. We may thus hope to bring the hated doctrine into favor, but a rigid analysis of motives might show us that there is also blended some anxiety to secure our own popularity. Men can never love a doctrine, and at the same time dislike the terms in which it is stated in the Bible.

So, too, the scriptural terms for sin, are too harsh for the refined ear of the present day. Those whom the Bible calls "proud" are styled in the improved dialect, "persons of taste;" the "covetous" are "careful men of business;" the fearful, who by their cowardice betray the cause of Christ, are transformed into "the modest and retiring;" "lovers of pleasure" are "social and agreeable;" and "liars" are "shrewd managers."

What a pity that Ananias had not fallen into the hands of apostles of this charitable school! Suppose he sold the land for four thousand dollars, and kept back one thousand: they would have apologized for him after this manner, "It was very wrong, but then you must take the '*circumstances*' into account. Ananias was only just converted. He was brought up a Jew, and the Jews love money. We cannot expect that the combined influence of nature, education and habit can be broken at once. It was natural that he should wish to lay by something for old age, or to help his children. The three thousand dollars is a large sum for one man to give—much larger than we apostles contributed to the common fund. Christ did not command His disciples to give all they had. As for the falsehood, it was rather a prevarication, for he did not say that he did not sell the land for any more than three thousand dollars, only that he received that sum for it, which was true. We ought not to conclude from this one circumstance that he is not a Christian; but his having done as much as he has, should be taken as an evidence of his sincerity. We must still consider him a good man."

But Peter, uncompromising in his devotion to the right, said, "Ananias, why hath Satan filled thine heart to lie to the Holy Ghost? Why hast thou conceived this thing in thine heart? Thou hast not lied unto men, but unto God;" and Ananias fell down dead. The fate of the first compromiser under the Gospel dispensation should be a warning.

The terms used in the Bible to designate the punishment of sin, are also going sadly out of use. The fashionable pulpit of to-day has but little to say about the "damnation of hell." The warnings of God are but little noticed, and men are sought to be won to Christianity by the beauties of poetry and rhetoric, and the soft blandishments of a higher style of social life.

We compromise when we attempt to regulate sin instead of prohibiting it altogether.

General commands sometimes have, in other parts of the Bible, limits set to their application. Where this is the case, the injunction and the limitation are to be taken together. They both rest upon the same authority. For instance, the general prohibition, "Thou shalt not kill," is limited in its application by this decree of equal authority, "Whosoever sheddeth man's blood, by man shall his blood be shed." But we have no right to make exceptions where God has made none. To make exceptions to a law, where and when we please, is equivalent to repealing the law.

No where in the Scriptures is the command, "Thou shalt love thy neighbor as thyself," limited in its application to those who are of our complexion. He whom Providence places within the reach of our kind offices, is our neighbor, whatever opinions he may hold, or whatever may be the land of his nativity.

Any thing that serves only to pander to the vices of our fellow-men cannot receive our countenance, directly or indirectly, without compromising. Whoever assists in obtaining for another a licence for the selling of spirituous liquors, will find in the great day of retribution, when God shall make inquisition for the blood of husbands, fathers and sons, slowly poisoned, tortured and put to death by strong drink, that a part of the woe pronounced against "him who putteth the bottle to his neighbor's lips" will fall upon him, to his eternal ruin.

Worldly conformity—adorning our persons in a way that tends only to inflame vanity and lust, cannot receive the countenance of him who would follow the Lord fully.

The temptation to compromise is one of the most subtle, as well as one of the most successful, employed by the arch-deceiver to neutralize the influence, and compass the ruin of the child of God. It is fabled that Achilles, having, when an infant, been immersed by his goddess-mother in the waters of Styx, so that he became invulnerable to mortal weapons, was at last slain by an arrow aimed at the heel, by which his mother held him—the only portion of his body that could be wounded. So, many faithful Christians, who were proof against the power of passion, and the seductions of the world, have, under the plea of increasing their influence, or of rendering religion less repulsive, gradually lowered down the standard of piety, and thus inflicted a heavier blow upon Christianity than could be given by all her enemies combined. No part of the world is so inaccessible to Gospel truth as those countries where the Greek and Romish Churches prevail. Mosheim thus describes the compromises by which the corruptions were established that have, for so many centuries, involved in moral gloom the Churches planted by the apostles, and watered by the blood of martyrs: "The rites and institutions, by which the Greeks, Romans, and other nations, had formerly testified their religious veneration for ficticious deities, were now adopted with some slight alterations by Christian Bishops, and employed in the service of the true God. These fervent heralds of the Gospel, whose zeal outran their candor and integrity, imagined that the nations would receive Christianity with more facility, when they saw the rites and ceremonies to which they were accustomed, adopted in the Church, and the same worship paid to Christ and his martyrs, which they had formerly offered to their idol deities. Hence it happened that in those times the religion of the Greeks and Romans differed very little, in its external appearance from that of the Christians. They had both a most pompous and splendid ritual. Gorgeous robes, mitres, tiaras, wax-tapers, crosiers, processions, lustrations, images, gold and silver vases, and many such circumstances of pageantry, were equally to be seen in the heathen temples and in the Christian churches.

No sooner had Constantine abolished the superstitions of his ancestors, than magnificent churches were everywhere erected for the Christians, which were richly adorned with pictures and images, and bore a striking resemblance to the pagan temples, both in their outward and inward form."

The wounds given to the Church, the body of Christ, by the horrible cruelties of Nero, and the savage fierceness of Domitian were soon healed, but those inflicted by compromising bishops and ministers, in their well-meant efforts to render the cross of Christ less offensive, remain uncured, and to all appearance, incurable.

The maxim, "Of two evils choose the least," has done immense service to Satan. Through the application of this, African slavery was first introduced upon this continent. Las Casas, bishop of Granada, was a kind-hearted man, with a high reputation for personal sanctity. His sympathies were deeply moved at witnessing the sufferings of the Indians under the cruel treatment of the Spaniards. The proud-spirited sons of the forest could not brook servitude, and they rapidly wasted away and died. The pious bishop, lacking the courage to denounce in suitable terms the wrong, proposed that the more patient and tractable African should be substituted. The avaricious Spaniards were but too ready to act upon the suggestion. From this compromise, made by a good, easy, timid bishop, have resulted already evils which no tongue can describe, and greater still are probably yet to come.

The experience of the past abundantly proves the falsity of the pleas usually urged in favor of compromising principle, that thereby some greater good can be effected, or some heavy calamity averted. If good cannot be accomplished without doing violence to one of the least of the commands of God, it had better go undone. If calamity cannot be averted without our departing, in the slightest degree, from the strictest rectitude, we had better suffer it patiently. Better for churches to go unbuilt, than for the followers of Jesus to cater to pride and covetousness. A community left entirely without the ordinances of religion, would be in a more hopeful condition than one where what is called the Gospel is preached in a way that gives countenance to prevailing sins. If, in all the South, not a minister or a Church could be found, there would be hope of the peaceful abolition of slavery. *A field had better lie fallow than be sown with tares.*

To the hope, delusive in reality, though apparently well-founded, of doing good by compromising, is often added the prospect of personal advantages to be realized. The compromiser, by carefully blending the bounds of right and wrong, expects to win the confidence of the lovers of righteousness without forfeiting the good-will of those who will not consent to abandon a course of sin. He usually enjoys the patronage of those in power who have favors to dispense, and offices at their disposal. Daniel Webster doubtless supposed that the way to the Presidential mansion lay between the abolitionism of New England and the slavery propagandism of South Carolina.

Compromising our religious principles is not only a sin in itself, but it generally includes a long catalogue of sins, such as contempt of the authority of God—distrust of the providential care of God—love of ease—of reputation; unbounded self complacency and moral cowardice.

Had David and the Hebrew children compromised, as they might easily have done, and found better reasons for it than compromisers usually have, the Bible would have wanted some of its most interesting illustrations of the care which God takes of those, who, leaving consequences to Him, dare to do right. The special interposition of God in behalf of His children is prevented by their failing when the crisis comes to hold fast with unbending firmness their integrity, looking to Him for deliverance. Fletcher mentions the case of a woman, who being awakened, was threatened with being burned alive if she went to meeting. She felt it her duty to go, and she went in the face of the most dreadful threatenings, and was converted. Coming home she found a fierce fire blazing in the oven, but her late infuriated husband, arrested by the Spirit of God, was on his knees pleading for mercy. Had she yielded to her fears in the hour of danger, the souls of both might have been lost.

Let us then, where our own ease or interests are at stake, be ever ready to make sacrifices for the good of others; and where fidelity to Christ is concerned, let us be like the break-water at the entrance of the harbor, defying the fury of the tempest, and affording protection to all within the circle of our influence.

This is a changing world, and men change as often as anything in it, and not always for the better. Highwrought notions of denominational excellence; posts of honor or profit gleaming in the distance; or some immediate acquisition of personal advantage, operate like magic power on certain minds; so that whoever undertakes to reform mankind at the present day, has a task which Gabriel might hesitate to touch.—Rev. J. D. Bridge.

We must not suppose a false doctrine harmless, merely because it has not been able to corrupt the heart of a good man.—Beattie.

FULLNESS OF JOY.

BY MRS. B. M. GILLEY.

It is the design of God that the peace which the believer receives through the Gospel shall be at all times, and under all circumstances, full, permanent, and uninterrupted. Hear the words of our Saviour. "These things have I spoken unto you, that my joy might remain in you, and that your joy might be full."

This fullness of joy is presented in the Bible, not only as the privilege of the believer, but its manifestation is required of him as a sacred duty. "Rejoice in the Lord always; and again I say rejoice." Hence we see, Christian, that just as far as you are destitute of this "fullness of joy," just so far you are disqualified for the great work to which God has called you. This fullness of joy does not, of necessity, imply the entire absence of external affliction. On the other hand, the design of the Saviour is that the peace-giving power of the gospel shall be rendered pre-eminently conspicuous in consequence of its filling the believer's cup of blessedness, even in affliction. How glorious the Gospel appears when it is seen to possess the power to cause the believer to rejoice in tribulation; and to render him, in the midst of persecution, famine, nakedness, peril, and sword, more than conqueror, through Him that loved him. The Bible does not promise to the believer freedom from physical suffering. It does, however, on the condition of simple faith, promise perfect peace, and entire fullness of joy. Consequently it proposes to bring the believer into such a relation to all physical suffering, that it shall not be a source of real unhappiness, but shall constitute one of the sources of that perfect peace into which steady and unwavering faith introduces the mind. Nor does fullness of joy imply the total absence of what may be called mental sorrows. Among the divine requirements we find a class of precepts like the following: "Rejoice with them that do rejoice, and weep with them that weep." To pour out our heart then for objects which demand tears of us, is not inconsistent with fullness of joy, but is rather essential to it. Tears poured out like water over sinners exposed to the pangs of the second death, and what may be called agonizing prayer for the redemption of lost men, are among the streams of pure and perfect blessedness which flow through a truly sanctified mind.

Nor does fullness of joy imply that the mind be always in a state of the highest conceivable ecstacy. The present circumstances and capacities of the mind do not permit it to be always in this state. There is, in a deep and pervading serenity of mind, a blessedness as full and perfect as in ecstatic joy. What then does fullness of joy imply? I answer: It implies the conscious absence of everything which would be to the mind a real evil. "All things work together for good to them that love God." What blessedness more pure, full, and perfect can we conceive of than this? In short, fullness of joy implies the same blessedness in kind and degree, as far as our capabilities permit, which Christ enjoyed when on earth. "Peace," says Christ, "I leave with you; my peace," that is the peace which I enjoy, "I give unto you." This, Christian, is the fullness of joy proffered to you in the Gospel. This is the blessedness which it is both your duty and your privilege to enjoy. This command and promise embrace everything which God sees necessary to our happiness. Did you ever reflect that when your joy is not full, and when the peace of God does not rule in your heart, that you are living in disobedience to the requirements of God? You have no more right to be filled with care and perplexity—you have no more right to let that "aching void" within remain unfilled with "joy unspeakable, and full of glory," than you have to blaspheme the worthy name by which you are called.

This fullness of joy in Christ is indispensable to the most energetic action in his service. "The joy of the Lord is your strength."

But just as far as the "peace of God" does not "rule in our hearts," so far we are weak and powerless in his service. If then, Christian, you would be "strong in the Lord, and in the power of his might," besiege the throne of grace, and, in the name of Christ, ask till your joy is full. "Whatsoever ye shall ask the Father in my name, He will give it you." Christian, "believest thou this?" If thou canst believe, all things are possible to him that believeth. While we thus ask God to meet all our necessities, we must present our whole being as a willing sacrifice to Him to be employed in his service. On no other conditions have we a right to ask or expect such fullness of the Lord. "Let us present our bodies a living sacrifice, holy and acceptable unto the Lord, which is our reasonable service." Christian, are you willing to do this? Are you willing to "suffer the loss of all things for Christ, and let "God dwell in you, and walk in you, and be your God, and you be his son or his daughter" for ever? If you can do this with all your heart, then in the name of the Lord let me assure you that "Because thou hast made the Lord, which is my refuge, even the Most High, thy habitation, there shall no evil befall thee, neither shall any plague come nigh thy dwelling." Surely He shall deliver thee from the snare of the fowler, and from the noisome pestilence. He shall cover thee with His feathers, and under his wings shalt thou trust; His truth shall be thy shield and buckler." Glory to God.

THERE are critical times of danger. After great services, honors and consolations, we should stand upon our guard. Noah, Lot, David and Solomon, fell in these circumstances. Satan is a footpad: a footpad will not attack a man in going to the bank, but in returning with his pocket full of money.

ANSWER TO PRAYER.—The following remarkable instance of answer to prayer, we give from the New York *Independent*. How the faith of this little girl reproves the unbelief of many who use words of prayer!

At the close of a prayer meeting in a country village, the clergyman observed that a little girl about twelve years of age remained upon her knees, when most of the congregation had retired. Thinking that the child had fallen asleep, he touched her, and told her it was time to return home. To his surprise, he found that she was engaged in prayer, and he said, "*All things whatever ye shall ask in prayer, believing ye shall receive.*" She looked at her pastor earnestly, and inquired, "Is it so? Does God say that?" He took up a Bible and read the passage aloud. She immediately commenced praying, "Lord, send my father to the church. Lord, send my father here!" Thus she continued for about a half an hour, attracting by her earnest cry the attention of persons lingering about the door.

At last a man rushed into the church, ran up the aisle, and sank upon his knees by the side of the child, exclaiming, "What do you want of me?" She threw her arms about his neck, and began to pray, "O, Lord, convert my father!" Soon the man's heart was melted, and he began to pray for himself—a gracious answer of peace to a prayer of faith from the lips of a child.

It was ascertained, afterwards, that the child's father was three miles from the church, when she commenced praying for him. He was packing goods into a wagon, and he felt an irresistible impulse to return home. Driving rapidly to his house, he left the goods in the wagon and hastened to the church, where he found his daughter crying mightily to God in his behalf, and he was then led to the Saviour.

OBSTINACY and a want of common sense, are two mental disorders for which logic provides no remedy.

A PURE CHURCH.

I NEVER see a new church edifice erected and dedicated to God's service, without thinking how glorious a thing it would be, if a new congregation could be formed on a truly Christian model; not chiefly in regard to its form of ecclesiastical polity, or to a faultless creed, or to the external seemliness of its devotions—things by no means unworthy of attention, or destitute of considerable influence on religious prosperity—but in the far higher regards of the deep piety of its members, and the entireness of their devotion to Christ's kingdom and glory. I have long since nearly despaired of seeing such a church in this dark world; yet I can see no insuperable obstacle, moral or physical, to its existence, and I am wholly sure that its example, and splendid successes, would usher in a new era. *A band of a hundred, or of fifty, or even of ten living* CHRISTIANS, *strong in mutual affections and confidence, and entire in their devotedness* to Christ and to the salvation of souls, would, I am confident, wield an amount of religious influence immeasureably greater than is usually exerted by our largest and most flourishing churches. As matters are too often managed, scarcely one in every four or five professors of religion ever attains to such elevation and maturity in piety as to be of much positive use to the cause, while all the rest require about as much effort on the part of the Church to keep them along as they contribute to the general movement. They are ever in bondage to first principles—to doubts and fears, and temptations, and bad habits, and besetting sins—evils which believing, courageous souls should dispose of very speedily, that they may "go on to perfection." While the vast majority are forever at or about this point of tantalizing equipoise, wasting much and contributing nothing of the spiritual resources of the Church—exciting at least as much of fear as of hope in the mind of charity itself, the sounder portion usually contrive to misdirect and squander away their moral force upon trifles, or in doing mischief. They glory in men or in sect more than in Christ and the truth. They thank God, and applaud themselves for being of a Church most distinguished for its stern orthodoxy, or its enlightened and large liberality—most venerable for its hoary antiquity, or most admirable for late improvements and new discoveries—most orderly or most zealous—most apostolic or most democratic.—OLIN.

PERSONAL CONSECRATION.—" Lo! I come," if this soul and body may be useful to anything, "to do thy will, O, God." And if it please thee to use the power thou hast over dust and ashes, over weak flesh and blood, over a brittle vessel of clay, over the works of thine own hands; lo! here they are, to suffer also thy good pleasure. If thou please to visit me either with pain or dishonor, I will "humble myself" under it, and through thy grace be obedient unto death, even the death upon the cross. Whatsoever may befall me, either from neighbors or strangers, since it is thou employest them, though they know it not, (unless thou help me to some lawful means of redressing the wrong,) I will not "open my mouth before the Lord," who smiteth me, except only to bless the Lord. Hereafter, no man can take away anything from me, no life, no honor, no estate; since I am ready to lay them down, as soon as I perceive thou requirest them at my hands. Nevertheless, "O, Father, if thou be willing, remove this cup from me; but if not, thy will be done." Whatever suffering hereafter may trouble my flesh, or whatever agonies may trouble my spirit, "O, Father, into thy hands will I commend my life, and all that concerneth it. And if thou be pleased, either that I live yet awhile, or not, I will with my Saviour, bow down my head." I will humble myself under thy hand; I will give up all thou art pleased to ask, until at last, I "give up the Ghost."—JOHN WESLEY.

PREACHING HOLINESS.

The following letter, written by Bishop George, to Rev. R. M. Evarts, when he was a Presiding Elder in the Genesee Conference, will, we think, repay a careful perusal:

August 14th, 1820.

My Dear Brother:—I have been writing to the Presiding Elders in the New England, New York and Genesee Conference, on one particular subject: that is, to request them, as far as possible to introduce the doctrine, the spirit and practice of holiness among their preachers, local and traveling, that the Heavenly influence may spread its energies among the membership; for there can be but little doubt but the members of our church will unite with us in pursuing and realizing this precious pearl when they find us sincere in doctrine and example. I have found in my experience as P. E., that this may be done with the most ease and success by introducing it into the Quarterly Conferences. There obtain the promise of all the official characters to commence the pursuit of it themselves, by prayer and fasting for this particular blessing, and then invite and lead their different charges into the possession of this special and Scriptural qualification for Heaven. Permit me to assign one or two reasons for this request. And first, we ought to do so for the sake of consistency. We read that the Methodists were raised up to be a holy people. The doctrines we preach, and the discipline we administer, call upon us to be a holy people, and while our practice is at war with our doctrines and discipline, we shall always appear to disadvantage among men of reason and intelligence. But my final and conclusive reason is this, that we may go on ourselves, and lead our people in a safe and pleasant way to Heaven; and also that we may see our fields of labor blooming with beauty, prosperity and glory; for we shall find a holy ministry, and holy people will in the general be useful in gathering souls to Christ. I hope you will pray for your sincere friend in the kingdom and patience of Jesus. Enoch George.

Persecution.—It must never surprise true Christians if they meet with the same treatment that the Lord Jesus met with. "Marvel not if the world hate you." It is not the utmost consistency, or the closest walk with God, that will exempt them from the enmity of the natural man. They need not torture their consciencies by fancying that if they were only more faultless and consistent, every body would surely love them. It is all a mistake. They should remember that there was never but one perfect man on earth, and that he was not loved, but hated. It is not the infirmities of a believer that the world dislikes, but his goodness. It is not the remains of the old nature that call forth the world's enmity, but the exhibition of the new. Let us remember these things and be patient. The world hated Christ, and the world will hate Christians.—Ryle.

Almost all the principal Churches within our bounds, are at this hour like the Pyramids of Egypt, each at once a temple and a tomb, crowded with spiritual mummies, sitting in silence amid all the chiselled grandeur of Sardonic magnificence, awaiting embalmed in the odor of a lifeless sanctity the vain hope of a resurrection they shall never see, while the preacher's voice, instead of being the deputed voice of the Son of God in its resurrection power, is smoothed and softened and lessened down to a reptile's whimper in these habitations of the dead.—J. McCreery.

Nothing proves more invincibly the immortality of the soul, the truth of religion, and the eternity of another life, than to see that in this life the righteous seldom receive the reward of their virtue, and that in temporal things they are often less happy than the workers of iniquity.—Calmet.

RULES FOR A HOLY LIFE.

1. Too much desire to please men, mightily prejudgeth of God.
2. Too great earnestness and vehemency, and too greedy delight in bodily work and external doings, scattereth and loseth the tranquility and calmness of the mind.
3. Cast all thy care on God, and commit all to His good pleasure; laud and praise, and applaud Him in all things, small and great. Forsake thy own will, and deliver up thyself freely and cheerfully to the will of God without reserve or exception, in prosperity and adversity, sweet or sour, to have or to want, to live or to die.
4. Disunite thy heart from all things, and unite it only to God.
5. Remember often and devoutly, the life and passion, the death and resurrection of our Saviour Jesus.
6. Descant not on other men's deeds, but consider thine own; forget other men's faults, and remember thine own.
7. Never think highly of thyself, nor despise any other man.
8. Keep silence and retirement as much as thou canst, and, through God's grace, they will keep thee from snares and offences.
9. Lift up thy heart often to God, and desire in all things His assistance.
10. Let thy heart be filled and wholly taken up with the love of God, and of thy neighbor; and do all that thou dost, in that sincere charity and love. The sum is:
1. Remember always the presence of God.
2. Rejoice always in the will of God. And,
3. Direct all to the glory of God.
—Archbishop Leighton.

Moments.—Every passing moment is furnishing the records of heaven, and filling up the pages of our history with good or evil, against the day of judgment.—Buckley.

Energy.—A man never knows what he is capable of until he has tried his powers. There seems to be no bounds to human capacity. Insight, energy and will, produce astonishing results. How often modest talent, driven by circumstances to undertake some formidable work, has felt his own untried and hitherto unconscious power rising up to grapple and to master, and afterward stood amazed at its own unexpected success.

Those circumstances, those people, enemies and friends, that provoke us to any noble undertaking, are our greatest benefactors. Opposition and persecution do more for a man than any seemingly good fortune. The sneers of critics develope the latent fire of the young poet. The anathemas of the angry church inflame the zeal of the reformer. Tyranny, threats, fagots, torture, raise up heroes and martyrs, who might otherwise have slept away slothful and thoughtless lives, never dreaming what splendid acts and words lay buried in their bosoms. And who knows but the wrongs of society are permitted, because of the fine gold which is beaten out of the crude ore of humanity?

Here is the truth worth considering. Are you in poverty? have you suffered wrong? do circumstances oppose you? are you beset by enemies? Now is your time. Never lie there depressed and melancholy. Spend no more time in idle whining. Up, like a lion! Make no complaint, but if difficulty overtake you, roar your defiance. You are at school, this is your necessary discipline; poverty and pain are your masters; use the powers God has given you, and you shall be master at last. Fear of failure is the most fruitful cause of failure. Stand firm, and you will not fail. What seems failure at first is a discipline.

Accept the lesson; trust the grand result; up and up again; strike and strike again, and you shall always gain, whatever the fortune of to-day's or to-morrow's battle.

REVIVALS.

BY THE EDITOR.

ONE of the most encouraging features in the revival of earnest Christianity that is going on in many places is, that the children of God are exercising a faith that knows no discouraging circumstances. Precious ingatherings of souls have taken place, where everything seemed to be in the way. But GOD'S SPIRIT knows no obstacle but unbelief.

ALDEN, in this county, has been visited by a gracious influence from above. A few praying ones met on week day evenings at the house of brother HARTSHORN, and the Lord set the seal of his approval by the conversion of several precious souls. The children of God were greatly quickened. Brother and sister HARTSHORN were prepared, by a special baptism of the Holy Spirit, for the heavy affliction that came upon them. And when their oldest child—a very interesting boy—was brought in mangled and torn by the machinery of a horse power into which he had fallen, they were prepared to endure the severe trial with a calmness and serenity surprising to themselves and to all their friends. The little sufferer lingered for about twenty-four hours, entirely conscious, but patient to a degree astonishing to all. To his mother, who was weeping over him, he said, with calmness, "Ma, don't cry : it don't hurt as bad as it did when I was in the machine." Not a cry escaped from his lips. "I love Jesus," he said, "I love every body," and his unsullied spirit took its flight to HIM who says, "Suffer little children to come unto me, and forbid them not, for of such is the kingdom of Heaven."

MATTERS OF EXPERIENCE.

The following letter, from one of the "expelled" ministers, will be read with interest:

DEAR BROTHER ROBERTS:—I feel it due to the cause of Christ to give to the readers of the *Earnest Christian* a few facts connected with our revival in Poter and Wilson. At the different points where I labor, about eighty have found pardoning mercy, and about thirty-five have experienced sanctification. The work is going on still. Among those who have obtained the blessing of sanctification are fifteen of the converts. Two sisters experienced this second blessing in two days after conversion. One sister in four days, and a brother in eight days after conversion. And the fifteen came out in this clear light within three weeks after their conversion. This is God's order, and what a powerful preventive to backsliding it becomes, by giving to these converts such a relish for the service of God, and such a Heavenward tendency! How much it increases their happiness and usefulness! We have marked the difference between old professors and converts in obtaining this grace, though we have seen converts go through a very great struggle, yet faith takes hold so readily with them, and the cleansing power comes down. We have an old pilgrim among us, Mother WRIGHT, as she is called. She is about seventy years of age, and is greatly rejoicing in God, and in the return of primitive power. This is, she says, as Methodism was fifty years ago. One sister, who had been a member of the Baptist church for six years, was lately converted, for she says she had never been before, and then in a few days was clearly sanctified, and is greatly rejoicing in the Lord, and laboring for souls. Another sister had been over twenty years a member of the Methodist Church without religion. She got justified and then was soon sanctified, and then went among her neighbors and talked with them about their souls, and at once the report went out that she was really crazy. Sister R., in Youngstown, was warned not to go to our meetings, that is, the meetings of those who go in for the life and power of religion. When we came here there was a great amount of opposition and prejudice against us, and she was troubled about what was duty, and one night she prayed for the Lord to show her which party was right, and that night she dreamed she saw two companies; one was smaller than the other; the smallest company, including myself, wife and a few others, were walking on a narrow plank path, surrounded with a peculiar light, and something said these Nazarites are right, go with them. And when she awoke she saw in her room the same light, and she came with us, and last New Years' day, which was Sunday, she came forward seeking full salvation; and, after a severe struggle, the blessing came, and when it came she saw distinctly the same peculiar light, and she is now rejoicing in God. Sister D., of Youngstown, for twelve years belonged to the Episcopal Church without religion, and when Brother D. was converted and joined the Methodist Church, hoping her spiritual state might be bettered, she also joined the Methodist Church, but she was in the same unsatisfied state still. Changing her forms of religion did not save her, and she sometimes would state her feelings to the ministers, and they would say, "O, sister, that is a temptation, you are a good Christian," and so she would quiet down again; and so it went on, until the last Bergen Camp-meeting, she went forward and sought justification, and experienced religion, and knew she had it, and knew she never had it before, and a few weeks ago she was brought out into entire sanctification. Before she was converted, she was full of prejudice against these straight pilgrims, and could not bear to have one of them come near her house. She says, last year, when Brother and Sister ROBERTS drove up to her house, and she ascertained who they were, she was so prejudiced against them, she started to leave and go to the neighbors, but Mother WRIGHT was there, and remonstrated with her, and urged her not to leave, and she, with the greatest reluctance, staid. She expected, from what she had heard, they would come in and abuse her, but she says they had not been in the house five minutes before she was really pleased with them, and that was the turning point with her religious life.

One feature of this work of the Lord is, that many, old and young, ranging in age from eighteen to seventy years of age, have given up tobacco, and know what self-denial is, in a practical sense. This is a reform that is greatly needed in the Church, among ministers and laymen, as well as in the world. God requires all to "cleanse themselves from all filthiness of the flesh and spirit."

W. COOLEY.

YOUNGSTOWN, April 6, 1860.

A "Regular Minister," writing us from a charge where was held a "General Quarterly Meeting," some months since, says:

MY BROTHER IN THE WAR:—You will be glad to learn that the work of the Lord is going on with power on this charge. Have now been steadily at the work ever since the General Quarterly Meeting, (14 weeks,) and and see yet no place to stop. Some seventy or eighty have been converted or reclaimed, and many members are *cleansed*. Praise the Lord!

We are receiving many such letters as the following. Coming as they do from those who are walking in the light, they encourage us to labor on, in the face of every difficulty, for the promotion of an earnest Christianity:

GOWANDA, March 26, 1860.

BROTHER ROBERTS:—Permit me, as a reader of the *Earnest Christian*, to tell you with what interest I peruse that valuable Monthly.

How glad I am that there are a few who do uphold an earnest, uncompromising Christianity.

May God bless their efforts to sustain it. O, may the followers of Christ gird on the whole armor, and go forth in the name of the Lord, to battle against the enemy of all righteousness! If we trust wholly in God, He *will* lead us on to certain victory, and strengthen us to build up the walls of Zion.

Our strength lies all in God; without it we can do nothing. Then, "Tarry at Jerusalem until ye be endowed with power from on high."

There, at the foot of the cross, may we await and receive the "Promise of the Father." Glory to God, this hour, for a full redemption. We are entered in, by a new and living way, even by the blood of Christ. I love the cross, the blood-stained cross. Yes, I love it, for by it I expect to gain Heaven.

My soul is *happy* in God. I know that my Redeemer liveth. I am the Lord's, and He is mine. One year I have lived, yes, lived. One year ago the 18th of this present month, as I knelt at the altar, seeking full salvation, Jesus came; He took away all filthiness and dross from my soul; He filled it with His love, peace and joy. Old things passed away, all became new in Christ. It is nearly four years since I first found Christ precious to my soul, but the past year has been so much better. Words cannot express the language of my soul.

It is to be all transformed into the image of Him who hath redeemed us; to follow Him whithersoever He leads me; to suffer with Him, that we may also be glorified together.

O, may I, indeed, be a living witness of the

power of Christ to save unto the uttermost, to be an earnest Christian.

Go on, Brother ROBERTS, and may your publication prove a blessing to thousands in leading them into the highway of holiness, and encourage those who are in the way to press on. We'll soon get home.

May God bless all those who are persecuted for His sake; yea, He will, for His promises are sure; theirs shall be the kingdom. Let us all stand fast in the liberty wherewith Christ hath made us free. Bless the Lord, O my soul; no mortal powers can bring us into bondage.

Your Sister in Christ, R. L. P.

THE REVIVAL IN ENGLAND.

We have been favored with the following extract from a private letter lately received in this city:

CHESHNUT, England, Feb. 10, 1860.

We have been most deeply interested in the revival going on in Ireland and Wales. A clergyman, from Belfast, gave a lecture here on the subject, which was very interesting. I do not see how we can doubt the special work of the Holy Spirit. I do not see why we should doubt God's willingness to quicken the hearts of men in these days, any more than in times past. At Testinvig, North Wales, where we spent last summer, there has been a most wonderful movement. The clergyman, who was averse to the revival, has now entirely changed his opinion. Two of the men who worked in the slate quarries were in deep mental distress on account of their sins. They could get no peace, and one day, at their dinner hour, agreed to go up on one of the hills, where they could be alone, for prayer. When they ascended the hill, instead of finding themselves alone, they found four or five hundred of their fellow workmen, all going up for the same purpose, and the prayers offered by that quickened multitude were wonderful to hear. The result is, that public houses are closed, or only opened for religious purposes, that the sale of Bibles and religious books has greatly increased, and the whole tone of the people entirely altered. Would that God would bring such a work about in our parish, and in our own hearts and homes. Mr. —— has joined the dissenters in having a union meeting once a month for the special supplication of the Holy Spirit. — *Christian Witness*.

TO CORRESPONDENTS.

We are always thankful for contributions of the right stamp for our Magazine. We have received several communications without the name of the writer. It is our choice, when we publish an article, to give, in all cases, the name of the writer. We have always felt an aversion for anonymous communications. If we have anything to say, we prefer to say it openly, and to meet the responsibility. We wish to publish nothing in our Magazine of which any one need be ashamed.

Some articles have been deferred for subsequent numbers. Of poetry we have a large stock on hand—more than we can use. Our object being—not simply to afford literary entertainment—but to assist earnest souls in gaining Heaven—to stir up the children of God to entire devotion to His service—to set up and defend the New Testament standard of piety. We can find room for but little poetry, and that must be devotional and of the higher order. Give us plain prose—stirring, searching truths.

Again we say, if you wish your contributions to appear, send your names with them. Our readers wish to know that the writers of the articles they read, show by their lives that they believe the doctrines they inculcate.

TO SUBSCRIBERS.

We take all the pains in our power to avoid mistakes in mailing the *Earnest Christian*. But if any occur, either through our fault or that of the Post Office Department, if you will inform us we will properly correct them.

We feel grateful for the interest that many of you have taken and are taking in getting new subscribers for us. Our list is already larger than we anticipated it would be when we started. But there are many more who would be benefited by taking the *Earnest Christian*, and who, if you should show it to them, would send on their names with the money. We can still supply back numbers for new subscribers. Please make a little effort to extend the circulation, and thus increase the usefulness of the *Earnest Christian*. To several offices we send but a single number. Can you not find some one among your neighbors, brother or sister, who wishes to share the benefit you receive from a perusal of its pages?

The following we take from a letter written to us, by one of our old preachers, now in Illinois:

"DEAR BROTHER ROBERTS:—Having been some fifteen years a member of the Genesee Conference, and having had special efforts made to get me connected with all the secret cliques of that Conference, but thanks to God, in vain, I could tell some facts that would make the Devil blush. I have often expressed my wish that something might be done to call back the Methodist Church to its original purity, and thousands more in the West are of the same mind. Many are looking to the traveling preachers about as the Papal Church does to their priest.

"But the best of the Church are anti-slavery, anti-secret-society men, and in favor of earnest Christianity, and pure Methodism.

"What we want is more light, and having seen one number of the *Earnest Christian*, we want more of the same with the *Independent*." L. B.

BROTHER ROBERTS:—The work of God is still going on in power on old Parma charge. Upwards of one hundred souls have commenced a life of prayer, and give evidence of conversion. Many others have been sanctified, and several of the young converts are groaning after the fullness of grace and love. We look for more fruit. Some 70 or 80 copies of the *E. C.* are taken on the charge, besides several copies of the *Beauty* and the *Guide*.

C. D. BROOKS.

A friend in New York writes us as follows, respecting a Minister there, whose piety and zeal God is honoring in the salvation of souls:

The Rev. H. GRATTAN GUINNES, the Presbyterian preacher from England, has been holding forth six days in the week, for most of the winter, in this devoted city. Thousands have rushed to hear him as often as he speaks, crowding every nook and corner and standing place in the aisles. The Churches where he preaches are frequently filled half an hour before the services commence.

He appears to be from 26 to 30 years old, but may be older; rather slender form and medium height; dark hair, rather pale visage, remarkable for its sensibility and loveliness of expression. His organization is sensitive and sympathetic. It is in his heart, and not in his brain, that his great strength lieth. He commences his services by a short invocation and reading a hymn, two lines at a time, which the congregation join in singing. He then reads a chapter or a part of a chapter from the Bible, on which he comments rather freely; then prays, standing with his face turned and his hands lifted towards Heaven. In this attitude he pleads with God for pardon, acceptance and justification through faith in the Beloved; and *pleads* as though he expected his prayer to be answered. After which, he announces his text and commences his illustrations, which are extempore, and with little or no exordium. His words seem to flow from a heart exuberant with love to God and love for the souls of men. Instead of a studied effort to show himself or to preach himself, his great aim seems to be to convince his hearers of the necessity of immediate repentance towards God, and faith on the Lord Jesus Christ. The thousands that constitute his audiences, seem more impressed with the impassioned zeal and ardor of the speaker, than with his well measured sentences and his graceful gestures. His illustrations are clear and forcible, and rather slightly resemble Mr. PHINNEY, except in sternness and severity. After having heard him once, you feel strongly inclined to hear him frequently. I understand that under his ministrations many have professed faith in Christ in the different Churches where he has labored. I can but involuntarily exclaim, Oh that many of our preachers, with more talent, would emulate his zeal!

Yours, &c. D. C.

MORAL ENTHUSIASM.

The following extract from the *Christian Inquirer*, a Unitarian paper, breathes a spirit which we are glad to believe is spreading among all the Churches of the land. Oh, that all who bear the name of Christ were intensely earnest in his service:

"If there is any one thing needed more than another, both in pulpits and in parishes, at this juncture, we believe it is moral enthusiasm. Truth is good, and theology is good, and morality is good, and criticism is good; but do let us have live preachers, live parishioners, live churches. It is good to be zealously affected in a good cause. Our cause is the noblest on earth—the cause of God, of Christ, of humanity. Strange that our words do not glow and burn when we speak of the astonishing theme of Christian salvation. Something more is wanted than fine rhetoric, or well-sifted learning, or human eloquence. Something more is wanted than emotional religion, which weeps and cries to-day, and goes the way of the world to-morrow. We do not know how better to characterize this much needed quality than to call it moral enthusiasm. It is the divine, the God-like waking up within us. Of how many preachers we can say, You are thoroughly prepared for your work, you have all the requisite education, general and professional. Oh! let there now be a precipitate of the heart in your sermons. Be not timid, but courageous; not faithless, but believing; not cold, but warm; muse, pray till the fire burns. If you preach sermons but fifteen minutes long, be sure they are live sermons, and not dead ones. Men are not saved by niceties and criticisms, but by the broad, plain, decisive truths of the gospel, believed, and preached, with all the mind and heart. 'Carry,' said one of our noble fraternity just translated, 'carry great matters with you, not corners and angles of subjects into the pulpit.' The machinery is all ready, the engine is on the right track, the ponderous cars are attached, but all is in vain unless our furnace is lighted, and our boiler heated.

"Moral enthusiasm! This is the want of the parish, too, as well as the preacher. Live parishes help to make live preachers, or, at least, do not kill those who are already alive, as dead ones do. All that many parishes need is not a new church, not a new pastor, nor the addition of new members, nor rich and influential persons, to make them flourish like the cedars of Lebanon, but more steam in the boiler. Let there be a baptism of the Holy Spirit. Let the tongues of fire again appear over each disciple. For never, never was there such want of a true, earnest, affectionate religion as now, in this new world, in this nineteenth century, in this perilous experiment of liberty, in this breaking up and passing away of old creeds and usages.

"Never was there a time when the high key and intense strain of the world required a more wide-awake and enthusiastic administration of the commanding interests of life. Not a noisy fanaticism, not a chafed and transient emotion, but a deep central life-glow, as of the steady beat of the heart, should move our words, and make our every motion and deed speak of the living and beautiful features of the human face divine. For what are all things in this world, that men most zealously labor for, compared with the spiritual interests of society, the victory of truth, the creation of a noble manhood, the beauty of holiness, the warm grasp of a tender and powerful humanity, and a lowly awe before the Infinite God? These are the gems of immortal worth, and it is not too much for us to live for them, it would not be too much for us to die for them."

THE EARNEST CHRISTIAN.

RELIGIOUS SENSIBILITY.

BY THE EDITOR.

Allow me to ask, beloved reader, are you earnestly striving to work out your salvation? You may inherit wealth. A fortuitous combination of favorable circumstances may render you famous. Nature may give you health and beauty. But neither friends, nor fortune, nor nature can bestow upon you eternal happiness; you will never go to heaven by accident. An effort is needed. The mightiest exertion of which you are capable is required. Hear what the Great Teacher has said, "Agonize to enter in at the strait gate, for many, I say unto you, shall seek to enter in, but shall not be able." You cannot commence too soon. You have not a longer period granted to you in which to prepare for eternity than is necessary. Time is flying on with tireless wing. Having commenced, with earnestness, the great work for securing for yourself a mansion in the skies, you have need of prosecuting it, till the end of your probation, with increasing intensity of purpose.

No matter with what alacrity the runner of a race begins, if he gives out before the terminus is reached, he does not win the prize. The blight that destroys the grain just before the golden eared harvest invites the reapers sickle is no less detrimental than the early frost that nips the infant blade. The emigrant who, having safely passed the dangers of the deep, is carried on shore to die, fails of realizing his golden visions, no less than he who, just as he was going on board, expired in the fatherland. So he who serves God long and faithfully but dies an apostate, misses heaven just as surely as if he had lived a sinner all his days. Over two thousand years ago, the Holy Ghost told the prophet Ezekiel to write: "But when the righteous turneth away from his righteousness and committeth iniquity, and doeth according to all the abominations that the wicked man doeth, shall he live? All his righteousness that he hath done, shall not be mentioned; in his trespass that he hath trespassed, and in his sin that he hath sinned, in them shall he die." Do not say that the self righteous is meant; for the sooner he turns from his spurious righteousness the better. If he holds on to that he must sink to ruin.

If you are thus in earnest, you will make religion the business of life. As the plant absorbs from air and earth and water only what is essential to its growth, and allows the noxious elements to pass untouched, so you will lay every providential occurrence under contribution to minister to your growth in grace. In all things you will aim to please God. Your feelings may fluctuate, but your outward life will present to the world a beautiful uniformity. You will do right at all times, and under all circumstances. In unswerving rectitude you will be like the old Roman of whom an enemy bore testimony, "That it would be easier to turn the Sun from his course, than Fabricius from the path of honesty." You may be devoid of comfort, but instead of neglecting your closet, you will visit it the oftener. The smouldering embers of the family altar may be nearly extinct, but you will only put on fuel the more carefully, and with the breath of prayer blow them into a flame.

Your corruptions may struggle hard for the mastery and, in fact, often prevail, but you will wrestle with them the more vigorously and call the more imploringly upon God for help, lest "these Sons of Zeruiah prove too hard" for you. He is not in earnest to secure his salvation, who, upon an interruption of his enjoyments becomes careless, prayerless, immoral and wicked.

We must here raise our warning voice against a practice but too prevalent. Many, as soon as they lose the power, think themselves fully justified in giving up the form of godliness. This is a great mistake. If a man faints it is not the best way to recover him to cut off his head. If your fire goes out you will not warm your room by petulantly throwing off the fuel and pouring on water. So, if your spiritual affections become languid, use incessantly the means of grace. Give yourself no rest. Stir up yourself to take hold of God. "Strengthen the things that remain, that are ready to die."

If you thus earnestly serve God, from deep seated principle, he will not leave you long without enjoyment. There will soon be a supernatural element introduced into your religion. It will not be a base morality, frigid and sparkling as the iceberg. Jesus says: "He that hath my commandments and keepeth them, he it is that loveth me, and he that loveth me, shall be loved of my father, and I will love him and will manifest myself to him.

Just here you will be exposed to danger in the opposite direction. You have complained of the want of feeling. You may now have so much that unless you are careful you will grieve the Holy Spirit, fall into darkness, and so your last state become worse than the first. God will let you see something of the magnitude of your eternal interests. And as President Edwards says: "Eternal things are so great and of such vast concern, that there is great absurdity in men's being but lightly moved by them." Your heart will be stirred to its lowest depths. The world will pronounce it excitement. Formality will decide that you are excited. And the Devil seizing an auspicious moment, will whisper to you, in the kindest manner, "may this not be mere excitement?" You reason with him. He is a shrewd logician—has had the benefit of six thousand years experience, which he well knows how to use. Overcome by his sophistry, you admit that, perhaps, it was excitement.

It is permitted by the prevailing code of fashion, for persons to become excited without losing caste on all subjects except religion. The editor of a leading journal, in describing the effect produced in a political meeting by singing a political song, says: "The audience wrought itself up into a perfect furore, and as the last words of the concluding stanza died away in a volume of sound, which made the very building shake, the whole assemblage rose to their feet *en masse*, and joined in a bust of cheering, again and again renewed, amid waving of hats, handkerchiefs and frantic demonstrations of delight." This was regarded as entirely proper. Men may become "frantic" in politics, without causing alarm or condemnation. But religious excitement is pronounced unbecoming in the highest degree. All unite in applying to it to the most opprobious epithets. Vital godliness has thus far had to make its way into the world under this great disadvantage. The Apostles were called "babblers," "fools," and said to be "mad," "drunk" and "beside themselves." Luther was styled a heretic, and Wesley, Whitfield and their coadjutors, fanatics and enthusiasts. The same weapon is still successfully wielded by the enemy of all righteousness. Many, whom the Spirit of God is endeavoring to lead into the full liberty of the Gospel, fail of making any considerable progress, because they shrink from this cross. They anxiously inquire if it is not possible to follow the Lord fully, without such manifestations of emotion as bring upon them the reproach of the world. Some bearing the Christian name look upon such manifestations with suspicion. They do not appear to be as much afflicted with the indifference and wordliness exhibited by many of the professed disciples of Christ, as with the overpowering feeling seen, at times, in a few.

This is the great impediment to the work of God, at the present time. The opposition, well-meant it may be, by many in the Church of Christ, to all uncommon manifestations of the Spirit's influence is, to-day, effecting more harm than the cavils of the skeptic and the sneers of the profane. Says an eminent living minister of the Presbyterian Church, " I have supposed, and do still suppose, that the great reason why revivals of religion have not been more deep, permanent and sin-subduing is, that the spirit has been unable to proceed beyond a certain limit in his work without meeting with a stern resistance on the part of multitudes of professors of religion and ministers. They seem in their unbelief, to have prescribed certain limits within which revivals should be kept; formed certain notions of order, and endeavored to confine the spirit down to a stereotyped mode of operation, ready to make common cause, and unite their hands in opposing the spirit, whenever he should step over into what they suppose to be the regions of disorder.

For myself, I am expecting, as soon as the Church will consent to it, and the ministry are prepared to lead the way, much deeper, more permanent, and sin-subduing revivals of religion than the world has ever seen. This must be if the world is ever to be converted."

.This is the testimony of a man of piety and learning, whose labors have, for many years, been highly blessed in promoting revivals of religion, both in this country and in England. He speaks from experience.

Our object in this article is two-fold. First. To persuade, if possible, all who fear the Lord, not to countenance this " stern resistance to the work of the spirit;" and secondly, to caution all who are endeavoring to follow the Lord fully, against grieving the Holy Spirit by allowing themselves to be tried with their peculiar exercises. In doing this we shall show that it is entirely proper, and to be expected, that those engaged in the service of God should manifest, at times, the deepest emotion.

While the earnest Christian will uniformly walk with the Lord by faith, and thus preserve an entire consistency of conduct, yet the depth of his emotions will vary. A continuance of the overpowering emotions that he sometimes experiences, would unfit him for the duties of life, and exhaust his physical frame. Paul could never have preached the Gospel had he always been so transported as not to know whether he " was in the body or out of the body."

Our first argument is drawn from the greatness of the danger to which sinners are exposed. They have wantonly violated the Divine law, which is holy and just and good. They have scornfully rejected all the overtures of mercy. God, who cannot lie, has said, " These shall go away into everlasting punishment. And the smoke of their torment ascendeth up forever, and ever; and they have no rest, day nor night!" I once saw a man who had violated the laws of his country and was awaiting his sentence to the State prison. Though a strong man he sobbed aloud, and for some minutes could not control himself so as to speak. No one who saw him could have pronounced his great grief extravagant. Shall then the sinner, whose crimes in the sight of God are of a far deeper dye, and who is exposed to a fate infinitely more dreadful, be thought to be unduly excited at the discovery of his guilt, though he should " roar by reason of the disquietness of his heart !"

An aged mother left the home of her youth and the graves of her kindred, and with tottering step crossed the Atlantic, that she might seek her son, in this land of plenty. She found him in a prison! I saw her as she reached her hand through the iron grating and grasped the hand of her loved though erring child; and then she turned away and sank to the ground, with a grief too big for utterance. He must be an unfeeling wretch who could ridicule the deep anguish of her broken heart. Who then will say that that Christian mother is fanatical, who seeing the child of her affections "condemned already," waiting only for the ministering spirits of the justice of the Almighty, to hurry him away to "outer darkness, where is weeping and wailing and gnashing of teeth," cries unto God, "with groanings that cannot be uttered," to stay the avenging sword, and send once more, to his obdurate heart, the convicting Spirit, to persuade him if possible to escape the damnation of hell? As the Bible is true, his danger is real, and hence no anxiety that she can feel is greater than the dreadfulness of the exposure will warrant.

But we prefer to let President Edwards speak on this point. As a philosopher and Divine, this country has never produced his equal. He was as pious as learned. Dr. Chambers says of him: "Looking to Edwards, we behold the most philisophical of all theologians, at the same time the humblest and holiest of men." Robert Hall pronounces him "The greatest man of the world." Through his labors many souls were brought to Christ. We do not subscribe to his Calvinistic views, but we do consider him as good authority on Christian experience. No one will hardly dare to charge this eminent Presbyterian Divine with either being fanatical himself or encouraging fanaticism in others. Edwards says, "There is one particular kind of exercise and concern of mind, that may have been overpowered by, that has been especially stumbling to some; and that is, the deep concern and distress that they have been in for the souls of others. I am sorry that any put us to the trouble of doing that which seems so needless, as defending such a thing as this. It seems like mere trifling in so plain a case, to enter into a formal and particular debate, in order to determine whither there be anything in the greatness and importance of the case that will answer, and bear a proportion to the greatness of the concern that some have manifested. Men may be allowed, from no higher a principle than common ingenuity and humanity, to be very deeply concerned, and greatly exercised in mind, at the seeing others in great danger, of no greater calamity than drowning or being burned up in a house on fire. And if so, then doubtless it will be allowed to be equally remarkable if they saw them in danger of a calamity ten times greater, to be still much more concerned: and so much more still, if the calamity was still vastly greater. And why then should it be thought unreasonable, and looked upon with a very suspicious eye, as if it must come from some bad cause, when persons are extremely concerned at seeing others in very great danger of suffering the fierceness and wrath of Almighty God, to all eternity? And besides, it will doubtless be allowed that those that have very great degrees of the Spirit of God, that is a spirit of love, may well be supposed to have vastly more of love and compassion to their fellow creatures, than those that are influenced only by common humanity. Why should it be thought strange that those that are full of the Spirit of Christ, should be proportionably, in their love to souls like to Christ; who had so strong a love to them, and concern for them, as to be willing to drink the dregs of the cup of God's fury for them; and at the same time that He offered up His blood for souls, offered up also, as their high priest, strong crying and tears, with an extreme agony, wherein the soul of Christ was, as it were, in travail for the souls of the elect; and therefore in saving them He is said to see of the *travail* of His soul. As such a spirit of love to, and concern for souls, was the spirit of Christ, so it is the spirit of the Church; and therefore the Church in desiring and seeking that Christ might be brought forth in the world, and in the souls of men, is represented, Rev. xii. as "a woman crying, travailing in birth, and pained to be delivered." The spirit of those that have been in distress for the souls of others, so far as I can discern, seems not to have been different from that of the apostle who travailed for souls, and was ready to wish himself accursed from Christ for others. And that of the psalmist—Ps. cxix. 53., "Horror hath taken hold upon me, because of the wicked that forsake Thy law." And v. 136, "Rivers of water run down mine eyes because they keep not Thy law." And that of the prophet Jeremiah—Jer. iv. 19—"My bowels! my bowels! I am pained at my very heart. My head maketh a noise in me! I cannot hold my peace! Because thou hast heard, O my soul, the sound of the trumpet, the alarm of war." And so, chap. xi. 1, and iii. 17, and xiv. 17, and Isa. xxii. 4. We read of Mordecai, when he saw his people in danger of being destroyed with a temporal destruction—Esth. iv. 1—"That he rent his clothes, and put on sackcloth with ashes, and went out into the midst of the city, and cried with a loud and bitter cry." And why, then, should persons be thought to be distracted, when they cannot forbear crying out, at the consideration of the misery of those that are going to eternal destruction."

"I have seen," says Finney, "a man of as much strength of intellect and muscle as any man in the community, fall down prostrate, absolutely overpowered by his unutterable desires for sinners. I know this is a stumbling-block to many; and it always will be as long as there remain in the Church so many blind and stupid professors of religion. But I cannot doubt that these things are the work of the Spirit of God. O that the whole Church could be so filled with the Spirit as to travail in prayer, till a nation should be born in a day."

God does not give any one this travail for souls continually, because no one could live under it; but every earnest and true Christian has it at times, and he that is led by the Spirit will have as much of it as he can well endure. Reader, if you have never felt it, you have good reason to fear that you have never yet been converted to God, and you cannot have the Spirit of Christ. And the apostle says—Rom. viii. 9—"Now if any man have not the Spirit of Christ, he is none of His."

The Spirit opens our eyes to the condition of sinners. In His light the threatenings with which the Bible abounds are clothed with terror. Have we, by any act of disobedience, brought ourselves within the range of the artillery of Sinai? Does the dark cloud of Divine vengeance hang over us? The consciousness of our condition can but be attended with the deepest anguish of Spirit. The soul thus exposed goes "mourning all the day long." The sweetest pleasures have lost their attractions.

Have we been rescued from our perilous condition by the strong arm of Him who is mighty to deliver? Do we see others, strangers, acquaintances, friends, relatives, in imminent danger of the same destruction which so recently threatened us? Does the compassionate Spirit of Jesus dwell within us? Then, how natural, how unavoidable is it that we should manifest, when alive to the condition of sinners, the deepest emotion.

Did Christ o'er sinners weep,
And shall our cheeks be dry?
Let floods of penitential grief
Burst forth from every eye.

When the ear is soothed with a variety of fine harmony, the soul is too often allured away from spiritual worship, even though a divine song attend the music.—WATTS.

BELIEVER, the more worldly business lies upon thy hand, the more need thou hast to keep close to thy closet. Much bnsiness lays a man open to many sins, many snares and many temptations.

Pure Christian humility has no such thing as roughness, or contempt; or fierceness or bitterness, in its nature; it makes a person like a little child, harmless and innocent; and that none need to be afraid of; or like a lamb, destitute of all bitterness, wrath, anger, and clamor, agreeable to Eph. iv. 31.

With such a spirit as this ought especially zealous ministers of the gospel to be clothed, and those that God is pleased to improve as instruments in His hands of promoting His work: they ought indeed to be thorough in preaching the word of God, without mincing the matter at all; in handling the sword of the Spirit, as the ministers of the Lord of Hosts, they ought not to be mild and gentle; they are not to be gentle and moderate in searching and awakening the conscience, but should be sons of thunder: the word of God, which is in itself sharper than any two-edged sword, ought not to be sheathed by its ministers, but so used, that its sharp edges may have their full effect, even to the dividing asunder soul and spirit, joints and marrow (provided they do it without judging particular persons, leaving it to conscience and the Spirit of God to make the particular application); but all their conversation should savor of nothing but lowliness and good will, love and pity to all mankind; so that such a spirit should be like a sweet odor diffused around them wherever they go, or like a light shining about them, their faces should, as it were, shine with it; they should be like lions to guilty consciences, but like lambs to men's persons. This would have no tendency to prevent the awakening of men's consciences, but on the contrary would have a very great tendency to awaken them; it would make way for the sharp sword to enter; it would remove the obstacles, and make a naked breast for the arrow.—Edwards.

God will not give his blessing to even a divine service, if not done in His own way, on principles of truth and righteousness.—Adam Clarke.

The most fatal ruins are, frequently, not those which come suddenly, but those which come progressively—by little and little—from step to step.

There is not a more fatal disease than a consumption; yet the consumptive patient is frequently so deceived respecting his disorder, because he is not in violent pain, and the progress of his disease is slow, that you can scarcely persuade him of his danger. Consumptive persons will plan and contrive for months and years to come, when they have not a week to live! Decay in religion is of this nature; it is a spiritual consumption. If a house receive a shock from a stroke of lightning, it may still be sound in the main, and may not require to be pulled down; but if a house begin to decay at the foundation, there is little hope but it must come down.—Cecil.

Self-Love.—Self-love is our most terrible enemy, because it is our nearest. Every one covets praise; but there is a strong self-love that has no bound, which is vanity; as there is, also, a feeble self-love which is moderate. We baptize the latter with the name of modesty. This is not a virtue, it is a natural quality, a simple mark of good sense. There is a great distance between modesty and humility. True humility is a miracle. A supernatural grace is necessary to impart to a minister. Nothing but love can remove self-love from the throne of his heart. Love is an ardent, passionate, pre-occupation, which withdraws from everything that is not allied to itself, from blame and from praise alike. Conversion essentially consists in love.—Vinet.

Love.—Let our love be firm, constant, and inseparable; not coming and returning like the tide, but descending like a never failing river, ever running into the ocean of Divine excellency, passing on in these channels of duty and a constant obedience; still being a river till it be turned into sea and vastness, even the immensity of a blissful eternity.—Taylor's Holy Living.

WHO ARE THE CHILDREN OF GOD?

BY NELSON C. LYON.

What an important question! It is one that should come home with force to the heart of every one who professes to be a follower of Christ. But who will answer it? Let the Word of God answer; for we must not judge. The inspired penman tells us that "As many as are led by the Spirit of God, they are the sons of God." It appears that our worship is based upon our being led by the Spirit; for the passage quoted implies that "As many as are *not* led by the Spirit of God, they *are not* the sons of God." If our being the children of God depends upon our being led by His Spirit, how important it is that we should be very careful to obey *all* its teachings.

What is it to be led by the Spirit? Where will it lead us? "He shall guide you into *all truth*, and teach you *all things*." Christ prayed, "Sanctify them through thy truth; thy Word is truth." If we are to be sanctified through the truth, and the Spirit guides us into all truth, it must, of course, lead us into sanctification; and if we are led by the Spirit, we shall be sanctified.

Perhaps you ask, "When?" Taking the Word of God for our guide, we reply, now; for, "Behold, now is the accepted time; behold, now is the day of salvation."

We are commanded to "Love God with all the *heart*, with *all* the *soul*, with *all* the *mind*, and with *all* the *strength*," and *surely* we cannot do that until our hearts are cleansed from all sin.

We cannot love God with all the heart, until our hearts are filled with love, and our hearts cannot be filled with love until they are emptied of all sin, till they are made pure. Being wholly sanctified, is nothing more or less than being cleansed from all sin; and "If we *confess* our sins, He is faithful and just to *forgive* us our sins; and to cleanse us from all unrighteousness."

Here is truth; that we must love God with all the heart, and at the *present* time; that we cannot do it until we are cleansed from all sin, or wholly sanctified; that, as the Spirit is to guide us into all truth, He will guide us into this truth. Also, that if we are led by the Spirit, we shall be cleansed from all sin *now*.

The Apostle prayed, "And the very God of peace sanctify you wholly; and I pray God your whole spirit, and soul, and body, be preserved blameless unto the coming of our Lord Jesus Christ. Faithful is He that calleth you who will do it." How can we be preserved blameless until we are first wholly sanctified? Certainly we *cannot* be, unless we say that sin is pleasing in the sight of God, and surely no one who believes the Word of God will say that it is; for He says that He "Cannot look upon sin with the least degree of allowance." "No unclean thing shall enter the kingdom of Heaven." It is evident, that before we can be preserved blameless, we must be made blameless, that is, pure in heart. Nothing that is defiled with sin can be blameless in the sight of a Holy God. "We are the temple of God; and if any man defile the temple of God him shall God destroy." Will not *sin* defile the temple of God?

We have proved, from the Word of God, that it is our privilege, and our duty, to be holy, and I ask, can we live year after year in a justified state, without going any farther? We have proved that if we are led by the Spirit, we shall be led into sanctification; that if we follow the teachings of the Spirit, and the Word of God, we shall be sanctified wholly, and preserved blameless unto the coming of our Lord Jesus Christ. Are those who have been professing to enjoy religion from five to forty or more years, and yet know nothing about sanctification—I ask with all charity—are *they* the children of God? Certainly they have not been led by His Spirit. Reader, hast thou obtained a *pure* heart? If so, thank God and take courage. Hast thou been many years professing to live justified in His sight, and yet hast thou not followed the teachings of His Sprit, or His Word, which says, "Be ye holy, for I the Lord your God am holy? If the latter case be your condition, *are* you a child of God? "Examine yourselves; *prove* your own selves; know ye not that Jesus Christ is *in* you, except ye be *reprobates?* "And if Christ be in you the body is dead because of sin." "Herein was the Son of God *manifested* to *destroy* the work of the devil." *Sin* is the work of the devil, and hence if Christ destroys the work of the devil, he must destroy sin. Reader, if Christ dwell in your heart, will he not destroy sin there? "If any man have not the Spirit of Christ, he is none of His." If we have the Spirit of Christ, we shall have its fruits also, which are "Love, joy, peace, long-suffering, gentleness, goodness, faith, meekness, temperance."

"Against *such* there is no law."

PRIDE.—Let none think themselves out of danger of spiritual pride, even in their best frames. Pride is the worst viper in the heart; it is the first sin that ever entered into the universe, is lowest of all in the foundation of the whole building of sin, and is the most secret, deceitful and unsearchable in its ways of working, of any lusts whatever. It is ready to mix with everything; and nothing is so hateful to God, contrary to the spirit of the gospel, or of so dangerous consequence; and there is no one sin that does so much to let the devil into the hearts of the saints and expose them to his delusions.—EDWARDS.

WE are apt to believe in Providence so long as we have our own way; but if things go awry, then we think if there is a God, He is in Heaven, and not on earth.—BEECHER.

HE that would pray with effect must live with care and piety.—TAYLOR.

THEY *have healed also the hurt of the daughters of my people slightly, saying peace, peace, when there is no peace.*

The prophet gives a thundering message, that they might be terrified, and have some convictions and inclinations to repent; but it seems that the false prophets, the false priests, went about stifling people's convictions, and when they were hurt or a little terrified, they were for daubing over the wound, telling them that Jeremiah was but an enthusiastic preacher.

Our hearts are exceedingly deceitful, and desperately wicked; none but the eternal God knows how treacherous they are. How many of us cry peace, peace to our souls, when there is no peace. How many are there that are now settled upon their lees, that now think they are Christians, that now flatter themselves that they have an interest in Jesus Christ! whereas, if we come to examine their experiences, we will find that their peace is but a peace of the devil's making; it is not peace of God's giving; it is not a peace that passeth human understanding. It is matter, therefore, of great importance to know whether we may speak peace to our hearts.

I know, by sad experience, what it is to be lulled asleep with a false peace. Long was I lulled asleep; long did I think myself a Christian, when I knew nothing of the Lord Jesus Christ. I went, perhaps, further than many of you do; I used to fast twice a week; I used to pray, sometimes, nine times a day; I used to receive the sacrament constantly every Lord's day; and yet I knew nothing of Jesus Christ in my heart. I knew nothing of inward religion in my soul.

O, if ye do not take care, a form of religion will destroy your soul; ye will rest in it, and will not come to Jesus Christ at all; whereas, those things are only the means and not the end of religion; Christ is the end of the law for righteousness to all that believe.—WHITFIELD.

EXPERIENCE
OF MRS. MINERVA COOLEY.

I WAS taught by a praying mother in the days of my infancy to lisp my evening prayer, and I never durst, before my conversion, close my eyes in sleep without first kneeling by my bedside, and saying my little prayer to God. But I do not remember to have been especially convicted for sin until after my tenth year, when I began to feel my need of salvation. During a series of meetings I went several times to the anxious seat. My heart was all broken down before the Lord, but I did not know how to cast my burden on Him, or how to exercise saving faith. After a time my deep convictions wore off, and I was encouraged by some to believe that God had pardoned my sins. But Jesus showed me by a vision of the night that I had settled down upon a false hope. After tenderly embracing me, he seemed to say to me, You think you are in the way to heaven, but you are in the way to hell: He then smiled upon me, and disappeared. When I awoke, it seemed to me that Jesus had appeared to me in person and told me that I was self-deceived. I now began in earnest to seek the Lord, and soon felt His power to save, and then how my young heart went out after others, especially the unconverted members of my father's family! I found some heavy crosses to bear, though they might appear trifling to persons of maturer years. I felt that God called me to labor, to do something for souls young as I was. I well remember the glory I used to feel in bearing the cross, and though Satan tried to prevent my doing certain duties, by telling me I was too young, yet my heavenly Father gave me grace and decision to put him to flight, and for a time led me by His Spirit in the path of obedience. I kept on in this way for a few years as well as I could, trying to follow Jesus according to the light I had, and sometimes I would feel so much of His presence as to quite overcome my physical powers; and then a great solemnity would pervade my mind for days, and I would feel such a sinking into God as I could not express. I read the lives of Hester Ann Rogers and Mrs. Fletcher, and greatly longed to see somebody deeply experienced as they were, to whom I could go for counsel, but I looked in vain to find them. O how I needed some spiritual guide to point out the dangers that beset my path, and guide my feet in the narrow way. Happy had it been for me had I kept on living near to Jesus. But after the lapse of a few years I commenced going in young company; and I proved, alas! that the society of the gay and thoughtless was no help to a life of faith. I now began to lay down my watch, and to neglect certain duties until I felt the light going out of my soul; and thus was I shorn of my strength, so that I had no power to labor, though I kept up an outward form, and attended regularly class and prayer meetings, and visited my closet three times a day; but O how little I knew of what it really was to be blessed! I felt a sort of satisfied feeling in doing those duties, because they were enjoined upon me, but my heart did not go out to God in them; it lay all unmoved and unwarmed within; though the divine rays were shining then as now, I had no faith to conduct them to my heart. I read the promises in God's holy word to His believing children, but I had no power to claim them as mine. I lived on in this way until in my nineteenth year I became the wife of an itinerant minister; and how little I then felt the responsibilities of a minister's wife! I thought I must please the people, and this I endeavored to do, by doing all that I thought was required of me; in visiting the members, taking part in the social meetings, in instructing the youth, in superintending Sabbath schools, and by being active in all the benevolent societies. I felt it a task to move, and thought when we went to a new station, if we could please the people the first year, they would want us back the second year;

and they generally did. Things passed on in this way until we went to the Springville charge, and Bro. Eleazier Thomas was appointed our Presiding Elder. With him holiness was a prominent theme, and he preached it wherever he went. Previous to this time, I do not recollect to have heard a sermon preached on this subject during all these years that I had lived so backslidden in heart though not in life. I did not know any one who could declare from a personal experience that there was power in Jesus' blood to cleanse the heart from all sin.

I had gone on measuring myself by others, and had thought I was as good as most in the Church; but sometimes I would feel the upbraidings of conscience, and some circumstance would lead to self-examination; and then I would feel that all was not right, and that I was not prepared for sudden death; but I had heard it many times said that we should have dying grace given to us in that hour, and that we did not need dying grace to live by. I tried to believe this, and would quiet my conscience and pass on. Yet I knew the Church was not what it ought to be, and was far from what it was in its earlier days of simplicity and power. I had read of those times, and could remember when a child, how the members went plainly dressed, and would kneel in the public congregation; and when assembled in love-feasts, the doors being shut, would enjoy seasons of great refreshing from the presence of the Lord. It did seem now as I looked over the state of the Church, and saw how its members tried to outvie each other in worldly conformity, and in building costly edifices to gratify the eyes of its fashionable worshippers, and saw so little humble piety and true Christian zeal for God, that Ichabod would soon be written upon the doorposts of our Methodism, for the glory was departing from her. At times I would see these things, and mourn over them, and would resolve to live nearer to God, and at times had some peace and rest, but it was only for a few moments. Thus I went on resolving and re-resolving to be more faithful, but without any real abiding change in my feelings, for about ten years.

And then, glory be to Jesus! it was my privilege to become acquainted with some Christians who walked in the clear light, and who felt it their duty to deal faithfully with souls. And these did not as others had done, flatter me, and encourage me to think I was doing well without any satisfactory evidences of my personal salvation. As I sat under the pointed preaching of some devoted ministers, the word came to my soul with searching, sifting power. And O how I saw that I was living on shadows without tasting the substance! Then, when I looked over my past life, and saw how little I had done with an eye to the glory of God; and how I had misrepresented Jesus, professing to be His disciple, and at the same time indulging in pride of life, and doing many things to gratify self, I felt like getting in the dust and thanking God that He had not removed the candlestick out of its place, and left me no space for repentance. About this time, while residing in Somerset, I was taken suddenly ill, and did not expect to live twenty-four hours; and keenly I then felt that the dying grace I had before expected would not be given when there were neglected duties unrepented of. I felt that I was not prepared to go into the presence of my Judge—I had not the wedding garment on. But God saw fit in His mercy to rebuke the disease, and to spare my life.

I then sought earnestly the forgiveness of all my backslidings, and felt that God did justify me freely, through faith in His name. I now felt greatly the need of more power to be useful, and was convicted for the blessing of entire holiness.

I resolved to seek it at the coming camp meeting which was soon to be held in Newfane. That meeting was rendered a great blessing to very many souls. The fruits of it will only be seen in eternity. It was the first that had been held in that region for fifteen years; and this would not have been, but for the untiring and persevering efforts of Bro. Joseph McCreery. It was there my soul entered the "Canaan of perfect love"—the land of rest from in-bred sin. On the last day of this meeting, a beloved sister—a mother in Israel, (wife of Dr. Israel Chamberlain) came to me and invited me to go into a tent where a few were seeking for entire holiness. I went in and found sister Hardy and Bro. William C. Kendall laboring with a few souls. I knelt with them, and was enabled by the help of God's Spirit to make an entire consecration of all I had to Him. And O how I saw the crosses coming up before me! One was to go home and profess it in the society where we then lived. I saw a little of what I should have to meet; there was very little sympathy with earnest religion in that place, only about a half dozen members out of seventy who met in class, and these were cold and formal, and my husband did not enjoy the blessing—but I said, Lord, I *will* confess it. Another was, to exhort in the public congregation, and another was to go home and labor with my mother, although she had long been a member of the Church, I felt sure she was not saved. A little before this she had been afflicted with severe illness; and I had stood by her bedside and saw her sinking, as I supposed, in the arms of death, and had not courage to speak to her about her soul.

The Lord pity such professors of religion! The reason this was such a cross to me, was, because religion was not a familiar subject in the family; and in how many professedly Christian families is this the case! Everything else, almost, is looked after, but the salvation of its members.

After promising the Lord I would take the cross every where with all the reproach, I felt the light breaking into my soul, and O what waves of light seemed to pass all through my inner and outer being. I was enabled by faith to put on Christ fully, and felt all through my soul such a glorious union with him. It was now my greatest delight to do His blessed will, and I began to feel such a sympathy for perishing souls, as I had never felt before. My soul was greatly burdened when I beheld the backslidings of God's people. At one time, for nearly a week so heavily did the state of the Church press upon me, that I was scarcely able to perform the common duties of the family. At length I was enabled to cast my burden upon the Lord. I went alone to the sanctuary, and entered the sacred desk, where I prostrated myself before the Lord, and earnestly besought Him to endue my husband with power from on high, to give edge and force to his truth as proclaimed from that desk —that the hearts of the people might melt under its burning power. I felt assured by the Holy Spirit my prayer was heard, and waited patiently expecting the answer. My burden was all gone, and with a light and happy heart I went about my work until the next Sabbath; and that day as I sat under the word, I thought I had never heard my husband preach with such freedom and power. I saw it was taking effect, and God manifested His presence in the class meeting, in a wonderful manner. Some fell under His power, and nearly all eyes were suffused with tears —it was the dawning of a new era to that society.

Glory, glory be to Jesus, who hears and answers prayer!

I felt it my duty to reprove sin wherever I saw it, in the Church or out of it, and this called down upon me bitter opposition. I met with trials and persecutions I had not expected, but O how graciously did the Lord sustain me, and cause me in every trial to triumph!

And O how I now felt that my husband as well as every minister of the gospel, needed the clear light in his soul, in order to teach others the way. And before our four days' meeting on Bear Ridge, I carried his case to the Lord, and got the assurance that He would save him fully at that meeting.

But the meeting passed on until the last evening, when the Lord laid upon me a heavy cross; but He gave me strength to bear it, although Satan suggested it would be very much out of place, and would injure the cause. I felt it my duty to go to him in the church, and ask him to come forward with others, and seek the blessing of holiness; for I felt that ministers must lay aside their dignity, and get down as low as others, to be fully saved.

I went to him, and we knelt together at the altar, and as we commenced praying, God began to show him his heart, and earnestly did he plead that the second work, the work of purification might be completed there. And that night, between the hours of eleven and twelve, while the now sainted William C. Kendall was lifting him up to the throne in earnest believing prayer, he experienced the inward crucifixion, the death of nature, and was enabled to testify clearly to the power of Jesus' blood to cleanse and purify the heart. And since that hour the ever blessed Jesus has been an abiding guest at our humble home.

O glory, glory be to His name, how He has sustained us while passing through trials, and He has enabled us to count it all joy when we fall into divers temptations, knowing that the trial of our faith worketh patience. Now I can say as did the apostle, I live, yet not I but Christ liveth in me. O what an amazing stoop of condescending grace to save so sweetly, so fully, a rebel soul like me. I find in Jesus my all every day, every hour, every moment, and like as the atom plays in the sun's beams, so my soul seems lost in God, and delights itself in the ocean of His love. O that I had an angel's tongue and a trumpet's voice to tell the world of God's redeeming love. O, how gently He bears me along, and unfolds to me daily the riches of His grace! My every wish and desire centers in Him, and the language of my heart is, O Jesus! I'll follow Thee everywhere, I'll go at Thy bidding, regardless of the world's flatteries or frowns, till Thou shalt sign my release and take me home!

QUALIFICATIONS FOR PREACHING.—When any one comes forward to offer himself as a laborer in the vineyard of the Lord, before he can be rightly assigned to any sphere, the question as to his spiritual character must be favorably decided, and then his sphere should be determined by his gifts. Which of the various gifts of the Holy Spirit have been conferred upon him? If none of them, who dare say that he is to be a minister of God, and a teacher of the souls of men? It is a manifest inversion of Christian order, when the commission of the Church is taken to be the authority to commence the exercise of spiritual gifts. In the New Testament the Church's only warrant for issuing her commissions is the known possession of such gifts; and this can only be proved by their previous exercise. Her work was not to create gifts, but from among the *gifted* brethren to select those whom the Lord had, by His own will and act, previously fitted for special offices. The ordination of the Church to the ministry was not a Christian's first authority to preach Christ; for that, opportunity and ability were authority enough; but the special eminence and usefulness of some among the company of preachers was the Church's warrant for separating them to the sole work of the ministry. If a commission from the Church be held to supply the place either of the Spirit's constraining call, or of His qualifying gift, His office in perpetuating the ministry is superceded. To do this effectually, it is not necessary to blot from creeds the expressions of right belief, but only to adopt in practice such regulations as will enable men without grace, or without gifts, by the use of ordinary professional preparations, to obtain a commission, and stand up as accredited stewards of the mysteries of God.—ARTHUR.

THE carnal minded cannot believe that there is any sure plan of driving out or keeping under one devil, except by calling in the aid of another.—HARE.

SINGING IN CHURCH.

How can we get persons to sing in our Churches? This is the inquiry that is being constantly made, not only in this city, but in many other places also. It ought not to be so. God requires his people to praise him, and especially in the sanctuary. By the mouth of the sweet Psalmist of Israel he said, "Whoso offereth praise glorifieth me," and David resolved accordingly, "I will bless the Lord at all times; his praise shall be continually in my mouth;" and invites all to do the same, "Sing praises to God, sing praises; sing praises to our King, sing praises; for God is the King of all the earth, sing ye praises with understanding;" and in other places he saith, "It is good to sing praises unto our God, for it is pleasant, and praise is comely; praise him in his sanctuary, praise him in the congregation of his saints." Praise constituted a very large part of the worship of the Jewish Church, and the Christians in apostolic times delighted in the same holy exercise. They waited not for the accompaniment of wind or stringed instruments, but in open air, in secret chambers, in prisons, or wherever any saints happened to be assembled, there they could sing a hymn. There was no straining after any artistic effect or scientific execution; but the plain song of piety ascended from earth to Heaven, in direct obedience to the command of the apostle to "offer the sacrifice of praise to God continually, that is, the fruit of our lips, giving thanks to his name." So, at a later period, in time of persecution, the early Christians were accustomed to meet a great while before day and sing praises to Christ as God. So, again, at a later period still, as we learn from Cave.

"When they (Christians) were at dinner, they sang hymns and psalms; a practice which Clement of Alexandria commends as very suitable to Christians, and a modest and decent way of praising God whilst we are partaking of his creatures. Saint Chrysostom also strongly pleads for it, that men should be careful to teach their wives and children; and which (singing) they should use at their ordinary works." Numberless testimonies to the same effect might be cited. The primitive Christians praised the "Lord at all times." So, again, at the times of the great Reformation, we have abundant evidence of psalmody and hymnology being common among Protestants. And from the glimpses which are afforded us of Heaven, it would seem that new songs of praise, "loud as from numbers without number, sweet as from blessed voices," will never die away from the lips of the holy and happy worshippers. Now the path of duty is plain. All must recognise it, and at the same time feel the need of united praise in church. But it may be asked, can any plan be devised to meet and overcome the difficulty complained of? We reply, most certainly. God has given all voices, some after one sort, some after another, but all have voices capable of improvement. Let, then, the heads of households practice plain singing at home; and, if "men," feeling indisposed to lead in this matter, will not prevent such pious exhortations of singing under their own roofs, "wives and children," sisters and brothers, maid servants and men-servants, will quickly draw all "men" out into family psalmody. Familiarized to it by fives, and by tens, and by scores in their private worship, what would check spontaneous joining (with or without choirs) in church? Accustomed to ecclesiastical music within their own family circle, where would any longer be such grave impediments as are now alleged to exist? Then we would also suggest that an effort should be made to get as many as possible of the people together to practice some two or three plain tunes by the ear during the intermediate week days. It could be done. Nature makes human beings vocal, and none refuse to sing any popular airs or national melodies when the occasion offers; and that they acquire by the ear, accomplish by practice. So it should be, and it could be, with sacred tunes if the spiritual pastor cordially called upon his flock to assemble in church or other suitable place for that exclusive purpose. In answer to an objection that may naturally arise to this plan, we would ask our readers to remember that among those who sang hosannas to the Lord, there might have been, and probably were, many false notes, many inaccurate and uncouth voices; yet our Saviour loved to hear them sing; and he declared, if they held their peace, the very stones would immediately cry out. Let us then be very careful how we silence any who would join in the act of praise, from the mistaken idea that they would interrupt others. "Let everything that hath breath praise the Lord, for His name only is excellent, His glory above Heaven and earth."—*Church Witness.*

FANATICISM. — Fanaticism is the child of false zeal and of superstition, the father of intolerance and of persecution; it is, therefore, very different from piety, though some persons are pleased to confound them. The pious man, always governed by humility and reason, implores and receives the succors of grace; and evidences this Divine nature by conducting himself with sweet humility and love, the genuine character of the first Christians. But the fanatic, big with pride, and full of himself, rejects reason, and takes the emotions of his own passions for those of grace; and far from conducting himself with Christian modesty and love, he follows the reveries of his imagination as if they were the inspirations of the Divine Spirit; he imitates the follies of enthusiastic fools, and if occasion offers, the cruelties of bloody persecutors. Let us cautiously guard against this excess, but let us not despise true zeal; for it differs as much from fanaticism as vigour, accompanied with health, differs from a delirium produced by a burning fever.—FLETCHER.

SUBSTITUTES FOR THE HOLY GHOST.

BY REV. A. A. PHELPS.

HAVING treated this subject in a former number in its application to the membership of the Church generally, we now proceed to notice some of the substitutes frequently made by the Christian ministry for the baptism of celestial fire.

1. *Education.* Many act as though they believed their erudition would measure their success more nearly than anything else. Their critical expositions and labored essays are dealt out with a master's hand, and regarded as the very quintessence of the gospel itself. In their estimation, the *intellect* is the devil's stronghold, against which their heaviest artillery is leveled. Logic is their principal weapon in the mighty war with sin and Satan. A perfect volley of arguments is hurled at the reasoning faculties, which may be robbed of every refuge of defense, and the heart remain the same dungeon of darkness—the same den of thieves—the same seat of Satan as before. This is surely the character of too much of our modern preaching. The intellect is fed, but the soul goes hungry away. The judgment is convinced, but the conscience is not effectually aroused and stung with the "arrows of the Almighty." There is a fearful tendency to be satisfied with the *light* without the *fire*—the *thunder* without the *lightning*.

2. *Eloquence.* True eloquence is the *power to move mind.* There is nothing unlawful in possessing such a power if employed in the right direction. Many, however, seem to rely more on their powers of oratory to move, than upon the unction of the Holy Spirit. A splendid elocution, and dazzling rhetorical flourishes, are prominent features of the sermon, which often have the effect upon the simple to make them pronounce the preacher a most "eloquent" man! A short extract from "B. M. A." of the *Guide to Holiness,* a few months

since, will forcibly illustrate this point: "We have seen the Redeemer of men so presented, that His friends scarcely knew Him. We have heard the gospel (as it was called) preached in such a way that we could think of nothing like it, but a grand display of spiritual pyrotechnics—rockets of imagination went streaming away into the heavens; all sorts of fires, from angel luminaries down, winding up in involved blazings of many-colored lights, and a terrific explosion, leaving us peering out into the darkness that followed, and asking, 'Where *is* Jesus?'"

3. *Orthodoxy.* It is a great thing, and very desirable withal, to be correct in doctrine, for God has made it a matter of no small concern as to what we believe. But theoretical and theological correctness is not *everything*. Indeed, for all practical and *saving* purposes it is *nothing* unless something else is superadded. Orthodoxy is the finished engine without the propelling *steam*—the perfect body without the animating and energizing *spirit!* It is not enough that the people be *indoctrinated*; they must be *stirred, melted, slain by the sharpness of the two-edged sword, and made gloriously alive from the dead by the power of the Holy Ghost!* It is not enough that a minister preach the *truth;* this he might do by asserting from morning till night that my name is *Alexander;* but who is made better by its announcement? Much truth may be preached and yet but very little be accomplished: *first,* because the most essential class of truths is not proclaimed; and *second,* because the truth itself, more than the Holy Ghost, is relied on for success. O this will never do! Let us have the truth —the simple truth—the whole truth, but let it come burning with the associated presence of the Infinite Spirit! Then it will cut its way to the heart of the King's enemy, and multiply its victories everywhere.

4. *Popularity.* Some preachers measure their success by their acceptability. Nearly the highest point of desirableness is reached if they have succeeded in preaching a considerable length of time without making any enemies. Having secured the good will of a large community, and established what they call a ministerial reputation, they seem to think that success henceforth is to be expected as *a matter of course.* Prosperity blinds their eyes, and they lose sight of the great fact that all their efforts will amount to nothing, or next to nothing, if unaccompanied by the Spirit's burning agency. A man that lives the nearest to God, and preaches with most of the unction of holy One, will not always or often be regarded with the greatest public favor. Such a man will "suffer persecution," for he must necessarily come in conflict with the darling sins of those who prefer to be let alone. To keep on good terms with everybody, a man must be composed of a peculiarly pliable material. It is seldom that a *popular* preacher is a *straight* preacher. So far from popularity answering as a substitute for the Holy Ghost, a man that would be fully led by this heavenly Guide, will probably be obliged to pursue a course eminently calculated to *diminish* his popularity. "Woe unto you when all men shall speak well of you; for it will doubtless be at the expense of your faithfulness to their souls, and of the anointing of the Holy Spirit.

What an amazing pity that the chosen heralds of mercy should so far reverse the order of Heaven as to presume to do anything in carrying out their great commission without a mighty baptism from on high! What wretched work they always make when they endeavor to dispense with the Holy Ghost! How Churches die off on their hands, and Infidelity, with unwonted boldness, stalks abroad over the fair fields of this favored land! How strangely weak appears the gospel as proclaimed by these polished theologians, in contrast with the mighty gospel of primitive times, and even of the present time, when announced by lips that are touched with celestial embers! It is too bad to find so many dead Churches over the land, but ministers should doubtless be sparing of their complaints unless they are quite certain that they have not contributed by their spiritless preaching to induce this very state of death. May God pity us! Amen.

RICHES NOT HAPPINESS.—The late Mr. Girard, when surrounded by immense wealth, and supposed to be taking supreme delight in its accumulation, wrote thus to a friend:

"As to myself, I live like a galley slave, constantly occupied, and often passing the night without sleeping. I am wrapped in a labyrinth of affairs, and worn out with care. I do not value fortune. The love of labor is my highest emotion. When I rise in the morning, my only effort is to labor so hard during the day, that when the night comes, I may be enabled to sleep soundly."

THE most you can do to a good man is to persecute him; and the worst that persecution can do is to kill him. And killing a good man is as bad as it would be to spite a ship by launching it. The soul is built for Heaven, and the ship for the ocean, and blessed be the hour that gives both to the true element.—BEECHER.

A PAINTER who was once reprehended by a cardinal, for putting so much *red* in the faces of St. Paul and St. Peter, answered: "It is to show how much they blush at the conduct of many who style themselves their successors.—ANON.

THERE is not a duty we are called to perform, not an evil temper we are required to vanquish, but we are directed in Scripture to seek for the aid of the Spirit of God, that our endeavors may be crowned with success.—VENN.

PERSONS may go to Church, receive the sacrament, lead honest, moral lives, and yet be sent to Hell at the last day.—WHITFIELD.

Do not complain of the *shoe* when the disease is in the *foot*.—A. A.

PREACHING.

I HAVE sometimes been tempted to speak thus from the pulpit: "My friends, I am as tired of sermons as you are; henceforth I will lay aside all pretensions to style, and speak to you as I do to a friend on the street. I will try to be simple, honest, true; telling you just what I think, and as I think it. I hope you will listen with attention and interest, as it is for your benefit, not my own, that I speak." But, on consideration, I saw it was better to make no such declaration, but to endeavor to act up to it. I have attempted it, but with how little success! The force of habit overcomes my best intentions; after a few minutes of simplicity, I again fall into declamation. But I do declare, that when I have been fortunate enough—let me speak more correctly and say—when I have been so far sustained from above as to remain simple and true, I have invariably enjoyed an unusual measure of peace of mind. I may add, that when I have suddenly checked myself in an affected delivery, and resumed a natural tone, I have seen drooping heads raised, wandering eyes fixed; my auditors thus taught me which was the right course.

Try it, Eusebius! Try it, and you will find the benefit of the change. You may fail the first time, but succeed the second. And you will succeed if you are in earnest, have real faith in the gospel, and love to souls. If the ministry is to you merely a profession, you will never be simple, because you are in a false position. Imitation of simplicity is as bad as imitation of dignity; both are disguises, and there can be no success in the pulpit without truth in principle and in practice.—REV. NAPOLEON ROUSSEL.

John the Baptist was a "burning and shining light." To shine is not enough—a *glow-worm* will do so; to burn is not enough—a *fire-brand* will do so.—SECKER.

BACKSLIDING IN OLD AGE.

BY THE EDITOR.

The pulpit and the religious press teem with admonitions to the young against backsliding. They are needed. The young Christian cannot be too much upon his guard. He is surrounded with dangers. His previous habits must be broken up. The associations formed prior to his conversion, cannot be continued without jeopardy. Invisible powerful foes are prowling about, plotting his destruction. He cannot tread too cautiously.

But it deserves to be remembered that those persons mentioned in the Bible as departing from God were generally men, who were, at the time of their defection, upon the down-hill side of life. Look at Moses. Exposed in his youth to the seductions found in the household of a heathen king, he remembered God, and retained his integrity. Vicious example was lost upon him. Ambition proffered her gilded baubles in vain. Passion tried its power to no purpose. He identified himself with a nation of slaves, choosing rather to "suffer affliction with the people of God, than to enjoy the pleasures of sin for a season.' In advanced life, just as he was ready to enter the promised land, he gave way to a spirit of vanity and impatience, and brought upon himself the displeasure of God, and though he was doubtless taken to Heaven, he was not permitted to enter the promised land.

Eli appears to have been eminently pious nearly all his days. It was not until he was "very old" that he "honored his sons above the Lord," and brought upon himself the malediction of Heaven.

See David. In his youth and through his prime, a man after God's own heart—in advanced life guilty of murder and adultery! and at a still later period giving way to pride and self-conceit—vices from which age is by no means exempt.

Consider the history of Solomon. The God of nature gave him wisdom above all men. The God of grace gave him another heart; and in a special sense the Lord loved him. Yet strange to say—"*it came to pass when Solomon was old*" that "his heart was turned from the Lord God of Israel." He yielded to a compromising spirit—the sin of old age. The altar and worship of Jehovah he never thought of forsaking; but in sinful compliance with the wishes of his wives, he gave countenance and support to the worship of false Gods. "And the Lord was angry with Solomon."

How many, who, in their younger days were noted for their uncompromising hostility to the fashionable follies and vanities of the world, find reasons, when their children come upon the stage of action, in favor of practices, which, when they walked in the light of the Spirit they strongly condemned. What a pitiable sight to see men in old age spending the remnant of their days in pulling down the edifice for the erection of which they devoted the strength of their manhood.

Old age is by no means exempt from the liability to backslide. There is danger when habits of piety are formed, that piety will degenerate into a mere habit. The body may retain its form long after vitality is fled—the embalmer's skill may keep it from corruption, so the form of devotion may be retained long after the spirit has departed.

SATAN'S ARTS.—Thou hast contended with Satan and hast been successful. Thou hast fought with him, and he has fled from thee. But, O, remember his artifices. Do not indulge the belief that his nature is changed. True, indeed, he is now very complacent, and is, perhaps, singing thee some syren song; but he was never more a devil than he is now. He now assaults thee, *by not assaulting thee;* and knows that he shall conquer, when THOU FALLEST ASLEEP.—UPHAM.

WITH CHRIST.

BY REV. WM. HART.

"Lord, remember me when thou comest into thy kingdom. And Jesus said unto him, Verily, I say unto you, today shalt thou be with me in paradise."—Luke xxiii, 42 and 43. In this chapter is recorded the closing scenes of the life of our Divine Redeemer. True to the purpose for which he left the shining seats above, we find him in the very agonies of death listening to, and answering prayer. No wonder we oft-times sing, "Jesus loves to answer prayer." And what a view does this give us, of the intense desire of Jesus to save the souls of men. Look at his sufferings, the cruel mockings and scourgings, his agony in the garden, his fainting under the cross as he ascended Calvary's mount, then the driving of the spikes through the quivering flesh, and above all this, and in the midst of all, the load of sin for a guilty world, and the hidings of his Father's face, causing him to cry out, "My God, my God, why hast thou forsaken me?"

While undergoing such sufferings, and accomplishing the work of redemption for a lost race, yet he finds time and inclination, to answer the prayer of the penitent thief. Infinite compassion! Wondrous love!

"O, for such love let rock and hills,
Their lasting silence break."

After Jesus was crucified, the first thing he did, was to pray for his murderers. "Father forgive them, they know not what they do." How perfectly his teachings and his character correspond. And if the Jews were led to say at one time, "Never man spake like this man," how much more might we say, never man died like this man. Or in the words of an Infidel, who, when contemplating the death and sufferings of Jesus, exclaimed, "If Socrates died like a philosopher, Jesus Christ died like a God." And like a God he answers the prayer of the penitent thief. "To-day shalt thou be with me in paradise." Who is this, nailed and expiring on the cross, that can use, such language as this? Who can thus open the gate of paradise, and give entrance into eternal glory?

He who is exalted a Prince and Saviour, to give repentance unto Israel, and the remission of sin. Well may we say with Thomas, and happy he who can look to the bleeding, dying Saviour, and with faith cry, "My Lord, and My God."

In the character of the two thieves, we have a striking illustration of the different effect produced by preaching the gospel of Christ. One of these dies hardened to the very last. He even joined the mockings of the rabble below, and railed on him saying, "If thou be Christ, save thyself and us." We should have expected, in such an hour as this, that his soul would have been in some degree humbled, enough so at least, to make a dying man refrain from insulting a dying man. The example of Christ, which has softened the heart of the other, has had an opposite effect on him. Making true the declaration of Scripture, that the gospel is to some, a savor of life unto life, while to others of death unto death. "The cross of Christ is to the Jew a stumbling block, and to the Greek foolishness, but to them who are saved the power of God, and the wisdom of God."

As far as we can learn from the narrative the circumstances of these thieves were similar. Both had the example of Christ before them, both had the same opportunity to learn and see, that he who was crucified was truly the Lord, and both would have found the same free grace in answer to prayer. Where then was the difference? One as he felt the movings of the spirit, yielded, and his heart was softened, and aided by these gracious influences, he made known the desires of his heart to Christ, and was saved. The other, having equally the first gentle movings of the Spirit, resisted, and by his voluntary perversity, grieved the Holy Spirit, and thus deprived himself of the only means which God could use to save him.

We see from this, that the greatest plagues will not humble men. Outward pains will never expel inward sins. How often God lays his hand upon us, and the racking pains of disease, and the scorchings of fever, bring us near the grave, and if our life is spared, we rise from the bed of suffering, with the same proud, unhumbled hearts. I once attended the funeral of a young man, who died of a loathsome disease. Decomposition progressed with such rapidity that the last look of mourning friends was prevented, and the coffin removed from the house during the services. The minister in alluding to the circumstances, remarked "If such a sight as this will not expel all levity and pride from the heart, I do not know what will." But a thousand such thoughts and sights never will. The gospel has presented a far different sight, by which to expel the pride of the heart, than the dissolution of this vile body. The burden falls, as the Cross of Christ appears in view.

"When I survey the wondrous cross,
On which the Prince of glory died,
My richest gain, I count but loss
And pour contempt on all my pride."

Look at that man doomed to die. See him in yon narrow cell, left to the corroding reflections of a guilty mind. The hour for his execution draws near. Eternity begins to unfold before his spiritual vision. But he nerves himself against any appearance of concern, and passes to the bar of God unhumbled and unsaved. What earthly condition can man be placed in, where the grace of humility would take root and grow, if not in circumstances like these? None. Nothing but Jesus' blood can wash away sin. The example of Jesus, and the history of the cross, is God's method of softening the hard heart. Hopeless, indeed, is that case, where these avail not. Apply then, oh! apply, for an interest in his blood, and the answer shall be given, and salvation received.

This penitent, who was this day to be with Christ, had outraged the law of his country, and died a criminal. But repentance and faith in his suffering Lord, took him to glory. David the adulterer and murderer, received again the pardoning seal of his Master's love. Peter, the swearer and perjurer, was pardoned, and with the rest received the pentecostal baptism. And Paul, breathing out threatenings and slaughter against the disciples, was arrested, converted, and made the chiefest of the Apostles. Omnipotent love can soften the hardest heart. No soul is so crimsoned with sin, but Jesus' blood can wash it white as snow.

Reader, dost thou desire to be with Christ, in the paradise of God? Learn then this prayer, "Lord, remember me."

MELANCTHON'S PORTRAIT OF A GOSPEL PREACHER.—He enters the house of God with a pious intention of preaching the unadulterated truth, and to present that which alone is useful and necessary, and not merely to delight the fancy of his hearers with human inventions, clothed in florid language. He disposes the matter of his discourse in a proper and natural order, and discusses it in a lucid and proper manner. He admonishes his hearers, and distinctly shows them how they may apply to themselves each truth. To impress it upon their minds, he employs clear and convincing argument, and illustrates it with appropriate examples, that every hearer may remember it well. He holds out motives, he rouses the feelings, he alarms them by denouncing the terrible threatenings of God, and awakens hope and confidence by the promise of His word. At one time he preaches the law, and then the Gospel, and explains the difference between them in the clearest manner. At one time he only explains the Scriptures, at another he addresses the heart and conscience vigorously—he excites the mind to activity, not by a mere sound of words, but by a solemn appeal to the affections. Such a preacher I knew well, it was MARTIN LUTHER.

BACKWOODS PREACHERS.

The following graphic description of backwoods preachers, furnished me by a friend, serves not only to illustrate the manner in which many preachers were manufactured in early days, but will convey some idea of their character and talents:

A Presbytery of the Cumberland Church had assembled in one of the valleys of the Cumberland range. It was a season of spiritual drought, and the Churches had suffered from famine. The members of the ecclesiastical body then collected in their semi-annual convocation, were mostly weather-beaten veterans—who had braved the earlier difficulties of the denomination to which they were attached, when, about twenty years before, it had seceded from the parent stock, to erect a banner in Zion with a new device. They were in all about twenty persons, of whom a little more than half were preachers, the rest ruling elders of congregations, who were there to represent the local interests of the Church sessions.

This meeting was at a solemn crisis; for the Church was troubled, and the way before her was shrouded in darkness. The love of many had waxed cold. Defections had occurred. Some—who were once masters in Israel had withdrawn, carrying off weighty influence and leaving perplexities behind.

Others were threatening to dissolve the Church unless radical changes were made in doctrines and polity. Alarming coldness prevailed in regard to candidates for the ministry, none having offered for several sessions, and those already in charge giving but little evidence of a disposition to advance or an ability to labor in the work which they had professed to love. Presbytery, however, was unusually full, nearly every Church session being represented and not one of the ordained ministers absent. The deliberations were opened, as usual, with prayer by the moderator, an aged servant of God; and it was observed by those skilled in such things, that there was great liberty given him when he entreated "that the God of the harvest, in infinite mercy, would send more laborers into his harvest."

The usual formalities being ended, the opening sermon was preached by the same person. His subject comprehended the character and importance of a call to the Gospel ministry, and was treated with much earnestness. The morning hour being ended, the body adjourned to early candle-lighting. A considerable crowd had assembled upon this novel occasion, and it was under their hospitable roofs that the members found welcome reception. Few, indeed, of the mountain cabins in the vicinity but what received one or more upon that occasion, glad to be permitted to talk of the Saviour to those who rarely had such opportunities of hearing the Gospel. Night brought them all back again to the house of gathering. It was a singularly wild and startling scene to one who has not mixed in the different phases of frontier life. The building in which the meeting was held was a plain log-cabin, the dwelling of one of the elders, and only selected on account of its being the largest in the vicinity. There were the beds and the furniture of the whole family, no unprolific one at that, stowed around a room but twenty feet square.

Upon those beds, and upon seats made by laying split puncheons upon cross logs, was seated the company of men, women, and children, ministers, delegates, and all, each glad to endure a process of compression for a few hours, in the expectation of an intellectual reward.

It had before been arranged that this night's meeting should be devoted to candidates for the ministry. A call was, therefore, made "to all who had felt impressions to preach to come forward and converse with Presbytery on the subject." Every one must undergo this peculiar ordeal who inclines to enter the ministry, and there are no traditions in the Church more entertaining than those which tell how the ministers who are now *burning and shining lights* made their first awkward and unpromising exhibit before Presbytery.

The call being made by the presiding officer, three persons arose to their feet. Of the first and second it will be unnecessary here to speak. The third had stood partly concealed in a dark corner of the room, while the others were relating the particulars which induced the Presbytery to accept them as probationers; but now he stepped forward and faced the moderator. His appearance excited a universal start of surprise even among that unsophisticated audience, accustomed to great peculiarities of dress and rudeness of manner. Let the reader imagine a person dressed in what is styled *copperas cloth ;* that is, a cloth home-spun, home-woven, home-cut, and home-sewed, dyed in that bilious hue which is formed by copperas, alum, and walnut bark, and made into coat, vest and breeches.

To this add brogans of home-tanned, red leather, tied with a leather thong, covering immense feet, made—both feet and brogans—for climbing hills, and you have the portrait of a *mountain boy ;* able at full run to scale a bluff, to live upon the proceeds of his rifle for support, and to whip any lowland fellow in the State. Such was the person who left his dark corner and came into the full blaze of the pineknot fire. He was weeping bitterly, and, having no handkerchief, the primitive arrangement for such cases provided was necessarily adopted. He stood silent for a minute, every beholder awaiting with intense curiosity the announcement of his business, then, clearing his throat, commenced, "I've come to Presby——," but a new flood of tears impeded his efforts to speak. The moderator kindly remarked, "And what did you come to Presbytery for, my good friend? Take your own time and tell us all about it; don't be alarmed; be seated; nobody will hurt you. Come, now, tell us what you come to Presbytery for." The stranger emboldened by this to commence again, even the third and fourth time, but could never proceed further than " I've come to Presby——," and the storm of his soul prevailed.

Here one of the members suggested that he had better retire with some one and communicate his wishes privately; for as yet no person imagined his true errand, but rather supposed that he was laboring under some spiritual difficulty, which he would needs have settled by the meeting. But to this hint he resolutely demurred, replying "that he'd get his voice d'reckly, please God;" and so he did; and he rose up, straightening his gaunt, awkward form, and then such words as passed his lips had never before rung through that assembly.

I shall not attempt—nor could I do it, for want of a report—to quote his own words; but the oldest minister present declared, years afterward, that they *scorched and burnt where ever they fell.* A sketch of his subject will be sufficient here. It seemed that he had lived all his days in ignorance and sin, without an hour's schooling, without any training either for this world or the next, without any knowledge of the affairs of humanity, having sprung up like one of the cedars on his own mountains, and with as little cultivation. Thus he had passed more than twenty years, laboring in a humble way for support, and at times pursuing the pleasures and profits of the chase.

A few months back he had accidentally fallen in with a traveling preacher, who had lost his way among the mountains, and, by several miles travel, had put him in the right track.

The minister, interested at the oddity of his appearance and his intense ignorance of everything religious, devoted the hour to a sketch of this world's condition, buried in sin, his own perilous state, and the value of his immortal soul, and concluded by kneeling with him, at the root of a tree, and pleading with God for his spiritual regeneration. They parted, and met no more, but the influence of that meeting parted not. The spirit which dictated the good man's effort, abode henceforward in the temple of his heart. A voice began to whisper in his ears, "Repent, repent; why will ye die?" A load, a weight of mountains, pressed upon his soul. Sleep forsook his eyelids. His axe rusted by the pile; his rifle hung, dust-covered, on the wall.

The simple-hearted neighbors, ignorant as himself, pronounced him deranged; the younger portion called it love; a few, not slanderous, but suspicious, thought, in a private way, it might be liquor. The man himself sought religious meetings, but they were few and distant, and he heard no echo to the voice within him, and he still returned hungry and dissatisfied.

The people of a certain town will not soon forget the apparition of that awkward and ill-dressed man who visited their churches, to plant himself in front of the pulpit, and to listen to the exercises with all that attention which the criminal upon the gallows bestows upon the distant horseman, who, perhaps, brings him the expected reprieve. It was in the midst of a camp meeting fervor that he at last found peace; and there his frantic ejaculation, "I've got it, I've got it!" was like the world-wide Eureka of the Syracusean, when his grand discovery first electrified his own breast.

Then he came home to tell his neighbors what the Lord had done for his soul. Forsaking all other duties, he wandered from cabin to cabin, and, wherever he found a hearer, he called upon him to forsake his sins. His ardor increased every day.

Soon his rude but forcible illustrations began to tell upon the hearts of those simple mountaineers, as the words of a second John Baptist, crying out, "Prepare ye the way of the Lord, make his path straight."

And yet he seemed to have no idea that he was called to preach. Such a thought as that of entering the ministry did not enter his breast. Although his heart overflowed with the one subject, and he declared his determination to speak that subject to others, so long as he lived, yet it was only as a friend counsels friend that he expected to do it—no more. How could he become a preacher? He couldn't read a hymn or a text; he hadn't means to buy decent clothing, or pay for a session's schooling. But he was guided right, for he fell in with a gentleman who was botanizing among his native hills, and had the good fortune to spend a Sabbath in his company. This man, a profound observer of human nature, and a friend of his species, was struck with the peculiarities of the case, and, although no professor in a religious way, yet he felt convinced that the hand of might was here. He, therefore, advised him to apply to some religious association, before which he could lay open his heart and be understood.

The result of this counsel we have seen in his coming to Presbytery, and presenting himself, a stranger to all, in the manner before described. This history, much elaborated, he gave out with a volubility that took away the breath.

The pine fire blazed low; the dipped and shapeless candles simmered themselves into torrents, unobserved by the hearers, while all sat spell-bound at the recital. With uncouth gestures, words barbarous as the African's, alternately crying and laughing, as he wandered from his first agony to his final triumph, and shouting till his voice rang back from the hill-side, the mountain boy enchained each heart, till its very pulsations might be heard. There was not a dry eye in the assembly. The grey-haired moderator sobbed aloud. The more excitable joined, from time to time, in his shouts, as the word of victory rung in their ears; and when, after a sentence of great length, he declared that "glory was begun in his heart," and that "God alone had done this work within him," not one who was experienced in such announcements but declared his convictions that it was even so—the hand of God was there.

A brief consultation ensued, and then

by general consent, George Willets was duly received as a candidate for the holy ministry.

THE BANK OF HEAVEN.

Tune—*Common Metre.*

I have a never failing bank,
    A more than golden store;
No earthly bank is half so rich—
    How then can I be poor?
    No earthly bank is half so rich—
    How then can I be poor?

'Tis when my stock is spent and gone,
    And I without a groat,
I'm glad to hasten to my bank
    And beg a little more.

Sometimes my banker, smiling, says
    "Why don't you oft'ner come?
And when you draw a little note,
    Why not a larger sum?

"Why live so niggardly and poor?
    Your bank contains a plenty;
Why come and take a one pound note?
    You might as well have twenty.

"Yea, twenty thousand, ten times told,
    Is but a trifling sum,
To what your Father has laid up,
    Secure for all his Sons."

Since then my banker is so rich,
    I have no cause to borrow,
I'll live upon my cash to-day,
    And draw again to-morrow.

I've been a thousand times before,
    And never was rejected;
Sometimes my banker gives me more
    Than asked for or expected.

And if you have but one small note,
    Fear not to bring it in;
Come boldly to this bank of grace—
    The banker is within.

All forged notes will be refused,
    Man's merits are rejected;
There's not a single note will pass
    That God has not accepted.

This bank is full of precious notes,
    All sign'd and seal'd and free—
Though many doubting souls may say,
    There is not one for me.

The leper had a little note—
    "Lord, if thou wilt thou can!"
The banker cash'd his little note,
    And healed the sickly man.

We read of one young man, indeed,
    Whose riches did abound;
But in this banker's look of grace,
    This man was never found.

But see the wretched dying thief,
    Hang by the banker's side,
He cried, "dear Lord, remember me!"
    He got his cash—and died!"

Christian Simplicity.—When on a certain occasion the pious Fenelon, after having experienced much trouble and persecution from his opposers, was advised by some one to take greater precautions against the artifices and evil designs of men, he made an answer in the true spirit of a Christian, "*Moriamur in simplicitate nostra,*" *let us die in our simplicity.* He that is wholly in Christ has a oneness and purity of purpose, altogether inconsistent with those tricks and subterfuges which are so common among men. He walks in broad day. He goes forth in the light of conscious honesty. He is willing that men and angels should read the very bottom of his heart. He has but one rule. His language is, in the ordinary affairs of life, as well as in the duties of religion, "My Father, what wilt thou have me to do?" This is Christian simplicity; and happy, thrice happy is he who possesses it.—Upham.

The *first* Adam was for self-advancement; but the *second* Adam is for self-abasement: the former was for having self *deified*—the latter is for having self *crucified*.—Secker.

There is a way to *keep* a man out of hell, but there is no way to *get* a man out of hell.—W. Secker.

WHO SHOULD PREACH.

When the Israelites were bitten by the fiery flying serpents, and the bite was inevitably fatal, Moses was directed to set up a brazen serpent, with the assurance that whosoever that had been bitten, looked upon it, should be healed. You can imagine how the first man who had felt its saving efficacy, flew to communicate the news to his brethren, and urge them to avail themselves of the remedy which had delivered him from death. Every man who was healed became immediately a herald of the glad tidings to others. Every one who was saved became a publisher of the salvation, or in other words, a preacher, until in a few minutes the news spread throughout the encampment, and in this sense every tribe was evangelized.

Allow me to illustrate the meaning of this term, as used by our Lord, by an occurrence of which I was an eye-witness. It so chanced, that at the close of the last war with Great Britain, I was temporarily a resident of the city of New York. The prospects of the nation were shrouded in gloom. We had been two or three years at war with the mightiest nation on earth, and as she had now concluded a peace with the continent of Europe, we were obliged to cope with her single-handed. Our harbors were blockaded. Communication coast-wise, between our ports, was cut off. Our ships were rotting in every creek and cove where they could find a place of security. Our immense annual products were moulding in our ware-houses. The sources of profitable labor were dried up. Our currency was reduced to irredeemable paper. The extreme portions of our country were becoming hostile to each other, and differences of political opinion were embittering the peace of every household. The credit of the government was exhausted. No one could predict when the contest would terminate, or discover the means by which it could much longer be protracted.

It happened that on a Saturday afternoon in February, a ship was discovered in the offing, which was supposed to be a cartel, bringing home our commissioners at Ghent, from their unsuccessful mission. The sun had set gloomily, before any intelligence from the vessel had reached the city. Expectation became painfully intense, as the hours of darkness drew on. At length a boat reached the wharf, announcing the fact that a treaty of peace had been signed, and was waiting for nothing but the action of our government to become a law. The men on whose ears these words first fell, rushed in breathless haste into the city, to repeat them to their friends, shouting, as they ran through the streets, peace! peace! peace! Every one who heard the sound repeated it. From house to house, from street to street, the news spread with electric rapidity. The whole city was in commotion. Men bearing lighted torches were flying to and fro, shouting like madmen, peace! peace! peace! When the rapture had partially subsided, one idea occupied every mind. But few men slept that night. In groups they were gathered in the streets and by the fire-side, beguiling the hours of midnight by reminding each other that the agony of war was over, and that a worn out and distracted country was about to enter again upon its wonted career of prosperity. Thus, every one becoming a herald, the news soon reached every man, woman and child in the city, and in this sense, the city was evangelized. All this you see was reasonable and proper. But when Jehovah has offered to our world a treaty of peace, when men doomed to hell may be raised to seats at the right hand of God, why is not a similar zeal displayed in proclaiming the good news? Why are men perishing all around us, and no one has ever personally offered to them salvation through a crucified Redeemer?—Dr. Wayland.

To *talk* of grace is good—to *taste* of grace is better.—A. A. P.

HOW FAR IS IT TO CANAAN?

"How far is it to Canaan?" said a friend. "Why," replied I, "the children of Israel found it a long way; for they traveled forty years in the wilderness. The most important thing is to know that we are in the way, for then the distance will get less and less every hour."

"How far is it to Canaan?" asks the doubting Christian; "for I am sadly afraid I shall never get there. My sins are a heavy burden to me, and I long to be rid of them, if indeed there is hope for such a one as I."

Go on, poor doubting Christian; take fresh courage, and quicken thy step. Canaan is not so far off but thou shalt reach it at last; and if thou couldst know how willing the Saviour of sinners is to receive thee, it would shed a sunbeam on thy dejected countenance. I have a word of comfort for thee, a cordial for thy heart:

"I, even I, am he that blotteth out thy transgressions for mine own sake, and will not remember thy sins."—Isa. xliii. 25.

"How far is it to Canaan?" asks the triumphant Christian; "for I long to be at home. I know that my Redeemer liveth, and because He lives I shall live also. My soul has made me like 'the chariots of Aminidab,' and I am impatient to behold Him face to face!"

Go forward, triumphant Christian, with the glorious ring of assurance upon thy finger. Cast not away thy confidence, which hath "great recompense of reward." But stay, I have a word for thee, which may be useful. Ponder it in thy heart:

"Let him that thinketh he standeth, take heed lest he fall."—1 Cor. x. 12.

"How far is it to Canaan?" inquires the afflicted Christian; "for I have lain a long while upon the bed of suffering. 'Wearisome nights are appointed unto me.' I am full of tossing to and fro unto the dawning day. 'O that I had wings like a dove! for then would I fly away, and be at rest.'"

Be of good cheer, afflicted Christian! The heavier the cross, the more pleasant will be the crown. If we suffer with Christ, we shall be glorified with Christ. I have a word to refresh thy fainting soul, and will now give it thee:

"The sufferings of this present time are not worthy to be compared with the glory which shall be revealed in us."—Rom. viii. 18.

"How far is it to Canaan?" asks the persecuted Christian; "for I am an outcast from my family, a stranger upon earth; like my Lord, I am 'despised and rejected of men.' 'Many are they that rise up against me,' and 'they hate me with cruel hatred.'"

Hold on thy way, persecuted Christian: it is a safe one, and a blessed one, yea, the one thy Redeemer trod before thee. Dost thou want a word of consolation? I will give it thee; lay it up in thy bosom:

"Blessed are ye, when men shall hate you, and when they shall separate you from their company, and shall reproach you, and cast out your name as evil, for the Son of man's sake. Rejoice ye in that day, and leap for joy: for, behold your reward is great in heaven."—Luke vi. 22, 23.

"How far is it to Canaan?" sighs the bereaved Christian; "for I am a lonely and desolate pilgrim. All that were dear to me upon earth are taken away. My tears have been my meat day and night, and my soul yearns for the land where 'there shall be no more death, neither sorrow nor crying.'"

Pass on, bereaved Christian; the more lonely thy pilgrimage, the more pleasant will be the company of the "shining ones" that await thee, and the sweeter thy reception at the end of thy journey. The Lord whom thou seekest hath a special care and pity for His desolate ones. Take these words with thee, and they may refresh thy spirit. For even though they be desolate—

"The redeemed of the Lord shall return, and come with singing unto Zion; and everlasting joy shall be upon their head: they shall obtain gladness and joy; and sorrow and mourning shall flee away."—Isa. li. 11.

"How far is it to Canaan?" asks the dying Christian; "for the swellings of Jordan are risen about my soul. Fearfulness and trembling are come upon me, 'and the terrors of death are fallen upon me.' Alas! I sink in deep waters: I shall not see the land that flows with milk and honey."

Look up, poor dying Christian; for yonder is the bright and morning Star; thy night is far spent, and the day is at hand. Is thine arm too feeble to be put forth for the book of God, then I must even hold it up before thine eyes. Look on these words, and let neither flood nor flame affright thee; be of good courage, for they are the words of Him who has promised, when flesh and heart fail, to be the strength of thy heart, and thy portion forever:

"When thou passest through the waters, I will be with thee; and through the rivers, they shall not overflow thee: when thou walkest through the fire, thou shalt not be burned; neither shall the flame kindle upon thee. For I am the Lord thy God, the Holy One of Israel, thy Saviour."—Isa. xliii. 2, 3.—Old Humphrey.

Revivals of Religion.—You well know that all our dependence for the conversion of sinners, the increase of holiness in God's people, and whatever else our ministry was appointed for, is on the promise of our blessed Lord that He would send His Holy Spirit to testify of Him; "to reprove the world of sin, of righteousness, and of judgment." The fulfillment of that promise began in the mighty works and blessed fruit of the day of Pentecost. In the midst of that outpouring of the Spirit, Peter pronounced it to be what the prophet Joel had predicted, viz: "It shall come to pass in the last days, said God, I will pour out my Spirit on all flesh." So, when in a few days after, "the number of the men that believed, (besides others) was about five thousand," in the single city of Jerusalem, it was the further progress of that prophecy. And let us mark that in that beginning of that fulfilment, all that we read of exhibits a rapid, powerful work of conversion, which arrested multitudes at once, and turned them instantly to Christ. The awakening was so mighty, that in the same day, thousands who, when it dawned, were at enmity with Christ, before it ended had confessed Him before men, and were regarded by apostles as new creatures in Him.

Say not there was miracle in those days. The Scriptures never set down the conversion of a sinner, the renewal of his heart, to miracle. "Begotten again by the word of God," as the instrument, and by the Spirit of God as the power, is the invariable testimony of Scripture. Miracle called attention to the apostles; miracle attested their credentials as God's messengers; miracle was the seal which certified their word to be the word of God. And those same miracles are as conclusive at this day as ever. And what the Spirit and the Truth, with miracle or without it, were then, they are still; so that if once they turned the hearts of the disobedient to the wisdom of the just, by thousands, in a day, in a single city, why may they not be expected to do the same now, in many cities and in all lands, where the gospel is preached?—Bish. McIlvaine.

Preacher's Defects.—The defects of a preacher are soon spied. Let a preacher be endued with ten virtues, and have but one fault, that one fault will eclipse and darken all his virtues and gifts, so evil is the world in these times. Dr. Justus Jonas hath all the good qualities that a man may have, yet by reason that he only often hemmeth and spitteth, therefore the people cannot bear with that good and honest man.—*Luther's Table Talk.*

Of what advantage is it to be *cried up* on earth by those about us, and *cried down* in heaven by those above us?—Secker.

REVIVALS.

BY THE EDITOR.

THE REVIVAL IN IRELAND.

WE have received "occasional reports" through our friend, Doctor HEATHER, of Dublin, which contain highly interesting accounts of the revival of religion in Ireland. We cannot, however, give much space in this number to extracts from the "papers" sent us, and we therefore take the following from the statement of Mr. WHITE, general missionary, whose position and observation enable him to speak intelligently about the "meetings" and the "revival" connected with them:

MY DEAR BROTHER:—At your request, I give you a few extracts from my journal, in reference to the great work of God which is at present spreading so gloriously over this land. And while we rejoice that God has poured out His Holy Spirit on all the Churches of His people—making no difference—we ought to thank Him that He has not overlooked our Society, but has abundantly blessed the labors of our agents in every place. Boasting is excluded forever from us or any people; but "praise is comely," and perhaps we have been more deficient in this than in any other duty.

July 22d, I visited Lurgan, and although there was no announcement made for anything special, the chapel was densely crowded with a deeply anxious congregation. The revival had commenced here: for a long time two Christian brethren had been earnestly pleading with God for the shower to come, and through discouragement and difficulties they prayed and labored on. Like Elijah, they looked toward the sea, and while others saw nothing but apparent drought, they beheld the promise of the coming shower, and it did come. While these brethren were holding a meeting one evening in our chapel, the Lord poured out His Spirit, and several sinners were cut to the heart, and cried aloud for mercy. The meeting continued till a late hour, when some went home rejoicing, and others in distress. These brethren retired too, but it was not to rest; for the work spread with amazing power, and many in several parts of the town were in deep distress in their houses, and sent for these brethren and others to pray with them. All the Churches were ready to fall in with the movement. Meetings for prayer were appointed in every place of worship; they were all crowded every night with anxious and prayerful congregations; and everywhere the same feelings were manifested, and the same glorious transformations effected.

This, my first night in Lurgan, was a very remarkable one. A multitude of newly converted souls were in the chapel, happy in God. Joy was depicted in their countenances; and their eyes, wet with tears, sparkled with delight, while they sung of Jesus, or heard of his love. Others appeared sad and downcast, while they audibly groaned out their distress into the ears of our compassionate Redeemer. Several, that night, found peace in believing.

"On the following Sabbath, the 24th, I preached in a field adjoining the town, and contiguous to our chapel, in Queen street, in the afternoon, at half-past three o'clock, to about *four thousand* of a congregation. While the Gospel was but simply proclaimed to them, there was deep solemnity, but no extraordinary exhibition of feeling. Some silently wept; others were deeply solemn and thoughtful; all seemed to feel that God was there, and speaking to them in His Word. Immediately after the sermon, the chapel was densely crowded at a prayer meeting. Several men—some of them stout-hearted sinners—fell before God to plead for mercy; and many of them were enabled to rejoice in a consciousness of pardon through Christ Jesus. This meeting lasted till near the time of preaching—at seven o'clock. At that hour, the house was again densely packed in every part; every foot of sitting and standing room was occupied by some one anxious to hear the Gospel; and many had to go away who could not get into the house at all. During the sermon, there was awful attention; every eye fixed; the tears falling like rain, and anon the stillness of the multitude broken by the sobbing of some burdened sinner. After the sermon, we proposed to offer prayer for all who were in distress on account of sin, when about *sixty, men and women, old* and *young,* fell prostrate before God to seek for pardon. The most of those in distress were young men and young women, in the prime of life, and among them some aged sinners. The meeting was very orderly, considering the multitude in distress. There was no screaming, but many loudly and bitterly wept before God. Singing and prayer were alternately engaged in till nearly two o'clock in the morning, when, I think, not less than sixty souls had entered into the liberty of the children of God.

"The work is still progressing in Lurgan. By a letter received from Brother PATTYSON, it appears that since the 3d of July last, when the revival commenced, more than a *thousand souls* have been converted in one chapel alone. They have not all connected themselves with us; but our Brother states that during the past three months *four hundred* have been added to the Society.

"I arrived in Clowes on Friday, the 9th September, and remained there till the following Tuesday, attending two meetings each day. The revival had begun and was progressing with great power for some weeks previous to this time.

"Brother WILSON, the Superintendent of the Circuit, on his return from the Conference, was deeply anxious about the work of God, and believing that He was as willing to bless souls in Clowes as in other places, he commenced to pray and labor for a revival of His work. He appointed as his first public effort, an *open air union prayer meeting* near the town, and invited the co-operation of Christian ministers of other denominations, with that of some of his own brethren in the ministry. About *four thousand* assembled on the occasion; the people were much impressed under the addresses of the speakers; a solemn stillness pervaded the assembly, and many were moved to tears; but nothing of a marked nature occurred.

"The evening I arrived in Clowes, I found Brother WILSON laid up from exhaustion, occasioned by hard labor and constant anxiety. The chapel was densely crowded in every part, and the large porch at the entrance was closely seated and crowded also. The meeting was commenced with singing and prayer, and then I addressed the people for a few minutes. While I was speaking, the sobbing of those in distress was audible. A great many fell before the Lord, crying for mercy. Several were stricken, and carried into the Society-room; some shrieked out in a most awful manner, and others, in comparative silence, sought mercy from the Lord.

"It would be impossible to say how many were saved at this meeting; every part of the house seemed filled with the glory of God. The Society-room was full of 'stricken ones,' all of whom went home happy. In the chapel were scores who were not prostrated, but who were in great distress; many of whom were delivered from the burden of their sins, and enabled to rejoice in God their Saviour. The meeting separated about one o'clock in the morning. The next day I had an opportunity of visiting a great many in their houses, who were either in great distress or happy in God. I was greatly struck with the wonderful change that had passed over the people; whole families of the very worst characters were saved; and, instead of drunkenness and swearing, now there are songs of praise and thanksgiving ascending from their dwellings.

"The following day—the Sabbath—was a very memorable time. At our morning service, at ten o'clock, we had a down-pour of Heavenly blessings. The congregation was very large, almost entirely composed of those who were happy in God. How easy was it to preach to them! How good was it to be there! At four o'clock in the afternoon, we held an *open-air service in the field*, where the former meeting was held. Between *four and five thousand* were there. Brother WILSON opened the meeting with praise and prayer. Mr. JOHNSTON, Wesleyan minister, read the Scriptures and prayed. Then, Mr. WILEY, from Belfast, a Presbyterian, addressed the meeting with great power. After which, I preached a short sermon on the sufferings of Christ for sinners, and the meeting was concluded with a short prayer meeting. It was a very solemn time. Many wept silently, others groaned in distress; one was stricken, and all seemed conscious that God was there. It was a beautiful, calm summer evening. It seemed as if God had hushed the winds, and arrested the rain, and curtained the sun with clouds, so that we worshipped with the greatest comfort. It was announced that our chapel, the Presbyrian Church, and the Wesleyan Chapel, were to be opened for prayer meetings, when the people retired from the field. As they moved down the slope of the beautiful hill leading to the town, a few friends commenced singing—

"All hail the power of Jesus' name!
Let angels prostrate fall;
Bring forth the royal diadem,
And crown him Lord of all!"

"The multitude joined with great earnestness in singing this beautiful hymn; and seldom did such music float on the evening air.

"I have read of the glorious march of armies after a victory, as they entered the capitol of their country with martial music, amidst the plaudits of the populace, and felt the blood course more quickly through my veins as I read of the glorious spectacle; but what is such a pageant when compared with such a a spectacle as this—*four thousand* men and women, from different parts of the country, of *different denominations*, many of whom had *never seen each other before*, all singing—

"Crown Him Lord of all!"

"It was, doubtless, music that angels bent down from their seats of glory to listen to.

"The multitude reached our chapel, Whitehall Street, and the living stream flowed into it till the body of the house, the galleries, aisles, porch, lobby, area, and every available spot of standing-room was crowded to suffocation. The living tide surged back again on the street; it moved toward the Wesleyan Chapel, which was soon crowded, then to the Presbyterian Church, which also was crowded to inconvenience, and many could not even obtain standing room anywhere."

It is computed that not less than *eighty thousand souls* have been converted to Christ during the time thus far of the revival's continuance.—*American and Foreign Christian Union Magazine, Dublin, Feb.* 28, 1860.

REVIVAL IN FRANCE.

A GREAT revival has taken place, recently, among the Roman Catholics, near Vesoul. In two or three villages, situated in the neighborhood of this place, nearly *a thousand souls* have left the Roman Catholic Church and turned to evangelical Protestantism. Other movements of this kind are announced in other localities.—*Letter from S. H. Grandpierre, of Cen. Prot. Soc. Evangelization.*

TO OUR FRIENDS.

WE are in immediate want of about two hundred dollars to meet liabilities we have incurred in trying to promote the work of the Lord. We ask our friends—the best in the world, for they are the friends of Jesus—to help us by getting subscribers for the *Earnest Christian*. We can still supply back numbers. Or, we will furnish it for half the year, commencing with the July number, for fifty cents for each subscriber. This is a good time to get us a few hundred new subscribers, either for the year or for half a year. We intend, by the blessing of the Lord, to keep up the high character of our Magazine, and we ask you to do good to us and to the cause of God, and to the souls of men, by assisting in extending its circulation. Address Rev. B. T. ROBERTS, Buffalo, N. Y.

TIDINGS FROM AN OLD PILGRIM.

THE following is an extract from a letter written by one of our old preachers:

DEAR BROTHER:—The first number of the *Earnest Christian* fell into my hands accidentally, and reminded me of the expression of my pious father on our first meeting after my conversion, "Now lettest thou thy servant depart in peace." On receiving the last three numbers, I could but say as the Dutch brother said of religion, "It grows better and better." For almost forty years I have tried to maintain the doctrines and Discipline of the Methodist Episcopal Church, the most of that time in the Genesee or East Genesee Conference. Through the grace of God I have been able to walk in the sunshine of the Gospel for the last thirty years, by the faith that—

"In danger knows no fear,
In darkness feels no doubt,"

though for the last fifteen years it has been against wind and tide. Though I now feel that my work is almost done, yet I am anew fired with the hope that our Israel may yet be redeemed. To God be all the glory.

We see our beloved brethren falling martyrs for truth, but we regard this as but sealing the truth for which you suffer. May God abundantly bless you in all your labors of love, and raise up thousands and millions to the Gospel standard of Holiness, through the instrumentality employed.

If martyrs are needed, you are now ready to be offered, and what little I can do to scatter broad-cast this light shall be done, though it is against prejudice and superstition that I never thought existed to so great an extent in the Methodist Episcopal Church.

An Old Itinerant,
LOOMIS BENJAMIN.

PERSECUTION.

IT is strange that the enemies of Holy Ghost religion do not learn from the experience of centuries that it can never be put down by any acts of persecution. Even error will live so long as it is persecuted. Direct assaults upon the religion of Jesus only tend to make it take deeper root in the heart of its votaries, and to commend it to the honest and magnanimous, whose nature it is to espouse the cause of the oppressed.

From the accounts we are receiving from different parts of the country of the persecutions that are raging against the friends of holiness, we judge that the number of those who are "living godly in Christ Jesus," are rapidly multiplying. The civil law prohibits the use of fire and fagot, of stocks and dungeons, but to one who has contributed his toils and prayers and money, for years, for building up the Church of his choice, excommunication may be as severe a test of constancy as sufferings in a more severe and dignified form. Hundreds of as pious and devoted Christians as can be found, have, in different places, in the Genesee Conference, been read out of their Church as withdrawn, without their consent. Others have been expelled for "contumacy," or disobedience to the order and discipline of the Church." This generally consists in attending religious meetings where their pastor does not like to have them, though they find them greatly blessed to the good of their souls.

The same work, as will be seen from the following letter, is going on in some places in the West.

FRANKLINVILLE, March 25, 1860.

REV. B. T. ROBERTS: — *Dear Brother*—I came here last Thursday, in time to get to a Church trial on Friday. Five persons (one whole family) were summoned to appear at the Church.

Charge—"Neglect of duty and disobedience to the Order and Discipline of the Church."

First Specification — Neglecting the public worship of God at the Franklinville Church, where you belong.

Second Specification — Neglecting to meet your class.

Two o'clock found them, the accused and a few of their friends, at the Church. After singing,

"A charge to keep I have,"

and prayer by the preacher, E. W., the trial commenced. The names of the accused were called over, and the charges read. The preacher then requested all to leave the house, with the exception of the accused, the committee and Secretary. The witnesses might retire to the Parsonage, and would be sent for as wanted. Their counsel, Rev. J. H. FAIRCHILD, could not be permitted to attend, because a member of another charge. The accused, not willing to be tried there, the preacher adjourned to the Parsonage, and proceeded with the trial. Meanwhile, we had a Love Feast, a time of rejoicing together—disturbed now and then by their officer coming in and summoning them one by one to appear at the Parsonage. About half-past four the preacher and committee came in. Our Love Feast went on. Five o'clock came, and we were dismissed by Brother FAIRCHILDS. It so happened Brother WILLIAM BISHOP had a good letter in his pocket, given by L. WHIPPLE, preacher in charge, which he denies giving. Brother WILLIAM says, "I suppose you know your own hand writing," and takes out the letter. I was standing near by, and noticed that Brother WILLIAM did not let go of it. I thought to myself, he is afraid to trust him, and thought I would watch. The preacher read the letter and looked up at Brother WILLIAM, and says, "You don't want this, it's mine," and jerked it out of his hands, and tore his name off, and then gave it up, Brother WILLIAM having got hold of it again. The preacher flatly denied jerking it. He said, "Brother WILLIAM jerked it out of *my* hands." What a scene! Some were wringing their hands and calling upon God to have mercy; others sank to the floor; while the preacher looked on, with a half laugh upon his face, seemingly indifferent to what he had done, and as if enjoying what was going on around him. Before he left the house, he denied no less than three times his tearing the letter, against the united testimony of eight or nine persons that saw it. The accused had been in the habit of holding meetings in the school houses around there, during the winter, where the people had been neglected by the ministry; and, as the result of it, some thirty or forty have been converted and sanctified. Little did I ever think it was coming to this.

Yours, in haste, J. G. T.

DYING GRACE.

THE religion of Jesus gives happiness and consolation under any and every circumstance of life. Christ intended that his followers should be happy. But its crowning excellence is found in its ability to afford joy and peace when all things else fail to comfort. We have seen the sinner on his death bed, wrung with anguish. Too often have we listened to the plaintive cries of the formalist for mercy, when he saw the time had come when he must bid farewell to this world, and enter upon an eternity for which he made no adequate preparation. But the earnest Christian, who has renounced the world and all its pomp and show, and trusted in Jesus for full salvation from sin, we have always found ready to go with holy triumph at the Master's bidding. The following account of the death of two of the members of the Free Methodist Church in Saint Louis, illustrates the value of a thorough work of grace in the soul. We need every hour of our life grace that would take us to Heaven.

"Among the first ripe fruit gathered by the angels, from the First Free Methodist Church of Saint Louis, was our very much esteemed Brother TWYFORD. Never can we forget the desperate struggle of our Brother while seeking the blessing of holiness before our separate organization, and his consistent, faithful and zealous deportment from that time until called as one of our first representatives to Heaven. While in the discharge of his duties South, and among strangers, a high ladder on which he was standing, gave way. By his fall, he received his death wound, breaking one or more of his limbs, and driving the bone of one arm into his body. His sufferings were severe, and he told the people he should die. But, said he, tell my brethren of Sixth Street Church, in Saint Louis, I am going home. Such was the testimony, and so great the triumph of our dear Brother, that a deep impression was made on the spectators, and some men of the world, who witnessed his sufferings and triumphs, said, with emotion, 'I could die for him.' Our hearts are made sad by our loss, while we doubt not that the hearts of angels were made glad.

J. W. REDFIELD.

"Last Sabbath our Church paid its last sad respects to the late Miss MARY FERGUSON, aged 21. She died on the first of May, of the protracted chronic disease, which for two years had been wasting her body, brightening her eye, and flushing her cheek with the fearful hectic, which hung out the sign of her coming funeral. To me, last Sabbath was a sad, solemn, and a rich day. I first saw MARY before our Church was organized. She was a member of the Methodist Episcopal Church. She was bright, beautiful, the beloved of all. She was very gay, and had been taught by ministers to believe that there was no harm in living the life of innocent pleasures and amusements. But God opened MARY'S eyes to see that her life did not comport with the Bible. In the honesty of her heart, she resolved at all cost, to be a Bible Christian. She put away her worldly conformity, sought and obtained a salvation that saved her from the love of these things; and ever after, her testimony was decided and clear for a salvation from all sin. Members of the Church, and even ministers, tried to persuade her to believe there was no harm in this worldly conformity. But MARY had chosen that good part, and she met and repelled all persuasion from both members and preachers, to return to a proud and fashionable life. On parting with her, last spring, and when, to all appearances she could remain on earth but a short time, I asked her, 'Do you now feel any misgivings for your thoroughness in laying aside all worldly conformity?' 'O, no,' said the dear one. 'O, how thankful I am that you dealt so faithfully with me. I expect to see you no more on earth, but I will come to meet you when you too shall follow me to the Spirit land. O, I shall be a star in your crown of rejoicing when we all meet in Heaven.'

This testimony and these assurances I then felt more than compensated me for all my toil and suffering through which I passed, and the vituperation heaped upon me by professed ministers of the Gospel. But, thank God, MARY is out of the reach of their influence, and the hope of meeting her a redeemed spirit in the land of the blessed, inspires me with consolation. Last Sabbath a large audience evidenced by their attendance at MARY'S funeral how greatly she was beloved, and how extensively she was respected. At the grave many of the members of Sixth Street, who seemed more to triumph than to mourn, sung a parting farewell—

"We'll be there, we'll be there,
　Palms of victory, crowns of glory
We shall wear,
　In that beautiful world on high."

On our way back to the city, it did seem that MARY was with us in the carriage, and we continued to sing for some time the same notes of triumph, while those in sympathy with MARY'S religion and Saviour, shouted aloud the praise of Jesus' love.

J. W. REDFIELD.

DOES CHRIST DWELL HERE?

THE following, from the *Sunday School Banner*, shows how the Spirit of God can and does operate to open the eyes of the blind, and bring them to feel the necessity of salvation:

Many years ago, a lady was seated, reading, in the veranda of her Burmese house, when suddenly she was startled by seeing a little, wild-looking boy standing before her, and asking, with great eagerness, "Does Jesus Christ live here?" He appeared about twelve years old. His coarse, black hair, matted with dirt, bristled up in every direction, like the quills of a porcupine; and the only covering about his person was a ragged cloth of cotton. "Does Jesus Christ live here?" he again asked, as he crouched at the lady's feet. "What do you want of Jesus Christ?" inquired the lady. "I want to see him: I want to confess to him." "Why, what have you been doing, that you want to confess to him?" "Doing!" repeated the boy: "what have I been doing? Why, I tell lies, I steal, I do everything that is bad. I am afraid of going to hell, and I want to see Jesus Christ, for I heard say, he can save us from hell. Does he live here? Oh, tell me where can I find Jesus Christ." "But, my poor boy," said the lady, "Jesus Christ does not save people from hell if they continue to do wickedly." "But I want to stop," answered the boy. "I want to stop doing wickedly; but I can't stop. I don't know how to stop. The evil thoughts are in me, and the bad deeds come out of evil thoughts. What can I do?" "Nothing," said the lady, "but come to Christ, like the rest of us; but you cannot see Jesus Christ now." Here she was interrupted by a sharp cry of distress from the poor boy. "But," she continued, "I am his humble follower and servant, and I can teach all those who wish to escape from hell how to do so." The joyful look of the wild Karen boy was beyond all description, as he exclaimed. "Tell me! oh, tell me! Only ask your master, the Lord Jesus Christ, to save me, and I will be your servant, your slave, for life. Do not be angry. Do not send me away. I want to be saved—saved from hell!"

The lady, you may believe, was not angry, and the next day she took him to the little bamboo school-house; and never was there a scholar, in any school or country, more anxious to learn "the truth as it is in Jesus." After some time, he was baptized; and then he went on daily improving in the knowledge of those things which belong to our salvation. Years passed away, and the gentle lady had gone to that happy home where sin and sorrow are known no more. The wild Karen boy had also changed from boyhood to youth, from youth to strong manhood, and then the hand of death was laid upon him. But while the strong man lay bowed down with sickness—while he tossed wildly to and fro upon his fevered couch—even then his heart was filled with precious memories of Jesus, and his lips uttered fragments of hymns and texts which he had learned in days of health.

"At last the parting hour arrived, when, without a sigh or struggle, his happy spirit passed away, to be forever with that Saviour whom he had sought with such eagerness."

THE EARNEST CHRISTIAN.

RELIGIOUS SENSIBILITY.

BY THE EDITOR.

Men ought to feel. God gives us sensibilities that we may feel. It is only by a long process of hardening that persons come into that fearful state described in the Scriptures as "being past feeling." If any thing should stir us, it is religion.

Every part of man's nature that can be moved—his fears and his hopes, his affections and his sympathies, his judgment, his sense of duty, his love of happiness, and his dread of suffering, of exposure and of shame—each and all are appealed to in the strongest manner by the Gospel of Christ, to lead erring mortals to return to their allegiance to God.

But the arch-enemy has succeeded not only in influencing many to resist the claims of their Maker, and to listen to his earnest appeals with indifference, if not with secret or open scorn, but to treat with contempt, and to overwhelm with opprobrious epithets, all who act as if they believe the awful truths which God has so clearly revealed. Insanity is one of the mildest terms employed to designate the state of those who are awake to eternal things.

In this number we propose to adduce some farther proof of the proposition we laid down last month. That, *It is entirely proper that the servants of God should manifest, at times, the deepest emotion.*

We need not repeat what we then said, that while the inward emotions of the child of God may vary, his outward life will preserve a consistent uniformity; however his feelings may fluctuate, he is unwavering in the discharge of duty.

In proof of the proposition, we call attention to *the greatness of the change that takes place when the penitent sinner becomes a child of God.*

"In witnessing," says a celebrated English philosopher,* "first the entreaties, and supplications, and tears, of a convicted, condemned, and repentant malefactor, prostrate at the feet of his sovereign; and then, the exuberance of his joy and gratitude in receiving pardon and life, no one would so absurdly misuse language as to call the intensity and fervor of the criminal's feelings enthusiastical; for however strong or even ungovernable these emotions may be, they are perfectly congruous with the occasion;—they spring from no illusion; but are fully justified by the momentous turn that has taken place in his affairs :—in the past hour he contemplated nothing but the horrors of an ignominious death, but now life and its delights are before him. It is true that all men in the same circumstances would not undergo the same intensity of emotion; but all, unless obdurate in wickedness, must experience feelings of the same quality. And thus, so long as the real circumstances under which every human being stands in the court of the Supreme Judge are clearly understood, and duly felt, ENTHUSIASM FINDS NO PLACE;—all is real; nothing is illusion."

The beggar may become a millionaire, the slave a king, with obedient nations at his feet, but this improve-

---

* Natural History of Enthusiasm, page 46.

ment in his condition is infinitely less than that which the sinner realizes when he is made an heir to "an inheritance incorruptible, undefiled, and that fadeth not away."

Julia was born of respectable parents, and carefully tended in her early years. Her mother was a prudent, pious woman, but she died when Julia was but twelve years of age. The father, soon after, took to drinking and gambling, and spent all the property he possessed. His daughter was brought into the midst of profligate associates, and became vicious and abandoned. In a fit of intoxication she married a worthless, dissipated fellow. When she was eighteen years old she was tried for perjury, convicted and sentenced to the Sing Sing prison for fourteen years. She was naturally intelligent, active, and energetic, and the limitations of a prison had a worse effect upon her than they would have had upon a more stolid temperament. In the course of a year or two her mind began to sink under the pressure, and finally exhibited signs of melancholy insanity. Friend Hopper had an interview with her at Sing Sing, and found her in a state of deep dejection. She afterward became completely deranged, and was removed to the Lunatic Asylum at Bloomingdale. He and his wife visited her there, and found her in a state of temporary rationality. They took her in a walk with them through the grounds; and she enjoyed this little excursion very highly. But when one of the company remarked that it was a very pleasant place, she sighed deeply, and replied, "Yes, it is a pleasant place to those who can leave it. But chains are chains, though they are made of gold; and mine grow heavier every day." Her temperament peculiarly required freedom, and chafed and fretted under restraint. Friend Hopper obtained permission for her to spend a day and night at his house in the city. The visit was found beneficial, and after a short interval was renewed. She spent several days in his family and conducted with the greatest propriety. He soon after applied to the Governor for a pardon, which was promptly granted. He next provided a suitable home for her. When all was arranged, Friend Hopper went out to the Asylum to carry the news. Fearful of exciting her too much, he asked if she would like to go into the city again to spend a fortnight in his family. She replied "Indeed I would." He promised to take her, and added, "Perhaps thou wilt stay longer than two weeks." At last he said, "It may be that thou wilt not have to return here again." She sprung up instantly, and looking in his face with intense anxiety, exclaimed, "Am I pardoned? *Am I pardoned?*" "Yes, thou art pardoned," he replied, "And I have come to take thee home." She fell back into her seat, covered her face with her hands, and wept aloud. Friend Hopper says, "This was the most affecting scene I ever witnessed." Obdurate, indeed, must be the heart of that man who could ridicule the deep emotion of this child of sorrow in this joyous hour.

But as great as is the difference between an eternity in perdition, and fourteen years in prison, so much greater occasion of rejoicing is there in the case of every sinner when God says to him by the Holy Spirit, "Thy sins, which are many, are all forgiven thee." We do not read that any of these events, which are admitted to justify tumultuous demonstrations of delight among men are noticed above, but our Saviour has said that " *There is joy in the presence of the angels of God over one sinner that repenteth.*"

He, then, that can witness with indifference, and coolly criticise, a scene that sends thrills of joy through all the ranks of the angelic hosts, has good reason to conclude that the veil is yet upon his heart,—that he has no just or proper sense of the magnitude of eternal things.

Well may Isaac Taylor say, "When those whose temper is abhorrent to religious services animadvert sarcastically upon the follies, real or supposed, of religionists, there is a sad inconsistency in such criticisms, like that which is seen when the insane make ghastly mirth of the manners or personal defects of their friends and keepers."

The application of the argument is easily made. Events that affect greatly our temporal welfare justify a manifestation of the deepest emotion. But our temporal bear no comparison to our eternal interests.

Therefore the service of God, affecting, as it does, our eternal interests, and those of our fellow men, renders a manifestation of the deepest emotion entirely proper.

We next adduce a few of the examples of Scripture in proof of our proposition. Let us first consider the case of Moses as recorded in Ex. xix, and Heb. xii, 21. God manifested himself to him upon Mount Sinai. And "there were thunders and lightnings, and a thick cloud upon the mount, and the voice of the trumpet exceeding loud; so that all the people that was in the camp trembled; and so terrible was the sight, that Moses said, I exceedingly fear and quake." Here was the emotion of fear manifested by trembling and quaking. The sinner, too, may well "tremble and quake," when the thunders of the law are sounding in his ear.

David was a man of great strength of body and of mind. In the height of his power he did not consider it derogatory to his dignity as a king, and a prophet, to give expression, publicly, to the highest transports of joy. Read the account of his bringing up the ark of the Lord, from the house of Obed Edom, to the city of David, as given in the iv. Chap. of the Second book of Samuel. "And David danced before the Lord with all his might; and David was girded with a linen ephod. So David and all the house of Israel brought up the ark of the Lord with shouting, and with the sound of the trumpet. And as the ark of the Lord came into the city of David, Michal, Saul's daughter, looked through a window, and saw King David leaping and dancing before the Lord, and she despised him in her heart. And Michal, the Daughter of Saul, came out to meet David, and said, How glorious was the King of Israel to day, who uncovered himself to day in the eyes of the handmaids of his servants, as one of the vain fellows shamelessly uncovereth himself!" To this irony David replied, "It was before the Lord. And I will yet be more vile than this, and will be base in my own sight." Are there none at the present day who would have united with Michal in saying that King David had disgraced himself? None, who seem to feel, like her, that they have to support the dignity of the Church? Let them take warning from her, for she bore her reproach all her days; while David realized the fulfilment of that Scripture, "He that humbleth himself shall be exalted."

Jeremiah was greatly troubled because of the defection of the religious teachers of the people. They amused their hearers with fine words, and cried, "Peace! Peace! when God had not spoken peace." Hear Jeremiah express his anguish, "Mine heart within me is broken because of the prophets; all my bones shake; I am like a drunken man, and like a man whom wine hath overcome, because of the Lord, and because of the words of his holiness."—Jer. xiii, 9. He knew what it was to be burdened for souls.

Daniel does not appear to have been wanting in intellect or nerve. The prospect of lodging in a den of lions did not frighten him. But on seeing a vision from the Lord he says,* "There remained no strength in me, for my comeliness was turned in me into corruption, and I retained no strength." His awe was so great that his physical frame could not bear up under it—he fell prostrate.

On the day of Pentecost, when the Holy Spirit was poured out upon the disciples, there were such manifestations of feeling, that the bystanders could account for on no other theory

---

* Dan. x, 8.

than that "These men are full of new wine."* There was such plausibility in the objection, that Peter felt called upon to enter into a formal argument to disprove it, "These are not drunken as you suppose, seeing it is but the third hour of the day."

When the Revelator, John, was favored with a manifestation of the Son of Man, in his glorified body, he thus describes the effect that it produced upon him: "And when I saw him, I fell at his feet as dead."†

He assures us that in Heaven, there is the deepest emotion among the worshipers that surround the throne, "And a voice came out of the throne, saying, Praise our God all ye his servants, and ye that fear him, both small and great. And I heard as it were the voice of a great multitude, and as the voice of mighty thunderings, saying, Alleluia; for the Lord God omnipotent reigneth."‡

Reader, if you have no sympathy with those who praise the Lord audibly in His sanctuaries below, how do you think you will be prepared to join above in this mighty tumult of praise?

No more, or clearer Scripture proof can be required to establish our proposition. If religion is the same in every age, and if under the Christian dispensation, the Spirit is to be poured out more abundantly than ever before, we may then expect, that those who are earnestly engaged in the service of the Lord, shall manifest from time to time the deepest emotion.

We refer, also, to the experience of those, who, in different branches of the Church of Christ, have been eminent for piety and usefulness.

The inquiry is often made, why, if this deep emotion is essential to the earnest Christian, do we not see it manifested among different denominations? Our answer is, that we do, among the eminently pious of all denominations. We will give you as many cases as our limits will permit. Luther, having gained the reputation of being one of the most learned men of his day, became awakened, by alarming providences, to his condition as a sinner. He solemnly determined to seek after holiness, as eagerly as he had pursued knowledge. For nearly two years he practised the greatest austerities, and discharged the most self-debasing duties. But he could find no peace. Sometimes his meditations on the divine justice and wrath, awakened such terrors in him, that his bodily powers failed him, and he sometimes lay motionless as if dead. He was found one day, on the floor of his cell, without any signs of life. "It is in vain," he says to Staupitz, "that I make promises to God; sin is always too strong for me." Staupitz told him to "look to the wounds of Jesus Christ to the blood which he has shed for you; it is then you will see the mercy of God."* He looked; and his deep emotions were followed by peace of conscience and joy in the Holy Ghost. But for these deep stirrings of soul, Luther had never been the Reformer he was.

Whitfield's life furnishes another example of the deepest emotion, first of penitence, then of joy. Had his conversion been of a superficial character, his name would not have gone down to posterity as the most successful preacher of modern times. Whitfield sought the Lord in earnest. He was accustomed to select Christ Church meadow as the scene, and a stormy night as the time, of his mental conflicts. He prostrated his body on the bare earth, fasted during Lent, and exposed himself to the cold till his hands began to blacken, and, by abstinence and inward struggles, so emaciated his body as to be scarcely able to creep up stairs. For seven weeks he labored under a severe illness. It was, in his own language, "a glorious visitation."† It gave him time and composure to make a written record and a penitent confession of his youthful sins—to examine the New

---

* Acts ii, 18. † Rev. i, 17. ‡ Rev. xix, 56.

* Life of Luther, by Cubitt, p. 44, 45.
† Stevens Miscellanies, p. 24.

Testament; and to seek, by prayer, for wisdom and for peace. The blessings thus invoked were not denied. "The day star," he says, " arose in my heart. The spirit of mourning was taken from me. For some time I could not avoid singing Psalms wherever I was, but my joy became gradually more settled. Thus were the days of my mourning ended." From that time, Whitfield was a joyous triumphant Christian, and the word which he preached was in demonstration of the Spirit and in power.

Mr. Flavel was an eminent minister of the Calvinistic school. His labors were greatly blessed. His works are still read with profit, by the devout of all denominations.* Mr. Flavel gives an account of a man that he knew, that was wonderfully overcome with divine comforts. It is supposed that he relates his own experience. He says "that as the person was traveling alone, with his thoughts closely fixed on the great and astonishing things of another world, his thoughts began to swell higher and higher, like the water in Ezekiel's vision, until at last they became an overflowing flood; such was the intenseness of his mind, such the ravishing tastes of heavenly joys, and such his full assurance of his interest therein, that he utterly lost all sight and sense of this world, and the concernments thereof; and for some hours, knew not where he was, nor what he was about; but having lost a great quantity of blood at the nose, he found himself so faint, that it brought him a little more to himself. And after he had washed himself at a spring, and drank of the water for his refreshment, he continued to the end of his journey, which was thirty miles; and all this while was scarce sensible; and says he had several trances of considerable continuance. The same blessed frame was preserved all that night, and in a lower degree, great part of the next day; the night passed without one wink of sleep; and yet he declares he never had a sweeter night's rest in all his life. Still the joy of the Lord overflowed him, and he seemed to be an inhabitant of another world. And he used, for many years after, to call that day one of the days of Heaven; and professed that he understood more of the life of Heaven by it than by all the books he ever used, or discourses he ever entertained about it."

In these deep experiences, is found the secret of the strength of these old divines, who shook the world in their day, and whose works are still exerting a benign influence far and wide.

The revival that took place under the labor of Edwards was characterized by the intensest feeling. No cold and heartless "submission to God" was regarded in those days as all the experience necessary to constitute the sinner a child of God.

He gives, with approbation, many instances of the manifestation of the deepest emotion. He says, *" Persons are first awakened with a sense of their miserable condition by nature, the danger they are in of perishing eternally, and that it is of great importance to them that they speedily escape, and get into a better state. Some have had such a sense of the displeasure of God, and the great danger they were in of damnation, that they could not sleep at nights. There have been some instances of persons that have had as great a sense of their danger and misery, as their natures could well subsist under, so that a little more would probably have destroyed them."

Of course this deep conviction was not produced in the minds of sinners without a corresponding depth of emotion in the hearts of believers. He represents that †" Some persons have had longing desires after Christ, which have risen to that degree, as to take away their natural strength. Some have been so overcome with a sense of the dying love of Christ to such poor, wretched, and unworthy creatures, as

---

* Edwards, vol. 3, 287.

* Edwards, vol. 3, pages 240, 1, 2, 3.
† Vol. 3, page 254.

to weaken the body. Several persons have had so great a sense of the glory of God, and excellency of Christ, that nature and life have seemed almost to sink under it; and in all probability, if God had showed them a little more of himself it would have dissolved their frame."

He gives, at considerable length, the experience of several individuals whose emotions were, at times, overpowering. We can find room for a brief account of only one, a young lady of "a rational understanding family." *" She was, before her conversion, of a sober and inoffensive conversation, and was a still, quiet, reserved person. She was first awakened by something she heard her brother say of the necessity of being in good earnest in seeking regenerating grace, together with the news of the conversion of a young woman. Her great terror," she said, was, " that she had sinned against God;" her distress grew more and more for three days, until, (as she said,) she saw nothing but blackness of darkness before her, and her very flesh trembled for fear of God's wrath. In prayer and reading the Bible she sought the Lord for a number of days. One morning, on awaking, these words came to her mind, " The blood of Christ cleanses from all sin;" they were accompanied with a lively sense of the excellency of Christ, and his sufficiency to satisfy for the sins of the whole world. Her mind was led into such contemplations and views of Christ, as filled her exceeding full of joy. All the next day she felt a constant sweetness in her soul. She had a repetition of the same discoveries of Christ three mornings together. One morning while in the enjoyment of a spiritual view of Christ's glory and fulness, her soul was filled with distress for Christless persons; and she felt in herself a strong inclination immediately, to go forth and warn sinners; and proposed to her brother to assist her in going from house to house. After this, seeing three persons lately converted, as they stepped in one after another at the door, so affected her, and so drew forth her love to them, that it overcame her, and she almost fainted; and when they began to talk of the things of religion, it was more than she could bear,—they were obliged to desist on that account. Soon after this she went to a private religious meeting, and her mind was full of a sense and view of the glory of God all the time; and when the exercise was ended some asked her concerning what she had experienced; and she began to give them an account: but as she was relating it, it revived such a sense of the same things, that her strength failed and they were obliged to take her and lay her upon the bed. Afterward she was greatly affected, and rejoiced with these words: " Worthy is the lamb that was slain." She endured unto the end and died triumphantly. He gives this and some similar cases as specimens of the experiences of those who shared in this gracious out-pouring of the Holy Spirit. It seems to have been a common thing among them for persons to lose their strength, as it is now termed.

He says, *" It is remarkable, considering in what multitudes of instances, and to how a great a degree, the frame of the body has been overpowered of late, that person's lives have, notwithstanding, been preserved, and that the instances of those that have been deprived of reason have been so very few, and those, perhaps, all of them persons, under the peculiar disadvantages of a weak, vapory habit of body. A merciful and careful divine hand is very manifest in it, that in so many instances where the ship has begun to sink, yet it has been upheld, and has not totally sunk. The instances of such as have been deprived of reason are so few, that certainly they are not enough to cause us to be in any fright, as though this work that has been carried on in the country, was not likely to be of beneficial influence, unless we are disposed

---

* Edwards, vol. 3, 260.

* Vol. 3, p. 284.

to gather up all we can to darken it, and set it forth in frightful colors."

This Presbyterian revival must have exceeded by far, in its effects upon the body, any that have taken place, of late years, among denomination in this country, to justify him in saying, "that in multitudes of instances, the frame of the body has been overpowered." Yet, it seems that nobody was killed, and but few became deranged. Edwards was not in the habit of using, in his narratives, the language of exaggeration.

"These things did not begin," he says, "in his day." * "They are not new in their kind; but are things of the same nature as have been found and well approved of in the Church of God before, from time to time."

We have a remarkable instance in Mr. Bolton, that noted minister of the Church of England, who being awakened by the preaching of the famous Mr. Perkins, minister of Christ in the University of Cambridge, was subject to such terrors as threw him to the ground, and caused him to roar with anguish; and the pangs of the new birth in him were such, that he lay pale and without sense, like one dead; as we have an account in the "Fulfilling of the Scripture," the 5th edition, p. 103, 104. We have an account in the same page of another whose comforts, under the sunshine of God's presence, were so great, that he could not forbear crying out in a transport, and expressing in exclamations, the great sense he had of forgiving mercy, and his assurance of God's love. And we have a remarkable instance in the life of Mr. George Trosse, written by himself, (who, of a notoriously vicious, profligate liver, became an eminent saint, and minister of the Gospel) of terrors occasioned by awakenings of conscience, so overpowering the body, as to deprive, for some time, of the use of reason.

Yea, such extraordinary external effects of inward impressions, have not only been to be found in here and there a single person, but there have also before now been times wherein many have been thus affected, in some particular parts of the Church of God; and such effects have appeared in congregations, in many at once. So it was in the year 1625 in the west of Scotland, in a time of great out-pouring of the Spirit of God. It was then a frequent thing for many to be so extraordinarily seized with terror in the hearing of the word, by the Spirit of God convincing them of sin, that they fell down and were carried out of the Church, who afterwards proved most solid and lively Christians.

Many in France were so wonderfully affected with the preaching of the Gospel, in the time of those famous divines, Farel and Viret, that for a time they could not follow their secular business. Many, in Ireland, in time of a great out-pouring of the Spirit there in the year 1628, were so filled with divine comforts and a sense of God, that they had but little use of either meat, drink or sleep, and professed that they did not feel the need thereof."

Edwards thus shows that these manifestations of emotions were common among earnest Christians. Of course, the devil was not pleased. Too general attention to religion was excited, and too many sinners were converted, for him to be very well satisfied. He stirred up all he could to talk against this way.

Manifestations and exaggerations were freely circulated. The ministers chiefly instrumental were freely charged with looking upon them as certain evidences of a work of the Spirit. This against a Calvanistic minister was a most serious charge, as according to their theory it could not, from any amount of evidence before one's death, be certainly ascertained that he was converted. If he fell away, the theory was that his apparent piety was not real.

Edwards defends these manifestations as follows: * "Another thing,

---

* Vol. 3, p. 286.

* Edward's Works, vol. 3, p. 343.

wherein I think some ministers have been injured, is in being very much blamed for making so much of outcries, faintings and other bodily effects; speaking of them as tokens of the presence of God, and arguments of the success of preaching; seeming to strive to their utmost to bring a congregation to that pass, and seeming to rejoice, yea, even blessing God for it, when they see these effects.

Concerning this I would observe, in the first place, that there are many things, with respect to cryings out, falling down, &c., that are charged on ministers that they are not guilty of. Some would have it, that they speak of these things as certain evidences of a work of the Spirit of God on the hearts of their hearers, or that they esteem these bodily effects, themselves, to be the work of God, as though the Spirit of God took hold of, and agitated the bodies of men; and some are charged with making these things essential, and supposing that persons cannot be converted without them; whereas I never yet could see the person that held either of these things.

But for speaking of such effects as probable tokens of God's presence, and arguments of the success of preaching, it seems to me they are not to be blamed; because I think they are so, indeed; and therefore when I see them excited by preaching the important truths of God's word, urged and enforced by proper arguments and motives, or as consequent on other means that are good, I do not scruple to speak of them, and to rejoice in them, and bless God for them as such; and that for this (as I think) good reason, viz: that from time to time, upon proper inquiry and examination, and observation of the consequence and fruits, I have found that these are all evidences that persons in whom these effects appear, are under the influence of God's Spirit, in such cases. Cryings out, in such a manner, and with such circumstances, as I have seen them from time to time, is as much an evidence to me, of the general cause it proceeds from,
as language; I have learned the meaning of it, the same way that persons learn the meaning of language, viz: by use and experience. I confess that when I see a great crying out in a congregation, in the manner that I have seen it, when these things are held forth to them that are worthy of their being greatly affected by, I rejoice in it much more than merely in an appearance of solemn attention, and a show of affection by weeping; and that because when there have been those outcries, I have found from time to time, a much greater and more excellent effect."

*"The most specious thing that is alleged against these extraordinary effects upon the body is, that the body is impaired and health wronged; and that it is hard to think that God, in the merciful influences of his Spirit on men, would wound their bodies and impair their health. But if it were so pretty commonly, or in multiplied instances, (which I do not suppose it is) that persons received a lasting wound to their health by extraordinary religious impressions made upon their minds, yet it is too much for us to determine that God shall never bring an outward calamity, in bestowing a vastly greater spiritual and eternal good.

Jacob, in doing his duty in wrestling with God for the blessing, and while God was striving with him, at the same time that he received the blessing from God, suffered a great outward calamity from his hand; God impaired his body so that he never got over it as long as he lived; he gave him the blessing, but sent him away halting on his thigh, and he went lame all his life after. And yet this is not mentioned as if it were any diminution of the great mercy of God to him, when God blessed him and called his name, Israel, because as a prince he had power with God and had prevailed.

We cannot determine that God never shall give any person so much

---

* Edwards, vol. 3, 282.

of a discovery of himself, not only as to weaken their bodies, but to take away their lives. It is supposed by very learned and judicious divines, that Moses' life was taken away after this manner; and this has also been supposed to be the case with some other saints.

Yea, I do not see any solid, sure grounds, any have to determine that God shall never make such strong impressions on the mind by his spirit, that shall be an occasion of so impairing the frame of the body, and particularly that part of the body, the brain, that persons shall be deprived of the use of reason. As I said before, it is too much for us to determine, that God will not bring an outward calamity in bestowing spiritual and eternal blessings; so it is too much for us to determine how great an outward calamity he will bring. If God gives a great increase of discoveries of himself, and of love to him, the benefit is infinitely greater than the calamity, though the life should presently be taken away. We cannot determine how great a calamity distraction is, when considered with all its consequences, and all that might have been consequent, if the distraction had not happened; nor indeed, whether (thus considered) it may be any calamity at all, or whether it be not a mercy, by preventing some great sin, or some more dreadful thing if it had not been."

* "It is easily accounted for from the consideration of the nature of divine and eternal things, and the nature of man, and the laws of the union between soul and body, how a right influence, a true and proper sense of things, should have such effects on the body, even those that are of the most extraordinary kind, such as taking away the bodily strength, or throwing the body into great agonies, and extorting loud outcries."

We have given large extracts from writers of other denominations. We have done this purposely. Our object has been to show that these manifestations of religious feeling that are of late so strongly opposed, have been common in thorough revivals, among those denominations that are freest from them now. We have room to fortify our position by only a brief reference to Methodist writers. These manifestations have been common among us as a denomination, from the beginning.

Almost all our books of biography and history abound with accounts of the extraordinary effects produced upon the body by the outpouring of the Spirit. I would refer the reader to Bangs' History of the M. E. Church, the Autobiographies of Finley and Cartwright, the Life of Benj. Abbott, Footprints of an Itinerant, by Maxwell P. Gaddis, and other biographical works.

I cannot forbear giving as a specimen, a few extracts from the account which Bangs gives of a wonderful revival that took place in 1775 and 1776.* He quotes from Asbury's Journal the narrative given by the Rev. Mr. Jarratt, a minister of the Church of England, who participated largely in that revival, and contributed by his labors to its advancement. Mr. Jarratt says: "I have no doubt but the work now carrying on is genuine; yet there were some circumstances attending it which I disliked; such as loud outcries, tremblings, fallings, convulsions. But I am better reconciled since I read President Edwards on that head, who observes, 'that whenever these most appears, there is always the greatest and the deepest work.'

There is another thing which has given me much pain; the praying of several at one and the same time. Sometimes five or six, or more have been praying all at once, in several parts of the room, for distressed persons. Others were speaking by way of exhortation, so that the assembly appeared to be all in confusion, and must seem to one at a little distance,

---

* Edwards, vol. 1, 528.

* Bang's History M. E. C. Vol. 1, p. 90, et. seq.

more like a drunken rabble than the worshiping of God; I was afraid that was not doing all things in decency and order. Indeed, Dr. Edwards defends this also. But yet, I am not satisfied concerning it. *But as this abated, the work of conviction and conversion usually abated too.*"

One of his correspondents, a local preacher, wrote him thus: "It is common with us for men and women to fall down as dead under an exhortation, but many more under prayer, perhaps twenty at a time. And some that have not fallen to the earth, have shown the same distress, wringing their hands, smiting their breasts and begging all to pray for them,"

Mr. Lee in an account which he gives of a revival in 1787, says: "Hundreds of the believers were so overcome with the power of God that they fell down, and lay helpless on the floor or on the ground; and some of them continued in that helpless condition for a considerable time, and were happy in God beyond description. When they came to themselves, it was generally with loud praises to God, and with tears and expressions enough to melt the hardest heart."

The next day, *" while the ministers were preaching, the power of the Lord was felt among the people in such a manner that they roared and screamed so loud that the preacher could not be heard, and he was compelled to stop. Many of the wealthy people, both men and women, were seen lying in the dust, sweating and rolling on the ground in their fine broadcloths or silks, crying for mercy."

CHRISTIAN CONVERSATION.—The eminently pious Rev. James Hervey, said, of fashionable society, "I hear much frothy and worldly chit-chat, but not a word of Christ; and I am determined not to visit those companies where there is not room for my Master, as well as for myself."

Bangs, vol. 1, 265.

GOD'S PRESENCE.

THE first want of our Christianity is a clearer recognition and a more perfect realization of God's actual presence and agency in all its conceptions and enterprises. Its greatest danger lurks, on the one hand, in a philosophising hard orthodoxy; on the other, in a sensuous, fastidious liberalism — the first insensibly losing, the last frankly discarding from its system the indwelling, co-working divinity. Meantime, every truly Christian aspiration that is felt among us cries aloud for the living God. Our helpless human nature turns away dissatisfied and disheartened from a religion which has no Divine manifestation to stir the soul and justify its hopes. Of philosophies and cosmogonies it has enough, or can make more; but it longs for a Divine presence, and will not endure the terrific solitude of a clime in which there is no God. In its desperate efforts to supply a want so intolerable, it creates divinities. The Israelites substituted a golden calf for Jehovah before he had been forty days withdrawn from their camp. It was not enough that they beheld the dark symbols of His presence on the dim, distant mountain top. They would see the cloud and the pillar of fire dwelling in the midst of them.

Natural religion, in all its aberrations, ever manifests its longings after Divine manifestations, that may make known, at least to the fears of men, the power and majesty of Heaven. Hence, it forms monsters hideous to the sight —Molochs to drink the blood of childhood—Juggernauts to be approved by martyrdom or self-immolations. The universal tendency is developed, though in less exaggerated forms, under the Christian dispensation. It is this, that in the absence or denial of the transforming energies of the Holy Ghost, deifies popes and hierarchies, and ordinances. It invests symbols and ceremonies with Divine attributes, and worships the wafer it has transformed into a crucified Saviour. Or, with an impiety yet more daring, as well as absurd, because it will not recognize God in revelation; and in Christ reconciling the world to Himself, it deifies man man and the universe, making all things living and brute, Divine, that it may reject the one only Divinity.

While we lament these deplorable errors, let us receive their lessons of instruction. They are spontaneous efforts, put forth by those who have lost God out of their Christianity, te save themselves from stark Atheism.—OLIN.

THE CROWN OF THORNS.

Translated from the German.

O sacred Head! now wounded,
　With grief and shame weighed down,
Now scornfully surrounded
　With thorns, Thine only crown;
O sacred Head! what glory,
　What bliss till now was Thine,
Yet, though despised and gory,
　I joy to call Thee mine.

What Thou, my Lord, hast suffered,
　Was all for sinners' gain;
Mine, mine, was the transgression,
　But Thine the deadly pain.
Lo! here I fall, my Saviour!
　'Tis I deserve Thy place;
Look on me with Thy favor,
　Vouchsafe to me Thy grace.

The joy can ne'er be spoken—
　Above all joys beside—
When in Thy body broken
　I thus with safety hide.
My Lord of life, desiring
　Thy glory now to see,
Beside Thy cross expiring,
　I'd breathe my soul to Thee.

What language shall I borrow,
　To thank Thee, dearest Friend,
For this, Thy dying sorrow,
　Thy pity without end!
O, make me Thine for ever,
　And should I fainting be,
Lord, let me never, never,
　Outlive my love to Thee.

And when I am departing,
　O, part not Thou from me,
When mortal pangs are darting,
　Come, Lord, and set me free!
And when my heart must languish
　Amidst the final throe,
Release me from my anguish,
　By Thine own pain and woe.

Be near when I am dying—
　Oh, show Thy cross to me!
And, for my succor flying,
　Come, Lord, and set me free.
These eyes, new faith receiving,
　From Jesus shall not move,
For he who dies believing,
　Dies safely, through Thy love.

MEEKNESS.—How difficult it is to be of a meek and forgiving spirit, when despitefully used. To love an enemy, and forgive an evil speaker, is a higher attainment than is commonly believed.

It is easy to talk of Christian forbearance among neighbors, but to practice it ourselves proves us to be Christians indeed.

The surmises of a few credulous persons need not trouble that man who knows his cause is soon to be tried in Court, and he openly acquitted.

So the evil language of the times need not disturb me, since, in the day of judgment my judgment shall be brought forth as the noon day.

DANCING.—When about twelve or thirteen years old, I learned to dance. I grew passionately fond of it. I lost the spirit of subordination, did not love work, imbibed a spirit of idleness, and, in short, drunk in all the brain-sickening effluvia of pleasure. I entered into no disreputable assembly, and in no one case ever kept any improper company. Nevertheless, dancing was to me a perverting influence. Let them plead for it who will, I know it to be evil, and that only.—ADAM CLARKE.

WE must believe God fully, or we shall profit little by a belief of Him in part.

Preaching in Another's Parish.

—In December 1772, Mr. Asbury went into Kent county, Maryland. "Before preaching," he says, "one Mr. R., a Church minister, came to me and desired to know who I was, and whether I was licensed. I told him who I was. He spoke great swelling words, and said he had authority over the people, and was charged with the care of their souls. He also said that I could not and should not preach : and if I did, he should proceed against me according to law. I let him know that I came to preach, and preach I would; and farther asked him if he had authority to bind the consciences of the people, or if he was a justice of the peace ; and told him I thought he had nothing to do with me. He charged me with making a scism. I told him that I did not draw the people from the Church, and asked him if his church was then open. He then said that I hindered the people from their work. I asked him if fairs and horse races did not hinder them ; and farther told him that I came to help him. He said he had not hired me for an assisstant, and did not want my help. I told him if there were no swearers or other sinners, he was sufficient. 'But,' said he, 'what do you come for?' I replied, 'To turn sinners to God.' He said, 'Cannot I do that as well as you?' I told him that I had authority from God. He then laughed at me, and said, 'You are a fine fellow indeed!' I told him I did not do this to invalidate *his* authority: and also gave him to understand that I did not wish to dispute with him; but he said he had business with *me*, and came into the house in a great rage. I began to preach, and urged the people to repent and turn from all their transgressions, so iniquity should not prove their ruin. After preaching, the parson went out, and told the people they did wrong in coming to hear me; and said I spoke against learning, whereas I only spoke to this purpose—when a man turned from all sin he would adorn every character in life, both in Church and state."—ASBURY.

Methodist Meeting in 1775.

—I was weak in body through riding so far in extreme heat and much exercised in mind, and did not know how I should be able to go through the labor of the day. We went to the chapel at ten, where I had liberty of mind and strength of body, beyond my expectation. After preaching I met the society, and was more relieved both in body and mind. At four in the afternoon I preached again, from "I set before thee an open door, and none can shut it." I had gone through about two-thirds of my discourse, and was bringing the words home to the present *now*, when such power descended that hundreds fell to the ground, and the house seemed to shake with the glory of God. The chapel was full of white and black, and many were without that could not get in. Look wherever we would, we saw nothing but streaming eyes, and faces bathed in tears ; and heard nothing but groans and strong cries after God and the Lord Jesus Christ. My voice was drowned amid the groans and prayers of the congregation. I then sat down in the pulpit ; and both Mr. S. and I were so filled with the divine presence that we could only say, This is none other than the house of God! this is the gate of heaven! Husbands were inviting their wives to go to heaven, wives their husbands : parents their children, and children their parents: brothers their sisters, and sisters their brothers. In short, those who were happy in God themselves were for bringing all their friends to Him in their arms. This mighty effusion of the Spirit continued for above an hour : in which time many were awakened, some found peace with God, and others His pure love. We attempted to speak or sing again and again ; but we no sooner began than our voices were drowned. It was with much difficulty that we at last persuaded the people, as night drew on, to retire to their own homes.—REV. THOMAS RANKIN.

TRUTH is the highest style of charity.

SECTARIAN STRIFE.

BY REV. S. COLLEY.

An Irishman, entering the fair at Ballinagone, saw the well-defined form of a large round head bulging out the canvass of a tent. The temptation was irresistable; up went his shillalah, down went the man. Forth rushed from the tent a host of angry fellows to avenge the onslaught. Judge of their astonishment when they found their assailant to be one of their own faction. "Och, Nicholas," say they, "and did ye not know it was Brady O'Brien ye hit?" "Troth, did I not," says he; "bad luck to me for that same; but sure if my own father had been there, and his head looking so nice and convanient, I could not have helped myself." Poor Paddy! true type of some controversial spirits; it is not in them to let the chance of a blow go by. They are of the brood of the vulture, not of the dove. "They scent the battle from afar." And many of the moot points for which they have done fierce fight, are so infinitesimally small that I would not give the turn of a button shank to get them infallibly decided.

Many contentions arise out of sheer misunderstanding. Disputants often become metaphysical according to the explanation given of metaphysics by the Scotchman who said: "Why, ye see, metaphysics is when twa mun are talking thegither, and the ane o' them dinna ken what he is talking about, and the ither canna understond him." Drs. Chalmers and Stuart must have been a "wee bit" metaphysical that day they got into a controversy about the nature of faith. Chalmers, compelled at length to leave his friend, said: "I have time to say no more; but you will find my views fully and well put up in a recent tract called 'Difficulties in the Way of Believing.'" "Why," exclaimed the astonished Dr. Stuart, "that is my own tract; I published it myself!"

That man was surely wise who prefaced every debate with, "Gentlemen, define your terms." During the Peninsular war, an officer of artillery had just served a gun with admirable precision against a body of men posted in a wood to his left. When the Duke rode up, after turning his glass for a moment in the direction of the shot, he said in his cool way: "Well aimed, captain; but no more; they are our own 39th!" The blunder has been repeated sadly too often in the armies of Jesus. With what fatal frequency have great guns of the Church, which might have battered down citadels of Satan, been misdirected against Christian brethren! There are surely deviltries enough in this world to shoot at without firing into each other.—*Household Magazine.*

The Light of the Spirit.—The promised baptism of the Holy Ghost is a flood of light, penetrating the darkest recesses of the soul, revealing its most concealed corruption.

It discovers dangers that were never before realized. It shows the perilous track of a wandering Church within the unhallowed precincts of sin. It compels the soul to shrink from and abhor the very things which before it has earnestly coveted. It trembles to see that the outward splendors of the Church, once deemed the reliable evidences of success, are but the attire of a harlot, both revealing and inviting illicit intercourse with a godless world.—Peck's Central Idea.

We are Laborers together with God.—Young converts often believe they should devote themselves wholly to God—in the ministry, perhaps—are unwilling—resist till the Spirit leaves them doubtful or blind. Such persons usually become mere formalists. They even fear to have more of the Spirit, lest this disagreeable conviction of duty may return.—Olin.

Whomsoever I please or displease, I will be faithful to God, to the people and to my own soul.—Asbury.

Human nature is too selfish to love justly.

SMALL SINS.

BY D. C.

God sees not as man seeth. Hence the great impropriety of calling anything that is contrary to the law of God a small sin. The only justification I can offer for the use of the term "small sin," is the poet's license.

Sin is a transgression of the law. The greatest commandment is, "Thou shalt love the Lord thy God with all thy heart, and with all thy soul, and with all thy mind." The second is like unto it: "Thou shalt love thy neighbor as thyself." This is the law. A violation of this is *sin*. It is breaking God's holy commandment. Murder, covetousness, and adultery, are only breaking the law. It is theft to take a penny that is not ours. It is only theft to take one hundred dollars. True, one is petit larceny, and the other is grand larceny, according to our criminal code; but both are *sin*. In the code of God we have no such nice distinctions. He who neglects to love God with all his soul, mind and strength, needs as much the atoning merits and righteousness of Christ to wash away his sins and make him meet for the inheritance of the saints, as does the one who steals, or who commits a murder. "The smallest sin," requires the atonement, and the darkest requires no more. There was no provision made in God's economy, for the pardon of sin, until the blessed son of God offered to take upon himself the sins of the human race. Adam's sin was only eating the fruit of one tree which was forbidden. One act of disobedience "brought death into the world." One act of impatience, or hastiness of spirits, kept the meek man Moses, after a pupilage of forty years in the land of Midian, from leading God's chosen Israel over Jordan into the promised land. One act of David's, the sweet singer of Israel, once the man after God's own heart, filled his soul with deepest sorrow, and caused the scalding tears of repentance to flow, while he cried "Restore to me, oh God, the joys of thy salvation." It was only one act of disobedience that brought the prophet, sent to prophecy against the Altar of Bethel, to a violent and untimely death.

How hard it was for Lot to obey when told to flee for his life, escape to the mountains, tarry not in all the plains. How ready to disobey: "See, this is a little place, may I not stop here," and thus he tempts God. Balaam is told not to go with the servants of Balack, and yet, after listening to the tempting offers of the servants of Balack, he again tempts God by asking permission to go with them, as though God was man that he should change. He loved the wages of unrighteousness.

Oh that we were wise, that we understood this, that we considered our latter end!

How hard it is for us to obey God and not lean to our own wills. We too often say in effect "this is a small thing, may we not indulge in it?" Yet we profess to be Christ's disciples, and to desire to do his will, and to be made wholly his. As soon as he touches our idols, health, friends, children, money or reputation, we at once cry out, "Oh, anything else but this affliction!" What brings the soul to a sense of its true condition, and especially the believer to a knowledge of the fullness of the Gospel of Christ Jesus, our Lord, is the taking away of broken stays and props, the removing of our Isaacs, and the prostrating of our bodies with disease. Or, what is most trying of all, He has suffered, or some of our brethren in the church have without his sufferance, blasted our good reputation that we had always maintained. Though we never had said much about it, yet we were in the habit of thinking of it rather complacently as a better qualification to do good than many others professed.

But, they are now all gone, nothing left, praise the Lord. Jesus wants to save us just now. "Whom I love, I chasten." Now we begin to desire of God that which we can find no where else. Glory to God for this bankruptcy; for it is just like him to take us now with all our poverty, without friends or character, or reputation, health, or money.

> "Now rest my long divided heart,
> Fixed on this blissful centre rest;
> Nor ever from thy Lord depart,
> With him of every good possessed."

Oh, how easy it is now to believe, to trust God—to do his will. We can now pray, and know that he heareth us. We now hear him say, "Ask what you will, and it shall be done unto you." Our prayer is not for any of those things that we have lost, for we find we are better off without them. We now pray to be kept by the power of God through faith unto salvation, ready to be revealed in the last time. What an astonishing effect chastening has had on us! How close to God it has brought us; how humble, and submissive it has made us; how our vision has changed; how wonderfully those little things have grown in a short time; how child-like we are; how we love the Lord, and those that persecute us; how willing to be anything or nothing! Glory to God for afflictions, for chastenings! Bless the Lord, oh my soul! all that is within me bless his holy name, forever and ever. Amen.

A GOOD ANSWER.—"How do you know," said an enlightened man to a poor ignorant savage of Kamschatga, "how do you know there is a God?" "How do you know," replied the savage, pointing to human footsteps near him, "how do you know that men have passed this way?"

CHRISTIAN GRACES.—Christian graces are like perfumes. The more they are pressed, the sweeter they smell; like stars that shine brightest in the dark; like trees, the more they are shaken the deeper root they take, and the more fruit they bear.

THE WEDGE OF GOLD.

AN army went forth, in the name of the God of Israel, to meet the enemy. They had conquered in other conflicts, and they were not less sure of victory. But the tide of success was turned against them. The sun went down, and cast his setting rays on the prostrate banners of Israel. Defeat had discouraged their hearts, and losses had weakened their hands. It was a time of mourning and humiliation.

Then went forth the voice of the Lord to the leader of the people—"There is an accursed thing among you!" There was no mention of its nature or its magnitude; but it was an iniquity and a transgression which could not be suffered to remain, except by the forfeiture of Divine favor and support. How must the heart of that devoted leader have throbbed, during the long night which intervened between the rebuke and the ordeal by which the transgression was to be disclosed! When the morning came, and the whole multitude were commanded to appear by tribes, what heart-searching must there have been! "Lord, is it I?" was the inquiry of all, in that time of fear and suspense.

The tribes passed in review, and Judah was taken. From the tribe of Judah, the Zarhites were taken. From the family of Zerah, the house of Zabdi was chosen. Step by step, the inquisition went on; and as the guilty one saw the precision of the choice, he became more and more conscious of his sin. Man by man, the sons of Zabdi came before the judge; and Achan at last stood forth, the author of the confusion, and the transgressor.

He had seen a goodly Babylonish garment, two hundred shekels of silver, and a wedge of gold, and had seized them for his spoils. Himself and his house suffered the penalty of the broken command, and the people witnessed a solemn and impressive vindication of the Divine law.

The Babylonish garment and the

wedge of gold have their admirers today, as well as when Israel was striving for her possession. The cloth is just as glossy and as richly dyed; the price is just as high now as then; the cost of its purchase precisely the same. It has different forms, woven by different artists, enriched by different ornaments, but all of them are produced in the workshops of Babylon, and by the hands of idolatrous artificers. The tinsel of the world is upon them. The glitter and the spangles of earth, her baubles and her gems, are seen flashing in the light of earthly pleasures. Be they never so rich and beautiful, be they never so costly and rare, they are nothing but Babylonish garments, and are not for the children of God.

The wedge of gold is wrapped up in the garment, as it was then. It is a tempting thing to look upon. The world has riches for its worshipers: and though the purchase-price may at last be an eternal loss, yet the wedge of gold will find the eager spoilsmen who will seize it as their reward. It is in every church, in every tent, in every heart, in some form or other; and if the work of searching were commenced, who would escape? If judgment should begin at the house of God, how many would be found with the wedge of gold lying deep in their hearts! Searching deep, the messenger would uncover the hiding-place, and display the transgression, the covetousness, and the idolatry of the professed follower of Christ.

Shall the wedge of gold be cast aside, and the Babylonish garment be destroyed, so that Israel may be blessed? If the Church should earnestly and humbly betake itself to heart-searching, in order to find out what hinders the full glory of the Divine blessing being poured out upon us, we should soon see the fruit in a work such as the world has not seen. The hindrances would be removed, the transgressions repented of, the Church purified from worldliness and pride, and the followers of Christ would appear in robes of righteousness, and with fine gold, not of Babylon, but tried in the fire, and stamped with the image of the Redeemer.—CHRISTIAN INTELLIGENCER.

PREPARATION FOR DEATH.—When you lie down at night, compose your spirits as if you were not to awake till the heavens be no more; and when you awake in the morning, consider that new day as your last, and live accordingly. That night cometh, of which you will never see the morning, or that morning of which you will never see the night. Let the mantle of worldly enjoyment hang loose about you, that it may be easily dropped when death comes to carry you into another world. When the fruit is ripe, it falls off the tree easily; so, when a Christian's heart is truly weaned from the world, he is prepared for death, and it will be be the more easy for him.

IT is quite possible for a man to possess the evidence of sanctification, who is temporarily destitute of joyful and rapturous emotions. But it is not possible for a man to possess such evidence, who is destitute of a living, operative and effective conscience. On no part of our nature does sanctification work greater effects than on the conscience. It may be said to give to it an intensity and multiplicity of existence; so that like the flaming sword of the cherubims it turns every way and guards the tree of life.—UPHAM.

HEAR ye, and give ear; be not proud; for the Lord hath spoken. Give glory to the Lord your God, before he cause darkness, and before your feet stumble upon the dark mountains, and while ye look for light, he turn it into the shadow of death, and make it gross darkness.—JEREMIAH.

OUR advancement in the Christian life may be said to depend upon one thing, viz: whether we wish to direct God, or are willing to resign ourselves *to be wholly directed by him.*—UPHAM.

PRIDE makes more slaves than oppression.

NO ALTERNATIVE.

BY M. H. FREELAND.

"He that is not with me, is against me; and he that gathereth not with me, scattereth abroad;" Matt. ii, 30.

According to this unequivocal declaration of the blessed Saviour, mankind is divided, with respect to their moral character, into two grand divisions—the good and the bad; the righteous and the wicked; believers and unbelievers; godly and ungodly; in short, those who are for God, and those who are against him. *Theoretically*, this division is emphatically true, as will be demonstrated to an assembled universe, when the books shall be opened, and the dead judged according to the deeds done in the body; but, *practically*, the accurate observer will discover the necessity of designating a third class in order to give a correct representation of the human family. It was, undoubtedly, at this would-be third class, that the Saviour aimed the searching declaration, "He that is not with me, is against me; and he that gathereth not with me, scattereth abroad;" for He that knew all things saw that there were such as would persist in declaring themselves as identified with a third class, (hence its practical existence,) notwithstanding the numerous Scripture tests that so plainly shows the impossibility of its existence; therefore, he was pleased to declare thus plainly and openly that all who were not with Him were against Him; that there was no such a thing as occupying neutral ground, being neither good nor bad—right nor wrong, for such was the position professedly occupied by those who professed to belong to the third classs. The real position and character of all such individuals, however, can always be determined by tests that compel them to identify themselves somewhere. As a general rule, they are found voting the devil's ticket every time.

Such are the proverbially *harmless* men of every community; who, never doing the devil any injury, are always pointed to as very consistent Christians—models of peace and loyalty. Such, too, are the devoted Pharisees—the worldly-wise and wordly prudent; yea, the worldly-policy men also. Here, too, we find that large class of individuals termed fence-men, who occupy such a position respecting every great political or moral question, that as soon as it is decided where the *majority* go, they instantly jump off and mingle with the throng. Hence, when the multitude cry "Hosanna to the son of David!" they too cry Hosanna the loudest, perhaps, of the multitude; and, when on the morrow the popular voice so changes as to cry, "Away with him! Crucify Him! Crucify Him!" their voices are again heard as loudly as before.

Again we find individuals of this third class assuming the inoffensive title of *conservatives*, professing to be in favor of the right every time, and every where, but always having some cause to advocate, or some end to gain, whether right or wrong. We hear such men crying out for peace and the exercise of charity, when some ultraist, all imbued with a sanctified recklessness, that dares do right though the heavens fall, hurls a blazing fire brand into the corn fields of the Philistines; thereby disturbing the enemy and endangering some "peculiar institution" of the devil, in which they have some personal or denominational interest. We ever find these careful souls blocking the wheels of radical reform in Church or State, preferring an unrighteous peace to a holy, righteous war. Failing to discriminate between a hot-headed fanaticism and a burning zeal for the right, they denounce agitators as enemies of the public good. Such men would not hesitate to beg pardon even of his Satanic majesty, should they accidentally disturb his repose with an arrow of truth, aimed at nothing, but which, unfortunately missing the mark, has fallen exactly into his dark dominion, and then forced the affrighted marksman to do penance for his offence.

These third-class individuals, though seemingly so inoffensive, are nevertheless, the most dangerous members of community; for there are always enough of them found to turn the scale whenever important decisions are to made; and, as remarked before, their vote is invariably cast on the side of wrong. Their habitual indecision begets a fearfulness that dares not face the foe; hence, you will either find them running, or cowardly seeking protection under the dark banner of wrong. Ah! how many benevolent schemes, and philanthropic purposes have been defeated by such non-committal kind of men! Their pathway is stained with the blood of their innocent victims; which in many instances their very *silence* has slain. Such men are more offensive to the Deity than the openly wicked. The words of inspiration concerning them is "I know thy works, that thou art neither cold nor hot; I would thou wert cold or hot. So then because thou art neither cold nor hot, I will spew thee out of my mouth." How fearful the denunciation, and yet how just. As we look over the land—especially the church, how many immortal souls we find posting their way down to ruin under this lukewarm influence! How many glorious revivals have been quenched by this time-serving spirit! Said a celebrated D. D. when interrogated as to his non-identification with a revival movement in progress, in his immediate vicinity: "I believe God is blessing his people and saving sinners, but I cannot endorse the *manner* in which the good is accomplished." Such excuses may be heard every where from men professedly occupying neutral ground. Alas! the result is too often as in the case alluded to; throwing an effectual barrier in the way of the work of God, or the success of the right in any form.

Reader, what is your position? Are you afraid to do what you know is right, lest some one should frown upon you and use his influence to blight your earthly prospects. Remember "He that is not *with* me, is *against* me." Who shall stand in this present evil hour? Who shall be numbered with that white-robed company, bearing palms of victory up the mount of God? They "that come up through *great tribulation,* having washed their robes and made them white in the blood of the Lamb." The walls of the new Jerusalem will never be scaled by cowards. The *fearful* and unbelieving will be without the gates to all eternity. God loves valiant hearted men who are not afraid to die. May the number be greatly increased all through the land! Amen.

"Since I must fight if I would reign,
Increase my courage, Lord;
I'll bear the toil, endure the pain
Supported by thy word."

EVIL COMPANY.—Sophronius, a wise teacher of the people, did not allow his daughters, even when they were grown up, to associate with persons whose lives were not moral and pure.

"Father," said the gentle Eulalia one day, when he had refused to permit her to go, in company with her brother, to visit the frivolous Lucinda, "father, you must think that we are very weak and childish, since you are afraid it would be dangerous to us in visiting Lucinda."

Without saying a word, the father took a coal from the hearth, and handed it to his daughter. "It will not burn you, my child," said he; "only take it."

Eulalia took the coal, and beheld her tender white hand black; and, without thinking, she touched her white dress, and it was also blackened. "See," said Eulalia, somewhat displeased as she looked at her hands and dress, "one cannot be too careful enough when handling coals."

"Yes, truly," said her father; "you see, my child, that the coal, even though it *did not burn you,* has nevertheless *blackened you!* So is the company of immoral persons."

HINTS TO PREACHERS.

The following hints to Preachers are from an old copy of the Wesleyan Methodist Magazine. They are said to have been given in the year 1713, to Dr. Andrew Gifford, by his grandfather. Though too quaintly expressed, in some instances, they contain many good thoughts and useful directions:

Discover no more of your method than what is necessary. Pass not any thing till you have bolted it to the bran. Use the mother-speech and tone, without affectation or imitation of any man; that you may not seem to act a comedy, instead of preaching a sermon. Clog not your memory too much; it will exceedingly hinder invention, and mar delivery. Be sure that you eye God, His glory and the good of souls; having, the day before, mortified self and man-pleasing. Let your words be soft, few and slow, and see that they come no faster than the weakest hearer can digest each morsel; pause a little and look in the child's eye till he swallow his bit.

Look to your affections most carefully, that they be not feigned; nor *forcedly* let loose to have their full scope; for then they will either overrun your judgment, or be a temptation to vain glory. Preach as if speaking or talking to the people. *Look on the people* and not on the walls or roofs; and look on the most mortified faces in the assembly. Let them know that your preaching is a *real talking with them*, whereby they may be provoked, as it were, to answer you again. Take heed of over wording any thing. Be sure that you have made the people thoroughly understand what is the good you exhort them to, or the evil you exhort them from, before you bring your motives and means. Touch no Scripture slightly, nor too many in the same discourse; but open the metaphors, and let one Scripture point out another—the one being a key to the other. Let the Scripture teach you, and not you it. Be sure that you feed yourself upon every passage with the people before you pass it, else it will do them little good, and you none at all. O, taste every bit. Take these four candles in order to find out what to say to the people. The Scriptures unbiassed; the thoughts and experience of good men; your own experience; and the condition of the people. Break off anywhere rather than run upon either of these two inconveniences—either to puddle or jamble together Spiritual things, or tire (by unreasonable prolixity) the weakest of the flock. Never pass over one point, provided it be a Spiritual point, when you have anything to say of it.

Let your doctrine, and the constant strain of your preaching, be about the chief Spiritual things; and let small controversies and external duties come in by the by.

Beware of (a servile adherence to) forms; neither be tied to any one method. Be always on the subject next your heart, and be not thrifty or careful what to say next, for God will provide. It will stink like kept manna, if preserved through distrust until the next day. Be sure that you extricate carefully, any Godly point you speak of, out of the terms of divinity, else it will freeze in your mouth and in the people's ears. Let there be no disfiguring of faces, nor snuffing in the nose, nor teazling in the throat, nor any antique gesture, pretended devotion, or made-up gravity; such things would make you look like a painted Pharisee, or a distracted man broke out of Bedlam. Do not care so much about what the people say of your doctrine, as whether you and it is acceptable to the Lord.

Do not conceive that your mere zeal or earnestness can prevail with the people, but the force of Spiritual reason, the evidence of Scripture, and the power of the Holy Ghost. Do not think that the hearers can receive as you conceive, and so make your comprehension the rule of dealing the bread of life; for so shall you only be admired, but not understood by others.

Let there be something in every sermon to draw perishing sinners to Christ. Take heed that your comparsions be not coarse, vulgar, and ridiculous; and yet be not too shy of homely ones. Study every Scripture you are to speak of beforehand, but do not overburden invention, or presume too much on your own parts. Beware of needless designs, needless heads, and innuendos. Shun apologies, for they always stink.

THE MYSTERIES OF THE FALL.

Before a man could understand his errors there are several mysteries which he must know. But each one of these mysteries, methinks, is beyond his knowledge, and consequently the understanding of the whole depth of the guilt of his sin must be quite beyond human power. Now the first mystery that man must understand is *the fall.* Until I know how much all my powers are debased and depraved, how thoroughly my will is perverted and my judgment turned from its right channel, how really and essentially vicious my nature has become, it cannot be possible for me to know the whole extent of my guilt. Here is a piece of iron laid upon the anvil. The hammers are plied upon it lustily. A thousand sparks are scattered on every side. Suppose it possible to count each spark as it falls from the anvil; yet who could guess the number of the unborn sparks that still lie latent and hidden in the mass of iron? Now, brethren, your sinful nature may be compared to that bar of iron. Temptations are the hammers; your sins the sparks. If you could count them (which you cannot do,) yet who could tell the multitude of unborn iniquities —eggs of sin, that lie slumbering in your souls? Yet must you know this before you know the whole sinfulness of your nature. Our open sins are like the farmer's little sample which he brings to market. There are granaries full at home. The iniquities that we see are like the weeds upon the surface soil; but I have been told, and indeed have seen the truth of it, that if you dig six feet into the earth, and turn up fresh soil, there will be found in that soil six feet deep the seeds of the weeds indigenous to the land. And so we are not to think merely of the sins that grow on the surface, but if we could turn our heart up to its core and centre, we should find it as fully permeated with sin as every piece of putridity is with worms and rottenness. The fact is, that man is a reeking mass of corruption. His whole soul is by nature so debased and so depraved, that no description which can be given of him, even by inspired tongues, can fully tell how base and vile a thing he is. An ancient writer said once of the iniquity within, that it was like the stores of water which it is believed are hidden in the depths of the earth. God once broke up the fountains of the great deep, and then they covered the mountains twenty cubits upward. If God should ever withdraw his restraining grace, and break up our hearts, the whole fountains of the great depths of our iniquity, it would be a flood so wondrous, that it would cover the highest tops of our hopes, and the whole world within us would be drowned in dread despair. Not a living thing could be found in this sea of evil. It would cover all, and swallow up the whole of our manhood. Ah! says an old proverb, "If man could wear his sins on his forehead, he would pull his hat over his eyes." That old Roman who said he would like to have a window into his heart, that every man could see within it, did not know himself, for if he had such a window he would soon have begged to have a pair of shutters, and he would have kept them shut up, I am sure; for could he ever have seen his own heart, he would have been driven raving mad. God, therefore, spares all eyes but his own that desperate sight—a naked human heart. Great God, here would we pause and cry, "Behold, I was shapen in iniquity, and in sin did my mother conceive me. Thou desirest truth in the inward parts, and in the hidden part thou shalt make me to know wisdom. Purge me with hyssop and I shall be clean; wash me and I shall be whiter than snow."—SPURGEON.

ALWAYS REJOICING.

ROM. v. 2.

"My days are gliding swiftly by,
  And I a pilgrim stranger,
Would not detain them as they fly,
  Those hours of toil and danger.

We'll gird our loins, my brethren dear,
  Our heavenly home discerning;
Our absent Lord has left us word,
  Let every lamp be burning.

Should coming days be cold and dark,
  We need not cease our singing;
That perfect rest naught can molest,
  Where golden harps are ringing.

Let sorrow's rudest tempest blow,
  Each chord on earth to sever;
Our King says Come, and there's our home
  For ever! oh, for ever!"

CHORUS.

"For oh! we stand on Jordan's strand,
  Our friends are passing over,
And just before, the shining shore,
  We may almost discover."

I HAVE observed that a word cast in by the by, hath done more execution in a sermon than all that was spoken beside. Sometimes also, when I have thought I did no good, then I did the most of all; and at other times, when I thought I should catch them, I have fished for nothing.—BUNYAN.

MEN will *wrangle* for religion; *write* for it; *fight* for it; *die* for it; anything but *live* it.

THE Father *purposed*, the Son *purchased*, and the Spirit *applies*.

TRIALS.

Are trials appointed and permitted by the Lord for the discovery of his people's sincerity? Then let none of God's people expect *a quiet station in this world*. Certainly you will meet with no rest here. You must pass out of one fire into another. And it is a merciful condescension of the Lord to poor creatures, thus to concern himself for their safety and benefit. "What is man that thou shouldest magnify him, and that thou shouldest set thine heart upon him; and that thou shouldest visit him every morning, and try him every moment?" O, it is a great honor put upon a poor worm, when God will every moment try him and visit him. It argues the great esteem the goldsmith has of his gold, when he will sit by the furnace himself, and order the fire with his own hand; when he pries so often and so curiously into the firing-pot to see that none of the precious metal upon which he has set his heart be lost.

Think it not then debasing to you to be so often exposed to trials. If God did not value you highly, he would not try you so frequently. What would become of you, if your condition here should be more settled and quiet than now it is? I believe you find dross enough in your hearts after all the fires into which God has cast you. Surely there is filth enough in the best of God's people to require all the trouble they have yet met with, and perhaps a great deal more. We fancy it a brave life to live at ease; and if we meet with larger respites and intervals of trial than usual, we are apt to say, "We shall never be moved," or "We shall die in our nest," as in Job xxix, 18; our hard and difficult days are over; but woe to us if God should give us the desire of our hearts in this. See what is the temper of these men's spirits who meet with no changes: "Because they had no changes, therefore they fear not God." O, it is better to be preserved sweet in brine than to rot in honey.—FLAVEL.

MESSAGES OF DYING SAINTS.

We customarily divide the pious into the living and the dead; and we think with interest of the influence still exerted over the living by those who, being dead, yet speak; and we sometimes sing, with aspiring spirits, the sweet lines—

"Give us the wings of faith to rise
  Within the vale and see
The saints above, how great their joy,
  How great their glories be."

O could we but hear from them! could we but get one message! we longingly but vainly exclaim.

But we overlook another division of the saints that lie between the living and the dead—the dying saints; and we slight their messages, delivered from the confines of eternity. Think of these favored ones, concerning whom it is said, "Precious in the sight of the Lord is their death; and "he shall make all their bed in their sickness." They have bid adieu to the world, they are ready to depart, and they wait all the days of their appointed time till their change shall come. They have finished their course; they expect their crown. They are midway from earth to heaven. They are a class, a division of themselves, and they make a large company; and are a standing order—as abiding as the living or dead. They are a part of the membership of every church— the members that never go to church nor sit at the Lord's table; but yet are earnest in prayers and fervent in spirit, serving the Lord, by their "faith and patience." Surely it must be the good pleasure of God to have this particular order of saints; it must be that the Master hath need of them; seeing they linger often so many weary months. Now what can be their mission? Are they here to be ministered unto altogether, or to minister to the living? For the latter purpose, we think, mainly; "none of us liveth unto himself, and no man dieth unto himself;" and no saint is here solely to be waited on, even when dying. These lingering, languishing, suffering ones are not useless, not a mere burthen. They are God's messengers to the busy, the active. "For us they languish, and for us they die." And what are their messages? What do they say to the living? What do they whisper to the worldly, to the ambitious, to the covetous, to the careworn? What do they testify to the dissatisfied? What comfort do they communicate to the disappointed? What words do they speak to their brethren who are in health, and can go to the sanctuary every Sabbath, and to the weekly prayer meeting? What do they say to the Marthas, the busy housekeepers, and what messages have they for those disciples who take undue thought about what they shall eat and drink, and wear? What special word have they for young Christians? What have they to witness concerning Christ? How do they regard death? Are they afraid of it? Is it gloomy to them? What is their estimate of the forms of godliness, compared with the power thereof?

These dying saints are continually sending out their messages, voiceless messages, most of them. Their sick chambers are sanctuaries, their pillows are pulpits, and every day of their stay is a hallowed day of rest, a holy Sabbath.—OBERLIN EVANGELIST.

OFTEN the water that is enclosed in a glass vessel appears to the unaided eye clear and pure. But if a ray of bright light suddenly strikes the vessel and illuminates it, we at once discover various impurities which before had escaped our notice. So our sins have many hiding places, which conceal them from the natural conscience. Hence we should ask God for light that we may find them out.—UPHAM.

"Just as the tree cut down, that fell
  To north or southward, there it lies;
So man departs to heaven or hell,
  Fixed in the state wherein he dies."

PITCAIRN'S ISLAND.

Of all the romantic and strange incidents connected with the story of the English Colony on Pitcairn's Island, there is nothing that touches the heart like the true, tender, deep and simple piety that seems to characterize the whole of that extraordinary community. Their pastor, the Rev. Mr. Nobbs, thus writes concerning the prosperity of the community:

"The community were never more harmoniously united than at the present time. There are eighty communicants, sixty scholars in the Sunday School, and fifty-five children in the day school; I am fully employed every day in the week either with the well or the sick, and I thank God, my avocations suit me, and I think I am suited to them."

His account of three deaths is very touching; the first of them is that of his own son:

"Sometimes his dear mother, flattered by the specious appearance of his insidious disease, hinted at the possibility of his being yet spared to us, but with a gentle shake of the head he would reply, 'No, dear mother, I feel I am rapidly approaching the grave; humanly speaking, my recovery is impossible, and that my dear father knows as well as I do; and if it is not improper to entertain such a wish, I would rather not return to health again; my desire and prayer is to depart and be with Christ, which is far better.' Such was the tenor of his discourse during the short time he remained with us; and he died strong in faith, giving glory to God.

An hour before his death he was seized with a violent spasm, which we thought would have carried him off, but he rallied again. Seeing his mother in tears, he said, 'Do not weep, mother; only one more such stroke and I shall be in the arms of my Saviour.' Shortly after he had another attack, and nothing remained but his attenuated form. The happy spirit had returned to join the glorified throng.

Daniel McCoy and his wife went to the northwest side of the Island in quest of fish. After descending to the rocks on a level with the sea, Daniel left his wife and re-ascended, intending to pass a small inlet; on doing so he fell, and his wife saw him fall; but there was the inlet between them, into which a heavy surf was running; it was to avoid this he had gone round, and in descending to the shore he fell. His wife had the presence of mind to call a lad at some distance, fishing, and despatch him to the village with the sad tidings that Daniel had fallen, but she did not know the extent of his hurt. She, being alone, plunged into the heavy surf which she had unfortunately persuaded her husband to avoid, and landing on the opposite side of the inlet, found him on the rugged beach of the shore, a corpse! Less than half an hour before, he had left her with a smile upon his countenance, for Daniel was always in a cheerful mood. What must have been the poor girl's agony, as she sat by her dead husband for more than an hour ere any could get to her assistance, I will not attempt to describe, but I will tell you what she did—on finding life extinct, she knelt down and prayed that God would give her grace so to live that she might rejoin her dear Daniel in heaven; 'for I am sure,' said she, (when speaking to me on the subject), 'that he was prepared for death, and that takes away the pain of my great loss.'

Three weeks after the demise of my son, death made another inroad amongst us. A little boy ten years old pierced his foot with a barbed arrow (used for taking fish from the holes among the rocks), which induced Tetanus; and in forty-eight hours after the terrible disease had manifested itself, his happy spirit fled to the realms of bliss. During the intervals of the violent spasmodic contractions of the suffering body, the dear child would speak of his blessed Saviour, and ask Him to take him to be with those who he took in his arms when on earth. The patient sufferer was aware that he could not recover, still he never expressed the least fear of death. At the time of his departure, I was praying with him, his parents and several others kneeling around his bed; the contraction relaxed from his jaws, he gave one slight shudder, and exclaimed in a clear audible voice, 'Lord Jesus, receive my spirit,' and then went to see Him as He is."—*Church Journal.*

WORLDLY AMUSEMENTS.

A SHORT time ago, we had a sermon in our church upon worldly amusements —a sermon good in itself, but which might be misunderstood by those who wished to do so. Now young Christians are greatly troubled on this score. Perhaps a few words of my experience might be good for those just commencing a Christian course. I was a very self-willed girl, and had been in the habit of doing just as I pleased, consulting my own inclinations in all things. At first I objected to joining the Church because I thought it would be a restraint; but as my love for Christ grew, I felt that I must obey or renounce my religion. I did not hesitate. I united with the Church, inwardly resolving that I would go to the places of amusement if I liked; and as there was no express prohibition, I felt the more liberty. Gradually a change came over me. The more I went to prayer-meetings the better I liked them. Teaching in Sunday-school was a delight to me. I looked forward to Sunday with fond expectation and desire. At length came an invitation to a small party. Shall I go? Why not? I did not expect to lead a hermit's life. Conscience said, "don't go." But a hankering after the party siezed upon me. I went. Of course I was asked to dance. I hesitated. Then I thought, "I have always thought there was no harm in dancing, why should I not dance?" I did dance, but I felt terribly uncomfortable. I went home, went straight to my closet, confessed to God that I had made a mistake, asked forgiveness, and promised, with His assistance, never to offend again in this particular. I have never since felt an inclination.

Now my dear young friends, take warning. If your heart is right, you will not, you cannot enjoy worldly amusements. If you do enjoy them, oh, beware. Gay parties and religious lectures, prayer meetings and theatres, do not agree. One must in time give way to the other. I do not say that no Christians ever go to such places; no, God forbid that I should be so uncharitable; but I do say that a Christian who does go is very apt to fall into a cold and languid state; to take less pleasure in religious duties, and after a while to find himself hesitating, (if the question comes,) to which he shall go, and finally giving the preference to the place of amusement. "Ye cannot serve two masters, for either ye will hate the one and love the other, or else ye will hold to the one and despise the other; ye cannot serve God and mammon."—*S. S. Times.*

THEY who do not acknowledge the Son of God incarnate, shall acknowledge Him when He comes as Judge in glory, even Him who now is abused in an inglorious body.—HIPPOLYTUS, A. D. 220.

A SINFUL life is a bitter pill. The sinner may coat it over with pleasure, but the flames of hell will melt the sugar-coat and leave it in all its bitterness to nauseate the ruined soul forever. —A. A. P.

HE that does not reason is a *fanatic;* he that will not reason is a *bigot;* and he that cannot reason is a *fool.*

PRAYER without study is *presumption;* but study without prayer is *atheism.*

WHEN the wolf is dead all the dogs give him a bite!

PEOPLE do not like to drink a river to get a drop of honey.

BLUEBEARD:

AN ALLEGORY FOR CHILDREN.

"It was in the olden time; no, I forget—it was not very long ago, when there lived in some land which I shall not name, a rich old baron whom we consider to be Bluebeard. He was slow in his movements, and heavy in his gait—indeed, some said that he limped. He had a long nose, a long beard, and a long name; his real name was Procrastination."

"I don't think I can remember it," said Rosey.

"The country people around shortened the title to 'Put-off,' for Procrastination is putting off till to-morrow what ought to be done to-day; so if you forget the long name, Rosey, you will easily remember the short one."

"Now this Baron Procrastination was wealthy, though how he had acquired his riches was rather a delicate question. If you have ever heard of him before, Lily, perhaps you can throw some light upon the subject."

"Mamma often says that 'Procrastination is the thief of time,'" replied Lily.

"A thief! oh what a shocking fellow!" cried Rosey.

"A shocking fellow he was, as you will see before I conclude my story. And yet, strange to say, though he was neither handsome, clever nor good, Baron Procrastination managed to get introduced into most respectable families. I rather think that I have seen him in this!"

"Oh!" exclaimed Rosey, opening her blue eyes very wide, "did he come with his long beard and all?"

"Don't interrupt so, Rosey," said Lily; "it is so tiresome to be stopped every minute; you can't be expected to understand an allegory."

"Rosey will understand me better, I hope, before my story is ended," said George, smoothing away with his hand an angry little furrow which appeared for a moment on the forehead of Rosey.

"There are many things which we all find it hard to understand; but gradually, with patience and attention, we find the meaning drawing upon us. Think of my hero as Baron Put-off, and you may remember that he is not quite a stranger.

"Well, as I said, this baron was received in many places as a visitor—in some he was even detained as a guest; and though something was generally missed wherever he had been, no one seemed to take warning by the past, or to see any harm in this Bluebeard.

"One day as the baron was sitting before his long mirror in the long hall of the long palace of Procrastination, in which he usually abode, stroking his long beard with a satisfied air, thus he held converse with himself:

"'For many a year I've meditated on the subject of taking a wife, and at length I have come to a decision on the matter. The town of Good Resolutions lies not far off: its citizens are handsome, prosperous and wealthy. It seems to me that I cannot do better than to than go there and win a fair bride; she is likely to have a rich dowry, and I am tired of dwelling here all alone.'

"So the baron pulled his long bell-rope, summoned an old servant, and ordered his coach to be brought to the door. A heavy, lumbering vehicle it was, rolling from side to side like a cradle, and drawn by four fat horses that moved at the pace of snails."

"I wish I'd been the coachman!" exclaimed Eddy; "wouldn't I have made them gallop! This slow old baron of yours, George, is not in my line; I'd have had nothing to do with such a sluggard!"

George only smiled, and went on:

"Miss Study-well was the fair lady to whom my Bluebeard first paid his addresses. She was pleasant looking and comely, as indeed all her countrywomen are, for Good Resolutions, as every one knows, are an uncommonly handsome race. The baron found her seated in a library, a large atlas spread open before her, her arm resting on a

Latin grammar, and a volume of history laid on her knee!"

"Oh! I'd never have gone near her!" cried Eddy.

"I think that you took her to school with you, George," said Lily. But Rosey looked puzzled still.

"So the baron wooed the lady, and won her, and a grand marriage feast they had. Etymology, Entomology, Zoology, and all the other ologies, were invited; the wedding cakes were decorated with goose-quills, and every one complimented the bride by going through the multiplication table!"

"The poor Good Resolution, Studywell, had not been one month married to Procrastination, when tidings came, alas! of her death! Of all the fortune which she was said to possess, nothing remained to her family, as a memorial of her, but blotted copy-books and an old dog's-eared grammar!"

"Oh!" cried simple Rosey, "how sorry her husband must have been!"

"It did not appear so," said George, "for he was soon again on his way, in his rumbling old coach, to the town of Good Resolutions. Again he wooed and won a fair lady, Miss Work-well, the cousin of his first wife. She was quick and lively in her manner, and rather peculiar in her dress. She wore as a brooch a red pin-cushion, with a thimble hanging from it as a pendant; her necklace was of reels of white cotton; scissors, needle-book and bodkin hung suspended from her waist."

Eddy glanced archly at Lily, as if suspecting that this Good Resolution might be some acquaintance of hers; but Lily looked down steadily on her knitting, and seemed to take no notice of the glance.

"Again," continued George, "there was a wedding and a feast, and soon afterwards the mysterious death of the bride! A broken-pointed pair of scissors, and a tangled skein of silk were sent to her family by Baron Procrastination, as relics of a Good Resolution now no more.

"Yet a third time came our Bluebeard to the town to wed. A sweet, smiling little fairy, was sitting in a jessamine bower, and weaving a wreath of the blossoms. She looked young, and bright, and happy, and her name was Please-my-Mother."

"Oh! that's *my* good resolution—mine!" exclaimed Rosey, a gleam of intelligence breaking over her features; "don't say that she married Put-off, don't!" and she grasped George's arm with an eagerness which set the others laughing.

"It seems almost a shame to say that she did, and yet such is my story," replied George.

"But Please-my-mother did not die like the rest?"

"When once given up to Procrastination, I fear that even she had a poor chance of life. She lived no longer than other Good Resolutions!"

"Well," exclaimed Eddy, striking his fist on the cushion, "I can only say this, that if Baron Put-off, or whatever you call him, found any one else silly enough to marry him, she deserved to disappear and be heard of no more, like that unfortunate Miss Studywell."

"I do believe, Master Eddy," laughed Lily, "that you smothered poor Studywell yourself, and that her blotted copy-books and dog's-eared grammar, are all in your school-box at this minute! But pray, George, go on with your story. Who was Baron Put-off's next bride?"

"A very sweet but quiet Good Resolution; one with gentle mien, and a soft, winning voice; one too good—oh! a thousand times too good to be given up by those who might have kept her!" George lowered his voice as he continued: "She might have made a home so happy; she might have smoothed every roughness away; but, alas! even sooner than those who had preceded her, died the gentle Good Resolution, Speak-kindly!"

A quick flush passed over the face of Lily, and she knitted on faster than before. George saw that his sister understood him, and, unwilling to inflict more pain, he passed on to Bluebeard's fifth bride.

"Rise-early was the next good Resolution who disappeared in the palace of Procrastination. The baron said that the chill of a winter's morning had killed the sprightly little dame; but I think that all who study the subject will agree, that had it not been for that sad fellow, Put-off, she might have been alive to this day."

"Were there any more wives?" asked Rosey.

"There was Help-others, one of the fairest and best to be found in the town of Good Resolutions. She was one whom everybody loved, and loud were the laments in her native place when she left it for the palace of Procrastination. After what had happened to Study-well, Work-well, Rise-early, Speak-kindly, and Please-my-mother, no one was astonished to hear that Help-others had died like the former brides; and every one in the town declared that Baron Procrastination should be flogged out of the parish if ever he ventured to come near a Good Resolution again!"

"I'd not have flogged him, but hanged him!" cried Rosey, fiercely, clenching her little hands. Her temper, as I have before hinted, was none of the gentlest or best, and she might have suggested some yet more terrible punishment for the killer of so many Good Resolutions, when her attention was directed to a tap at the door, and Sarah, her nurse, appeared at the entrance.

"Miss Rosey, it is time to go to bed."

"Oh, how tiresome!" exclaimed the little girl with impatience; "I am sure that it's not seven o'clock yet!"

"I heard it strike some minutes ago," observed Lily, "just as George was finishing off poor Rise-early."

"So, now, Go-to-bed-early must have her turn," said Eddy, with his good-humored smile.

"It doesn't matter, I don't choose to go yet," cried Rosey; "nurse may come back in half an hour."

"Mistress particularly desired that you would not be late," said Sarah, to her spoilt little charge.

"Ah, ha!" exclaimed Eddy, rubbing his hands, "there's Baron Procrastination running away with Please-my-mother! He has got hold of a Good Resolution, and will smother her dead in a minute! Oh, Rosey! run, run, or she is lost!"

Rosey burst into a merry laugh, jumped down from George's knee, and giving hurried kisses to her brothers and sisters, scampered out of the room, exclaiming, "No, no, I was just in time to save her! Old Bluebeard shan't kill Please-my-mother!"

"We must not go on with the story while poor little Rosey is away," said Eddy.

"No; and I think that I should set to my Greek," observed George, "or the Good Resolution Study-well may suffer from our evening's amusement."

"And I suppose," said Lily, taking up her volume, "that for the sake of both Study-well and Please-my-mother, I should read over my portion of Hume."

"Let me see, what Good Resolution can I keep from being smothered?" cried Eddy. "I told Rosey, before I went to school, that I'd make her a little paper box to hold her needles and pins; and oh! dear me! Help-others has been all this time shut up a prisoner in the palace of Put-off! Just lend me your scissors, Lily, and I'll have her out in a trice!"

HEAVEN A HOME.—Chrysostom, when banished, said to a friend, "You now begin to lament my banishment, but I have done so for a long time; for since I knew that heaven is my country, I have esteemed the whole world as a place of exile. Constantinople, whence I am expelled, is as far from Paradise as the desert whither they send me."

JOHN WESLEY preached forty thousand sermons, and traveled two hundred and twenty thousand miles.

"MILLIONS for Mars, but mites for Jesus," is the worldly maxim.

WE must already be wise to prize wisdom.

REVIVALS.

BY THE EDITOR.

NOTHING rejoices us more than to see the work of God moving on in power at all seasons of the year. This is one peculiarity of the thorough work He is carrying on in many places. When a person, saved to the uttermost, is enabled to sing—

> "No changes of season or place,
> Can make any change in my mind,"

he is then prepared to labor successfully for the salvation of others. Such men and women the Lord is raising up. Wherever they are found there will be a religious interest.

Last Saturday and Sabbath it was our privilege to attend the first Quarterly Meeting of the *Free Methodist Church* of Rochester. God was there. All said it was one of the best meetings they ever attended. In the evening, several penitents, all broken down, came to the altar; some professed to find peace, and all expressed the determination not to rest until they have the assurance of sins forgiven. A good work is begun in Rochester, which will, we trust, go on until a multitude of souls are saved. Rev. J. K. TINKHAM, of the Methodist Episcopal Church, was present, and rendered efficient service. Brother TINKHAM thinks it is hardly worth while to expend large sums of money to send delegates across the ocean to testify our love for Christians, when we can do it right at home.

DEDICATION AT ALBION.

EVERY provision made for preaching the gospel to the masses is a matter for congratulation.

The tendency of the exclusive system upon which most of the churches in the cities and large towns in Western New York are conducted, is to alienate the masses from religious worship. In a church where a few have their pews which they occupy as a right, the many will not feel like intruding; nor will they consent to advertise their poverty from Sabbath to Sabbath by occupying seats reserved for the poor.

Hence, we are glad to chronicle the success which has crowned the effort to build a Free Church in Albion.

The Rev. L. STILES, who, with others, was expelled by the Genesee Conference, at its last session, for doing his duty as a Christian minister, was invited by the great majority of the church at Albion, which he had served with great acceptability for the two previous years, to continue his labors among them as a minister of Jesus Christ, and he accepted the invitation. Rather than have any disturbance, they gave up the church property, to which they were legally entitled, and proceeded at once to purchase a lot and erect a house of worship. This house was, yesterday, dedicated to the worship of God by the Rev. E. BOWEN, D. D., of the Oneida Conference of the Methodist Episcopal Church. His sermon, on holiness, based upon 1 Cor. vi. 20, "For ye are bought with a price," etc., was most able and impressive, and it made a profound impression upon the vast congregation in attendance. It was judged that some 1,300 persons were in attendace. Many went away unable to find standing room. In the evening, the Rev. B. J. IVES delivered one of his powerful appeals from the words, "We will go with you, for we have heard that God is with you." The thrilling shouts of the people showed that the truth had fell upon ears capable of appreciating it.

The house thus dedicated is a substantial structure, 101 feet by 55. The audience room—the largest in the place—pleasant and and commodious, will seat about 1,000 persons. A basement, the whole size of the building, entirely above ground, affords pleasant and convenient rooms for class and prayer meetings and Sunday school. The lecture room in the basement will hold about 600 persons. The house is plainly and neatly furnished, and lighted with gas.

The cost of the whole has been, in round numbers, about $10,000. The whole has been paid or provided for. About $4,500 were raised yesterday and last evening. For this result great credit is due to the Rev. B. J. IVES, through whose indefatigable exertions the whole amount called for was secured.

The meeting continued over the Sabbath. Rev. Mr. IVES preached with more than his usual power to a congregation as large as could be packed into the spacious church, and the sacrament of the Lord's supper was administered to some 440 communicants.

Mr. STILES has collected a large and intelligent congregation—a devoted, pious, working church, and with their present facilities for doing good, the best results may be anticipated.

FROM ST. CHARLES, ILLINOIS.

A brother writes us—"Please say to the friends of Jesus that the first General Quarterly Meeting ever held in the West by the Pilgrims, took place at St. Charles on the 19th and 20th of May. Many rejoiced that they had lived to see this day. One brother, coming up to this feast from an adjoining town, testified, in the Love Feast, that when he drew near the sacred spot, he felt as though he had struck the borders of Canaan. It was a glorious day for the Pilgrim band in the West. Glory to God for a salvation that saves the people."   E. O.

The following letter, from a brother at the East of this, whom we have never seen, and who has never been exposed to our influence, will show how what are called Nazarites are made. Let one be fully saved and take an uncompromising stand against all sin, and at once the most opprobrious epithets are applied to them. Let all such remember the word of the Lord, "If when ye do well, and suffer for it, ye take it patiently, this is acceptable with God." Let all then be borne with *meekness* and *humility*.

REV. B. T. ROBERTS:—*Dear Brother*—It is persecution that urges me to write to you. I was born in the year 1841, in the town of Malling, West Kent, England. I became very much attached to the Methodist society, but, my parents being very much opposed to them, would not let me attend many of their means of grace, and, of course, I was trained up in the Church of England, and taught to read prayers. At the early age of nine, I loved to mingle in the grog shop and taste of the poison. I wandered far from everything that was good, and very far from God our common Father. Yet, I would go to Church and read prayers. Three years ago my father and mother thought that they would try America. While on the Atlantic ocean, a dreadful storm arose, and we all expected a watery grave. It was a very dark night, over four hundred souls on board—most all using forms of prayer. Some continued to repeat their prayers several times, and others would gather together in groups and worship the Holy Virgin Mary, while I was fast asleep. But my sweet repose was broken by a huge wave which broke to pieces against the vessel. What a time was that! Too dark to read prayers; expecting every moment to perish, my mind was agitated as to what prayer could I offer, what sacrifice could I make. At length, I prayed, "Lord, save me till I land, and then I will serve Thee!" The storm decreased, but the vow was made. We safely reached the shore, but the conviction followed me, and for almost a year I was striving against the Spirit, but at last I yielded, and sought after Christ who saves me now, day by day, by His precious blood. I had never before realized what it was to seek after Christ. My seeking was all in vain, till I sought with all my heart, and gave up everything for the sake of Christ. It was early in the morning when I went to the hay shed to feed my cattle. I felt that the Lord would hear my prayer there. I prayed, but no relief. I examined my heart, and gave up everything for the Saviour, got on my knees, uttered a few words, and O how Jesus blessed my soul! Yes, Jesus set me free! Glory to God! I cried, "The power of sin and Satan is removed, and I am free!" Then the Lord set me to work. I had a father who opposed me, and a mother who ridiculed me, and a brother who mocked me, and a sister who thought I was crazy. But these did not move my integrity. Jesus had taken full possession of my soul. I continued to pray for them, talk with them, and prayed with them. Whilst at a camp-meeting, I made a covenant with God that I would never leave off praying for them. God had promised to hear and answer prayer. So I struggled on. Sometimes, at midnight, I would pour out my soul's desire, and get my faith made stronger while praying for my friends. Were those prayers useless? No! I trust the Lord was pleased, though they scoffed at me, and told me that my religion was too severe; they do not think so now, for God has had mercy, and they all have attained the precious faith. Jesus saves us day by day, through His all redeeming grace, and we are a family bound for Heaven and immortal glory. We expect to urge our way through, and when these mortal bodies fail on earth, we shall be clad with immortality.

We worship God according to our conscience. They have tried to use me up by calling me a Nazarite, and the pastor has told me that he was sorry that I was getting to be a Nazarite. He said that the devil was at the bottom of Nazaritism, but I am willing to follow Christ through evil as well as good report. I want to show to the world that I have Christ found within, the hope of glory. I very often think if I was older I would do more for the Saviour, but when I speak in prayer-meeting, and talk about pride, the ruling sin in our Church, the brethren tell me that I am too young to advise older ones, and then I often think of David and Goliah. I want to live peaceably with all men. But I pray day by day that God will make me valiant for the truth. There is quite a number in C. that would like to hear you preach. We pray for your welfare—hope that you will be successful in rooting out the sins that are so prevalent. We are expecting to come out to your camp-meeting, if you have one. A little band of Christ's flock meet together in C. on every Wednesday night to worship. We are censured. The pastor is trying to break up the Wednesday evening prayer meetings, but we trust in God, and fear not what man can do unto us." A.

GENERAL CONFERENCE OF THE METHODIST EPISCOPAL CHURCH.

THIS body closed its labors on the 4th of June. Though the session was protracted but little was done. An intense interest was felt in most portions of the Church, that its connection with Slavery might cease. Its position upon the "vexed question" has been most inconsistent. Denouncing slavery as a sin, they yet welcome slaveholders without stint to its communion. It is supposed that there are now, in the Northern division of the M. E. Ch., at least ten thousand slaveholders communicants in the Church. Private members, class leaders, stewards, local preachers, and even traveling preachers hold slaves!

To these it must be quite a relief to have the present Chapter, which forbids official members and ministers to hold slaves, substituted by the one adopted by the late General Conference, which forbids nothing, but "*affectionately admonishes*" all our preachers and people to keep themselves pure from this great evil, and to seek its extirpation by all lawful and Christian means."

"Affectionate admonition" must exert a greater potentcy than it was ever yet known to possess, if it frees the Church from "this great evil." The case of GORSUCH and others of a similar stamp, almost persuade us that Methodist slaveholders would bear a little serious scolding, before they would part voluntarily with their slaves!

It is a matter of profound regret, that the Church founded by JOHN WESLEY, should occupy so inconsistent a position in relation to a system which he fearlessly denounced as the "sum of all villianies." If slavery be a sin, as we believe, and as the General Conference declares, then let the "accursed thing" be put out and no longer find a sanctuary in the Church. But if the M. E. Church intends to tolerate it let her boldly take the stand assumed by the Church south, that "the relation of master and slave when established by law, is one with which the Church as such has nothing to do." Then the meed of consistency at least, can be awarded her. What would be thought of a Church that should pronounce against gambling in the strongest terms, and then freely admit gamblers without repentance or reformation to her communion?

We look upon the action of this General Conference upon the slavery question as decisive. We fear that the M. E. Church will never be free from slavery, so long as the states uphold it within which her influence extends.

APPEAL CASES.

Great dissatisfaction is felt at the disposition of several appeal cases that were brought before the General Conference. Some ministers in whom the community has no confidence, guilty, in the judgment of those who knew them well, of real immoralities, were restored. The Genesee Conference matters were passed over with as little attention as possible. Petitions came in from some fifteen hundred members, asking that the judicial action of that Conference might be thoroughly investigated. The Genesee delegates professed great willingness to have their doings thoroughly examined. A committee of one from each Conference was appointed for that purpose. Just as they were getting ready to enter upon their duties, a determined effort was made by the Genesee Conference delegates, and their partisans, to get the Committee discharged. Suspicious as this effort to shut out the light must look in the eyes of every impartial person, it nevertheless succeeded. THE COMMITTEE WAS DISMISSED.

Of the six appeal cases, two only were entertained. On one of them, an appeal from a sentence of censure, the Committee were equally divided. The other was sent back for a new trial. What there is to try is a mystery, as all the facts are admitted.

We must confess that we felt greatly disappointed. The hope had been indulged that these difficulties would be investigated with such thoroughness and impartiality, as would entitle the decision to respect. If we have been wrong in our teaching, or spirit or practice, we feel anxious to know it. No person can possibly be so solicitous as we are, to be convinced that we are out of the way, if this is really the case. But such proceedings convince us only that there is in certain quarters a great dread of LIGHT, and that other considerations weigh more heavily with the authorities of the Church than the disposition to do justice, and to judge righteous judgment.

We trust our friends will give us their sympathies and their prayers, and we will do the best we can, under the disadvantageous circumstances we are placed in, to promote the Redeemer's kingdom, waiting for the revelations of the last day to set all right.

Should any of our readers desire more particular information respecting these matters, if they will send us eight three cent postage stamps, we will in return, forward them a copy of our trial, and of the proceedings of the Laymen's Convention, and then they can read and judge for themselves.

THE following from an English paper, the Oldham *Chronicle* for May 26th, 1860, shows that the spirit of persecution is not confined to any age or country. It will be manifested in one form or another, whenever and wherever there is a revival of spiritual religion.

IMMURING A WOMAN IN THE IMBECILE WARD FOR BEING CONVERTED.—It may be easily imagined that on the first introduction of Christianity amongst heathens, they would look upon its professors with feelings of mingled pity and contempt. Even when Paul was pleading the cause of his Master before Agrippa he was accused of being beside himself, but it is something astonishing at the present day to learn that people are charged with being mad when they become religious. This has, however, recently happened in Middleton, England. About a month ago, a young woman, named Hannah Lee, a reeler, employed at Messrs. Schofield and Buckley's factory, Hall Yard, and residing with her brother-in-law, John Wrigley, Swindell's Buildings, went to a religious service at the Primitive Methodist Chapel, Mount Pleasant. It was a revival meeting, and Hannah Lee found her way to the penitent form. She was converted that night along with the town crier, James Tagg, and several others. She then began to pray aloud in the family, morning and evening, and to ask a blessing before and after the meals, to the no small astonishment and annoyance of her brother-in-law and his wife. Nothing of the kind had ever been known in the family before, and this unwonted introduction of prayer into the house was deemed a sure sign of madness, both by her sister, Mrs. Wrigley, and the master of the house, Mr. Wrigley. The neighbors also became alarmed for the young woman's wits, and therefore a jury of women was called, and sat in solemn conclave on the case at the Trowell Inn, where they came to the conclusion that Hannah Lee was mad, and must be immured in a lunatic ward. With a perfect conviction of their own power to act in the matter, and with no doubts as to their own sanity, some of the jury went as a deputation to Mr. Ramsden, the relieving officer, and after making him acquainted with their verdict, requested him to give a certificate for her removal as a lunatic to the female imbecile ward of the Oldham workhouse. Mr. Ramsden, at length, convinced the sane jurors that they had really no power to decide in the matter, and informed them that before he could give an order for the woman's removal he must have a medical man's certificate of her insanity. Nothing daunted by this unlooked-for information, they still hoped for success in ridding the neighborhood of a woman who was insane enough to pray aloud and be converted. So the aid of Mr. Knott, the medical officer of the Middleton district, was called into requisition, and he proceeded to subject her to the necessary scrutiny in order to determine her state of mind. He asked her how she was; to which she replied that she was very well, but a great sinner; and after hearing the statements of Hannah Lee's brother-in-law and her sister, and satisfying himself that it was a case of insanity, he made out the necessary certificate for her removal to the imbecile ward as an insane person. Armed with this formidable instrument from one of the officers of the Oldham Union, the next step was how to get the dangerous praying woman out of the district, so as to immure her amongst people bereft of reason. To accomplish this object as neatly as possible, Hannah was persuaded that there was a tea party at Royton, and her sister invited her to go along with her and another, because Royton was their native village. They set out and took care to have the certificate along with them. They passed along by the Union workhouse, and when they were at its gates persuaded her to call in with them, when they produced their certificate, and she was immured in the female imbecile ward as a mad woman. This is upwards of a fortnight ago. But some knowledge of the case reached Mr. Wright, one of the Middleton guardians, who had seen Hannah Lee attending a place of worship, and he therefore came up to the workhouse to see what condition she was in. He found that she was perfectly sane in every respect, and was corroborated in that view by Mrs. Fletcher, the matron of the ward. Mr. Wright then procured the poor woman's discharge, and during the last week she returned to Middleton, but not to her sane sister's house. She went to reside at another place near to them, where we suppose praying aloud, and asking a blessing upon her food, are not deemed to be tokens of insanity. On her entrance into the factory, to commence her usual work again, her old companions in the mill welcomed her back by singing, "Was dead, and is alive again; was lost, and is found."

REVIVAL IN IRELAND.

At the close of February "the good work of revival still continued to extend over several parts of the island."

At the close of last year, it was estimated that not less than *eighty thousand souls* had had been converted since the revival began. We read of one "open air prayer meeting," in Clones, of four thousand people!

In counties where the courts formerly convicted scores each term, for crime, the record now reads only "Nil"—no indictments. A general missionary laboring in that revival says:—"I was greatly struck with the great change that had passed over the people; whole families of the very worst characters were saved; and instead of drunkenness and swearing, now there are songs of praise and thanksgiving."

Whenever the historian of these revival scenes touches the antecedent agencies, he is sure to say—"God's people believed in prayer; they stirred up their souls to cry mightily to God; and then, ere they were aware, their assemblies were moved; the glory of God seemed to fill the place, and many are converted."

Who shall set limits to the power of the Holy Ghost, coming in answer to such prayer as honors God?—*Oberlin Evangelist.*

CAMP MEETINGS.

These have fairly commenced. We attended one last week at Eagle, Wyoming county, N. Y. There were only a few tents, but a large number of people were on the ground, especially on the Sabbath, and an untold amount of good was done.

To-day, the Bergen Camp Meeting commences. We trust that the Divine power to save may be more signally manifested than even at any of the previous meetings which have been held upon this ground. Thousands, all over the land, can testify of Spiritual blessings received at the Bergen Camp Meetings. They have been as the gate of Heaven to multitudes of souls. Reader, do you make it a point annually to attend a feast of tabernacles? If not, you cannot commence the practice too soon. It is not possible to devote a week to better purpose than to self-examination and the worship of God. At Camp Meeting you will meet persons of mature piety, whose faith and experience you may render very serviceable to yourself. By all means, go to Camp Meeting. Take your family with you, and leave the world behind. Look for large blessings, and you will not be disappointed.

HALF YEAR SUBSCRIBERS.

Any persons wishing to provide themselves with religious reading of the first order, will be furnished with the *Earnest Christian* for the last half of the year, commencing with this number, for fifty cents. Will not our friends see what they can do in adding to our list? To those who wish the volume complete, we will still furnish the back numbers. Send on your orders.

THE EARNEST CHRISTIAN.

VOL. I.   AUGUST, 1860.   NO. 8.

JAMES BRAINERD TAYLOR.

BY THE EDITOR.

God is no respecter of persons. He makes for all the same conditions of salvation. *Without* HOLINESS *no man shall see the Lord*. The HOLY SPIRIT may operate in a thousand different modes for the awakening of men, but all who gain Heaven become the subjects, while on earth, of the same radical change from nature to grace, and they invariably exhibit the same holy tempers in the varied circumstances in which they are called to move. The routes by which they came to the "strait gate" of conversion may be different, but all the pilgrims to Mount Zion paid the same tribute, parted with all their sins, passed through the same low, narrow door—and traveled the remainder of their lives in the same narrow way, which soon becomes the *highway* of *holiness* cast up for the ransomed of the Lord.

Education and outward circumstances have less to do with religious experience than is commonly imagined. God undertakes to be the teacher of his children. He impresses upon all who are willing to learn the same great lessons. "If any man," Catholic or Protestant, Episcopalian, Presbyterian, Baptist or Methodist, "lack wisdom, let him ask of God, that giveth to all men liberally and upbraideth not; and it shall be given him." One breath of the Holy Spirit can root from the mind long cherished theories which no arguments could overthrow. The Holy Ghost can instantaneously lead the sincere inquirer into the permanent enjoyment of a state of grace, which his creed and his teachers most emphatically pronounce unattainable in this present life.

When professing Christians give themselves up fully to be led by the Spirit of God, then, and not till then, will be found in their experience and in their lives, the unity for which the Saviour prayed. They will differ probably more than they do now in circumstantials, while there will be a substantial agreement in all essentials. A formal religion will be characterized by a cold uniformity, but wherever real piety prevails there are "diversities of operations," but the "same *Spirit*." God's works are marked by variety. All men possess the same essential attributes, yet no two of the millions who comprise the human family can be found who are in all points alike.

JAMES BRAINERD TAYLOR belonged to a denomination in which the doctrine of HOLINESS as a distinct work of grace attainable instantaneously by faith, was not only not taught, but most positively denied. He was born in Haddam, Connecticut, in 1801. His parents were Episcopalians. In his early youth he was gay and careless, fond of the dance, and of the festive party. Awakened through the instrumentality of an elder brother, at the age of fifteen, he made a public profession of religion, and united with the Congregational Church. He commenced at once the faithful discharge of his duties as a Christian, and appears to have steadily grown in grace. As a Sabbath school teacher, he engaged in the instruction of children, and rendered himself efficient and useful. He soon felt called upon to devote himself to the work of the ministry, and at the age of nineteen commenced with zeal to receive the literary qualfications deemed essential to a minister of the Gospel by the church to which he belonged. He did not, however, suffer his piety to decline, but endeavored daily to grow in grace. He established a prayer meeting in a destitute neighborhood, led Bible classes, visited from house to house, and strove to do all the good in his power to the souls of men.

But he was not satisfied with his progress in the divine life. The Spirit of God in the absence of human teaching, convicted him of the necessity of a deeper work of grace—of being cleansed from inbred sin. In a letter to a friend, after noting a precious season he had recently enjoyed, when "Heaven and its glories appeared in view," and his soul was "joyful," he says: "I am tired of living *by halves*; God says, 'Son, give me thy heart.' I answer, O for an entire surrender,—I long for complete deliverance from remaining corruption, for *sanctification in soul, body and spirit*, for that *perfect love* which casteth out all fear; and until I attain this, I shall feel that I shall be unfit to be a minister of Jesus Christ."

On the 23d of April 1822, the longing desires for full salvation begotten within his heart by the Holy Spirit were fully satisfied. After a solemn consecration of all to God, he felt that Christ did indeed come and take possession. But we will let him give that experience in his own language. In speaking of the "great and wonderful things" which God had done for his soul, he writes as follows to a friend:

"Shall I tell you? My tongue could not, much less my pen express, the loving kindness of the Lord to me, who am less than the least of all his mercies. 'Eternity is too short to utter all his praise.' But I may tell you some of the merciful dealings of the Lord to my soul.

You will doubtless recollect how often I have complained to you of the littleness of my attainments in the divine life; how much of sin was still remaining within me, notwithstanding my profession, that I had crucified the world, the flesh, and the devil. I have had keener sorrows for indwelling sin, than I ever experienced before conversion. O the distress which I have felt on account of pride, envy, love of the world, and other evil passions, which have risen up and disturbed my peace, and separated between God and my soul. But the Lord heard my cries and groans, and was witness to my tears and my desires for holiness. I pleaded and wrestled with him, and praise to his name! after six long years I found what I had so long and earnestly sought. It was on the 23d day of April, 1822, when I was on a visit at Haddam, in Connecticut. Memorable day! The time and place will never, no, never, be forgotten. I recur to it at this moment with thankful remembrance. For then, through the great power and love of our Lord, my feet were set in a large place.

I cannot give you the particulars better than by making an extract from my journal:

"For some days I have been desirous to visit some friends, who are distinguished for fervor of piety, and remarkable in the happiness which they enjoy in religion. It was my hope that by associating with them, and through the help of their prayers, I might find the Lord more graciously near to my soul. After my arrival, I took up a hymn book, where I found a hymn descriptive of my situation. The perusal of this increased my desire that the Lord would visit me, and fill me with the Holy Ghost—my cry to him was, "seal my soul forever thine," I lifted up my heart in prayer that the blessing might descend. I felt that I needed something which I did not possess. There was a void within, which must be filled, or I could not be happy. My earnest desire then was, as it has been ever since I professed religion six years before, that all love of the world might be destroyed—all selfishness extirpated—pride banished—unbelief removed—all idols dethroned—everything hostile to holiness, and opposed to the divine will, crucified; that holiness to the Lord might be engraved on my heart, and evermore characterize my conversation. My mind was led to reflect on what would probably be my future situation. It recurred to me, I am to be hereafter a minister of the Gospel. But how shall I be able to preach in my present state of mind? I cannot—never, no, never, shall I be able to do it with pleasure, without great overturnings in my soul. I felt that I needed *that*, for which I was there, and for a long time had been hungering and thirsting. I desired it, not for my benefit only, but for that of the church and the world. At this very juncture I was most delightfully conscious of giving up all to God. I was enabled in my heart to say, here, Lord, take me, take my whole soul, and seal me thine—thine now, and thine forever. "If thou wilt, thou canst make me clean." There then ensued such emotions as I never before experienced—all was calm and tranquil, silent, solemn—and a heaven of love pervaded my whole soul. I had a witness of God's love to me, and of mine to him. Shortly after, I was dissolved in tears of love and gratitude to our blessed Lord. The name of Jesus was precious to me, "'Twas music in my ear." He came as king and took full possession of my heart; and I was enabled to say, " I am crucified with Christ; nevertheless, I live; yet not I, but Christ liveth in me." Let him, as King of kings and Lord of lords, reign in me, reign without a rival for ever. But this is not all—since that blessed season I have enjoyed times of refreshment, in which I have gained *nearer* access to God. I have enjoyed his presence from day to day. Not one I believe has passed, in which I have not had the witness in myself, that I am born from above. O the peace which I have had, and joy in the Holy Ghost! It has flowed as a river. I have been happy in my Lord; I have exulted in the God of my salvation. But I ascribe all to his grace. The Lord hath done great things for me, whereof I am glad, and for which I would praise his name. Not unto me, not unto me! I am nothing—Jesus is all. To his name be the glory! He is the author and finisher of faith. I know and am as fully assured of my acceptance with God as I can be of my own existence—that is, if love, joy, and peace, are evidences of reconciliation. I have a hope full of immortality. The perfect love of God casteth out all fear of death, of the grave, of judgment, of hell. Filial fear—fear of offending my heavenly Father and my brethren, possessed me. Surely I am a miracle of grace—a sinner saved by grace, free grace, sovereign grace, almighty grace. I feel that I love the Lord, because he first loved me. And, even now, I am favored with the gracious presence of *Emmanuel*. How suitable and delightful is the *name—God with us!*—yes, and *formed within us*, the hope of glory.

I find the Scriptures increasingly delightful. I read no book with so much pleasure. It is indeed not a *dead letter* but *spirit* and *life*. Divinity is stamped on its pages; and when carried home to the heart, its truths are life and power.

In closet duties you doubtless find most pleasure. Here I too find the heavenly manna. My soul has had Gospel measure in my evening's retirement. 'Tis here the Christian comes at the *essence* of religion, while he holds intimate communion with heaven, and partakes of joys sublime and substantial, such as the world knoweth not, the unrenewed never taste. But they are real; they are pure; they are foretastes of good things to come, earnests of future endless bliss.

The prospect before me is a pleasant one. I have no anxiety about the future. My only wish is to know what my heavenly Father will have me to do. I have indeed the ministry in view. I believe that the great Head of the Church has called me to prepare for it. But whether he will count me worthy to be put into it, is not for me to decide. *I* would not determine. He may see fit to remove me hence before I shall have finished my course of study. Pleasing thought, if it be his will! With some he has dealt thus, and so taken them from rendering service below, to render a perfect service above. But whether my life be protracted or shortened, my enquiry is, Lord, what wilt thou have me to do? "Speak, Lord, for thy servant heareth." I am not my own keeper; neither would I be at my own disposal. "Godliness with contentment is great gain." I trust that I have won this prize. Pray that I may keep and finish my course with joy."

The light thus received was not covered up. The Holy Spirit which had led him into this state of grace, taught him also the necessity of complying it to the glory of God.

In a letter to another friend, he writes:

"I am ready to testify to the world that the Lord has blessed my soul beyond my highest expectations. People may call this blessing by what name they please, *faith* of *assurance, holiness, perfect love, sanctification*—it makes no difference with me whether they give it a name, or no name, it contains a blessed reality, and, thanks to my Heavenly Father, it is my privilege to enjoy it—it is yours also, and the privilege of all to enjoy the same, and to go beyond anything that I have ever yet experienced."

Had he continued to walk in all the light that God gave him, there is no doubt but that he might have been eminently useful. He felt that he ought to abandon his preparatory studies and enter at once upon the work of preaching the Gospel, for which he had a passionate longing. He came near forming the resolution to do so. But "judicious" friends dissuaded him from it. In consequence of following their advice he never enjoyed the privilege, for which he sighed, of preaching Christ to his fellow men. When will Christians learn that it is not only safe to follow the *Spirit* of the *Lord* themselves, but to allow others to do the same? No one should engage in preaching the Gospel without adequate preparation. But the one great qualification is the anointing of the *Holy Spirit*. Without this the well chosen words of the learned minister will be but as "sounding brass or a tinkling cymbal." With this the most illiterate man that God ever sent out with the message of salvation, will be instrumental in leading his fellow-men Christ. Had James Brainerd Taylor with his good, natural gifts, and his deep experience in the things of God, been permitted, in accordance with what we cannot but regard as the promptings of the Holy Spirit, to go out and preach, he might have been instrumental in the salvation of thousands of souls. But through the mistaken counsel of those whose advice he felt bound to follow, he suppressed the longing of his sanctified heart, and continued some five years longer to study for the ministry, until consumption marked him as its victim.

As he had been honest in his decision, God did not withdraw the blessing he had received. He continued to walk in the light of full salvation, enjoying sweet communion with God. He says of his enjoyments while in college, "My seasons of prayer in the evening, have been times of *special* blessing, indescribable, sometimes *full of glory*. My heart broke with the longings it had to live to and for God —rejoiced that Christ was in me the hope of glory." As disease was doing its work upon his body he writes to a friend: "Think of me as one blessed of God, and happy though an invalid." His end was peaceful and triumphant. In the last letter dictated by him a short time before his departure, he says: "Symptoms of disease all tending to announce my departure.

I wish to say now that I am peaceful. The prospect of changing worlds is is pleasant."

And thus, before his course of study was ended, and he permitted to preach that Gospel which he had found to be the power of God to his salvation, was this devoted servant of Christ called home to his reward.

In his experience we see how the Holy Spirit will lead honest souls into the enjoyment of spiritual blessings, of which they had, prior to receiving them, no adequate conception.

PATERNAL DUTY.—The father who plunges into business so deeply that he has no leisure for domestic duties and pleasures, and whose only intercourse with his children consists in a brief word of authority, or a surly lamentation over their intolerable expensiveness, is equally to be pitied and to be blamed. What right has he to devote to other pursuits the time which God has allotted to his children? Nor is it an excuse to say that he can not support his family in their present style of living without this effort. I ask by what right can a family demand to live in a manner which requires him to neglect his most solemn and important duties? Nor is it an excuse to say that he wishes to leave them a competence. Is he under obligation to leave them that competence which *he* desires? Is it an advantage to be relieved from the necessity of labor? Besides, is money the only desirable bequest which a father can leave his children? Surely, well-cultivated intellects; hearts sensible to domestic affection; the love of parents and brethren, and sisters; a taste for home pleasures; habits of order, regularity, and industry; hatred of vice and vicious men; and a lively sensibility to the excellence of virtue—are as valuable a legacy as an inheritance of property—simple property, purchased by the loss of every habit which would render that property a blessing.—WAYLAND'S MORAL SCIENCE.

MILDLY JUDGE YE OF EACH OTHER.

Mildly judge ye of each other,
  Be to condemnation slow;
The very best have got their failings,
  Something good the worst can show!
The brilliant sun hath spots of darkness
  On his radiant front they say;
And the clock that never goeth,
  Speaks correctly twice a day.

Do not mock your neighbor's weakness,
  When his random whims you see,
For perhaps he something like it,
  Every day beholds in thee.
Folly leavens all our natures;
  Soundest metal hath its flaws;
And the rigid stoic scorner
  Is no wiser for his saws.

Every mortal hath his hobby;
  It may foolish seem to you,
But remember! bright or simple,
  You have got your hobby too.
Let a fellow-feeling warm you,
  When you criticise your friend
Honor virtue in his actions,
  In yourself his virtues mend.

Think not those whom mortals honor
  Are the best the earth affords,
For no tongue of praise doth blazon
  Forth the deeds which God rewards.
There are fish behind in ocean,
  Good as ever from it came:
There are men unknown, as noble
  As the laureled heirs of fame.

Mildly judge then of each other,
  Be to condemnation slow,
For the wisest have their failings,
  Something good the worst can show.
The sun himself hath spots of darkness
  On his radiant brow they say;
And the clock that never goeth,
  Speaks correctly twice a day.

WE commend the following noble sentiment, from a heathen philosopher, to timid Christians.—"Heaven hath given me virtue—man cannot hurt me."—CONFUCIUS.

"I'LL REST WHEN I GET HOME.—While I was walking through a street in the city of———, a few days ago, I passed a man whose head was whitened and body bowed by the hardships of not less than sixty years. His limbs trembled under their heavy burden, and with much apparent effort he advanced but slowly. I overheard him talking in a low and subdued voice, evidently mourning over his weariness and poverty. Suddenly his tone changed, and his step quickened, as he exclaimed " I'll rest when I get home."

Even the thought of rest filled him with new life, so that he pursued with energy his weary way. To me it was a lesson. If the thought of the refreshing rest of home encourages the careworn laborer, so that, almost unmindful of fatigue and burdens, he quickens his step homeward, surely the Christian, journeying heavenward, in view of such a rest, should press onward with renewed vigor.

This little incident often comes to my mind amid the perplexing labors of the day, and stimulates me to more constant and earnest effort. Each laborer toiling in his Master's vineyard, bearing the heat and burden of the day, can say, "I'll rest when I get home." Here let us be diligent in the service of our Lord, remembering that our rest is above. Fellow-traveler, are your burdens grievous to be borne, so that you are ready to faint in the way? Jesus says, "Come unto me, all ye that labor and are heavy-laden, and I will give you rest." To rest from toil is sweet; to rest from sin is heaven.

THE HEATHEN.—A clergyman traveling in a stage coach was asked by one of the passengers, if he thought pious heathens would go to Heaven. "Sir," said the clergyman, "I am not appointed judge of the world, and consequently cannot tell; but if you get to Heaven, you shall either find them there, or a good reason why they are not."

A SOLEMN THOUGHT.—Very few men better knew the human heart than Whitfield. He seemed to know all the thoughts and feelings of his hearers, and the best way in which to meet them. He once preached in Scotland, from the text, "The door was shut"—Matt. xxv, 10. A respectable lady who heard him sat near the door, a considerable distance from the pulpit, and observed two showy and trifling young men who appeared to turn the solemn appeals of the preacher into ridicule; she heard one of them say in a low tone to the other, "Well, what if the door be shut, another will open." In a very few minutes, to the surprise of the lady, Mr. Whitfield said, "It is possible there may be some careless, trifling person here to-day, who may ward off the force of this impressive subject by lightly thinking, 'What matters if the door be shut? another will open.'" The two young men looked at each other as though they were paralyzed, as the preacher proceeded: "Yes, another door will open: and I will tell you what door it will be; it will be the door of the bottomless pit—the door of hell!—the door which conceals from the eyes of angels the horrors of damnation."

FRESHNESS OF THE BIBLE.—"The fairest productions of human wit," remarked Bishop Horne, "after a few perusals, like gathered flowers, wither in our hands, and lose their fragrancy, but these unfading plants of Paradise become, as we are accustomed to them, still more and more beautiful; their bloom appears to be doubly heightened, fresh odors are emitted, and new sweets extracted from them. He who hath once tasted their excellencies, will desire to taste them again; and he who tastes them oftenest, will relish them best."

I FEAR to speak it, but it must be spoken, that even martyrdom itself, when suffered for admiration and applause, profits nothing, but is blood shed in vain?—ST. JEROME.

THE BIBLE VIEW OF JUSTIFICATION.

BY REV. W. COOLEY.

There has been on the hearts of many of God's people a painful conviction that the standard of Christian experience has been lowered down to a fearful degree, to accommodate the feelings and professions of formal and worldly members of the Church. We are safe only when we make the Bible our standard of experience.

No one lives in a state of justification who commits sin of any kind, great or small, for the commission of sin vitiates our justification: "For whosoever shall keep the whole law, and yet offend in one point, he is guilty of all." To live free from the commission of actual sin, is not, as some suppose, peculiar to entire sanctification, but is the condition of the lowest state of justification. We cannot violate the law of God in some of the smaller matters, or omit known duties of any kind, or refuse to walk in the light given us, and be free from condemnation. The idea that we can perform some duties and omit some, love God some and the world some, or divide our service between Christ and Belial, and be accepted with God is a great and fatal error, which is destroying multitudes of souls: for "Ye cannot serve God and Mammon." We may know we are accepted by God as definitely and certainly as we can know any fact in relation to our being; and where this evidence is wanting there is something wrong, some self-indulgence, or cherished idol, or neglect to meet the full claims of God upon us; and these uncertain Christians have this experience:

"'Tis a point I long to know,
  Oft it causes anxious thought,
Do I love the Lord or no?
  Am I His or am I not?"

But God's children can all say from an honest, but rejoicing heart,

"We by His Spirit prove,
  And know the things of God—
The things which freely of His love
  He hath on us bestowed."

The justified soul feels and endorses what the Bible says in relation to this state, which is, "There is, therefore, now, no condemnation to them which are in Christ Jesus, who walk not after the flesh, but after the Spirit." "Awake to righteousness and sin not." "Whosoever abideth in Him, sinneth." "Whosoever is born of God, doth not commit sin." "He that committeth sin, is of the devil." The economy of God does not allow us to be Christians and sinners; to be justified and condemned, to be saved and unsaved at the same time. "He that hath my commandments and keepeth them, he it is that loveth Me," and, "Whomsoever doeth not righteousness, is not of God."

The fruits of justification are peace, joy, the witness of the Spirit, a relish for Spiritual things, for Spiritual meetings, for Spiritual conversation, for Spiritual reading, for communion with God, for the Bible standard of experience, realizing that it is God's standard and must be right; and a *desire* to know and do the will of God. A justified person will have a relish for the Lord's vineyard, and will possess power to do execution in this work—not the power, the girding power, that moves out and onward the entirely sanctified soul, and fills it with holy courage and boldness, to wage an uncompromising war against all sin; but power to win souls to Christ. The peace and joy of of this state are Heavenly, and at times very great, but still it is not that *deep* and *full* enjoyment which fills and ravishes the purified heart.

The experience of most justified persons has been very uneven, up and down, back and forward, sinning and repenting, happy and then unhappy, free and then in bondage again; and now, why is it so? The principal reason is, many fail to see and follow the Divine order. Above and beyond this, living without committing sin is a state of purity, of likeness to God, of freedom from all inward or heart sin, so that the lust of the flesh, and all roots of bitterness are removed, and the foes of the child of God are all without the heart. The strong man is not only bound, but his goods are all destroyed, and the soul is emptied of sin. As the Word says, "But now being made free from sin, (which includes all inward sin,) and become servants to God, ye have your fruit unto holiness, and the end everlasting life." "That we might serve Him without fear, in holiness and righteousness all the days of our life." "That ye may be perfect and entire, wanting nothing." The order of God is for justified souls to "go on unto perfection." And the Spirit will lead such unto this mature state, if it is not grieved or repelled away from the heart. It is a matter of universal experience that, after conversion, unholy inclinations, the rising at times, under provocations of anger, revenge, envy, and sometimes pride and love of the world will be felt in the heart. The existence of these, in a somewhat latent state, as they are found in the believing heart, does not prove a backslidden state, for he may and will have the witness of the Spirit that he is justified, as these feelings and inclinations never destroy his justification, unless he allows them to obtain the ascendancy, and controlling power over him, and thus cause him to cherish and follow them. So long as he keeps, by grace, which he may, victory over them, he will find in his soul a settled hatred to every kind of sin. There are some justified persons, who, not understanding the nature and attainability of this state of purity, may retain justification, by constant praying, watching, and wrestling, in order to keep victory over these inward foes, without pressing on to secure a definite and desired state of purity. Such grieving the Spirit ignorantly, are borne with and blessed of God, but how little do they know of real freedom? But such as have light on this subject, and understood their duty in reference to holiness, can keep justified only by pressing on after freedom from all sin, for if we close our eyes to the light we shall walk in darkness, and the favor of God shall be withdrawn from us. The reason so many Church members have lost the witness of the Spirit, and are left with only a dry form of religion with now and then a degree of conviction, is, they have failed to observe the Bible rule, to go on to a mature state. Many have left their first love and are obliged to confess, if they speak honestly, that they are not where they once were, but are greatly under the shadows of this world, with weaker faith and love than they had years ago; longing for the comfort and joy of past experience, without seeming to know the cause of this dead and desolate state. But many of these have yet a form of godliness, but the power is gone, and what is still worse, many of them either deny it or do not desire it. What a sad truth it is that multitudes, through resting in justification, have wrecked on the rocks of sin, and are now as much in the broad way to destruction as any that may be found. One great necessity for holiness is seen in its power to prevent apostacy. How active the Church should be to prevent this settling down into a state of dead formality, and especially its ministers and sanctified members should lose no opportunity, nor cease from any possible effort to arouse the slumbering thousands in our Zion from this dangerous and uncertain state. The pious and conscientious laborer in the Lord's vineyard, has found that it is much harder to make a saving impression upon the mind of the formalist, bolstered up by his profession of religion, than upon the mind of the man who never was converted. But some of these have tender hearts and longing desires for the former bliss, but how faint and feeble are their efforts to regain it. They say—

"Thy secret voice invites me still,
 The sweetness of thy yoke to prove;
And fain I would; but though my will
 Seems fix'd, yet wide my passions rove;
Yet hindrances strew all the way;
I aim at Thee, yet from Thee stray."

Nothing but repentance, confession and faith in Christ, will bring such to God's favor.

SCRAPS FROM DR. REDFIELD.

SAY JUST WHAT YOU MEAN.

A FEW years ago I met with an honest German who had been a resident of our county but a few years. Had been converted and sanctified about four years when I heard him relate his experience substantially thus:

"Mein bredren, ven I vas to vork for mine masther 'pout four years ago, I t'inks I bees von poor miserable sinner, an' I shall goes to hell. Den I feels so pad I cannot eat—I cannot shleep; so I goes out to te parn, und I brays so loud an' hart as I can, and I feels no petter yet, py and by mine master comes out and say, 'Shacop, you musht shtop! you vill kill yourself.' Put I says, 'I cannot sthop! I musht have rest to my soul!' Den mein sisther comes out an' tells me to get up, I shall kill myself; put I dells her, 'I shall not sthop, for I musht have rest to my soul!'

Den I goes up onto de hay, and I prays an' prays all night, and ven de morning light comes in, I feels *God* did convert my soul; and I shumps up, an' shlaps my hans, and cries, 'Clory to *Cot!*' Den I says, 'O! mein *Cot*—I vants ev'ry pody to haf dis coot relishion; an' I t'inks vere shall I go first? So I t'inks I vill go to de shoemaker's, an' tell him all apout it. So I t'inks I vill go and get mein poots, an' take 'em down and get 'em mended, and dat vill pe a coot vay to pegin to talk mit him. So ven I has got shtarted, I t'inks de *Spirit* say to me, 'Shacop, vot you doin' mit your poots? You don't care apout gettin' dem mended—vat, den, does you vant de shoemaker to t'ink you comes to get de poots mended, ven you pees on'y goin' to talk about de religion!' Den I says, 'O! mein *Cot*—I has not got de relishion 'nough yet.' Den I goes right back to de parn, and I prays an' prays all night, and den de *Lort* gif me de sanctification! and den I could go midout mein poots, and tell de man vat I cum for—to talk apout de relishion; and not make pelief I vants my poots mended, ven dat aint vot I come for."

A CONVERSION OF THE OLDEN TIME.

AN old physician brought up in Massachusetts when Methodism was young, and whose father was of the old Calvinistic school, said to me:

"When I was a schoolboy of 18, I was sent off to an Academy; and while there I became deeply concerned for my soul; and so much so that I could not attend to my studies. So I resolved to return home, and ask father what I should do. My father seemed gratified to see the state of my mind. I asked father if it would if be right for me to pray. 'By no means,' said my father, 'for the prayers of the wicked are an abomination to the *Lord*. But if the *Lord* should convert you, you then might pray.' I then asked father if I could go to a meeting where a Methodist was going to preach. He answered, 'O no, my son, these are the false teachers prophesied of, who would come in the last days, if possible deceiving the very elect.' I dared not disobey my father, and in my distress, thinking I was probably a reprobate, took a razor and went to the stable to cut my throat, and then I should know the worst of my case. Well, I went to the stable, unbuttoned my shirt collar, and raised the hand to take my life. But each time I felt a power to pull my razor from my throat, and then I thought, 'I shall have to give it up, for I cannot kill myself.'

Soon, hearing that another Methodist meeting was to be held, I resolved to go without asking father, and then I should not be guilty of disobedience.

"A GREAT many believers walk upon the promises of God's call in the way to Heaven, even as a child upon weak ice, which they are afraid will crack under them, and leave them in the depth."—TRAILL, 1690.

IT is better to be a humble worm than a proud angel.—FLAVEL.

"AND THEN."

A story is told of a very good and pious man, whom the Church of Rome has enrolled among her saints on account of his great holiness. He was living at one of the Italian universities, when a young man, whom he had known as a boy, ran up to him, with a face full of delight, and told him what he had been long wishing, above all things in the world, was at length fulfilled, his parents having just given him leave to study the law; and that thereupon he had come to the law school in this university on account of its great fame, and meant to spare no pains or labor in getting through his studies as quickly and as well as possible.

In this way he ran on a long time, and, when at last he came to a stop, the holy man, who had been listening to him with great patience and kindness, said—

"Well! and when you get through your course of studies, what do you intend to do then?"

"Then I shall take my doctor's degree, answered the young man.

"And then?" asked St. Filippo Neri, again.

"And then," continued the youth, "I shall have a number of difficult and knotty cases to manage, and shall catch people's notice by my eloquence, my zeal, my learning, my acuteness, and gain a great reputation."

"And then?" repeated the holy man.

"And then," exclaimed the youth— "why then, there can't be a question; I shall be promoted to some high office or other; besides, I shall make money and grow rich."

"And then?" repeated St. Filippo.

"And then," pursued the young lawyer—"then I shall live comfortably and honorably in health and dignity, and shall be able to look forward quietly to a happy old age."

"And then?"

"And then," said the youth—"and then—and then—I shall die."

Here St. Filippo again lifted up his voice, and again said—"and then?"

Whereupon, the young man made no answer, but cast down his head and went away.

This last "and then," had pierced like a flash of lightning into his soul, and he could not get quit of it. Soon after, he forsook the study of the law, and gave himself up to the ministry of Christ, and spent the remainder of his days in godly words and works.— ARCHDEACON HARE.

An unrenewed man may be kept from the commission of some sin, not because there is a principle of grace within him, but because of *some providential restraint* without him, or upon him; for it often falls out, that when men have conceived sin, and are ready to execute it, Providence puts on them the fetters of restraint, and hinders them from so doing. This was the case with Abimelech, Gen. xx, 6: "I withheld thee." And though such persons so restrained have not the good of such providences, yet others have; for by it much mischief is prevented in the world, which otherwise would break out; and to this care of Providence we owe our lives, liberties, estates and comforts in this world.—FLAVEL.

THE SWORD OF THE SPIRIT.—The Scriptures are called "the Sword of the Spirit," because they derive all their power from the Spirit. In themselves, they are like a sword sheathed and lying upon the ground; they are a dead letter; they convey no spiritual energy; they carry with them neither conviction nor consolation: whether read or preached, they are equally without effect. Paul was convinced with the Scriptures before his conversion; but could not see in them that Jesus was the Christ; nor could he learn from them the temper and the disposition of a child of God.—SIMEON.

THAT young man who drinks, bets, swears, gambles, and idles away his time, is on a thin place on the ice.

THE PASS OF DEATH.

It was a narrow pass,
  Watered with human tears,
For death had kept the outer gate
  Almost six thousand years.
And the ceaseless tread of a world's feet
  Was ever in my ears—
Thronging, jostling, hurrying by,
  As if they were only born to die.

A stately king drew near,
  This narrow pass to tread,
Around him hung a gorgeous robe,
  And a crown was on his head;
But death, with a look of withering scorn,
  Arrested him and said:
"In humble dress must the king draw near,
For the crown and the purple are useless here."

Next came a man of wealth,
  And his eye was proud and bold,
And he bore in his hand a lengthy scroll,
  Telling of sums untold;
But death, who careth not for rank,
  Careth as little for gold—
"Here that scroll I cannot allow,
For the gold of the richest is powerless now."

Another followed fast,
  And a book was in his hand,
Filled with the flashes of burning thought
  That are known in many a land;
But the child of death quailed to hear
  Death's pitiless demand,—
"Here that book cannot enter with thee,
For the bright flash of genius is nothing to me."

Next came a maiden fair,
  With that eye so deeply bright,
That stirs within you strange sweet care,
  Should you meet on a summer night;
But death, ere the gentle maid passed through,
  Snatched away its light—
"Beauty is power in the world," he saith,
"But what can it do in the Pass of Death?"

A youth of sickly mien
  Followed in thoughtful mood,
Whose heart was filled with love to God
  And the early brotherhood;
Death felt he could not quench the heart
  That lived for others' good,—
"I own," cried he, "the power of love,
I must let it pass to the realms above!"
              SCOTTISH GUARDIAN.

NO REPENTANCE—NO PEACE.—Have you ever heard of the great clock of St. Paul's in London? At mid-day, in the roar of business, when carriages, and carts, and wagons, and omnibuses, go rolling through the streets, how many never hear that great clock strike, unless they live near it. But when the work of the day is over, and the roar of business has passed away—when men are gone to sleep and silence reigns in London—then, at twelve, at one, at two, at three, at four, the sound of that clock may be heard for miles around. Twelve!—One!—Two!—Three!—Four! How that clock is heard by many a sleepless man! That clock is just like the conscience of the impenitent man. While he has health and strength, and goes on in the whirl of business, he will not hear his conscience. He drowns and silences his voice by plunging into the world. He will not allow the inner man to speak to him. But the day will come when conscience will be heard, whether he likes it or not. The day will come when its voice will sound in his ears, and pierce him like a sword. The time will come when he must retire from the world, and lie down on the sick bed, and look death in the face. And then the clock of conscience, that solemn clock, will sound in his heart, and, if he has not repented, will bring wretchedness and misery to his soul. Oh, no! write it down in the tablets of your heart—without repentance, no peace!—J. C. RYLE.

EDUCATION. — Thewald thought it very unfair to influence a child's mind by inculcating any opinions before it should have come to years of discretion, and be able to choose for itself. I showed him my garden, and told him it was my botanic garden. "How so?" said he, "it is covered with weeds." "Oh," I replied, "that is because it has not yet come to its age of discretion and choice. The weeds, you see, have taken the liberty to grow, and I thought it unfair in me to prejudice the soil in favor of roses and strawberries." — COLERIDGE.

"BURNING AND SHINING."

BY REV. A. A. PHELPS.

It is the highest ambition of some persons to *shine* in the world. But theirs is the glitter of empty show, ignoring the charms of the gospel, and deifying the opinions of men. There are also many that *burn* in the world; but it is with the fires of passion rather than the quenchless zeal inspired by the Holy Ghost. They that burn with ambitious desires, and shine only to show off themselves to better advantage, are the enemies of the cross and the servants of the devil. If we shine at all, we must shine for God; and if we burn at all, it must be for the honor of his matchless name.

To burn is not enough—to shine is not enough; we are to be "burning and shining lights" in this crooked and perverse generation. There are demands for all the light we can shed, and all the fires we can kindle. To say nothing of the mantle of midnight darkness that enshrouds the hapless millions of paganism proper, how terrible is the gloom that veils the acknowledged land of light, and holds in ignorance of spiritual things ten thousand souls for whom the Saviour died! A superficial observer could hardly be made to credit the amazing amount of darkness and dullness that prevails, especially in our populous towns and cities. Many of the inhabitants of these need to be taught the first principles of the Gospel, and the work is so great in extent and difficult in itself, as to require a patient continuance in well-doing—a following up of effort after effort, and blow after blow, till the righteousness of God "go forth as brightness," and sinners shall behold "a light upon the road that leads them to the Lamb."

But it is not in the capacity of spiritual teachers alone that we are to shine for God. By the sweetness of our tempers, the simplicity of our testimony, the sacredness of our conversation, and the sanctity of our entire lives, we are to shed a halo of light around us that shall reveal the indwelling Divinity, and richly exemplify his "glorious grace!" Let no one imagine that the charms of personal character, the lavish bestowments of nature, or the polish of a classical education will answer at all as a substitute for the light of a heart-experience in the deep things of God. If any would shine to the honor of Jesus' name, he must first *burn* with celestial fire! The *light* must be but an emanation from the *heat*. God has united these two elements not only in *nature*, but in *grace*. And what he "hath joined together let no man put asunder." There is feeling—emotion—*fire* in the salvation of the Gospel, as principle, reason and light. We are to be so clothed with the power of the Spirit, that we shall burn our bigness through every circle in which we are called by the Providence of God to move. It is doubtless our privilege to call down the awakening influences of the Holy Ghost on those with whom we mingle, and compel them to feel the force of our faith and the fervor of our spirit. And who shall say that our *privilege* in this respect is not our bounden *duty?*

We are to shine with "borrowed rays divine," and shine with purest love. Love is the very center and essence of our holy religion. It is this that warms the heart, energizes the soul, overleaps difficulties, melts down icebergs, weeps over sinners, and goes out in yearning entreaties and earnest efforts for their salvation. It is this that will give unction to our spirits, point to our words, and access to the hearts of others. This is the mighty impulsive power that urges onward the minister of Jesus in the toils and trials that thicken on his path. It is love that brought the Saviour from above to rescue ruined man. "The heaven of heavens is love;" and the sanctified heart is chiefly distinguished by the fact that it is made "*perfect in love!*" The love of Christ is a quenchless flame in the home where it dwells. It is this that makes Howards and Wilberforces, and Wesleys, and starts them out into the moving masses of mankind, to spread greater terror and dismay among the devotees of the devil, than did Sampson's foxes among the Philistines when they set their corn on fire. May the Head of the Church fill us with this heaven-born element, and send us out to burn and glow, to live and labor, to fight and conquer!

RULES FOR MORAL WARFARE.

BY REV. T. L. CUYLER.

A SIMPLE "yes," or an emphatic "no," may cost you a fortune—may cost you a troop of friends—may cost your political promotion—may cost you your character—may cost you your soul! How many a public man has had his whole career decided by his course in some trying emergency, or on some one great question of right. He is led up into the mount of temptation where some gigantic iniquity bids him bow down and worship it, and promises in return "all the world and the glory thereof." From that mount of trial he comes down a hero or a fool. The die is cast. If he has honored justice and truth, then justice and truth will honor him; if not, his bones will be left bleaching on the road to a promotion he can never reach.

That was a hard struggle for Nathaniel Ripley Cobb, of Boston, when he decided to accumulate no more than $50,000 during his life, and to give all the surplus to the treasury of the Lord. But after the noble resolution was once taken, selfishness was a conquered lust in that man's breast forever. He had come off more than conqueror. How many a minister of Christ has been charged upon and overcome by this accursed spirit of "wordly wisdom!" He was put to the decisive test, not in Nero's judgment hall, or before Agrippa's tribunal: not before a Popish inquisitor, or in sight of Smithfield's fires of martyrdom. But in his quiet study, when some timid friend counseled a treacherous silence in pulpit on some vital question of right, his "yes," or his "no," has either called from his Master the precious benediction, "Well done, good and faithful servant," or else the fearful anathema, "Ye were ashamed of me and of my truth, and of thee will I be ashamed before my Father and his holy angels!" We all have our moral Marengos and our Waterloos, where we win or lose the crown of Christian character. When those decisive conflicts come on between our conscience on the one hand, and some selfish scheme or Satanic iniquity on the other, then try to remember a few simple rules of moral war:

1. Never change your position in sight of an enemy. This was a fatal policy to the allies at Austerlitz. It has cost many a disgraceful defeat in spiritual warfare.

2. Never place on guard a doubtful or a questionable principle. Your sentinel will be sure to betray you.

3. Never abandon the high ground of right for the low lands of expediency. Before you are aware, you will be swamped in the bottomless morass of ruin.

4. Get your moral armor from God's Word; and "put on the *whole* armor." An exposed spot in character may admit the fatal weapon of the foe. Ahab was wounded through the joints of his harness. Do not mind blows in the face. Heroes are wounded in the face, cowards in the back.

5. But whether wounded by foes or deserted by friends, *never surrender*. It is said that none of the old Imperial Guard survived the wreck of Waterloo. Toward the sunset of that long, bloody day, when the surviving remnant of the Guards was summoned to lay down their arms, the scarred veterans of fifty victorious fights cried out, "The Old Guards can die, but they never learned to surrender!" The glorious CAPTAIN OF OUR SALVATION could die for us, but he could not desert us. Blessed is he who is found faithful! He shall wear the crown of amaranth in the paradise of God.

No Middle Course in Religion.—Often do we hear remiss professors strive to choke all forward holiness by commending the golden mean. A cunning discouragement; the devil's sophistry! The mean of virtue is between two degrees. It is a mean grace that loves a mean degree of grace; yet this is the staff with which the world beats all that would be better than themselves. What! will you be singular—walk alone? But were not the apostles singular in their walking, a spectacle to the world? Did not Christ call for this singularity, what do ye more than others? You that are God's peculiar people, will ye do no peculiar thing? Ye are separate from the world, will ye keep the world's road? Must the name of a puritan dishearten us in the service of God? St. Paul said in his apology, "by that which they call heresy, so worship I the God of my fathers;" and by that which profane ones call puritanism, which is indeed zealous devotion, so let my heart desire to serve Jesus Christ.—Old Puritan Writer.

Christian Comfort.—Let the course of tribulation be what it will, "in Me ye shall have peace." How is it then, perhaps you will ask, that Christians are not always rejoicing? How is it that we so often see them bathed in tears, and scarcely hear anything for their sighs and complaints? It is easily enough to be accounted for. It is because they love the world and the things of the world so much that they have no room or relish for divine consolations. To be sure, where Christ is there is always ground for comfort; but Christians are not always fit to be comfortable. They may, through mere inattention to spiritual things, or too fond attention to temporal possessions and enjoyments, be so sadly declined as to require reproof rather than comfort; and what they want Christ gives.—Lavington.

It is perfectly well understood, or if not, it should be, that almost any husband would leap into the sea, or rush into a burning edifice to rescue a perishing wife. But to anticipate the convenience or happiness of a wife in small matters, the neglect of which would be unobserved, is a more eloquent proof of tenderness. This shows a mindful fondness which wants occasion in which to express itself. And the smaller the occasion seized upon, the more intensely affectionate is the attention paid.—Horace Bushnell.

Outside and Inside.—"Two things a master commits to his servant's care," saith one—"the child and the child's clothes." It will be a poor excuse for the servant to say at his master's return,

"Sir, here are all the child's clothes, neat and clean; but the child is lost!"

Much so with the account that many will give to God of their souls and bodies at the great day:

"Lord, here is my body; I was very grateful for it; I neglected nothing that belonged to its content and welfare; but as for my soul, that is lost and cast away forever,—I took little care and thought about it!"—Flavel.

Sensible Prayer by a Boy.—A little boy, one day, had done wrong, and was sent, after parental correction, to ask, in secret, the forgiveness of his Heavenly Father. His offense had been passion. Anxious to hear what he had to say, his mother followed him to the door of his room. In lisping accents she heard him ask to be better, never to be angry again, and then, with child-like simplicity, he added, "*Lord, make ma's temper better, too!*"

"Oh, blessed is he who can divine
  Where real right doth lie,
And dares to take the side that seems
  Wrong to man's blindfold eye!

Oh, learn to scorn the praise of men!
  Oh, learn to love with God.
For Jesus won the world through shame
  And beckons thee his road.
      —Roman Breviary.

EVIL WHISPERING.

BY JOHN WESLEY.

Oh that all you who bear the reproach of Christ, who are in derision called Methodists, would set an example to the Christian world, so called, at least in this one instance. Put ye away evil speaking, tale bearing, whispering: let none of them proceed out of your mouth! See that you " speak evil of no man;" of the absent, nothing but good. If ye must be distinguished, whether ye will or no, let this be the distinguishing mark of a Methodist: " He censures no man behind his back; by this fruit ye may know him." What a blessed effect of this self-denial should we quickly feel in our hearts! How would our "peace flow as a river," when we thus "followed peace with all men!" How would the love of God abound in our own souls while we thus confirmed our love to our brethren! And what an effect would it have on all that were united together in the name of the Lord Jesus! How would brotherly love continually increase, when this grand hindrance of it was removed! All the members of Christ's mystical body would then naturally care for each other. "If one member suffered, all would suffer with it;" " if one was honored, all would rejoice with it;" and every one would love his brother " with a pure heart fervently." Nor is this all: but what an effect might this have, even on the wild, unthinking world! How soon would they descry in us what they could not find among all the thousands of their brethren, and cry, (as Julien the apostate to his heathen courtiers,) "See how these Christians love one another!" By this chiefly would God convince the world, and prepare them also for his kingdom; as we may easily learn from those remarkable words in our Lord's last, solemn prayer: "I pray for them who shall believe in me, that they may be one, as thou, Father, art in me and I in thee,—that the world may believe that hou hast sent me." The Lord hasten the time! The Lord enable us to love one another, and not only "in word and in tongue, but in deed and truth," even as Christ hath loved us!

ALONE AT THE JUDGMENT.—There is no escape alone or in the crowd at the judgment day. It is not a multitude amid which we may hide ourselves and escape notice. At that solemn tribunal, each man will be as transparent before the searching eye of the Son of God, as if that man and Jesus were the only twain in the whole universe: such will be the intense light of that day, that one reason why the lost will call out for the hills to cover them, and the mountains to shadow them, will be that they cannot bear the intensity of that searching and unutterable splendor; and such will be the dread silence of that moment, that each man will hear the pulsations of his own heart, and if that heart be unregenerate, each pulse will sound a keath-knell to his hopes and prospects forever. There is no escape in the crowd; there is no escape by wealth; there is no escape by talent; there is no escape any way; for "how, if we neglect so great a salvation," says the apostle, as satisfied that there is no escape whatever, "shall we escape?—Dr. CUMMING.

NO COMPLIMENTS IN PRAYER.—We have heard some prayers which were designed to affect the hearer, rather than to reach Heaven. The following characteristic anecdote of John Randolph is a keen rebuke of the practice:

In one of his spells of repentance and sickness, he was visited by a minister, who, at his request prayed for and with him. The minister began in this wise: "Lord, our friend is sick. Thou knowest how generous he was to the poor, and what eminent services he has rendered to his country, and how is among the honored and great men of the earth—"

"Stop, stop," said the impatient Randolph—" no more of such stuff, else the Lord will damn us both."

ART THOU CHRIST.

Art thou content to take to Christ for thy only Lord and King, to govern and guide thee by his laws and Spirit, and to obey him when he commandeth the hardest duties, and those which most cross the desires of the flesh? Is it thy sorrow when thou breakest thy resolution herein; and thy joy when thou keepest closest in obedience to him? Wouldst thou not change thy Lord and Master for all the world? Thus is it with every true Christian. But if thou be a hypocrite, it is far otherwise. Thy mayest call Christ thy Lord and thy Saviour, but thou never foundest thyself so lost without him as to drive thee to seek him, and trust him, and lay thy salvation in him alone; at least thou didst never heartily consent that he should govern thee as thy Lord, nor resign thy soul and life to be ruled by him, nor take his word for the law of thy thoughts and actions. Doubtless thou art willing to be saved from hell by Christ when thou diest, but, in the meantime, he must command thee no further than will consist with thy credit or pleasure or other worldly ends! And if he would give thee leave, thou hadst far rather live after the world and the flesh, than after the Word and the Spirit. And though thou mayest now and then have a notion or purpose to the contrary, yet this that I have mentioned is the ordinary desire and choice of thy heart. Thou art, therefore, no true believer in Christ; for though thou confess him in words, yet in works thou dost deny him, "being abominable and disobedient, and unto every good work reprobate."—BAXTER.

THE BAPTISM OF THE HOLY GHOST OF FIRE.

THERE is a spiritual baptism, to which we ought to aspire, "Baptised into Christ," "Baptised with the Holy Ghost." This is peculiar language. The formula, "baptised in the name of the Father, and of the Son, and of the Holy Ghost," means not merely christening or taking upon one's self the christian name; it signifies this higher baptism. We are baptised unto God as we are unto Christ. Not merely is the name of God a portion of the formula; the spirit of God is the transfusing element. In true baptism, the font is not hewn out of marble or fabricated of silver. Our baptistry is the universe; the baptismal flood is God, and Christ, and the Holy Spirit. We are plunged in the mighty influences of truth. It is a fiery baptism,—one that melts and refines us; one that sheds warmth and vivacity through our souls; one that disperses the darkness of the mind and gives rest and peace to our natures. Daily as the sun baptises the earth with light, yearly as it baptises it with verdure, so ought we to be baptised with the power of God.

Whatever we may think about water baptism, let us not forget the baptism with the Holy Ghost and fire. Let us strive for the baptism of Christ, even as Paul did for the resurrection. —JUDD.

SECRET RELIGION.—God is often lost in prayers and ordinances. "Enter into thy chamber," said he, "and shut thy door about thee." "Shut thy door about thee," means much; it means shut out not only frivolty, but business; not only the company abroad, but the company at home; it means, let thy poor soul have a little rest and refreshment, and God have opportunity to speak to thee in a still small voice, or he will speak in thunder. I am persuaded the Lord would often speak more softly if we would shut the door.—CECIL.

TRUE felicity is, when any one is as happy as to find out and follow what is the proper bent of his genius, and turn all his endeavors to exert himself according as that prompts him.

CENSORIOUSNESS.

BY REV. A. A. PHELPS.

THERE is a great deal of misapprehension and senseless talk about a censorious spirit. If a brother has not "charity" enough to apologize for sin, and mantle the general "works of the devil," there are many religionists who are ready to charge him with "sour godliness," "censoriousness," etc. They forget that the purest love that ever awakened the heart throbs of divine compassion, is at infinite and irreconcilable odds with sin in every degree and kind; and the nearer the love of the Christian approaches to the love of Christ, the more hearty will be his disapproval of everything opposed to God. It is simple nonsense to talk of a holiness that has no rebuke for sin and no opposition to Satan. Plainness and earnestness of speech are not necessarily censoriousness of speech. The "whole counsel of God" includes the "thunders of the law" as well as the messages of mercy. The sinner must be alarmed — awakened — broken in spirit, before he is ready to appropriate the special *promises* of the Gospel. And he that would largely succeed in taking captives for Jesus must learn to vary the tactics of war to meet the peculiarities of a thousand different cases. It is no sign that a man is censorious because sinners become enraged under the burning truth he utters; and as little so, because backslidden church-members rail out against the faithful utterance of God's ambassadors, and join their influence with the open enemies of the cross. It is a cheap way they often have of apologizing for their own meagerness in religion, to erect a very ordinary standard of piety, and then stigmatize all that rise above it as censors, fanatics, or fools! With such epithets, applied to such persons, and with such a spirit, we have not the least possible sympathy. There may be real censoriousness indulged to some extent by very excellent people, who have taken it on by imperceptible degrees. We can see some points of danger here, even with those of the deepest devotion to God. Indeed, their scrutinizing and painful views of the sad condition of things may render them even more liable to what Caughey has denominated a "sore conscience," and this may lead to overwrought notions of the state and duty of others. Our sober conviction is that among the earnest Christians of this section, there is but *little* to condemn as real censoriousness. Should any of our brethren or sisters, however, be inclined to depreciate either the state of justification, or entire sanctification, the suspicion of danger would be awakened in a corresponding degree. We confess we have observed a *tinge* of something which has suggested a word of caution, and those who know us understand that we *dare* give it, even at the hazard of being thought *conservative*. *We* think there is demand for review and revision of one's theology, when he comes to regard the great blessing of inward purity as only a small attainment compared with the other "gifts" of the Spirit, which it is the believer's privilege to enjoy. And if he is disposed to look or talk suspiciously of those who, while they are clear in the blessing of perfect love, are convinced of the superior importance of the *graces* of the Spirit to the *gifts* of the Spirit, and of the concerns of the *soul* to those of the *body*, there is doubtless a touch of censoriousness, if not of fanaticism also. If these hints shall fall under the notice of any who find themselves leaning in the direction indicated, we ask them to move cautiously; and while they are careful to walk in *all* the light revealed, let them be equally careful to shun the false glare of lights that are *not* revealed. We can never effectually lead on souls to the very depths of love, if we allow ourselves by any means to get ahead of the Spirit. Whatever we think, or do, or say, let us forever remember that salvation from sin is the great thing to be sought, to be lived, and to be pressed upon the attention of all.

PARTIALITY.—There are some people that must never be blamed; and again there are some that must never be praised. There is a sort of step-motherish disposition running through all the world. God alone is no respecter of persons. Every one of us is conscious that some people can do to us or to ours, with impunity, things which, were another to attempt them, would anger us in an instant. It is "Jacob have I loved, but Esau have I hated," from generation to generation. In the household, in society, in the business and the literary world, it is the same. One must be lauded and loved for everything, another for nothing. At home, while the children are little, the disposition is seen—there is a pet and there is a scapegoat in almost every family. Among the grown up sons and daughters, and brothers and sisters, it is still the same. "What do you *mean* by such conduct, you wicked Esau?"—"It was not I, but Jacob that did it."—"Oh! very well. I don't think there is any harm done, after all." This is the way. Sometimes it is the wife, sometimes it is the husband, that must not be blamed. No matter what the favorite does, if a reflecting word is uttered, somebody is angry and ready for a fight. You must bear anything and everything from the favorite, and never presume to complain—for how can the favorite be wrong? He will not be found so, you may depend on *that;* and you will yourself meet with the condemnation which you think that he deserves. You will find it your cheapest way to suffer in silence if the favorite has injured you. Life, as well as the household, has its favorites; and it is in vain for any to seek for justice against them. They must not be blamed, nor shamed, nor thwarted; they must be allowed to help themselves to the lion's share of everything.—MILWARD.

MONDAY, 20TH DEC. 1742.—We laid the first stone of the house. (At Newcastle.) Many were gathered from all parts, to see it; but none scoffed or interrupted, while we praised God, and prayed that he would prosper the work of our hands upon us. Three or four times in the evening, I was forced to break off preaching that we might pray and give thanks to God. When I came home, they told me the physician said, he did not expect Mr. Meyrick could live till the morning. I went to him, but his pulse was gone. He had been speechless and senseless for some time. A few of us immediately joined in prayer; (I relate the naked fact;) before we had done his sense and his speech returned. Now, he that will account for this by natural causes, has my free leave; but I choose to say, this is the power of God.

Thursday, 23*d*.—It being computed that such a house could not be finished under seven hundred pounds, many were positive it would never be finished at all; others that I should not live to see it covered. I was of another mind; nothing doubting, but as it was begun for God's sake, he would provide what was needful for the finishing of it.

Saturday 25*th*.—The physician told me he could do no more; Mr. Meyrick could not live over the night. I went up and found them all crying about him; his legs being cold, and (as it seemed) dead already. We all kneeled down, and called upon God with strong cries and tears. He opened his eyes and called for me; and from that hour, he continued to recover his strength, till he was restored to perfect health. I wait to hear who will disprove this fact, or philosophically account for it.—WESLEY'S JOURNAL.

I HAVE been charged with "small preaching." This is a new phrase to me, but I suppose it means my condescending to dwell upon those "minute points" of Christian experience, usually taken up in a more florid and eloquent style. But have you never read that striking sentiment of Galen, "In physic nothing is little." A little error there, may occasion fearful mischiefs; so a small mistake in soul's concernments may occasion everlasting ruin. An *error* respecting conversion is *ruinous, damnable*, if the person die in it. "Except a man be born again, he cannot see the Kingdom of God." This is a decision of tremendous import. Now the object to be attained by faithful preaching is, to tear away the veil, so that the deluded conscience may be enabled to look the deception fully in the face. It is not, however, that kind of preaching which you call "eloquent," that is adapted to acccomplish this.—CAUGHEY.

OBEDIENCE THE PRICE OF FREEDOM.

BY S. K. J. CHESBROUGH.

To obey is better than sacrifice. How few have learned this important lesson! All through our Zion, the cry is heard, "I am not free." Why not, dear reader? Has the Gospel lost any of its power? We want to enjoy the freedom that belongs to the child of God; but we are unwilling to pay the price. Many of us once knew what it was to be God's free men and women. But alas, we feel creeping over us "the spirit of bondage again to fear." We struggle at times to get free. The price, or cost of this freedom is set before us in God's word. Obedience. A short command, but comprehending all. God is our Father. He offers us salvation, and adoption into his family, to make us "joint heirs of Jesus Christ," "our elder brother." This adoption, however is conditional. "We must continue in his words," walk in all his holy commands. "Walk after the Spirit; or, in other words, *we must obey*. Perfect obedience brings perfect freedom. We forget sometimes our individuality. Satan often entraps us here. We are members perhaps of some church or band, He appears to us in the form of "an angel of light," and arrays before our mind the glorious and precious promises given to the Church. The next step is easily taken. I am a member, therefore they are mine; when at the same time we are conscious of neglect of duties, of shrinking from the cross, of a fearfulness in walking in all the light that has shone upon our heads, of a dread of being considered too forward, or a secret coveting of the praise of men. At times we have arisen above these things, but soon relapsed again into bondage! The trouble arises from our forgetting that the Church is composed of individuals and that I, even I, cannot claim one of these promises or blessings, *as mine*, until I have complied with the conditions. We look to others instead of looking to Jesus. We lean upon one another, instead of leaning upon that arm that is alone able to save. Oh! when will we, as individuals, seek for ourselves the fulfillment of the promises in us? Many of our pilgrims are to-day in bondage, because they have refused to "go forward." Many have professed to be freely justified. God has set before them, a higher state of grace, but for fear of the opinions of men they have hesitated; the Spirit has been grieved; to-day they mourn over their leanness, "I am not free." Beloved reader, obey God, and "go forward," believe in Jesus, Consecrate *all*. (Oh! may God show you what is implied in the expression "My little all to give.") You can then claim the promises as yours, by simple faith in Jesus.

Again, others have felt the cleansing blood. They have walked in the light, have grown in grace, and have power with God; but to-day they are as "weak as other men." Why? Because they have not obeyed. The path of the just is as the shining light, shining more and more. The light shone very bright. Then new heights, depths, lengths and breadths were spread out before them. To experience them required a more perfect burial of self, new sacrifices, new crosses and more self-abandonment. "The shrinking flesh complained." They shrank, ceased to obey the command "go forward," and now instead of going through the length and breath of the land, they are in bondage. How emphatic the words of Jesus. "Ye shall know the truth, and the truth shall make you free" " Walk in the light." " Deny thyself, take up thy cross and *follow me.*" Oh! this following Jesus everywhere. "Ah!" says one, " be careful." Jesus says, " I am the way, the truth, and the life." Glory to God! No fear of fanaticism here. " If we abide in Jesus, and his words abide in us, the Spirit will guide us into all truth." If we live near to Jesus, and follow obediently, " gladly leaving all below," we shall never be ashamed or confounded. Reader, are you free in Jesus ? Are you obeying fully ? Remember we are not only judged for the improvement of what we enjoy, but shall be called into account for not receiving all that was offered to us. Begin just now a life of obedience. Obey. Ye shall know the truth; and the truth, not the Church, nor the pilgrims, *but the truth*, shall make you free. Glory to God!

THE "IRREPRESSIBLE CONFLICT."

BY REV. J. A. WELLS.

He that is not for me is against me; and he that gathereth not with me scattereth abroad.—Matth. xii, 30.

The wise sayings of Jesus, though mysterious, and, often apparently absurd, harmonize with the unfoldings of human experience from age to age. He knew what was in man—knew all the deep-laid principles of human nature, and the secret causes which can ever develop themselves in the endless diversified character and condition of our race. Many of his "hard sayings" have long since received the full demonstration of experience.

One of those uncomprehended verities is the entireness of devotion demanded by the law of God—the impossibility of any common ground of neutrality between God and the world, on which a man may stand and be on friendly terms with both. The character of God on the one hand, and the character of the world on the other, is so imperfectly understood, that most men are led to suppose that they may, in some way, please God, while they are in full sympathy with the world. The teaching of Jesus is radical on this point. "No man can serve two masters:" "He that is not for me is against me." His character of pure, spotless holiness cannot tolerate, in his own dominions, a character which does not harmonize with it. Infinite love, guided by Infinite intelligence, is essential to the glorious ideal which the Scriptures give us of God. It is His fixed and unalterable determination, that love and purity shall be the prime characteristic of every sentient being in all his moral empire. He never will compromise holiness, or yield one ray of its glory from his brow. Wherever the eye of His omniscience penetrates, whatever responsible being resists the universal sway of His holiness—His law in all its claims, must encounter the fire of his Infinite displeasure. He never can change. All that is unlike God, must itself change, or suffer the consequences of a contest with the Infinite.

The world is opposed to God. Man is fallen and unholy. By nature he has no common sympathy with God. The whole force of his inclination is the opposite of what the law of God requires. God may have mercy on a wicked world and spare it for a time; but, He can never change His character so as to harmonize with it. He may institute a way of salvation, by which individual men may be redeemed from the fall and brought to harmonize with His holiness; but He can give them no salvation without bringing them into harmony with His holiness. He may bridge the gulf of moral distance between himself and fallen men by the mysterious, glorious atonement. So that man may travel over the awful void and harmonize with God; but He can never come down in his character towards that of a sinful world to harmonize with man.

All saved men are made harmonious with God. They are in full sympathy with him. They know Him and themselves. They recognize, as never before they became saved men, the irreconcilable difference of spirit between God and a fallen world. They hate sin; they love holiness. There is no longer a harmony between them and the world. They are all harmonious with God, angels, and the redeemed; but, intensely opposed to all that opposes God.

Can a company of men, called a Christian Church, composed in part of those who have the Spirit of God, and in part of those who have the spirit of the world, live and work together in the labor of the Lord, harmoniously, without a change on either part? To effect such a result, is the almost universal attempt of the ecclesiastical organizations of the present age. The impossibility of the supposed harmony may be seen in the light of gospel principles.

1. The Spirit of God and that of the world can never harmonize.

2. Men who are of God have the Spirit of God. Their sympathies and their actions are in accordance with the mind of God.

3. The spirit of the world is in direct antagonism to the Spirit of God. "The carnal mind is enmity against God." The world will resist every movement of God to set up and advance His kingdom, and establish righteousness in the earth.

4. The men of the world are in full sympathy with the world. "He that will be the friend of the world is the enemy of God." Hence, the impossibility of a harmony of spirit between saved men and those not saved, is obvious.

Men of the world will never do the Lord's work. They may appear to be much engaged in promoting the cause of God, but the real motive, the true cause of their actions, is something radically different from an enlightened purpose to do the work of the Lord. They have no hearty intention of bringing mankind to submission and full sympathy with all the mind of God; God living, reigning, loving, all through the soul of man; God speaking, planning, acting, in all the activities of the outer man, is a conception too pure and glorious for men of the world. Yet, nothing less than the realization of this glorious conception in human experience, is the true object of the work of the Lord. Christ will reign on earth as He reigns in Heaven. All men who have His spirit must labor to extend His kingdom, to bring human hearts into full submission to His sway. Men not in sympathy with God will never do this work. Their highest aims terminate in self. The gratification of some constitutional propensity or sentiment is the limit of all that they will do. They never think of losing sight of self and letting Christ be all in all.

The men who have the spirit of Jesus will labor to promote the real work of God according to the best intelligence which they have. They constantly desire only the holy, perfect will of God. Their souls are in loving harmony with God. They will labor to promote the same object which Jesus died and lives, intercedes, and reigns to promote. They will not be diverted from this to some other object.

The more fully the Spirit of Christ takes possession of His people, the more vigorous is their contest with the world. Christ is intensely desirous of bringing a lost world to himself. He is intensely opposed to all sin. The whole force of His Infinite might moves in the direction of saving the lost, and of bringing them into entire harmony with all the mind of God. As men are brought in harmony with Him, they feel the same hatred of sin—the same love for souls—the same concern for the lost—the same intense anxiety that men should be brought into harmony with all the mind of God. Hence, the boldness, energy, ardor and perseverance, with which they contend against the spirit of the world, increase with the depth of their union with Christ. The more of the Spirit of Christ a man has, the more he feels as Christ feels. The wider a man is removed from sympathy with the world, the more violent will be the conflict of spirit between him and the world. "Marvel not if the world hate you; it hated me before it hated you." "If ye were of the world, the world would love its own, but, because ye are not of the world, therefore, the world hateth you."

It is the purpose of God to redeem the earth to himself. He has undertaken it; and He will accomplish His purpose. The earth is promised to the Son as his inheritance. He must reign till He triumphs over all. The conflict will wax hotter and hotter, till the harps of God proclaim the final victory of Emanuel, and Jesus stretches forth His sceptre as King of Kings and Lord of Lords. The opposition of spirit between the men of God and the men of the world, can never be less. Deep in the nature of man, the nature of the wicked world, and the nature of God, is laid the foundation of the "*irrepressible conflict.*" It has been a conflict ever since the plan of redemption has operated in the world, and cannot cease till the Triumphant Son has put all enemies under His feet. With the Almighty infusing His own Spirit and power into His followers, and leading them forward against the world; and, with the world in irreconcilable hostility against God, there is no possibility of a peace, till the day that it is proclaimed in Heaven, "The kingdoms of this world have become the kingdoms of our Lord and of His Christ; and He shall reign forever."

The world will never cease to fight against God, while any strength remains in it to continue the conflict. It is its nature to fight God. "The carnal mind is enmity against God." It is the nature of God's Spirit to hate sin. The men in whom God's Spirit reigns are in love with holiness and in enmity with sin. They must be so by an unalterable law of their nature. Hence, the conflict is *irrepressible*. It cannot cease. No power in Heaven, earth, or hell, can stop it. It is daily culminating to its glorious consummation. The Sun of Righteousness is rising to annihilate earth's darkness and shine forever.

Every effort to quiet agitation will prove a failure. The men of God will never cease from their efforts to carry on the real work of God. The desire to quiet agitation implies that the mind is not in enlightened sympathy with God. God is the originator of the conflict. A soul in harmony with Him goes heartily with him to the very heat of the strife, never desiring that it should be less till victory turns on the Lord's side.

The conflict will drive the men of God nearer to God, and the men of the world to fortify themselves more and more in the principles of the world. God's people will become holier and more like God; and the men of the world will develop, more than ever, their unlikeness to God. Those who, at the present time, oppose the work of God—the promotion of holiness—will go farther and farther away from the principles of the gospel. They have taken a position against God, and the contest will drive them to strengthen themselves by becoming more and more grounded in their first principle, which is deadly hostility against God. The history of the Christian Church is full of examples of apostacy, wreck and ruin, which began by opposition to what was supposed to be unimportant matters, but, which were, truly, the works of God. When a man sets himself to oppose the works of God, he little thinks where he will end; but, unless he retrace his steps, he is sure to go far into the "gall of bitterness and the bond of iniquity."

The nature of the conflict is spiritual. It is to be decided whether the power of darkness, on the one hand, shall reign to the depravation and ruin of man's entire being; or, whether, on the other hand, God shall reign to his salvation, and elevate him morally, intellectually and physically, to that position that will be pleasing to God. The victory is sure. Jesus shall reign on earth and in Heaven, God over all. His faithful followers will share with Him the victory and triumph and glory, and rest forever and ever. There are toils, sufferings, conflicts and struggles here, but treasures and perfect blessedness forever afterwards. Poverty, scorn and death are for us in the militant state, but robes, palms, crowns and thrones when we triumph with the Lord. O, for a greater baptism of THE SPIRIT to arm us, nerve us, inspire us, as we press on in the IRREPRESSIBLE CONFLICT.

SEED TO THE SOWER.—There are two ways of treating the seed. The botanist splits it up, and discourses upon its curious characteristics; the simple husbandman eats and sows; sows and eats. Similarly there are two ways of treating the gospel. A critic dissects it; raises a mountain of debate about the structure of the whole, and the relation of its parts; and when he is done with his argument, he is done. To him the letter is dead; he neither lives on it himself, nor spreads it for the good of his neighbors. He neither eats nor sows. The disciples of Jesus, hungering for righteousness, take the seed whole; it is bread for to-day's hunger aud seed for to-morrow's supply.

IF we duly join faith and works in all our preaching, we shall not fail of a blessing. But of all preaching, what is usually called Gospel preaching is the most useless, if not the most mischievious; a dull, yea, or lively harangue, on the sufferings of Christ, as salvation by faith, without strongly inculcating holiness. I see, more and more, that this naturally tends to drive holiness out of the world.—JOHN WESLEY.

THE AWAKENING.

BY JAMES G. CLARK.

See them go forth like floods to the ocean,
  Gathering might from each mountain and glen,
Wider and deeper the tide of devotion,
  Rolls up to God from the bosoms of men.
Hear the great multitude mingling in chorus,
  Groan as they gaze from their crimes to the sky,
"Father, the midnight of death gathers o'er us,
  When will the dawn of redemption draw nigh?"

"Look on us, wanderers, sinful and lowly,
  Struggling with grief and temptation below,
Thine is the goodness in everything holy,
  Thine is the mercy to pity our woe.
Thine is the power to cleanse and restore us,
  Spotless and pure as the angels on high,
Father, the midnight of death gathers o'er us,
  When will the dawn of redemption draw nigh?"

Gray hairs and golden youth, matron and maiden,
  Lovers of Mammon, and followers of fame,
All with the same solemn burden are laden,
  Lifting their souls to that One mighty name.
"Wild is the pathway that surges before us,
  On the broad waters the black shadows lie,
Father, the midnight of death gathers o'er us,
  When will the dawn of redemption draw nigh?"

Lo! the vast depths of futurity's ocean,
  Heave with Jehovah's mysterious breath,
Mortals, press on, while the deep is in motion,
  Jesus is walking the waters of death.
Angels are mingling with men in the chorus,
  Rising like incense from earth to the sky,
"Father, the billows grow brighter before us,
  Heaven, with its mansions, eternal draws nigh."

PURITY, soberness, distributing onr property amongst the poor are nothing, without love. Satan trembles to see in us that true, lowly love which we bear to one another; he grudges us this harmony, for we thus display that which he himself was not able to retain.—GREGORY.

THE CAUSE.

BY M. H. FREELAND.

The question is not unfrequently asked, "Why do so many turn back after commencing a life of devotion to God?" The answers to this question have been as various as the minds that have given it their serious consideration. Our Calvinistic brethren give as their final reply, "They never were converted, else they would have continued faithful. God never commences a work without finishing it." But they forget, meanwhile, that the great work of individual salvation is subject to human volition; that God never resorts to *coersive* measures when dealing with the human will. That the answer given by those of the Calvinistic school, is, however, true to a very considerable extent, must be admitted by every careful observer. For, undoubtedly, multitudes who are gathered within the pale of the Christian Church during seasons of revival, have never known the joys of pardoned sin, no conclusive evidence having ever been given by them of a radical change of heart—of their being new creatures in Christ Jesus. 'Tis true that, while the tide of revival influence is high, they float along with the current and seem to know something of the saving power of grace; but no sooner does the time of testing come, than it is found they have no root in themselves, and they quickly wither away. But it is not exclusively to this class that we allude when speaking of those who turn back, but also, and more particularly, to those who actually experience a knowledge of sin forgiven—of pardon sealed. For we believe it is possible for a saved soul to fall into sin and thus become alienated from God and be lost to all eternity. Nor would we restrict our inquiries to those who have barely become experimentally acquainted with the first principles of the Gospel, as it is a sad fact that individuals have fallen from a state of grace far in advance of justification. There is, undoubtedly, one cause more than any other that occasions the fearful apostacy from the real life of God in the soul, everywhere so painfully visible. While minor causes exist, this stands preeminent, viz.: *resting in present attainments.* Here lies the "Enchanted Ground" where Bunyan's Pilgrim fell asleep and lost his roll. There is no such thing as attaining a state of religious experience in this life as leaves no more enemies to be overcome, no more victories to be gained. Infinite as its originator, the glorious scheme of redemption provides an inexhaustible store for the constantly increasing capacity of finite beings. And to suppose one's cup of bliss complete in the hour of conversion, or at any subsequent period, is to suppose the infinite can be exhausted by the finite. But absurd as such a supposition may appear in theory, it is taught, practically, to an alarming extent. Bible religion is something that cannot be retained without constantly increasing. It is diffusive in its nature, and as naturally tends to permeate the entire being of its possessor, as does the leaven hid in three measures of meal to leaven the whole lump. It is of the utmost importance that individuals just commencing in the service of God, should be well informed at this point. How, often we hear the remark, "I supposed, when I was converted, there was nothing more to be done or suffered, only to rejoice in God all the day long. Hence, when temptations came, they found me all unprepared to meet them, and before I was aware, I cast away my confidence and became an easy prey to my subtle foe." What need of nursing fathers and mothers to instruct the babes !

Nor is it less important for those just entering the land of rest from inbred sin, the land of perfect holiness, to be well instructed at this very point. It is so natural to suppose *all* is gained with this important victory, that very many stop on the shores of Jordan, instead of going up to *possess* the goodly land before them. Hence their experience becomes stereotyped in its character, and is destitute of that freshness and vigor it once possessed. As we look around do we not find many of this class among those professing holiness. There is a deplorable lack of power evidenced in all they do. Their testimonies seem to savor of the manna gathered over night. Unlike St. Paul, they count themselves to have apprehended. Nor do they leave the things that are behind and press forward to the things that are before. The Apostle was found reaching forward, hence he was able to say he had kept the faith. The Bible standard is, "to be filled with *all* the *fullness* of *God*." Where then is the end? "Be not drunken with wine wherein is excess, but be ye *filled* with the *Spirit*." But let an individual begin to take possession of the legacy bequeathed to him in the Word of God, and Satan comes up at once and whispers the caution, "You are going too fast." Indeed, this caution is repeated at every successive step, and almost invariably through the instrumentality of a professor of religion. Ah, what multitudes have relaxed their exertions, and gradually fallen into a state of luke-warmness by yielding to this suggestion!

Who believes the Bible? Who takes that sacred book as the *will* of God to *them*? Such truths as have been tested by our fathers are received; but what an inclination there is to reject what we have not *seen* tested by actual experience. We read that the records there are for examples to those who follow after; but let any one teach, for instance, that the faith experienced by the ancient worthies, as recorded in the eleventh of Hebrews, is still attainable, how quick the cry of "fanaticism" will be heard in response, and that, too, by many who have known much of the deep things of God. But the Apostle did not teach thus; on the contrary he taught that God had provided some *better thing* for *us*, i. e., for those under the Gospel dispensation. There is, however, great reproach inseparably connected with receiving by faith *all* Jesus has died to purchase. It costs something to be *saved*, to be sanctified wholly, *body*, *soul* and spirit, and to be preserved blameless unto the coming of our Lord. Mr. Bramwell, a man rarely equaled in depth of experience says, "I am persuaded many turn back after receiving the cleansing touch, and the cause generally is their not determining to receive the *whole*." Let us beware how we set down anything as fanatical that bears the broad seal of God's eternal truth, for in so doing we shall invariably find the light waning in our own souls as a result. Let us not make void the law through *tradition*. God cannot deny himself. "Give kind words to all," says Bramwell, " but *tarry* for none." The standard of Bible religion has been fearfully lowered during the ages past; and nothing but a faith that

" Laughs at *impossibilities*,
And cries '*it shall be done*,'"

will ever enable the friends of Jesus to raise it again. Let the same stamp of salvation be enjoyed as was possessed in the early age of the Christian Church, and the same determined opposition will, undoubtedly, be made to it by the hosts of hell. And will any other stamp of salvation, or a less degree of it than that which the early Christians possessed, ever redeem the world from the dominion of Satan to Jesus Christ? Let us not forget that we live in the dispensation of the Holy Ghost, ushered in by the day of Pentecost. The power then felt and retained for centuries by the Church, is the power we need in this age of infidelity and spurious religion, to meet the devil with. Who can *scripturally* assert that the Holy Ghost is a less efficient agent to-day than eighteen centuries ago? Ah, follower of Jesus!—professed Pilgrim to Canaan!—the inheritance is yours, all yours. You and I may be filled with *faith* and the Holy Ghost. Glory be to God.

" Faith, mighty faith, the promise sees,
And looks to that alone,
Laughs at impossibilities,
And cries '*it shall be done*.' "

SELF EXAMINATION.

BY FLAVEL.

It will never repent you that you have prayed and mourned, that you have trembled and feared, that you have searched and tried; nay, it will never repent you, that God has tried you by thousands of sharp afflictions and deep sufferings, if after all, your sincerity may be fully cleared up to the satisfaction of your soul: for, in the same day in which your sincerity shall be cleared, your title to Christ will be made as clear to your soul as your sincerity is. You may then go to the promises boldly, and take your own Christ into the arms of your faith and say, "My Beloved is mine and I am his." Yea, you may be confident that it shall be well with you in the judgment of the great day, for "God will not cast away the upright man." If his word clears you now, it cannot condemn you then.

O, what an ease it is to the soul when the fears and doubts that hang about it are gone—when a man sees what he is, and what he has in Christ and the promises—what he has to do, even to spend the time between this and heaven in admiring the grace of God that has delivered him from the ruining mistakes and miscarriages by which so great a part of the professing world are lost to all eternity.

CHINA.—Dr. Wentworth writes, under date of April 24th, 1860: "Brother Lo Ting, while preaching in the streets of the city (Fuh Chau) was surrounded by a crowd of Chinese, who said: 'You say you are not afraid of idols; we will now take you to a temple and you shall break one of the idols to pieces, and then we shall see whether it has not power to revenge itself.' While they were hurrying him along with insults and derisive shouts, he said: 'I do not fear your idols of wood and stone, and mud, and will show you that I do not by smashing any number of them to pieces if you will give me a written agreement that I shall not be harmed by any man for so doing. *I'll risk the gods, but I dare not risk you.*' The crowd dropped off and let him go. Brother Hu Long-Mi, our first Chinese itinerant, stated that last Sunday, while in the country preaching to our little class of church members, his heart sank within him to see the multitude working in the fields, in all directions, where his message could not reach them. Soon a violent thunder shower came up and drove many of them into the house where he was preaching. He made them sit down, and for once he preached to a large congregation of them."

HYPOCRISY.—Let all that profess religion be uniform and steady in the profession and practice of it without politic reserves and by-ends. O, take heed of this Laodicean neutrality and indifferency which Christ hates. Be sure your ground be good, and then be sure you stand your ground. The religion of time-servers is but hypocrisy. They have sluices in their consciences which they can open or shut as occasion requires. Every fox will at least have two holes to his den, that if one be stopped he may escape at the other. The hypocrite poises himself so evenly in a mediocrity, that—as it was said by Baldwin, "Let Antony win, let Augustus win, all is one;" so, let Christ win, or let antichrist win, he hopes to make every wind that can blow serviceable to to waft him to the port of his own interest. The hypocrite has always more of the moon than of the sun, little light, many spots, and frequent changes. It is easier to him to bow to the cross, than to bear the cross; to sin, than to suffer.—FLAVEL.

AM I sincerely resolved to follow Christ and holiness at all seasons, however the aspects of the times may be towards religion? Or do I carry myself so warily and covertly as to shun all hazards for religion, having a secret reserve in my heart to launch out no further than I may return with safety, contrary to the practice and resolution of upright souls?

REVIVALS.

BY THE EDITOR.

BERGEN CAMP MEETING.

Five years ago when Rev. L. Stiles was Presiding Elder of Genesee District, we purchased in Bergen, Genesee Co., N. Y., twenty-five acres of land, the most of which was covered with magnificent forest trees of primeval growth, for a Camp Ground. Mr. Stiles and ourself became personally responsible for the payment thereof. By some effort, with the efficient assistance of Seth M. Woodruff and Rev. A. Hard, we succeeded, in a short time, in getting enough pledged to cancel our obligation. The most of these pledges have been met, leaving only from one to two hundred dollars yet unpaid.

The annual Camp Meetings upon this ground, have all been seasons of deep religious interest. Here thousands of fluctuating Christians have been led on into the higher grades of Christian experience, and have had their wavering minds

> "Settled and fixed
> With all the weight of love."

The meeting this year was thought by many to be the most profitable one ever held upon this ground. There were, it is estimated, at least one hundred tents, most of them of large size. We notice that from year to year, there is an increase, on the whole, in the size of the tents. Nearly every tent is a prayer tent. It is found that much more good is accomplished in this way than by setting apart a few exclusively for religious services. The tents were unusually well filled. On the Sabbath the attendance was very large. It would seem as if the whole of the densely populated country, with its thriving villages for twenty miles around, turned out *en masse*. There were probably ten thousand persons on the ground.

The preaching was in demonstration of the Spirit and in power. There was no attempt at display, no historical or philosophical essays were read, no studied declamation upon the greatness and power of the Church, but point-blank shots were sent from the stand day after day, to the hearts and consciences of the hearers. The sermon Sabbath morning from that veteran of the cross, Rev. Asa Abell, was one of the most eloquent and powerful we ever listened to. The services throughout were eminently spiritual. A good number of conversions took place, and many sought and obtained the blessings of a clean heart; and the graces of believers generally, were quickened. Eternity alone can unfold the amount of good that was done.

The best of order generally prevailed. This we have found to be almost always the case where God's Spirit has worked in power. The multitude as they came upon the ground, seemed awe-struck, listened with attention, and, at the close of the services, departed in silence. Almost the only instances of a wilful departure from becoming decorum that have come to our knowledge, have been, we are sorry to say, among those Methodist ministers, whose object in attending, seems to be to obtain material which will enable a wild imagination by misrepresentation, exaggeration, and false coloring, to so mould over and paint, as to throw contempt upon the whole proceedings. It took a fallen arch-angel to make a devil; and it takes a backslidden minister to ridicule meetings which God honors with the salvation of souls. It is with the hope of preventing, in the future, conduct disgraceful alike to the ministry and the Church that we pen these remarks.

ST. CHARLES CAMP MEETING.

From Bergen a company of seven of us went via the N. Y. Central, Lake Shore, and Mich. Southern R. R's to Chicago, on our way to attend this meeting. We had a pleasant time on the cars. We cheerfully commend this route to any of our friends at the west desirous of visiting the east, or *vice versa*. The track was in good condition, the cars convenient, and the running up to time. In all our travels we find no Rail Road that we think is quite so pleasant and safe to travel on as the New York Central. There is a double track all the way from Buffalo to Albany, and these are always kept smooth and in fine order. The cars are all that could be desired, and the conductors uniformly courteous and obliging. Such is the skillful management of this road, that accidents are of rare occurrence.

We found the Camp Meeting located about

a mile from Wayne Station on the Galena road, thirty-five miles west of Chicago. It was held in a fine grove, owned by brother James Laughlan, who not only generously gave the use of the ground, but kindly entertained us, and a host besides. There was about thirty tents upon the ground — the largest number several informed us, that they had seen of late years at a Western Camp Meeting. As we came upon the ground, we plainly perceived that God was among the people. At once we felt at home. Strangers are brought nigh by the blood of Christ. Dr. Redfield, whose labors for the promotion of holiness have been greatly blessed in Northern Illinois, had charge of the meeting. He was assisted by as promising a body of young ministers as we ever saw together— men of grace, gifts, and physical vigor, who will yet leave their mark for good upon the world. Here, as at Bergen, God carried on his work in power. The people were in earnest, and they were blessed accordingly. Many entered into the rest of perfect love. Perhaps as much good was accomplished as at any Camp meeting we ever attended. At different times there were marked displays of the Divine presence. One evening in particular, the power of God rested upon the congregation in awful grandeur. Conviction was general, and the altar was filled with weeping penitents, agonizing in prayer for deliverance from sin. Some of the most interesting cases of conversion occurred, that we ever witnessed. Two young men who came upon the ground to sell liquor were arrested by the Spirit of God. Loud and earnest were their cries for mercy. Soon, he who delights to save the chief of sinners, came to their relief, spoke peace to their souls, and made them unspeakably happy in the assurance of sins forgiven.

One young man, converted on the evening when the power of God came down in such a wonderful manner, was indeed a miracle of saving grace. In relating his experience he said in effect, as nearly as we can recollect— "My mother was a pious woman. She often prayed for me, but I became very wicked. I wandered far from God. Last year I joined a company that went to Battle Hill in Canada, to dig for enchanted gold. The gold, it is said was buried with magic rites in the revolutionary war. To get it we were told that we must burn the Bible, and sell ourselves body and soul to the devil. I consented. I went to a sister's and a borrowed a Bible and stood by and saw it burned. I have been upon the very verge of hell. But O, the infinite mercy of God. He has had pity upon me, and pardoned my sins." His narrative was interrupted by floods of tears. No one who listened could doubt the genuineness of his conversion, or sufficiently adore that grace which had snatched him as a brand from hell.

LETTER FROM DR. BOWEN.

The following letter from that veteran of the cross, Dr. BOWEN, we lay before our readers *with his consent.* If all our aged ministers, who mourn over the worldly Spirit that claims control of the church, would thus boldly speak out, the best results would follow. God bless those who are "valiant for the truth!"

Dear Brother ROBERTS:—I have not forgotten the very kind and respectful invitation you gave me, soon after the "*Earnest Christian*" started its eventful career, to become a contributor to its columns; and though I have not found time to do it, on account of an unusual press of other matters, hitherto, yet, as I am beginning to be a little relieved about these days, I shall soon, I trust, be able to send you something.

If there ever was a time when there was occasion for the friends of "Christianity in earnest," to rally around that only evangelical and saving form of religion, and plead its waning cause, we have unhappily fallen upon that period. "How has the gold become dim, and the most fine gold changed." "Yea, truth faileth; and he that departeth from evil maketh himself a prey." I am glad, Brother ROBERTS, that God has thrust you out into this field: not that there was any occasion for it, or that some of your brethren should have been the guilty instruments of bringing it about; but that you have been led, in the order of Providence, to improve the occasion which has arisen to proclaim an earnest Christianity to the people.

I like the "*Earnest Christian.*" I like it much. It is the very thing for the times. Its matter and manner, its spirit and style, its character and course, so congenial with its object and title, must open its way into a wide circle of inquiring readers, and render it an efficient instrumentality in advancing the cause of holiness. Its adaptation to meet an important demand of the times in which we live—times when the manifestations and spirit of religion are being restricted to mere forms, and even these tied down to the Procrustean bedstead of "Church order," could scarcely be exceeded. We are fast approximating a state of things, in which the prevalence of clerical pride and profligacy and forgetfulness of God, must call for another Wesleyan revival. And who, or what is to be the instrument of inaugurating and carrying forward such a work? Officialism will never do it. There is nothing in its boasted "law and order, its famous conferences and councils, its mighty self-magnified, wonder-working prestige, that can bring us back to our primitive simplicity and purity of life. We must have a live man, and a pure press, to lead the van; "and who knoweth whether thou art come to the throne" of obloquy and martyrdom—"for such a time as this?" There must be a breaking away from forms and authorities—a plunging into the simplicity and spirit of the pure Gospel—however "irregular," or "contumacious" it may appear, and a relying on God alone for the accomplishment of the great ends and purposes of the Christian ministry. An unshackled ministry, and a press independent, must be put in requisition, even in defiance of "the powers that be," if necessary, or Popery will take the world.

Affectionately Yours,
ELIAS BOWEN.

CALL FOR HELP.

THE following letter, coming from a distant place and from an entire stranger, we give to our readers. It will encourage earnest Christians to learn how the Spirit is moving upon honest hearts in different sections of the country. We have made arrangements for a preacher to go to the place referred to, and we shall expect soon to hear of a gracious revival of God's work there.

REV. B. T. ROBERTS:

Dear Brother in Christ:—Though an entire stranger to you, I have been led to address you by letter. I saw in the *Independent* an account of your trial and expulsion from the Methodist Episcopal Church, which most deeply interested me, while it excited my feelings of sympathy in your behalf. At this you will not be surprised, when I make known the fact that not many months previous I had been silenced by the Minister in meeting, (a meeting for prayer and speaking,) for speaking as the Spirit gave me utterance. I was urging holiness upon God's people who were carnal, and who I knew were hedging up the way of a revival. This being the second time I had been silenced, I was led to unite, with one other who was one in spirit with me, in holding meetings where we could be free. From that period to the present, we have kept up our meetings, and in all weathers, have met three times each week, the Lord meeting with us in power. We are still members of the Methodist Episcopal Church, but we have *come out* from her sins, and no doubt would be expelled if we should speak as formerly in the Church. I have been charged with breaking up revivals even, by my prayers; so I thought the path of duty led me to pray where such charges could not be made. Last winter I saw in the North-Western *Christian Advocate* an account of a Minister holding meetings in St. Charles, Illinois, and heard, through the *Earnest Christian*, further particulars concerning this meeting, which set me on fire, and made me thank God and take courage. I involuntarily exclaimed, after reading the article in the *Advocate*, "These are my people—I am one of them." And, by further reading of your excellent paper, I am confirmed in what I then believed. But, to be brief, I will say that about two months since, this sister and I engaged a house to hold our meetings in, having previously held them at our own houses alternately. The school house, at which we now hold our meetings, is in the centre of the town, and on Main street. There we meet and pray, and there talk as directed by the Holy Spirit. Our meetings are well attended, and the number is increasing at each succeeding meeting. And I am now assured that if one of your Ministers were to come to this place and hold a meeting, there would be a most glorious revival of religion. The people are *hungry* for the *truth*—yes, *starving* for it—many of them so much so as to listen with manifest interest even to a weak and stammering woman. The meetings are so largely attended, and there is such apparent eagerness to hear that I feel bewildered with the responsibility; yes, overburdened—and I write to you for help. Could you not send us a Minister? If you know of one who could make the sacrifice of coming to this place, and you would direct him to come, I will say his reward will be sure, both temporal and spiritual. The Church here is dead, as a body, spiritually, and seems likely to remain so. The smooth sermons that are preached are evidently hardening the people, and unless sinners all around are reached through some other instrumentality, they will remain unsaved. I regard the people called Nazarites as reformers of the genuine stamp, and believing so, as I have for years past, that a reformation is needed in all the Churches, I am anxious to have one visit this community and labor. In writing to you, I am not insensible to the fact that it could scarcely be expected that you should, upon the suggestion of an entire stranger, take the responsibility of sending a Minister to this place. But with all the probabilities against your doing so, I thought I would make the effort, and I would be clear. I have been a traveler in the King's Highway for the last seven years, and feel experimentally the power of Jesus' blood to cleanse from all sin. Believing you to be spiritually minded, and consequently in a special sense led by the Spirit, I have an unwavering confidence that in the matter under consideration you will be led right, and if no Minister comes, I shall think it is all right, believing that the Lord will show you your duty. I praise my Redeemer that He condescends to teach me and make known His will to me in all matters with which I have any concern, and so He does to all who follow Him and who walk in the light. Pray about this, my brother, and all will be right. I feel that I am a sheep without a shepherd, and there are many such these perilous times. Please write me a letter; I shall be so thankful to you for any instruction or advice.

Sincerely yours, in the bonds of Christian love. E. E. B.

FREE METHODIST CHURCH IN BUFFALO.

BUT few are aware of the religious destitution that prevails in our cities. The prevailing rage for splendid Churches, with the pews rented or sold, has the effect of driving the masses from the House of God altogether.

The Buffalo *Christian Advocate* said in 1855, and things have not materially changed for the better since, "We have in Buffalo about forty Protestant Churches. These reach, and influence more or less, about twenty thousand of our eighty thousand people. This leaves sixty thousand either unprovided for, or to Catholic influence. It may be safe to calculate that forty thousand of our inhabitants attend no place of worship whatever." * * *
"Thousands do not attend any of our Protestant Churches, for the simple reason that no sittings are designated for them. Our sanctuaries are built for the few, and not for the many. Pews rented and sold ever alienate the masses from the place of worship." Just think of this! FORTY THOUSAND of the inhabitants of Buffalo who '*attend no place of worship whatever!*'" One great cause is *the want of* FREE CHRCHES. Thus, while we are making a great ado about the conversion of the heathen abroad, it would seem that they are growing up by the thousand under the very shadow of our magnificent, tall - steepled, aristocratic Churches! "Sittings may be designated" in a pewed Church for those who have not the inclination or ability to pay for one, but who is willing, by occupying them, to advertise, from Sabbath to Sabbath, his poverty or indifference?

In reference to the spiritual condition of the Churches, the same paper said, in March, 1859, in an article headed "Religious Interest in Buffalo: "We have none; we have no more than is usual through the year. We do not intend to convey the idea, by the above heading that there is any special movement among us, or that there are any very marked efforts towards getting souls converted, or keeping those converted who are already in the Church. The great movement among us, is, we judge, to determine how far the Church can go back to the world, and save its semblance to piety, devotion and truth. Hence, many, many Church members have become the most frivolous and pleasure-loving, and folly-taking part of our town's-people. They love, give and sustain the most popular worldly amusements, such as dancing parties, card parties, drinking parties, masquerade and surprise parties, and have no disposition to come out from the world, and to be separate from it. All this may be seen, read and known in more or less of the Buffalo Churches."

This is the testimony of an eye-witness. Mr. ROBIE has, for a long time, been a resident of Buffalo, and, at the time of writing the above, he was a local preacher, belonging to one of the city Churches This is not the testimony of an old-fashioned Methodist, who might be regarded as prejudiced—but of a friend of the prevailing order of things—one who was never suspected of being tainted with "Nazariteism."

We send missionaries to Italy and to Turkey. Why? Have they not the gospel? Yes, Have they no Christian Churches? They have Churches planted by the Apostles, illustrated by the virtues and enriched by the blood of martyrs. Have they no ministers? They have a ministry, educated for their office—claiming their authority by unbroken lineal descent from Peter, and Paul, and James. Why, then, do we, at great expense, send missionaries there to stir up strife, and awaken persecution? The reply is, that 'their religion is a mere form, insufficient to save the soul.' And what better, according to Mr. ROBIE, is the Protestant religion of Buffalo?

1. *No very marked efforts towards* GETTING SOULS CONVERTED.

2. *Nor to keep* SOULS CONVERTED.

3. *" The great movement* is to determine how far the Church can go back to the world and save its SEMBLANCE to piety, devotion and truth." Real piety not at all cared for—its *semblance* only is sought.

4. " Many of the Church members have become the most frivolous and pleasure-loving part of our town's-people."

5. "They give and sustain dancing parties, card parties, drinking parties, masquerade and surprise parties, and have no disposition to come out from the world."

Now, we ask, in all candor, are not the devotees of the Greek and Roman Churches quite as likely to gain Heaven as such Protestants?

Is not a Free Church needed in this city, not only to reach some of the " forty thousand who attend no place of worship whatever," but to elevate the standard of piety among the Churches, and to provoke them to love and good works?

Our labors in the Church on Thirteenth street, kindly furnished us by Mr. JESSE KETCHUM, have been greatly blessed. Some sixty or more, we judge, have been converted the past year—more, we heard it stated by a member of the Young Men's Christian Union, than in all the other Churches in the city, in the same time. The work is still going on. Conversions are frequently occurring. Last Sunday evening some six adults were forward seeking religion, and three of these were very clearly converted. We expect to keep up the meetings on Thirteenth Street, and to drive the battle on there more vigorously than ever. But this Church is located in the suburbs—some two miles from the heart of the city. We also need a location more central.

In accordance with what we believe to be the will of God, we have purchased a brick building suitable for a Church. It was formerly used for a theatre. It costs us thirty-five hundred dollars, and about five hundred dollars will be needed to put it in a proper condition. Towards it we have turned in our house and lot in Buffalo, valued at fifteen hundred dollars, leaving us for the present homeless. We shall give the whole of this, cheerfully, if needed. For the balance, we depend upon the liberality of the friends of Jesus. About five hundred dollars was paid or pledged at the Bergen Camp-Meeting. One sister gave a gold watch chain, and another a gold watch. Two thousand dollars are still unprovided for. We can depend upon but little in Buffalo, as our friends there are poor. If any of the readers of the *Earnest Christian* feel that it would be pleasing to God, we should be glad to have them send on their contributions for this purpose. Any sum from one dollar to a hundred, will be thankfully received. Can you devote your missionary money to a better object? For whatever you give in this direction you may expect a speedy return in a rich harvest of souls. We trust that those who have given us pledges, will send on their moneys as soon as possible, as we have been obliged to borrow to make the payments, and we need still more to pay for seats and repairs. Brothers, sisters, on your knees please ask the question. "Lord, what wilt Thou have me to do?"

NOTICE FOR CAMP MEETING AND CONVENTION.

A Camp Meeting will be held at Pekin, Niagara county, N. Y., twenty miles north of

Buffalo, about forty rods from the depot, to commence on Thursday, 16th of August. A convention will be held at Pekin, for the purpose of adopting a Discipline for the Free Methodist Church, to commence at the close of the Camp Meeting, Aug. 23d. All societies and bands that find it necessary, in order to promote the prosperity and permanency of the work of holiness, to organize a Free Church on the following basis, are invited to send delegates:

1. Doctrines and usages of primitive Methodism, such as the Witness of the Spirit, Entire Sanctification as a state of grace distinct from justification, attainable instantaneously by faith. Free seats, and congregational singing, without instrumental music in all cases; plainness of dress.

2. An equal representation of ministers and members in all the councils of the Church.

3. No slaveholding, and no connection with secret oath bound societies.

Each society or band will be entitled to send one delegate at least; and an additional one for every forty members. The committee appointed by the convention at Bergen, will meet at Albion, the 15th of Aug. at 9 o'clock A. M.

WESTERN LAYMEN'S CONVENTION.

This was held in Wayne, Du Page County, Illinois, July 2d, 1860. It was well attended, and its action was harmonious, interesting and important. Substantially the same ground of complaints exists as at the East. Old and reliable members, of undoubted piety, who have done as much or more than any others for the prosperity of the Church, have been expelled on frivolous pretexts, or read out as "withdrawn," without their consent. The real difficulty is, they are simply old-fashioned Methodists, who cannot in conscience give their support to the peaceable reign of formalism and worldly policy in their respective Churches.

The following resolution was unanimously adopted:

Resolved, "That our attachment to the doctrines, usages, spirit and discipline of Methodism is hearty and sincere. It is with the most profound grief that we have witnessed the departure of many of the Ministers, from the God-honored usages of Methodism. We feel bound to adhere to them, and to labor all we can, and to the best possible advantage, to promote the life and power of godliness. We recommend that those in sympathy with the doctrine of holiness, as taught by WESLEY, should labor in harmony with the respective Churches to which they belong; but where this cannot be done—where they cannot do their duty without continual strife and contention, we recommend the formation of Free Methodist Churches, as contemplated by the late Convention held in the Genesee Conference in the State of New York."

Some eighteen preachers — most of them young men of promise — were authorized by the Convention to go out under its auspices and labor for the salvation of souls.

It was decided to hold a Camp-Meeting at Wayne, on the same ground on which it was held this year, to commence on Wednesday, the 12th of June, 1861. They also concluded to hold one this fall, the time and place to be hereafter designated. We expect to see great results from this Convention.

After the Camp-Meeting, we held meetings at St. Charles, Clintonville, Kishwaukee, Franklinville, Marengo, Bonus, Woodstock and Queen Ann. In each of these places we found large and attentive congregations, and living Christians, in earnest to save themselves and others. God has begun a glorious work in Northern Illinois. The country is one of the finest we ever saw. May a revival of pure religion sweep like fire all over these splendid prairies!

OUR SELECTIONS.

In each number we give short articles, taken from old standard authors of different denominations. These extracts cost us, generally, quite as much, and often more labor than would be required to furnish original articles. But we think it better to let these old divines speak, than it would be to say the same things ourselves, even if we were capable of saying them as well. They show very plainly, that the self-denying religion we are endeavoring to inculcate is no new thing. We are glad to see that many of these articles find their way in the Church papers. We hope they will do good. In a single paper edited by a regular conference minister, we noticed some six articles taken from our pages. We tender our thanks for even this indirect acknowledgment of the merits of the *Earnest Christian.*

THE EARNEST CHRISTIAN.

SANCTIFICATION NOT IDENTICAL WITH REGENERATION.

BY E. BOWEN, D. D.

Dear Brother Roberts:

We still hail the arrival of your excellent monthly, "*The Earnest Christian*," with feelings of the liveliest interest. The exhibition and advocacy of Christianity in earnest, or of pure Wesleyan Methodism, to which it is pledged and devoted by the very title it bears, have strikingly characterized its course thus far, in every successive number. We are highly gratified to observe in it both the spirit and the teachings of our sainted founder. Especially are we pleased with this complexion of it at a time when worldliness and formalism are becoming so prevalent in the Church, and our distinguishing characteristics — the element of "Scripture holiness,"—is fast falling into disrepute among us.

There was a time when "holiness to the Lord," was the motto of our Church. The pulpit, the social gathering, and the private circle, dwelt upon it as a most delightful theme; and many among us, both preachers and people, enjoyed the precious attainment of full salvation. Such was emphatically the case in our own Conference a few years ago. Hamlin, of precious memory, said to me the last time he visited us, that we were the banner Conference with regard to this subject.

But O, alas! "Our silver has become dross, and our wine mixed with water." Few are now the witnesses of perfect love, particularly among the ministry; and many actually oppose, nay, ridicule it, as a matter of fanaticism and delusion. And this they do, partly "because they know not the Scriptures, neither the power of God," and partly to keep themselves in countenance in their stand-stillism, or rather in their retrogressive movements. Shade of Wesley! And has it come to this? Must thou look down upon thy own children and see them trample upon the doctrine of holiness as taught by thee, with the clearest illustration of it in thy long life before their eyes; and the voluminous published works in which thou hast established it by the Scriptures, in their hands? And that too within less than three-quarters of a century after thy death? And must thou see them do all this while they still continue to call themselves by thy name, and boast thee as their founder and pattern?

True, our standards of religion, both doctrinal and experimental, remain unchanged. And an intimation of a departure from these old land-marks was somewhat obscurely given by the Bishops, in their quadrennial address at the last general Conference. But no further notice was taken of it. The whole matter was passed over as a thing of no consequence. We were not even "advised," to "return to our first love," or "go on to perfection," in fulfillment of our ordination vows. How strange! How discouraging to the friends of "Old-fashioned Methodism!" And what are we to infer from all this? In our opinion, the failure of the General Conference to rebuke the innovation alluded to in the address of the Episcopacy, virtually inaugurates the old Moravian heresy of the identity of entire sanctification with the new birth, as an article of our creed; and that henceforth little is to be expected, either from our preachers, or our press, in support of the genuine Wesleyan perfection. We must now look, we cannot help thinking, for real experimental holiness, nay, for the life and power of religion generally, to be scouted among us as mere animal excitement, or wild enthusiasm, in the manner of the famous Genesee Conference "Pastoral," of which you so justly complained.

But we will not "give up the ship," for holiness—the life and soul of our holy religion—is immortal, and destined to exist forever. "Many waters cannot drown it, nor the fires" (of persecution) "consume it." It is a living, quenchless flame, which God himself has kindled in the Church. And we greatly rejoice, since so little can be hoped for from our worldly-minded officialism in "spreading Scripture holiness over the land," or "driving away the strange doctrine" of the identity of sanctification with regeneration which has infested our borders for a while past—we greatly rejoice, we say, in this view of the state of things among us—that "*The Earnest Christian*" is in the field, "doing battle for the Lord," and nobly laboring, in connection with a few coadjutors in the same work, to promote the blessed cause of a living Christianity, and bring back a declining Church to her primitive purity and power, This "new school Methodism," as you rightly named it, must be put down; or the life of the Church will soon become extinct, and "Ichabod will be written upon our door-posts!" We do not draw this gloomy picture of the Church because we have any pleasure in contemplating her spiritual decline, or feel the least degree of satisfaction in spreading her pitiable condition before the world. Far from it. "Our heart's desire, and prayer to God for Israel is, that they might be saved" from their sins, and from the calamities that await them on their account. And to aid in effecting this most worthy object, we propose in the few brief paragraphs that shall follow, to exhibit the fallacy of the arguments by which it is attempted to sustain the Count Zinzendorf notion of Christian perfection that she is so greedily drinking in, and to indicate the irrefragable grounds on which the orthodox or Wesleyan view of the subject must forever rest.

For the enemies of holiness to deny the doctrine, *in terms*, would be impolitic. All Christian denominations hold it in some form. They are aware a far more deadly wound can be given it by confounding it with regeneration, or the new birth. Whether they are aware of it or not, Satan, their great prompter in this matter, knows that by arresting the work of grace at the point of conversion, many will be utterly destroyed. Some, by discovering in themselves "the remains of the carnal mind," which they had been taught to believe were wholly extirpated by the new birth, will be led to give up their hope altogether; supposing that they could not have been converted at all: while others will lose their justification, and sink into a backslidden state by failing to "go on to perfection," in obedience to the divine command, or to seek an attainment which they imagine they already possess.

Among the arguments by which the "new school" divines attempt to sustain their Moravian theology, those dawn from the analogy of regeneration to the natural birth of a child, the perfection of the works of God, and their own negative experience, are the chief. A brief examination of these, therefore, will furnish no unfair specimen of the weakness of their cause.

The arguments drawn from the analogy of regeneration to a natural birth, they deem conclusive; lugging it in on all occasions, and proclaiming it as decisive of the question in dispute.

The idea is, that "the possession of a perfect human nature by the new-born child—the full-grown man differing from the infant only in the degree of the developement of his parts and powers—proves the possession of a perfect Christian nature by the young convert—the mature, or perfect Christian, differing from "the babe in Christ," only in the developement of his Christian graces. In a word, that nothing but growth, developement, expansion, is necessary to constitute the young convert a perfect Christian; the same as an "infant of days," a full grown man. But this argument loses all its force when viewed in the light of the following considerations:—

1st. Analogy proves nothing any way. It only serves to illustrate some assumed fact, proposition, or sentiment, and render it more obvious and intelligible to the understanding. 2. It is never intended to bear at all points, or to go on all fours, as the expression is; but simply to aid us in the discovery, or presentation of truth, by some particular resemblance which one thing bears to another—a thing that is well understood, to one that is obscure and difficult of comprehension. 3. Though the analogy of the birth of a child to the conversion of a soul, be drawn out or extended to every conceivable point of resemblance, (which, by the by, no rules of interpretation or construction would justify,) still, a *distinction* between regeneration and sanctification, rather than their identity with each other, would be established by the process; for there is something to be removed from the natural child after it is born into the world—something that pertains to its pre-existent or unborn condition—and that something, let it be remembered, unclean, and fatal to the life of the child except it be taken away, is analogous to "the remains of the carnal mind" in the new born soul.

The argument drawn from the perfection of the works of God, is equally groundless and futile. This argument runs thus—" What God does, he does to perfection—not at the halves, but to perfection, i. e. completely; finishing it all up at once. Consequently, we are saved from all sin, and constituted perfect Christians by the work of regeneration, or the new birth. Now, we have no difficulty in admitting the fact of the perfection of the works of God; but we deny the conclusion drawn from it. The perfection of the works of God is one thing; the process by which they are carried on, distinctly another. The work of God in the creation of the world, was perfect; but he did not do it all at once. He was six long days about it—doing it, so to speak, at the halves or piecemeal. So, time is required, in the divine economy, perhaps days merely, it may be weeks, or months, to consummate the work of entire sanctification. Yet, there is perfection, both in the work, and in the manner of its accomplishment. The perfection of the works of God does not depend upon the manner in which they are wrought; whether it be instantaneous or gradual, at once or at successive periods, in a single whole, or in various additional parts or parcels; only so that the method employed be adapted to secure the proposed end.

The only remaining argument of our new divinity teachers, for the identity of entire holiness with the work of regeneration, which we propose to examine in this article, lies in their own negative experience, and is easily disposed of. They tell us that "the great second blessing" we talk of, or the being cleansed from "the remains of the carnal mind," subsequently to "a change of heart," is something they have never experienced, and therefore it cannot be true. But this argument, if argument it may be called, is almost too trifling to be entitled to notice. If it prove anything, it proves too much. "The world that lieth in wickedness," has never experienced religion at all. And does this prove that there is no religon? How then does the non-experience of the second blessing, as we call it, prove that there is no such blessing attainable? That many among us, perhaps all who maintain the heresy we are opposing here, have never experienced the witness of perfect love, is too true, we fear; and lamentable as true. Yet, their negative experience of this attainment, invalidates neither its authority, nor its importance. It still remains a doctrine of the holy Scriptures, a prominent feature of our beloved Methodism, and an indispensable acquisition to the candidate for heaven. A fair specimen of the character and use of the argument founded on negative experience, may be seen in the following anecdote: "A Paddy, being accused of a criminal act, and told that half-a-dozen witnesses saw him do it, replied, by way of vindicating himself from the charge, "Indade, and I can bring twice that number who didn't see me do it."

It only remains to indicate the grounds of the doctrine of a clear and important distinction between the two states of grace, denominated sanctification and regeneration. We shall not enlarge here, however, but simply refer the reader to the Holy Scriptures and the standard authorities of the Church, Wesley in particular, with but a very few accompanying remarks.

If believers are wholly sanctified at the time, and by the process of regeneration, what mean the following *precepts*, with many others of the same kind, addressed to them in the word of God? "Let us go on unto perfection"—"Let us cleanse ourselves from all filthiness of the flesh and spirit, perfecting holiness in the fear of God."

What mean such *promises* as the following: "I will sprinkle clean water upon you, and ye shall be clean; from all your idols, and from all your filthiness will I cleanse you." "His name shall be called Jesus, for he shall save his people from their sins." And why those *prayers* offered by, and for believers, for the blessing of full salvation? "Create in me a clean heart, O God, and renew a right spirit within me." "The very God of peace sanctify you wholly; and I pray God your whole spirit and soul, and body, be preserved blameless to the coming of our Lord Jesus Christ." "Sanctify them through thy truth; thy word is truth." Would the inspired penmen employ precepts, and promises, and prayers in reference to a work of grace which had been superceded by a previous work upon the heart—a work already accomplished in the believer?

That our standard authors teach the doctrine of a distinction between sanctification and regeneration, no one, we believe, is prepared to deny. They are all unanimously agreed upon the subject; and some of them are very full and explicit. See Wesley's "Plain Account"—his sermon on "Sin in believers"—also one on "Let us go unto perfection," with here and there a narrative, a comment, a biographical sketch or allusion scattered all through his "Works," in which he has presented the subject in all its various bearings—doctrinal, experimental, and practical—as one of vital importance to the interests of religion.

The cavil that Wesley was not infallible, and therefore we are not bound to follow him in this matter, does very little credit either to the head or the heart of its author. The *Scriptures* are infallible, and until we can overthrow his interpretation of these in the premises, let us be manly enough to forbear to attempt to hide our love of sin under his fallibility. It will be time enough to reject the doctrine he so ably advocates and proves, when we shall have given a better interpretation of Holy Writ upon the question at issue, and sustained it by better arguments.

We shall only add, that this blessed Scripture doctrine of the verity and importance of the great " second blessing," so called, is corroborated by actual experience. " A cloud of witnesses"—of living, intelligent, competent " witnesses"—have testified their own happy experience of the blessing; and what is all the negative experience in the universe compared to this? They have borne witness to this delightful state of grace through a long succession of years, some of them—they have done it in prosperity and in adversity, in sickness and in health, living and dying—and there is no law, authority, or power, in heaven, earth or hell, that can impeach their testimony.

PRESUMPTION.

BY J. G. TERRILL.

Definition: Unreasonable confidence. Webster.

It is not presumption to venture as far as the word of God will allow; it *is* presumption to refuse to go as far as the word of God says we must. Jesus says, "Whatsoever things ye desire when ye pray, believe that ye receive them, and ye shall have them." John says, "And this is the confidence that we have in him, that if we ask any thing according to his will, he heareth us; and if we know that he hear us, whatsoever we ask, we know that we have the petitions that we desired of him." Charles Wesley sang:

"If what I wish is good,
And suits the will divine,
By earth and hell in vain withstood,
I know it shall be mine.
Here then I doubt no more,
But in his pleasure rest;
Whose wisdom, love, and truth and power,
Engage to make me blest."

When in seeking for any blessing at the hand of God, the suppliant having performed the conditions, it is *not* presumption for him to take the words of Jesus, and say I receive it now, "through the blood of the Lamb."

It *is* presumption for that one to come into the presence of God with a known idol in his heart, that he is unwilling to give up. "If I regard iniquity in my heart the Lord will not hear me." It is *not* presumption to cry, "Create in me a clean heart," but it *is* presumption of the most fearful kind to neglect seeking for it, when we know God's will. It is *not* presumption to say "I'll stay here till I get it," but it is presumption to wilfully go one moment without it. God says, "Now," and we please him when we say "Now." I once saw a man, a minister of the Gospel, at the altar, seeking for the blessing of Holiness. We staid with him until two o'clock in the morning; he would *not* say, "I'll stay till I get it." Afterwards, he put it three months ahead; nine have passed, and he can not claim it.

It is *not* presumption to "go straight for God," and leave consequences with him. It *is* presumption to run as near to God as we think it will do, and not discommode the devil, and then "let God take care of his own cause."

It is not presumption to offer "to be a wedge for Jesus," to dare to go in and throw down the fence that has been the seat of "*trimmers between the two*" for years, but it is presumption to dare to pass them by, calling "it a light thing," and not warn them of their danger.

It is *not* presumption to dare to meet the scorn, the contempt of the worldling, the hatred of the disturbed, but half awakened Pharisee, the jealousy of the cold-hearted; but it *is* presumption to *dare* to falter for a moment on account of them.

It is not presumption for the minister of the Gospel to say, "Lord I'll lean on thee," but it *is* presumption to undertake to handle the edge-tools of God without his help.

It is not presumption for that young preacher to throw himself into the hands of the Lord, and "lay like clay in the hands of the potter;" but it is presumption for him, after God has given him a mind, a Bible, and a Holy Ghost to "lead him into all truth," to idle away his time by lounging around until the hour of his appointment comes, and then think of leaning on the Lord. *You will get hurt.*

It is *not* presumption for the children of God, in time of vengeance from the hand of the Lord to throw themselves like a Moses *into the gap*, but it is presumption in time of refreshing from the hand of God, for any one to make light of the work, or of those engaged in it, or to get in the way by bad counsel or opposition. May God help us. Amen.

ONE IN JESUS.

BY MRS. M. F. KENDALL.

The last prayer of Jesus before he entered the garden of Gethsemane to drink the bitter cup of a *world's* transgressions, was for those whom the Father had given him. And he adds, "Neither pray I for these alone, but for them also which shall believe on me through their word; that they all may be one; as thou, Father, art in me, and I in thee, that they also may be one in us; that the world may believe that thou hast sent me." "I in them, and thou in me, that they may be made perfect in one."

O! what *infinity* of *love* is breathed through this whole prayer! A fit climax to the gospel scheme, whose crowning beauty must fill every mind with the most exalted conceptions of God's love to man. What *could* be done *more* for us—made one with each other, and then with the Redeemer, our blessed Saviour, the Almighty Father! And as if this perfection of all love, was the last effort of Divinity to entrance, and save an unbelieving world, he adds yet again—"that the world may know that thou hast sent me, and hast loved them as thou hast loved me." What inimitable condescending *love!*

This plain, simple test—"perfect in one," was, and is ever to be, then, the sure mark of the disciples of Jesus, *by which* the world may judge of the reality of their professed faith. And now in a matter so important, so all-absorbing to those who are intent on eternal life, let us carefully and honestly enquire.

In what are we to "be one?" Is it to be one in theory in our doctrinal views of God's word? If so, but a tithe of the professed Christian world, ever were or will be members of the great family of Christ. All history and experience contradict this, for we have the record of a multitude of those who lived and died in Jesus, belonging to different branches of the Church. Is it then, to be united merely in our efforts to save others lost in sin? No, this is not it, for even among those who can agree in their theology, there is discord here. And taking the whole Church, in no one thing is there greater diversity of feeling than in this.

Is it to be so united that the worldly goods of all are held in common? Let the results of the many associations among Christians professedly established for this end, answer the question. There have been many "mutual aid" societies, but who ever heard of them as a *fruit* of being *one in Jesus.* They were never cemented together by love to God, as in the old Apostolic Church, nor did they ever prove to the world, that their members were "perfect in one." The record of their effects upon Christians, and upon the world, tells us that they were ever a most fruitful source of hatred, envy, and discord.

Ah! the secret of being "one," lies not in any one or all of them. It is a power that no human wisdom can counterfeit. Men may embrace theories that are perfect, and may make their views of truth harmonize, while their hearts are as opposite as the poles, and full of hatred. They may band together in great numbers to secure union of effort in carrying out their plans for making disciples to their faith, but pride or self-love is the main-spring of their zeal, and the world only beholds a *semblance* of union. They may form societies and raise funds for mutual benefit, but experience proves that here the only bond of "brotherhood" is a love that requires some *dowry* to render the object worthy of being loved or relieved.

Through all these we make a fruitless search for the element which Jesus infused into the hearts of those who left all to follow him. These were to be one as the Father and the Son were one—"as thou Father, art in me, and I in thee"—so "I in them." This unfolds the whole mystery: *Jesus in us.* When the Son of God is revealed in our hearts we cannot *but be one.* Does one ask here, how then are we to know he is in us? We answer by the fruit we bear, as well as "by the Spirit which he had given us."

And now then as we have ascertained where this perfection of union does *not exist,* let us find if we can, where it *does.* Who are one in Jesus? If we are *in Jesus* and he in us, our hearts will unite in love for each other, and for sinners. So that whatever doctrines we hold, founded on God's word, or whatever are our notions of the best means of saving souls, love for the perishing, swallows up every minor consideration, and we have no room for controversy. United in Jesus, no self reigns to the exclusion of our brother, in gratifying our wants. We love to share what we have with those who have not. The end of our ambition is not to secure position or enjoyment, or a name, but to further the cause of God in the earth. To do this, we can give a farm as soon as a shilling, when we are convinced God demands it. We live not unto ourselves, but unto God. When we thus become one, we put forth as much effort to save the poor as the rich—we love the bond as well as the free—we will sacrifice as much to save outcasts, reckless in sin, as to save genteel sinness. We that are *truly one* love those most who bear most of the *image of Jesus*—we do not love becuuse we are loved alone, but because we see that which is to be loved. And this in no wise excludes that love for souls which will lead us even to peril our lives for their salvation. We can possess and exercise both, in obedience to that law of the divine mind which necessarily loves best that which bears most of its own likeness. We are one in Jesus who love to bear spiritual burdens for each other, and for the work of God. We love to weep with those who weep and rejoice with those that rejoice—their griefs are ours, their joys are ours, and we watch over each other in love, jealous only lest we grieve the Holy Spirit, and offend God. We live to build each other up in Christ, and we rejoice in proportion as we see the impress of the Master in each other. No jealousy lest one become more a favorite than ourselves. "In honor, preferring one another."

We cannot receive honor one of another—we know no titles of distinction, but those God has made. We remember that the nobility of heaven, are the weak "chosen" to confound the things that are mighty, and things which are not to bring to nought the things that are."

How many of us who profess to be pilgrims to Mount Zion, bear these marks of the love which is in Christ Jesus? We fear the siftings of reproach and persecution will leave but a handful, who can be measured by the standard which Jesus himself raised. How many are there who are willing to be counted as the filth and off-scouring of all things—who glory in tribulations—who have gladly suffered the *loss of all things* for Jesus' sake—who are ready for stripes and imprisonment—yea, who count not their lives dear unto themselves, so they may finish their course with joy? There *are* those in *these* days, bless God! who can answer these questions, and answer them right. All these things the Holy Ghost witnesseth they are able to do, and some of them they *have done,* Glory to God in the highest! And as Jesus said, "The world hath hated them because they are not of this world." They are accused of causing strife and divisions—of dividing families and neighborhoods—of rending Churches and Conferences—of casting out devils by Belzebub, the prince of the devils. But while they have, in all these things, been learning how to sympathise with Jesus, in the dreadful load he bore, they have had the presence of the promised Comforter to sustain them. Jesus says of them, "I am glorified in them." "And the glory which thou gavest me I have given them, that they may be one, even as we are one!" They have tasted of this glory even here, and found it bearing the soul far beyond the reach of their foes. They *love* their enemies. From the depths of their souls they can say, "Father forgive them, they know not what they do." There is love that none but God can bestow. And then to seal this glorious union with each other and with Christ, we have the promise that we shall be with him, where he is, that we may behold the glory given him of the Father. Blessed union, begun on earth—to know no barrier but sin to its everlasting growth and perfection! Exhaustless love!

> This is the grace must live and sing
> When faith and hope shall cease,
> And sound from every joyful string
> Through all the realms of bliss.

TRUSTING IN JESUS.

BY ALFRED SULLY.

Trusting in a Saviour's blood—
  O, my Father, here I pray,
Plunge me in the healing flood,
  Cleanse and wash my sins away;
Make, O make me pure and white
  In that fount that gushed for me,
Fit to be an angel bright,
  And to dwell above with thee.

Trusting in a Saviour's love—
  Father, now I come to thee,
Send to me the heav'nly dove,
  Set me from earth's trammels free;
Cleanse my heart and make me pure;
  Give to me a spirit new,
And oh, help me to endure
  All on earth I may pass through.

Guide me thro' the valley deep,
  Thro' the dark and tangled wood,
O'er the mountain's rugged steep,
  Till I come where Jesus stood.
'Till I come to be like him,
  Filled with thy own beauteous love,
Freed from every mortal sin—
  Fit to dwell with thee above.

HE is happy whose circumstances suit his temper, but he is more excellent who can suit his temper to any circumstances.

ARE YOU SAFE?

It is no infallible sign that we are not ourselves the sons of perdition, because people regard us as the children of God, and because our external deportment seems to justify their opinion. For among those who are respected, and reputed as blameless characters, among churchmen and those who are apparently devout, nay, even among those who frequent the Lord's Table, may be found such as are rushing onward to destruction. In congregations where the Gospel is preached, Satan entraps individuals in the snare of religious self-deception, as well as in the pits of infidelity and ungodliness. Among those to whom the dreadful words will be addressed, "I never knew you," not a few will be found, who with good reason, are able to say, "Lord have we not eaten and drunk in thy presence? have we not prophesied in thy name? and in thy name done many wonderful works?" The disciples were aware of this; and hence, on the Lord's informing them, that there was one among them who was accursed, they were by no means satisfied with being merely in their Master's immediate vicinity. "Lord," they ask one after the other, deeply concerned and grieved, "Is it I? Is it I?" Let us follow their example in this respect, and not seek at a distance those who shall eventually perish. Let us commence the inquiry within our own walls, and not exclude ourselves from those whom we regard as being possibly the deplorable people in question. On the contrary, let each first examine himself. It is not only those who openly revolt, and swear allegiance to the enemies of God and his annointed, who are hastening to perdition, but there are also others, with the Bible in their hands, and the name of Jesus on their lips, who will finally perish.—KRUMMACHER.

REPUTATION is often got without merit, and lost without fault.

A BITTER BUT HEALTHFUL MORSEL.

BY THE REV. WILLIAM ARNOT.

"Whoso loveth instruction, loveth knowledge; but he that hateth reproof is brutish.—Prov. xii, 1.

Reproof is not pleasant to nature. We may learn to value it for its results, but it never will be sweet to our taste. At the best it is a bitter morsel. The difference between a wise man and a fool is, not that one likes and the other loathes it—both dislike it—but the fool casts away the precious because it is unpalatable, and the wise man accepts the unpalatable because it is precious. It is brutish in a man to act merely according to the impulse of sense. We are not so foolish when the health of our bodies is at stake. When we were children indeed, if left to ourselves, we would have swallowed greedily the gilded sweetmeat that sickened us, and thrown away the bitter medicine which was fitted to purge disease from the channels of life; but when we became men, we put these childish things away. Day by day, in thousands of instances that concern this life, we accept the bitter because it is salutary, and reject the sweet because it destroys. Would that we were equally wise for higher interests! "I hate him; for he doth not prophecy good concerning me," (1 Kings xxii, 8;) there, in the person of that ancient Israelitish king, is humanity in the lump and without disguise. Grown men lick flattery in because it is sweet, and refuse faithful reproof because it is unpleasant. The best of us has much to learn here; and yet we think that, by pains and prayer, Christians might make large and rapid progress in this department. No advancement will be attained without particular and painstaking trial; but such trial will not be labor lost. Paul reached his high attainments not by an easy flight through the air, but by many toilsome steps on the weary ground; smaller men need not expect to find a royal road to spiritual perfection. "Herein do I exercise myself," he said, "that I may have a conscience void of offence." What he obtained only by hard exercise, we need not expect to drop into our bosom. Here is an exercise ground for Christians who would like to grow in grace. Nature hates reproof; let grace take the bitter potion, and thrust it down nature's throat, for the sake of its healing power. If we had wisdom and energy to take to ourselves more of the reproof that is agoing, and less of the praise, our spiritual constitution would be in a sounder state.

Some of the reproof comes directly from God by his providence and in his word. This, if there be a right spirit of adoption, it is perhaps easier to take. So thought David. When he found that a terrible rebuke must come, he pleaded that he might fall into the hands of God, and not into the hands of man. Still these chastenings are painful, and wisdom from above is needed to receive them aright. But although all are ultimately at the disposal of the Supreme, most of the reproofs that meet us in life come immediately from our fellow-men. Even when it is just in substance and kindly given, our own self-love kicks hard against it; and, alas! the most of it is mixed with envy and applied in anger. Here is room for the exercise of a Christian's highest art. There is a way of profiting by reproof, although it be administered by an enemy. It is in such narrows of life's voyage that the difference comes most clearly out between the wise and the foolish. A neighbor is offended by something that I have said or done. He becomes enraged, and opens a foul mouth upon me. This is his sin and his burden; but what of me? Do I kindle at his fire, and throw back his epithets with interest in his face? This is brutish. It is the stupid ox kicking everything that pricks him, and being doubly lacerated for his pains. It is my business and my interest to take good for myself, out of another's evil. The good is there, and there is a way of extracting it. The most unmannerly scold that ever came from an unbridled tongue may have its filth precipitated and turned into a precious ointment, as the sewerage of a city, instead of damaging the people's health, may as a fertilizer become the reduplicator of the people's food. The process is difficult, but when skillfully performed it produces a large return. When Shimei basely cursed David in his distress, the counsel of a rude warrior was, "Let me go over and take off his head." This was merely a brutish instinct—the beam that lay not on the solid, rebounding, by the law of its nature, to the blow. But the king had been getting the good of his great affliction. At that moment he had wisdom, and therefore he got more. He recognized a heavenly Father's hand far behind the foul tongue of Shimei; he felt that the rebuke, though cruelly given, contained salutary truth. He occupied himself not with the falsehood that was in it, in order to blame the reprover, but with the truth that was in it, in order to get humbling for himself. "Let him alone," said the fallen monarch, meekly; "let him alone and let him curse, for the Lord hath bidden him," Here is wisdom. It is wise to receive correction from God, although it come through an unworthy instrument. Although the immediate agent meant it for evil, our Father in heaven can make it work for good.

SCOPE OF MIRACLES.—The Gospel miracles differ from all others in their nature and frequency, and in the disinterestedness which characterized them. Neither the Saviour nor his disciples ever wrought a miracle for their own personal benefit. Dr. Carson well says:

"Trophimus have I left at Miletum sick." Did you, Paul? And why did you leave him sick when you possessed the power of working miracles? Why were you so profuse of your miracles in Melita, while you are so sparing of them among your best friends? For the very reason of showing that miracles are rather for the proof of the Gospel, shan for the private benefit even of the heirs of glory. God is sovereign in this as well as in everything else. Jesus healed the ear of the high priest's servant, while Paul did not heal his friend Trophimus. The apostles exercised their power, not by their discretion or caprice, but by the suggestion of the Holy Spirit. This, then, is a providential fact, the record of which, though to human wisdom trifling, is yet of great importance to the children of God. They are not to expect that they will always be free from sickness, or that their sickness will be soon dismissed. They have reason to trust that God will always be with them, and will turn every thing to good for them. But they must submit to him as a sovereign who gives no account of his matters.

NOTHING can avail or save, if Jesus is not ours. If you, my readers had any commensurate idea, how much you need him, you would throw open every avenue to admit him. Gladly would you divest yourselves of that which is the dearest and most precious to you, in order that you might possess him. Nay, you would risk your very lives, much more the vain delights, and empty honors of this world, in order to gain him. There exists no compensation for the want of Jesus, and the cleansing efficacy of his blood. The most specious tissue of austerities, of morality, and devotional exercises, can not supply his place. It is only a more handsome dress for a delinquent, and not the wedding garment for the invited guest.—KRUMMACHER.

TEMPTATIONS, when we meet them at first, are as the Lion that roared upon Sampson; but if we overcome them, the next time we see them we shall find a nest of honey within them. —BUNYAN.

SILENCE seldom doeth harm.

GROWTH IN GRACE.

BY DODDRIDGE.

Do you find divine love advancing in your soul? Do you feel yourself more and more sensible of the presence of God? and does that sense grow more delightful to you than it formerly was? Can you, even when your natural spirits are weak and low, and you are not in any frame for the orders and ecstacies of devotion, nevertheless find a pleasing rest, a calm repose of heart, in the thought that God is near you, and that he sees the secret sentiments of your soul, while you are, as it were, laboring up the hill, and casting a longing eye toward him, though you cannot say you enjoy any sensible communications from him? Is it agreeable to you to open your heart to his inspection and regard, to present it to him laid bare of every disguise, and say with David, "Thou, Lord, knowest thy servant?" Do you find a growing esteem and approbation of that sacred law of God, which is the transcript of his moral perfections? Do you inwardly "esteem all his precepts concerning all things to be right?" Psalm cxix, 128. Do you discern, not only the necessity, but the reasonableness, the beauty, the pleasure of obedience; and feel a growing scorn and contempt of those things which may be offered as the price of your innocence, and would tempt you to sacrifice or hazard your interest in the divine power and friendship? Do you find an ingenuous desire to please God, not only because he is so powerful, and has so many good and so many evil things entirely at his command, but from a veneration of his most amiable nature and character? and do you find your heart habitually reconciled to a most humble subjection, both to his commanding and to his disposing will? Do you perceive that your own will is now more ready and disposed in every circumstance, to bear the yoke, and to submit to the divine determination, whatever he appoints to be borne or forborne? Can you "in patience possess your soul?" Luke xxi, 19. Can you maintain a more steady calmness and serenity, when God is striking at your dearest enjoyments in this world, and acting most directly contrary to your present interests, to your natural passions and desires! If you can, it is a most certain and noble sign that grace is growing up in you to a very vigorous state.

AN AWFUL WARNING.—The Baltimore *Clipper* of June 1st, has the following: We heard yesterday, from an entirely satisfactory and responsible source, the particulars of an occurrence which can only be looked upon as an instance of Divine rebuke for taking the name of the Almighty in justification of a falsehood. We refrain from mentioning names through consideration of the parties, who are respectable persons, residing in the south-western section of the city. It appears that a few days since the aunt of a young girl about eighteen years of age, accused her of having been guilty of some misconduct, which she positively denied, and on being again accused, she called upon God to strike her blind if she was not telling the truth. In a moment after, according to her own statement, a film seemed to pass before her eyes, and in the course of five minutes she was totally blind, and has continued sightless ever since. The afflicted victim of her own impiety confessed that she had called upon her Maker to justify her in what was a falsehood.

The Madison (Iowa) *Plaindealer* says that a poor miserable wretch living near Farmington, in Van Buren County, while horribly blaspheming God on Saturday last, for withholding rain from his suffering crops, was suddenly struck with palsy, and almost immediately died.

ONE always receiving never giving, is like the stagnant pool, in which whatever remains corrupts.

WOMAN'S INFLUENCE.

BY MISS L. S. CLEMENT.

Sister in Christ—Did you ever consider the weighty influence you are exerting either for or against the cause you have espoused? Did you ever reflect upon the fathomless depths of the consequences which will arise from your individual influence: that if directed to the promotion of the highest good of your fellow-beings you will call into action the noblest energies and highest powers of which humanity is susceptible? Did you ever think that in every soul with whom you come in contact in your daily walks, there is a power for good, or evil, that may tell upon generations yet in the remote future; that an action of which *you* are hardly conscious, may make an indelible impression upon others—an impression which may affect their future destiny, and the destiny of the world? Perhaps you think your *sphere* is *so* limited, and your influence *so* small that it does not matter. You may think your sex shields you from the exercise of this unbounded influence; but, Sister, you are laboring under a serious mistake. If your direct influence does not extend beyond your own family circle, you may *there* wield a power that shall shake the world.

Your sex brings you into the closest contact with the mind in its most impressible state, and you are fearfully accountable for the impressions you make. Have you a brother? You are, perhaps, unconscious of the power you exert over him. Your gentle influence has restrained him when his impetuous nature has rebelled against parental authority. He may *affect* contempt for your religion, but in his heart he respects you for it, and your pious example and earnest prayers may yet lead him to seek the "Pearl of great price," and the life which might otherwise have been a curse to the world, may, in the service of the Redeemer, win many souls from sin. He may become a bright star in your crown of rejoicing.

Perhaps your earnest zeal in the cause of God may stimulate a father, who, worn and weary with the strifes and turmoils of life, is ready to lay down his watch, to renewed diligence in the Master's service. His counsels and prayers first led you into the narrow way, and, when treading the slippery path of youth, he anxiously guarded your footsteps, enabling you to shun the snares of the tempter, and now, trusting that your feet are firmly planted on the Rock, he feels safe in your counsels, and relies upon your spiritual strength to aid him in his journey home.

Sister, is your destiny linked with one whom you have promised to love, honor, and keep in sickness and health, for whom you have promised to forsake all others, and keep thee only unto him so long as ye both shall live? Your influence may determine the character of your husband. If he is a stranger to Christ, your life of devotion, your patience amid trials, your resignation in affliction, and your faithfulness in the discharge of duty, may win the heart over to the service of his Maker, which the most stirring appeals from the pulpit have failed to reach. Has your husband heard and obeyed the command of the Master, "Go ye into all the world, and preach the Gospel to every creature?" Your sympathy and counsels may do more to encourage and sustain him in his heaven-appointed labors, than all the world beside. Are you repining at your lot in being cast out upon the world with no permanent abiding place? are you sighing for the happy home, and its delightful associations, in which you spent your childhood? Do you meet him with whom you have promised to labor for the building up of Christ's kingdom in the world, with murmurs and complaint?

These will do more to fetter his spirit and hinder his usefulness, than all the scorn and contempt that an ungodly world could heap upon him.

And your influence may rob him of many a bright star that would otherwise shine in his crown of rejoicing.

Sister, have you calmly folded your hands, and quietly sat down content to see others labor in the vineyard of the Lord, while you are sighing that you have not a more extensive field to labor in? What though your position is an obscure one? your influence is just as potent in your sphere, as though it were a more exalted one. If you first discharge the duties which devolve upon you in your humble station faithfully, and the Father sees that you are fitted for a broader field of usefulness, he will open the way for you. But if you already possess wealth, station, and talent, they only add to the extent of your influence. How important then that it be wholly on the right side. In order to have your influence over others all that it should be, regard must be had, not to the outward deportment alone, but to the outward adornings which every one can observe, and which exert an influence wherever you go. "They are known and read of all men." Christ said to his disciples, "Ye are not of the world, but I have chosen you out of the world," and again the Apostle Paul says, "Be not conformed to this world, but be ye transformed by the renewing of your mind; that ye may prove what is that good, and acceptable, and perfect will of God."

Then, Sister in Christ, let us awake, and in spite of position, circumstances, or means, let our whole influence be to the building up of Christ's Kingdom in the world. "For so an entrance shall be ministered unto you abundantly into the everlasting Kingdom of our Lord and Saviour Jesus Christ.

It is better, said Antisthenes, to fall among crows than flatterers, for those only devour the dead, these the living.

God hath often a great share in a little house.

All are not thieves that dogs bark at.

STRIVE TO ENTER IN AT THE STRAIT GATE.

"Strive to enter in at the strait gate." And in order thereto, settle it in your heart, and let it ever be uppermost in your thoughts, that if you are in the broad way, you are in the way that leadeth to destruction. If many go with you, as sure as God is true, both they and you are going to hell! If you are walking as the generality of men walk, you are walking to the bottomless pit! Are many wise, many rich, many mighty, or noble, traveling with you in the same way? By this token, without going any farther, you know it does not lead to life. Here is a short, a plain, an infallible rule, before you enter into particulars. In whatever profession you are engaged, you must be singular, or be damned! The way to hell has nothing singular in it; but the way to heaven is singularity all over; if you move but one step towards God, you are not as other men are. But regard not this. It is far better to stand alone, than to fall into the pit. Run then with patience the race which is set before thee, though thy companions therein are but few! They will not always be so. Yet a little while, and thou wilt come to an innumerable company of angels, to the general assembly and church of the first-born, and to the spirits of just men made perfect."

Now, then, "strive to enter in at the strait gate," being penetrated with the deepest sense of the inexpressible danger your soul is in, so long as you are in the broad way—so long as you are void of poverty of spirit, and all that inward religion which the many, the rich, and the wise, account madness. "Strive to enter in," being pierced with sorrow and shame for having so long run on with the unthinking crowd, utterly neglecting, if not despising that "holiness without which no man can see the Lord." Strive, as in an agony of holy fear, lest "a promise being made you of entering into his rest," even that "rest which remaineth for the people of God," you should nevertheless "come short of it." "Strive, in all the fervor of desire, with "groanings which cannot be uttered." Strive by prayer without ceasing; at all times, in all places, lifting up your heart to God, and giving him no rest, till you "awake up after his likeness," and are "satisfied with it."

"Strive to enter in at the strait gate," not only by this agony of soul, of conviction, of sorrow, of shame, of desire, of fear, of unceasing prayer; but likewise by ordering thy conversation aright, by walking with all thy strength in all the ways of God; the way of innocence, of piety, and of mercy. Abstain from all appearance of evil; do all possible good to all men; deny thyself, thy own will, in all things, and take up thy cross daily. Be ready to cut off thy right hand, to pluck out thy right eye, and cast it from thee; to suffer the loss of goods, friends, health, all things on earth, so thou mayest enter into the Kingdom of Heaven!—JOHN WESLEY.

DR. ARNOLD once observed of a bad pupil and his instruction, "It is very often like kicking a football up hill. You kick it upwards twenty yards, and it rolls back nineteen. Still you have gained one yard, and then in a good many kicks you make some progress. Here is genuine encouragement for the teacher placed among the rough and rude. It is not in the nature of instruction and correction wholly to be thrown away.

"IF we work on marble, it will perish; if we work on brass, time will efface it; if we rear temples, they will crumble into dust. If we work upon immortal minds, if we imbue them with high principles, with just fear of God and their fellow men, we engrave on these tablets something which no time can efface, but which will brighten to all eternity."

SOME professed Christians have nothing belonging to the sheep but the skin.

THE POWER OF THE HOLY GHOST.

IF the amazing revival which characterized the last century be viewed merely as a natural progress of mental influence, no analysis can find elements of power greater than have often existed in a corrupting and falling Church, or than are found at many periods when no blessed effects are produced. Men equally learned, eloquent, orthodox, instructive, may be found in many ages of Christianity. It is utterly impossible to assign a natural reason why Whitefield should have been the means of converting so many more sinners than other men. Without one trace of logic, philosophy, or any thing worthy to be called systematic theology, his sermons, viewed intellectually, take an humble place among humble efforts. Turning again to his friend, Wesley, we find calmness, clearness, logic, theology, discussion, definition, point, appeal, but none of that prodigious and unaccountable power which the human intellect would naturally connect with movements so amazing as those which took place under his word. Neither the logic of the one, nor the declamation of the other, furnishes us with the secret of their success. There is enough to account for men's being affected, excited, or convinced; but that does not account for their living holy lives ever after. Thousands of pulpit orators have swayed their audiences, as a wind sways standing corn; but, in the result, those who were most affected differed nothing from their former selves. An effect of eloquence is sufficient to account for a vast amount of feeling at the moment; but to trace to this a moral power, by which a man, for his life long, overcomes his besetting sins, and adorns his name with Christian virtues, is to make sport of human nature.

Why should these men have done what many equally learned, and able, as divines and orators, never did? There must have been an element of power in them which criticism cannot discover. What was that power? It must be judged of by its sphere, and its effects. Where did it act? and what did it produce? Every power has its own sphere. The strongest arm will never convince the understanding; the most forcible reasoning will never lift a weight, the brightest sunbeam will never pierce a plate of iron, nor the most powerful magnet move a pane of glass. The soul of man has separate regions, and that which merely convinces the intellect may leave the emotions untouched; that which merely operates on the emotions may leave the understanding unsatisfied, and that which affects both, may yet leave the moral powers uninspired. The crowning power of the messenger of God, is power over the moral man; power which, whether it approaches the soul through the avenue of the intellect or of the affections, *does* reach into the soul. The sphere of true Christian power is the heart—the moral man; and the result of its action is not to be surely distinguished from that of mere eloquence by instantaneous emotion, but by subsequent moral fruit. Power which cleanses the heart, and produces holy living, is the power of the Holy Ghost. It may be through the logic of Wesley, the declamation of Whitefield, or the simple common sense of a plain servant woman, or laboring-man; but whenever this power is in action, it strikes deeper into human nature than any mere reasoning or pathos. Possibly it does not so soon bring a tear to the eye, or throw the judgment into a posture of acquiescence; but it raises in the breast thoughts of God, eternity, sin, death, heaven and hell; raises them, not as mere ideas, opinions, or articles of faith, but as the images and echoes of real things.

We may find in many parts of the country, where much has been done to dispel darkness and diffuse true religion, that some of the first triumphs of grace were entirely due to the wonderful effects produced by the private and fireside talking of some humble Christians, who had themselves gone to the throne of Grace, and waited there until they had received the baptism of fire.

In proportion as the power of this one instrument is overlooked, and other means are trusted in to supply its place, does the true force of Christian agency decline; and it may without hesitation be said, that when men holding the Christian ministry habitually and constantly manifest their distrust in the power of the Holy Ghost to give them utterance, they publicly abjure the true theory of Christian preaching. It is according to the authority of its Author, delivering a message from God—a message through man, it is true—but not delivered through the excellency of man's speech, not under the guidance of man's natural wisdom; a message, the effect of which does not rest upon the artistic arrangement, choice, and ardor of words, but upon the extent to which its utterance is pervaded by the Holy Ghost.—ARTHUR.

A BEAUTIFUL THOUGHT.—When I gaze into the stars, they look down upon me with pity from their serene spaces, like eyes glistening with tears, over the little lot of man. Thousands of generations, all as noisy as our own, have been swallowed up by time, and there remains no record of them any more; yet Arcturus and Orion, Sirius and the Pleiades, are still shining in their courses, clear and young as when the shepherd first noted them from the plain of Shinar. What shadows we are, and what shadows we pursue!—THOMAS CARLYLE.

RULE OF FAITH.—A belief that in all things, and at all events God is to be obeyed; that there is the essential distinction of holiness and sin in all conduct, both within the wind and in external action, and that sin is absolutely a dreadful evil; that *that* must not be done which must be repented of; that the future should predominate over the present.—FOSTER.

ENTHUSIASM.

When the Holy Spirit is in full union with a Church, and when a Church is in full communication with the influences of the Holy Spirit, there will be proportionate compassion, tenderness and concern for the souls of men; and these will be excited and developed in a higher degree than could be accomplished by the mere sympathies of humanity. It deserves to be exhibited on the face of the skies, in letters as bright and vivid as rainbows, that, on the supposition that a soul is in real danger of being lost, no excitement of the emotions however high, no anguish of feeling however intense, is either extravagant or enthusiastic. The enemies of religious emotion brand this excitement with the epithet of enthusiastic; but it is only in proportion as they diminish the amount of danger which produces it. It must, however, be admitted that there is, in connection with this subject one state of religious emotion which well deserves to be called enthusiasm—weak, vain and empty enthusiasm. It *is* enthusiasm to fancy facts concerning the soul which are not testified in the Scriptures; it is enthusiasm to fancy that a soul is under the influences of the Spirit, when there are no fruits of the Spirit: it *is* enthusiasm to expect a thing strongly without using the appointed means; to expect a soul to go to heaven who neither walks nor seeks the way thitherward; to expect a mysterious process of forced conversion to take place in the dying hour; and to hope there is no danger to the soul, when the Scriptures declare that it is in danger of eternal perdition. The men who indulge in these fancies and expectations, and oppose enthusiasm, are themselves fanatics the most wild and extravagant.—DR. JENKYN.

ONE half our forebodings of ill to our neighbors are but our *wishes*, which we are ashamed to utter in any other form.—LANDON.

DIVINE GUIDANCE.—Though the Divine dispensation of spiritual aid is no longer miraculous, the presence of Christ no longer visible, for we "walk (wholly) by faith, not by sight," still that aid is not less real, that presence not less abiding. The Spirit ever "helpeth our infirmities." Our Divine Master has promised to " come unto them that love Him, and keep His saying," and to manifest himself to them. He speaks to them, though not in a literally audible voice. He leads them, not less really than of old, though not literally, by the hand; for " as many," says the Apostle Paul, " as are led by the Spirit of God, they are the sons of God." If we look earnestly we shall see Him; if we listen attentively we shall hear His voice.—WHATELEY.

DIFFICULTIES.—Wait not for your difficulties to cease; there is no soldier's glory to be won on peaceful fields; no sailor's daring to be shown on sunny seas, no trust or friendship to be proved when all goes well. Faith, patience, heroic love, devout courage, gentleness, are not to be formed when there are no doubts, no pains, no irritations, no difficulties. The highly favored are they who amid tribulation are patient, amid rebuffs are meek, amid chastisement are resigned, amid pains are courageous, amid provocations are gentle, amid enemies are full of love, amid doubts hold fast the faith, amid sorrows find joy in God.

MYSTERIES.—Those who profess, by simplifying and explaining the mysteries of the Christian religion, to make Faith easy, destroy in effect the very nature of it, considered as a duty; for there is surely no virtue in assenting to Euclid's propositions or anything denonstrable to the understanding. Such men in endeavoring to widen the strait gate, are guilty of much the same fault with those who turn aside from it in disgust. The latter will not believe what they find it impossible to explain; the former are resolved to explain what they find themselves compelled to believe.—ARCHBISHOP WHATELEY.

EXPERIENCE OF FRANCES D. BYRNS.

The first five years of my life, I was the only child of *good*, but over indulgent parents. They professed religion, but will, I think, agree with me in saying, they were then very worldly. I was never taught to pray; yet I did sometimes; though I was too proud to kneel. I do not remember hearing much about religion in my early days, though I knew my parents professed it, because my father asked a blessing at the breakfast table; and when the minister came the large Bible was handed him and he read and prayed with us. But glory be to God a *very great* change has taken place in our family since then. I can remember having but few serious thoughts when a child. I told a wicked lie once for which I felt very bad and could not rest till I had confessed it to my mother.

While in a class-meeting at a very early age, I felt bad because my mother trembled and wept when she spoke. But I knew not the cause of it.

I went to Sunday school at an early age, and was generally prompt in attendance. I loved to excel in reciting verses from the testament, but I did not realize the true object of the Sunday school, and no one taught me. Perhaps the teachers did not have time, as it took so long to hear so many recite.

I distinctly remember admiring the rich and gay clothing of some of my teachers, and thinking one morning when my aunt wore a new bonnet with flowers, "I should not think she would like to kneel down this morning." It was then prayer time. Alas! how many think it of small importance what example is set before *children*. At another time when the Superintendent was asking questions upon the lesson, the verse came up, "But I say unto you, that every idle word that men shall speak, they shall give account thereof in the day of judgment." He then asked the school if we thought it was really so: and I said, (honestly) I did not think it was; and he said he guessed not.

Thus was my natural inclination to speak idle words left unchecked. Yet I thank God I ever went to Sunday school, for those lessons there learned now appear like an unsealed book.

I grew up with an unhappy fretful disposition, seeking enjoyment in trying to out-do some one in making fun, as I termed it. O, what a snare did this prove to me in after years! I reached my thirteenth year before I remember having any conviction for sin. There was at the time a protracted effort being made for the salvation of souls in our village. I attended several of the meetings, and though no one spoke to me on the subject, I felt myself to be a great sinner. And when the invitation was given for those seeking religion to take the front seat, I went. I wept bitterly, and told them my determination to find my Saviour. But the next day Satan tried to shame me out of it, and made great use of my proneness to trifling conversation. I could not shed a tear during the first part of the day, but in the afternoon I went to meeting; and again my heart was melted. After a season of prayer, while they were singing, "My God is reconciled, his pardoning voice I hear," the preacher said, if we would believe it, it would *be* so. I thought I can do that, and for a moment felt relieved. But I thought it could not be that the work was done so quickly, but that I must feel very bad a great while, so I kept on seeking. But I no longer felt the weight of sin, and think I was converted that afternoon. I now felt that Jesus smiled upon me—that I was his child. Still I do not remember to have had much of the *glorious joys* of salvation for more than three years after I made a profession of religion. I thought my life must be different—that I ought not to get angry nor laugh so much, now that I professed to be a Christian. and many were the resolutions I made in my own strength. Of course I could not keep them alone, and it seems to me now, I never thought of looking to Jesus. Being large of my age, I had begun to go among young people some, before my conversion, and they seemed to like me just as well after it.

Gradually I found myself more and more entangled with the vain things of earth. I often think, with regret, I was about that time instrumental in two young persons making a profession of religion when they knew *very little*, if any, of the *power of saving grace* in the heart. Alas! the almost blind leading the totally blind. O, how we cling to the world! Yet, "If any man love the world, the love of the Father is not in him." Thus I lived on, conforming more and more to the world-giving way to bursts of anger—or when things suited, in indulging too much in levity. For a whole year after my conversion, I refused or failed to pray in public. The bell ringing for prayer-meeting seemed to say, "Come pray, come pray." And I would resolve "I will," but when there the cross seemed *so heavy*, and I did not understand the way of looking to God for help to bear it. Finally, by a mighty effort, I *did* take the cross, and for a time was justified. During all this time I had been to class meeting, and would weep and tell that I had been trying "to carry religion in one hand, and the world in the other," and would resolve not to be so rude for the week to come—not to get impatient again. But as often did I break my good resolutions.

About a year and a half after I had professed to be a follower of Jesus, a seminary was built in our village, and school opened. Here the young and gay assembled, and I wished to be as lively as any one, if not *more* so. Again the cross was presented, and very humiliating it was too, to kneel in prayer-time before all the students. Well, at first I made the excuse to my mother, when she asked me concerning it, that the seats were too close together. But soon they were placed farther apart, so that I had no excuse. A short time afterward I resolved in class-meeting, I *would do it*, and for a few mornings following I did. I must have had a little influence then, for a young sister who sat near me would kneel when I did; but my example the rest of the time was so bad, I grew ashamed of kneeling, and she gave it up also. I tried to persuade myself it was not duty. For another year I lived in the known omission of duty—ceased to repent of my "little sins," went to class, told a fair story, and was loved by a large circle of friends. About this time, Brother Wells came to our place to labor, and once in a class meeting after I had spoken so smoothly, he asked me if I was doing every known duty? I thought a moment, and the Spirit of God, true to its work, said very distinctly, "You do not kneel in chapel."

But I quickly replied, "It isn't duty," and told him I did not think of any I was neglecting, or something to that effect. O! God, why was I not cut down when thus cumbering the ground! He told me to revolve it in my mind during the next week, and see if I could not find something I was leaving undone. And I did think of it, but did not consent to do it till the next watch-night, when I solemnly promised God, I *would*. During that winter some of those with whom I had been so intimate, did not attend school, and I was mercifully thrown under the benign influence of a young sister who had, a few months previous, received the blessing of holiness. Glory be to God! I think I was justified a part of the time, but if anything *personal* was said upon the subject of dress or any such thing, I would immediately rebel. Still the Spirit of God was at work in my heart, and I saw I was far from being right. Thank God for light.

But in the spring the dear sister left me, and again I sought my intimate friends among the ungodly. I was once more as light and trifling as ever, though I did religious duties, and was thought to be a consistent Christian.

At times, 'tis true, I felt my sinfulness, and once said to my near friend, O, I feel so wicked! But she kissed me, and said something about my being so *good*. Thus was my pride fed and I glided along. At this time I took an active part in two exhibitions at the seminary, which seemed to kill all the spirituality I had remaining. What will the reader think of a follower of the "meek and lowly Jesus," appearing before a gazing crowd, dressed in white, and wearing a wreath of flowers, and a long white veil, to *represent religion?* At another time, with painted face and arms, decked with feathers, &c., representing an Indian maiden? O, my Father how couldst thou bear with me? Yes, many precious hours have I spent in preparing my dress, and committing compositions to memory, just to feed my pride—to gain the applause of the multitude. I remember thinking one afternoon when going on the stage to rehearse the dialogue, "What if God should so convict me that I should be compelled to fall down here and cry for mercy on the night of the exhibition?" Though the teachers who superintended these things professed religion, yet it was no excuse for me. I knew very well it was wrong, after I had commenced, but thought I had such a prominent part it would be a pity to break it all up. So I *persisted* in it. But glory to Jesus! soon after this I obtained *salvation*, and no longer felt any desire to gain the applause of the world. Yes, many grateful hearts often praise God for the well-known "Black Creek Camp Meeting," or in other words, "The Independent Laymen's Camp Meeting." As it was only a few miles from home, I went, intending to stay but one day. I felt that I was very good that morning, for I did not realize my true condition in the sight of God. I had concluded that it was *policy* to cultivate a good disposition—not to *show* impatience when I *felt* it—for I wanted to be amiable and have many friends. But a wicked, proud heart lay beneath the unruffled surface. It was service time when we reached the encampment, and the loud Amens from happy saints, found no sympathy in me. I grew more and more astonished, but the light was beginning to shine into my darkened soul. Glory, glory to Jesus for conviction.

At night I felt too wicked to return home, and my parents consented to let me stay as long as I wished. Bless the Lord for that. One morning, I strayed into a class meeting where truly they had such salvation as I never had heard of. "I would praise thee, where shall I thy praise begin?" Sister Kendall who led the class asked me several heart-searching questions, and among other things said, "I *know* you are not in the clear light or you would not wear that ring." O, how sinful I felt as those holy sisters looked at me, and I began to break down before the Lord. Plain dealing was just what I needed. I had been told I was so good, too long already. I was soon seeking justifying grace, trying to humble myself before God, the young people from our town looking into the tent with astonishment I suppose. I went mourning that day till toward evening, when the light broke in, and God did bless my soul. I must have promised to give up the world then, for I was justified. But I soon drew back, and the next morning when questioned again in class, I sobbed out, " O I can't dress *plain*." Now I never dressed very costly, but every time I knelt down to pray, something would strive with me to give up those needless flowers and ribbons at home. And I wore my hair curled, which I saw would not do for me, if I would get into the light. Finally after some struggling, I was enabled to consecrate my little all, to break off my ring, to arrange my hair in a manner more becoming a Christian, and to promise I *would* trim my bonnet when I should reach home. My soul was now happy in God, my Father. Truly I tasted the joys of salvation. But frequently my past exam ple came before my mind with such force, that I would almost despair, give way to doubts, and thus bring the shadows over my soul. Yet the Lord did bless and save me, and *now* I see he was leading me. I left the camp ground feeling rather sorrowful, yet little dreaming what awaited me in the future. I began to fulfill my promises to do duty, and the light of God shone more and more. The next Sabbath, I committed myself to seek definitely the blessing of sanctification. A number of professed Christians had received great good at the camp meeting, and we had powerful prayer meetings. Some three weeks after the camp meeting closed, in one of these glorious meetings, I was enabled to consecrate myself more fully to Jesus, to look to Him as a *perfect Saviour*, and the great work was wrought. O glory to God in the highest. What light and glory streamed into my soul as soon as I believed. 'Tis vain to try to express it, but thank God many have felt the same.

It is nearly a year since I commenced to walk the highway of holiness. I am very sorry I have not been more faithful. I remember the dark hours that have followed when I have neglected duty or compromised. O, it seemed as if I never could smile again. When Jesus had done *so much* for me, to think I would ever shrink from the cross or cover up its glorious reproach. But at such times I had to confess and seek the fountain again. O yes! the all-cleansing fountain that never is empty or shallow. Glory to Jesus for salvation. I wish I could tell how I have triumphed over everything at times. When my dear parents thought I would be crazy, and many things conspired to crush my soul then it was that Jesus stooped to earth, filled my soul with glory and carried me above. It did seem sometimes that I did not breathe the air of earth, so far did my soul soar above all its trials. But it was not always so: Ah! no, I have sometimes let these things trouble me. It was *so hard* to take a course which my own parents and relatives could not approve! If I could only be a *consistent* Christian, not so *unlike* every body else, if I would only dress so as not to *attract attention*, and not go to certain (blessed) meetings, then all would go well. But I must believe till Jesus says otherwise.

I did my heavenly Father's will. 'Tis nothing to boast of, for I came very near compromising several times, and once I did. But God's children prayed, and he answered prayer, and I was enabled to retrace my steps, and walk the narrow glorious way. I went to Jesus and asked him to undertake for me. And he did; bless his holy name! The tide of opposition was rolled back, and for months I have been permitted to follow God as I saw fit. I doubt not many think me stubborn and self-willed. But Jesus knows how hard it was. He knows how much I suffered mentally. *He knows I loved* to obey my parents, when I could obey *him* at the same time. O yes! I kept a standing wish for sometime that I might please Jesus and my mother too. But I finally gave it to Him, for it seems as though one were not satisfied when wishing for anything. And now this sunny afternoon, it seems to me I could walk with Jesus upon this sinful earth, and never grow weary. O, may I ever walk in white! I know it soils easily, but by keeping close to Jesus' precious wound, the blood will keep my garments as white as snow. How I long to see the work of God go on. I want to be kept in the dust at my Saviour's feet, lost to self and the world; but O, let Jesus reign without a rival. Yes, give me Jesus! I can *say* and *feel it* too.

"Let the winds blow high, or the winds blow low,
'Tis a pleasant sail to Canaan. Hallelujah!"

WATCH AND PRAY. — Watching without prayer were but an impious homage to ourselves. Prayer without watching were but an impious and also absurd homage to God.—FOSTER.

BIGOTRY.

God sometimes puts our desire for his glory to the test, by bringing under our eyes signal and extensive usefulness by other hands than our own, or those of our party. Can we say, "I therein do rejoice, yea and will rejoice?" Or do we refuse to "wish him God speed" whom God has sent? Are we slow to believe the laborer which God has owned? Dare we repine, when God has blessed? Are we cold when many hearts are made to glow with "the love of God shed abroad" therein? Are we unthankful when "one" who is not of us, "converteth a sinner from the error of his way, and that saveth a soul from death and hideth a multitude of sins?" When God causeth others to triumph in Christ, and maketh manifest the savor of his name by them, do we sullenly refuse to join in the joyous procession? Do we refuse to unite in the symphonies of angels when they rejoice over one sinner that repenteth, because that sinner repenteth not at our bidding, but at some other voice not tuned to our key, or not shaped to our form of words? Have we to accuse ourselves in any measure of these godless discontents? O tell it not in Gath! Publish it not in the streets of Ashkelon! Genuine bigotry would rather see men sink into perdition, than consent that they should be saved by another hand. What foe to the Gospel! Who would not wish to see it detroyed?—Thomas Quinton Stow.

Dead Worship.—In a Christian land men become Christians by profession. And while the life is decent, and the Church attended, all things pass off mighty well. But it happens these genteel professors are the very troops of Ezekiel's army, before it was quickened; covered well with plump flesh and fair skin, yet no breath was in them; ranged well in rank and file, bone comes to his bone, and at a distance they seem a famous army; but on a near approach all are dead men. No life is found among them, because the Holy Spirit has not breathed upon them.

So fared it in the prophet's day, and so fareth it now. A Christian army still appears, with many decent soldiers of kindly flesh and skin, and, when exercised at church, are ranked well in order; bone comes to his bone, and a *noise* of prayer is heard, but no breath of life is found, no presence of the Lord bestowed, no quickening aids imparted, no cheering consolations granted. It is a dead scene of worship, conducted like an undertaker's funeral, with a very cloudy face, and yawning entertainment.—Berridge.

Faith.—A stranger to the life of faith makes a sport about believing, and thinks no work so easy or so trifling. He wonders why such *gentle* business should be called the *fight* of faith? why the chosen twelve should pray for faith, when every human brain might quickly furnish out a handsome dose?

For my part, since first my unbelief was felt, I have been praying fifteen years for faith, and praying with some earnestness, and am not yet possessed of more than *half* a grain. You smile, sir, I perceive, at the smallness of the quantity; but you would not if you knew its efficacy. Jesus who knew it well assures you that a single grain, and a grain as small as mustard-seed, would *remove a mountain;* remove a *mountain* load of guilt from the conscience, a *mountain*-lust from the heart, and a *mountain*-load of trouble from the mind.—Berridge.

Satan's great design is eternally to ruin souls; and where he cannot do that, there he will endeavor to discomfit souls by busying them about the secret decrees and counsels of God, or by engaging them in such debates and disputes as neither men nor angels can certainly and infallibly determine, that so he may spoil their comforts, when he cannot take away their crown. —Brooks.

THE BOY MARTYR.

It was at Antioch, about three hundred years after the birth of Christ, that the deacon of the Church of Cæsarea—the place from which the devout Centurion of the Roman army sent for St. Peter—was subjected to the most cruel tortures, in order to try his faith, and force him to deny the Lord who bought him with His own precious blood. The martyr, amidst his agonies, persisted in declaring his belief that there is but "one God, and one Mediator between God and men, the man Christ Jesus." His flesh was almost torn to pieces; the Roman Emperor Galerius himself looking on. At length, weary of answering their taunting demands that he should acknowledge the many gods of the Heathen, he told his tormentor to refer the question to any little child whose simple understanding could decide whether it were better to worship one God, the Maker of the heaven and earth, and one Saviour, who was able to bring us to God, or to worship the gods many, and the lords many whom the Romans served.

Now, it happened that a Roman mother had approached the scene of the martyr's sufferings, holding by the hand a little boy of eight or nine years old. Pity, or the desire of helping the sufferer, had probably brought her there; but the providence of God had ordained for her an unexpected trial. The judge no sooner heard the martyr's words than his eye rested on the child, and pointing to the boy from his tribunal, he desired the Christian to put the question he proposed to him.

The question was asked; and to the surprise of those who heard it, the little boy replied, "God is one, and Jesus Christ is one with the Father."

The persecutor heard it, but far from being either softened or convinced, he was filled with fresh rage.

"It is a snare," he cried: "O base and wicked Christian! thou hast instructed that child to answer thus."

Then, turning to the boy, he said more mildly, "Tell me, child, who taught you thus to speak? How did you learn this faith?"

The boy glanced up to his mother's face, and then replied: "It was God's grace, that taught it to my mother; and when I sat upon her knee a baby, she taught me that Jesus loved little children, and I learned to love Him for his love to us."

"Let us see now what the love of Christ can do for you," cried the cruel judge; and at a sign from him, the lictors, who stood ready with their rods, after the fashion of the Romans, instantly seized the poor trembling boy. Fain would the mother have saved her timid dove, even at the expense of her own life. She could not do so; but she could whisper to him to trust in the love of Christ and to maintain the truth. And the poor child, feeble and timid as he was, did trust in that love; nor could all the cruelty of his tormentors separate him from it.

"What can the love of Christ do for him now?" asked the judge as the blood streamed from that tender flesh.

"It enables him to endure what his Master endured for him and for us all," was the reply.

Again they smote the child to torture his mother.

"What can the love of Christ do for him now?" they asked again. And tears fell even from heathen eyes as that Roman mother, a thousand times more tortured than her son, answered;

"It teaches him to forgive his persecutors."

And the boy watched his mother's eye as it rose up to heaven for him, and he thought of the sufferings of his dear Lord and Saviour, of which she had told; and when his tormentors inquired whether he would not now acknowledge the false gods they served, and deny Christ, he steadfastly answered, "No! there is no other God but one; Jesus Christ is the Redeemer of the world. He loved me, and I love Him for his love."

Then, as the poor child fainted between the repeated strokes, they cast the quivering and mangled little body into the mother's arms, crying, "See what the love of Christ can do for him now."

And as the mother pressed it gently to her own bleeding heart, she answered:—

"That love will take him from the wrath of man to the peace of heaven."

"Mother," murmured the gasping child, "give me a drop of water from our cool well upon my tongue."

"Child, thou shouldst not have time to receive it, ere it was here thou shouldst be drinking of the river of life in the paradise of God."

She spoke over the dying; for the little martyr spake no more; and thus the mother continued: "Already dearest, hast thou tasted of the well that springeth up to everlasting life, the grace of Christ given to his little one; thou hast spoken the truth in love; arise now, for the Saviour calleth for thee. Young, happy martyr, for His sake, may He grant thy mother grace to follow thy bright path!"

The boy faintly raised his quivering eye-lids, looked up to where the elder martyr was, and said again, "There is but one God, and Jesus Christ whom He has sent;" and so saying, he died.

THE BOY PREACHER OF LOUISIANA.

MARK BOATNER CHAPMAN is now in his fourteenth year. He was born in Clinton, Louisiana, where his parents still reside. About two years ago he was received in the church; very soon after this he commenced instructing his father's servants on the afternoon of every Sabbath. His custom was to read a chapter and comment upon it, having first closely studied the chapter, consulting Benson, Clark and Wesley on every passage.

He at length began, says a writer to the Memphis *Advocate*, to speak in the love-feasts and class-meetings; then to pray in the public congregation. His appearance is that of the merest boy; and he seems wholly unconscious of any superior gifts or attainments. He now preaches regularly every Sabbath at his father's place, near the town. His parents have refused to allow him to enter the pulpit and supply the place of the regular minister on Sabbath, although he is often solicited to do so. He does nothing without permission from his parents. He attends school and joins in all the amusements of the boys of his own age; he is a mere child everywhere, save when preaching. On last Sabbath I sat under his ministry, and have seldom been more edified and delighted with a sermon. His style is chaste, his words fitly and happily chosen. The nicest critic would not detect a grammatical error; his manner is earnest, and his pathetic appeals reach all hearts. Occasionally his feelings overwhelm him, and he gives way to floods of tears.

The most gifted lawyers, doctors and divines have heard him with astonishment and delight. I confess that it is most wonderful, and to me incomprehensible. When I heard him, he preached from the text, "How long halt ye between two opinions?" He preached from notes, sometimes seeming to forget that his notes were before him. His subject was arranged with perfect system; and most logically treated. When through with his sermon, he closed the book and gave a brief and touching exhortation, under which I could, with others, but weep. His public addresses, published, have attracted much attention, and should he live, he must, in his onward course, leave a broad wake on the tide of morals. Such is the character of the "Boy Preacher," whose wonderful precocity is without a parallel.—N. O. CRESCENT.

THOU art not the more holy, though thou be commended; nor the more abject, though thou be dispraised.—KEMPIS.

One Brick Wrong. — Workmen were recently building a large brick tower, which was to be carried up very high. The architect and the foreman both charged the masons to lay each brick with the greatest exactness, especially the first courses, which were to sustain all the rest. However, in laying a corner, by accident or carelessness, one brick was set a very little out of line. The work went on without its being noticed, but as each course of bricks was kept in line with those already laid, the tower was not put up exactly straight, and the higher they built the more insecure it became. One day, when the tower had been carried up about fifty feet, there was heard a tremendous crash. The building had fallen, burying the men in the ruins. All the previous work was lost, the materials wasted, and worst still, valuable lives were sacrificed, and all from *one brick laid wrong* at the start. The workman at fault in this matter little thought how much mischief he was making for the future. Do you ever think what ruin may come of one bad habit, one brick laid wrong while you are now building a character for life? Remember, in youth the foundation is laid. See to it that all is kept straight.

There are many persons who would willingly be Christians, and eminent Christians too, if Christianity were limited to great occasions. For such occasions they call forth whatever pious and devotional resources they have, or seem to have, and not only place them in the best light, but inspire them, for the time being, with the greatest possible efficiency. But on smaller occasions, in the every-day occurrences and events of life, the religious principle is in a state of dormancy, giving no signs of effective vitality and movement. The life of such persons is not like that of the sun, equable, constant, diffusive and beneficent, though attracting but little notice; but like the eruptive and glaring blaze of volcanos, which comes forth at remote periods, in company with great thunderings and shakings of the earth; and yet the heart of the people is not made glad by it. Such religion is vain; and its possessors know not what manner of spirit they are of.— Upham.

Temptation.—It is usual with the devil in his temptings of poor creatures, to put a good and bad together, that by show of the good the tempted might be drawn to do that which in truth is evil. Thus he served Saul; he spared the best of the herd and flock, under pretence of sacrificing to God, and so transgressed the plain command. But this the apostle said was dangerous, and therefore censureth such as in a state of condemnation. Thus he served Adam; he put the desirableness of light, and a plain transgression of God's law together, that by the loneliness of the one, they might the easier be brought to do the other. O, poor Eve, do we wonder at thy folly? Doubtless we had done as bad with half the argument of thy temptation.—Bunyan.

That love which accompanies salvation is like the sun. The sun casts his beams upward and downward, to the east and to the west, to the north and to the south; so the love of a saint ascends to God above, and descends to men on earth; to our friends on the right hand, to our enemies on the left hand; to them that are in a state of grace, and to them that are in a state of nature. Divine love will still be working one way or another.— Brooks.

Before we have God with us in outward labor, we must seek Him and obtain His direction and promise of help in secret. O, if thy heart were more in the closet, it would be more full of hope in the Church of God, where thou oughtest to act the man always.

Kirwan says that a pious Scotchman used to pray, "O, Lord, keep me right; for thou knowest if I go wrong, it is very hard to turn me."

STAND TO YOUR POST.

BY M. N. DOWNING.

IF ever there was a time when the friends of the cause of God both among the ministry and laity should *love* religion, it is now. We are on the eve of a great battle; yea, it has commenced. The issue is truth and righteousness. It is between the reign of a deadly formalism, and the life and power of godliness in the soul. The world is in commotion. Church and state are rocking with excitement; and we say, rock away, if Satan is only routed, and his kingdom demolished.

The Church of God has fallen asleep a number of times since its establishment. Every time she has awoke to see her danger—how far down the stream of formalism she has floated—and how near the precipice she has reached,—there have been heart-rending cries, groans, tears, convulsions, noise, and commotion while striving to regain her former position. Some of her priests have clothed themselves in "sackcloths and ashes," and have mourned before God on account of their sins—on account of indolence, carnal prudence, worldly policy, love of praise and position, and God has restored them to His favor. Others have been aroused, but only to mock and deride, and cry "fanaticism," and "crucify him," and to float on to the vortex of eternal woe, with their craft freighted with immortal souls for whom Christ died. The Church asleep! One of her seasons of slumber has been during nearly a half of a century just past. Many will say this is unrighteous judgment, but the thousands of formal ministers and members that throng our churches, will ere long be obliged to assent to the awful truth. Could the shrieks of the lost—those who have gone to the world of woe from the cradle of formalism,—break upon our ears, they would utter the same assent. Asleep! and, as such a state is one in which men dream, dream of happiness, of prosperity, and awake to the sad consciousness that it was only a dream. So has the Church on account of her outward appearance, and her amount of machinery, been dreaming of prosperity. Behold her numerous and costly edifices, well filled with intelligent hearers. But pause! Look inside. What do you see? Her *splendid* choir of singers. Who *are they?* Many of them are worldlings, who, not unfrequently until past the midnight hour, are reveling in the ball-room, the ante-chamber to hell. Yet they come to church on the Sabbath, and monopolize that part of divine worship which belongs to the children of God. Look again! What do you see? A concourse of people, who, by their profession represent Jesus Christ. Who, by their profession are a *peculiar* people. But is their profession true? Were we to class them off as God does in his word, where would they appear? On the side of the worldling, decorated and adorned with all the paraphernalia of the world!

She has been dreaming of prosperity on account of her refined and educated ministry, too many of whom spend most of their time in their studies, writing essays, which are brought to the Church, spread out in the *Bible*, and prayers offered that God would help to preach the Gospel!

Dreaming of prosperity on account of her wide-spread mission fields, her literary institutions and her wealth; all of which are means of diffusing light, but light is not salvation. Where, in our home lands is her *life*, her *power*, her *glory?* Where are they who are joined to God? Who "know Jesus, the fellowship of his sufferings,—being made conformable to his death?" There are a few. The Church has some life and power, and why? Because she is awaking, and God is again coming to Zion. She feels his awful tread. All denominations are feeling his power. Volcanos are bursting, and sending their thunderbolts into the sepulchre of the dead, whose bones begin to *stir*, causing commotion! The wheels of God's car are rolling in fire! Devils are aroused, believe and tremble. Sinners are being awakened and converted. Backsliders are returning home to God. The lukewarm are embarking either for the region of iceberg formalism or the sea of divine love, while what saints there are, are shouting for the battle of our God, who "is a man of war." Yes, God is coming! Hallelujah! Apostolic times are returning. The millenium may not be far distant, for the light is rapidly spreading, and Protestantism is making wide paths into the Romish Church. But whether it is far or near, one thing is certain— God's work is reviving—a work of faith and power. God will have a remnant—all have not bowed the knee to Baal—the Church is on a rock, the devil cannot get it, for "the gates of hell shall not prevail against it." Bible *truth*, so long crushed to earth, is rearing its head and winning its victories. The banner of the Prince of Peace, dyed in His own blood is waving over the valiant band who know no retreat. Victory or death is the watchword of those who sing as they march through Immanuel's land,

"Thy saints in all this glorious war
Shall *conquer* though they *die*."

A soldier of the Cross can stand amidst the din and strife of battle, with an unblanched cheek; and though the crack of human superstructures may be heard, he prays "ride on, O God of power!"

Then brother, sister, stand at *your* post, for you have a post if you are a child of God. Do not be alarmed at the roar of battle. God's order must and will prevail; and if men hedge up the way of God, think it not strange if you see sights and hear wonders. God's ways are not as ours. Stand at your post as a faithful sentinel, and never yield, for the battle is the Lord's and victory will turn on Zion's side. Some of you have preached and labored, and groaned, and have "earnestly contended for the faith once delivered to the saints," all alone, and that for years, while the missiles of the devil have fallen thick and fast around you. But thus far the Lord has led you on. Then raise your Ebenezer, and take courage, for as that man of God, who fell on the plains of Africa, declared, "though a thousand fall, Africa shall be redeemed;" so it may be said of the work of God throughout these lands; it shall go on though a thousand feel the knife of an ecclesiastical guillotine. In a spiritual contest some must go ahead. Some must fall. Some must hear the cry of "lo! a fanatic," an ".enthusiast." But happy are such, for the "Spirit of glory and of God rested upon them."

Stand at your post, brother, sister, and never leave it to do the duty of some one else, for in so doing you will be overcome. Individualism is the order of battle that must be observed. Never leave *your* post to follow a deserter, for if any become afraid and draw back, they draw back to perdition, which you cannot afford to do. Better stand until, if need be, you are shot down, and your final reward will be a voyage on the sea of eternal bliss. STAND AT YOUR POST.

DEEDS.—Deeds are greater than words. Deeds have such a life, mute but undeniable, and grow as living trees and fruit trees do; they people the vacuity of Time, and make it green and worthy. Why should the oak prove logically that it ought to grow, and will grow? Plant it, try it; what gifts of diligent, judicious assimilation and secretion it has, of progress and resistance, of *force* to grow, will then declare themselves.—CARLYLE.

IT is said that where the most beautiful cacti grow, there the venomous serpents are to be found at the root of every plant. And so it is with sin. Your fairest pleasures will harbor your grossest sins. Take care; take care of your pleasures. Cleopatra's asp was introduced in a basket of flowers; so are our sins often brought to us in the flowers of our pleasures.

REVIVALS.

BY THE EDITOR.

PEKIN CAMP MEETING.

THIS has been a very successful meeting The number of conversions have been greater, we think, than has been usual at camp meetings in late years. The attendance is large— very large—considering how busy farmers are, getting in their grain and preparing to sow their wheat. The Rev. DANIEL WORTH, recently confined in jail in North Carolina, for the crime of selling *Helper's Impending Crisis*, and sentenced to one year's imprisonment, was present, and gave an interesting account of his experience among slaveholders; and on another occasion preached a most pointed and effective gospel sermon. Friends of liberty have helped him to money to pay his bonds. God bless him, and make him instrumental in creating a greater hatred of slavery of all kinds, and enable him yet to lead many souls to Jesus.

FROM a recent number of the London *Quarterly Review* we learn that the religious movement in Sweden has been attended with the most extraordinary results. Out of a population of 2,500,000, the lowest estimates place the number of converts which have been made at 250,000. Everywhere meetings for worship and reading the Scriptures are being largely attended; and what may seem most remarkable, is, that the great mass of human means employed in this work has been the pious efforts of laymen, inspired for their noble work not by the love of fame or lucre, but by the meek and holy spirit of their divine master. The moral consequences of this religious movement have been exceedingly gratifying. Drinking has so far ceased that two-thirds of the distilleries have been closed. In the parishes bordering on Russia, where nearly every man was guilty of smuggling, hundreds of persons have returned the duties of which they had defrauded the government, in many cases even selling their property to obtain the money.

ABYSSINIA BECOMING CHRISTIANIZED.

SOME months ago the Bishop of Jerusalem sent a supply of Bibles to the King of Abyssinia in his own language. He received them with great joy, and began at once to distribute them, telling the priests to whom he gave them that henceforth they must teach the people out of this book in the vernacular. The missionaries who labor there have gained a great influence over the mind of King Theodorus. They build roads and bridges, introduce useful arts of all kinds, distribute Bibles, and recommend the truth by their conversation and their lives. The King has so far recognized their civil services as to raise them to the rank of nobles. He has recognized them to be right in those points where the doctrines of the Bible differ from the traditions of the Abyssinian Church, and in token of it has received the sacrament of the Lord's Supper with them.

REVIVAL IN NEWTONLIMAVADY.

A YOUNG woman was stricken down in the Roman Catholic Chapel on Sunday morning, the 14th instant, and the doors were immediately closed to prevent her screaming being heard by those outside. Another young woman, a Romanist, was stricken down here on Saturday last, in her own house. Her father was sent for, and, on his arrival, he began to pray for the "Blessed Virgin to come to banish the evil spirit" out of his daughter; but she still cried, "None but Jesus—none but Jesus," much to the annoyance of those present, who wished her to pray to some favorite saint, instead of Jesus, who alone can do poor helpless sinners good. Meetings are held here every evening, and are well attended by all parties, Romanists included; but a great many of the latter are prevented from attending, as meetings are held in the chapel every evening to prevent any of the poor creatures attending where Scriptural knowledge can be obtained. But, thank God, Rome is daily losing her power over the deluded people in this place.

THE following letter from one of the preachers employed by the late Western Convention, shows the good that is already being realized. We are satisfied that immediate results should be looked for in every meeting.

REV. B. T. ROBERTS :

Dear Brother :—Since the camp meeting, I have been exploring. God has been with us.

and no meeting has been a barren one, for I have learned to ask and believe for present results, and we have them. At our first meeting, fifteen came forward as seekers—all were adults. One was soundly converted—two thoroughly sanctified, and several backsliders reclaimed. At the next appointment, five rose for prayers—not barely to ask others to pray for them, but pledging to pray for themselves, and to die in the struggle or get salvation. We have held no meeting yet where God has not at the first assembling so far removed prejudice from the public mind as to get a place to set his seal, at least, in convicting power. The people, thus far, plead at each appointment for Bible preaching, and we promise them, thus far, to send them somebody that enjoys religion, that will talk Bible, and that will labor for the salvation of souls.

Another discovery that we make is this: That God has laborers standing all the day idle, and for the reason assigned long since, "because no man employs us." They are not prepared to read a lecture upon the stars, and hence they are not encouraged to labor for God. I firmly believe that God is able, and will man his own work, if he is allowed his choice of implements. He wants burden-bearers, axe-men, not many log-rollers, breaking plows, harrows, sowers of seed, bearers of water, dressers of the vineyard, pruning hooks, reapers, binders, flails and threshers.

Oh, that God could have his own way in these matters, then would our earth blossom as the rose, and in no distant season bring forth its fruit unto holiness, and secure us with the end, everlasting life. D. T. S.

CHURCH FESTIVALS.

THE Gospel represents that there is to be, after death, a difference such as imagination can scarcely conceive, between the fate of sinners and the fate of Christians. The one shall dwell in mansions prepared for them by Christ, in the palace of the "King of Kings." They shall enjoy the society of the pious and holy, redeemed from earth—of angels that never sinned, and God shall wipe away all tears from their eyes. There the scorching sun shall never beat upon the aching brow of toil, nor the pale moon shed her rays upon the couch of suffering, for the glory of God shall lighten that blessed place, and there shall be no more death, neither shall there be any more pain.

"Fair land, could mortal eyes,
But half its charms explore,
How would our spirits long to rise,
And dwell on earth no more!"

On the other hand "the wicked shall be turned into hell," where "the smoke of their torment ascendeth up for ever and ever." Their companions shall be devils and damned spirits, "the fearful and unbelieving, and the abominable and murderers, and whoremongers and sorcerers, and idolaters, and all liars," all of whom the unerring *word* declares "shall have their portion in the lake which burneth with fire and brimstone, which is the second death."

"O, what eternal horrors hang
Around the second death."

This difference of condition is not the result of caprice or chance, or unavoidable necessity. It springs from a real and voluntary difference in the character and conduct of men while on earth.

The traveler to Heaven, with his loins girt about, steadily pressing forward in the face of every difficulty and danger, is very unlike the careless passenger floating thoughtlessly but surely down the stream of time to perdition. The faithful picture which the Holy Ghost has drawn of the adopted children of God, bears no resemblance to the children of the Wicked One. The Bible describes Christians as "a peculiar people." They have "come out" from the ungodly, and are "separate." They are not "conformed to the world."

Transformed by the renewing of their minds they "walk not after the flesh, but after the Spirit." They are crucified with Christ, dead unto sin, seeking no longer the pleasures of the world, but denying themselves and taking up their cross daily and following Jesus. They have renounced the hidden things of dishoner, by never "doing evil, that good may come." They seek, not the pleasures of the world, but the peace of God which passeth all understanding, and the joy of the Holy Ghost.

Most, if not all, of Christian churches, both those which still flourish, and those which have gone to decay, commenced their career upon these principles of self denial. Two centuries ago, and the founders of some of the most fashionable churches of the present day were stigmatized as *puritans*, on account of the austerity of their manners.

The Methodists set out with the avowed object of spreading Scriptural Holiness over these lands. They were a simple-hearted, plain, earnest people. In the face of much opposition and persecution, they relied upon the co-operation of the Holy Ghost. Their success proved that their reliance was not in vain. To obtain the necessary means for carrying on the work of the Church, the appeal was simply made to the love the people had for Christ. It is but a few years since, even in the city of New York, but a single Methodist Church could be found where the pews were rented or sold. Now, even in the rural districts, free churches, where the poor can have the Gospel preached to them are the exception and not the rule.

When once a divergence from the right course is commenced, no human eye can foresee where it will end. From the mammoth depot of the Central Railroad in Buffalo, two trains start out, and for a little time they run in the same direction, and apparently side by side. By little and little they diverge—soon they lose sight of each other—and in twenty-four hours the passenger upon one finds himself among the fertile prairies of Illinois or Wisconsin, while the traveler upon the other is winding his way among the mountains of Massachusetts, or is swallowed up in the sea of human beings that throng the metropolis. So when an individual or a church turns aside from the narrow path, no one can tell how fast or how far they will go in a direction opposite to that in which they at first set out.

We have seen, with sorrow, the unholy plans that have been adopted to raise money for holy purposes. We have borne our testimony against all the contrivances resorted to for the purpose of beguiling the enemies of God into an involuntary support of his precious cause. We expected that according to the laws of spiritual declension, those who adopted, in order to raise money for the church, the expedients of oyster suppers and festivals, grab-bags and lotteries, and post offices where "fun is sold cheap, and dealers in that commodity are invited to come and purchase," would go on from bad to worse, but we must say that the latest plan devised to raise money for the support of the church, took us utterly by surprise. It was carried out in Buffalo, the seat of the late General Conference, and it took place only a few weeks after the delegates left, while yet the savor of their influence remained.

"CLAM BAKE AND CHOWDER."

For a few days previous to the great festival held by the Methodist Episcopal Church in Buffalo, large hand-bills, with the above heading, were posted up throughout the city. The following notice was published in the daily papers:

"M. E. CHURCH FESTIVAL.—Next Thursday a grand festival of the Methodist Episcopal Church is to inaugurate "Clinton Forest," the newly fitted-up picnic-grove at Black Rock, on the line of the Niagara Street Railroad. In many features the affair will be quite an extraordinary one. The great incident of the occasion will be an old-fashioned "Clam Bake and Chowder," upon a large scale, which will be a great novelty in these parts. One or two of the military companies are expected to attend, and the Twilight Serenaders will assist a fine band in enlivening the occasion with music. A large delegation from Lockport is looked for to attend the festival, as the Central Railroad Company has consented to bring an excursion party at half-price."

We did not attend. When we made a profession of religion, a number of years ago, we ceased attending such places. Of course, we cannot speak of the occurrence from personal observation, but the following account from the Buffalo *Courier* of August 4th, we think is worth preserving. The editor, who was present, appears to have heartily enjoyed the festival, of which he speaks in the following complimentary terms:

"CLAM BAKE AND CHOWDER. — The spot selected for the clam bake was Clinton Forest, situated about half a mile from the road. This place, containing about twenty acres, was surrounded by a neat board fence, and ten cents demanded from each visitor for admission within the enclosure. Within we found thousands of people, some ventilating their garments on swings, some playing games of different descriptions, hundreds eating ice-cream, coffee, ham, fowls and other substantials, while the great mass opened, swallowed or gorged themselves with clams. Clams was the cry—from every corner came the echo, clams! clams! and the odor and flavor of clams went up and down odorous as exquisite ottars, and fragrant as a back kitchen about dinner time. The heroic FERGUSON presided over the clams, within an enclosure of plank, and with his head wreathed in a towel, and his delicate waist spanned by a clean apron, he looked the very god Epicurus, as he intrepidly ladled out the chowder, and courageously burned his fingers in his mortal haste. (*Entre nous* the chowder was superb.)

"At other points on the grounds were many tables, spread with delicacies of all sorts, behind which handsome women added their voices to urge on appetite; flower tables were many, where young and pretty damsels waylaid pecunious young men with their eyes, and persuaded them into floral purchases; ice-cream booths, where shillings were exchanged for the frigid luxury, accompanied with parallelogrammatic sections of sponge cake; there were other places where money could be laid out to advantage in many ways, but of them we remember none. At the rope-walk, a building which appeared to us to be a mile long, a large crowd had collected, and to the music of two bands were jumping about and perspiring to their heart's content, which privilege cost each dancer the sum of ten cents. The atmosphere in this place was so intensely hot and high flavored, that we positively failed to get the programme of the dances.

"In the main grounds, the Union Cornet Band, with their new instruments, delighted the crowds with their music, while the Twilight Serenaders were kept musical all day long, by the voices of women and girls, who surrounded them with a rampart of charms, denying their egress without some specimen of their vocal attributes. The singers fairly made themselves hoarse with their efforts. All was hilarity and enjoyment throughout the afternoon, everybody appearing to be happy just in proportion as they had absorbed clams, (and here arises the question of the relation of good humor to baked clams. Perhaps the gentlemen who took the money at the gate will inform us.) We call particular attention to this new social meteor, in consequence of hearing some gentlemen who never were considered musical, successfully attempting the "Star Spangled Banner," with variations, about thirty rods from Clinton Forest, where a contraband lager beer merchant had opened his wares. No one will be unkind enough to intimate that the music came from the lager. No!

"The festival altogether was a success, and has initiated a new order of excursions, which we hope will be followed up. The receipts at the gate were over four hundred dollars, we understand, and at the different booths, &c., several hundred dollars more. The proceeds are for the benefit of Niagara Street Methodist Church, and will prove a great assistance to them in paying off the debt of the church. The ladies, particularly, deserve the highest encomiums for their efforts and attempts to make the festival a model one, and carrying it on to triumph."

The person who stood at the door of the rope-walk and collected "ten cents" of each one who attended the "dance," is, we understand, a member of one of the M. E. Churches in the city, and the proceeds, after "paying for the music," went for the benefit of the church. There will, quite likely, be a revival of dancing, when the church becomes its patron, and when any one can dance " to his heart's content" for only "ten cents!"

The "chief priests" of old, *would not permit the money which Judas received for betraying Christ to go into the treasury of the Lord.*

The object of this "festival," was to raise money to pay off the debt of the Niagara Street M. E. Church. This Church once highly prosperous, when "holiness" was a common theme among its members, has been declining for several years. The members were taught that this lack of prosperity was not occasioned by a decline of spirituality, but by the want of a better edifice. The church was remodeled, and made one of the most splendid in the city. All the money was raised that could be raised by the sale of pews—by taxing the members to the utmost of their ability, and by making one of the largest liquor dealers in the city trustee and treasurer. Still the debt of the church was augmented to eight or nine thousand dollars.

Many of the members, we have no doubt, disapprove in their hearts of these unchristian proceedings, but they are so accustomed to obey their preacher that they fall in with his wishes, faintly whispering to their souls,

"The evil which I would not, that I do."

In the name of our common Christianity, we protest against all these contrivances for raising money. If the cause of God cannot be sustained in any other way let it go down.

1. All these expedients for obtaining funds for the Church are based on the assumption that the Church is in a state of hopeless apostacy. St. Paul in 1st Tim., 3d chapter, gives it as one of the marks of "men of corrupt minds, reprobate concerning the faith," that they are lovers of *pleasure, more than lovers of God*, HAVING A FORM OF GODLINESS *but denying* THE POWER thereof." "*From such*," he says, "TURN AWAY."

2. They foster and encourage vice for the sake of pecuniary gain. What better are they in principle than the indulgences of the Romish Church?

3. They tend to sap the foundations of morality. If the Church may "do evil that good may come," why may not the individual? Personal gain is thus made the standard of action instead of the immutable principles of right and wrong.

4. They lead to practical Atheism. They say in effect that God cannot save us, and now we must go to the world for help.

5. They lead souls to hell. Many a Church member who has, for years, stood out against the seductions of pleasure and the blandishments of the world, has out of *love for the Church*, been induced to go to those festivals, "lost his *first love*," sank down into dead formalism, and gone from the bosom of the Church to the fires of perdition. Many a penitent has had his convictions dissipated, and many a doubter has gone away saying that religion is all a humbug and a farce.

CONVENTION AT PEKIN.

ABOUT eighty laymen and fifteen preachers met in convention, at Pekin, Niagara County, N. Y., on the 23d of August, to take into consideration the adoption of a Discipline for the "FREE METHODIST CHURCH." Quite a discussion took place as to the propriety of effecting, at present, a formal organization. When the vote was taken, all but seven—five preachers and two laymen—stood up in favor of organizing immediately.

In considering the provisions of the Discipline presented by the committee, every new feature was scanned most closely and critically. The deep interest and close scrutiny of the intelligent laymen who were present as delegates, must have convinced any one that that church is a great loser which excludes them from her councils. After a careful examination, item by item, the Discipline, as agreed upon, was adopted with singular unanimity. It was as surprising as delightful to notice the similarity of views entertained by men who think for themselves, coming from different parts of the country.

The doctrines agreed upon are those entertained by Methodists generally throughout the world. An article on sanctification, taken from Wesley's writings, was adopted. As a difference in views upon this subject is one cause of the difficulties that have occurred in the Genesee Conference, it was thought best to have a definite expression of our belief.

The countenance given of late by Methodist ministers in this region to Universalists, by affiliating with them—supplying their pulpits, and going without rebuke to their communion—rendered it necessary, in the judgment of the convention to have an article, drawn from the Bible, on future rewards and punishments.

The annual and quadrennial conventions are to be composed of an equal number of laymen and ministers. The episcopacy and presiding eldership are abolished. Class leaders and stewards are chosen by the members, and the sacred right of every accused person to an impartial trial and appeal is carefully guarded.

Several searching questions relating to personal experience and his purpose to lead a life devoted to God, must be proposed to every individual offering to join the church; and upon an affirmative response, he is to be admitted with the consent of three-fourths of the members present at a society meeting.

It is not the intention to try to get up a secession. On the contrary, as much as in us lies, we shall live peaceably with all men. The wicked expulsion of several ministers, for no other crime than simply trying to carry out their ordination vows, and the cruel refusal of the General Conference to grant us the hearing of our appeals, guaranteed to us in the most solemn manner by the Constitution and Laws of the Methodist Episcopal Church, and the violent ejection from the Church of many of its most pious and devoted members, whose only offence was that of sympathising with us, as we are trying to endure "the afflictions of the Gospel," have rendered it necessary to provide a humble shelter, for ourselves, and for such poor, wayfaring pilgrims as may wish to journey with us to heaven. We are very firm in the conviction that it is the will of the Lord that we should establish free Churches—*the seats to be forever free*—where the Gospel can be preached to the poor. We have this consolation—and it is a great one—that if our effort is not for the glory of God, and does not receive His approval, *it cannot succeed.* And if it is not for His glory, we most devoutly pray that it may fail in its very incipiency. We would rather be covered with any amount of dishonor than have the cause of God suffer. We have no men of commanding ability and influence to help on the enterprise—no wealth, no sympathy from powerful ecclesiastical, or political, or secret societies; but all these against us—so that if we succeed, it must be by the blessings of Heaven upon our feeble endeavors. We cannot avail ourselves of any popular excitement in favor of a reform in Church government—or against slavery; but we are engaged in the work, always unpopular, and especially so in this age, of trying to persuade our fellow-men to tread in the path of self-denial—*the narrow way that leadeth unto life.*

The new discipline will be ready probably in two or three weeks. It will be about the size and form of the old Methodist Disciplines, and will be furnished at two dollars a dozen, or twenty-five cents for a single copy.

Orders may be addressed to B. T. ROBERTS, Buffalo, N. Y.

A SOLEMN BALLAD.
CONTAINING MORE TRUTH THAN POETRY.

THE silks brought to this country, exceed in value, by eight millions of dollars, all the flour that we send abroad. During the year 1855, $1,374,077 worth of coin left our ports, and cigars valued at $3,311,935 were brought in. Of beef, tallow, hides and horned cattle, we sold for other countries only $2,214,544 in the last commercial year, and during that time we bought brandy to the amount of $3,241,408.

Three leading principles have we,
  An Orion's belt of stars,
To guide the nation of the free:
  Silks, brandy and cigars.

Were battle here, we'd bravely fight,
  And would not shrink for scars;
But oh—we'd tremble should we miss
  Silks, brandy and cigars.

We fear the loss of trash, and smoke,
  And rum, much more than wars;
We're ripe to fight—but can't give up
  Silks, brandy and cigars.

Americans, ye are not now
  Like your old pa's and ma's;
They gave up tea, and with it, too,
  Silks, brandy and cigars.

But you go on—lock'd fast and tight,
  Twixt French and British bars;
Selling your birthright—and for what?
  Silks, Brandy and Cigars.

THE EARNEST CHRISTIAN.

THE DIFFERENCE BETWEEN REGENERATION AND SANCTIFICATION.

BY REV. WM. COOLEY.

We understand by regeneration, that change of heart resulting from being born of the Spirit, which makes its subject a new creature; and by entire sanctification that cleansing of the heart from all inward corruption, which constitutes it holy. This entire sanctification is a work wrought in the heart subsequent to regeneration, and not in conjunction with it. Regeneration is only a partial renovation of the heart, while sanctification is an entire work as far as purity is concerned. The necessity of this subsequent work grows out of the fact, that the heart is not freed from all the carnal nature when it is regenerated. What remains is *inbred sin, inward sin, sin of the heart,* of desire, feeling and volition, such as the roots of pride, of anger, jealousy, envy, or love of the world; and not actual sin, or the sin of the life. Though these are found in the heart after regeneration, grace gives us victory over them, and we commit sin only when we let these get the mastery over us. Some find it quite difficult to understand such distinctions, but they agree with the Bible and with experience. In vindicating this view, we shall present the testimony of the Bible and of able divines, and also the experience of Christians. Paul in addressing the Church at Corinth says in 2 Cor. 7, 1: "Having therefore these promises, dearly beloved, let us cleanse ourselves from all filthiness of the flesh and spirit." From all outward pollution of the flesh if there is any; and then from all pollution of the spirit, which includes all inward sin. These Corinthians were justified persons. Paul call them "*dearly beloved.*" In verse 4th, he says "great is my glorying of you." Though some of this Church had been backslidden, Paul's first letter corrected them, and he now says, in verse 9th: they had sorrowed after a godly sort, and then mentions the result of this sorrow, " yea, what clearing of yourselves, yea what zeal, etc. In verse 16, he says, "I rejoice therefore, that I have confidence in you in all things." The conclusion is, these must have been justified persons, who needed to be fully cleansed. Paul prays for the Thessalonian Church in a way to teach this doctrine. 1 Thess. v, 23. "And the very God of peace sanctify you wholly; and I pray God your whole spirit, and soul and body, be preserved blameless unto the coming of our Lord Jesus Christ." These were Christians, partially sanctified, but not wholly, and Paul prays that they might be sanctified wholly. Sanctification begins with regeneration, and thus all justified persons are partly sanctified. These were to be entirely sanctified and then kept so,— " preserved blameless."

Gal. v, 17: "For the flesh lusteth against the Spirit, and the Spirit against the flesh; and these are contrary the one to the other." Mr. Wesley says, "He is speaking to believers, and describes the state of believers in general when he says, "the flesh lusteth against the Spirit, and these are contrary the one to the other."

Nothing can be more express. The apostle here directly affirms that the flesh, evil nature, opposes the Spirit, even in believers; that even in the regenerate there are two principles, contrary one to the other. Ser. vol. 2, p. 109. The apostle speaks of a class of persons in 1 Cor. iii, 1—2, whom he denominated carnal in a sense, and yet they were babes in Christ. Mr. Wesley thinks they were believers.

Paul speaks in Heb. xii, 15, of "roots of bitterness spring up and troubling them," in connection with the duty to follow holiness, which leads us to conclude, (though it may refer also to other things,) that it must have reference to inward sin. 1 John i, 9,—"If we confess our sins He is faithful and just to forgive us our sins, and to cleanse us from all unrighteousness." This means He will pardon us, and then He will cleanse our hearts. Christians are addressed in the Scriptures as though they needed a higher state of purity. "And every man that hath this hope in him purifieth himself, even as he is pure." 1 John, iii, 3. "Be ye holy for I am holy." "Be ye therefore perfect, even as your Father in heaven is perfect." "Sanctify them through thy truth, thy word is truth." "Leaving the principles of the doctrine of Christ, let us go on to perfection." "This is the will of God, even your sanctification." "That ye may be perfect and entire, wanting nothing." "Always laboring fervently for you in prayer, that ye may stand perfect and complete in all the will of God." The apostles gave evidence of inward sin, which sometimes got the mastery over them, before they "*were filled with the Holy Spirit*," and entirely sanctified, as they evidently were on the day of Pentecost.

We will now consider some objections to this doctrine. "If any man be in Christ, he is a new creature: old things are passed away; behold all things are become new." 2 Cor. v, 17. This passage means that a great change has taken place in conversion, so that the power of the old man is broken, and the views and feelings are greatly changed, but it cannot mean that this is done in an absolute sense, for the physical and mental powers remain much as they were before. Mr. Wesley says, "But we must not so interpret the apostle's words as to make him contradict himself. And if we will make him consistent with himself, the plain meaning of the words is this: His old judgment concerning justification, holiness, happiness, indeed concerning the things of God in general, is now passed away: so are his old desires, designs, affections, tempers, and conversation. All these are undeniably become new—greatly changed from what they were. And yet though they are new, they are not wholly new. Still he feels, to his sorrow and shame, remains of the old man, too manifest taints of his former tempers and affections, though they cannot gain any advantage over him, as long as he watches and prays." Ser. vol. 1, p. 112. Some have understood 1 Cor. vi, 11, which mentions the word sanctified before justified, as opposed to this view, but the term is simply used not in the sense of holiness, but in its lower meaning of separation from sinful uses. Dr. Clark says, "It means ye are separated from idols to be joined to the living God."

An objection of this character is sometimes made, "God never does a partial or imperfect work." This objection is not valid, as we propose to show. He might have created the world in a moment of time, but he was six days in doing it. He was four thousand years in introducing the scheme of redemption into our world. When our Saviour raised Lazarus from the dead, he left part of the work to be done afterwards, which was "loose him and let him go." He led the blind man out of the town and then partially cured him, so that he saw men as trees walking, and then he put his hands again upon his eyes, and he was restored, and saw every man clearly. Mark viii, 23. There are steps or degrees in the personal salvation of every soul. The enlightening of the mind, the conviction of guilt, the penitence, the faith exercised, the conversion of the soul, the witness of the spirit, the subsequent growth in grace, the entire sanctification of the heart, the subsequent growth in love, and enlargement of the heart, and increase in power and faith. It is so in the natural world. The work God does there is not all done at once, for there is the small sprout, and then the tree, the germinating seed, the stalk, and the full corn in the ear, the rose-bud, and then the beautiful flower. In religious experience there is the babe in Christ, and the perfect man. These illustrations are used to show the two states, and not the length of time in passing from one state to the other.

We will now introduce the testimony of several prominent writers, beginning with Dr. Dempster; he says, speaking of sanctification, "Between this state and mere regeneration, the distinction should be accurately defined. You ask in what then does regeneration consist? Simply in this threefold change, viz: justification, partial renovation, and divine adoption. Above and beyond this great change stands that of *Christian Perfection.* Do you then demand an exact expression of the difference? It is this, the one admits of controlled tendencies to sin, the other extirpates those tendencies. That is, the merely regenerate has remaining impurity, the fully sanctified has none. The difference between these two states is, therefore, moral, not physical—owing not to one being more largely developed than the other, but to one being *more pure* than the other. Beyond sanctification there is no increase in purity, but unceasing increase in expansion."

Says Mr. Wesley, "When does inward sanctification begin? In the moment a man is justified, yet sin remains in him, yea the seed of all sin, till he is sanctified throughout." Plain Account, p. 48. "By sin, I here understand inward sin, any sinful temper, passion or affection; such as pride, self-will, love of the world, in any kind of degree, such as lust, anger, or peevishness; any disposition contrary to the mind which was in Christ." Ser. vol. 1, p. 109. "And it is most certain that there does still remain even in the hearts of them that are justified, a mind that is in some measure carnal, a heart bent to backsliding, a propensity to pride, anger, revenge, love of the world, yea and all evil, a root of bitterness, which if the restraint were taken off for a moment, would instantly spring up; yea, such a depth of corruption, as without clear light from God, we cannot possibly conceive, if you think it (inbred sin) does not remain, you certainly have not considered the length and breadth, and height and depth of the law of God." Wesley's Ser., vol. 1, p. 119 and 113.

Richard Watson says, "That a distinction exists between a regenerate state, and a state of entire and perfect holiness will be generally allowed. Regeneration we have seen, is concomitant with justification; but the apostles in addressing the body of believers in the churches to whom they wrote their epistles, set before them, both in the prayers they offer in their behalf, and in the exhortations they administer, a still higher degree of deliverance from sin as well as a higher growth in Christian virtues. Two passages only need be quoted to prove this: 1 Thes. v, 23. "And the very God of peace sanctify you wholly, and I pray God your whole spirit and soul and body be preserved blameless unto the coming of our Lord Jesus Christ. 2 Cor. vii, 1. "Having these promises, dearly beloved, let us cleanse ourselves from all filthiness of the flesh, perfecting holiness in the fear of God." In both these passages deliverance from sin is the subject spoken of; and the prayer in one instance, and the exhortation in the other, goes to the extent of the entire sanctification of the *soul* and *spirit* as well as the *flesh* or *body*, from all sin; by which can only be meant our complete deliverance from all spiritual pollution, all inward depravation of the heart, as well as that which expresses itself outwardly by the indulgence of the senses, is called filthiness of the flesh." Theological Inst. vol. 2, p. 450.

Mr. Fletcher says, "We do not deny that the remains of the carnal mind still cleave to imperfect Christians; and that when the expression "carnal" is softened and qualified, it may in a low sense, be applied to such professors as these Corinthians were, to whom St. Paul said, "I could not speak to you as to spiritual."

Dr. J. T. Peck says, "We hazard nothing in asserting that true Christians may, and often do know, that they have the remains of carnal nature within them, while at the same time, "the Spirit itself beareth witness with their spirits that they are the children of God." The more they improve in religious experience, until wholly sanctified, the more they see of the evils of their own hearts. Their tendency to sin is not so great, because they are living nearer to God, but because they know more of it. Their spiritual vision is constantly becoming clearer, and hence they detect depravity in their own souls, which was before unknown to them. Is not this incontestably so? Who are they who have the deepest sense of inward corruptions? Who have most mental agony upon the discovery of their unlikeness to Christ? Certainly not those who have departed from the faith; not those who seldom pray in earnest—whose lives are yielded a sacrifice to the world. "No, they are surely those who live nearest to God in a justified state; who are most constant and devout in the use of the means of grace." Central Idea, p. 77.

Bishop Hedding says, "The justified soul finds in himself the remains of inbred corruption, or original sin: such as pride, anger, envy, a feeling of hatred to an enemy, a rejoicing at a calamity which has fallen upon him."

Dr. Bangs says, "That after a sinner is justified freely by his grace, he is made deeply sensible, and perhaps more so than ever, of the impurity of his nature, we freely admit; not indeed because he is more impure, but because the light of God's Spirit shining into his soul, now more clearly discovers to him the native impurity, the roots of bitterness within." In another article we propose to consider the experience of many intelligent Christians on this question.

THE BEAUTIES OF THE WORLD TO COME.

Beautiful Zion built above,
Beautiful City that I love;
Beautiful Gates of pearly white,
Beautiful Temple, God its light.

Beautiful Trees for ever there,
Beautiful Fruits they always bear;
Beautiful Rivers gliding by,
Beautiful Fountains never dry.

Beautiful Light without the sun,
Beautiful Days revolving on,
Beautiful Worlds on Worlds untold,
Beautiful Streets of shining gold.

Beautiful Heaven where all is light,
Beautiful Angels clothed in white,
Beautiful Songs that never tire,
Beautiful Harps thro' all the Choir.

Beautiful Crowns on every brow,
Beautiful Palms the conqueror's show,
Beautiful Robes the ransomed wear,
Beautiful All who enter there.

Beautiful Throne for God the Lamb,
Beautiful Seats at God's right hand,
Beautiful Rest all wanderings cease,
Beautiful Home of perfect peace.

Psalm xlviii, 2; Isaiah lii, 1; lx, 19, 20, 21; Hebrews iv, 9; II Peter iii, 13, 14; Revelations iv, 7; 21, 22 Chap.

WITH the same height of desire that thou hast sinned, with the like depth of sorrow thou must repent; thou that hast sinned to-day, defer not thy repentance till to-morrow: he that hath promised pardon to thy repentance, hath not promised life till thou repent. —QUARLES.

REV. JOHN SMITH.

BY REV. A. A. PHELPS.

I have just closed the life of Rev. John Smith, of the British Wesleyan Conference. It forms an 18-mo. volume of 324 pages, besides nearly a hundred pages of introductory matter by Dr. James Dixon, which is both sound and suggestive. The body of the work was written by Rev. Richard Treffry, Jr., who has shown himself an able biographer. The subject of the memoir was one of the most pious and useful ministers of his or any age. His career was short, but full of labors and signal conquests for God. His zeal was as intense as his faith was invincible. Having neither time nor inclination to dabble in worldly speculations, he fixed his eye on the one great object of the Christian ministry, and pursued it with a devotion that swallowed up every power of his being. He was on the track of *souls*, and O how bitter his grief when he failed to rescue them from ruin's brink and lead them to the "fountain filled with blood!" But he *did* succeed in plucking thousands from death and hell, and helping them on in the way to heaven. It ought to be remarked, that one great element of his success was the energy with which he strove to create a fund of power in the Church. He did this by constantly urging believers on to holiness. Indeed, his uniform way of working, like that of the celebrated Caughey, was to have two revivals go on simultaneously—one among sinners and backsliders, the other among justified Christians. A revival occurring under such circumstances, has a three-fold advantage. First, the Church itself is made holy and happy and stable. Second, the members of a Church thus baptized and sanctified, are clothed with such power that more sinners are actually converted than would otherwise be the case. Third, the converts stand a thousand times better chance to live, by being thus fanned by gracious breezes around them and urged on themselves to the depths of perfect love. How much better it seems for a minister of the Gospel to imitate the example of such men as Smith, Nelson and Bramwell, (who all drank into the same spirit) in waving the banners of salvation on the watch-tower of Zion, marshalling the soldiers of Christ to an earnest contest with the prince of darkness, and then joining in the shout of victory over the retreating legions of Satan, than to be throwing obstacles in the way of their ever gaining a victory, and if perchance a few intrepid heroes should lead the way to a bloody slaughter in the "army of the aliens," to have him rally his sleepy forces and unite his influence with theirs in suppressing the rising joys of their more valiant-hearted comrades!

We conclude this hasty sketch with an extract from the biographer, at the close of Mr. Smith's labors on the Nottingham circuit: "Such was the closing scene of Mr. Smith's regular ministry, in a circuit most tenderly endeared to his own heart, and in which his name will long be remembered with deep emotions of gratitude and reverence. Of his usefulness, during the four years of his residence here, it is impossible to form any adequate estimate. A gentleman intimately acquainted with the circuit, and in every other respect qualified to form a correct calculation, states it as his opinion, that there are now in its societies not fewer than four hundred persons, who were converted to God through Mr. Smith's immediate instrumentality. And if to this extraordinary number, we add those cases in which his ministry was powerfully blessed to neighboring circuits, and the other instances in which he was in a still more extended, though less palpable and direct way, the instrument of good in his own circuit,—we have an amount of spiritual service to the Church, as the result of one man's labor, such as, in so short a period, has very rarely been surpassed. Upon the supposition that his principles were really incorrect, and his modes of effort unscriptural, the marvellous character of his usefulness is strikingly enhanced. What must have been the might of that piety, which in spite of fundamental and practical error, achieved such an incalculable mass of good! What the energy of that faith which, with such serious hindrances, succeeded in bringing down heavenly influence so extensive and powerful! Nay, rather, we are compelled to say, "Blessed is the error which tends to lead such multitudes to the knowledge of the truth! honorable is the heresy which establishes countless believers on their most holy faith! sacred is the extravagance which from every side calls wandering sheep into the fold of Christ! and happy, thrice happy is the man who, with the brand of error, heresy, and extravagance affixed to his character at a human tribunal, returns to God to be enshrined and exalted, as a radiant and spotless star, forever and ever!"

IF the members of churches are to be not Christians, but "respectable persons," if their piety is to be not the reverent upturning of the finite eye to the Infinite God, but a fluctuating accommodation to the religious fashions of the day—that goes once to Church, or twice, as is the mode, that subscribes to missions, and gets up sales for charitable purposes, or does not, as is the mode—then they may indeed remain for a time, and even do their work and get their reward; but the first blast of millennial Christianity will sweep them utterly away. The Tyrians chained Appollo to the statue of Dagon, but Alexander laid their towers in the dust all the same! Revolution is fearful; the unchained masses, foaming, maddened in atheistic frenzy, are fearful; but Christianity chained in the temple of mammon is the most fearful of all.—BAYNE.

THE TRUE WISDOM.

A MAN may know all about the rocks, and his heart remain as hard as they are; a man may know all about the winds, and be the sport of passions as fierce as they; a man may know all about the stars, and his fate be the meteor's, that, after a brief and brilliant career, is quenched in eternal night; a man may know all about the sea, and his soul resemble the troubled waters, which cannot rest; a man may know how to rule the spirits of the elements, yet know not how to rule his own; a man may know how to turn aside the flashing thunderbolt, but not the wrath of God from his own guilty head; he may know all that La Place knew—all that Shakspeare knew—all that Watts knew—all that the greatest geniuses have known; he may know all mysteries and all knowledge, but if he does not know his Bible, what shall it avail? I take my stand by the bed of a dying philosopher as well as of a dying miser, and ask of the world's wisdom, "What shall it profit a man if he gain the world and lose his own soul?"

I despise not the lights of science; but they burn in a dying chamber as dim as its candles. They cannot penetrate the mists of death, nor light the foot of the weary traveler on his way in that valley through which we have to pass. Commend me, therefore, to the light which illumines the last hour of life—commend me to the light that, when all others are quenched, shall guide my feet to the portals of that blessed world where there is no need of the sun, and no need of the moon, and no need of any created lights, for God and the Lamb are the light thereof. Brethren, leave others to climb the steps of fame—brother, sister, put your feet upon the ladder that scales the sky; nor mind though your brows are never crowned with fading bays, if you win, through faith in Jesus, the crown of eternal life.—DR. GUTHRIE.

CONFIRMATION OF SCRIPTURE.

The following interesting article, from an exchange, shows the bearing of the discoveries at Nineveh on the teachings of the Bible:

The discoveries of Layard at Nineveh, though curious and instructive in all respects, are most important from the light they throw on Scripture. In reading the narrative of the bold explorer, we seem to be transported back to the days of the Hebrew prophet, for substantially the same manners and customs prevail in Messopotamia now as did three thousand years ago. There are still the lodges in the cucumber gardens which Isaiah describes; the oxen still tread out the corn; the vessels of bulrushes may still be seen; and the wild asses of the desert, so poetically alluded to by Job, still watch the traveler from a distance, pause for him to draw near, and then gallop away to the shadowy horizon. To realize the Old Testament, Layard should be read. The ancient portion of the Bible ceases to be the dim, far-off record it has heretofore appeared; light gleams all along its pages; its actors live and move before us; we become ourselves sharers in the story; and the past, for the moment, is vivified in the present.

The confirmation of the truth of the Scripture derived from the sculptures of Nineveh is not less remarkable. The bas-reliefs on the walls of the palaces, now just restored to light, after being entombed for nearly two thousand years, verify perpetually the Hebrew Bible. There is still to be seen the wild bull in the net mentioned by Isaiah; the Babylonian princes in vermillion, with dyed attire on their heads described by Ezekiel; and warriors bringing the heads of their enemies in caskets, to cast them down at the palace gates, as was done with the seventy sons of Ahab. There, too, are painted shields hung on the walls of besieged towns, as we are told by the Jewish prophet, he beheld at Tyre. There are the forts built over against the beleaguered city; the king placing his feet on the necks of the captive princes; and the idols of the conquered carried away by the victors, precisely as described by Hosea and other sacred authors. There are also the Assyrian Gods, still the same as when their portraits were drawn five-and-twenty centuries ago—cut from the trees of the forest, decked with silver and gold, fastened with nails, and clothed with purple and blue. The very star to which Amos alludes is yet on those palace walls, above the horned cup of the idol, though the worshippers have been dead for thousands of years, and though the wild beasts as predicted, have made their lairs there.

Even the enormous circumference which Jonah gives to the walls of Nineveh is fully corroborated. The three day's journey of the prophet is still required to make the circuit of the great ruins on the east bank of the Tigris, for the people of Messopotamia build their cities as the Hindoos still construct theirs. First one king erected a palace, around which grew up a town; then a new monarch built one, for fresh air on the verge of the open country, whither soon followed another town; and this process was repeated till several contiguous cities were decaying and being erected, all passing, however, under the general name, and covering together an extent of ground which would otherwise be incredible. The light thrown on Scripture, the confirmation afforded to the Bible by these recent discoveries at Nineveh, is so remarkable, that it almost seems as if that ancient city, after being buried, had been allowed to be disinterred solely to confound the folly of modern skepticism.

BODILY infirmities, like breaks in a wall, have often become avenues through which the light of Heaven has entered to the soul, and made the imprisoned inmate long for release.

HE THAT WINNETH SOULS IS WISE.

BY REV. JAMES MATHEWS.

PAUSE a moment, my brother, and think of this. Not he that winneth honors, not he that gains a position in the world, or the Church, but "he that winneth souls." How many have forgotten this! Young men of promise, whom God called out of the world, made wise unto salvation, and sent into the vineyard to work for him, have labored for a little time, then forgetting that the only wisdom was to win souls, turned their eyes to a college course, and left the field—turned away from the great work, and instead of laboring to pull men out of the fire, began to work for a degree, as though death would forbear to call any away until they were prepared to warn them. What has been the result? They have gained the prize—gone out titled—able to please the fancy of wise men, to round a period, frame a sentence, speak correctly, and gesture faultlessly. Men applaud and sink down to the regions of woe under their preaching.

There are many to-day, called of God to proclaim the gospel, who are shrinking from it. Ask them why? "Oh," they say, "we know so little." So thought Gideon Ously: He would say, "Lord, I am a poor, ignorant creature; how can I go? Then it would rush into his mind, "Do you know the disease? "O yes, Lord, I do!" "And do you not know the cure?" "O yes, glory be to thy name! I do." Then go and tell them of the disease and the cure." He did so, and his works say *he was wise*, for he won souls.

"If that man is the best physician who performs the most cures, that is the best preacher who brings the greatest number of souls to God."

A course of study never made a man mighty to pull down the strong holds of the devil. "God has chosen the weak things of the world to confound the mighty, and things that are not, to bring to nought things that are." When a man cries out, "Who is sufficient for these things?" and wrestles with God for help, makes his closet his study, his Bible his hand-book, and goes through the college of Jesus—then the degree he takes will be of some use. He that denies himself, wrestles with God in mighty prayer, and takes hold on the horns of the altar, holding on by persevering faith, will take a degree that will fit him for service. God makes A. M's. "*All is yours.*" The man of God knows it, and cries, "*All is mine.* Now Father, give me souls,"—and he wins them. Such a man is wise.

There are hundreds of learned men in the ministry to-day, who win everything but souls. Large churches are built for them, they win applause, preferment, congregations, fortunes, but souls never.

Why? Not because they do not labor. They travel, write, lecture and preach all the time, and are really earnest men. But they do not aim to win souls. They wear themselves out lopping off branches, instead of striking at the root of the tree of evil; building up a party, or establishing some favorite notion of church order, instead of insisting on repentance, deep and self-killing—leaving all to follow Jesus or no salvation,—and so win members to the Church perhaps, but no souls to Christ. Yet they talk of repentance; *so does the Universalist.* They talk of faith in Christ; *so does the Antinomian.* They preach, but not as did the apostle, "warning every man, and teaching every man in all wisdom, that they may present every man perfect before God," or they would reap, as did the apostle, *souls daily.* St. Paul was a leader of the sect of Nazarenes, (so called,) and had he been possessed of worldly policy, he would have first attempted to make the movement a popular one. Not so did he act. He boldly struck for souls, and won them. Would to God men did so to-day, instead of piping the tune "Popularity," with soul-saving accompaniments. Look at the fathers; they sought souls, won them; counted not their lives dear unto them, so they might pull men out of the fire. They were wise men. God gave them seals to their ministry. The names of many wise men, who have won souls are written on God's calendar. Their memory is precious. And some such we have to-day, but how few, compared with the thousands called "Heralds of the Cross." Yet, there is here and there one, thank God! What is the secret of their success? *Knee work!* Yes, my brother, KNEE WORK! The closet can tell of wrestlings, and importunate pleadings, as did Fletcher's, and that old man, who, when going to preach said, "I will not go, except the Lord goes with me."

Young men, in the name of God I appeal to you. We are called to win souls. Shall we do it? Can we bear to be drones here, and then hear the master say, "Take ye the unprofitable servant, and cast him into outer darkness?"

Brothers, let us band together to win souls. Let it be before you ever. Pray, agonize for the mighty power of the Holy Ghost. Get this first—God will show you what to do next. You will then study as those who have to give an account.

Be wise—never rest—but with the sword unsheathed rush into the battle and take spoils for Jesus.

"Herein is my Father glorified, that ye bear much fruit, so shall ye be my disciples."

HUMILITY.—It is worthy of remark, that soon after Paul was converted he declared himself "unworthy to be called an *Apostle*." As time rolled on and he grew in grace, he cried out, "I am less than the least of all *saints*." And just before his martyrdom, when he had reached the stature of a perfect man in Christ, his exclamation was, "I am the chief of *sinners*."

COME TO JESUS.

Sinner list; a voice is speaking
   In sweet tones of love to thee;
Through thy soul's deep silence breaking
   With its holy melody;
And each tuneful cord is waking
   With its echoes, "Lovest thou me?"

Hear those accents sweetly pleading,
   As they whisper, "Come to me;"
Mark that side, now freshly bleeding,
   See how truly, earnestly,
That One's voice is interceding
   For thy soul: 'Tis all for thee.

Thou hast hitherto neglected,
   In thy deep iniquity,
That sweet voice; else ne'er reflected
   Who it was thus spake to thee;
Surely thou has oft suspected
   It was he who died for thee.

Mark him in his holy calling,
   Kneeling in Gethsemane;
Note the sorrow so appalling
   Which he suffered there for thee!
Till his sweat like blood was falling
   From his brow—and all for thee!

Canst thou now that cross reviewing,
   Watch his silent agony?
See that saving blood imbuing
   With its hue the accursed tree?
By thy sins each pang renewing,
   When those pangs are all for thee?

Hear that cry so agonizing,
   "Why hast thou forsaken me?"
Heed that prayer so sympathizing,
   "Lord forgive, they know not me!"
See him whom thou art despising,
   Suffering, dying thus for thee.

Come to Jesus! Come believing,
   Come in true humility;
Jesus loves to be receiving
   Sinners such as thou must be.
Come to Jesus—he forgiving
   Waits to pardon all like thee.

BE DEFINITE.

BY ALEXANDER.

SEEKERS of perfect love! Suffer a word of exhortation from one who would fain assist you in entering the narrow way.

1. Be definite in your *conviction of real want*. A vague and ill-defined desire will not avail. You want to be *cleansed from all sin, and filled with all the fulness of God*. Nothing *less* will answer, and nothing *different*. Try to get on your naked heart and conscience, a burning sense of the precise facts in the case. It is the Spirit that must produce this conviction, but put yourself in the way to receive the light, and welcome the most painful disclosures which that Spirit may make. Remember the searching truth will not *injure* you, though its penetrating edge may *hurt*. You need never expect to *blunder* into the "King's highway." If your heart shall ever exult in the triumphs of full redemption, it will be after you have seen the dark depravity of your nature, and been filled with unutterable longings for inward purity. Open your eyes then, to see the very worst. Lay bare your bosom to the "sharpness of the two-edged sword." Do not dare to shrink away from the most humiliating revelations of the Holy Ghost, but rather cry out from the depths of your yearning heart, "*Spirit of burning come!*"

2. Be definite in your *committal* for the blessing. Some are so accustomed to deal in generalities that nobody can tell what they are after, and I have sometimes thought it doubtful whether they themselves know. They are forever expressing a desire for "more religion," or a "deeper work of grace." But what do they mean by that? *How much* "more religion" would they have? How much *deeper* would they have the "work of grace?" This looseness, my brethren, will never answer for those who intend to have their religion amount to anything. If you are *not justified*, you do not want "more religion,"—you want *religion!* If you *are* justified your wants can never be adequately expressed by such general phrases; you now want inward purity—entire holiness—perfect love! Not a "deeper work of grace," but *salvation from all sin*, ought to be the burden of your prayers and testimonies, till you get the thing itself. Bring your heart up to this definite point, and make it your "one idea," and you will succeed without the shadow of a doubt. Besiege the throne of grace for a *clean heart*, and utterly refuse to accept of any substitute. Be not shy of using the language of Inspiration to express your convictions. Bible terms are good enough for anybody. If you are really in earnest for purity, tell God of it in all the simplicity of a hungry child; and tell it to the deeply devoted that they may unite their supplications with yours in helping you to secure

"A heart in every thought renewed,
And full of love divine."

A PLACE FOR PRAYER.—"Where do you find a place to pray in?" was asked of a pious sailor on board of a whaling ship.

"Oh," he said, "I can always find a quiet spot at the mast-head."

"Sam, do you find a spot for secret prayer?" asked a minister of a stable-boy.

"Oh, yes sir; that old coach is my closet, and it is the best spot on earth."

Where there is a heart to pray, it is easy enough to find a place.

IT is in vain for the bird to complain that it saw the corn, but not the pitfall. So it will be vain for sinners to plead company and allurements, by which they have been enticed to undo their souls for ever. The God of Spirits, the God of all flesh, will not be put off with any excuses or pretences when he shall try and judge the children of men.—BROOKS.

NOBODY SAVED.

BY REV. A. A. PHELPS.

'Twas Tuesday evening, and I made my way to the General Class Meeting in the beautiful village of L———. Quite a large number were present, and probably thirty to forty gave in public testimony as the representatives of Christ. Some spoke of happy seasons in other days; some expressed their hopes for days to come. Some descanted very cooly and logically on the general character and benefits of Christianity. Some knew religion to be good, although they had lost its sacred flame—its soul-moving vitality; yet they would not sell their *hope* of heaven for ten thousand worlds! Some rejoiced in anticipation of greeting in the kingdom above, friends who had "passed on before." Some spoke extensively of living beneath their privilege—coming short of God's glory—making crooked paths—doing many things they ought not to do—having dark days, weak faith, etc., though cherishing very strong *desires* to serve the Lord and find their way to heaven. But of all this number, no one spoke of the joys of present and full salvation, through the atoning Lamb.

As I sat, and mused, and listened, the question was forcibly impressed: Is there nobody saved? And the response came echoing back, "Nobody saved! nobody saved!" But why should the fact exist that requires such testimony to be given? Why should any so live as to be compelled to tell the heart-rending story that falls on our ears from time to time? Are there not abundant provisions made to help us out of all the difficulties in which sin has involved us? Is there not an infinite ability, willingness and *desire* on the part of God to lead his children out into a large place, where the light of salvation unceasingly shines? Many would like to be saved, but in all their pleadings they seem tacitly to cherish the idea that they are invoking a cruel tyrant who keeps shoving them away from the cross and is loth to grant their petitions. The case, however, is far otherwise. The fact is, *every one enjoys as much salvation as he really proposes to enjoy.* Not that we are to make a divinity of our *will;* but the God of redemption is *waiting* to be gracious—*anxious* to pour upon us all the riches of his grace. Salvation is provided. Its terms are plain and reasonable. All may meet them. Jesus beckons us to the gushing fountain and the cleansing blood. The Holy Spirit enlightens, melts and moves. All heaven is in favor of our complete deliverance from sin; and if we are not saved, it is plainly because *we will not be saved;* we prefer another course. If this be true, how fearful our responsibility, and how inexcusable all our complaints of darkness and leanness of soul!

RETALIATION—The great apostle of the Gentiles felt himself under a painful necessity to rebuke Peter in the presence of the whole Church. He had recorded that rebuke, too, in one of his epistles. It was thus to be handed down to every age as a permanent and humiliating evidence of the wavering inconstancy of his fellow-laborer.

Peter, doubtless, must have felt acutely the severity of the chastisement. Does he resent it? He, too, puts on record long after, in one of his own epistles, a sentence regarding his rebuker, but it is this—"*Our beloved brother* Paul!"

Speak of the faults of others only in prayer; manifesting more sorrow for the sin of the censorious and unkind, than for the evil inflicted on yourselves.

Retaliate! No such word should have a place in the Christian's vocabulary. Retaliate! If I cherish such a spirit towards my brother, how can I meet that brother in heaven? "But ye have not so learned Christ."

"APOSTACY from God begins at the closet door."—MATTHEW HENRY.

THE LAND OF RUINS.

Above all other countries in the world Palestine is the land of ruins. It is not that the particular ruins are on a scale equal to those of Greece or Italy, still less to those of Egypt. But there is no country where they are so numerous, none in which they bear so large a proportion to the villages and towns still in existence. In Judea it is hardly an exaggeration to say, that while for miles and miles there is no present life and habitation, except the occasional goatherd on the hill side, or gathering of women at the wells, there is yet hardly a hill-top of the many in sight, which is not covered by the vestiges of some fortress or city of former ages. Sometimes they are fragments of ancient walls, sometimes mere foundations and piles of stone, but always enough to indicate signs of human dwellings and civilization.

These countless ruins, of whatever date they may be, tell us at a glance that we must not judge the resources of that ancient land by its present depressed and desolate state. How often is the question asked by eastern travelers, can these stony hills, these deserted valleys, be indeed the land of promise, the land flowing with milk and honey? Could they ever have supported such a teeming population as the Israelites?

The country must have been very different when every hill was crowned with a flourishing town or village, from what it is, since it ceased to be the seat not only of civilization, but in many instances even of the people who fertilized it.

The entire destruction of the woods which once covered the mountains, and the utter neglect of the terraces which supported the soil on steep declivities, have given full scope to the ruins, which have left many tracts of bare rock, where formerly were vineyards and cornfields. The loss of foliage has hindered rain, and so has exposed the country in a greater degree than formerly to the evils of drought. The forests of Bethel, of Sharon, of Hereth, the thicket wood of Ziph, and the forests which give their name to Kirjath-jearim, the city of forests, have long since disappeared. Palm trees, which are now all but unknown on the hills of Palestine, formerly grew with myrtles and pines on the almost barren slopes of Olivet, and groves of oak though never frequent, must have been far more common than now. The very labor which was expended on these barren fields in former times has increased their present sterility. The natural vegetation has been swept away, and no human cultivation now occupies the terrace which once took the place of forests and pastures.

It should also be borne in mind that Palestine, in contrast with the waterless deserts which skirt it on the south and east, must have appeared like an oasis of uncommon fertility. It was emphatically a good land, a land of brooks of water, of fountains and depths that spring out of plains and mountains, not as the land of Egypt, where thou sowest the seed, and waterest with thy foot as a garden of herbs, but as a land of mountains and plains, which drinketh water of the rain of heaven. This mountainous character, this abundance of water, both from natural springs and from the clouds of heaven, this abundance of milk from its cattle on a thousand hills, of honey, from its forests and its thymy shrubs, was absolutely peculiar to Palestine among the civilized nations of the East. Feeble as its brooks might be, though doubtless they were then more frequently filled than now, yet still it was the only country where an Oriental could have been familiar with the image of the Psalmist: "He sendeth the springs into the valleys, which run among the hills." These springs, too, however short-lived, are remarkable for their copiousness and beauty. Not only in the East, but hardly in the West, can any fountains or sources of streams be seen so clear, so full grown, even at their birth, as those which fall into the Jordan and its lakes, through its whole course, from north to south.

"IT IS WRITTEN."

We cannot fail to be struck, in the course of the Saviour's public teaching, with his constant appeal to the word of God. While, at times, He utters, in His own name, the authoritative behest, " Verily, verily, *I* say unto you," He as often thus introduces some mighty work, or gives intimation of some impending event in His own momentous life, "These things must come to pass that the *Scriptures be fulfilled*, which saith." He commands His people to " search the Scriptures," but He sets the example, by searching and submitting to them Himself.

Whether he drives the moneychangers from their sacreligious traffic in the temple, or foils his great adversary on the mount of temptation, he does so with the same weapon, " It is written." When he rises from the grave, the theme of his first discourse is one impressive tribute to the value and authority of the same sacred oracles.

The disciples on the road to Emmaus listen to nothing but a *Bible lesson*. " He expounded unto them in all *the Scriptures* the things concerning himself."

If an infallible Redeemer, " a law to Himself," was submissive in all respects to the "written law," shall fallible man refuse to sit with the teachableness of a little child, and listen to the Divine message?

There may be, there *is*, in the Bible, what reason staggers at: " We have nothing to draw with, and the well is deep." But "Thus saith the Lord," is enough. Faith does not first ask what the bread is made of, but *eats* it. It does not analyse the components of the living stream, but with joy draws the water from " the wells of salvation."

Reader! take that Word as " the lamp to thy feet, and the light to thy path." In days when false lights are hung out, there is the more need of keeping the eye steadily fixed on the unerring beacon.

Make the Bible the arbiter in all difficulties—the ultimate court of appeal. Like Mary, " Sit at the feet of Jesus," willing only to learn of Him. How many perplexities it would save you! how many fatal steps in life it would prevent—how many tears!

" It is a great matter," says the noblest of modern Christian philosophers, " When the mind dwells on any passage of Scripture, just to think how *true it is*."

In every dubious question, when the foot is trembling on debatable ground, knowing not whether to advance or recede, make this the final criterion, " What saith the Scripture?" The world may remonstrate—erring friends may disapprove—Satan may tempt—ingenious arguments may explain away; but, with our finger on the revealed page, let the words of our Great Example be ever a divine formula for our guidance. " *This* commandment have I received of my Father!"

ABOUNDING IN FAITH.

Faith has won its grandest conquests on straightened and sorrowful fields. If the strength and joy of believing are proportioned to the weight of the crosses for it—and such a rule as that does appear to have place in the spiritual economy—then it is in some such post of perplexity as a Cæsar's household, some age of persecution or close corner of peril, that we must look for the bravest witnesses to truth. So keenly has this been felt by some adventurous souls, that they have positively longed for fiercer onsets of trial than our common and easy fortunes bring, giving their religious constancy a chance to prove itself invincible. Sir Thomas Browne, with his unbounded veneration, had an appetite so hungry for this stimulus to trust, that he says, in one of the passages of his Treatise on the Religion of a Physician, " I bless myself and am thankful that I lived not in the days of miracles, and that I never saw Christ nor his disciples; for then my faith would have been thrust upon me, and I could not have enjoyed that greater blessing promised to all that see not and yet believe." He envies the old Hebrews their title to the only bold and noble faith, since they lived before the Saviour's coming, and gathered their confidence out of the mystical type and obscure prophecies. Modern society does not abound in instances of such enthusiasm for believing. More persons seem to be asking what is the minimum of faith that can be made to serve for safety—how much knowledge will release them from here, and divine indulgence there—than how affluent a measure they may be privileged to keep in reserve. We eulogize virtues that flourish only in a favorable soil and climate. We palliate and excuse the deficiency, when honesty is missing in the household of Cæsar—in seats of power, or wealth, or folly, in office or at court, in Washington or in Paris. We forget that the current piety of the Church, of society, and of the market sinks and dwindles inevitably, unless it is replenished by the energy of those valiant examples which will dare to bear testimony and be true in the very palaces of power, and fashion, and mammon.—Rev. F. D. Huntington.

DECISION OF MRS. FLETCHER.

I was now about nineteen years of age, and soon after, my parents having an intention to go to Bath for a season, proposed that I should spend that time at Bristol, as I was now thought to be consumptive. I gladly embraced the offer, as a merciful providence. I accordingly went to Bristol, where I remained seven weeks. Mrs. Downes (late Miss Furley,) showed me much kindness. Indeed, I was in some sense committed to her care by my parents, who had for years been acquainted with her family. I spent much of my time with Mrs. Ryan and Mrs. Clark, and I trust in some degree partook of their spirit. After my return home, I clearly discovered that I still conformed too much in my appearance to the spirit and fashions of the world; but I plainly saw a renunciation of that conformity would give my relations great offence. I loved my parents, and feared to disoblige them. I sought for arguments to quench that little spark of light which was kindling in my soul, conscious they could not see in my light, and knowing that obedience to parents was one of the first duties. I did so far quench it that I put on again many of the things I had thrown off. My acquaintance took much notice of me, and I was so afraid of losing their good opinion, that I had no power to reprove sin, or even to refrain from joining in light or trifling conversation when in company. But I soon discerned the danger consequent on their approval, and therefore determined to weigh well what was most likely to please God, and by that abide.

I prayed for direction, and saw clearly that plainness of dress and behaviour best became a Christian, and that for the following reasons:—

First. The apostle expressly forbids *women professing godliness to let their adorning be in apparel;* allowing them no other ornament than that of a *meek and quiet spirit.*

Secondly. I saw the reasonableness of the command, and proved it good for a proud heart to wear the plain and modest livery of God's children.

Thirdly. It tended to open my mouth; for when I appeared like the world, in Babylonish garments, I had its esteem, and knew not how to part with it. But when I showed, by my appearance, that I considered myself as a stranger and foreigner, none can know (but by trying) what an influence it has on our whole conduct, and what a fence it is to keep us from sinking into the spirit of the world. For there is no medium: they who are conformed to the fashions, customs, and maxims of the world, must embrace the spirit also, and they shall find the esteem they seek: for the world will love its own. But let them remember also that word, *The friendship of this world is enmity with God.*

Fourthly. I saw myself as a steward, who must render an account for every talent, and that it was my privilege to have the smiles of God on every moment of my time, or penny of money which I laid out.

Fifthly. I saw clearly that the helping my fellow creatures in their need, was both more rational, and more pleasant, than spending my substance on superfluities; and as I am commanded *to love my neighbor as myself,* and to consider all done to the household of faith as done to Christ, surely I ought not only to suffer my superfluity to give way to their necessity, but also (as occasion may require) my necessities to their extremities.

Sixthly. But it is not only the talent of money, but of time, which is thrown away by conformity to the world, entangling us in a thousand little engagements, which a dress entirely plain cuts through at once.

Seventhly. The end usually proposed by young persons in their dress is such as a devout soul would abominate. A heathen may say, It will promote my being comfortably settled in life; but I believe the Lord appoints the bounds of our habitation, and that *no good thing shall be withheld from those who walk uprightly.* I have therefore nothing to do, but to commend myself to God, in holy obedience, and to leave every step of my life to be guided by his will. I will therefore make it my rule to be clean and neat, but in the plainest things, according to my station; and whenever I thought on the subject, these words would pass through my mind with power, *For so the holy women of old adorned themselves.*

As soon as I saw my way clearly, I ventured to open my mind to my father concerning dress, as I had done before with regard to public places; entreating him to bear with me while I endeavored to show him my reasons for refusing to be conformed to the customs, fashions, and maxims of the world. He heard me with great patience; and as I loved him tenderly, it came very near me to oppose him. My trials increased daily. I was perplexed to know how far to conform, and how far to resist. I feared, on the one hand, disobedience to my parents, and on the other, disobedience to God.

My dear mother had sometimes expressed a belief that it would be better for the family if I were removed from it, lest my brothers, who were younger than I, should be infected by my sentiments and example. Yet she did not see it clear to bid me go; but rather wished me to depart of my own accord. The furnace now became hot; but I did not dare to come out without the Lord. Indeed, could there have been any amicable agreement between us, and that I had my parents' leave to live elsewhere, I would gladly have accepted it. I even made some distant proposals of this kind, but they never saw it good to concur. Providence thus overruled my desire for wise ends: and to run away from my father's house, I could not think of. I was twenty-one years of age, and had a small fortune of my own. I saw myself on the verge of a material change, and it was easy to discern that my father's house would not long be a refuge for me; but in what manner I should be removed, or what trials I might yet have to go through, I could not tell. The continual language of my heart was, *I am oppressed: Lord, undertake thou for me.*

One day my father said to me: "There is a particular promise which I require of you; that is, that you will never, on any occasion, either now, or hereafter, attempt to make your brothers what you call a Christian." I answered, (looking to the Lord,) "I think, sir, I dare not consent to that." He replied, "Then you force me to put you out of my house." I answered, "Yes, sir, according to your views of things, I acknowledge it; and, if I may have your approval, no situation will be disagreeable." He replied, "There are many things in your present situation which must be, I should think, very uncomfortable." This I acknowledged, and added that if he would but say he approved of my removal, I would take a lodging which I had heard of at Mrs. Gold's, in Hoxton-square; but that no suffering could incline me to leave him, except by his free consent. He replied with some emotion, "I do not know that you ever disobliged me wilfully in your life, but only in these fancies; and my children shall always have a home in my house." As I could not but discern a separation would take place, (though I knew not how nor when,) I judged it most prudent to take the lodging, that in case I should be suddenly removed, I might have a home to go to; which I preferred to the going into any friend's house as a visitor. I also hired a sober girl, to be ready whenever I might want her. I informed my mother, a short time after, of the steps I had taken. She gave me me two beds, one for myself, and a little one for my maid; and appeared to converse on it in a way of approval. Something, however, seemed to hold us, on both sides, from bringing it to the point.

For the next two months I suffered much; my mind was exercised with many tender and painful feelings. One day my mother sent me word, I must go home to my lodgings that night. I went down to dinner, but they said nothing on the subject, and I could not begin it. The next day, as I was sitting in my room, I received again the same message. During dinner, however, nothing was spoken on the subject. When it was over, I knew not what to do. I was much distressed. I thought, if they go without saying anything to me, I cannot go; and if they should not invite me to come and see them again, how shall I bear it? My mind was pressed down with sorrow by this suspense. Just as they were going out, my mother said, "If you will, the coach, when it has set us down, may carry you home to your lodging." My father added, "And we shall be glad to see you to dinner next Tuesday." This was some relief. I remained silent. When the coach returned, I ordered my trunk into it; and struggling with myself, took a kind of leave of each of the servants, as they stood in a row in tears, in my way out of the house. About eight o'clock I reached my lodging.

It consisted of two rooms, as yet unfurnished. I had neither candle nor any convenience. The people of the house I had never seen before, only I knew them by character to be sober persons. I borrowed a table and a candlestick, and the window seat served me as a chair. When bolting the door, I began to muse on my present situation.

I am, said I, but young—only entered into my twenty-second year. I am cast out of my father's house. *I know the heart of a stranger;* but, alas! how much more of it may I yet have to prove! I cried unto the Lord, and found a sweet calm overspread my spirit. I could in a measure act faith on these words: "When thy father and thy mother forsake thee, the Lord shall take thee up." The following reflections also arose in my mind: I am now exposed to the world, and know not what snares may be gathering around me. I have a weak understanding, and but little grace. Therefore, now, before any snare has entangled me, I shall form a plan for my future conduct, and endeavor to walk thereby. First, I will not receive visits from single men, and in order to evade the trial more easily, I will not get acquainted with any; I will, as much as possible, refrain from going into any company where they are. Secondly, I will endeavor to lay out my time by rule, that I may know each hour what is to be done: nevertheless, I will cheerfully submit to have these rules broken or overturned, whenever the providence of God thinks fit to do so. And thirdly, I will endeavor to fix my mind on the example of Jesus Christ, and to lead a mortified life; remembering, "He came not to be ministered unto, but to minister."

SPIRITUAL LIBERTY.

It has probably come within the observation of many persons, that there is a form or modification of religious experience, which is denominated "Liberty." Hence, in common religious parlance, it is not unfrequently the case that we hear of persons being "in the liberty," or in the "true liberty." These expressions undoubtedly indicate an important religious truth, which has not altogether escaped the notice of writers on the religious life. The account which is given by Francis de Sales of "liberty of spirit" is, that *it consists in keeping the heart totally disengaged from every created thing, in order that it may follow the known will of God.*

To this statement of De Sales, considered as a general and somewhat indefinite statement, we do not find it necessary to object. Certain it is, that he who is in the "true liberty" is "disengaged," and has escaped from the enslaving influence of the world. God has become to him an inward, operative principle, without whom he feels he can do nothing, and in connection with whose blessed assistance he has an inward consciousness that the world and its lusts have lost their inthralling power. Liberty—considered in this general sense of the term—is to be regarded as expressive of one of the highest and most excellent forms of Christian experience. And we may add further, that none truly enjoy it in this high sense but those who are in a state of mind which may with propriety be denominated a holy or sanctified state; none but those whom God has made " free indeed." We proceed now to mention some of the marks by which the condition or state of true spiritual liberty is characterized. Nor does there seem to be much difficulty in doing this, because liberty is the opposite of inthralment; and because it is easy, as a general thing, to understand and to specify the things by which we are most apt to be inthralled.

(1.) The person who is in the enjoyment of true spiritual liberty is no longer inthralled to the lower or appetitive part of his nature. Whether he eats or drinks, or whatever other appetite may claim its appropriate exercise, he can say in truth that he does all to the glory of God. It is to be lamented—but is, nevertheless, true—that there are many persons of a reputable Christian standing, who are subject, in a greater or less degree, to a very injurious tyranny from this source. But this is not the case with those who are in the possession of inward liberty. Their souls have entered into the pleasures of divine rest; and they can truly say they are dead to all appetites, except so far as they operate to fulfil the original and wise intentions of the being who implanted them.

(2.) The person who is in the enjoyment of true spiritual liberty is no longer inthralled by certain desires of a higher character than the appetites—such as the desire of society, the desire of knowledge, the desire of the world's esteem, and the like. These principles, which in order to distinguish them from the appetites, may conveniently be designated as the propensities, or the propensive principles, operate in the man of true inward liberty as they were designed to operate, but never with the power to enslave. He desires, for instance, to go into society, and in compliance with the suggestions of the social principle, to spend a portion of time in social intercourse; but he finds it entirely easy, although the desire in itself considered may be somewhat marked and strong, to keep it in strict subordination to his great purpose of doing everything for the glory of God. Or, perhaps, under the influence of another propensive tendency,—that of the principle of curiosity—he desires to read a book of much interest, which some individual has placed before him; but he finds it entirely within his power as in the other case, to check his desire, and to keep it in its proper place. In neither of these instances, nor in others like them, is he borne down, as we often perceive to be the case, by an almost uncontrollable tendency of mind. The desire, as soon as it begins to exist, is at once brought to the true test. The question at once arises, Is the desire of spending my time in this way conformable to the will of God? And if it is found, or suspected to be at variance with the divine will, it is dismissed at once. The mind is conscious of an inward strength, which enables it to set at defiance all enslaving tendencies of this nature.

(3.) A man who is in the enjoyment of true religious liberty will not be inthralled by inordinate domestic or patriotic affections, however ennobling they may be thought to be—such as the love of parents and children, the love of friends and country. It is true that spiritual liberty does not exclude the exercise of these affections—which are, in many respects, generous and elevated—any more than it condemns and excludes the existence and exercise of the lower appetites and propensities. It pronounces its condemnation and exclusion upon a certain degree of them, or a certain intensity of power. When they are so strong as to become perplexities and entanglements in the path of duty, then they are evidently inconsistent with the existence of true spiritual freedom, and in that shape, and in that degree, necessarily come under condemnation. I have, for instance, a very near and dear friend, who is exceedingly worthy of my affections; but if my love to him leads me—perhaps almost involuntarily—to seek his company when my duty to my God and my fellowmen calls me in another direction, and if I find it difficult to subdue and regulate this disposition of mind, it is evident that I am not in the purest and highest state of internal liberty. I have wrongly given to a creature something which belongs to God alone.

(4.) When we are wrongly under the influence of disinclinations and aversions, we cannot be said to be in internal liberty. Sometimes, when God very obviously calls us to the discharge of duty, we are internally conscious of a great degree of backwardness. We do it, it is true; but we feel that we do not like to do it. There are certain duties which we owe to the poor and degraded, to the openly profane and impure, which are oftentimes repugnant to persons of certain refined mental habits; but if we find that these refined repugnances which come in the way of duty, have great power over us, we are not in the true liberty. We have not that strength in God, which enables us to act vigorously and freely. Sometimes we have an aversion to an individual, the origin of which we cannot easily account for; there is something unpleasant to us, and perhaps unreasonably so, in his countenance, his manners, or his person. If this aversion interferes with, and prevents, the prompt and full discharge of the duty which, as a friend and a Christian, we owe to him, then we have reason to think that we have not reached that state of holy and unrestrained flexibility of mind which the true idea of spiritual liberty implies.

(5.) The person is not in the enjoyment of true liberty of spirit, who is wanting in the disposition of accommodation to others in things which are not of especial importance. And this is the case when we needlessly insist upon having everything done in our own time and manner; when we are troubled about little things, which are in themselves indifferent, and think, perhaps, more of the position of a chair than of the salvation of a soul; when we find a difficulty in making allowance for the constitutional differences in others, which it may not be either easy or important for them to correct; when we find ourselves disgusted because another does not express himself in entire accordance with our principles of taste; or when we are displeased and dissatisfied with his religious, or other performances, although we know he does the best he can. All these things and many others like them, give evidence of a limited mind that has not entered into the broad and untrammeled domain of spiritual freedom.

We may properly add here, that the fault-finder—especially one who is in the confirmed habit of fault-finding—is not a man of a free spirit. Accordingly, those who are often complaining of their minister, of the brethren of the church, of the time and manner of the ordinances, and of many other persons and things, will find, on a careful examination, that they are too full of self, too strongly moved by their personal views and interests, to know the true and full import of that ennobling liberty which the Saviour gives to his truly sanctified ones.

(6.) The person who is disturbed and impatient when events fall out differently from what he expected and anticipated, is not in the enjoyment of true spiritual freedom. In accordance with the great idea of God's perfect sovereignty, the man of a religiously free spirit regards all events which take place—SIN ONLY EXCEPTED—as an expression, under the existing circumstances, of the will of God. And such is his unity with the divine will that there is an immediate acquiescence in the event, whatever may be its nature, and however afflicting in its personal bearings. His mind has acquired as it were, a divine flexibility, in virtue of which it accommodates itself, with surprising ease and readiness, to all the developments of Providence, whether prosperous or adverse.

(7.) Those who are in the enjoyment of true liberty are patient under interior temptations, and all inward trials of mind. They can bless the hand that smites them internally as well as externally. Knowing that all good exercises are from the Holy Spirit, they have no disposition to prescribe to God what the particular nature of those exercises shall be. If God sees fit to try, and to strengthen, their spirit of submission and patience by bringing them into a state of great heaviness and sorrow, either by subjecting them to severe temptations from the adversary of souls, or by laying upon them the burden of deep grief for an impenitent world, or in any other way, they feel it to be all right and well. They ask for their daily bread spiritually, as well as temporally; and they cheerfully receive what God sees fit to send them.

(8.) The person who enjoys true liberty of spirit is the most deliberate and cautious in doing what he is most desirous to do. This arises from the fact that he is very much afraid of being out of the line of God's will and order. He distrusts, and examines closely, all strong desires and strong feelings generally, especially if they agitate his mind, and render it somewhat uncontrollable; not merely or chiefly because the feelings are strong; that is not the reason; but because there is reason to fear, from the very fact of their strength and agitating tendency, that some of nature's fire, which true sanctification quenches and destroys, has mingled in with the holy and peaceable flame of divine love. John the Baptist, no doubt, had a strong natural desire to be near Jesus Christ while he was here on earth, to hear his divine words, to enjoy personally his company; but in the ennobling liberty of spirit which the Holy Ghost gave him, he was enabled to overrule and suppress this desire, and to remain alone in the solitary places of the wilderness.

(9.) He who is in true liberty of spirit is not easily excited by opposition. The power of grace gives him inward strength; and it is the nature of true strength to be deliberate. Accordingly, when his views are controverted, he is not hasty to reply. He is not indifferent; but he replies calmly and thoughtfully. He has confidence in the truth, because he has confidence in God. "God is true;" and being what he is, God can have no fellowship with that which is the opposite of truth. He knows that, if his own sentiments are not correct, they will pass away in due time; because everything which is false necessarily carries in itself the element of its own destruction. He knows too, that if the sentiments of his adversaries are false, they bear no stamp of durability. God is arrayed against them; and they must sooner or later fall. Hence it is, that his strong faith in God, and in the truth of which God is the protector, kills the eagerness of nature. He is calm amid opposition; patient under rebuke.

(10.) The person of a truly liberated spirit, although he is ever ready to do his duty, waits patiently till the proper time of action. He has no choice of time but that which is indicated by the providence of God. The Saviour himself could not act until his "hour was come." When he was young, he was subject to his parents; when he was older, he taught in the synagogues. In his journeyings, in his miracles, in his instructions, in his sufferings, he always had an acquiescent and approving reference to that providential order of events which his heavenly Father had established. On the contrary, an inthralled mind, although it is religiously disposed in part, will frequently adopt a precipitate and undeliberate course of action, which is inconsistent with a humble love of the divine order. Such a person thinks that freedom consists in having things in his own way, whereas true freedom consists in having things the right way; and the right way is God's way. And in this remark we include not only the thing to be done, and the manner of doing it, but also the time of doing it.

(11.) The possessor of true religious liberty, when he has submissively and conscientiously done his duty, is not troubled by any undue anxiety in relation to the result. It may be laid down as a maxim, that he who asserts that he has left all things in the hands of God, and at the same time exhibits trouble and agitation of spirit in relation to the results of those very things (with the exception of those agitated movements or disquietudes which are purely *instinctive*,) gives abundant evidence, in the fact of this agitation of spirit, that he has not really made the entire surrender which he professes to have made. The alleged facts are contradictory of each other, and both cannot exist at the same time.

Finally. In view of what has been said, and as a sort of summary of the whole, we may remark that true liberty of spirit is found in those, and in those only, who, in the language of De Sales, "keep the heart totally disengaged from every created thing, in order that they may follow the known will of God." In other words, it is found with those who can say, with the apostle Paul, that they are "dead, and their life is hid with Christ in God." The ruling motive in the breast of the man of a religiously free spirit is, that he may, in all cases, and on all occasions, do the will of God. In that will his "life is hid." The supremacy of the divine will—in other words, the reign of God in the heart—necessarily has a direct and powerful operation upon the appetites, propensities and affections; keeping them, each and all, in their proper place. As God rules in the heart, everything else is necessarily subordinate. It is said of the Saviour himself, that "he pleased not himself," but that he came "to do his Father's will."

Another thing, which can be said affirmatively and positively, is, that those who are spiritually free are led by the Spirit of God. A man who is really guided by his appetites, his propensities, or even by his affections, his love of country, or anything else other than the Spirit of God, cannot be said to be led by that divine Spirit. The Spirit of God, ruling in the heart, will not bear the presence of any rival, or competitor. In the heart of true liberty the Spirit of God rules, and rules alone; so that he who is in the possession of this liberty does nothing of his own pleasure or his own choice. That is to say, in all cases of voluntary action, he does nothing under the impulse and guidance of natural pleasure or natural choice alone. His liberty consists in being free from self; in being liberated from the dominion of the world; in lying quietly and submissively in the hands of God; in leaving himself, like clay in the hands of the potter, to be moulded and fashioned by the divine will. Natural liberty may be said to consist in following the natural sentiments; in doing our own desires and purposes, which naturally throng in upon the soul and take possession. It is like a strong man, that is under the complete control of his irregular passions. Spiritual liberty consists in passively, yet intelligently and approvingly, following the leadings of the Holy Ghost. It is but a little child, that reposes in simplicity and in perfect confidence, on the bosom of its beloved mother. Natural liberty combines, with the appearance of liberty, the reality of subjection. He who has but natural liberty is a slave to himself. In spiritual liberty, it is just the opposite. He who is spiritually free has entire dominion over himself. Spiritual liberty implies, with the fact of entire submission to God, the great and precious reality of interior emancipation. He who is spiritually free is free with God. And he may, perhaps, be said to be free in the same sense in which God is, who is free to do every thing right, and nothing wrong.

This is freedom indeed. This is the liberty with which Christ makes free. This is emancipation which inspires the songs of angels—a freedom which earth cannot purchase, and which hell cannot shackle.—UPHAM.

BAD BOOKS AND EVIL COMPANY.—Sir Peter Lely made it a rule never to look at a bad picture, having found by experience that whenever he did so his pencil took a tint from it. Apply the same rule to bad books and bad company.

"THE Soul and Body make a man; the Spirit and Discipline make a Christian."—WESLEY.

TRUE AND FALSE HUMILITY.

IN the whole catalogue of Christian virtues, there is, perhaps, none which is so decisive a mark of a renewed nature, as a meek and lowly mind.

"It is reported," says Robert Hall, "of the celebrated Austin of Hippo, that being asked what was the first thing in religion, he said Humility. When asked what was the second, he answered Humility; and what was the third, he still returned the same answer, Humility!"

Yet there is no trait which is more often counterfeited. It is made to consist in a demure or downcast look, or an abject posture—in externals which imply only a humiliation and self-degradation, while they cover up a heart full of pride and of duplicity. It is well, therefore, to understand what is *not* and what *is* genuine Humility.

It is *not* meanness of spirit. The idea of meanness properly includes that of selfishness. A man is called mean, when, for the sake of some petty advantage, he will sacrifice the interests, or disregard the feelings of others. From such meanness, humility is at the farthest remove, as it is opposed to all arrogance and assumption, and of course forbids the slightest trespass on the rights and feelings of the humblest human being.

But, perhaps, by meanness is meant timidity, or cowardice, a want of spirit or resolution in maintaining one's rights. Here, too, the term applies not at all. Humility never forbids the firm maintenance of personal rights. Indeed a man whose modesty and principle lead him never to ask more than his just due, will often be most firm in maintaining that against intended injustice.

Nor does humility consist in self-contempt. It is not opposed to a just self-respect. Some make this mistake, because they confound self-respect with pride and self-conceit, whereas the two states of feeling are not only distinct but incompatible. A conceited man can not have a true self-respect, for the flutter of self-conceit blinds his mind to really valuable qualities.

Nor does humility require a man to think meanly of himself; to think himself the most ignorant or wicked of mankind. A wise and good man can not think so. He knows better. He can not believe himself the most ignorant of his race, any more than he can believe himself the wisest or the best. Nor does humility require of us any such thing.

Nor does humility require a man always to speak in dispraise of himself. This is a habit with some Christians. But it is a bad habit, and one which springs more often from a subtle spiritual pride than from real humility.

There is a vast deal of self-conceit in those *public confessions* which some modern preachers have urged upon their followers, and which their disciples naturally enough at last got to be fond of. It was an easy way to become conspicuous. A man had but to confess himself "the greatest of sinners," and he was thought the greatest of saints. This is all hypocrisy. These men, who get up in public meetings, and abuse themselves so, would be very angry if anybody else charged them with the very sins which they are confessing.

Let us not be misunderstood, as if we meant to imply that confessions are *never* called for. Alas! sometimes the cause of truth demands them, when they are most galling to our pride. Sometimes a guilty conscience, or the sentiment of the Christian community, outraged by a public scandal, compels us to rise in the great congregation and confess our sins with sorrow and shame. But unless the interests of religion require it, it is better to keep silent, and confess our sins to God alone. For often there is as much pride in speaking evil of ourselves as in speaking good. The conceit lies in talking of ourselves at all. Fenelon, with his rare knowledge of the human heart, says: "It is not safe to speak of ourselves unnecessarily, either good or evil."

Thus humility never requires us to say or think anything of ourselves which is not in accordance with the exact truth. Its only caution to any one's self-respect is, "not to think of himself more highly than he ought to think; but to think soberly." That is, we are to see ourselves as we are, and regard ourselves as we deserve, no more and no less.

What then *is* humility? We define it by its opposites. It is opposed to all forms of pride—to pride of birth, beauty, wealth, or fashion, to pride of intellect or of character. It is opposed to extravagant self-esteem, as shown in an insufferable air of superiority; in a positiveness of opinion, and impatience of contradiction; or, more good naturedly, though not less offensively, in a condescending and patronizing manner. It is opposed to that self-confidence which makes a man headstrong and obstinate; and to that irritable vanity which cannot bear to hear anybody praised but itself, and which constantly oozes out in low envy and detraction.

Humility consists in *unaffected modesty*—in a modest estimate of our talents and our importance in the world, and in a deep consciousness of our weakness and moral imperfections. It consists, too, in careful deference to others —to age, to superior station, and longer experience, and to the characters and feelings of all. As such it is allied to instinctive delicacy of feeling, that nice sense of propriety, which constitutes the indescribable charm of ingenuous youth, and of the female sex, and from which all true refinement springs. Above all, it consists in that deep humiliation, that sense of guilt and nothingness which becomes a worm in the presence of the Great God.—N. Y. EVANGELIST.

SHOULD any attempt to praise you, dart immediately to God, "Lord, I am thine; save me!"—JOHN NELSON.

WE had better be saved in a storm, than lost in a calm.—JOHN NELSON.

ONCE MORE, ST. PATRICK NO ROMANIST.

The following testimony to the Catholicity of the first Prelate of all Ireland, is useful in its way, and may be added to the others before given: The oldest piece of writing in the Irish tongue is called " St. Patrick's Defence, or Breastplate." It is a prayer written when St. Patrick was going to Tara, to preach before the king and nobles; and at that time the people in Ireland were Pagans, and he feared he should be killed. Now it is remarkable that St. Patrick should have written such a prayer, and not mentioned the name of the Virgin Mary in it! Yet we find there is not one word addressed to her in the whole prayer. Hear the prayer:

"At Tara, to-day, the strength of God pilot me—the power of God preserve me—may the wisdom of God instruct me—the eye of God watch over me—the ear of God hear me—the word of God give me sweet talk—the hand of God defend me—the way of God guide me. Christ be with me—Christ before me—Christ after me—Christ in me—Christ under me—Christ over me—Christ on the right hand—Christ on my left hand—Christ on this side—Christ on that side—Christ at my back—Christ in the heart of every one to whom I speak—Christ in the mouth of every person who speaks to me—Christ in the eye of every person who looks upon me—Christ in the ear of every person who hears me at Tara to-day." —Austin.

Display in Devotion.—Dr. Wayland says: "If we keep on in our present course, building expensive churches and keeping up our expensive worship, our population will all be heathen, both within the church and without."

"His hand the good man fastens on the skies,
And bids earth roll, nor feels her idle whirl."

GOD KNOWN BY LOVING HIM.

BY MADAME GUYON.

'Tis not the skill of human art,
Which gives me power my God to know;
The sacred lessons of the heart
Come not from instruments below.

Love is my teacher. He can tell
The wonders that he learnt above;
No other master knows so well;—
'Tis love alone can tell of love.

Oh! then, of God if thou wouldst learn,
His wisdom, goodness, glory see,
All human arts and knowledge spurn,
Let love alone thy teacher be.

Love is my master. When it breaks,
The morning light, with rising ray,
To thee, O God! my spirit wakes,
And love instructs it all the day.

And when the gleams of day retire,
And midnight spreads its dark control,
Love's secret whispers still inspire
Their holy lessons on my soul.

"My conception of heaven," said Robert Hall to Wilberforce, "*is rest.*" "Mine," replied Wilberforce, "is love; love to God, and love to every bright and holy inhabitant of that glorious place." Hall was an almost constant sufferer from acute bodily pain; Wilberforce enjoyed life, and was all amiability and sunshine; so that it was easy to account, says Mr. Gurney, "for their respective conceptions of the subject." What a mercy that both these conceptions are true.

Yes, both *are* true; and the union of rest and love, perhaps, conveys within a small compass, the most correct idea of the heavenly state.

The life of faith, when faith is perfect, is a very simple one. The principle of faith is to the soul, considered in its relation to God, what the principle of gravitation is to the physical universe; uniting all, harmonizing all, but always without confusion and noise, and with the greatest simplicity of operation.—Guyon.

TRUE RADICALISM.

"RADICAL" is a term of reproach. To apply it to a preacher, is one of the surest ways of injuring his reputation and his usefulness with multitudes. But in the true sense of the word, every preacher ought to be radical—he ought to go to the root of the matter. Baxter's advice, given on the very last page of his "Reformed Pastor," is just as good now as it was two centuries ago. "Strike," he says, "at the great radical sins."

We fear that our modern preachers are too much given to lopping off the branches, and thus promote the vigor of the poison tree that is rooted in every heart, while they dream that they are destroying it. Pruning sends the vigor of the tree downward, and causes many new fibres of relf-righteousness to start, which not only root the tree more firmly, but soon manifest their power in causing a more vigorous growth of branch and foliage than that which was pruned away. There can be no reformation of character, no newness of life in this fallen world, until selfishness is uprooted. Against it the preacher of righteousness must direct his most vigorous efforts. When it is eradicated, all the growth of depravity will wither and die.

But how shall the preacher strike at radical sins? To hack at the root of a tree, only deforms instead of destroying it. And there are those who "cry aloud and spare not," yet only drive their hearers to new and worse forms of depravity. To make a hypocrite or religious formalist of a careless sinner, is only bringing a more monstrous growth from the old root. Everything depends upon the spirit of our radicalism. We may go down fearlessly to the lowest rootlet in the heart, if we go with the true gospel implement. Paul wrote to the Corinthians, "I determined to know nothing among you but Jesus Christ and him crucified." That was radicalism, one-ideaism. But it resulted in the upbuilding of a noble church. Let us, with godly simplicity, strike at the selfishness of the heart with the truth of a crucified Saviour. Let us convince men of sin by presenting the great sin-offering — then we shall not lead any to self-righteousness or hypocrisy. Neither shall we repel or offend any. But we shall, by Him who was lifted up from the earth, draw men to repentance, faith and love, to holiness and heaven.

DISCOURAGEMENT.

BY THE EDITOR.

ARE you a child of God? Then what right have you to yield to discouragement? A desponding heart is the almost certain harbinger to defeat. An army that goes into battle with the expectation of being conquered, was never known to be victorious. If you have doubts about your acceptance with God, get them settled. On your knees repent, consecrate, believe! Rest not till satisfied that you are sincerely and entirely and forever set apart to do and suffer the will of God in all things. Look for the evidence of your acceptance. Get it. It is for *you*. Be assured that you enjoy the divine favor. Put on at once the whole armor of God. Inquire not as a matter of form, but with a sincere desire to obtain a reply, Lord what wilt thou have me to do? Get an answer. Then go to work. Never suffer yourself to be discouraged. Discouragement to one who is doing the work of the Lord, is of the devil. It should be resisted like any other temptation. He will try to discourage you,

1. *In relation to your own religious experience.*

When God lets us see the fullness of our spiritual graces in comparison with those which he has promised in the Bible to work in his children, there is, with the light, a sweet encouragement to press forward, and in all humility, yet boldness, claim all that we see necessary to render us useful and happy.

But when Satan, transformed into an angel of light, holds up a high standard, it may be the Bible standard of religion, there is a depressing influence exerted upon the mind, and in taunting tones he may be heard to say, "Now it is of no use; you may as well give up; you can never meet the requirements of God." Resist the temptation. God is no respecter of person. Go to Him in confidence. Do not be denied.

> Is not His grace as mighty now
> As when Elijah felt its power,
> When glory beamed from Moses brow
> Or Job endured the trying hour?

Obtain the complete mastery over the world, the flesh and the devil. Never be discouraged,

2. *In your business.* Suppose it does go wrong. If you are the Lord's, that should not trouble you. It may be that you have too heavy a load to carry to march with much rapidity through

> Immanuel's ground,
> To fairer worlds on high.

If the Lord lightens your burden, should you complain? If your business is right in itself, and tends not to deprave and undo, but to benefit your fellow men, and it is that which the providence of God points out for you to pursue, follow it to the glory of God, and you will have all of this world that is necessary for you. Your main object is to lay up treasures in Heaven. Keep that clearly in view, and however the minor matters of this world go, you will steadily prosper in your great undertaking. The sainted Payson prayed, that if the Lord had any temporal prosperity for him, He would withhold it and grant him grace instead! Imitate this devotion, and every disappointment that in the providence of God comes upon you, will be a great success. Then do not be discouraged,

3. *In laboring for the salvation of souls.*

Here there is much to discourage. Men are hard. They love sin. They love the world. It is difficult to get them converted. It is still more difficult to keep them converted. But there is also much to encourage. The Spirit of God is Almighty. He can melt the hardest heart. His efficacious assistance is promised to all who earnestly seek it. Rely upon the Holy Ghost. He will never disappoint you. Just as certainly as you lean upon Him you will be successful in laboring for souls. Sinners will be convicted whether they desire it or not. The wicked may rage, formalists may divide and oppose, but some honest souls will be saved.

Are you a minister? Has God called you to preach? And are you discouraged? *You* who should be rallying the hosts of God to battle, and infusing a spirit of courage into the most timid! Shame on you. Read over your commission. It concludes with "And lo, I am with you always, even unto the end of the world." John afterwards saw Him who uttered these words, and he had upon his vesture and upon his thigh a name written King of Kings, and Lord of Lords. *He* with you! and you discouraged? It seems incredible. I thank my Saviour that we do not know in these days what a feeling of discouragement is. Our name is cast out as evil—bandied about by the tongue of calumny and defamation. Ministers with whom we were once associated by tenderest ties, and whom we still love, and would be glad to serve, exert all their influence to prevent our usefulness. The grossest misrepresentations and caricatures of us, and of our meetings, are published in the public journals. To say a good word for us is often as much as a man's reputation is worth. Many, whose convictions and sympathies are with us, are fearful and faint-hearted. Yet in the midst of all we never had a lighter and more joyous heart. Discouragement is a stranger to us. We are doing the work of God, and we must succeed. Mighty obstacles, like mountains of mist, vanish as we approach them. For the encouragement of others to do this whole duty fearless of consequences and to the glory of Divine grace, we feel bound to say, that it is our deliberate conviction that more souls have been saved through our instrumentality, during the past two years, than during the ten years we stood connected with the Conference, though then our labors were blessed quite as much, we believe, as those of our brethren generally.

Do not be discouraged. If you meet with difficulty, or opposition, or persecution, face it manfully. Look up. Discouragement is of the devil. Have nothing to do with it.

CALLED TO PREACH.

BY THE EDITOR.

You will, of course, do all you can to help save others if you are yourself a child of God. His Spirit within will prompt you to it. You will delight in this work. Many, as soon as they are really saved, think, because they feel this desire to do good to the souls of men, that they are therefore called of God to preach. Do not let the devil get you here. By setting unwary souls to looking at this, and weeping over it, and praying over it, he often keeps those busy in doing nothing, who otherwise might labor efficiently in building up the Redeemer's Kingdom. Embrace the first opportunity to persuade your neighbors to seek the forgiveness of their sins. Make opportunities. If you are really called of God to preach, the fruit of your labors will render it evident both to yourself and to the spiritually-minded of your acquaintance. But a pulpit cannot help you. If you cannot speak to exhortation and edification, and comfort, without a license, you cannot with. Parchments do not make scholars. A certificate from the church for the sun to shine, would not make it any brighter or warmer. Standing two feet above the congregation, with a desk before you, and a license in your pocket, will not make your thoughts clearer, nor your heart warmer, nor give your words a greater power to lead erring men to Christ. Do not then be troubled about your call to preach. Labor where you are, and as you are, as God directs. If He wants you to bear weightier burdens, He will in His providence lay them upon you soon enough. Complaining that your are not sufficiently put forward, will neither help you nor the cause of God. The tree is not all the while asserting its right to grow, but it demonstrates it by making the rain, and the sunshine, and the frost, and the tempest, contribute to its growth. Do not wait for somebody to make an opening, or get a congregation for you. Go to work. If God calls you to preach you will have no difficulty in securing a congregation, whether you have a license, or take a text or not. If you are moved by the Holy Ghost it will be apparent. You will have something to say that will benefit somebody. God never sends a messenger without putting a message in his mouth.

THE ROMAN SENTINEL.—When Pompeii was destroyed, there were many buried in the ruins of it, who were afterwards found in different situations. There were some found in deep vaults as if they had gone thither for security. There were some found in lofty chambers. But where did they find the Roman sentinel? They found him standing at the city gate with his hand still grasping his war-weapon, where he had been placed by his captain; and there where the heavens threatened him; there where the earth shook beneath him; there where the lava stream rolled, he stood at his post, and there, after 1,000 years had passed away, was he found. So let Christians learn to stand to their duty, willing to stand at the post on which their Captain has placed them, and they will find that grace will support and sustain them.

THE powerless Christian *ought to be felt* to be as great a misnomer as the forceless thunderbolt.—REV. S. H. PLATT.

TURNED OUT, ARE YOU?

Are you turned out of the house? Well, how do you like it? How do you feel? How do you bear it,—meekly, patiently, humbly,—as Christ did, as the prophets and the apostles? This turning out of house and home is no uncommon thing. Christ told his disciples, when turned out of a house or city for truth's sake, to shake off the dust of their feet, as a testimony against the opposers and persecutors.

Madame Guyon was turned out of house, into prison,—even a cold, damp dungeon; for adhering to truth! Baxter was served in a similar manner. Bunyan was turned out of house and home, and turned into prison twelve years, in which time he wrote the immortal "Pilgrim." Most all God's faithful servants are turned out, sooner or later. Some are turned out of Union prayer-meetings, for opening their lips for the dumb, and for witnessing to a full salvation. Editors are often turned out arbuptly, unceremoniously, for dealing "all the words of this life" boldly. Missionaries of the Cross, the humble followers of Jesus —in Kentucky Brother Fee and his associates were violently turned out of their peaceful dwellings, in mid-winter, for declaring "*all the words of this life*" in meekness and love. Our beloved brother Worth, in N. C., was not only turned out, but turned into prison, for preaching Jesus, for "remembering those in bonds as bound with them." What sayeth the Lord of glory?—"Think not I am come to send peace on earth: I came, not to send peace, but a sword." "They that will live godly in Christ Jesus shall suffer persecution." "Behold, I send you forth as sheep in the midst of wolves."

Hear what Paul says:—"I reckon that the sufferings of this present time are not worthy to be compared with the glory that shall be revealed in us. Nay, in all these things we are more than conquerors, through him that loved us. For I am persuaded, that neither death, nor life, nor angels, nor principalities, nor powers, nor things present, nor things to come, nor hight, nor depth, nor any other creature, shall be able to separate us from the love of God, which is in Christ Jesus, our Lord." Rom. viii, 18; 37—39.

"But what are all our sufferings here,
If, Lord, thou count us meet,
With all the enraptured host to appear,
And worship at thy feet."—GOLDEN RULE.

THINK GENTLY OF THE ERRING.

Think gently of the erring one,
O, let us not forget,
However darkly stained by sin,
She is our sister yet.

Heir of the same inheritance,
Child of the self-same God,
She hath but stumbled in the path
We have in weakness trod.

Speak gently to the erring ones,
We yet may lead them back;
With holy words, and tones of love,
From misery's thorny track.

Forget not, mortal, thou hast sinned,
And sinful yet may'st be;
Deal gently with the erring heart,
As God hath dealt with thee.

TOBACCO AND RUM are no doubt shortening the lives of our fellow citizens and bringing more diseases upon the human body than any other cause that can be named by the most learned physician.

"There is infinitely more poison in one paper of tobacco than in the tin-foil that surrounds a hundred. If anybody doubts this let them hold a sheet of white paper over the smoke that curls up from burning tobacco, and after a pipefull or a cigar has been devoured, scrape the condensed smoke from the paper, and put a very small amount on the tongue of a cat, and they will see her die by "strokes of paralysis" in fifteen minutes."

REVIVALS.

BY THE EDITOR.

RUSHFORD CAMP MEETING.

THIS was held near the village of Rushford, Alleghany Co., N. Y., the last of August, and the first of September. We reached the ground on Friday, and staid until Monday morning. The attendance was good, though the farmers of that region were very busy in securing their crops. A large congregation was in attendance upon the Sabbath, and the preaching of the Word was listened to with marked attention. Conversions took place in the altar, and in the various prayer-rings on the Sabbath; but how many we do not know. But the great benefit of these meetings is found in their inciting Christians to seek a deeper experience in the things of God. They come in contact with those who have drank more deeply than themselves at the fountain of salvation, and seeing the beneficial results, they are thus encouraged to drink more freely at the waters of life. Some were sanctified, and the meeting was, as far as we can learn, a profitable one.

There is a good band of Earnest Christians at Rushford. They have purchased the old Methodist Church, and intend to consecrate it again to the worship of God. We trust it may be in time to come, as it has been in years past, the birth-place of many redeemed souls.

AURORA CAMP MEETING.

THIS was held in a pleasant oak grove, on the banks of the Fox River, about two miles from the city of Aurora, Illinois. There were upon the ground twenty-six large tents, well fitted. The attendance from the adjoining city, villages and country was large.

I believe nearly all the preachers professed to enjoy the blessing of holiness. Their appearance upon the Camp Ground justified their profession. They worked in the pulpit, in the altar, and in the tents, as if their only aim was to save souls. There was a point and directness in their labors that we have seldom seen equalled. The result was glorious. We never attended a more successful Camp Meeting. Prejudices gave way, and many who went there out of curiosity, went away to pray, and to lead a new life.

The pastor of the M. E. Church in Aurora, as we were informed from several reliable sources, publicly gave his people to understand that if they wished to remain members of the M. E. Church, they must not participate in this Camp Meeting. Yet the strength of the church was there, we should judge; and many were greatly blessed. Two of their local preachers rendered efficient assisttance. We love to witness these exhibitions of Christian unity.

It is impossible to sum up in figures the results of a religious meeting. Converts may be numbered by the hundred, when, owing to the superficial nature of the work, real injury rather than good was done. On the other hand, through the life-long devotion of a soul fully sanctified to God, an untold amount of good may be accomplished in a meeting that is seemingly a failure. At this Camp Meeting the work was, as far as could be judged, deep and thorough. There was a parting with idols. Men gave up their tobacco, and women gave up their jewelry, and came to Christ for grace to save them both inwardly and outwardly.

In one afternoon meeting, some sixteen gave explicit testimony that the Lord had, in that meeting, cleansed their hearts from all sin. We dismissed the meeting, but it continued on without intermission until ten at night.

Two who came forward while we were singing the doxology, were fully saved, (as none could doubt who heard their testimony, and witnessed their rejoicing in Christ,) before the singing was finished. A lady who stood weeping at the altar, hesitated to go forward for fear she should "be turned out of church." A local preacher, belonging to the same church with herself, encouraged her to go, if she felt it her duty to do so. As she went, she deliberately consecrated herself fully to God's service, whatever the consequences might be. The Lord met her as she fell upon her knees, and in an instant almost, she bounded upon her feet, and went shouting through the altar, giving testimony that no one could doubt, that the Lord had saved her from her sins, and filled her soul with glory. That meeting will never be forgotten. It was thought by those best qualified to judge, that there were at least fifty or sixty who received the blessing of pardon, and more than twice that number who sought and obtained purity of heart during the Camp Meeting. One man who started to go home before the meeting closed, had his buggy kicked to pieces by his horse. He and his wife returned to the camp ground, and one of them experienced the blessing of holiness, and the other was converted.

AURORA, ILLINOIS.

THIS is a beautiful city of about eight thousand inhabitants, situated about seventy miles south-west, I believe, from Chicago, on both sides of the Fox River. It has the appearance of an enterprising business place. The afternoon the Camp Meeting closed, we preached in the public park, on the east side of the river, to a large and attentive congregation. The truth appeared to take effect. The next day we held another meeting there, and one sinner deeply pricked to the heart, came forward to seek salvation. We had another meeting there the next day, and again in the same place on the Sabbath. The large congregation listened with intense interest, and we do not know when we ever saw more deep feeling manifested in a congregation, than while our companion in labor, as well as in life, related what God had done for her, and exhorted the weeping multitude to become partakers of the like precious faith. We also held several meetings in a hall, which were well attended, and with good results. Some obtained, we trust, the blessing of purity, and many were encouraged to lay themselves out for usefulness in the cause of God.

We also preached at St. Charles, and Geneva, on the green, to attentive congregations. One middle-aged man, of some prominence, who had been seeking the Lord without getting an evidence of pardon, said he would lay aside his Masonic badge, and break off his connection with the lodge. The Lord spoke peace to his soul. The next day his wife was triumphantly converted to God. We have seldom seen any one manifest more gratitude for plain dealing than he did, after he renounced all, and obtained the assurance that God received him.

From Aurora we went, by invitation, to WHEATON. This is a new, beautiful village, on the open prairie, about twenty-five miles west of Chicago. Here the Wesleyan Methodists have a college. Their Annual Conference was in session at the time of our visit; and at their request we preached in the evening in the College Chapel. The Lord graciously assisted us to enforce the claims of holiness to the personal and earnest attention of all—especially of ministers of the gospel. It was one of the best meetings we ever attended. This Conference is made up, we should judge, of earnest, honest men, who have entered the ministry not for the sake of the loaves and fishes—but because they believe God has called them to it—men who hate sin and oppression, and love righteousness. They deeply felt their need of that spiritual power found only in connection with purity of heart. Such a time of breaking down among ministers we never witnessed before. Some of their strongest men wept like children. We doubt if there was one among them that did not feel determined to experience holiness, live holiness, and preach holiness the rest of his days. Several came out very clearly in its enjoyment before we left.

The President of the college, a Congregational Doctor of Divinity, endorsed the doctrine, and said he was not a stranger to the experience of this state of grace, and hoped to come again into its enjoyment. He had read our "Trial" with care, and bid us God speed in our work. We shall be greatly disappointed if the Wesleyan Methodist Church within the bounds of the Illinois Conference does not double its membership, and more than double its spiritual strength the coming year. Our visit to Wheaton will long be cherished among our most pleasing recollections.

AT MOUNT PLEASANT, Ogle Co., we held a grove meeting, commencing on Thursday, and continuing over the Sabbath. The meeting was a profitable one, and the fruit will, we trust, long remain. We went, we were told, within forty miles of the Mississippi. The prairies were most magnificent. In some directions, as far as the eye could range, not a tree nor a bush could be seen. The immense growth of corn, and the countless stacks of grain, attest the great fertility of the soil.

BONUS GROVE MEETING.

WE never were in a place where heaven and earth seemed quite as near together as at that meeting. There is a fire kindled on that beautiful prairie that will not soon be extinguished. Among other narrations of experience to which we listened with interest, was that of a local preacher from Belvidere. He experienced the blessing of holiness at Wheaton at the meeting referred to. He said on going home, he told his wife what God had done for him. Greatly affected, she fell upon her knees, and sought the same blessing. He felt as if he ought to go to a neighbor's, a very wicked man, and a bitter enemy of his, who had forbidden him his house. "But," said he, "I thought I could go in if the house was bolted and barred." He went. His neighbor came to the door. "O," said the brother, "I have something good to tell you!" "Something good to tell me," said the man in astonishment. "Yes; the Lord has sanctified my soul, and I now love HIM with all my heart; and I love you!" "O," said his neighbor, the tears streaming down his face, "I once enjoyed the blessing of the Lord upon my soul, but now I do not know as there is any mercy for me!" He finally promised to go to the brother's house to a prayer meeting.

GOWANDA INDIAN CAMP MEETING.

THIS was held on the Reservation, about six miles from the village of Gowanda. To our great regret we were unable to be present, as it took place at the same time of the Aurora meeting. We understand that they had a very profitable time, and that about one hundred were converted. Dr. Redfield was there through the meeting.

SUSPENSION OF REV. GEORGE FOX.

WE understand that this devoted brother has been suspended from the ministry in the Wisconsin Conference. His chief offence, we understand, was circulating the *Earnest Christian*, and writing for the *Northern Independent* a favorable notice of the dedication of the Free Methodist Church in Albion.

BUFFALO.

THE Lord is carrying on his work in the Free Methodist Church, under the labors of brother James Mathews. Believers are being sanctified, and sinners are getting converted from time to time. The congregations are large and attentive. Brother M., besides preaching twice at the Church, keeps up an out-door service every Sabbath on the dock. Hundreds flock to hear the Word. The congregations are uniformly quiet, orderly and attentive, and a feeling of seriousness has been manifested by many. Some have walked up from the dock to the Church, a distance, we should judge, of from two to three miles, that they might have the prayers and assistance of God's people in seeking the salvation of their souls.

DEDICATION.

THE second Free Methodist Church of Buffalo, located on Pearl street, just above Eagle street, will be dedicated to the service of Almighty God, on Friday the 19th of October, at 2 o'clock, P. M. Preaching, also in the evening, and the meeting will continue over the Sabbath. The friends of an earnest Christianity are cordially invited to attend.

We need very much the money that our friends have pledged to assist us in paying for this Church, and about four times as much besides. On the strength of these pledges we have made engagements which *must* be met. Brother, sister, will you not without delay, send us the money you have promised? And if any one who has not subscribed, would like to contribute some of the money with which the Lord has entrusted them, to help open a place where the Gospel may be preached to the poor, any remittance that they may send us, would be thankfully received. Have you paid your missionary money this year? If not, here is an opportunity to appropriate it where, without doubt, a large and speedy return may be looked for in a rich harvest of souls. Send by mail, directed to B. T. Roberts, Buffalo, N. Y.

THE EARNEST CHRISTIAN.

WE feel gratified to our Heavenly Father for the success with which he has crowned our efforts to establish a magazine devoted to the fearless advocacy of an uncompromising, earnest Christianity. Our success has so far exceeded our anticipations, that we are unable any longer to furnish back numbers to the commencement of the volume. We can still supply subscribers from July to the end of the year. Send on your orders. The price for the last half of the year is fifty cents *in advance*. We shall continue the publication of the *Earnest Christian*. It may now be regarded as a fixed institution. It is the child of prayer and faith, and God gives it favor in the eyes of His people. We expect all our old subscribers will continue with us, and we request them to renew their subscriptions at an early date.

We also want a large list of new subscribers. We should be glad to commence the next volume with ten thousand subscribers.

AGENTS.

To enterprising agents, male or female, who will devote their time to canvassing for new subscribers, we will pay a liberal commission. We want every county in the land canvassed. Those desiring to canvass for new subscribers, may send on their applications. Good recommendations will be required from those who are strangers to us.

The character of THE EARNEST CHRISTIAN will remain the same. It will not be denominational or sectarian, but filled with solid, substantial matter, calculated to promote the life and power of godliness—*the holiness without which no man shall see the Lord*.

PROSPECTUS.—THE FREE METHODIST.

OUR friends are urging us to establish a weekly paper. We feel the need of it as much as any one can, but we are not willing to undertake it unless we can get assurances that it will pay its way. If we can get enough subscribers to warrant it, we will commence on the first of Jan. 1861, the publication of a weekly of the size of the *Northern Independent*. We cannot edit it, but we know of a suitable man who can.

It shall be the object of our paper to oppose *sin* rather than *churches*, and to advocate *principles* rather than *men*. While it will seek to treat every subject with the utmost fairness, and to defend the right with *unblushing fearlessness*, it will studiously avoid a mere "war of words" carried on in the spirit of bitterness. By the grace of God we mean to make it a "terror to evil doers, but a praise to them that do well." It shall advocate an uncompromising Christianity, whose characteristic elements are faith, and love, and power, and whose requirements are the universal renunciation of sin and the consecration of all to God. In short, we design to make it a *salvation* journal, spiced with bits of burning experience and enforcing a type of religion that *saves the soul*.

It will not be so "lady-fingered" as not to meddle with the great moral questions of the day. On the subject of intemperance in all its departments, and of oppression in all its phases, it will ring out the clarion notes of truth, and endeavor to merit the respect of *real men*.

Let all that sympathise with the above sentiments, male and female, exert themselves at once to get up and send on a large list of subscribers for "THE FREE METHODIST." *We want ten thousand at least!* The subscription price will be *one dollar a year*, payable always in advance. Direct all orders to

REV. A. A. PHELPS,
Holley, Orleans Co., N. Y.

DISCIPLINE OF THE FREE METHODIST CHURCH.

OUR unexpectedly protracted visit to the west has occasioned a longer delay in the publication of the Discipline than we anticipated. It is partly printed, and we trust will be ready for distribution soon after this meets the eye of the reader. Orders are coming which will be filled just as soon as possible.

A BRAVE BOY.

For the information of some of our young readers, we would mention that Holland, or the Kingdom of the Netherlands, is the most level part of Europe, and much of its surface is lower than the sea, which is prevented from overflowing the land by vast dykes or embankments.

There was once a little Hollander, who though a very child in years, saved many of his countrymen from destruction. The legend, for history has hardly stooped to chronicle the deed, informs us that this lad, on his return from school, passing along a sequestered road, and looking with childlike curiosity at a great dyke, saw, breaking through, a small stream of water, which, as it oozed, carried away some particles of the bank. It was the small beginning of what might be a frightful end — some such catastrophe as sweeps away, before its relentless tide, our southern homes. The boy had simply present to his mind the sense of danger; before he could reach assistance, it might be too late, and he felt that the remedy was with him and must be promptly applied. Our hero left the highway, and clambering to the spot, planted himself in the very breach of danger, and thrust his little hand into the increasing aperture; to his joy he found it closed the avenue, and all was right. A few hours, at worst, he deemed would bring some passer-by to his relief; but though he strained eye-balls and hearing, no wayfarer greeted his senses. The evening would surely find some stray wanderer, or perchance they might be passing on the opposite side and not perceive him. He tried his voice, but this soon failed him, and night came; to him, brave boy,

"The night came on alone."

As darkness closed around him, we can well imagine, tears found their way down his cheeks. Doubtless, too, there came before him the image of home—of the waiting brothers and sisters, the anxious parents. With that thought would come the recollection of the lessons of piety received from a mother's lips; of the prayers she had taught him on her knee; and to his cry for help and strength would succeed a holy and abiding trust. All unused to such exposure—wearied, hungered, strained with the compulsion of his attitude, his little arm paining and swelling—all these increasing through the long watches of that night, what else was his support? No mere animal endurance could have sustained this anguish for half that time; and yet, till day-break, and searching friends brought relief, this faithful sentinel withstood it all! When, recovered from this and the peril of succeeding sickness, he was asked if during that long night he had felt no fear? His answer tells of true patriotism: "No, no! I knew God would preserve me for preserving others."

LITERARY NOTICES.

GUIDE TO HOLINESS.

This standard Monthly comes to hand, freighted as usual with solid matter upon the most important theme. The *Guide* has done, and is doing a good service to the cause of holiness. It is published at one dollar a year by H. V. Degen & Son, 456 Washington St., Boston, Mass.

THE BEAUTY OF HOLINESS.

This, too, is devoted, as its title indicates, exclusively to the subject of holiness. It takes a strong, Scriptural position upon the subject of slavery, advocating a holiness that cannot consist with oppression. It is ably conducted by Mr. & Mrs. French. Its influence is good in promoting heart religion. Published at one dollar per annum, by Rev A. M. French, 48 Beekman St., New York.

THE GOLDEN RULE.

We are glad to form the acquaintance of this vigorous, earnest periodical. It is the most outspoken advocate of an uncompromising Christianity among all the religious journals of our acquaintance. It speaks in bold utterances against the fashionable, pleasure-loving, tobacco-using pro-slavery religion of the day. Its editor is evidently a man who does not fear to declare the whole counsel of God. It is published monthly in newspaper form at fifty cents a year for a single copy—one hundred copies for twenty-five dollars. All orders should be addressed to Rev. David F. Newton, editor. Box 1212, New York.

THE AMERICAN MONTHLY,

Including also *The Household Magazine*, and *Beadle's Home Monthly*. Edited by Rev. S. H. Platt. This is the best miscellaneous Magazine for family reading with which we are acquainted. It is conducted with ability, and has a "religious" and Sunday School department. It is published at one dollar twenty-five cents a year, by H. M. Platt, 5 Beekman St., New York.

THE EARNEST CHRISTIAN.

VOL. I.   NOVEMBER, 1860.   NO. 11.

SANCTIFICATION EXPERIENCED.

BY REV. WM. COOLEY.

It is proper that we should attach great importance to the light we receive from Christian experience, and especially if this experience is our own. An experience that leads to a holy life, and that is in harmony with the plain teachings of the Bible, must be a safe guide in matters of salvation, and becomes an incontestible argument in favor of its truth. Arguments which oppose positive experience have but little power to convince. When experience is clear and positive, no mere theory, however plausible, can induce the conscientious man to throw it aside as false. It is really a matter of great surprise, that an intelligent Christian should ignore the experience of holiness, or deny any important facts in such experience, when so large a number of members of the Christian church declare it to have been their personal realization.

There are three points in the experience of sanctification. The first is the felt presence of *inbred sin* in the heart after conversion. The second is, a conviction of unlikeness to God, or a want of purity; and then the instantaneous cleansing of the heart from all its corruption, or inbred sin, by the Holy Ghost. These three facts will be found in every clear and definite experience of holiness. We have found this true in all the cases with which we are acquainted. Who knows of any experience against these facts? What man can say he has never felt since his conversion, any risings of anger, pride, love of the world, or unholy ambition? The existence of inbred sin, after conversion, can no more be disproved by experience, than it can by the written word. Who ever has received a clear experience of freedom from inbred sin in a gradual way? Who among the many experiences published to the world, or among the thousands of living witnesses have testified to any such thing? It is allowed that there is a vast amount of defective experience. That experience which falls short of entire sanctification, can no more disprove this high state of grace, than the unconverted man's defective experience can disprove the doctrine of regeneration. In arraying our experience against any doctrine, we should be careful to see whether it really is against it, or only falls short of the standard claimed.

We will give, in a condensed form, the experience of a large number of Christians, eminent for intelligence, good sense, and long years of devotion and integrity in the service of God. Our design in presenting these examples, is to show the uniformity of *conviction* of inward depravity, and its removal by faith in Christ, in an *instantaneous* manner.

Dr. Adam Clark in a letter to Mr. Wesley says, "Since I was justified, I have in general expected and prayed for that inestimable blessing, a heart in all things devoted to God, which, soon after I received pardon, I found to be indispensably necessary; but meeting with little encouragement in my pursuit after it, I obtained it not. Here, (meaning in the Bradford Circuit,) the good Lord was pleased to give me a sight of the unspeakable depravity of my heart; and one time in particular, in such a measure, that the distress I felt was as painful in sustaining, as it would be difficult in describing. * * Soon after this, while earnestly wrestling with the Lord in prayer, and endeavoring self-desperately to believe, I found a change wrought in my soul. * * * But my indulgent Saviour continued to support and encourage me, and enabled me with all my power to preach the glad tidings to others, so that I soon saw more of the effects of the travail of my Redeemer's soul than I had ever seen before. Glory be to God through Christ."

Mr. Fletcher had a clear experience of entire sanctification, and rejoiced in it many years. While he was in a justified state he felt the need of the removal of the remains of the carnal nature, which he expresses in the following manner: "My heart is hard! O wretched man that I am, who shall deliver me from this heart of unbelief." "But I see my heart is full of deceit. I mourn deeply for my corruptions, which are many and great."

Mr. Wesley had a deep experience of the things of God, and without any doubt experienced and enjoyed holiness, for he preached it himself, and urged his ministers to do the same everywhere; but he has not left as full a record of this work in his own heart as we could desire; but in reference to the need of it, in about four months after his conversion he examines himself to see if he was a new creature in Christ Jesus. He says of a new creature, meaning in a high sense, "His love, and joy, and hope, his sorrows and fears, have all respect to things above. * * * I dare not say I am a new creature in this respect. For other desires often arise in my heart, but they do not reign. I put them all under my feet through Christ which strengthens me." Speaking of the fruit of the Spirit he says, "I find a measure of peace, long-suffering, gentleness, meekness, temperance; others I find not, nor have I such a peace as excludes the possibility either of fear or doubt. When men have told me I have no faith, I have often doubted whether I had or no. And those doubts have made me very uneasy, till I was relieved by prayer and the Holy Ghost, nor the full assurance of faith, much less am I, in the full sense of the words, in Christ a new creature. I nevertheless trust that I have a measure of faith, and am accepted in the beloved. I trust the hand-writing that was against me is blotted out, and that I am reconciled to God through His Son."—*Wesley's Journal, vol.* 1, *p.* 112.

Mr. Carvosso says of himself, "My inward nature appeared so black and sinful, that I felt it impossible to rest in that state. Some perhaps will imagine that this may have arisen from the want of the knowledge of forgiveness. That could not be the case for I never had one doubt of my acceptance. At length one evening, while engaged in a prayer-meeting, the great deliverance came. I began to exercise faith, by believing I shall have the blessing now. Just at that moment a heavenly influence filled the room; and no sooner had I uttered or spoken the words from my heart, *I shall receive the blessing now*, than refining fire went through my heart, illuminated my soul, scattered its life through every part, and sanctified the whole."—*His Life, pp.* 32 *and* 38.

"Mr. Bromwell," says his biographer, "being obedient to the teaching of the Spirit, it was not long before he was convinced of the necessity of a further work of grace upon his heart. He now saw that it was his privilege to be *cleansed from all sin*.' 'I was for some time deeply convinced of my need of purity, and sought it carefully with tears, and entreaties, and sacrifice; thinking nothing too much to give up, nothing too much to do or suffer, if I might but attain this pearl of great price. * * * When in the house of a friend at Liverpool, whither I had gone to settle some temporal affairs, previously to my going out to travel,

I was sitting,' said he, 'as it might be on this chair,' pointing to the chair on which he sat, ' with my mind engaged in various meditations concerning my affairs and future prospects, my heart now and then lifted up to God, but not particularly about this blessing, heaven came down to earth; it came to my soul. The Lord, for whom I had waited, came suddenly to the temple of my heart; and I had an immediate evidence that this was the blessing I had for some time been seeking. My soul was then all wonder, love, and praise. It is now about twenty-six years ago; I have walked in this liberty ever since. Glory be to God! I have been kept by his power. By faith I stand.'"— *His Life, p.* 36.

Father Reeves says, "I believe the ever blessed Lord is carrying on His own work of grace in my poor soul, because I never felt the corruption and awful depravity of my own heart and life as I do now." Again he says, "For several weeks past my soul has been longing for a clearer testimony from the Spirit of my entire sanctification. I pleaded hard with the Lord for it, through the precious blood of Jesus; and glory be to my Heavenly Father, He very soon granted me the desire of my heart, though so unworthy, and filled my soul with perfect love."—*His Life, pp.* 112, 114.

Thomas Welch says, after his conversion, " If an evil thought was at any time injected, or *the remains of the old man* began to stir, I had immediate power to resist and overcome them." Again he says, after praying earnestly for the presence and fullness of God, " O how plentifully did the Lord pour his love and consolation into my soul! I am amazed at the goodness and long suffering of God toward me."—*His Life, pp.* 50, 156.

Mrs. Fletcher says, "I know Him mine, *but other things had life in me,* though not dominion over me! Again I said in my heart, *Thy will be done! Thy will be done!* And in that I felt my rest. In the same moment brother Gilford changed prayer into praise, telling the Lord He had heard and answered; He had set me at liberty, and now he would praise Him. This surprised me, as I had not given the least sign, by either word or motion, of what I had felt within. He concluded his prayer with that act of praise. He asked me how I felt myself? I could not fully tell; but that I found that the love of the will of God had brought an unspeakable peace into my soul; but that I did not feel joy, only a rest in that thought, *the Lord reigneth,* and *His will shall be done.*" Again she says, " But above all I felt such a simplicity, such a hanging on the Lord Jesus, that self seemed annihilated, and Jesus was my all. The nothing into which I felt myself sunk, and the great salvation I seemed to possess in Jesus, were such as I cannot explain."—*Mrs. Fletcher's Life, p.* 46.

Hester Ann Rogers says, "I had a deeper sense of my *impurity* than ever; and though by grace I was restrained from giving way outwardly, yet I felt such *inward* impatience, pride, fretfulness, and in short, every ill temper, that at times I could truly say, I was weary and heavy laden." Again she says, " But now Lord, I do believe; this moment thou dost save. Yea, Lord, my soul is delivered of her burden, I am emptied of all; I am at thy feet, a helpless, worthless worm; but I take hold of Thee as my fullness."— *Her Life, pp.* 40, 45.

Mr. Bromwell says of Ann Cutler, " In a short time she received pardon, and her serious deportment evinced the blessing she enjoyed. It was not long before she had a *clearer sight into her own heart;* and, though she retained her confidence of pardon, she was made deeply sensible of her need of perfect love. * * * In the same year of her finding mercy, the Lord said, '*I will, be thou clean*.' She found a sinking into humility, love, and dependence upon God. At this time her language was, ' Jesus, I love Thee with all my heart.' * * * After this change, something remarkable appeared in her countenance—a smile of sweet composure. It was noticed by many as a reflection of the divine nature, and it increased to the time of her death."

Says the Biographer of Gideon Ouseley, "When he had become saved by grace from the guilt and power of sin, he resolved to be a Christian in earnest. He was instructed by the ministers of the Methodist preachers to go on to higher attainments in the life divine; to 'press toward the mark for the prize of the high calling of God in Christ Jesus;' and he longed to love the Lord his God with all his heart, and with all his soul, and with all his mind. * * * He therefore concluded that the privilege of a matured Christian was distinct and clear. ' O God,' he would say, 'clease me from all filthiness of the flesh and spirit, that I may perfectly love Thee, and worthily magnify Thy holy name.' * * * He ' cried mightily to God,' to use his own words, and after a short, but severe struggle, he proved that 'the blood of Jesus Christ His Son, cleanseth from all sin. * * * He now ' rejoiced with joy unspeakable and full of glory.' * * * Mr. Ouseley was now supremely happy, or to use his own words, 'as happy as the day is long.'"—*His Life, pp.* 68, 70.

Benjamin Abbott, after hungering and thirsting for full salvation for a time, says he prayed at family prayer, " Come Lord, and sanctify me, soul and body. That moment the Spirit of God came upon me in such a manner that I fell flat to the floor, and lay as one struggling in blood, while my wife and children stood weeping over me. But I had not power to lift hand or foot, nor yet to speak one word. I believe I lay there half an hour, and felt the power of God running through every part of soul and body, like fire consuming the *inward corruptions of fallen depraved nature.* When I arose and walked out of doors, and stood pondering these things in my heart, it appeared to me that the whole creation was praising God; it also appeared as if I had got new eyes, for everything appeared new."—*His Life, p.* 38.

We have before us a book denominated the " Riches of Grace," containing the Christian experiences of sixty-two living witnesses. We have found nothing in these experiences contrary to what we advocate in this article; that there is, after conversion, carnal inclinations that are in the way of loving God with all the heart; and that these inclinations are instantaneously removed by faith in Christ; but a uniform testimony confirming these facts. We select from this volume the testimony of the following eminent Christians.

Bishop Hamline says, " He saw that in his heart were the roots of many evils, which, though they could not grow while under the reign of grace, yet were ever ready to spring up under the least declinings of faith and love." Again he says, " All at once he felt as though a hand, not feeble, but omnipotent, not of wrath, but of love, was laid on his brow. He felt it not only outwardly, but inwardly. It seemed to press upon his whole being, and to diffuse all through and through it a holy, sin-consuming energy. As it passed downward, his heart as well as his head was conscious of the presence of this soul-cleansing energy, under the influence of which he fell to the floor, and in the joyful surprise of the moment cried out in a loud voice."—*pp.* 13, 18.

Mrs. Bishop Hamline says, speaking of her efforts to obey God, "There was much of self-confidence, and of effort to work out a righteousness of my own, * * * while unbelief was still so much the habit of my soul, that I feared to offer praise, lest I should express what I did not feel. * * * The heavens seemed bowed almost to my reach, and every breath bore upward the prayer, O Lord, give me a clean heart! I had laid all on the altar, and so intensely was I occupied in watching the sacrifice till it should be consumed, that I dreaded even the salutation of a friend, lest my heart should be for a moment diverted from its object. * * * I found around me a few of those who were used to pray with and for me. One of them, a dear sister, began to exhort me to look up. I did look, and quick as thought was spoken to my inmost soul, 'If you ask bread, will He give you a stone?" A glimpse of the fullness of God was at the same instant presented to my now opened eyes, and glory to God brake from my lips, which had so long refused to speak His praise. I wondered at myself, but had no idea that I had received the long-sought blessing. * * * About an hour after, the congregation assembled at the stand, (as this was at Camp-meeting,) for preaching. As I was kneeling, during the first prayer, I thought, I shall meet sister ——— on the ground in the morning, and in spite of the tempter, I will say I am an heir of God; and at the thought my soul filled and overflowed with unutterable bliss. My heart had become like the full vessel, which runs over with the slightest motion. That was indeed a new life, in which hallelujas rose spontaneously from a heart so long unused to notes of joy."—*p.* 288.

Dr. Upham says, "The principal difficulty, as I daily examined my heart to see how the case stood between my soul and God, seemed to be a consciousness, while other evils were greatly or entirely removed, of the remains of selfishness. Indeed, at this particular time, the selfish principle, or rather the principle of self-love, and its inordinate and unholy exercises, seemed to be stimulated to unwonted activity. The remains of every form of internal opposition to God appeared to be centred in one point, and to be presented in one aspect." Again he says, "The soul seemed to have gathered strength from the storm which it had passed through on the previous night, and, aided by a power from on high, it leaped forward, as it were by a bound, to the great and decisive mark. I was distinctly conscious when I reached it. * * * I was then redeemed by a mighty power, and filled with the blessing of perfect love. * * * There was calm sunshine upon the soul. The praise of God is continually upon my lips."—*pp.* 25.

Mrs. Upham says, "But I had come to the Bible to receive and believe it all, and my eye fastened on the promise of our Saviour, 'Blessed are they that hunger and thirst after righteousness, for they shall be filled. Blessed, sweet promise, my heart swells with emotion while I repeat it. While pleading this promise, kneeling before God with the words upon my lips, I felt a sweet assurance that my prayer was heard; a sensible peace entered into my soul. I arose and returned to my Bible with new emotion. Now I saw and believed. * * * But after this peace or love entered into my soul, nothing moved me."—*pp.* 437.

President Mahon says, "In regard to my early experience as a Christian, I would say, that that experience had two prominent characteristics, a desire, inexpressibly strong, to be entirely consecrated to the love and service of God." Again he says, "In a moment of deep and solemn thought, the veil seemed to be lifted, and I had a vision of the infinite glory and love of Christ, as manifested in the mysteries of redemption. * * * My heart melted and flowed out like water. The heart of stone was taken away, and a heart of love and tenderness assumed its place."—*p.* 46.

J. J. Pettee, of N. E. Conference, says, "I felt convicted of the remains of sin in my heart, and deeply convinced of my need of holiness." Again he says, "The fullness of the promise assured me that God was ever on the giving hand—willing, ready, waiting; this reduced it to the present tense. Here infinite benevolence met the suppliant, and cut short the work in righteousness. The blessing was mine, I felt I possessed it; it made me contented. * * * A mighty comfort pervaded my heart; a mighty peace rolled through my soul."—*p.* 34.

James Brainard Taylor says, "I have had keener sorrow for indwelling sin, than I ever experienced before conversion. O the distress which I have felt on account of pride, envy, love of the world, and other evil passions, which have risen up and disturbed my peace." Again he says, "At this very juncture I was most delightfully conscious of giving up all to God. I was enabled in my heart to say, here Lord, take me, take my whole soul, and seal me thine—thine now, and thine forever. 'If thou wilt thou canst make me clean.' Then there ensued such emotions as I never before experienced—all now was calm and tranquil, silent, solemn, and a heaven of love pervaded my whole soul. I had a witness of God's love to me, and of mine to Him."—*His Life*, p. 85.

Mrs. Fanny L. Bartlett says, "O the agony of that hour, in which God showed me all I could bear of the remains *of inbred sin!* My convictions exceeded those before my conversion, which caused me to feel that the pains of hell got hold upon me. I was riveted to the spot, and had no idea of giving up the contest until my spiritual foes were all vanquished. The duties and crosses connected with a life of holiness were presented to my mind, and the Holy Spirit seemed to propose the definite inquiry, *Will you make these sacrifices?* My heart replied, by the grace of God *I will*. At that moment I made a full surrender, and in the twinkling of an eye, those never to be forgotten words were applied to my heart, 'Though your sins be as scarlet, they shall be white as snow.' A sweet calm overspread my spirit. I bathed in the sea of inexpressible delight."—*Her Life*, p. 15.

Mrs. Cordelia Thomas says, "I realized in a manner never before experienced the contamination of sin, and the odiousness of it in God's sight. * * * Pride and anger were sins which easily beset me." Again she says, "Conscious, through the illumination of the Spirit, that I was saved, 'faith being the substance of things hoped for, the evidence of things not seen.' I was not filled with extatic delight, but Christ gave me rest in that hour. He took me out of the pit. A new song was put into my mouth. I declared to all around, 'This is the way I long have sought.'"—*Her Life, pp.* 20, 28.

We will close this article with a quotation from Dr. G. Peck's work on Perfection. He says, "Is it not presuming too far to suppose that those who have professed this high and holy state were mistaken—that they do not understand the character of their own experience? To say nothing of those among ourselves who have made professions of this kind, and have given the most indubitable proofs of their sincerity, let us refer to Messrs. Fletcher, Bramwell, Carvosso; Mrs. Rogers, Mrs. Fletcher, Lady Maxwell, and a host of others who have died in the faith. All these explicitly declare that they received a distinct witness of this *second blessing;* that while in a justified state they felt the workings of inward corruption; they sought by prayer and faith for deliverance, and obtained a clear and satisfactory evidence of entire sanctification, so that they reckoned themselves dead indeed unto sin, and alive unto God through Jesus Christ! They now had the witness of perfect love, distinct from the witness of pardon which was communicated on their justification. Now shall we say they mistook the operations of their own minds? This we might do if there was anything in their experience contrary to the word of God; or if they had in other instances exhibited signs of mental aberration, or incorrigible enthusiasm, we might be justified in supposing that they were self-deceived. But of the persons above named we can form no such conclusion. In all they say on other points, reason and the true spirit of the Gospel are predominant. Why should we conclude them entirely beside themselves here? Indeed, if the Gospel remains the same that it was in the days of John and Paul, we have good reason to conclude them in their sober senses even in their highest professions."

THE JOY OF THE CROSS.

BY MADAME GUYON.

Long plunged in sorrow, I resign
My soul to that dear hand of thine,
   Without reserve or fear;
That hand shall wipe my streaming eyes;
Or into smiles of glad surprise
   Transform the falling tear.

My sole possession is thy love;
In earth beneath, or heaven above,
   I have no other store;
And though with fervent suit I pray,
And importune thee, night and day,
   I ask thee nothing more.

My rapid hours pursue the course
Prescribed them by love's sweetest force,
   And I thy sovereign will,
Without a wish to escape my doom;
Though still a sufferer from the womb,
   And doomed to suffer still.

By thy command, where'er I stray,
SORROW attends me all my way,
   A never failing friend;
And, if my sufferings may augment
Thy praise, behold me well content,
   Let *sorrow* still attend.

It costs me no regret, that she
Who followed Christ, should follow me;
   And though where'er she goes,
Thorns spring spontaneous at her feet,
I love her, and extract a sweet
   From all her bitter woes.

Adieu! ye vain delights of earth,
Insipid sports and childish mirth,
   I taste no sweets in you;
*Unknown delights are in the Cross,
All joy beside, to me is dross;*
   And Jesus thought so too.

The *Cross!* Oh, ravishment and bliss—
How grateful e'en its anguish is;
   Its bitterness how sweet!
There every sense, and all the mind,
In all her faculties refined,
   Taste happiness complete.

Souls, once enabled to disdain
Base, sublunary joys, maintain
   Their dignity secure;
The fever of desire is passed,
And love has all its genuine taste,—
   Is delicate and pure.

Self-love no grace in sorrow sees,
Consults her own peculiar ease;
   'Tis all the bliss she knows;
But nobler aims true Love employ,
In self-denial is her joy,
   In suffering her repose.

Jesus, avenger of our fall,
Thou faithful lover, above-all
   The Cross have ever borne!
Oh tell me,—life is in thy voice,—
How much afflictions were thy choice,
   And sloth and ease thy scorn!

*Thy choice and mine shall be the same,
Inspirer of that holy flame,
   Which must forever blaze!
To take the Cross and follow Thee,
Where love and duty lead, shall be
   My portion and my praise.*

SOME ONE MUST PRAY.—A man of learning and talent, but an unbeliever, was traveling in Manilla on a scientific expedition. He was escorted by a native, and, as they were about to start, the native, with the refined politeness which characterizes the Orientals, requested the white stranger to pray to his God.

This was probably the only thing he could have been asked to do without being able to comply; and on his declining, the native said;

"Well, *some* God must be prayed to, so you will excuse me if I pray to mine."

   "Full many a shaft at random sent
   Finds mark the archer never meant."

So it was in this case. The unbeliever was rebuked by a heathen, and the man of science who had gone there in quest of natural curiosites, returned, having found the "pearl of great price." His next visit is to be as a missionary to preach Christ.

A HINT TO MOTHERS.

*"There's music in a mother's voice,
More sweet than breezes sighing,
There's kindness in a mother's glance,
Too pure for ever dying."*

MOTHERS, how do you adorn your little ones: modestly? When about to costume your daughter for the parlor, the social circle, or the sanctuary, do you turn to the map of maps, to wisdom eternal? to Romans xii, 2; 1 Tim. ii, 9; 1 Peter v, 3? Or do you lay aside the heavenly chart, let popular fancy take the lead? Many of you manifest a commendable scrupulosity and scriptural consciousness in your *own* personal decorations. Your apparel is, in the main, modest, plain, simple, economical, Gospel-like. Meanwhile, you *tip off* your little ones gaudily and fashionably—allow them to gratify their fancies to the utmost! Mothers, how is this? What right have you to bedeck your offspring in butterfly costume, gay and costly finery, any more than yourselves?

Have *you* not just as good a right to follow the fashions and follies, yourselves, in expensive adornments, "gold, pearls, and costly array," which God forbids, as you have to allow your daughters to do so? What's the difference in the sinfulness or criminality?

God holds parents responsible for the conduct of their children, for their influence at home and abroad. Mark the case of Eli.

The tendencies of this worldly conformity in dress, are evil, and only evil.

Furthermore, very many parents allow their sons and daughters to read novels, romances, sip at the muddy, corrupting streams of the popular weeklies and monthlies—the Godeys, Harpers, Leslies, Ledgers, Leaders, Mercurys, and the whole batch of these locusts, lice, flies and frogs of Egypt! And do these parents *begin* to realize that the guilt and consequences of this undue license given to those under their charge, rests upon their own shoulders? Beloved, the Lord holds you responsible for the deeds of your little ones.

Again, very many parents that suffer their little ones to kill time on these debasing, soul-destroying influences, would not be seen, on any account, poring over these reptiles, these serpents in the grass! Parents, rest assured, God, by-and-bye, will bring this whole matter into judgment. And even in this life, you may sip the wormwood and the gall, or reap the whirlwind.

This sinful apathy of yours, this criminal neglect of wholesome parental discipline, may bring down your gray hairs with sorrow to the grave.

"God is not mocked; whatsoever a man soweth that shall he also reap. He that soweth to the flesh, shall of the flesh reap corruption."

"Train up a child in the way he should go, and when he is old he will not depart from it."

*"Mothers, your cause is holy, 'tis to guide the erring,
To lead the blind, and make the deaf to hear;
To win to virtue those who, vice preferring,
Plunge in the slough of crime without a fear."*
—GOLDEN RULE.

"BY reflecting on an odd book, "The general delusion of Christians with regard to Prophecy," I was fully convinced of what I had long suspected,

1. That the Montanists in the second and third centuries, were real, scriptural Christians; and 2. That the grand reason why the miraculous gifts were so soon withdrawn, was not only that faith and holiness were well nigh lost, but that dry, formal orthodox men, began even then to ridicule whatever gifts they had not themselves; and to decry them all, as either madness or imposture."—WESLEY.

PRAYER.—It is not the place of prayer that God examines; nor is it the words that God primarily regards; it is not the form in any sense that avails;—it is the intense and ardent desire breathed from the depths of the heart into the ear of God, which God answers exceeding abundantly above all that we can ask or think.—CUMMING.

WORSHIP.

BY THE EDITOR.

Is God worshiped in our Churches? This may seem a strange question. But we ask it in all seriousness. If so by whom? By all present? To assert that, would be to assume that worship consists in decently sitting for an hour within consecrated walls. Then the gambler, the libertine, the swindler, is a worshipper. But he certainly does not intend to bear that character.

Prayer and praise are acts of worship. But how many pray in the solemn assemblies of Protestant Churches? How many assume even the outward attitude of prayer? The Psalmist says, "O come let us worship and bow down, let us kneel before the Lord our Maker."

The Bible teaches that men ought to pray, *meekly kneeling upon their knees.* It furnishes a not very flattering example of standing in prayer, for the Pharisee "stood and prayed. His prayer like too many we have heard men make in that position, was more of a self-complacent speech than a prayer. While listening to such addresses, we have been often reminded of what an eastern editor said of a prayer made upon some public occasion by Edward Everett, when he was a preacher. "That it was the most eloquent prayer that was ever offered *to* the Boston people."

"It is not all gold that glitters," but real gold shines nevertheless. An attitude of devotion may be assumed by an undevout person, but we very much doubt whether any one ever offered fervent prayer whose position of body, indicated the greatest listlessness and indifference, unless circumstances rendered such position unavoidable.

Dr. Adam Clarke says, "I suppose the grossly absurd and perfectly ungodly custom of sitting during prayer is out of the question. It was so perfectly unlike every thing that was becoming in divine worship, and so expressive of a total want of reverence in the worshipper, and of that consciousness of his wants, and deep sense of his own worthlessness that he ought to have, that the Church of God never tolerated it, *a custom that even heathenism itself had too much light either to practice or sanction."* Who, then, prays in public worship? The minister says "Let *us* pray:" but who heeds the invitation? One of our preachers of the primitive stamp, after vainly striving to induce his people to unite with him in prayer gave up in despair, and instead of the usual formula he prefaced his public devotions, with the phrase "LET ME PRAY."

Singing is a part of worship. But in our Protestant Churches who sings? Usually does one in ten of the congregation? Is not this part of worship generally in the hands of merely professional singers?—Of persons who do not even profess to be Christians? Can any one suppose that God is pleased with this vicarious worship? The leading singers are frequently paid for their services—sometimes in money—sometimes in deference and submission. In some places it is the custom, in time of singing, for the congregation to arise, turn around, and stand in respectful silence before the choir during their musical performances. Whether the object is, that the choir may sing to the congregation or that the congregation may pay their homage to the choir, we could never determine.

God is a Spirit: *and they that worship him, must worship him in spirit and in truth.* With what propriety then can heartless ceremonies, performed for pay, be called worship? We send missionaries to the poor heathen, who, fastening a written prayer to a wind-mill imagine that at every revolution acceptable worship is paid to the divinity to whom it is addressed. Who can say of merely mechanical performances of sacred rites, that one kind is more pleasing to God than another? Who can say that prayer or praise, when offered upon the arms of a wind-mill, will not meet with the Divine approbation just as readily as when it is uttered by the unpurged lips of one who does not mean a word he says, but whose only desire is that he may play his part well?

When God is lost sight of—when the Holy Spirit's aid is not earnestly implored "to help our infirmities," and to teach us "what we should pray for as we ought, and to make intercession for us with groanings which cannot be uttered," when the house of God becomes merely a place of fashionable resort for genteel people upon the Sabbath, then imposing ceremonies that dazzle the imagination and please the taste may exert a restraining influence upon some, but can we in the light of the Scriptures call any thing worship that does not spring from the heart?

> Vainly we offer each ample oblation;
> Vainly with gifts would his favor secure;
> Richer by far is the heart's adoration,
> Dearer to God are the prayers of the poor.

A WORTHY CONFESSOR.—It was a fine reply which Basil, of Cæsarea, made when the Emperor Valens sent by his prefect, endeavoring by threats to compel him to receive acknowledged Arians into the fellowship of the Church. The prefect demanded whether he alone, when all others obeyed the Emperor, dared to wish to have any other religion than that of his master. Basil replied, that he had nothing to be afraid of; possessions, of which men might deprive him, he had none, except his few books and his cloak. An exile was no exile for him, since he knew the whole earth was the Lord's. If torture was threatened, his feeble body would yield to the first blows; and as for death, that would only bring him nearer to God after whom he longed. The prefect gave up the case. It was vain to threaten such a man.

TEMPER.—Too many have no idea of the subjection of their temper to the influence of religion and yet what is changed if the temper is not! If a man is as passionate, malicious, resentful, sullen, moody, or morose, after his conversion as before it, what is he converted from or to.—J. A. JAMES.

DRINKING POISON.

LAST week Dr. Cox delivered a couple of lectures in the Lecture Room of Dr. Pressly's Church, Alleghany, that should alarm the drinkers of beer and liquors, and awaken concerted movement throughout the entire community against the farther progress of the drinking habits that have been so greatly revived among us. Because, if the Dr. be a true man, as he is generally supposed to be, and if the tests are reliable, which can be easily determined, most of what is now drunk under the names of beer, whiskey, brandy, and wine, is nothing less than diluted poison—and not so very diluted after all.

He pronounced a specimen of *Lager beer*, from one of the most popular establishments for that kind of manufacture in Allegheny, to have in its ingredients *tobacco*, instead of hops. A bottle of *whiskey*, obtained from one of the most respectable liquor dealers in Pittsburg, was found to contain a large amount of *sulphuric acid*. With respect to *brandy*, he said that instead of being made from wine, its base was generally *bad whiskey*, containing *sweet spirits of nitre, sulphuric acid, lead, lime, chloroform,* and other ingredients. In *wine* he had found *arsenic*. *Sulphate of zinc* was very common in *gin*. *Strychnine* was a most wonderful stimulant, and would make one barrel of liquor go as far as four. He had examined a specimen of imported old *Cogniac*, and discovered it to have whiskey as a base, with *fusil oil, sulphuric acid, chloroform, pepper, &c*. In view of these facts why will people continue to use such maddening and death-dealing preparations any longer? And why is the community so regardless of such fearful ruin?—PITTSBURG PRESBYTERIAN BANNER.

THOSE who pretend to live by faith when they are spiritually blind and dead, do but deceive themselves.—BELLAMY.

REFLECTIONS.

BY REV. JAMES MATHEWS.

SOLD myself for naught! Bound up here in these miserable chains of my own forging. O! wretched man that I am—who shall deliver me. Jesus once delivered me—that first time when I came a trembling sinner to the footstool of mercy, loathing myself, and repenting in dust and ashes. Oh! I could believe then and there the joy that filled my soul, when God whispered *Peace*. O! how the remembrance increases my agony. I thought in that hour that I never should be moved. I determined, O how resolutely, to serve God and him only, all the days of my life. It was all light then, gloriously light. As I read the blessed word, it opened to my understanding, and there I read of the inheritance of the children of God—that "Land of rest from inbred sin," and my heart was drawn toward it; yes, the light was very clear. I understood the meaning of being sanctified wholly, soul, body, and spirit, in that hour. O! the yearning of my soul after that state can never be told. You that have felt it know. For a while I trembled on the verge, until my heart cried out,

"By faith I plunge me in that sea."

O! how glory flooded my soul. I leaped as an hart. Hallelujahs burst forth, and I exulted in perfect freedom. Yes, I knew then for myself the power of Jesus to save to the uttermost. Would to God I could stop now, for memory goads me. Must I, can I write it. *I will;* it is my only hope. I went out, rejoicing as a strong man to run a race. That night one came to me, (O that I could forget it,) a member of the church, an old man, a class leader; he took my hand, and told me he rejoiced with me. Then I praised God aloud out of a full heart; again he told me, he was glad to find me in such a good way, (I could not think why I felt so strangely while he was speaking, I know now.) "But, said he, "you will need to be careful, very careful. I have been on the mountain where you are, and it is a dangerous place; now I rest, I live in the valley." I did not then know the difference between the valley of humility, and the valley of sin. I know now to my sorrow.

Again he said, "You say you are sanctified. I do not doubt your sincerity, but then we are so likely to be mistaken, you may enjoy the blessings of entire holiness, but I would not say anything about it; wait awhile, if you find you can live it, why then on proper occasions, profess it, but be very careful. I have been a member of the church forty years, and never professed it, and there is no one in our church that does." O! my God, I listened, I could not account for my feelings; chilliness crept over me, and I felt as though death was near.

Next day, in meeting, I rose to tell what God had done for my soul, and right before me sat the old man; his counsel flashed across my mind, and after stammering a few words I sat down, with, O such a weight upon my heart; I went home, but not to rest; that night my thoughts troubled me; I tossed restlessly from side to side, and felt that I had been ashamed of Jesus, —had suffered man to make me fear. I was reproved in that hour. And now what could I do? I resolved to go and confess it, but I found pride had been sown again in my heart; there was opposition to this within me, but I went to the meeting, and instead of obeying the Spirit, suffered my feelings to check me. The next meeting I felt but little, then I gave way to impatience, then to peevishness, at last to passion, and so forth from step to step, until I became a poor miserable backslider. I see now where my feet began to slide, O! that I could recall the past. O! that I could retrace my steps. Can God have mercy upon me? May I dare come to him again? O is there any hope for me? Lord have mercy upon me. I will return. No, I have tried so many times and failed. What shall I do? God help me.

There was the Prodigal; he wandered into sin, so have I. He felt his degradation, so do I. He saw his folly, so do I. He cried, "I am not worthy to be called thy son," this I feel. He went towards his home, so will I. I will, I will. Father I have sinned, Oh forgive me. Thou didst receive the Prodigal, wilt Thou not receive me? Thou wilt, I dare believe. Father! I come. Thou dost invite, thou dost. I come, Father. Thou dost accept.

"Hallelujah! Father's reconciled—
For me the house must now rejoice,
My Father owns his child."

So much as you have of pride, so much you have of the fallen angel alive in you. So much as you have of true humility, so much you have of the Lamb of God within you. Could you see with your eyes what every stirring of pride does to your soul, you would beg of every thing you meet to tear the viper from you, though with the loss of an hand or an eye. Could you see what a sweet, divine transforming power there is in humility, what an heavenly water of life it gives to the fiery breath of your soul, how it expels the poison of your fallen nature, and makes room for God to live in you, you would rather wish to be the footstool of all the world, than to want the smallest degree of it.—LAW.

A WONDERFUL MISSION.—The mission of the American Baptist Union among the Karens in Burmah has a wonderful history. Only thirty years ago the first convert was baptized, and now the number of church members is over fifteen thousand, and the natives under regular Christian instruction amount to more than one hundred thousand. The station at Toungoo was commenced seven years ago by a native preacher, and in two years there numbered in that place two thousand converts. Prosperity still attends it. Will the churches withhold funds when God is thus pouring down his blessings?

WHICH WILL YOU HAVE?

Your finery, your fashionable dressing, your ear jewels, breastpins, finger-rings, your flounces and gay artificials, your costly attire, or Jesus, the blessed Saviour, the gift of power, the fruits of the Spirit, love, joy, peace, gentleness, goodness, a pure conscience, a sweet, holy, heavenly joy, all that is lovely and of good report, a sure hope of life eternal? Which will you have, sister? which will you choose? You can have one or the other, as you please, but not both—no man can serve two masters.

Whom will you serve? the god of fashion, or the Lord of Lords, King of Kings, the Holy One of Israel?

" What is beauty? Not the show
Of shapely limbs and features. No,
These are but flowers
That have their dated hours,
To breathe their momentary sweets, then go.
'Tis the stainless soul within."

Says Joshua, "Choose you this day whom ye will serve; * * * but as for me and my house, we will serve the Lord." Josh. xxiv: 15.—GOLDEN RULE.

DISPUTE WITH THE DEVIL.—Never a word, a single syllable; the very instant he whispers in your ear, say, "Get thee hence, Satan."

An excellent writer remarks, "If you would not be foiled by temptation, do not enter into a dispute with Satan. When Eve began to argue the case with the serpent it was too hard for her; the devil, by his logic, disputed her out of Paradise. Satan can mince sin, make it small, and varnish it over, and make it look like virtue. Satan is too subtle a sophister to hold an argument with him. Dispute not, but fight. If you enter into a parley with Satan, you give him half the victory."

DIVINE truths are like chain-shot, they go together, and we need not perplex ourselves which should enter first; if any one enter, it will draw the rest after it.—ANDREW FULLER.

BACKSLIDERS.

BY FINNEY.

No class of persons make so much trouble for a minister. If he preaches so as to commend himself to their conscience, he hurts their feelings, and they oppose him. If he preaches so as to satisfy their feelings, then their conscience condemns him, and they have no confidence in his honesty. You come down to their standard, and they know you are wrong.

There is no such thing as pleasing them by preaching.

If you crowd the truth home to them, they will grumble, and call it harsh and personal. If you do not preach so as to cut them to the quick, they know that it is wrong, and they will say, "That will never do, we shall never get awake by such preaching as this, the minister is as much asleep as we are, and we never can get along so."

Thus they will always feel uneasy, let the preaching be as it may.

A minister ought not to conciliate the feelings of professors who are in a backslidden state, by any compromise, but he ought to tear open their hearts, and pour in the burning truth, till he can drive them out from their bed of slumber and death.

Backsliders are the *most hypocritical* of all people. They neither serve God nor the devil, sincerely. They have forsaken the devil, so that they no longer serve him with singleness of heart, and have given themselves to God, but now they do not serve him. They are hypocrites on both sides. Neither God nor the devil can trust them.

THE reason why many seek to be saved from the carnal mind, and do not obtain the blessing, is, because they have secretly backslidden, and have forfeited the divine favour. If they were correctly acquainted with their own state, they would first seek to be justified by faith in Christ Jesus.
—BRAMWELL.

PAUL'S ESTIMATE OF HEAVEN.—In speaking of the glories of the eternal world, the rapture of the Apostle does not escape him as a sally of the imagination, as a thought awakened by the sudden glance of the object; he does not express himself at random from the sudden impulse of the moment, but in the sober tone of calculation. "I reckon," he says, like a man skilled in this spiritual arithmetic, "I reckon," after a due estimate of their comparative value, "that the sufferings of the present time are not worthy to be compared with the glory that shall be revealed."

No man was ever so well qualified to make this estimate. Of the sufferings of the present world he had shared more largely than any man. He had heard the words of God, and seen the vision of the Almighty, and the result of this privileged experience was, that he desired to escape from this valley of tears; that he was impatient to recover the celestial vision, eager to perpetuate the momentary foretaste of the glories of immortality.—HANNAH MORE.

THE formalist may, from legal fears and mercenary hopes, be so strict and conscientious in his ways, as to think himself a choice good man. And the *enthusiast*, from a firm persuasion of the pardon of his sins, and the love of Christ, may be so full of joy and love, zeal and devotion, as to think himself a most eminent saint; but there is nothing of the nature of true holiness in either; for it is *self*, and nothing but *self*, that is the principle, centre, and end of all this religion.—BELLAMY.

IT may be found, upon strict inquiry, that there is not a grace of the Holy Spirit which does not possess a portion of every other grace. Yet faith is not love, nor hope, nor joy, nor longsuffering, nor gentleness, nor goodness, nor patience; each has a distinctive character; and yet each is so blended with the other, that in dissecting one, you must cut through the veins of all.
—ANDREW FULLER.

Do Good. — Thousands of men breathe, move and live, pass off the stage of life, and are heard of no more. Why? They did not a particle of good in the world; and none were blessed by them, none could point to them as the instruments of their redemption; not a word they spoke could be recalled, and so they perished; their light went out in darkness, and they were not remembered more than the insects of yesterday. Will you thus live and die, O man immortal? Live for something. Do good, and leave behind you a monument of virtue that the storm of time can never destroy. Write your name in kindness, love and mercy, on the hearts of thousands you come in contact with, year by year, and you will never be forgotten. No, your name, your deeds, will be as legible on the hearts you leave behind, as the stars on the brow of evening. Good deeds will shine as the stars of heaven.—Dr. CHALMERS.

MOTIVES TO HOLINESS.—A man who has been redeemed by the blood of the Son of God should be pure. He who is an heir of life should be holy. He who is attended by the celestial beings, and who is soon—be knows not how soon — to be translated to heaven, should be holy. Are angels my attendants? Then I should walk worthy of their companionship. Am I soon to go and dwell with angels? Then I should be pure. Are these feet soon to tread the court of heaven? Is this tongue soon to unite with heavenly beings in praising God? Are these eyes of mine soon to look on the throne of eternal glory, and on the ascended Redeemer? Then these feet and eyes and lips should be pure and holy, and I should be dead to the world and live for heaven.—ALBERT BARNES.

DUTIES AND EVENTS.—Duties are ours—events are God's. This removes an infinite burden from the shoulders of a miserable, tempted, dying creature.—CECIL.

HEATHEN BOYS.—A missionary in the East Indies was giving away tracts, when a little boy, about eight years old, asked for one. At first he was refused, for tracts were then very scarce. But the child begged so hard, that one called "The Way to Heavenly Bliss" was given him. Some days passed, and the little fellow came again with the same request. "But have you read the other?" he was asked. "Yes," said he; and standing before the missionary and several heathens, he repeated the whole tract from the title to the end. Well done, poor little heathen boy.

Thus we see that books and tracts reach the dark spots of the earth, and like rays of light serve to guide some from among the heathen to heaven.

GOD'S CHILDREN are like the stars, that shine brightest in the darkest night. Like torches, that are the better for beating, like grapes, that come not to the proof till they come to the press. Like trees, that drive down their roots further, and grasp the earth tighter by reason of the storm. Like vines that grow the better for bleeding. Like gold, that looks the better for scouring; like glow worms, that shine best in the dark. Like Juniper, that smells sweetest in the fire. Like the Pomander, which becomes more fragrant for chafing. Like the Palm Tree, which proves the better for preserving. Like the Chamomile which spreads the more as you tread upon it.

You may as well think to be saved for being good musicians, physicians, or astronomers, as for being learned divines, if your knowledge cause not holy love, it may help others to heaven, but it will be but vanity to you; and you will be as sounding brass, or a tinkling cymbal. You glory in a lifeless picture of wisdom; and hell may shortly tell you, that you had better have chosen anything to play the fool with, than with the notions and words of wisdom mortified.—BAXTER.

SECRET SINS.

Of all sinners, the man who makes a profession of religion, and yet lives in iniquity, is the most miserable. A downright wicked man, who takes a glass in his hand, and says, "I am a drunkard, I am not ashamed of it," he shall be unutterably miserable in worlds to come, but brief though it be, he has his hour of pleasure. A man who curses and swears, and says, "That is my habit, I am a profane man," and makes a profession of it, he has at least some peace in his soul; but the man who walks with God's minister, who is united with God's church, who comes out before God's people, and unites with them, and then lives in sin, what a miserable existence he must have of it! Why, he has a worse existence than the mouse that is in the parlor, running out now and then to pick up the crumbs, and then back again to his hole. Such men must run out now and then to sin; and O! how fearful they are to be discovered! One day, perhaps, their character turns up; with wonderful cunning they manage to conceal and gloss it over; but the next day something else comes, and they live in constant fear, telling lie after lie, to make the last lie appear truthful, adding deception to deception, in order that they may not be discovered.

"O! 'tis a tangled web we weave,
When once we venture to deceive."

If I must be a wicked man, give me the life of a roystering sinner, who sins before the face of day; if I must sin, let me not act as a hypocrite and a coward; let me not profess to be God's, and spend my life for the devil. This way of cheating the devil is a thing which every honest sinner will be ashamed of. He will say, "Now, if I do serve my master I will serve him out and out, I will have no sham about it; but if I do not, if I live in sin, I am not going to gloss it over by cant and hypocrisy." One thing which has ham-stringed the church, and cut her very sinews in twain, has been this most damnable hypocrisy. O! in how many places have we men whom you might praise to the very skies, if you could believe their words, but whom you might cast into the nethermost pit if you could see their secret actions. God forgive any of you who are so acting! I had almost said, I can scarce forgive you. I can forgive the man who riots openly, and makes no profession of being better; but the man who fawns, and cants, and pretends and prays, and then lives in sin, that man I hate, I can not bear him, I abhor him from my very soul. If he will turn from his ways, I will love him, but in his hypocrisy he is to me the most loathsome of all creatures. 'Tis said the toad doth wear a jewel in her head, but this man hath none, but beareth filthiness about him, while he pretends to be in love with righteousness. A mere profession, my hearers, is but painted pageantry to go to hell in: it is like the plumes upon the hearse and the trappings upon the black horses which drag men to their graves, the funeral array of dead souls. Take heed above every thing of a waxen profession that will not stand the sun; take care of a life that needs to have two faces to carry it out; be one thing, or else the other. If you make up your mind to serve Satan, do not pretend to serve God; and if you serve God, serve him with all your heart. "No man can serve two *masters;*" do not try it, do not endeavor to do it, for no life will be more miserable than that. Above all, beware of committing acts which it will be necessary to conceal.—Spurgeon.

"Beware of self-dependence. The first step in spiritual declension is thus:—"Let him that *thinketh he standeth!*" The secret of real strength is this:—"Kept by the power of God!"

The road ambition travels is too narrow for friendship, and too crooked for love.

INDUSTRY IN MINISTERS.

The pious Christmas Evans, when he was about putting off his harness, thus wrote to a young minister: "I am old, my dear boy, and you are just entering the ministry. Let me now, and here, tell you one thing, and commend it to your attention and memory. All the ministers that I have ever known, who have fallen into disgrace, or into uselessness, *have been idle men*. An idle man is in the way of every temptation. Temptation has not to seek him; he is at the corner of the street, ready and waiting for it. In the case of a minister of the gospel, this peril is multiplied by his position, his neglected duties, the temptations peculiar to his condition, and his superior susceptibility. Remember this, *stick to your book*. I am never much afraid of a young minister, when I know that he can, and does, fairly sit down to his book. There is Mr. ——, of such unhappy temper, and who has such a love to meddle with everything; he would long ago have been utterly wrecked, but his habits of industry saved him."

Let no merchant in the town—no lawyer—no physician of your acquaintance—no farmer of your parish—be more industrious than you, in their calling. Give not a day of your life, but for its worth. Industry will keep you always busy and always at leisure. It will give you time for everything, and enable you to do everything in its time, and to perfect everything you undertake. It will aid you in writing short sermons. It will bless you and your people, and the Church, in a thousand ways.

And examples for your imitation you will find in Luther, Calvin, Baxter, Wesley, in every man, in every department of life, who has risen to high position among his fellows. Shepherd, himself a great preacher, used to say: " God will curse that man's labors who goes idly up and down all the week, and then goes into his study on Saturday. When his friends sought to persuade Newton, then upwards of eighty years old, to preach no more, he replied, " I can not stop; what! shall the old African blasphemer stop while he can speak?"—Dr. Murray.

Prayer.—A man cannot be a true believer, a child of Christ, unless he be a man of prayer. For what the breath is to the body, prayer is to the soul. If the breath gasp and be faint, the body grows out of order; and if prayer be slack and unfrequent, the soul becomes diseased. If breath ceases, life is at an end; and if prayer ceases, all hope for the soul perishes. As soon as we give over communing with God, Satan enters in, and begins to commune with us. Man can never walk alone: if he choose not the better part, to walk with his God, he must choose to walk with God's adversary and his own. That man would but be persuaded, " Prayer is man's best work!"— Luther.

Recognition in Heaven.—"I must confess, as the experience of my own soul, that the expectation of loving my friends in heaven, principally kindles my love to them while on earth. If I thought I should never know them and consequently never love them after this life is ended, I should number them with temporal things and love them as such; but I now delightfully converse with my pious friends in a firm persuasion that I shall converse with them forever; and I take comfort in those that are dead or absent, believing that I shall shortly meet them in heaven, and love them with a heavenly love.— Baxter.

A mortified spirit is such, without indignation against scorn, without revenge against injuries, without murmuring at low offices, not impatient in troubles, indifferent in all accidents, neither transported with joy, nor depressed with sorrow and is humble in all his thoughts.—Jeremy Taylor.

ARE YOU SAVED?

BY M. N. DOWNING.

READER! of all questions this is the most important. The interest involved is weighty and eternal. You are to live forever, either with the blood-washed millions, or in the land of deepest shade, the world of woe! Do not evade the question, but bare your heart to the searching light. You are hastening to the judgment. Probation with you will soon close, when your second life, or "second death," bounded only by the coming years of *Him* whose attribute is eternity, will commence. "These shall go away into everlasting punishment, but the righteous into life eternal."

In whatever else you may be deceived, you cannot afford to be deceived in reference to your soul's eternal welfare. It will be *too bad* for you to dream of heaven; its jasper walls, its pearly streets, its crowns, its palms, its glorified inhabitants, and wake up in hell! Oh, it will be *too bad*. What a *sting*, what a *gnawing*, what an eternal *anguish* will it be. Oh, my soul is stirred, my head is sick, my heart is faint, while beholding the *wreck* of the vast multitude of immortal minds, capacitated to enjoy heaven, the concentration of all that is *good;* but who with the same capacities must take up with the concentration of all that is unlike *God*—banished "from God and the glory of his power," and locked up in eternal night, where fiends forever dwell, who curse

"Almighty God, and curse the Lamb, and curse
The earth, the resurrection morn, and seek,
And ever vainly seek, for utter death."

God, angels, ministers, Christians, *engage* in stirring the millions in and out of the churches, who only need to die to be damned! God help me to *write the truth*. Others may soar, others may abound in flowery sentences, others may write to make display, and to see their names in print; but oh, Thou discerner of the thoughts and *intents* of the heart, I *must* and *will* write for *Thee!* Help thou author of *truth!* Thou Judge of quick and dead!

Again I ask, especially you who are orthodox in your creed, are you saved? That you may better answer the question, I will ask you a series of others.

1. Have you ever had the "*witness of the Spirit*" that you were a child of God?

Not do you profess religion and belong to a church; not how many sacrifices have you made, how many means of grace have you attended; not do you desire to gain heaven at last; but do you *know*, by the Spirit of God, that you have been converted? The "witness of the Spirit" is the only *sure* evidence that we have been saved. This is the sealing of the work. "The Spirit *itself* beareth witness with *our* spirit that we are the children of God. This is not a flight of the imagination, something we think we have, when we have it not. It is not a *seeming* to be right, a *thinking* we are right, but it is *knowing* we are right, "by the Holy Spirit given unto us." It is an inward consciousness produced by the Spirit of God, of the removal of guilt and condemnation, so that we no longer feel the load of sin. Our souls are free. Notwithstanding the enormity of our past transgressions, we feel *innocent* before God. This is accompanied with peace of mind. The breast no longer heaves the burdened sigh; the aching heart no longer throbs with disquieted emotion, but all is peaceful, calm and serene. Now

"The Spirit answers to the blood,
And tells me I am born of God."

Was this your experience when you professed religion? If so you were converted to God; if not, you were not converted to God; and if this has not been your experience since you professed the religion of Jesus Christ, let me tell you, in love for your soul, *you have never been converted to God*. We are aware some may take exceptions to this close dealing; but the time is upon us that "judgment must begin at the house of God." You had better know the truth *now*, and get right with God while you *may*, than to face it when the cold earth is making its deathly rattle over your coffin, and your spirit stands undressed before your final Judge. The conversion of the soul to God is the greatest work that can be done for man. That it might be accomplished, the crimson blood of the Incarnate God ran freely, crying, "Mercy's free!" Then it is not a "cunningly devised fable," but a *reality*, wrought by the Holy Ghost, so that they who are saved can say,

> "What we have felt and seen,
> With confidence we tell;
> And publish to the sons of men,
> The signs infallible."

The doctrine of the "*witness of the Spirit*" is clearly taught in the bible, and corroborated by the experience of every one who has been truly born of God. It has been lost sight of too much. It is a part of the faith for which the church is exhorted "earnestly to contend." Strike it out and there is no use of preaching to sinners. Strike it out and the system of Christianity is worthless. What! shall we tell the sinner that by the righteous judgment of the Most High he is doomed to everlasting destruction from the presence of God, and from the glory of His power? Shall we alarm him with guilty fears by the terrors of the Lord, and then tell him, that notwithstanding he *may* be saved, he need not expect an assurance of his present salvation, for he cannot have it, but only hope he is saved?

What consolation is it to the awakened sinner, who stands trembling between two worlds with a lively sense of his unholiness, the wrath of a holy God abiding upon him, and the fiery billows rolling beneath him, to be told in that hour that he cannot *know* when his sins are cancelled, wrath turned away, and the smiles of a reconciled Father beaming upon him? Such a docrine has proved the ruin of more souls than the "Age of Reason." The hardened sinner wants to *know* when God is reconciled; and he *may* know, yea he *does* know, for "he that believeth on the Son of God hath the witness in himself." "And because ye are sons, God hath sent forth the Spirit of His Son into your hearts, crying, "Abba, Father." Can a person cry "Abba, Father," by the Spirit of Christ and not *know* it? Again, "For ye have not received the spirit of bondage again to fear, but ye have received the spirit of adoption, whereby we cry Abba Father." The Spirit itself bearing witness with our spirit that we are the children of God. Do not these passages teach an inward *assurance* of a state of acceptance with God? Verily!

If the foregoing has been your experience, we ask,

2. *Have you retained it?* Is it your present experience? Remember the inquiry is, *are* you saved, not have you been. You are walled in by a profession, a church relation it may be, or even an official position; you may be a class-leader, a steward, or a preacher. Have you peace with God? Have you joy in the Holy Ghost? Do you know from day to day that you are a child of God? Let us see; before you could obtain peace with God, you had to renounce the devil and all his works, the vain pomp and glory of the world. Are they still renounced? Since your conversion you have felt the necessity of more *fully* renouncing the world. Have you done it? and do you do so now? Since you were converted you have seen that you could not wear some articles of dress, or adorning, and retain your justification. Have you laid them aside? Perhaps you have seen that the business in which you were engaged did not please God, and that you must give it up in order to enjoy religion. Have you done it? Old habits you must renounce. Have you renounced them? If you cannot answer these interrogatories in the affirmative, you cannot claim, on bible ground, to be a Christian. Hear what God says: "If any man draw back, my soul shall have no pleasure in him." Heb. x, 38. "Jesus Christ, the same

yesterday, to-day, and forever." Hence His *command*, as well as his promise, is *immutable*. We may change our views of God's requirements; we may shift them to circumstances, but "the word of the Lord endureth forever!" Think of this, you who take back part of the price. Remember the case of Ananias and Sapphira.

Again, God never gives light for nought. What he shows us to be His will *must be done*. His Spirit and His word agree. His word says, "without holiness no man shall see the Lord." Has the Holy Spirit written this upon your heart? It has if you have been converted, and have walked in the light of this grace a great length of time. This is the Divine order in the process of redemption. The Spirit first awakens the sinner, then if he yields to the claims of God, it pardons and regenerates him, and that not only *instantaneously*, but, as far as his apprehension is concerned, *simultaneously*. If this is your experience, a great work has been wrought; one that cannot be retained, and knowingly break one of the least of God's holy commandments. Yet you are not *fully* saved. From guilt and condemnation you are fully saved, but you have *felt* the need of something more being done; of being cleansed from inbred corruption. You have felt under provocation a rising contrary to love. It may have been pride, or anger, or impatience. This is *experience*. We may split theoretical hairs until we are gray, and it will not change the word of God.

The testimony of all who have been freely justified, while living in the enjoyment of this state, is that they have felt these things, prior to their entire sanctification, call them what we may. The state of the heart subsequent to justification, and prior to entire sanctification, is expressed by the use of various terms, such as "the remains of the carnal mind," "native depravity," "inbred sin," &c. It matters not so much what terms are used to express the state, as it does to be *saved from it*. God *wants* to save us from it. Has He convicted you for this second work? What have you done? You felt its need, not only to save you to the uttermost, but to impart unto you *power* to do or suffer the will of God. Have you obeyed the dictates of the Spirit, and sought for this blessing? If not, you are not now freely justified. No one can refuse to take what God holds out and be clear. Here is where many make shipwreck of faith. They have the light, they feel their need, but they fail through fear and unbelief to enter into this second rest. They settle down and try to pacify themselves; talk of peace, but it is the peace of death, for there can be no true peace without obedience to God. They lose their love for souls, and power to reach them. Is this your state? if so, you are not saved. Awake! renew your consecration, and again take Christ and the cross.

Again, if you have experienced this second work, we ask,

3. Have you retained it? If not, you are not now justified, unless you have aroused and are hastening with all possible speed to return. Some have imbibed the idea that one may fall from a state of entire sanctification into justification. This, in the nature of things, cannot be. One cannot fall from a state of *purity* but through transgression of some point of God's law, which is sin, for "sin is the transgression of the law." If one fall through disobedience, law is transgressed; if through doubt, law is transgressed, for "what is not of faith is sin," and "without faith it is impossible to please God." Then if law is transgressed condemnation ensues, and whoever is condemned is not in Christ Jesus, for "there is therefore now no condemnation to them that are in Christ Jesus, who walk not after the flesh but after the Spirit." If not in Christ Jesus, not justified. If not justified, not in the way to heaven; the truth is not in them, neither have they spiritual life, for Christ is "the *way*, the *truth*, and the *life*." This is a fine point, and in the defence of which my opinion may conflict with some of deep

experience, but I think not when I am rightly understood. The *witness* of the state of entire sanctification may not be equally clear at all times, and yet the *state* is equally clear of itself, at all times, while it is retained. There are a variety of emotions or conditions of the soul which are consistent with a state of purity, such as "*heaviness* through manifold temptations," *sadness* on account of the unbelief of the church, *sorrowfulness* on account of the wickedness and doom of the unsaved around. These are all consistent with a state of purity; yea, I should doubt the existence of purity without them more or less. But those who are but little disciplined in the school of Christ may regard these emotions as evidences of the absence of purity. But not so. Christ was pure, and yet he was sad; he was sorrowful, yea he wept, groaned, cried aloud. But it was not for himself, but for others. When one is weeping for others, he is not weeping for himself, neither is he rejoicing, and yet he may be pure. When a soul first enters into perfect rest, it is in neither a state of heaviness, sadness, nor sorrowfulness; but perfect peace, clear light, and it may be, great joy. But because these other emotions may subsequently exist, they do not argue that we have lost purity. But, on the other hand, if we are willing and obedient, they argue that purity exists. Now, in the case of one who has entered into perfect rest, if while willing and obedient, yet in great heaviness, they were asked if they had the witness of purity, they might say, "It is not as clear as it has been." This may be said in truth, and yet we think it would honor God more if they would say, "though my faith is being tried, yet I know that I am all the Lord's."

In reference to this point I conclude by saying that he who is entirely sanctified, has, amidst the varied emotions of soul, mortal conflicts, and under all circumstances, the testimony of his own spirit that he is *wholly given to God*, and here he stands by faith.

Is this your experience? Are you *now* living in obedience to God? Are you willing to die in your present state? It requires no more purity to stand before the searching eyes of Christ at the judgment, than it does to live for Him on earth. If you do not dress your soul with the spotless robe in this world, it never will be dressed but with the drapery of "blackness and darkness for ever." Hasten to the blood and be washed. Of whatever name or denomination you are, hasten to the blood, for God has not one standard for you, and another for some one else; but all who are to compose that church which Christ is to present to his Father, must be "without spot or wrinkle, or any such thing." Glory to Jesus! He is mighty to save, strong to deliver, powerful to redeem!

"His blood can make the foulest *clean*,
His blood avails for *me*."

Eternity.—Solemn and important was the advice given by Robert Hall, "Walk, as it were, upon the borders of the ocean of eternity and listen to the sound of its waters, till you are deaf to every sound beside." O, if we always did this, what different persons we should be to what we are now, "in all manner of holy conversation and godliness." Archbishop Tillotson, when his brethren were all preaching on "the times," asked permission to discourse on eternity.

Religion is the tie that connects man with his Creator, and holds him to his throne. If that tie be sundered or broken, he floats away a worthless atom in the universe, its proper attractions all gone, its destiny thwarted, and its whole future nothing but darkness, desolation, and death.

Allowed Evil.—It is dangerous to tolerate the least evil, though prudence itself may require it, because toleration in this case, raises itself insensibly into permission, and permission soon sets up for command.—Dr. Clarke.

FORMALISM.

The following, which we clip from an editorial of the *North Western Christian Advocate*, shows that the evils which we have attempted to remove are so great and so widely spread as to admit no longer of concealment. We have found that it is dangerous business to war against formalism. We fear it is too strongly intrenched to be easily dislodged. We should not be willing to guarantee the safety of that minister who wars against the fashionable, time-serving religion of the day, with that vigor and earnestness that promises success.

In our Saviour's time some longed for his coming, who opposed him most bitterly when he made his advent. So is it at the present day. Many who deplore the dignified, soul-killing formality that prevails, when a revival of real, spiritual religion breaks out, array themselves against it with all their might. Perhaps there are circumstances connected with it that tend to humble pride, and that bring reproach. Or perhaps the instruments that God is pleased to use to carry on his work, are persecuted and reviled, "thrust out of the synagogues," and have "all manner of evil spoken of them falsely for Christ's sake." The disposition which leads one to "garnish the sepulchres" of the righteous dead, and to stone the living, is still extant. Happy is he, who, where God works, is not found fighting against him.—Ed.

"How unconsciously it creeps upon us! A brother said in a social meeting a few days ago, that he had his religious principles as strongly fixed as ever—that he was constant in the performance of duty, but when he closed his prayers it seemed to him he felt much as when he subscribed a business letter, *Yours respectfully*. It was a business transaction, done in business hours, and in a cool, business way! We fear it is the experience of thousands. They suffer no external duty to be overdue; no *promise to pay* goes to protest; no item goes over; but, instead of the warm, hearty gush of the affection—instead of the heart-yearning of desire; instead of the outcry of a wanting soul for a needed blessing, the prayer is a cool record of receipts, acknowledging certain blessings, and an invoice of wants, while the Saviour's merits are mentioned as the valuable consideration, and the *Amen* rounds off with the cold " *Yours respectfully* " ring to it. The heart goes not into the worship—the principles of right are there as moorings holding the soul from evil, but we need the warmth. Our preaching is too cold, too devoid of appeal and exhortation, of reference to personal experience. There is the same cold " *Yours respectfully* " in the address to the people. Style is faultless, doctrine orthodox, sentiment evangelical, manner finished, but the sympathies are untouched, no soul is stirred, no heart is melted. Formalism has erected an ice barrier between the preacher and his auditors. Can he reach them to lead them to Christ while it remains?

How formal are our songs! Oh, for one good hearty song sung by a whole congregation with hearts full of love! Oh, for strains in which harmony and praise are alike perfect! Our remembrances of sacred song, those which linger longest and most sweetly in our memory, are they not of sweet lyrics, sung by whole audiences, or by sweet voices in home's hallowed circle? Were they the cold songs from lips which have never professed Christ, but which now "lead our praises?"

There is no war between full harmony and full hearts, between perfected music and perfected devotion. We want it much. Give it to the people, oh ye who have the sacred trust in charge.

At our family altars how little have we of earnest pleading with God! How tame our prayers! We do not ask that home may be made a Bethel. Formalism chills into cold propriety what should be earnest and simple.

The *heart* cannot be satisfied without a religion of emotion. Love, joy, hope, peace—these are not quieted with syllogisms, nor feed upon formulas. The heart cries out for food. Do not give it a stone.

"Denying the power" has been the bane of many a church which had a blameless form. Shall it be so of ours? Men and brethren, there is danger that it may."

NOW!

To-morrow, and that mind immortal might be filled with burning thoughts of time wasted, life lost, and an eternity of misery secured. "*Now* is the accepted time." *Think now.* 'Twould be awful to begin to think of the soul when beyond the reach of mercy. Think of a Saviour's love; of the prayers and tears, and groans that have ascended up to God on your behalf. Can you wade through these to hell? Think of it. What a remembrance. What a worm to know the soul lost forever. And then, think forward. O! forever —to reap the reward of my neglect forever. You cannot bear the thought. Would you avoid it?

Act now. Just now. It is yours. Bless the Lord, the present moment is yours, to be saved in. You have often thought about getting religion *some time*, but have put it off to a more convenient season. But you meant to get it. And yet to-day you are unsaved. Don't delay another moment, you see the danger. He who means to be saved to-morrow, drops into perdition, for to-morrow never comes. We must be saved *now*, or lost forever.

Seeker of Entire Holiness, when do you expect to obtain it? You have sought long — yes, so long that you are quite used to it. It has become a form to pray for a clean heart. Years roll around and find you praying to be cleansed from all unrighteousness. How long do you mean to have it so? Do you say, "I shall be cleansed in God's time." That time is *now*.

Come to the altar *now*. Lay the sacrifice on it. Bind it there, *now*. And the fire will fall and consume it. Glory to God.

A word to you who are saved *now*. Never let the Devil persuade you from doing your duty in the present. You know sometimes the Spirit of the Lord has brought you up to a cross, and instead of taking it up, you *meant* to do it. *Now* is the only time.

Never be put back by the enemy, but live, work for God by the moment, and soon you shall hear the word.—*Now* come up higher. Hallelujah.

Do Duty.—Consult duty, not events. We have nothing to do but to mind our duty. All speculations that tend not to holiness are among your superfluities; but forebodings of what may befall you in doing your duty, may be reckoned among your sins; and to venture upon sin to avoid danger, is to sink a ship to avoid pirates. Oh, how quiet, as well as holy, would our lives be, had we learned that single lesson. To be careful for nothing, but to do our duty, and leave all the consequences to God! What madness for silly dust to prescribe to infinite Wisdom! To let go our work, and meddle with God's! He hath managed the concerns of the world, and of every individual person in it without giving cause of complaint to any, for above these five thousand years. And does he now need *your* counsel? Nay, it is *your* business to mind your own duty.—Dr. Annesley.

Trials.—Didst thou part with thy trials, thou wouldst part with some of thy choicest blessings. Not that trials are in themselves blessings, but it is the pathway in which the Lord walks when he comes to bless.

WARNING.

"Hast thou not reason? Canst thou not so much as once soberly think of thy dying hour? or of whither thy sinful life will drive thee then? Hast thou no conscience? or having one, is it rocked so fast asleep by sin, or made so weary by an unsuccessful calling upon thee, that it is laid down and cares for thee no more? Poor man! thy state is to be lamented. Hast no judgment? Art not able to conclude that to be saved is better than to burn in hell; and that eternal life, with God's favor, is better than temporal life in God's displeasure? Hast no affection but what is brutish? what, none at all? no affection for the God that made thee? none for his loving Son that has showed his love, and died for thee? Is not heaven worth thy affection? O, poor man! which is strongest, thinkest thou, God or thee? If thou art not able to overcome him, thou art a fool for standing out against him. 'It is a fearful thing to fall into the hands of the living God.' He will gripe hard; his fist is stronger than a lion's paw; take heed of him, he will be angry if you despise his Son; and will you stand guilty in your trespasses, when he offereth you his grace and favor?

Consider thus with thyself: Would I be glad to have all, every one of my sins, to come in against me, to inflame the justice of God against me? Would I be glad to be bound up in them, as the three children were bound in their clothes, and to be as really thrown into the fiery furnace of the wrath of almighty God, as they were into Nebuchadnezzar's fiery furnace? Would I be glad to have all and every one of the ten commandments to *discharge* themselves against my soul,—the first saying, 'Damn him, for he hath broken me;' the second saying, 'Damn him, for he hath broken me?' &c. Consider how terrible this will be; yea, more terrible than if thou shouldst have ten of the biggest pieces of ordnance in England to be discharged against thy body, thunder, thunder, one after another! Nay, this would not be comparable to the *reports* that the law (for the breach thereof) will give against thy soul; for those can but kill the body, but these will keep both body and soul; and that not for an hour, a day, a month, or a year, but they will condemn thee for ever.

Mark, it is *for ever*, FOR EVER. It is into *everlasting* damnation, *eternal* destruction, *eternal* wrath and displeasure from God, *eternal* gnawings of conscience, *eternal* continuance with devils. . . . . . If it were but for a time, even ten thousand years, there would be ground of comfort, and hopes of deliverance; but here is thy misery,—this is thy state *for ever*, here thou must be *for ever*. When thou lookest about thee, and seest what an innumerable company of howling devils thou art amongst, thou shalt think this again,—this is my portion *for ever*. When thou hast been in hell so many thousand years as there are stars in the firmament, or drops in the sea, or sands on the sea-shore, yet art thou to lie there for ever. O! this one word, EVER, how will it torment thy soul!

Consider and regard these things, and lay them to thy heart, before it be too late. O! I say, regard, regard, for hell is hot. God's hand is up! The Law is resolved to *discharge* against thy soul! The judgment day is at hand! The graves are ready to fly open! The trumpet is near the sounding! The sentence will ere long be past, and then you and I cannot call time again."

"Friends, I have given you but a short touch of the torments of hell. O! I am set, I am *set*, and am not able to utter what my mind conceives of the torments of hell! Yet this let me say to thee, Accept of God's mercy through our Lord Jesus Christ, lest thou feel that with thy conscience which I cannot express with my tongue, and say, 'I am sorely tormented in this flame.'"
—BUNYAN.

PIC-NIC RELIGION.

It is on the increase, the order of the day. Conviviality is the *ultimatum*, the first and the last. " Let us have a jolly time, eat, drink, and be merry, for to-morrow we die."
Curtail in the least the joyfulness of the little folks or the great folks? Not for the world. Our joy is increased with their joy. We delight evermore to see parents and children, teachers and pupils, on the wing of happy, joyful extacy, always abounding in cheerful vivacity. But how is this joyfulness to be, save in the Lord, in all purity and loveliness ; save in seeking *first* the kingdom of God and his righteousness ; things true, honest, just, pure, lovely and of good report ? The question is whether this pic-nic or convivial religion is gospel, pure, undefiled, such as meets the emergencies of the day, and is well pleasing in the sight of Heaven. It is more than possible that pic-nics may be harmless, the amusements connected therewith, the relaxation also, lawful and healthy: but *are* they so ? Are pic-nics profitable, spiritually or religiously, the way they are generally managed ? Do they tend to reform, enlighten the mind, convict and convert the soul ? Instead of exerting a saving, salutary influence, do they not frequently prove detrimental to spiritual life and hope ? The excitement for weeks is more or less dissipating, swallowing up every thought of the soul's welfare. Children are on fire for a spree,—and what else are very many of these pic-nic excursions but sprees or frolics ?

We rejoice to see a waking-up on this question. A valuable correspondent of " The Boston Recorder " inquires whether Satan is not spreading his net hereabouts; whether there is not now an excess of this pic-nic and sleigh-ride development in our religion, and whether we are not losing sight of the spiritual in the animal : All false religions seek to attract interest by amusements and animal gratifications.

The worshippers of the golden calf sat down to eat and drink the oblations to their new god, and then rose up to play. And a bait of sensuality in some form has always been the lure to heathen worship. Popery has always followed in the same line. Even its Sabbath-worship connects a dance with the mass. And throughout the whole structure of that "mystery of iniquity," the sensual and the comic are interwoven with the pomps and ritual of worship. And one of the most common methods by which decay advances upon sound churches is by pleas of amusements to give an attractive and hilarious character to religion—which usually are so many pleas for conformity to the world.

I am not unaware of the value of a cheerful religion. I respond to the reasonableness of the command to "rejoice evermore." And yet I read that the "joy *of the Lord* is your strength," and that our rejoicing must be in God to make it a religious joy. It is not a religious joy, where professedly religious men indulge in gratifications that are worldly, sensual, and frivolous.

" There is a path that leads to God ;
All others go astray."—Golden Rule.

REV. JOHN WINEBRENNER.

BY THE EDITOR.

The lives of persons eminent for piety and for devotion to the cause of God belong to the church at large. Though, more perhaps from the prevailing bigotry of the day, which would forbid one to cast out devils if he follow not us, than from choice, his services may be bestowed chiefly upon the denomination to which he belongs, yet all branches of the Church of Christ are benefited by his labors. His example is not lost. Even those who oppose him will be aroused to activity by his persevering zeal and his faithful love. The apostle tells us to hold such in reputation as regard not their own lives for the work of Christ.

Such a man was Rev. John Winebrenner. He was educated in the German Reformed Church, of which at the age of twenty-three, he became a minister, having received a collegiate and theological training for this purpose. But he did not enter the ministry as a mere profession. In his twentieth year he was powerfully converted and made unspeakably happy in a Saviour's love. His heart yearned for the salvation of his fellow men. Settled in the year 1820, over three German Reformed Congregations, one in Harrisburg, and two in the country, he at once commenced laboring for a revival. God owned his efforts—poured out His Spirit upon his congregations, and many were brought to a knowledge of sins forgiven. A violent opposition against the work, and against the minister that God was pleased to employ to promote it, followed. He was persecuted and annoyed in almost every possible way. This continued for five years, and resulted in his final separation from the German Reformed Church.

He continued to labor as before for the salvation of souls. "He preached" says the editor of The Church Advocate, "that all men must repent or perish, that they must be regenerated or lost, and used great efforts and manifested a most ardent zeal to bring the unconverted, whether members of the church, or non-professors, to immediate submission to God. To this end he not only preached, but held prayer meetings, anxious meetings, experience meetings; praying and laboring with anxious and sin-sick souls; pointing them direct to Christ for salvation.

These were the things that gave offence and disturbed the peace of the churches of his charge; and no remonstrance, no threats, no persecution or opposition that these carnal professors of religion, whether Elders of the Churches, or influential members, or brethren in the ministry, could offer, could move him from his fixed purpose, or cause him to desist an hour from laboring to secure the salvation of his hearers; and when every other effort failed them, they locked the doors of the meeting houses against him." He then went to the Court House. But such was the influence of his opposers that they succeeded in getting this locked against him. He then preached from the steps of the churches —in the lumber yards, and market places; and held prayer meetings in private houses with those who became convicted under his preaching. This continued for some time. The work spread through the adjacent villages and country. The converts, numbered by scores and hundreds, were associated together, and the pastoral charge was left with young ministers whom God raised up through the labor of this devoted Evangelist.

In the year 1830, Elder Winebrenner, and his co-adjutors associated the minister and elders of their churches together for general and united co-operation. This was the origin of the denomination which has taken the name of "The Church of God." They are evangelical in their doctrines. One of the most striking of their peculiarities is that of practising, as a religious ordinance, "the washing of the saints' feet"—a practice which it is much easier to ridicule than it is to prove to be contrary to the word of God. They number at present about thirty thousand scattered throughout Pennsylvania, and the western states. They are, we should judge, a devoted pious people, laboring to gain Heaven. They have a weekly organ, "The Church Advocate," published at Lancaster, Pa. It is much more decidedly religious than church papers usually are. It is edited by Rev. E. H. Thomas, in a good spirit and with ability. To this paper we are chiefly indebted for the facts in this article.

Elder Winebrenner, lived down the calumny that his opposers heaped upon him. The editor referred to says, "No man perhaps in the past or present generation, has been more persecuted, more calumniated, at least on the continent of America, than Elder Winebrenner, though no man has been more self-sacrificing for the good of others, or has accomplished more real good in his day, than he; no man ever had warmer friends, or more bitter enemies. But he lived to triumph over all opposition, and died embalmed in the memory of his many true-hearted brethen."

On the 12th of September last, in the 64th year of his age, he exchanged the cross for the crown. His end was peaceful and triumphant. To one of his preachers he said in his last hours, "Brother, preach Jesus while you have health!" "O! the glory of preaching Jesus in health." "Tell the brethren to stick together." "*Stand up for Jesus!*" "*Stand up for Jesus!*"

ORIGIN OF THE FREE METHODIST CHURCH.

The Free Methodist Church had its origin in necessity and not in choice. It did not grow out of a secession, nor out of an unsuccessful attempt to bring about a reform in the government of the Church. Those concerned in its formation never expected a separation from the Methodist Episcopal Church, until they were unjustly excluded from its pale. They sought redress at the proper tribunal. It was not granted. Even a candid hearing was denied them. Thus thrown out, and the possibility of a restoration being cut off, and believing that God still called them to labor for the salvation of souls, they had no alternative but to form a new organization. In doctrine, discipline, and spirit they were Methodists, and hence they could not offer themselves to any other denomination.

The issue on which they were thrust out was between dead formalism, and the life and power of godliness, and so they could not feel at home with those branches of the Methodist family into whose formation other questions mainly entered.

Jesus has always had a people—a plain, humble, earnest people—to preach the Gospel to the poor, and to spread scriptural holiness throughout the world. We believe the Methodists were raised up for this purpose. God was with them, and gave them great success in saving souls.

But as they grew strong and wealthy, pride, and a love of popularity crept in among them. The Discipline was too generally unheeded. It became obvious to the most casual observer, that there was, among many of the ministers and members of the Methodist Episcopal Church in the United States, a very wide and growing departure from the original spirit of Methodism. This departure is also seen in the alterations that have been recently made in the Discipline.

In 1852 the rule requiring our houses of worship to be built "*plain and with free seats*," was effectually neutralized by adding the words, "wherever practicable." Conformity to the world was greatly encouraged in 1856 by repealing *the law* which had stood in the Discipline from the first, forbidding the reception of members until they had laid off "superfluous ornaments," and substituting a simple exhortation to "conform to the spirit of the apostolic precept," as though plain commands of God could be violated without violating their spirit.

In the Genesee Conference this departure from the old paths was hastened by the connection of several of its prominent members with secret societies. These, bound together by a tie unknown to the rest of the body, and laying their plans in the strictest secrecy, formed a solid nucleus, around which the formal and the aspiring naturally rallied. A portion of the Conference wished to adhere to primitive Methodism. They loved the doctrine of holiness, and preached it with success. Their labors were prospered, and their services were sought for. While they had the countenance of the bishops they were unmolested.

At the General Conference of the M. E. Church, held in 1856, the bishops took a decided stand against the enactment of a law excluding slave-holders from the church. The secret-society worldly-policy members of the Genesee Conference, some of whom had been radical abolitionists, sided with the bishops, on the slavery question. At its next session, thirty of them combined together not to take work unless Rev. L. Stiles, and Rev. I. C. Kingsley —men whose sympathies and labors were for the promotion of spiritual religion—were removed from the cabinet. They were transferred, and their places supplied by such men as the thirty (who, with their adherents, were henceforth known as "The Regency,") could render subservient to their purposes.

But the work of holiness went on. Dead and formal ministers were in no better demand than before. At the next session of the Genesee Conference; in a secret meeting held by the regency, they voted to bring Rev. B. T. Roberts, and Rev. W. C. Kendall to trial. Charges were preferred. Mr. Roberts was voted guilty of "immoral and unchristian conduct" for publishing in the *Northern Independent,* in an article entitled "New School Methodism," things that were not in that article, or in any other that he ever wrote.

His character was then passed, and he was sent out to preach. For the want of time Mr. Kendall's trial was deferred. At the next Conference, held in Perry, in October, 1858, secret meetings of the regency were held, as had been done at the two preceding sessions. Mr. Roberts was charged with "contumacy," for publishing and circulating a second edition of "New School Methodism," and a pamphlet signed by "George W. Estes," which gave a short account of the trial of the year preceding. On this charge, and on the testimony of only one witness, whose veracity was fully impeached, Mr. Roberts was expelled from the Conference, and from the M. E. Church. Mr. McCreery was also expelled at the same time on the same charges.

Called of God to preach, they could not cease because the human authority with which they had been invested was thus taken away. The members of the church who had witnessed their labors and their spirit, thought they should still endeavor to save their fellow men.

One hundred and ninety-five prominent laymen met in convention at Albion, Dec. 1st, 1858, and passed resolutions, expressing their entire and unabated confidence in the expelled preachers, and recommending them to continue to labor for the salvation of souls.

At the next session of the Genesee Conference, held at Brockport, in Oct. 1858, Reverends L. Stiles, C. D. Burlingham, J. A. Wells, and W. Cooley, were expelled for "contumacy," in sympathizing with those who had been expelled the year preceding. Reverends J. W. Reddy, and H. H. Farnsworth, were located for the same cause.

Members of the Church who manifested an active sympathy with the expelled preachers, were themselves expelled in large numbers. Many were, without their consent, and contrary to their wishes, read out by the preachers as "withdrawn." Among both these classes were many of undoubted piety, and of long standing in the church, who had contributed largely by their money and their influence to its prosperity, and whose love for it was unabated.

Fifteen hundred members of the M. E. Church, within the bounds of the Genesee Conference, respectfully petitioned the General Conference, at its session in Buffalo, in May, 1860, to investigate the judicial action of the Genesee Conference. A committee of forty-two was appointed for this purpose. A memorial setting forth the grievances complained of, and affidavits and documents substantiating the complaints, were presented. A determined effort to get the committee discharged was made by the partisans of the majority of Genesee Conference. *The committee was discharged,* and *investigation was suppressed.*

The appeal cases were summarily disposed of. That of the Rev. C. D. Burlingham, who, from the time of his expulsion, desisted from all public efforts to do good to the souls of men, was, without the shadow of a reason, sent back for a new trial. Upon the first appeal of Mr. Roberts—that from the verdict of reproof—the committee stood equally divided. The other appeals were not entertained, though the constitution of the M. E. Church declares, in the most emphatic manner, that the General Conference shall *not deprive* the ministers *of the privilege of appeal.*

The same General Conference authorized the preachers to go beyond the bounds of their charge to obtain a committee to try their members.

Under this new rule the work of expulsion went on. Pious men, long known for their strong attachment to Methodism, who were too conscientious and God-fearing, to give their sanction to what they believed to be great iniquities, were excommunicated.

Committees, imported from a distance for the purpose, expelled, after the mockery of a trial, devoted men of God. All hope of a change for the better being cut off, and it being evident that the authorities of the Methodist Episcopal Church were determined to put down what devout souls believed to be the work of God, a convention of laymen and ministers met at Pekin, Niagara Co., N. Y., on the 23d of August, 1860, and adopted the following form of Discipline.

We do not wish any to subscribe to it unless they believe it will be for the glory of God and the good of their souls. We have no desire to get up simply a large church; but we do hope that our societies will be composed, *exclusively*, of those who are *in earnest to gain heaven*, and who *are determined, by the grace of God*, to live up to the requirements of the Bible.

Where societies already organized design to unite with the Free Methodist Church, we recommend that they adopt the Discipline as a whole; and then, that each member be admitted in his individual capacity, as provided for in section third of chapter first, entitled " Of receiving members into the Church."

It is of the greatest importance that those who come into the new organization be of one heart and one mind.— *Introduction to Discipline.*

WORLDLINESS.

With the increase of nominal Christians, there is always an increase of conformity to the world; and the world appears better that it did to Christians, not so much because *it* has changed, as because *they* have changed; the wild beasts and the tame ones dwell together, not so much because the leopards eat straw like an ox, as because the ox eats flesh like a leopard. *Ephraim he hath mixed himself among the people;* the people have not come over to Ephraim, but Ephraim has gone over to them; the people hath not learned the ways of Ephraim, but Ephraim hath learned the manners of the people. This is too much the case in the Vanity Fair of the world at the present time; there is not such a marked and manifest distinction between the church, and the world as there should be; their habits, maxims, opinions, pursuits, amusements, whole manner of life, are too much the same; so that the Pilgrims in our day have lost the character of a peculiar people, not so much because they have become vastly more numerous than formerly, as because they have become conformed to the world, not like strangers, but natives of Vanity Fair.

The great temptations of the church in our day is that of entire, almost unmingled worldliness; formalism and worldliness are too sadly the types of our piety; we are in imminent danger of forgetting that our life is a pilgrimage, and that this is not our rest.— CHEEVER.

CLOSING WITH CHRIST.—Salvation is not waiting till some miracle is wrought before we come; nor till we have made ourselves different from what we are now; it is instant closing with Christ: first, for his forgiveness, as our Priest; next, for his teaching, as our Prophet; lastly, for peace, accounting Him as our complete and accomplished righteousness, as our great God, our Sovereign and gracious Ruler.—CUMMING.

REVIVALS.

BY THE EDITOR.

So rigid was the discipline among the old Spartans, that a campaign was looked upon by them in the light of a pleasant duty. So it is with every real Christian. His best days are when he is putting forth the most vigorous efforts for the salvation of men. He loves revival scenes. The cry for mercy of the convicted sinner, groaning under the load of his sins, and the shouts of the redeemed, fall like sweet music upon his ear. We are never so happy—never so raised above the world—as when God condescends to use us as his "battle-axe to break in pieces the nations" of sinners and to "destroy kingdoms" of darkness.

But a revival to be a blessing and not a curse, must be accompanied with the purification of the church. The old Pharisees made proselytes, but they were twofold more the children of hell than themselves. So it is with the converts of a cold, dead, formal, fashionable church. Among the old members are many who were once soundly converted, and who, when they were poor, and when their church was persecuted and dispersed, really enjoyed religion. These are generally, unless they are living in the secret commission of flagrant sin, sufficiently in sympathy with salvation not to oppose it very bitterly. But when unrenewed men in large numbers get into the church and take the reigns of government into their hands, then the opposition to the life and power of godliness becomes too formidable to be successfully encountered. Then the Sanctuary of the Most High is turned into a market place where the right of worshipping God is sold by auction to the highest bidder. Then fairs and festivals, pleasure rides, oyster suppers and sociables, become the order of the day. True religion is treated with ridicule, and those who enjoy it are stigmatized as fanatical or superstitious.

A genuine revival is one that leads its subjects to get right with God and man, that leads the stout-hearted to bow in humble submission at the feet of Jesus. Brother, would you enjoy a revival? Begin at once to search your own heart. Get right at any cost. Wherein you have wronged any one in his character or property, make confession and restoration to the utmost of your ability. Consecrate yourself fully to God for all coming time. Get the baptism of the Holy Ghost upon your soul. This will give you a spirit of prevailing prayer. You will love souls. Your efforts will be attended by divine power and be crowned with success. God grant you, dear reader, a gracious revival in your own heart, in your family and in your church!

DEDICATION OF THE SECOND FREE METHODIST CHURCH OF BUFFALO.

THIS interesting event took place on Friday the 19th of October. Rev. DR. REDFIELD offered the dedicatory prayer, and Rev. L. STILES preached the dedication sermon. It was a soul-stirring discourse, full of moving thoughts of God and salvation. DR. REDFIELD preached in the evening and on the Sabbath. The congregation kept increasing till on Sabbath evening the house was well filled. The edifice is a plain, unpretending brick building, pleasantly and commodiously fitted, and capable of seating from five to six hundred people. We never felt so sensibly that God owned any place as that. His glorious presence has filled the temple every time we have met there for His worship. IT IS FREE. Glory to God! there is one place in the heart of this large wicked city where the poor may have the Gospel preached to them; one place where the auctioneer's voice is not heard converting the house of God into a house of merchandise; one place where the Gospel will, we trust, be preached without fear or compromise, where it will be in order for God's people to get blessed.

To secure it has cost us sacrifices which but few can appreciate, and exposed us to calumnies which we would not have thought Satanic malignity could infuse into human minds. But we are glad that it is done. We have no doubt but that it will be the spiritual birth-place of hundreds if not thousands of souls. Jesus smiles upon the enterprise and that is enough.

PROSCRIPTION GOING ON.

THE following extract from a letter from Brother D. B. INGRAHAM, well known to many of our readers in this section, shows that the spirit which thrusts men out of the church for doing their whole duty, is not confined to

Genesee Conference. Brother INGRAHAM has long maintained the character of a consistent straight forward Christian. He was much petted by the church, until he experienced the blessing of holiness. We hope that all others who are called upon to suffer in a similar manner, will exhibit the same spirit of meekness and forbearance. "If ye be reproached for the for the name of Christ, happy are ye."

PAWTUCKET, R. I.

DEAR BROTHER ROBERTS:—We need all the helps we can have down here in this region, especially at this time, as we are called to pass through some peculiar trials. We have been expelled from the M. E. Church. A Bill of charges was presented, Brother INGRAHAM accused, tried, condemned and executed, without a *counsel* or *one witness*. The committee consisted of *five members* all *prejudiced* as well as the *witnesses*. We thought we could sympathise with you and Brother McCREERY when we were out there, but we just begin to realize what sympathy means. There are a number of the church who feel bad, and who are disposed to stand out, and if necessary, be driven from the bosom of their home. We have had a Friday evening prayer meeting at my house since *last fall*. The preachers say to the members you must not attend *them*—just the same spirit as is found in Genesee Conference. But, my dear Brother, amidst it all my soul is resting sweetly in the arms of my blessed Jesus. Oh, how he saves me! Not the first rising of resentment against the Brethren, all is love, and I am enabled through grace imparted to say as did Christ, "*Father forgive them*." I think we hardly know God or ourselves until we are put to the test and placed in the crucible. Well, Brother R., bless God, help me praise him for his goodness, to me so unworthy. Oh, how thankful I ought to be that God permitted me to become acquainted with the Pilgrims, and especially yourself and Brother McCREERY.

Bless God that through these mediums my eyes were opened and the way, the narrow way, was shown me.

Yours, in Christian bonds,
D. B. INGRAHAM.

The following, from a highly responsible source, gives a little insight into the character of the men who proscribe them who sympathise with us, and who dare to labor with us for the salvation of souls. The letter is from Illinois, where, as we informed our readers in our last, we had the privilege of spending several weeks most delightfully in the vineyard of the Lord.

AURORA, Oct. 15th, 1860.

DEAR BROTHER AND SISTER ROBERTS:—With regard to the Camp-meeting, I think it was the best I ever attended. It lives with me yet, and when I reflect how you both labored for unworthy me, it sends a thrill all through me, and an involuntary groan escapes me. I trust it was not all in vain. You speak of a lady who feared she should be turned out of the church if she went in the altar. I am going to see if she will not subscribe for the EARNEST CHRISTIAN and FREE METHODIST. You mention two local preachers who assisted at the Camp-meeting.

When Brother J.'s character was brought up, Brother W., a conference preacher, objected to it because he had taken part in the Camp-meeting, and when the votes were called for, Brother A., the presiding elder, thought the yeas had it; and then it was moved that it should be taken by a rising vote, when nine rose in favor, and Brother W. and one other man against him. Brother J. was not there. Brother M.'s character was called up next, to which Brother W. also objected, and asked him if he did not take part in said Camp-meeting. Brother M. arose and confessed that he did exhort there twice—did the best he could, was not sorry for it, for the Lord blessed him in it. He confessed also that when another opportunity presented itself, he should do the same if he knew he would be turned out of the church the next minute. Then Brother W. asked him if he recognized Brother ROBERTS as a minister of the Gospel. His answer was that he did, and that he believed him to be a holy man of God, and that Brother ROBERTS would find in Brother M. just as true and faithful a friend when he was a thousand miles away, as when close at hand. Then the vote was taken, and no one rose against him. Brother B. and J. H., and Brother S. were turned out of the stewardship, and three others of the *right stripe* were put in their places. When Sister S. heard that Brother W. objected to Brothers M.

and J. she thought he had better be careful, or like Mordecai he might build a gallows to hang himself on.

Brother M. followed up a report until he came to where Brother W. had been insulting a young Sister in the church, from the 2d of February until the 20th of March, and then went to Brother Q. with it, and they two went to Conference whither Brother W. had gone, and got him, Brother A. and Brother S. together, to whom he confessed the whole. They took from him his Agency, and the Conference gave him a station. And we suppose if it had been Brother ROBERTS, he would have been expelled from the Conference and from the Methodist Episcopal Church.

We *feel* thankful to the Almighty for sending Brother and Sister ROBERTS, Brother TINKHAM, and Sister SMITH to the West. We believe it will be a blessing to us in time and in eternity, and our prayer is that the Lord will direct their steps here again, and that *speedily*. *

The result in the above case was what might have been anticipated. When the General Conference restores to the ministry such men as were restored at its recent session, it cannot be expected that an Annual Conference will deal with its members for insulting ladies.

THE following from a highly esteemed brother, a member of one of the Eastern Conferences, breathes the right spirit. Were all, or even a majority of the Conference, thus devoted to the right, the necessity for a new organization would not exist.

DEAR BROTHER ROBERTS:—Believing that the Free Methodists are now well organized into a body by themselves for all the high and holy purposes for which the Saviour has established his church on earth, I desire to be better informed concerning them; for if they are such a people as are described in the New Testament, they are my people, and their God is my God for ever.

I have long desired and prayed that old-fashioned Methodism, or pure Wesleyanism, both experimental and practical, might again revive and stand out before the world, baptized with hallowed fire, and shining like the sun at mid-day. And I have always held myself in readiness to identify myself with a people of this type of piety, whether rich or poor, few or many.

I am no stickler for a name, but I do love and earnestly contend for the highest state of moral piety to which the church can attain in this life; and whenever I find a person who enjoys this grace, he is my brother.

The church may have numbers and wealth, and churches many and fine; but if she lack purity of heart and life, she is a dead letter. O, for a Holy Ghost people, a church full of fire and power!

In the last number of the EARNEST CHRISTIAN you say, "Many whose convictions and sympathies are with us, are fearful and fainthearted." I pity such, and pray that they may have better hearts and courage to live up to their convictions in the church or churches where they belong, let the consequences be what they may. They may be persecuted, suspended from the ministry, or turned out of the church; but what of it? "The foundation of God standeth sure," and he who stands thereon stands securely; he shall never be moved.

Our God has given a great many in the different churches the light to see the truth and their duty with reference to it; but fear or shame holds them back from embracing it. Such should feel the danger of their position, and arise at once and walk in the light as it shines upon them, lest it go out in darkness, and they lose their way.

Brother ROBERTS, fight on, though clouds and tempests rise around you; the battle is the Lord's, and his truth shall triumph. "Greater is he that is in you, than he that is in the world."

I want a Discipline as soon as it is ready, and the EARNEST CHRISTIAN another year; and also the "Free Methodist." I like the proposed plan of the paper very much.

The Discipline I presume will furnish me all the needful information concerning the church, but I should be glad to hear from you if you can find it convenient to write.

Truly yours, *

THE brother—a local preacher—at the East who wrote the following, is drawn towards us just as many others are, whom we have never seen in the flesh. The Lord blesses him, saves him fully, and then his heart is drawn out towards us.

Dear Brother Roberts:—I want you to send me one dollar's worth of Free Methodist Disciplines, as soon as you can, for I think it will be congenial to my spirit. God converted me over twenty years ago. In a short time after I called on Jesus to wash my sins all away. And he did; glory to his name! I am a Free Methodist, for Christ made me so. I take a good many scoldings and threatenings for trying to publish this free salvation to others, and for sympathy with the persecuted. But God is with me. Bless his name. All we know about the people called *Nazarites* out your way, we get from the Independent and your welcome Monthly, which I gratefully receive. I hope God will bless it to thousands in our world. Some of our traveling preachers here call you Nazarites very bad names, but the Holy Ghost has impressed it on my heart that you are my people, and I long to get out there to see some of the despised ones. I think if Brother Roberts will keep us posted about the meetings out there, and let us into some light where they are, we shall yet have more knowledge of this way and people; for, Brother Roberts, be assured that the element is out here in many hearts, and we pant to be free. I know of many here that want to be free, and it is all we can do to wait. I am glad, and thank God that the time is come when he is about to raise up a free and holy people. Brother R., I will do the best I can to get more subscribers for the Earnest Christian this winter, if you continue to publish, and I hope you will. I think God will bless your efforts in that. I should like to give you a history of our camp-meeting, but I have not space. Oh how it was managed to crush out the Spirit! Not one conversion, as we could learn; and no wonder, the inclement weather. But oh what pains to stop all the working of the Spirit for fear we should get out of *order*. God forgive, is our prayer. Now, Br. Roberts, I must close. I shall weary you, but my heart is full. Keep us posted as much as possible. I send you one dollar in this; please to forward me the books as soon as you get them.

The following is from the pen of one whose writings upon religious experience we used to read with pleasure and profit in other periodicals. We shall gladly welcome her contributions to our columns. Our readers may expect to hear from several new and valuable correspondents in our forthcoming volume. How we thank our God for putting it into the hearts of his children to write us such letters.

District Parsonage, Oct. 10, 1860.

Rev. B. T. Roberts:—*Dear Brother*—We are delighted with your magazine, and pronounce it unequivocally the best religious periodical in the nation. We recommend it to others as having no rival, and believe no one can read its pages without spiritual profit. Its original articles are concise, pointed, searching, and will compare in a literary point of view with any other in the land. Its selected articles display rare talent and research, and bring out from the mines of olden literature, the rich ore of the masters in theology and spirituality. In short I am more and more pleased with it, and bid you good speed in spreading spiritual holiness over these lands. The Lord help you to deal lusty blows at formalism, and worldly conformity; drawing the division line between a Church party religion, and a Holy Ghost salvation. So that all shall see there is a difference between him that serves God, and him who serves Him not.

I have been unwell all summer, and have written nothing until recently. Shall send you a manuscript soon. Love to Sister Roberts, and believe me in sympathy with the little ones of Christ's flock, who are persecuted for His sake.

Yours, in the fellowship of Saints.

THE FREE METHODIST DISCIPLINE.

The demand for this has been so great that we have been unable as yet, to fill the orders as fast as they come in. Our binders have good facilities which they are using to the best advantage. We hope soon to get enough ahead to promptly supply all that may be called for. We published all that we supposed would be needed for the two years to come, but about one-half are gone already, and we apprehend that we shall soon be obliged to issue a new edition.

The heaviest cross we ever took up was in doing what we were satisfied was our duty in regard to getting out this Discipline. We hope none will adopt it unless they intend by God's grace to live up to it, and to such we have no doubt but that it will prove a great blessing.

THE EARNEST CHRISTIAN.

PREACHING.

WE take the following from an article in the March number of the *Atlantic Monthly*, entitled "Is the religious want of the age met?" It is a corroboration from an unexpected source of the views which we have set forth in this magazine, of the inefficacy of the ministry of the present age.—ED.

The prevailing impression among the ministry appears to be, that the man who cannot write "an able doctrinal discourse" is but an inferior man, fit only to preach in an inferior place; and that it would be a great gain to the Church, if scholarship were only so general that the standard of the universities could be applied, and only Phi-Beta-Kappa men allowed to enter the ministry. No doubt, those who incline to this view are quite honest, and not unkindly in it. But those who think this, grievously misunderstand the necessities of the age in which we live. Reading men know where to find better reading than can possibly be furnished by any man who is bound to write two sermons weekly, or even one sermon a week; and to train any corps of young men in the expectation that any considerable fraction of them will be able to win and to maintain a commanding influence in their parishes mainly by the weekly production of learned discourses, is to do them the greatest injury, by cherishing expectations which never can be realized. * * * It is not worth while for any man to go into the ministry who cannot relish the Apostle's invitation, running thus: "I beseech you, therefore, brethren, by the mercies of God, that ye present your bodies *a living sacrifice*, holy, acceptable unto God, which is your reasonable service." If that seem not reasonable, ay, and exceedingly inviting too, better let it alone. All men cannot do all things. Better raise extraordinary potatoes than hammer out insignificant ideas. You do not see the connection? you were a Phi-Beta-Kappa man in college, and know that you can write better than many a man in a metropolitan pulpit? Very likely; but we of the few go to church to be made better men, and not by fine writing but by significant ideas, which may come in a homely garb, so they be only pervaded with affectionate piety, but which can come to us only from one who has laid all ambitious self-seeking on the altar of God. There is a power of persuasion in every minister who follows God as a dear child, and who walks in love, as Christ loved us, which the hardest heart cannot long resist,—which will win the congregation, however an individual here and there may be able to harden himself against it. You think that the great power of the pulpit is in high doctrine, presented with a metaphysical precision and acuteness. We have no disparagement to offer of your doctrinal knowledge, nor of your ability to state it with metaphysical precision and hair-splitting acuteness. But we know, from much experience, that there is a divine truth, and a fervor and power in imparting it, with which God inspires the man who is wholly devoted to Him, in comparison with which the higher achievements of the man who lacks these are trumpery and rubbish. Many, *many* men have failed in the ministry, are failing in the ministry every day, because their principal reliance has been upon what they deem their thorough mastery of the soundest theories of doctrine and of duty. They were confident they could administer to minds and hearts diseased the certain specific laid down in the book, admeasured to the twentieth part of a scruple. Confident in their theoretical acquisitions, they could not comprehend the indispensable necessity of a large experience in actual cases of mental malady. And for want of such experience, it was absolutely impossible that they should be *en rapport* with the souls they honestly desired to benefit. Can you heal a heart-ache with a syllogism? There is no dispensing with the precept and prescription,— "Weep with those that weep!" "Be of the same mind one toward another!"

Theories of doctrine and of practice are not without their value; but the minister who is merely or chiefly a theorist, whether in doctrines or in measures, is an adventurer; and the chances against him are as many as the chances against the precise similarity of any two cases presented to his attention,—as many as the chances against the education of any two men of fifty years being precisely alike, in every particular and in all their results. The soul's problems are not to be solved by theories. Such was not the practice of the Great Physician; "*surely He hath borne our griefs and carried our sorrows.*" Theories shirk that. "*In all their affliction, He was afflicted; in His love and in His pity, He redeemed them.*" And precisely in this way his ministers are now to follow up his practice. Our age is growing less and less tolerant of formality,—less and less willing to accept metaphysical disquisition in place of a warm-hearted, loving, fervent expansion of the Word of God, recommended to the understanding and to the sensibility by lively illustrations of spiritual truth, derived from all the experience of life, from all observation, from all analogies in the natural world,—in short, from every manner of illumination, from the heavens above, from the earth beneath, and from the waters which are under the earth. God is surely everywhere, and hath made all things, and all to testify of Him; and the innumerable voices all agree together.

And when this is both understood and felt, what rules shall be given to guide and control the construction and the delivery of discourses? Shall we say, The people must be brought back to the old-time endurance—ay, *endurance*, that is the word—of long-drawn, laborious ratiocinations, wherein the truth is diligently pursued for its own sake, with an ultimate reference, indeed, to the needs and uses of the hearer, but so remote as rarely to be noticed, except by that very small fraction of any customary congregation who may chance to have an interest in such doings,—some of whom watch the clergyman as they would the entomologist, running down a truth that he may impale it, and add one more specimen to his well-ordered collection of common and of uncommon bugs? Our neighbors in the South do better than this; for they hunt with the lasso, and never throw the noose except to capture something which can be harnessed to the wheels of common life.

No, the people are not going back to the endurance of any such misery. They have found out that still-born rhetoric is by no means the one thing needful, and care far less for the *art* of speech than for the *nature* of a holy heart. They want a man to speak less of what he believes and more of what he feels. The expectation of bringing the people again to endure prolonged mataphysical discriminations, spun out of commonplace minds, cobwebs to cloak their own nakedness and universal inaptitude, if indulged, is absurdly indulged. The whole Church is sick of such trifling. She knows well that it has made her most unsavory to those who might have found their way into the temples of God, or kept their places there, but for the memory of an immense amount of wearisome readings from the pulpit,—too often a vocabulary of words seldom or never found out of sermons,—a manner of speech which, when tried by the sure test of natural, animated conversation, must be pronounced absurd and abominable. It is a wonder of wonders, that, in spite of such drawbacks, an individual here and there has been reclaimed from worldliness to the love and service of God.

The student-habits of the clergy most naturally lead them to prefer the formal statement, the studied elaboration of ideas, which their own training cannot but render facile and dear to them. And there is here and there a man who, in virtue of extraordinary genius, can infuse new life into worn-out phrases,—a man or two who can for a moment or for an hour, by the very weight and excellence of their thoughts, and because they truly and deeply feel them, arrest the age, and challenge and secure attention, in spite of all the infelicities of an antiquated style and an unearthly delivery. But in this age, more than ever before, we are summoned to surrender our scholastic preferences and esoteric honors to the exigencies of the million. And the men of this generation have, without much conference, come with great unanimity to the determination that they will not not long endure, either in or out of the pulpit, speakers who are dull and unaffecting, either from want of words, ideas, or method and wisdom in the arrangement of them, or lack of sympathies,—and especially that they will not endure dull declamation from the pulpit.

If any man really wish to know how he is preaching, let him imagine himself conversing earnestly with an intelligent and highly gifted, but uneducated man or woman, in his own parlor, or with his younger children. Would any but an idiot keep on talking, when, with half an eye, he might discern TEDIOUS, wrought by himself upon the uncalloused sensibilities of his hearers?

How long ought a sermon to be? As long as you can read in the eye of seven-eighths of your audience, *Pray, go on*. If you cannot read that, you have mistaken your vocation; you were never called to the ministry. The secret of the persuasive power of our favorite orators is in their constant recognition of the ebb and flow of the sensibilities they are acting upon. Their speech is, in effect, an actual conversation, in which they are speaking for as well as to the audience; and the interlocutors are made almost as palpably such as at the "Breakfast Table" of our dramatic "Autocrat." In contrast with this, the dull preacher, falling below the dignity and the privilege of his office, addresses himself, not to living men, but to an imaginary sensibility to abstract truth. The effect of this is obvious and inevitable; it converts hearers into doubters as to whether in fact there be any snch thing as a religion worth recommending or possessing, and preachers into complainers of the people as indifferent and insensible to the truth,—a libel which ought to render them liable to fine and punishment. God's truth, *fairly presented*, is never a matter of indifference or of insensibility to an intelligent, nor even to an unintelligent audience. However an individual here and there may contrive to withdraw himself from the sphere of its influence, truth can no more lose her power than the sun can lose his heat.

The people, under the quickening influences characteristic of our age, are awaking to the consciousness, that, on the day which should be the best of all the week, they have been defrauded of their right, in having solemn dulness palmed upon them, in place of living, earnest, animated truth. Let not ministers, unwisely overlooking this undeniable fact, defame the people, by alleging a growing facility in dissolving the pastoral relation,—a disregard of solemn contracts,—a willingness to dismiss excellent, godly, and devoted men, without other reason than the indisposition to retain them. Be it known to all such, that capable men in every department of life were never in such request as at this very hour; and never, since the world began, was there an audience so large and so attentive to truth, well wrought and fitted to its purpose, as now.

PLEASE YOUR HUSBAND?

Do you wear jewelry to please your husband; do you, sister, wear that breastpin to please your husband? Well, will this pleasing your husband please Jesus? Which do you prefer to please: your husband or your Saviour? who "For you bore the shameful cross and carried all your grief?"

"What's the harm, pray, in wearing a modest gold breastpin?"

What's the harm, sister, in wearing any ornaments of gold? Why did the Holy Spirit say: "Whose adorning let it not be that outward adorning * * * of wearing of gold," &c.,—see also 1 Tim. ii, 9. If it is right for you to wear a gold breastpin, why not also gold ear-rings, gold wristbands, tip off from top to toe in gold, even to nose-jewels like the heathen? The Bible makes no distinction between much gold or little gold: "He that offendeth in one point is guilty of all." It's the little foxes that destroy the vines; it's the little leak that sinks the ship; it's the little spark that kindles the flames. "Behold how great a matter a little fire kindleth." Sister, you profess to be a Christian, enjoy the inner life,—what is the effect of your example on the lambs of the flock? What says Christ of those who offend or cause to stumble "one of these little ones." Read Matth. xviii, 6—8.

But you wear the gold breastpin to please your husband! Sister, beware of this trap of Satan, *beware,* lest like Sampson you are shorn of your locks. "He that loveth father or mother more than me, is not worthy of me; and he that loveth son or daughter more than me, is not worthy of me. And he that taketh not his cross and followeth after me, is not worthy of me."

"At his command, we must take up
  Our cross without delay;
Our lives—and thousand lives of ours—
  Can ne'er his love repay.

"Each faithful suff'rer Jesus views
  With infinite delight:
Their lives to him are dear; their deaths
  Are precious in his sight.

"To bear his name—his cross to bear—
  Our highest honor this!
Who nobly suffers now for him,
  Shall reign with him in bliss.

"But should we, in the evil day,
  From our profession fly,—
Jesus, the Judge, before the world,
  The traitor will deny."—GOLDEN RULE.

STRONG BELIEVERS.—Luther was a tower of strength, because his whole trust was in the Lord. Baxter was a burning flame, because he lived hard by the mercy-seat, whereon the glory dwelt between the cherubim. Whitefield was "the voice of one crying in the wilderness," because like John, his crying was, "Behold the Lamb of God!" Chalmers foamed like a cataract because the deep rapids came rushing down upon him from the everlasting mountains. Hall's words were all moulten in the furnace where his faith was tried with fire. These were great preachers, because they were *strong* believers; and they were strong believers because they loved the truth, kept their hearts with all diligence, and walked in the light of heaven. There is no age in which *such* preachers would not have power. — ECLECTIC REVIEW.

RELIGION in the hands of self, or corrupt nature, serves only to discover vices of a worse kind, than in nature left to itself. Thence are all the disordered passions of religious men, which burn in a worse flame, than passions only employed about worldly matters; pride, self-exultation, hatred and persecution, under a cloak of religious zeal, will sanctify action, which nature, left to itself would be ashamed to own. —LAW.

OPINIONS OF EMINENT MEN RESPECTING THE BIBLE.

A Book which Sir Isaac Newton esteemed the most authentic of all histories; which by its celestial light illumes the darkest ages of antiquity; which is the touchstone whereby we are enabled to distinguish between true and fabulous theology—between the God of Israel, holy, just, and good, and the impure rabble of heathen Baalim; which has been thought by competent judges, to have afforded matter for the laws of Solon, and a foundation for the philosophy of Plato; which has been illustrated by the labor of learning in all ages and countries, and been admired and venerated for its piety, its sublimity, its veracity, by all who were able to read and understand it.—*Bishop Watson.*

There never was found in any age of the world, either philosopher, or sect, or law, or discipline, which did so highly exalt the public good as the Christian faith.—*Lord Bacon.*

There is no book upon which we can rest in a dying moment, but the Bible.—*John Selden.*

There are no songs comparable to the Songs of Zion; no orations equal to those of the Prophets, and no politics like those which the Scriptures teach.—*Milton.*

There is no book like the Bible for excellent wisdom, learning and use.—*Sir Matthew Hale.*

It is a matchless volume; it is impossible we can study it too much, or esteem it too highly.—*Hon. Robert Boyle.*

To a person who asked that profound thinker, John Locke, which was the shortest and surest way for a young gentleman to attain to the true knowledge of the Christian religion, in the full and just extent of it, he replied,— 'Let him study the Holy Scriptures, especially the New Testament; therein are contained the words of eternal life. It hath God for its Author; Salvation for its End: and Truth, without any mixture of Error, for its matter.'

I have carefully and regularly perused the Holy Scriptures, and am of opinion that the volume contains more sublimity, purer morality, more important history and finer strains of eloquence than can be collected from all other books, in whatever language they may have been written.—*Sir William Jones.*

In every generation, and wherever the light of revelation has shone, men of all ranks, conditions, and states of mind, have found in this volume a correspondent of every movement towards the better felt in their own hearts. The needy soul has found a supply, the feeble a help, the sorrowful a comfort! yea, be the recipiency the least that can consist with mortal life, there is an answering grace ready to enter. The Bible has been found a spiritual world, —spiritual, and yet at the same time outward, and common to all. You in one place, I in another, all men somewhere or at some time, meet with an assurance that the hopes and fears, the thoughts and yearnings that proceed from, or tend to, a right spirit in us, are not dreams of floating irregularities, no voices heard in sleep, or spectres, which the eye suffers, but not perceives. As if on some dark night a pilgrim, suddenly beholding a bright star moving before him, should stop in fear and perplexity. But lo! a traveler passes by him, and each, being questioned whither he is going, makes answer. "I am following yon guiding star!" The pilgrim quickens his own steps, and presses onward in confidence. More confident still will he be, if by the way-side, he should find here and there ancient monuments, each with its votive lamp, and on each the name of some former pilgrim, and a record, that there had he seen or begun to follow the benignant star!—*Coleridge.*

The Bible is by far the most inexhaustible book in the world, even laying aside its Divine origin altogether.

For its great antiquity, simplicity of narrative, splendor of poetry, and wise and holy injunctions, there is no work once to be compared with it.—*James Hogg.*

In this world we are children standing on the bank of a mighty river. Casting our eyes upward and downward along the channel, we discern various windings of its current; and perceive that it is now visible, now obscure, and now entirely hidden from our view. But being far removed from the fountain whence it springs, and from the ocean into which it is emptied, we are unable to form any conceptions of the beauty, usefulness, or grandeur of its purpose. Lost in perplexity and ignorance, we gaze, wonder, and despond. In this situation, a messenger from Heaven comes to our relief, with authentic information of its nature, its course, and its end; conducts us backward to the fountain, and leads us forward to the ocean. This river is the earthly system of Providence; the Bible is the celestial messenger; and Heaven is the ocean in which all preceding dispensations find their end.—*Dwight.*

A single Book has saved me; but that book is not of human origin. Long had I despised it; long had I deemed it a class-book for the credulous and ignorant; until, having investigated the Gospel of Christ with an ardent desire to ascertain its truth or falsity, its pages proffered to my inquiries the sublimest knowledge of man and nature, and the simplest, and at the same time the most exalted system of moral ethics. Faith, hope, and charity, were enkindled in my bosom; and every advancing step strengthened me in the conviction, that the morals of this book are as superior to human morals, as its oracles are superior to human opinions.—*M. L. Bautain.*

A person who tells you of the faults of others, intends to tell others of your faults.

AMAZING GRACE.

Dr. Tyng is writing a series of articles for one of the New York papers, in which we find the following incident that occurred in his pastoral experience. It illustrates the power of Divine grace to subdue the strongest will, and also shows the power of gentleness, of a wife's gentleness, to bring a husband near the Saviour's feet. As the account is true, it will be read with the more interest:

"Many years since, a gay and fashionable pair lived near me and attended my ministry. The wife was beautiful, social and admired. The husband was rich and worldly, and delighted in the admiration which, in society, his wife received. They lived a reckless, gay, and worldly life. Except in the worship of an occasional Sunday morning, they knew nothing of religion, and cared nothing for what they heard even then. But in the wonders of grace this gay and fashionable woman was converted there, and in the most open and decided manner renounced her life of folly, and cast her lot among the followers of the Lord. Her sudden change of life and purpose intensely enraged her unconverted husband, who had no sympathy with her, and could not understand her. He tried in every possible manner to overthrow her plans, and drive her from her choice. He forbid her union with the church, in any personal act. He watched at the gates of the church-yard to prevent her entrance by force. So far was this hostility carried, that at last she found access to the church for her appointed baptism only through the window in the rear. Thus matters went on for weeks, every day bringing me some new tidings of his violence and her sufferings. How much their domestic affairs were known to others, I never knew. The people and the generation have since passed away. Their young children are now mature, and several of them parents themselves.

Some weeks of this new history had

passed, when late one evening, after I had retired to my chamber for the night, my door-bell was violently pulled, and a messenger said Mrs. —— desired to see me immediately. I dressed myself and went, anticipating some scene of violence, and simply saying to my wife where I was going, in case I might be prevented from returning. The streets were solitary and still. As I ascended the steps, the door was quietly opened to me, and I was directed to the parlor, where, to my surprise, I found the two sitting together on the sofa, with no other person present. The man looked up to me in an agony of tears, as in astonishment I sat by his side and asked an explanation. "Oh, sir," he cried, "can I be saved, can I be saved?" "Yes, surely," I answered; "but you amaze me—what has led you to this?" "This angel," he replied, with eagerness,—" you know how I hated her religion. But you do not know how I hated you. I thought you the blackest of human beings. You had broken up my happiness, you had destroyed my peace, you had separated my family, you had alienated my wife from me. I laid it all to you. I was intensely enraged with you. I have several times watched for you at night with the intention of killing you. But it is all over now. I am thankful to see you. But this angel wife—I have cursed her, I have persecuted her in every way. I have beaten her, I have pulled her down by her hair; and she has received it all in silence and meekness. She has never said one unkind word in reply; but she has prayed for me and loved me. And I can stand it no longer. I am miserable, because I am so guilty. I have rebelled so horribly. I have been loved and treated so affectionately. Can I be saved?" The wife sat silently and heard the whole,—and then gently said, "My dear husband seemed so distressed to-night, that I took the liberty to send for you." How fresh and vivid is that whole scene before me as I write, with all its incidents and details, which I will not describe. With what delight did I preach the Saviour's love to this lost one thus at last aroused by that love to see his own voluntary and aggravated guilt!

We passed more than an hour thus together, and closed our conversation with earnest prayer. Blessed indeed was the result. The strong man armed had found a stronger than he, who had taken from him all his armor wherein he trusted, and spoiled his goods. He was subdued by love, converted by Divine power. He too came into the Saviour's flock, and on the side of Jesus. How changed the mad one became, "sitting at the feet of Jesus, clothed, and in his right mind." He witnessed among us for years a good confession; —he was honored and beloved in the church;—a pattern of gentleness and fidelity at home and abroad. After some years of earnest Christian life on earth, his course was finished and his rest attained. I have since hardly passed the house in which they lived without recalling to my mind this whole remarkable scene—that peculiar display of grace—that voluntary wanderer, and the wonderful love and mercy which in so much rebellion he received. He assumed all the responsibility of the guilty wandering upon himself. He learned to give all the glory of his recovery to that amazing grace, which had plucked him as a brand from the burning, and loved him when he was dead in sins."

ANY movement by the oppressed to recover their rights, will be resisted by those who have oppressed them; but *suffering*, and *persecution*, in a cause which the love of GOD and MAN requires, should be *fearlessly met and resolutely borne.*—BASCOM.

DEFECTIVE RELIGION.—A religion that never suffices to *govern* a man, will never suffice to save him; *that* which does not sufficiently distinguish one from a wicked world, will never distinguish him from a perishing world. —HOWE.

SECRET PRAYER.

Men never take so firm a hold on God as in secret. Remember Jacob.

Thou shouldst pray alone, for thou hast sinned alone, and thou art to die alone, and to be judged alone. Alone wilt thou have to appear before the judgment seat. Why not go alone to the mercy seat? In the great transaction between thee and God, thou canst have no human helper. You can be free before God. You are not going to tell him any secret. You may be sure he will not betray your confidence. Whatever reasons there may be for any species of devotion, there are more and stronger reasons for secret devotion.

Nothing is more embarrassing and disturbing in secret prayer than unpropitious circumstances. Great attention ought always to be paid to this point. "Enter into thy closet," says Christ. He says not *a* closet, nor *the* closet, but thy closet. The habit of secret communion is supposed to be formed. The man is supposed to have a closet—some place to which he is accustomed to retire for prayer—some spot consecrated by many a meeting there with God—some place that has often been to him a Bethel. The Saviour uses the word to mean any place, where, with no embarrassment either from fear or pride of observation, we can freely pour out our heart in prayer to God. No matter what are the dimensions of the place, what its flooring or canopy. Christ's closet was a mountain, Isaac's a field, Peter's a house top.

Go not to thy closet to say prayers. Oh! I wish obsolete could be written against that phrase, "saying prayers." It were as proper to speak of saying phrases. If, when in thy closet, thou feel nothing, say, "Oh, God, I feel nothing—no gratitude, no contrition." God likes truth.

It is in the closet, and not in the crowd, that men become acquainted with God! Oh, how it lightens the pressure of a calamity, relieves the loneliness of death, and breaks the shock of the entrance to eternity.

To become remiss in secret devotion is to become tired of God.

What an argument we have for secret prayer, in the example of Christ, who seems to have been in the habit of retiring to very solitary places, for the purpose of personal communion with God, and especially for prayer. Yes! He who knew no sin, needed no forgiveness, and whose mind was not liable to be diverted and distracted, as ours is, maintained secret prayer. Though the habit of his soul was devotion, and every breath bore upon it, and wherever he was, he held perfect and uninterrupted communion with the Father, yet he was wont to seclude himself to pray. With these advantages over us, he felt the necessity of it; and, with the business of the world's redemption to attend to, he found time for it. This example speaks volumes to us all. Was it necessary for him and not for thee, poor, guilty, exposed sinner, who hast a God to propitiate, a soul to save, a heaven to obtain? Was it practicable for him, and canst thou, durst thou, say it is not for thee? Canst thou not find a secrecy, or make a solitude? And if the day is not thy own, is not the night? That was the Saviour's time for prayer, and the cold mountain-top was his oratory.

The Scriptures do clearly teach that secret prayer ought not only to be daily—"give us us this day our daily bread"—but often through the day. Daniel and David prayed three times a day at least. "To pray frequently, is to pray fervently."—Nevins.

A Witness for Jesus.—Mary Dyar who was hung in Boston, in 1660, for being a Quaker, on her way to the gallaws said, "This is to me an hour of the greatest joy I could enjoy in this world. No eye can see, no ear can hear, no tongue can utter, and no heart can understand, the sweet incomes, or influence, and the refreshings of the Spirit of the Lord, which now I feel."

PRAYER.

BY REV. JOHN B. GRAHAM.

PRAYER is the key of the Kingdom of Heaven. It opens the celestial gates. It unlocks the store-house of divine grace.

Prayer is the keeper of the human heart. It admits the truth into the chambers of our imagery—into the secret things of the spirit of a man.

Prayer like rest or music, brings an evenness and serenity over the mind. It calms the soul till it becomes like the countenance of the benign Saviour. It imparts a peace which the world cannot give nor take away. The spritual part of man ascends in prayer, as upon the wings of a dove, to the sky, enters into the presence of God, and returns to earth with the radiance and tranquility of heaven about it.

Prayer for ourselves is the entrance to every good gift, and it elevates and purifies the suppliant.

But when the saint prays for others, the bond of perfectness, the generous emotions of unbounded love, makes him resemble the divine Advocate with the Father, the interceding Spirit of God. The good man thus goes abroad in his desires towards the family of his great Parent, like an angel on his ministrations here below.

What has prayer not done? What mountain, what natural impossibility has it not removed and cast into the sea? Has not God often spared a city or a people at the prayer of one holy person? Are not the children of God the salt of the earth which preserves it from corruption? Do not the prayers of the saints prevent the Holy One from leaving it to dissolve by the force of its own enmities and discord? Shall not the cries of the martyrs proceeding from beneath the altar arouse the Judge of the quick and the dead? The prayers of holy men have hindered God's judgments, and again they have hastened them. Prayer has quenched his wrath, and inflamed it. It has repelled the mightiest temptations, and chased away the evil one from his prey. It has procured the ministry of angels to supplant the attendance of devils. For sickness it has brought health; for barrenness, fruitfulness; for death, life.

Prayer has given nerve and constancy to the timid and weak virgin to resist the fire, and the rack, and the cord of demoniac inquisitors.

It has made torments, however sharp, appear easy; afflictions however protracted, brief; dangers, however formidable, unseen and unheeded. What cannot prayer do?

And then how suitable this work is to our nature, and how accommodated to our diversified circumstances. It is not the cumbrous and and imprisoned body that need act in this work. We need no eloquence but that of the unfortunate and needy beggar. A sigh may contain a prayer; a groan, a tear, a cast of the eye, may each wrap up many petitions. The current of thoughts is like the incessant flowing of a mighty river, and each thought may be a prayer. Oh! how niggardly the soul that cannot spare a few drops. Faith is like the sun upon the river of the human soul. It turns a certain portion of the stream of mind into celestial desires, which ascend to heaven and come down again in fertilizing showers of blessed influences upon this parched world, causing the desert to rejoice and blossom as the rose.

But some prayers are like the sluggish and creeping mists that hang over the stagnant marsh. They are not sufficiently rarified by holy fire. They proceed from formal, unthinking, unbelieving souls. They are as unpleasant breath in the nostrils of God. He smells no sweet savour of faith and love. They turn back upon the false, unfeeling suppliant, without ever reaching the skies.

What can an indifferent prayer do? Can it save a soul from death? Can it even vanquish a sinful passion, or obtain a piece of bread? If men must be in earnest to bespeak effectually benefits from men, how much more from God? If the paltry concerns of sense and time be worth fervency and importunity, how much more the one thing needful.

God hates a cold prayer worse than none at all. For it is pouring contempt on those things on which he himself has put more value by the death of his Son, and the intercession of his Spirit, and his own eternal concern about them, than he hath put upon the globes, and crowns, and sceptres of imperial kings—upon the hidden treasures of golden mountains, or the pomp and fame of conquests. Oh! then, dear reader, pray in faith, for

"Prayer is the Christian's *vital* breath,
The Christian's native air;
His watchword at the gate of death,—
He enters Heaven by prayer."

FAULT FINDING.—To find fault with others requires neither commanding talents, nor a high state of piety. It is much easier to idly look upon the tireless endeavors of active Christianity to do good, and to show wherein they might have done better, than it is to improve upon their example. He who is most ready to examine others, will generally be found most backward to examine himself. If we are faithful to our own convictions we shall have too much to do at home, to become "busybodies in other men's matters." He who scrutinizes the conduct of his fellow Christians with the greatest severity is not unfrequently least able to bear such scrutiny himself. Many have been excommunicated for the faithful discharge of duty, by those who deserved to be themselves excluded from the pale of the Christian Church for real crimes. Before we can attain to the stature of perfect Christians we must have less tongue, and more *heart work*. *Speak not evil one of another, brethren.*

THE WORLD.—As you love your souls, beware of the world; it has slain its thousands and tens of thousands. What ruined Lot's wife? The world. What ruined Judas? The world. What ruined Simon Magus? The world. And "what shall it profit a man, if he gain the whole world and lose his own soul?"–MASON'S REMAINS.

READING.

The principles of holy living extend, in their application, not only to the affections and the ordinary outward actions, but to every thing.

For instance, in the matter of *reading*, he who has given himself wholly to God, can read only what God permits him to read.

He cannot read books, however they may be characterized by wit or power, merely to indulge an idle curiosity, or in any other way to please himself alone.

If we look to God for direction in the spirit of humility, we may reasonably hope to be guided aright in this thing as in others. As a subordinate means of such guidance, it is proper for us, not only to exercise our own judgments with care, but to consult the opinions of religious friends and teachers.

In the reading of religious books, I think this may be a suitable direction, namely, to read but little at a time, and to interrupt the reading by intervals of religious recollection, in order that we may let the Holy Spirit more deeply imprint in us the Christian truths to which we are attending.

When the state of recollection turns our minds from the truths of the book to the object of those truths, so much so that our desires are no longer upon the book, we may let it fall from our hands without scruple.

God, in the person of the Holy Ghost, becomes to the fully renovated mind, the great inward teacher. This is a great truth.

At the same time we are not to suppose that the presence of the inward teacher exempts us from the necessity of the outward lesson. The Holy Ghost, operating through the medium of a purified judgment, teaches us by the means of books, especially by the word of God, which is never to be laid aside.—FENELON.

MEN are generally deserted in adversity. When the sun sets, our very shadows refuse to follow us.

LEAN ON JESUS.

When thy spirit is opprest,
Sad and weary, longs for rest,
Burden'd with the weight of sin,
Foes without and fears within.

Anxious cares press heavily,
Dreaded ills thou may'st not flee,
Lean on Jesus, He can cheer,
He can dry each falling tear.

None can such relief afford,
None sustain thee like thy Lord,
He can soothe thy fainting heart,
He can peace and joy impart.

Chase thy anxious fears away,
Turn thy darkness into day;
He removes sin's heavy load,
With His own most precious blood.

Clothe thee in the beauteous dress
Of His spotless righteousness,
Guide thee with His gentle hand
Safely to the promised land.

Fit thee now the cross to bear,
Then a glorious crown to wear;
Lean on Jesus, trust His word,
Lean, O! lean upon thy Lord.

DRUNKEN WOMEN.

There is a great and growing evil in this city, but one of such a delicate nature as to almost forbid being dragged into public print. I refer to the increasing and lamentable habit, now so common, of the indulgence by ladies in intoxicating drinks. I do not refer to those who do wrong from necessity, but that other class who have rich husbands and homes, that might be made happy. A larger number of this class are steadily diving deeper and deeper into dissipation every year than many persons greatly interested in their welfare even imagine. I have heard recently of several distressing cases of this kind, and to-day I learn that the wife of a well known citizen, reported to be very wealthy, has been sent to the Lunatic Asylum, in the hope that she may, with returning reason, be enabled to overcome the terrible temptation which intoxicating liquors have of late had for her. Her husband's name is almost as familiar in some parts of the South as it is here.

It is unwise to attribute this growing evil to one cause, for there are a variety in operation. A few may be named, and the reader must make such use of them as an intelligent conscience may urge.

Reputable physicians seem to be falling into the habit, more and more, of advising alcoholic remedies, either frankly and above board, or under the disguise of Tonics, Tinctures, and bitters. Scarcely a religious newspaper of any name or sect can be taken up which does not contain advertisements of these same mischievous agencies, with "Reverend" certifiers, *ad nauseam*. The editors of respectable medical journals, and the publishers of the same, lend their aid towards the introduction of wines, and beers, and brandies into the families by whose patronage they live; thus prostituting their influence to vile purposes for the sake of a few dollars they receive from the advertisement of the same. To show the extent to which these things are practised we take up a medical periodical, for July, of this city, issuing from the establishment of a name which for half a century has commanded the respect of the whole community; the editor an old man of learning and culture, and high position in his profession and his church; such men we say, are found introducing to the knowledge of their readers "Pure liquors for the use of the sick," and telling where such a brand of gin and such a quality of whiskey can be had; showing, however, some little deference to public decency, by saying: "So long as people will take domestic medicines, they ought at least to discriminate the good from the bad."

How is it possible to "discriminate" between good and bad London Dock Gin and Philadelphia Whiskey and French Cordials, when all are bad;

when the use of any of them for a short time tends to set up a desire for more, which no man of intelligence and who has any respect for himself or truth will deny? How many men and women under the habitual use of Tonics and Bitters and Beers and Cordials, have waked up at last to the fearful truth that "they cannot do without them—must have them," let our asylums and prisons and poor-houses testify; and let ruined families and blasted reputations and broken hearts the land over confirm the terrible record. He, and he only, is safe from a drunkard's death who never tastes a drop of anything that can intoxicate.—THE JOURNAL OF HEALTH.

THE QUARTER-DOLLAR SIN.

Rev. DANIEL LINDLEY, after an absence of forty years—more than half of the time passed as a missionary in Africa—returned to this country and returned to Athens, Ohio—the home of his childhood—the theatre of his youthful days. He trod again the old Campus, walked through the old college halls, stood upon the *cliff*—the rocky rostrum of college boys. He examined the old paths, and inquired for the companions of his youth. Changes had passed upon every scene. He was asked to preach at night, and to give some account of his life in Africa. At the close of the services, a very respectable and aged gentleman approached, and desired him to take a walk.

They passed on, and, when they had reached a somewhat retired place, the gentleman turned, and said:

"Brother Lindley, if a man has ever done wrong—has committed a sin—don't you think he should confess it?"

"Why, yes," said Mr. Lindley, "if thereby he may glorify God; if it will make amends to the party wronged, or do good to the party who sinned."

"Well, that is just what I think. I am in that predicament. I have long desired and prayed for an opportunity to make a confession and amendment to *you*. When we were boys together, fifty years ago, we were playing together. You dropped a quarter of a dollar, and I snatched it up, and put it in my pocket. I claimed it as my own, and kept it. It was, perhaps, a little, mean, dirty trick: and it has worried and troubled me ever since."

"Oh, it was a small matter, and I have no recollection of it," said Mr. Lindley.

"Ah, you may call it a small matter, but it has been a mighty burden for me to bear. I have carried it now for fifty years; I would not carry it fifty more for all the gold in California. And suppose I had to carry it for fifty thousand years, or for all eternity! No, sir, it is no small matter; it has been growing bigger and heavier, and I want to get rid of it. I have no doubt you have forgotten it, but I could never forget it. I have not, for the last fifty years, heard your name mentioned, or the name of your father, or any of the family, but that *quarter* has come in connection. Why, the very buttons on your coat—every thing that is *round*, represents a quarter. The moon and stars are magnified and illuminated quarters. You need not call it a little sin; if it was, it has grown mighty to plague me; and deservedly too."

With this the gentleman took from his pocket-book a five-franc piece, worn bright and smooth, and said:

"I wish you to take this; it belongs to you, it is rightfully yours, and will be no burden to you. And if this is not enough, I will give you more."

Mr. Lindley accepted it, and the gentleman raised himself erect, and drew a long breath, as a man would who has thrown off a heavy load. He was at last relieved.

The sense of guilt is enduring and tormenting, and can only die or be relieved by repentance, confession, amendment, or atonement. It needs not that it be the theft, fraud, or wrong, amounting to a thousand, ten, twenty, fifty, or a hundred thousand dollars, in order that the soul be oppressed by its burden; a twenty-five cents—a *quarter of* a *dollar sin*—may become larger than the globe, weightier than many worlds, with a punishment like the sin of Cain—*unendurable.*—N. Y. OBSERVER.

EXPERIENCE OF MRS. EUNICE COBB.

AT a grove meeting which we held last spring near Marengo, Illinois, our attention was attracted to an aged female, whose plain dress, devout appearance, and clear, explicit testimony to the power of Christ to save to the uttermost, bespoke the pilgrim to Mount Zion. We learned that it was Mother Cobb, of whose earnest uncompromising piety we had heard much in that region. The following account of her experience, which was published in the Christian Advocate and Journal, in 1847, has been forwarded to us, and will we trust be made a blessing to our readers.—ED.

Soon after I was converted I felt conviction for a deeper work of Grace, and a fervent desire for full redemption in the blood of the Lamb. Sometimes I felt as though I had almost obtained that great blessing, then I would lose my grief and for sometime live without my accustomed deep feeling. Still I continued to pray for the blessing.

After a time that man of God, G. Fillmore, came to our circuit. He preached the doctrine of holiness so plainly and powerfully that my heart became all alive for that perfect love of God that casteth out fear.

Now I was powerfully tempted. It was suggested to me that I was so ignorant and unworthy, that God could not bestow such an inestimable blessing upon me. I thought all my friends would shun me, and that all would despise me; and the powers of darkness gathered so thick about me, that I was already in despair. The struggle I now felt was a fearful one. I felt that I could no longer live without this blessing; I therefore resolved in the strength of the Lord, that I would not rest till I had obtained the prize; now I was willing to become anything or nothing for Christ sake. In that moment, my prayer, my struggle, my unutterable longing was gratified; praise took the place of prayer, my full soul, dissolved in love and praise, seemed as wax before the fire; then was that "new name" written upon my heart, which no man knoweth save he that receiveth it. In a moment I saw that this was sanctification, but quick as thought it was suggested, "Do not speak of it, for no one will believe you; it is only a blessing, and you have been blessed a great many times;" but blessed be God, who enable me to resist the devil and claim the blessing! My peace was "like a river." In the morning with streaming eyes I was enabled to tell the dear friends in love-feast that I had received a great blessing from the Lord. I had not strength fully to profess the blessing. O, it seemed such a great thing to profess sanctification! I had never heard any say they enjoyed sanctification, and it appeared to me that no one could believe me, if I professed it. For a number of weeks in every prayer and class-meeting, I told it as well as I could, and not say sanctified. After another conflict with the powers of darkness, I was strengthened fully to profess what God had done for me. Thanks be to God for ever for victorious love!

A beloved sister said to me, "I am sorry you have made such a profession, I am afraid you will wound the cause." I replied, my blessed Master, who has enabled me to testify of his goodness, is able to keep me; for it is not I that live, but Christ that liveth in me. When I reached home, my Bible, my Hymn Book, were full of holiness, and upon the walls and door-posts I could read holiness; all praise be to God and the Lamb for ever, that when we fully believe with the heart, we may then make confession with the mouth unto salvation. By faith, faith only, I received this precious treasure, and by simple faith I held it fast. Now my fellowship is with the Father, and with his Son Jesus Christ, and I am anxious that all the world should taste the riches of his grace. O,

 The arms of Love that compass me
 Would all mankind embrace.

About this time several in our village experienced religion, and I commenced praying in earnest for my unconverted companion. God convicted; but still he refused to yield, and he pointedly opposed me; yet I told my friends he would be converted—that I could claim that promise. "The unbelieving husband is sanctified by the wife." To this promise my soul clung for a long time, rejoicing and praying without ceasing, until the time of our Camp Meeting, when his long captivated soul was set at liberty. He, however, made no profession till a few weeks after the meeting, at which time our neighbors came in to rejoice with us, that "the dead was alive, and the lost was found." When Rev. J. Dempster, came in, he said "you have no need of a physician," and he added "you remind me of a merchant in Rochester, who, on being converted rushed into the street, swinging his arms, inviting every one as he went to come to Jesus, just now come to Jesus, just now come to Jesus."

Now I went from house to house, and tried to persuade the people to embrace religion. Every one rejoiced with me for the wonderful work which God had wrought. Instead of being neglected, as I had been tempted to believe I should be, every one seemed to have confidence in me. Some sent for me to their homes, others would call me in when I was passing, to inquire concerning what God had done.

Occasionally I had some difficulty in ascertaining duty, and I have found it vastly important carefully to guard my heart, lest Satan should find an entrance. On one occasion, having been in great distress for about an hour, and all access at a throne of Grace appearing to be cut off, I retired, opened my Bible, knelt and read, "Ye are they who have continued with me in my temptation; ye that sit down with me in my kingdom." The cloud broke, and O, what a bright light shone all around me! Then I felt as though I could convince a world of the divine realities of religion. Glory to our great deliverer, who set me in a large place! I now felt it my duty to be decidedly plain in dress. Going one day to church I met a lady dressed in the height of fashion; I was tempted, and it was suggested to my mind, "Why should I be so plain and singular when I can have those fashionable articles just as well as others? nay, and my friends feel mortified to observe my old dress? All as in a moment I seemed to see a robe displayed before me, which outshone the sun in brightness. I cried out, farewell all earthly grandeur, while a voice seemed to say, "Be thou faithful unto death, and I will give the a crown of life."

 Dear Saviour, let thy beauties be,
  My soul's eternal food;
 And grace command my heart away,
  From all created good.

My heart is grieved when I witness lightness and trifling among those professing godliness. Surely we must have the spirit of Christ, or we are none of his. We read that "Jesus wept," but where do we read that Jesus laughed and trifled?

On one occasion it was suggested to me, "you have given way to temptation; you have been impatient; you may now give up this great blessing," and while I was crying mightily to God, these words came to my mind, "cast not away, therefore, your confidence which hath great recompence of reward," and again my enemy was vanquished. Glory be to God that we have an advocate with the Father, Jesus Christ the righteous!

Our physician called upon me about this time, saying he wished me to take a number with me, and visit and pray with a young man who was lying sick in our village, and so low that medicine had ceased to effect him, adding that if prayer would not raise him he must die. We went, he took no notice of us; but there was a mighty spirit of prayer given to us; faith lent her realizing light, and I felt constrained to say that the young man would recover, and be thrust out to preach. In a few days he was able to be removed a hundred miles to his father's house, and some time after I learned that he was standing upon the walls of Zion, a faithful ambassador for Christ. At a Camp Meeting in Indiana, I heard Brother J. Armstrong, and Brother Griffith, preach their last sermons. The effect was glorious. Many where so cut down that they could not move. Such weeping, such shouting, such displays of the power of God I never witnesseth before.

When Dr. Ruter came out to preach Brother Armstrong's funeral sermon, I inquired if there were many in the Conference who enjoyed the blessing of sanctification. He replied that now Brethren Griffith and Armstrong were gone he feared there were few who enjoyed sanctification. How lamentable that a preacher of the Gospel should lack a blessing so essential! How can such a one with satisfaction to himself feed the flock of God? O, let the constant cry of the church be, "give us a holy ministry! I thank God that the witnesses of this great grace are becoming more numerous. Many can now say from happy experience that the blood of Christ cleanseth from all sin. O, may this blessing become common, yea, general! Lord, hasten the glorious time!

From the moment in which I received the blessing of perfect love, I have ardently desired to do all in my power, and am constantly inquiring, "Lord, what wilt thou have me to do? I have found by blessed experience that "labor is rest, and pain is sweet," when we see God in everything. O, if every professor would arise and assert his liberty, what a great turning to God there would be among sinners! My Bible teaches me to visit the widows and fatherless in their afflictions, and to keep myself unspotted from the world. All this by the grace of God I am striving to do; and the Gospel, the blessed Gospel! I am doing all I can to sustain it, and send it abroad to every destitute corner of the earth.

It is now twenty-three years since I experienced this blessing, and my way is brighter, and brightening still. I find that all things work together for my good. O, how delightful to cast every care upon Jesus, knowing he careth for me! O what green pastures, what still waters! How I love to dwell in the house of the Lord.

I have felt frequently a wish to send forth my experience in the Christian Advocate and Journal, but knowing my unfitness to write, I have deferred it from time to time; but impelled by a sense of duty, I have at length written as above, praying that the grace thus shown me, may encourage others to embrace this fullness of the blessing of the Gospel.

LOSS OF THE SOUL.

If you get not the soul's attachments to the world loosened before death, there will ensue such a rending and agony upon your departure, as no loss of country, of wife or children, can be compared with, and, if you take not a cool forethought of the future, nor prepare to meet it, there will come such a brood of fears, such a wreck of hopes, as no improvident spendthrift ever encountered. O! ye sons of men, if these things are so, and ye tread every moment upon the brink of time, and live upon the eve of judgment, what avail your many cares, and your unresting occupations? Will your snug dwellings, your gay clothing, and your downy beds, give freshness to the stiffened joints, or remove the disease which hath got a lodgment in your marrow and in your bones? Will a crowded board, and the full flow of jovial mirth, and beauty's wreathed smile, and beauty's dulcet voice, charm back to a crazy dwelling the ardours and graces of youth? Will yellow gold bribe the tongue of memory, and wipe away from the tablets of the mind the remembrance of former doings? Will wordly goods reach upward to heaven, and bribe the pen of the recording angel, that he should cancel from God's book all vestige of our crimes? or abrogate the eternal love by which sin and sorrow, righteousness and peace are bound together? Once more, ye sons of men, hear me for your honor and your interests' sake; and give ear as you value the love of Christ and the majesty of God. It is as sure as death and destiny, that if you awaken not from this infatuation of custom and pleasure, at the calls of God your Saviour, the habitations of dismal cruelty, endless days and nights of sorrow, shall be your doom. O! could I lift the curtain which shrouds eternity from the eye of time, and disclose the lazar-house of eternal death, what sleeper of you would not start at the chaos of commingled grief?—EDWARD IRVING.

GROWING IN GRACE.—I was considering how it was, that so many who were once filled with love, are now weak and faint. And the case is plain: the invariable rule of God's proceeding is "From him that hath not, shall be taken away even that which he hath." Hence, it is impossible that any should retain what they receive, without improving it. Add to this, that the more we have received, the more of care and labor is required, the more watchfulness and prayer, the more circumspection and earnestness in all manner of conversation. Is it any wonder, then, that they who forget this, should soon lose what they had received?—WESLEY.

PRIDE is as loud a beggar as want, and a great deal more saucy. When you have bought one fine thing, you must buy ten more that your appearance may be all of a piece; but it is easier to suppress the first desire than to satisfy that which will follow it.—BENJ. FRANKLIN.

FATE OF THE APOSTLES.

Do you complain of hardships? See how the apostles fared. Do you think you ought to have an easy time in old age, and die surrounded by weeping friends? Read the fate of the apostles. Job says of the wicked, "They spend their days in wealth, and in a moment go down to the grave." David says "There are no bonds in their death; but their strength is firm. They are not in trouble as other men; neither are they flayed like other men."

But the apostles, those holy men of God, not only endured bitter persecutions though life, but the most of them met with a violent death.

St. Matthew is supposed to have suffered martyrdom, or been put to death by the sword at a city in Ethiopia.

St. Mark was dragged through the streets of Alexandria, in Egypt, till he expired.

St. Luke was hanged upon an olive tree in Greece.

St. John was put into a cauldron of boiling oil at Rome, and escaped death. He afterwards died a natural death at Ephesus, in Asia.

St. James the Great was beheaded at Jerusalem.

St. James was thrown from a pinnacle or wing of the temple, and then beaten to death with a fuller's club.

St. Philip was hanged up against a pillar at Heirapolis, a city of Phrygia.

St. Bartholomew was flayed alive by the command of a barbarous king.

St. Andrew was bound to a cross, whence he preached to the people till he expired.

St. Thomas was run through the body by a lance, at Coromandel, in the East Indies.

St. Jude was shot to death with arrows.

St. Simeon Zelotes was crucified in Persia.

St. Mathias was first stoned and then beheaded.

BE temperate in all things.

WESLEYAN METHODISM.

We are confident that we shall do our readers a favor in presenting to them the following article, which we take from the *North British Review*, an able journal of Presbyterian proclivities. It breathes a commendable spirit of liberality. We hope that some, at least, who read it may be stirred up to imitate the ceaseless activity of the founder of Methodism in doing good. Who, like him will consecrate themselves fully to the Lord? There never was a greater demand for LABORERS in the Lord's vineyard than at the present time. Reader, will you go to work for God?—ED.

In the year 1785, well nigh half a century after the rise of Methodism, a sapient society in London discussed, for three nights in succession, this question: "Have the Methodists done most good or evil?" The disputants do not appear to have been either a company of free-thinkers, or a set of frolicsome and reckless young men. It seems to have been a grave and earnest affair. Thomas Olivers, of whom Southey, in the Life of Wesley, gives such an interesting sketch, joined the society to be present at the debate, and his speech on the occasion was published long afterwards in the form of a pamphlet. How the question was decided we do not know; nor is it of any consequence. It is the discussion, not the decision, of the question that is at all curious. That serious men should at that date have made this a subject of prolonged debate, is not a little remarkable. We cannot but think that, in our own day, Methodism is better understood and better appreciated. Looking at its extensive labours at home and abroad, and estimating—if it can be estimated—the value of its services to the human race, we might smile at, but should never think of discussing, the question which the London sages so laboriously debated. Doubtless, there are still whole classes of men who would promptly give their vote against Methodism. Infidels would do so; so would Papists; so would the enemies and revilers of evangelical religion; and so, we fear, would many who consider themselves zealous Christians in that church which the Wesleys loved so well and treated so tenderly. We are told by John Wesley, that up till the time when he commenced field-preaching, he thought it "almost a sin to save souls out of a church;" so there are some who seem to think that it is almost a sin—if, indeed, it be not an impossibility—to save souls out of the Church of England; and that it is both almost and altogether a sin to detach them from her communion. But among intelligent and earnest Protestants, who will, of course, treat such pretensions with derision, there can, we imagine, be only one opinion as to the debt which the world owes to Methodism. That debt we cordially acknowledge, without qualification or reserve. We do not say, of course, that we are prepared to subscribe all its dogmas, or to approve of all its ecclesiastical regulations. It might be easy enough to find things in the Wesleyan creed and organization to which we should be disposed to take exception; but this does not hinder us from expressing our hearty admiration of the zeal and devotedness with which Methodism has prosecuted the great work of promoting the best interests of mankind.

Our readers will have no difficulty in discerning, that the special ground of our esteem for this branch of the Church of Christ is the amount of good which it has done to the souls of men. Indeed, it is only when we look at man as an immortal being, and take eternity into our reckoning, that we can duly appreciate the services of Wesleyan Methodism. We cheerfully admit that it claims our respect and gratitude upon other grounds. It has done much to elevate and civilize the lower orders of society in England and elsewhere, and thus to diffuse elements of order and stability through our social system. By its efforts multitudes in heathen lands, who, a few years ago, were debased and brutal savages, are now "sitting clothed, and in their right mind." It has produced many men of distinguished talent, and the literature emanating from its book-room, has neither been scanty in amount nor contemptible in quality. But we strongly feel that Wesleyan Methodism would be unfairly treated if it were tried by such standards of judgments as these. For however great may have been the material, or social, or intellectual benefits flowing from its labours, these were rather the incidental accompaniments of the Christianity which it sought to diffuse than the direct object of its efforts and aims. If it were the main business of a church to polish and refine human society, to add extensively to the stock of general literature, to maintain a body of dignified, well-bred, and scholarly ecclesiastics, or even to frame an orthodox creed, and construct symmetrical systems of divinity, and exhibit a stately and harmonious development of correct ecclesiastical order, we might probably be of opinion that Methodism must retire from competition with some other denominations. But it was not any of these things which it set before it as its leading object. "Your business is to save souls," was Wesley's pointed and oft-repeated admonition to his preachers. And if this be, in truth, the primary and principal mission of the Church of Christ, then we cannot but regard Methodism as having, from the first, done the great work of the Church vigorously and well. And the more adequately we realize the incalculable value of immortal souls, the higher will be our estimate of all that Wesleyanism has done, and is still doing for their welfare.

It is not necessary that we should affirm that the erection of the Wesleyan Institute was the very best thing that could have occurred in England at the time when it arose,—that it was better, for example, than would have been an extensive revival of true religion in the Establishment, or better than if some one or more of the Non-conformist bodies had taken the place and performed the part which fell to Wesley and his coadjutors. But, if the religious condition of the Church was such as to call for supplementary efforts for the Christianization of the people, and if none of the other ecclesiastical systems afforded them, then we are surely not only at liberty, but bound to rejoice in the rise of Methodism, and to look with complacency upon its progress.

The annals of Methodism form a curious chapter in the ecclesiastical history of England. The reign of the second George is a singularly dreary and uninviting period to contemplate, both as respects the political, and social, and religious, character of the nation. Corruption rioted in all the public departments of the state; a withering Socinianism infested the Church, and, as a consequence, gross immorality and avowed irreligion widely prevailed. Nor did evangelical religion fare much better among the Dissenters in England than in the Established Church. The fervent piety of the early Non-conformists had grievously declined ; and many of the ministers had lapsed, or were fast lapsing, into a virtual and practical, if not an open and professed Socinianism, and many of the people into utter ungodliness. It was at the time when the gloom seemed to be deepening all around, and every source of illumination becoming hopelessly obscured, that a light dawned at Oxford, which, faint and struggling at first, soon shed its rays into the surrounding darkness, and ultimately did not a little to dispel it.

The Wesleys sprang from a good stock. The parents had been educated as Puritans, though they subsequently "conformed." The Father—the rector of Epworth—was a diligent and conscientious minister. The mother—like so many mothers of eminent men—was remarkable for strong sense, high principle, deep piety, uncommon natural talent, energy, and force of character,

It is easy to prophecy after the event; but one feels disposed to say, that the sons of such a woman could hardly turn out mere ordinary men.

Under deep religious convictions John and Charles Wesley, with three or four kindred spirits, formed at Oxford about one hundred and thirty years ago, what was called, in derision, the "Holy Club," and they were nicknamed "Methodists." Braving the storm of ridicule, —that most formidable of all modes of assault against educated young men, —they resolutely held on their course. Prominent even then, as ever after, was the distinctive aim of Wesley, to which we have before adverted. And, as their work went on, the broad and placid surface of ecclesiastical routine was stirred; the waters were put in motion, and though there might be here and there, a turbid eddy visible, yet even the wildest rush of the torrent was infinitely preferable to the sluggishness and stagnation which reigned before. The Wesleys and Whitfield were soon surrounded by listening thousands, many of them men for whose souls no one had hitherto cared, and on whose ears now fell, for the first time, the warnings and offers of the Gospel. Church dignitaries fretted and fumed at these disorderly proceedings; though they might have remembered that, as Wesley says, " one pretty remarkable precedent of field-preaching" is to be found in the Sermon on the Mount. But with all their reverence for the Church, these fervid evangelists were not to be driven from their labour of love, even by a bishop's frown. "You have no business here," said the Bishop of Bristol to Wesley, "you are not commissioned to preach in this diocese." "My Lord," said Wesley, " my business on earth is to do what good I can. Wherever, therefore, I think I can do most good, there must I stay so long as I think so. At present I think I can do most good here, therefore here I stay." The pulpits were generally shut against them; but this, instead of silencing, only drove them the more to preach in the open air, where tens of thousands listened to their message, who never would have entered within the walls of a church to hear it.

But the frown of the regular clergy, was far from being the only or the most formidable opposition, which the early Methodists had to encounter. They were violently persecuted,—and the narrative of these persecutions is one of the strangest chapters in their history. It is sad to think that, in a Christian land, those who were preaching the Gospel of the grace of God, and who could have no other aim or object than the good of their hearers, should be assailed and put in peril of their lives by fierce and brutal mobs, composed of men and women who had themselves been baptised into the Christian Church, and who called themselves Christians. We read, till we are absolutely sickened with the details, of Methodist preachers being hustled, pelted with stones and filth, dragged by the hair of the head through the streets, and trampled bleeding in the mire; of men and women plundered and maltreated; of soldiers sentenced, one to receive two hundred, and another five hundred lashes, for attending a Methodist meeting, *when off duty,* etc., etc. We might fill pages with the hideous recitals, and yet the worst would remain to be told. No honourable mind can learn, without indignation and disgust, that these abominble atrocities were, in many cases, openly encouraged by the gentry and the clergy; not unfrequently by some of both these orders who were in the Commission of the Peace, and occasionally by some of *both* these orders, who were at the moment in a state of intoxication. " We find and present," said an English jury, when receiving—or rather when throwing out—the depositions of some of the sufferers, " We find and present Charles Wesley to be a person of ill-fame, a vagabond and a common disturber of his Majesty's peace, and we pray he may be transported!"

When scenes like these occurred in England, one cannot be surprised to read of men and women present at a Methodist meeting in Ireland, being "beaten without mercy;" the preacher being knocked down, " one thrusting a stick into his mouth, another tramping upon his face, swearing that he would 'tread the Holy Ghost out of him,'" etc., etc. It is pleasing to us, as North Britons, to think that though Wesley might occasionally have to complain of a Scottish congregation, "which seemed to know everything and to feel nothing," no similar proceedings disgraced our Presbyterian country. Meanwhile, fed continually by the untiring labours of its founder and the preachers appointed by him, and organized by the sagacity and administrative talent which so pre-eminently characterised him, the system of Methodism began to take shape and consistency. Wesley was not content, like Whitefield, simply to Christianize great multitudes of men. He would not leave the "babes in Christ" to walk alone, or find support to their tottering steps wherever they could; whether from the clergy, or in the chance fellowship of private Christians. He surrounded each of them with suitable counsel, and provided needful superintendence,—thus linking the several parts of the mechanism together by a strong yet flexible chain. With a zeal which burned like a fire, and consumed every personal feeling of reluctance or self-indulgence; with a courage which braved the most appalling dangers; with a determination which bore him right onward over obstacles which would have staggered the timid and repulsed the feeble; with a capacity for work which hardly knew weariness or claimed repose, and a capacity for administration, which moulded with plastic skill the rough materials with which he had to deal, into form and symmetry; with a heaven-inspired devotedness which breathed the spirit of his Divine Master,—"My meat is to do the will of my Father, and to finish His work;" and with a band of ardent coadjutors, whom he raised up, or rather whom God raised up, to second his efforts and to share his toils; and above all, with the blessings of the Most High upon his and their labours, Wesley soon had thousands belonging to his societies, and calling themselves without scruple by the once despised name of Methodists,

But we are to keep it full in view, that in all this, John Wesley never intended to establish a separate ecclesiastical community, or to detach his converts from the Church of England. This pregnant and remarkable fact should at least exempt him from the imputation of ambitiously aiming at making himself a name as the founder of a sect. But it deserves careful consideration on many other grounds. His resolute and tenacious clinging to the Established Church, and his desire to frame his own institute—or rather to regulate his *societies*—so as to give scope to this strong attachment, and harmonize, if possible, with this fond adherence, materially affected the constitution of the Wesleyan system, and modified its course. Indeed, the relation of Wesley and Wesleyanism to the Church of England, is one of the departments of this subject which deserve special attention. As to Wesley himself, it is certain that, amid obloquy and insults heaped upon him for half a century, and fierce opposition to his efforts for the salvation of souls, he cherished an undying love for the Church, and was most unwilling to become, or to be called, a separatist. No man was more tender of her reputation or more anxious for her welfare. No man with a spirit so high as Wesley's, and, as has been sometimes alleged, so imperious and impatient of contradiction, could, unless animated with profound reverence and affection, have borne the treatment which he had to endure from his mother church and her clergy, without being driven into hostility and hatred. Towards her, at least, he largely manifested that charity which " suffereth long and is kind," which " envieth not, doth not behave itself unseemly, seeketh not her own, is not easily provoked, thinketh no evil, beareth all things, believeth all things, hopeth all things, endureth all things;" and, in this respect as in so many others, his mantle has, to a wonderful extent, fallen upon his successors. Even in the state of separation, into which the Church did so much to *force* them to enter, they have cherished towards her, feelings not merely of forbearance, but of kindness and good-will, which have been but coldly acknowledged and but scantily reciprocated.

We remarked that Wesley's stanch adherence to the Church had an important bearing upon the constitution of his societies. It followed from it that Methodism, as it came from the hands of its founder, was not properly *a Church*, but *a society within a Church;* not a distinct and complete ecclesiastical institute, but an auxiliary, or supplement, or appendage, to the national institute already existing. Thus, he admonishes his preachers to attend the Church at least two Sundays every month, and denies that the service of the Methodists is "public worship," in such a sense as to supersede the Church service. "It presupposes public prayer, like the sermons at the University." "If the people put ours in place of the Church service, we *hurt* them that stay with us, and *ruin* them that leave us." In harmony with these views, so frequently and forcibly expressed, was the constant declaration of Wesley, that his preachers were mere laymen, having no right to administer the sacraments, or to assume the designation of ministers, or clergy, or the title of *reverend*.

From all this it follows that the Wesleyan system was not framed after what was in reality—or even after what appeared to its founder to be—the New Testament model of a Church, just because it was not designed to be a Church at all. It was constructed piece-meal, as experience required, and as new emergencies called for new provisions. The Conference, the District, and Quarterly, and Leaders' Meetings, the Circuit and Superintendent, the Class and its Leader, Itinerancy and Lay Preaching,—these and other parts of the vast machinery of Methodism, were instituted, not primarily or professedly, because Scripture expressly prescribed them as necessary component parts of, and as together constituting, the external economy of a Church of Christ, but because they were deemed important auxiliaries, and useful arrangements in carrying on, *in the bosom of the Church of England*, the great work of converting sinners, and building up believers in their most holy faith. Hence it occurs, that intelligent and candid Wesleyans, like the biographer of Dr. Bunting, freely admit that "Methodists do not profess to rest their ecclesiastical policy upon any *jus divinum*."—P. 84, note. It is interesting to observe how, in spite of Wesley's fond predilections, and strong prejudices, and resolute struggles, and firm will, and sovereign authority, his societies were gradually falling, even in his own day, into a distinctive ecclesiastical mould, and admitted an organization which paved the way for a separate denominational existence. Some lament that he did not bind his societies indissolubly to the Church: we can only marvel at the tenacity with which he clung to her. What was anticipated by others, and dreaded by himself, occurred soon after his death. Yet so reluctant were many, even then, formally to withdraw from the Establishment, that we find, in the life of Dr. Bunting, that when he was on probation in the Macclesfield Circuit, 1803, " service during church hours not having been yet introduced into the Methodist Chapel, he was able frequently to attend the vigorous ministry of Mr. Horne"—an Episcopal minister—"and he communicated occasionally at his church."

Ere we pass from the Methodism of Wesley's day, and the career of that extraordinary man, we have a few additional remarks to offer. We have seen that Wesley did not owe his success, in any measure, to the exhibition of a new church, claiming to be more scriptural and complete in its constitution than the existing Establishment.

Nor did it flow from the promulgation of new doctrines, although so obsolete had the old doctrines become in many parishes, that we read of the people, in one place, engaging in high debate as to what religion the preacher (Wesley) was of, some averring that he was a Quaker, others insisting that he was an Anabaptist, till a village oracle solved the problem and settled the controversy, by pronouncing him to be a Presbyterian Papist.

Nor did Wesley attract men to him by speaking smooth things, and crying, "Peace, peace," while there was no peace. He and his fellow-laborers proclaimed the total depravity of the natural man, and the absolute necessity of the great and thorough spiritual change called conversion, and offered to their hearers a free and present salvation through an all-sufficient Saviour. Under God, we ascribe Wesley's success, *instrumentally*, to that noble characteristic which pre-eminently distinguished him, and which has distinguished all great men, and been productive of all great achievements, the characteristic of *hard work*. It was not by the magic of genius that he won his triumphs. Universally, indeed—at least the exceptions are marvellously few— it has been by strenuous, persevering toil—by *sheer hard work*—that even great men have achieved great results.

So it was with Wesley. When we read his journal and letters, we discover the secret of the spread of Methodism, in so far as it depended upon human instrumentality. For example, under the date of Friday—not *Sunday*, be it observed—the 11th July 1765, when he was in his sixty-third year, we have this record, "Preached at five; again at nine, in the new house at Stokesley; came to Gainsborough a little before twelve, and preached immediately; then rode on to Whitby, and preached at seven." Writing from Dumfries, on June 1st 1790, he says, "I doubt I shall not recover my strength till I use the noble medicine, preaching in the morning." Well may Mr. Bunting exclaim, "To think of an early morning preaching"—*i. e.*, at five A. M.—"curing the ailments of a man in the eighty-eighth year of his age!" All the pages at our disposal might be filled with similar illustrations of this splendid capacity for work.

And these labours of Wesley and his confreres were carried on amid many outward discomforts. We have referred to the persecutions which they endured, but they had other hardships to encounter. "Brother Nelson," said Wesley, one morning about three o'clock, to his companion, as they lay on the floor. where they had lain every night for near three weeks, one of them having a great coat for a pillow, and the other "Burkitt's Notes on the New Testament;" "Brother Nelson, let us be of good cheer, 1 have one whole side yet, for the skin is off but one side." Then look at Mr. Thomas Taylor, paying 3s. a week for room, fire, and attendance in Glasgow, often telling the landlady not to provide anything for dinner, dressing himself a little before noon, and walking out, then coming in to his "hungry room with a hungry belly," thus making her think that he had dined out, and so saving his credit. We read of an entry in the society book of a certain city to this effect, "7s. 6d. for turning the assistant preacher's coat to make it fit the second preacher." In the Bradford Circuit book 1770, the whole annual income of the preacher for food, clothes, books, and all other necessaries, *for himself and his family*, is stated to be less than L. 33. Assuredly it could not be for filthy lucre that *any* man, educated or not, could engage in a work of which the wages amounted to such a pittance as this. These circumstances made the hard work of the early Methodist preachers harder still. Yet we find Wesley labouring after the fashion now indicated, from day to day, and from year to year, through more than half a century. It is truly a noble spectacle to contemplate, such a long lifetime of toil, expended in such a cause. We must not, of course, say that it absolutely *deserved* succes, but we do say that it was the most likely of all things to obtain it.

And when treating of this subject, we may observe that the example of Wesley has been extensively followed by his successors. No one, indeed, will affirm that they have universally or generally manifested a zeal and assiduity equal to his. Had they done so, there would scarcely, we believe, have been at this moment, a man, woman, or child, in England, ignorant of the way of salvation. This, however, was not to be expected. Men like Wesley are not so rife. But there is ample evidence of the possession by others of an admirable aptitude for work. "My circuit," wrote John Bennet in 1750, "is one hundred and fifty miles in two weeks, during which time I preach thirty-four times, besides meeting the societies and visiting the sick," Half a century later, "Brother Solomon Ashton" describes his *walks* and labours in the Lancaster circuit. "Eighty-two miles and eleven sermons the first week; forty-three miles and nine sermons the second," and so on. "This," he adds, "was my first month's work on foot. The fatigue of walking and talking, rain by day, damp beds by night, etc., have caused me to suffer very much in health." During the two years which young Bunting spent in the Oldham circuit, " he preached six hundred and twenty-eight times in his own circuit, and twenty-two times out of it." In his four years of probation, " he preached thirteen hundred and forty-eight times." We are told of an old gentlemen, still surviving, who " walked with Adam Clarke, during the three years of his residence in London, six thousand miles, heard him preach nine hundred sermons (eight hundred and ninety-eight of which were from different texts)." Work like this carried on for a long course of years, and over the whole empire, could not fail, by the blessing of God, to be extensively successful.

In sketching, however rapidly, the history of Methodism, one loves to linger upon the character and career of Wesley. He lived so long and bulked so large, that it is not easy to lose sight of him. Fettered as he was by his devoted allegiance to the Church of England, hampered and hindered as was his rare talent for organising, by the fear of invading existing ecclesiastical authority, yet impelled irresistibly onwards by his ardent zeal for the conversion of sinners, and his anxious concern for the growth in grace of his converts, this great evangelist went resolutely on, doing most energetically the work to which he felt himself called, preaching the Gospel, tending and training his spiritual children, and providing for the oversight and government of his rapidly multiplying societies. We follow his footsteps with unflagging interest for upwards of sixty years, from the days of the "godly club" at Oxford, onwards to the time when, in 1790, he presided over his last Conference, and when the circuits in the British dominions numbered 119, served by 313 preachers, and comprising 77,000 members; and, in addition to these, there were 97 circuits, 198 preachers, and 43,000 members in the United States. With what feelings must the venerable Wesley have contemplated the prodigious results of his apostolic labours! Before another Conference, he had entered into his rest and reward; and when *at length* he rested from his labours, of few men that ever lived could it be said with so much truth and emphasis, that "his works do follow him." "There may come a time," said Southey, some forty years ago, " when the name of Wesley will be more generally known, and in remoter regions of the globe, than that of Frederic or of Catherine." Assuredly that time has already come.

Wesley passed away; but the vast mechanism which he had constructed did not fall in pieces or come to a stand. The hopes of enemies, and the fears of friends, were alike disappointed. Another Wesley, indeed, could not be found, nor could any one stand in the same relation to the societies which he had formed. It was impossible, there fore, to perpetuate such an autocracy as he had exercised, and if it had been possible, it would not have been desirable. But the Conference which had met annually for almost half a century, through which, and in whose name, Wesley had governed the societies, and which he had formally designated, by the legal Deed of Declaration, his successors in power, now firmly grasped —if we must not say the *sceptre*—at least the *helm*, and the good ship moved steadily forward in her course. She did not, indeed, escape some stiff gales, which now and then rent a sail, and snapped a spar, and on more than one occasion severely tested the sea-worthiness of the vessel, but she bore bravely on; and though she sometimes reeled and staggered in the storm, she never foundered, nor, though once or twice very near the breakers, did she ever run aground.

In looking at Methodism after the death of Wesley, we miss, of course, the grand central figure—the master-spirit which had so long directed all its movements; and the men whom he left behind must have missed him much more. They would feel every hour the want of his sagacity and authority in counsel, his skill and promptitude in administration, his energy and unquenchable ardour in action. But it was not merely that his seat of supremacy was empty, and that the blank was sorely felt. There were grave questions, which a respectful deference to his feelings and authority had kept in abeyance while he lived, and, we were about to say, *reigned*, which now urgently clamoured for a settlement. Were the tens of thousands who had grown up in the bosom of Methodist families, or had been converted by Methodist preachers, both of which classes had scarcely known, and had never valued any other religious services than those held in Methodist chapels—were they still to profess a nominal adherence to the Church of England, and were they to deny themselves, or suffer themselves to be deprived of sealing ordinances within what they could not but esteem their *own* communion? They had in the Wesleyan preachers the only ministers of the Gospel from whom they had ever derived spiritual benefit; were they to go to others, of whom they knew nothing, and who might possibly refuse and repel them, for the sacraments of baptism and the Lord's Supper? They had hitherto yielded to Mr. Wesley's wishes; but was the glaring anomaly to continue? In short, was Wesleyan Methodism to be *a church*, or was it to be a mere appendage or supplement to the English Establishment? The moment was critical, the question vital. Warm and wide-spread discussion took place as to whether the sacraments should be administered in Wesleyan chapels, and by Wesleyan preachers; and it required all the cautious wisdom of the Conference to prevent an explosion. The danger was averted by the adoption of a prudent "Plan of Pacification," which permitted, under certain regulations, the sacraments to be administered; and thus was Wesleyan Methodism launched as a distinct and independent branch of the Church of Christ.

THE cruelest magistrates seldom are very bloody or persecuting, but when a worldly or proud clergy stirs them up to it. And all the heresies that ever sprang up in the church, do seem to have done less harm on one side, than by pretences of unity, order and government, they have done on the other. O how unspeakably great have been, and still are the church's, sufferings, by a proud and worldly clergy, and by mens abuse of pretended learning and authority.—BAXTER.

IT is certainly a parodox that we are naturally desirous of long life, and yet unwilling to be old.

IT is one of the worst of errors to suppose that there is another path of safety beside that of duty.

REVIVALS.

BY THE EDITOR.

A REVIVAL of pure religion is the work of God. Whatever human instrumentalities may be employed in its promotion, so far as the work is genuine, it is *Divine*. Every real convert is born of the *Spirit*. There may be proselytes where the influence of the Holy Ghost is scarcely recognized or felt. But when souls are really saved, and fitted for Heaven, there God works in a supernatural manner. His Spirit melts, subdues and changes sinful hearts. He influences man to yield—working in him to will—and then enables him to carry out the good resolutions he has formed, working in him to do of his good pleasure. Would you see a revival. Then be *filled* with the *Spirit*. Just as certainly as you are, souls will be brought to Christ through your efforts. But in order to do this you must,

First. Consecrate yourself fully to God.

The Spirit never dwells in a divided heart. There may be zeal where self reigns. And zeal may bustle about, build churches and parsonages, endow colleges, and make a display before the world, but it alone cannot save souls. The present age does not need more activity so much as it needs more deadness to the world, more of a spirit of unreserved consecration to God, his truth, and his cause. How few are there who *listen always* to the *voice* of *God*, who dare stand by his truth when it is unpopular to do so? How few are there so fully given up to God as to act up to their own convictions of right at all times and in all places? Does not *expediency*, instead of conviction of right, control the actions of most professing Christians, and ministers of the Gospel? So long as this is the case, revivals of religion will be superficial in their nature, and limited in their extent.

Second. You must lead a life of self-denial.

He who would live in the Spirit must mortify self. He who lives in sensual indulgence need not expect to have any considerable measure of the Spirit of God. "Sensual, not having the Spirit," is a brief but truthful description of too many who come around the altars, and occupy the pulpits of Christian churches. Ministers may defend with ramparts of subtle logic and plausible sophistry, the pleasure ground on which the church and the world meet in in loving embrace, but he who would have the Spirit of God, must not come down upon the plains of Ono.

PREACHING.

THE London *Christian Observer*, on the question, "Why preaching does so little good," asks:

"Is it not because, while the world has apparently come nearer to the Church, the Church has really drawn nearer to the world? It seems as if a mutual approximation had taken place, and a mutual sacrifice had been made; but in truth the sacrifice has been chiefly on one side, and that on the wrong side. Things which are, perhaps, not unlawful in themselves, have become a snare to the great mass of professors of religion. The world has smiled upon them, and they have too often been fascinated."

Some instances of the inconsistency of Christians, such as taking great pains to attend a fashionable concert of music one evening, and the next deterred by fear of taking cold from attending church or lecture close at their doors, are cited, and then the writer proceeds:

"And when the world sees such conduct on the part of Christian neighbors, what other inference can they be expected to draw from it than that professing Christians do not believe what they profess; that their religion is but a cloak, which hangs loosely upon them, and which they are glad at any time to cast off, in order that they may enjoy the pleasures of sense? This is one great cause which serves to neutralize the effect of the most earnest and faithful ministrations of the Christian Sabbath and sanctuary. It is doubted whether the minister means what he says, when he denounces the love of the world, and of the things of the world; because they who profess the greatest attachment to his ministry are so little affected by his preaching. And if he who thus preaches begins himself to descend to any kind of frivolities, then he may preach like an angel, without ever converting one sinner from the error of his ways."

TOUCHING INCIDENT.

SOME two or three weeks since, a little girl in West Newton, predicted her own death.

When apparently in her usual health, she was suddenly taken with croup, and died the same night, exclaiming just before her death: "Do you see the angels over there? they have come for me." The following communication from a valued correspondent narrates an incident of a similar touching and remarkable character, and equally well authenticated:—*Boston Journal.*

"*Out of the mouths of babes and sucklings hast thou ordained praise.*"—PSALM viii. 2.

Jennie Sharp, only daughter of Elisha B. Pratt, Esq., of this city, died Feb. 3, 1857, at the age of three and a half years, after a short illness. A few weeks since she arose early in the morning and got into her mother's bed, saying "Mother, I dreamed that I saw God, and he asked me to come and live with Him." "What did you say to Him, my child?" "I told him, I do not want to leave my dear father and mother, and my dear little brothers." Her father then asked her, "What did God say then?" "He said," she replied, "You may stay with them a little longer." A short time before her death, she whispered to one of her playmates, then visiting at the house, "I am going to be an Angel." It was an affecting sight when this beautiful creature lay in her coffin— surrounded by flowers—her small hands clasped on her bosom—and her little chair by its side, in which her fond parents would never see her more.

Hast thou gone up to God on the wings of the morning,
Ere sin cast a shadow, or grief woke a sigh—
While fresh to thy young eye the world was just dawning,
And bright shone this beautiful dome of the sky?

Didst thou see Him, whom heavenly hosts are adoring—
Whom Sages and Saints longed to see—but in vain—
Who veil'd his own glory, our lost race restoring,
And rose from the dead in his glory again?

God is love. He came down to the little one's dwelling,
And he spake in a *still small voice* to her ear,
As He spake on the Mount—when the storm had ceased swelling,
And the earthquake and fire—to Elijah, the seer.

For the Angels of childhood are always beholding
The face of our Father in Heaven, we know—
And the words which she breath'd a great truth were unfolding—
"I shall soon be an Angel!"—And is it not so?

Weep no more! that thy lovely and lov'd one is taken
Like rending the chords of the heart though it seem,—
For the death-robe of earth laid aside and forsaken,
She is happy with Him whom she saw in her dream!

FREE METHODIST CONVENTION.

THE first session of the Eastern Convention of the Free Methodist Church was held in Rushford, Alleghany Co. N. Y. It was composed of fourteen lay delegates, and fourteen preachers. The district chairmen were authorized to employ ten other preachers. Still all the places that called for preachers could not be supplied. Men full of faith and the Holy Ghost, who seek not their own ease or profit, but the salvation of souls, are in great demand. Though in its infancy, the Free Methodist Church could profitably employ a hundred such men. In the work of soul-saving —in trying to reach the masses, and lead them by the way of the Cross to Heaven, there is too little competition among the "leading denominations" of our country.

There appears to be a very general tendency to display. Fine edifices, fine musical instruments, fine singing, and fine sermons, are all the rage. Be it ever the business of the Free Methodists to preach the Gospel to the poor, and hold out to all the self-denying doctrines of Christ.

THE WEEKLY PAPER.

THE propriety of starting one at present was very fully discussed. The want of having a medium in which the many misrepresentations of our actions and motives can be corrected, is very generally felt. But the financial risk is considerable.

A weekly paper at the present time would almost unavoidably involve us in controversy. Those who are leaving no means untried to destroy us, have put so many weapons into our hands, that might be employed to our advantage and their discomfiture, that the temptation to use them would, we fear, be irresistable. But to beget and foster a controversial spirit among the people of God would be a great calamity. What we most need is, *a general, deep, and thorough revival of religion.* A rehearsal of the wrongs we have suffered, and of the misdeeds of others, will not be very likely to save souls. If we stick to this, the

Lord will be our defence. *Salvation will God appoint for walls and bulwarks.* So we look upon the worst of encouragement to start a weekly paper at this time, as providential. As soon as the Lord puts it into the hearts of those who have the means to supply what is necessary to place the enterprise upon a safe basis, a weekly paper will, we have no doubt, be commenced. From eight hundred to a thousand dollars are needed to buy type, press, and other fixtures. A committee consisting of A. W. Perry, D. E. Tyler, George Worthington, G. W. Holmes, J. Handley, Rev. A. F. Curry, Rev. J. W. Reddy, W. H. Doyle, E. S. Woodruff, Rev. T. W. Read, Charles Denny, and Seth M. Woodruff, was appointed to raise the above amount for this purpose. The pilgrims of the west were invited to participate in this enterprise.

THE APPOINTMENTS

Were made by a committee of five laymen and five preachers, as follows:

GENESEE DISTRICT.—Chairman. Holley—to be supplied. Albion—Rev. L. Stiles, Kendall, M. N. Downing. Rochester and Chili—Daniel M. Sinclair. Buffalo, Thirteenth Street—James Mathews. Second Free Methodist Church—supplied by S. K. J. Chesbrough and others, Cary and Shelby, J. B. Freeland. Asbury—to be supplied. Carlton and Yates—supplied by A. C. Leonard. Alden—to be supplied. Pekin, Tonawanda—Porter and Wilson, Russell Wilcox, Judah Mitchell, Arthur King, and Isaac Williams.

ALLEGHANY DISTRICT.—A. F. Curry, Chairman. Alleghany—A. F. Curry. Wales and Springbrook—Ephraim Herrick. West Falls—supplied by Levi Metcalf. East Otto—supplied by Otis Bacon. Rushford—J. W. Reddy. Gowanda and Collins—to be supplied. Chemung—T. W. Read, Henry W. Spears. Perry—A. A. Phelps. Cadiz—supplied by A. B. Mathewson.

A. A. Phelps was ordained deacon. The preachers went to their appointments with, we believe, the determination to have revivals of religion. May the Great Head of the Church abundantly bless their labors for the salvation of souls.

MIRACULOUS GIFTS.

AMONG many other things charged upon those who, in western New York, are trying to "walk in the light," is that of claiming the exercise of miraculous powers or gifts in the theological sense of the term. We know of no one who makes any such pretensions. In our judgment, the best way to meet such charges, is with silence. The attempt to repel them clothes them with an importance to which they are not entitled. But the late convention thought otherwise. They judged that it was best to make the effort to set ourselves right before the public. So they passed the following resolution, which was introduced by Rev. L. STILES.

" *Resolved.* That we, as individual members of this convention, do not believe that miraculous gifts in the commonly received theological sense of the term, are for us as Christians at the present day, to be obtained or exercised; nor do we believe that the gifts of healing, of working miracles, of prophecy of discerning of spirits, of divers kinds of tongues, and the interpretation of tongues, as miraculous gifts or powers, are any of them attainable by any of the children of God at the present day."

A great deal of the misunderstanding on this subject has arisen from a misconception of the meaning of the word miracle, in the theological sense of the term. Any special and marked interposition of God in behalf of his children, is denominated by some a miracle. It may be wonderful, but in the theological sense of the term it is not miraculous.

A miracle, in the theological sense of the term, is defined by Watson to be "An effect or event contrary to the established constitution or cause of things, or a sensible suspension or controlment of, or deviation from, the known laws of nature, wrought either by the immediate act, or by the concurrence, or by the permission of God, *for the proof or evidence of some particular doctrine, or in attestation of the authority of some particular person.*"

The canon of Scripture is complete. We are not to look for any new revelations of the will of God. Hence no miracle will be performed for the confirmation of any new doctrines. As mighty wonders will yet be wrought as any of which our earth has heretofore been the theatre—the dead shall be raised, and the living changed, the earth and all its works shall be burned up, and the elements shall melt with fervent heat, but these will not be miracles, in a theological sense. In the philosophic sense, "A miracle is an effect which does not follow from any of the regular laws of nature, or which is inconsistent with some known law of it, or contrary to the settled constitution and cause of things."

It must be obvious to every careful reader of the Bible, that God designs that miracles should, in this sense, be continued in his church till the end of time.

THE REV. E. BOWEN, D. D., has just sent us a very able article on the subject of "SPIRITUAL GIFTS." It was not received in time for this number, but will be found in our next. This article alone is worth the subscription price of the magazine for a year.

THE EARNEST CHRISTIAN.

WITH the present number closes the first volume of the *Earnest Christian.* We would record our gratitude to God for the assistance He has so graciously afforded us. Its publication was commenced without subscribers, and without contributors, but, as we believed, at the call of God. The success has, so far, exceeded our most sanguine anticipations. But few ministers have acted as agents, or subscribed for themselves. On the contrary many have used all their influence to prevent its circulation. But by the blessing of the Lord it has lived. From the first the subscription list has been steadily increasing. Our friends have done nobly. They have our warmest thanks. We trust they will not be weary in well doing. Will you not at once send your subscription and get a neighbor or friend to subscribe also? We ought to have at least twice as many subscribers for the next volume. If our friends will work as hard for us for *one* month as we have for them the past *twelve*, it will be done. Do you say, "*It shall be done?*" Then set to work forthwith to send us three or four times as many subscribers from your post-office, as have taken the *Earnest Christian* there the past year.

NEW CONTRIBUTORS.

WE expect several new, pious, and able contributors for the next volume. We have no desire to present a list of eminent names merely for show. A person may write well on many subjects, and yet write very poorly on experimental religion. A clear understanding of the subject is the first qualification to good writing. Then a deep feeling of its importance will enable one of even small literary pretensions to write to edification. He who sees clearly and feels deeply, will generally write well. But however skillful one may be in the construction of sentences, if he write merely for the sake of writing, it will generally be to but little purpose. Hence the reason why so many titled divines write so poorly, if at all on experimental piety. They are not at home. They understand neither what they say, nor whereof they affirm. They give mere theories. But theories do not feed hungry souls. We must have a deep, heartfelt experience to lead others into the highway of holiness.

> What we have seen and felt,
> With confidence we tell.

Our readers may expect to find in our pages the contributions of those who are in earnest. Encourage them and encourage us, by giving their productions a wide circulation. One can write just as easily, and generally a good deal better for ten thousand, than for a few hundred. We shall do our utmost to make the second volume of the *Earnest Christian* still better than the first has been, and many of our subscribers have thought that a single number was worth the subscription price for a whole year.

RENEW.

Do it *at once.* Do not put it off. Do not wait for an agent to call upon you. Send on your dollars. It will not take you five minutes to write a letter, and the postage will only be three cents. So do not wait for any body. We wish to know just as soon as possible, how many to publish for the next volume. Be particular to write your name, post office, county, and state, very plain. Be your own agent. And if you can get any of your neighbors to subscribe, send on for them.

PAY IN ADVANCE.

FOR our own safety, as well as for the benefit of our subscribers, we shall be obliged to adhere strictly to advance payment. If you have not a dollar at hand, you had better borrow it of some one near to you than owe it to us at a distance. We endeavor to "pay as we go," but to do this we must have payment in advance from our subscribers.

SPECIMEN NUMBERS.

IF any of our readers will send us the Post Office address of any persons, that will probably subscribe another year for the *Earnest Christian,* we will send them a specimen number gratis. *Send on the names at once.*

www.ingramcontent.com/pod-product-compliance
Lightning Source LLC
LaVergne TN
LVHW041606070426
835507LV00008B/154